Imperfect Sens

IMPERFECT SENSE

Imperfect Sense

THE PREDICAMENT OF MILTON'S IRONY

VICTORIA SILVER

PRINCETON UNIVERSITY PRESS
PRINCETON AND OXFORD

STUART LYNDS SILVER 1951–1980

atque in perpetuum, frater, aue atque uale

For Christopher W. Grose,
whose Milton this is

CONTENTS

PREFACE

NOT JUST Milton but authors generally live in fear of their reception, so I will follow the incorrigible practice of my subject by prefacing what I have to say. Certainly if no one ever wished *Paradise Lost* longer than it is, as Dr. Johnson insists, then I show some audacity in writing a long book about the very peculiarities which drove Johnson to make his remark. There are several reasons for this, and perhaps the most considerable of them has to do with the caliber of criticism Milton's work continues to enjoy: I don't think anyone can write credibly about him without incurring, however subliminally, an immense and immediate debt to the interpretive tradition established by his readers—readers who have seen far more deeply into the poet's words than is usual. Originality here is not only impossible but also undesirable, because it refuses a history of such rare if sometimes perverse insightfulness. It is proper and inevitable, then, that I would take William Empson's acknowledgment for my own, since the result of my inquiry—if not the process—was the same: "The book," he writes, "carries many obligations, as it largely consists of reporting the ideas of previous critics and then using them."[1] Indeed, in offering a solution to the problem they expose, one can only attempt yet once more to describe the occasions, or rather the provocations, which have moved those ideas.

My particular intellectual debts are made obvious less by specific references than by the kind of question I engage and the nature of my response—in short, what I look for in Milton—which makes the book more essay than work of scholarship. This could also explain to the adventitious reader why it may seem to do nothing much, because the argument addresses a phenomenon so seemingly impalpable yet pervasive as irony. Because of the sense in which they understand his justification, many Miltonists do not regard the poet's expressions as deliberately, designedly ironic—conflicted, contradictory, dubious perhaps, but not ironical—a view which threatens to leave my very topic in the lurch. By contrast, many Romanticists almost assume such irony, are at least unimpressed by the claim, since their own writers are seen to discover precisely this conceptual turn, and to adapt its apparent novelty to their own poetic ends. So how should one go about proving the calculated presence of irony, that order of meaning always wrapped in fresh disguises; and how could one hope to create any interest in an argument whose broad outlines at least are already known?

As a historian of a kind, my response to this quandary has been to seek the sources of irony not only in what Milton wrote, but also in the intellectual culture to which he belonged and especially its new theologies, in which *Para-*

dise Lost by its very matter participates. At that time in Europe and Britain (not to mention the Middle East and North Africa), theology was still understood as a species of grand theory, in its idea of the divine necessarily encompassing the order of human being and truth, the status and character of nature and history, and the range of human possibility. But this new sort of theology never proposes to talk about the mind of God, which Milton is often thought to do. Instead, it addresses deity from the human standpoint—how the divine is made known to us and how we should understand and speak about that knowledge which *Paradise Lost* pointedly calls "the ways of God." As Calvin observes, to know God is to know ourselves, with theology delineating that inextricably mutual relation. Yet in saying so, he does not fall prey to the notion of some correspondence between divine and human, negative or otherwise, that might collapse the picture we hold of God with deity per se. In the writings of Luther and Calvin (as against some of their more scholastic or, in Milton's scornful phrase, syntagmatic followers), the hidden God's difference from us is consummate and ineffable even as it creates the most palpable, particular qualities of human life. I will argue that it is this abiding, sometimes anguishing, distinction between creator and creature which fosters the apparent eccentricities of *Paradise Lost*; and as I see it, the success of my argument will lie in how well it accounts for those qualities which continue to perplex and divide the poem's readers just as Milton himself does, with whose notorious character its vagaries are presumptively identified.

On this head, Montaigne remarks that, in the conceptual affairs of humanity, we are inveterately caught between two modes of understanding: "Just as no event and no form completely resembles another, neither does any completely differ. What an ingenious medley is Nature's: if our faces were not alike we could not tell man from beast: if they were not unalike we could not tell man from man. All things are connected by some similarity; yet every example limps and any correspondence which we draw from experience is always feeble and imperfect."[2]

Between them, the reformers do for religion what Montaigne does for philosophy, which is to make the lived experience of its inadequacy the sole restraint on our habitual and promiscuous pursuit of likeness. There could be no rationality, no human knowledge without the instrument of analogy; yet each argues that it is a device easily subject to abuse, especially in those benighted suppositions and speculative flights which either tacitly deny or openly disdain the intractable constraints of our condition. And for Luther and Calvin as well as Montaigne, the means of curbing such analogical hubris consist in a reciprocal exerting of distinctions. The "ingenious medley" of human perception, forever tossed between likeness and difference, in their hands becomes a critical principle not unlike irony itself, which we would do well to observe in reading the literature of this sceptical and abruptly self-conscious age.

I have tried to implement that recognition in the conduct of my argument, if only because irony like any other human expression cannot be confined to a single meaning or effect but remains as various as its use. Milton's practice of irony is not Kierkegaard's or Goethe's; nor is it the same as Luther's—most demonstrably in the politics with which it is allied. Yet in order to picture the special intelligence and dimensions with which he endows his master trope, I have had recourse to other writers, ancient and modern, whose dialectics show some instructive affinity with the writings of both Milton and the reformers: preeminently Wittgenstein and Stanley Cavell but also Adorno and Benjamin, and of course the Judaic and Christian scriptures, as read by what are called Old and New Testament theologians—Milton's own vantage. Their implicit and stated presence in the book is meant to elucidate only, and not Milton's position alone, but the whole refractory problem of injustice that occupied him as long as he lived. From disparate beginnings, injustice engenders in every one of them a certain morality of knowledge at odds with what passes for truth; and this profoundly humane conception takes at once an interpretive and an expressive form.

For it is no coincidence that the philosophical writers I have named articulate that understanding in ways their several communities have found incongruous, untrue, and even outrageous, rendering them all dissenters as well as prophets in the seventeenth-century sense of that word—as people who newly interpret the relationship between humanity and truth. For each modern, the very language of argument is idiosyncratic and difficult, values of expression shared by Jeremiah, Luther, and John Milton. As T. S. Eliot declares, after Johnson: "In Milton there is always the maximal, never the minimal, alteration of ordinary language. Every distortion of construction . . . every idiosyncrasy is a particular act of violence which Milton has been the first to commit. There is no cliché, no poetic diction in the derogatory sense, but a perpetual sequence of original acts of lawlessness."[3] And these writers experiment with their own idiom and disciplinary conventions for much the same reason Milton does: namely, the desire to transfigure fundamentally the meaning things have for us—to work out our salvation through words or, as the *Investigations* say, to show the fly the way out of the bottle.[4] Irony for Milton is the expressive means and salient difficulty he uses to accomplish this unexpected sort of justification, which revises rather than confirms our habitual notion of things. Yet it is hardly an innovation in European literature: tragic irony first exposed the abyss between the human and the absolute, inciting in its audience a kind of conceptual and moral therapy through the salutary emotions Aristotle calls pity and fear. And the goal of that therapy was the reflective knowledge of the Delphic dicta, so apposite for Milton's argument in *Paradise Lost*: *meden agan*, "nothing in excess," and *gnothi sauton*, "know yourself"—that is, in Walter Burkert's fuller rendering, "know that you are not a god."[5]

The book's first chapter addresses the ideas his readers have had of Milton's justification in *Paradise Lost*, a preliminary scrutiny almost conventional to a certain kind of Milton study since Empson or even Walter Raleigh. Like Empson's introduction, it acknowledges the significance of those passions and conflicts which congregate around Milton's God, anticipating how the argument of subsequent chapters will respond to them. The second chapter initiates that argument by examining the precedent hiddenness of the reformers' God, how it underlies Luther's formative concept of justification and religious experience more largely, and how the boundary or "distinction" between divine and human is peculiarly manifest in the way Luther and Calvin each interpret deity's expressions of itself, both textual and historical. The third chapter takes up this ironic model of revelation in Milton's polemical and doctrinal writings, describing the way the tracts educe meaning from his world—how they argue God and truth are made known to us. It is appropriate to mention here that I regard the *Christian Doctrine* as Milton's:[6] in the end, the circumstantial grounds on which we authenticate the content, as against the material, of such historical documents are ideological and aesthetic, as anyone who edits Shakespeare knows all too well. In lieu of other evidence, we are assessing the identity of a text by the known characteristics of an author's work; and I for one find the intimacy between Milton's writings and this theological treatise remarkable because remarkably helpful, even as I must refrain from pronouncing on the exact causes of that intimacy. Certainly, theology does not diminish or circumscribe Milton's imaginative resources any more than it does Dante's, although that judgment has been obliviously levied on both.

The book's second half brings Milton's complex understanding of the relationship between creator and creature, deity and its revelation, to bear on his poetics and *Paradise Lost* in particular, loosely following the sequence in which its dramatis personae are introduced to us. Thus the fourth chapter explores the ironic implications of the speaker's self-portrait in the proems, and how the predicament to which he alludes motivates his attempt at justification, affecting every aspect of the story he tells. The fifth chapter is devoted to Satan's tragedy, and the cataclysm accompanying his shocked recognition of Milton's God, which precipitates the fatal cycle of antipathy and suffering consequent upon the creature's apostasy from its creator. The sixth chapter belongs to Adam and Eve, examining how they bear the image of God in light of this distinction between deity and the world, an imaging which articulates the expressive order of creation and shows the immediacy or self-evidence of prelapsarian truth to be the delusion of sin itself. The book ends where Milton ends *Paradise Lost*, in hope, not resolving the dilemma of understanding which the poem poses but perhaps describing it again to good effect.

Notwithstanding my eccentricities, or perhaps because of them, I owe much to many but to some especially. At Columbia, Kathy Eden, (formerly) Margaret Ferguson, Robert Hanning, Jean Howard, David Kastan, Michael Seidel, and Edward Tayler gave encouragement when I sorely needed it, not to mention a job twice or three times. Jim McMichael and J. Hillis Miller did nothing short of save the proverbial day. I remember with gratitude Cyrus Hoy and Joseph Summers, as well as the late John Wallace, whom I miss. Like gods in the machine, Stanley Fish and Victoria Kahn have momentously intervened in my professional life to keep me from willful disaster. Michael Leib and David Loewenstein generously offered me a forum at the Newberry Library Milton Seminar, and still more timely support when it seemed least warranted. The UCI Humanities Center kindly came up with funding at a critical juncture in the process. My editor, Mary Murrell, proved that miracles have never ceased by managing, against all odds, to get the whole damn thing published. Without the ardent intelligence and sympathy of Jayne Lewis, I would not have been able to go on. And only by the constant, unequaled, and much-tried engagement of Richard Kroll with every sentence on every page, is there a book here worth reading. The debt I owe my parents is incalculable, like their loss.

ABBREVIATIONS

(The Revised Standard Version is the biblical translation used throughout the book.)

CC   *Calvin: Commentaries*, ed. and tr. Joseph Haroutunian (Philadelphia: West-
        minster, 1958).

CM   *The Works of John Milton*, ed. Frank Patterson et al. 17 vols. (New York: Colum-
        bia U P, 1931–38). [Columbia Milton]

CR   Stanley Cavell, *The Claim of Reason*. (Oxford: Oxford U P, 1979).

LM   *The Poems of John Milton*, ed. John Carey and Alistair Fowler. (London:
        Longman, 1968). [Longman Milton]

LW   *Luther's Works*, ed. Jaroslav Pelikan and Helmut T. Lehmann et al. 55 vols.
        (Philadelphia and St. Louis: Fortress and Concordia, 1955–76).

ND   Theodor Adorno, *Negative Dialectics*, tr. E. B. Ashton. (New York:
        Continuum, 1973).

OTT   Gerhard von Rad, *Old Testament Theology*, tr. D.M.G. Stalker. 2 vols. (New
        York: Harper & Row, 1962–65).

PI   Ludwig Wittgenstein, *Philosophical Investigations*, tr. G.E.M. Anscombe.
        (New York: Macmillan, 1953).

IMPERFECT SENSE

CHAPTER ONE

Introduction

꞉══◆══꞉

THE PREDICAMENT OF MILTON'S IRONY

Caught as we are between possibility and mortality, irony remains a quintessentially human expression that, without platitudes, conveys the perplexity of our condition. This is especially the case when irony is taken to the extremes of absurdity or extenuation, since these manage to ridicule that most fundamental of human dogmas, namely, our pretension to something grander and finer than mere animal existence. For even as irony expresses the rueful if distinctive impulse to reflection or consciousness of ourselves *as* creatures, our very attempts at that perspective tend to leave us lost in Swiftian loathing at the unangelic thing we find, in terror of what looks like our own bestial futility. Of course, absurdity has always inspired such revulsion at our creatural nature, designed as it is to deliver us from the rational delusion of human preeminence. Yet more tacitly or more insidiously, so do the endless placating, temporizing, casuistical rounds we make in the opposite direction, invoking 'mere humanity' to excuse our seemingly invariable failure to improve ourselves. I mean the unctuous irony of rationalization, when we devote all our ingenuity to the task of avoiding thoughtfulness, and whose point is how we debase and betray our peculiar intelligence in thus refusing responsibility for what we have made of human being.

But intelligence, however it is expressed, remains our obligation as creatures, and the one quality capable of rendering this existence meaningful, memorable, artistic in the ancient sense. And for the most part, we invoke irony both more kindly and scrupulously to assess just this intelligence, in the desire to better if not transcend human nature as we find it, and at the same time to acknowledge the finitude of the creature on which human vanity appears doomed to founder. That is why irony and drama show such an entire affinity for each other, because drama is the mode of representation most completely capturing not just the sense but the intimate sensation of this tension integral to human being—between our aspirations and our actualities. When Aristotle says that epic, like tragedy, is a *mimesis* or imitation of an action, he is distinguishing this dimensionality that attends any populated, diversified account of our experience: it is the genius of drama as an expressive mode to imagine and depict the human predicament much like we undergo it, projected as the perpetually latent mean-

ing that figurative persons must encounter and negotiate—forever latent because forever contingent upon the humanly inevident and incalculable train of
motive and circumstance. For no matter how resolute or pointed, drama makes
for an uneasy, restless literature just as irony does an uneasy, restless meaning.

These observations may seem entirely superfluous to *Paradise Lost*, which is
not a drama, at least in the conventional sense, and whose idiom is explicitly
cast as a justification, which we generally take to mean a positive assertion of
truth—God's ways being truth, as Milton reminds us. Understandably, then,
critics both friendly and hostile to what his speaker relates about the loss of
Eden and all our woe have supposed the poem to be anything but dramatic or
ironical, incapable of surprise or self-criticism. With ever more sophistication
and nuance, they have tended instead to read it as symbolic and propositional—
a poetic tractate if you will; and it is this supposition which ensures that there
isn't much middle ground of opinion where Milton is concerned, with the readers of the poem either vindicating or condemning what it more or less figuratively asserts, and loving or hating its author accordingly. Without seeking to
exonerate Milton of what he says there (although it will inevitably appear that
way), I would like to show that *Paradise Lost* is both dramatic and ironical in
some perhaps surprising and self-conscious ways. Yet I also want to suggest that
this is why there are, broadly speaking, two Miltons to be found in Milton
studies and why people tend to evolve such exclusive and opposed ideas of
them. It is telling, I think, that we never get so exercised over what we presume
to be Shakespeare's notion of things (unless we are George Steiner or Wittgenstein). But then, Shakespeare's meanings are dramatical and, as such, too
oblique and manifold to give indelible offense. But Milton and his poem have
been offending someone or other for more than three hundred years.

Needless to say, this project of arguing Milton's irony is by no means incidental to yet one more reading of *Paradise Lost*, which I will give in a somewhat
episodic fashion, the better to explain how the dramatic and ironical aspects of
the poem are created not so much despite, but because we know the outcome
of the story. For irony not only causes there to be two Miltons; it is the reason
that there are two Gods in Milton's poem—one tedious and repellant, the other
unremittingly if only vicariously delightful, and both the source, or rather the
occasion, of some extraordinary poetry. In relating the two—Milton with Milton's God—I am of course enlisting William Empson, without whose book I
could not proceed.[1] For as one admiring critic has described Empson's place in
Milton studies, his offense was "to take seriously and to force us to take seriously
the idea that Milton truly thought that God's ways needed justifying, that this
was a hard, not an easy thing to do, and that a case could also be made for the
other side."[2] And Empson's triumph, like his Milton's, was "a triumph of the
will, a work of extraordinarily perverse dedication"—"to try to keep us from
thinking that Satan's grandeur can be *easily* dismissed, or that God's goodness
can be *easily* cleared."

I would like to take up our understanding of Milton where Empson left off—with the *uneasy* significance of *Paradise Lost* and that perdurable human need to justify God's ways—and will begin by stating the obvious: that we usually undertake to justify something only when we suffer an injustice, by which I mean an incoherence, a challenge or conflict in our experience of the world. For whether or not they go by that name, our religious commitments tend to respond not to our ease but to our difficulties with things, on those occasions when the ordinary would seem to behave not just extraordinarily but wrongly—defying reasonable expectation and eluding that mastery of our circumstances to which we presume. Crises like these make us fearful but also reflective, self-conscious, moving us to pursue the justification, the right conceiving or ordering of such experiences, precisely because we cannot as creatures tolerate the uneasiness left in their wake. So rather like Lord Macaulay's Francis Bacon, or Hugo von Hofmannsthal's Lord Chandos, we make an enduring scandal of the discovery that the familiar remains unknown or perhaps unknowable at its core, because we dearly want to assume that human expectation and human understanding are one and the same, when they are not. Indeed, our human predicament is chronic, ineluctable surprise at the discrepancy between these dimensions of our experience, which we are obliged daily to witness as expectation outstrips understanding even in the smallest things. This aspect of being human is what irony enacts for us. And while there is something really wonderful and hopeful about the fact that we are always learning what we do not know, yet as thinking and time-bound creatures, we are unable to leave our existence to what feels like chance. So we worry it endlessly, which is why we are also religious.

Yet when we think about religion at all these days, we do not tend to regard it as an account of humanity's inveterate uneasiness in the world. We are most inclined to suppose that it is some sort of positive, exclusive representation of what we cannot see or prove, that is, the absolute nature of things as it affects us in this life—a metaphysical statement variously credible, variously mythic or symbolic, to which we adhere devoutly or thoughtlessly in some degree of "implicit faith." Seen in this narrow, prejudicial way, religion is indeed ideology, a perverse frame of thought by which we situate ourselves in the world to hopeful and ruinous effect, precisely because we refuse to distinguish our religious notions from the truth. For as the rationalist bias runs, truth is the sole prerogative of science and its emulators, which is one reason why Marx and Freud insist on calling their explanations of our predicament by that name, although they address the human subject no less evaluatively than religion or philosophy, and no more rigorously or systematically. But as anthropologists have kept reminding us in recent years, there isn't an *essential* difference between "civil" and "savage" modes of thought—between "science," "religion," and "magic" so-called. Their distinction is real, but it must be argued in other terms than axiomatic truth, and not in such a way as to bolster once again the delusion of one's superiority over the other.

Be that as it may, most humane sciences are religious in one undeniable respect, namely, that their concern lies with the obscure causes of our condition. For even when we dignify human being by making our own effects the grand object of inquiry, there is the lurking suggestion that our study aims to repair something gone awry with our world—something that still keeps us poised and uncertain here. In different respects, Empson's writings and Milton studies in general could be said to acknowledge this congenital need for reparation, each wanting to dispel their own discomfort at what they read, as well as any injustice this uneasiness may have promoted toward its ostensible cause. Mind you, I am not suggesting that the offense we take at what Milton or Empson argue in itself justifies or refutes what they say. I want only to ensure that the difficulty their ideas or language poses does not lead us to restrict our criticism to the authors alone. For it should also make us reflect on the sources of uneasiness in ourselves: that is, we should not only be scrutinizing what we suppose to be Milton's justice or Empson's truth, but in turn what exactly it is *we* expect these things to be and with what justification. Of course, such self-consciousness is irony's art; and in *Paradise Lost* it compels us to consider not simply what John Milton thinks is right and true, good and just (as though this were something perfectly feasible to know in itself), but equally to reflect upon what we ourselves assume them to be and how it is that we continue to be surprised by sin. Empson takes some pains to make this fact clear—that critics have always felt thrown back upon themselves by Milton's poem, for the simple reason that it has the temerity to represent God. And representing God, we feel, entails nothing short of asserting God's own truth (although, if we look again, Milton himself never quite proposes that for his poem). It is as if *Paradise Lost* were to say, without preface or apology: *this* is the nature of deity and the essential order of things, *this* the shape of history, *this* the nature of man and particularly womankind, *this* the extent of knowledge we should seek, *this* the type of polity to which we should conform. Because the poem is almost inordinately intellectual, looks as though it were defining universal order, and relies upon a primal religious myth to do its business, we respond to *Paradise Lost* not as we would to art or fiction or any such self-mitigating expression, but as though we were in the presence of a philosophical proposition—a truth claim.

In its tendency thus to confound our ideas and expectations, the poem a little resembles its great source in the Judaic scriptures, about which Erich Auerbach has remarked that they too seem to make an exclusive, "tyrannical" demand that we accept their world as objectively, irrevocably the case for us.[3] In other words, by the very nature of their subject, we are bound to read the scriptures as though they legislated our universal condition as human beings, not just their own meaning or the status of believers. And Auerbach describes our trepidation and reluctance in the face of such perceived coercion with a political metaphor Samuel Johnson would appreciate—someone who dreaded *Paradise Lost* as he would God Almighty; that is, Auerbach observes that the Judaic scriptures "seek to subject us, and if we refuse to be subjected we are rebels" to the truth about ourselves.[4] We get something like this impression from Milton's poem—that there is a comparable stake in his justifying, that his truth allows us no choice but submission or offense because of what we assume him to be doing with it. In 1757, William Wilkie anatomized this offensiveness of *Paradise Lost* from a position to which we are perhaps less alive nowadays:

> This art [of epic poetry] addresses itself chiefly to the imagination, a faculty which apprehends nothing in the way of character that is not human, and according to the analogy of that nature of which we ourselves are conscious. But it would be equally impious and absurd to represent the deity in this manner, and to contrive for him a particular character, and method of acting, agreeable to the prejudices of weak and ignorant mortals. In the early ages of the church, he thought fit to accommodate himself, by such a piece of condescension, to the notions and apprehensions of his creatures: but it would be indecent in any man to use the same freedom, and do that for God, which he only has a right to do for himself. The author of *Paradise Lost* has offended notoriously in this respect; and, though no encomiums are too great for him as a poet, he is justly chargeable with impiety, for presuming to represent the Divine Nature, and the mysteries of religion, according to the narrowness of human prejudice: his dialogues between the Father and the Son; his employing a Being of infinite wisdom in discussing the subtleties of school divinity; the sensual views which he gives of the happiness of heaven, admitting into it, as a part, not only real eating and drinking, but another kind of animal pleasure too by no means more refined: these, and such like circumstances, though perfectly poetical and agreeable to the genius of an art which adapts every thing to the human mode, are, at the same time, so inconsistent with truth, and the exalted ideas which we ought to entertain of divine things, that they must be highly offensive to all such as have just impressions of religion, and would not choose to see a system of doctrine revealed from Heaven, reduced to a state of conformity with heathen superstition.[5]

Wilkie's objections to the poem raise a problem more fundamental to its undertaking than the anthropomorphism of Milton's God, or the notorious materiality of Milton's heaven. For they concern the very place of imaginative art in his kind of religion, where almost any human expression of the scriptural deity cannot but transgress against its prohibition on graven images: that is, we are idolatrous not only in presuming to give a face to the hidden God of Isaiah, but also because we ineluctably make that face like our own, inasmuch as all human representation is drawn from human understanding. And poetry as the idiom most deliberately iconic not only misconceives but flagrantly violates this theological decorum. Implicitly, as Wilkie sees it, the only seemly language for divine things is theology's own—abstract, allusive, and honorific. Nor is he the only critic to think so, since readers from Alexander Pope to David Daiches have bemoaned Milton's tactlessness, his lack of grace or sublimity in representing this God. Indeed, if nothing else, Wilkie's distaste for *Paradise Lost* proves that, for a long time after Milton wrote, the world remained a religious if not a theopathic place, with a deeply reverent sense of how divinity and divine things should be depicted. Yet Milton himself was no folk poet, no religious primitive. So we ought to find it disconcerting that someone of his sophisticated piety would reduce God Almighty to a character in a poem, much less expect us to see deity in the peculiar figure of the Father, who would seem to succeed only in proving Dryden's suspicion that Milton must have been on the side of the devil. Then again, who but John Milton would ever have presumed to do such a thing, as Walter Raleigh remarks: " 'This man cuts us all out, and the Ancients too,' Dryden is reported to have said. But this man intended to do no less, and formally announced his intention. It is impossible to outface Milton, or to abash him with praise."[6]

Never mind that, like nature itself, Raleigh suggests Milton can do nothing in vain, even when he appears to be suborning the one true God to his version of truth. Such egotism only reinforces our impression that *Paradise Lost* intends to subject us, since unlike Wilkie but entirely like Milton himself, we are disinclined to separate his poetic from his theological decorum and are thus unable to extricate Milton's art from his religion. So we associate the great argument of Milton's poem with the speeches of Milton's God, yet are appalled at what ensues for us as readers when we do so, since Milton's God has the effect not only of making his truth unpalatable but also of rendering its justification injurious, intolerable. I need hardly mention that once Empson renewed this question of the poem's difficulty, Stanley Fish, Joseph Summers, Northrop Frye, and Arnold Stein more or less immediately took it up by examining the reflexive character Milton gives his images in *Paradise Lost*. But neither they nor Empson were the first to try to reconcile readerly disdain with consummate artistry in his case: Samuel Johnson's *Life of Milton* was there before them.

More than almost anyone before or since, Dr. Johnson has the uncanny ability to say, without flinching or digressing, whenever Milton's poem strays into the difficult—or what Johnson himself prefers to call the peculiar, the outrageous, or the implausible.[7] That is because Johnson as a critic possesses something like an innate decorum of ideas, a normative sense of how the good and just, the right and true, ought to appear to us. Yet he observes this instinctive classicism in a manner wholly unlike Addison, whose rage for Miltoniana made him the poet's posthumous impresario, not just his apologist. But if Dr. Johnson is devoid of the latter's suavity and self-consequence, not to mention his graciousness (in the sentimental picture of Addison honoring the poet's memory by relieving an indigent Milton daughter),[8] that is because John Milton genuinely disturbs him, with the result that the *Life* is acute, even febrile in its sensitivity to its subject and so endlessly if wrong-headedly perspicacious: "Bossu is of opinion that the poet's first work is to find a *moral*, which his fable is afterwards to illustrate and establish. This seems to have been the process only of Milton: the moral of other poems is incidental and consequent: in Milton's only it is essential and intrinsick. His purpose was the most useful and the most arduous; *to vindicate the ways of God to man*; to shew the reasonableness of religion, and the necessity of obedience to the Divine Law."[9] Johnson evidently departs from Empson in thinking that Milton's "essential and intrinsick" moral is made perfectly clear and obvious to us, an effect created by what he (and many critics after him) describes as a stringent, calculated, almost syllogistic economy of poetic meaning—not a jot or tittle of verse free from the task of justifying God's ways to us. And this should interest us, for Johnson finds *Paradise Lost* a thesis-ridden poem, which may partly explain his sense of its "arduousness," not simply for the poet but for the reader, neither of whom are permitted anything in the way of diversion from its great and painful argument. In *Paradise Lost*, he tells us, we get no gratuitous or at least unencumbered flights of imagination; we have withheld from us the delights of sheerly voluptuous verbalizing; and (anticipating Eliot) we are obliged to forego the pleasures of any passion which is not rational.[10]

What with such an implacable argument, and such a remote and repulsive subject as deity, divine law, and the precipitance of human corruption and death, it is hardly surprising that Johnson would be moved famously to remark that no one ever wished *Paradise Lost* longer than it is: "Its perusal is a duty rather than a pleasure. We read Milton for instruction, retire harassed and overburdened, and look elsewhere for recreation; we desert our master, and seek for companions."[11] Johnson apparently feels about the poem the way Adam and Eve do the Lord's curse: namely, as an indictment operating upon him like necessity. And in such excruciation he speaks for many subsequent readers, who see Milton in Milton's God not so much for what the Father says in condemning his creatures as for how he says it—ruthlessly, intractably, *inhumanely*. Implicitly, Johnson says that we are oppressed by the poem in a fashion not unlike the way Milton in his blindness notoriously oppressed his daughters; that is, we too are placed in involuntary servitude to an obsessive, domineering text which repels our sympathy, if not our entire understanding.

Such readerly durance is the effect Johnson analyzes when he says that the poem's argument is not circumstantially discovered but rather imposed ineluctably upon us, in a relentless amplification of human sinfulness. Seen this way, *Paradise Lost* is scarcely suitable reading for someone of Johnson's poignant and melancholy temper. Yet is Milton's argument really the bitter pill he feels thus obliged to prescribe to us, or does Johnson actually recoil at his own interpretation of the poem? The latter must be true to some extent or other—that despite Milton's supposedly Draconian mastery of his poem's meanings, the dreadfulness of the argument that Dr. Johnson bravely, stoically approves is at least partly the work of his own critical art. Yet I would contend that this sort of displaced, vicarious authorship of *Paradise Lost* by its readers occurs with such strange consistency as to render it a notable literary phenomenon, one worthy of attention and scrutiny. For how could it happen that an argument so patent and tendentious, so doctrinaire and exacting, is susceptible of the utterly un-Miltonic meaning Johnson chooses to give it? Let us allow for the moment that Milton was unlikely to part company entirely with those religious and political opinions to which he devoted the most public portion of his writings through the 1670s, and which, as he considers them true, he associates with the revelation of his God. Let it also be allowed that he intends *Paradise Lost* to perform the work of right understanding or justification of its readers that Milton had declared from early on to be the office of poetry. Yet despite these probabilities, Johnson's version of Milton's life and text manages selectively to convert *Paradise Lost* into a pusillanimous palinode, a recantation for its author's career as an advocate of dissent, republicanism, and regicide. For by Johnson's own account, it was a career spent in the poet's flagrantly defying the more natural and decorous, and presumably kinder and gentler, order of human things which the divine institution of monarchy ordains for us—an outrage Milton perpetrated upon the state and his betters, among his peers, in his home and within his writings.

Moreover, as a high churchman and a royalist, it is Johnson's joke that the person thus coercing daughters and readers alike is a noisy but not a very notable libertarian who tyrannizes over almost everyone, with the sole exception being his copious indulgence of himself. Indeed, in the *Life*, the only real latitude shown to others is exercised not by Milton but by sundry royalists and Charles II especially, who at his restoration forbears to prosecute the poet equally for his manners and his crimes, even as that artful traducer of God and king tries to slink out of justice's reach. And when Johnson gets down to reading *Paradise Lost* itself, he predictably finds the same generosity expressed by that "Supreme King," the title Johnson prefers for Milton's God, who elects to restore an unworthy humanity in a fashion altogether reminiscent of the Stuart noblesse oblige just celebrated. Taken altogether, the *Life* succeeds admirably in showing us a *Paradise Lost* upholding that divine yet reasonable authority, that beneficent paternal power exercised by monarchs toward their subjects, which Milton had slandered in his tracts apparently to his ultimate regret, repenting thoroughly in his own life where his Satan would not. And no doubt because he is a great and subtle classicist, inexorably defining the universal canon of value, Johnson effectively bypasses the peculiar embarrassments of the dissenting poet in favor of God the transcendent king and rational epitome: that is to say, God in a kind of immaculate conception vicariously begets all decorum, truth, and beauty in Dr. Johnson's *Paradise Lost*—vicariously, because Johnson makes the "moral sentiments" of the poem original to the supernal author of Genesis, and so exempt from the taint of Milton's nonconformist views.[12]

It follows that whatever Johnson finds good about the poem, he finds good about English monarchy and the Anglican God, such that the poet becomes their virtual amanuensis. And what he condemns in the conduct of the poem is what he predictably abhors in Milton himself, which is that willful idiosyncrasy and self-indulgence, that want of proper deference to the authority of nature and custom, and—although Johnson can almost bring himself to applaud its effects—that "uniform peculiarity of *Diction*, a mode and cast of expression which bears little resemblance to that of any former writer, and which is so far removed from common use, that an unlearned reader, when he first opens his book, finds himself surprised by a new language."[13] For reasons not entirely distinct from the classical unity of aesthetic, moral, and political value, Johnson allocates to Milton all blame for his poem's perversities and innovations, while praising Genesis for its sublimity and truth, from which (he concludes) piety alone prevented the poet's deviating. It is Milton's personal flaws which create *Paradise Lost*'s errors of expression, although these are not so grievous as to mar irretrievably the poem and its putative moral; only the man is beyond the pale (as Eliot concurs). But man and text are clearly a source of unease for Johnson, compelling him to reconcile the poem's indubitable achievement with his aversion to its author. For when they are kept inseparable in the way Milton most probably intends (given all the autobiographical excursus linking his political to his poetic professions), then *Paradise Lost* constitutes a real threat and affront to Johnson's ideas—precisely because he supposes Milton to be offering up God's own truth. Of course, this enthusiastic presumption on Milton's part would be nothing if the poem he wrote weren't itself too considerable an object to be dismissed by someone of Johnson's taste and intelligence. But as it stands, the sheer marvelousness of *Paradise Lost* requires him to engage in some vindicating of his own.

So he sets about saving the appearances of Milton's poem in order that its stature lends legitimacy to neither the regicide nor its author's theological opinions nor Cromwellian policy more generally, but instead proves the necessity of obedience against Milton himself, whose incorrigible dissent from the decorous and the true is used to separate the poem from the poet's errors. And while Johnson thus diverts the ingenious artistry and vast intellectual apparatus of *Paradise Lost* into the service of a conforming God and king, in the same breath he damns Milton himself for a lifetime of practices "founded in an envious hatred of greatness, and a sullen desire of independence; in petulance impatient of controul, and pride disdainful of superiority."[14] And with this lesson for the attentive reader: that John Milton in life offers a truer fable about human presumption than even *Paradise Lost*, as someone whom study never made pleasant or wise, whose justification of God's ways recoils back upon himself, and whose fixed and unrelenting mind could not preserve him from self-contradiction, or what is worse, impudence.

I offer Samuel Johnson's unease with the poem and his attempts to obviate his discomfort for a number of reasons, first if not foremost because his version of *Paradise Lost* flies utterly in the face of that self-justification to which we usually regard Milton as bound by the fact of the Stuart restoration in 1660. Read in this light, the poem can still be understood as a sort of roman à clef, but in a different sense than Dr. Johnson intends. As Alisdair MacIntyre has had occasion to put the case—and with as little sympathy as Johnson himself could wish—this different vindication entails a Milton "who does not have to justify the ways of God to man in general, but has to reconcile the hidden fact that God rules with the manifest fact that Charles II rules and the saints do not."[15] In thus ridiculing what he presumes to be Milton's professed intimacy with eternal providence—that is, given the poet's failures in the way of merely ordinary prediction—MacIntyre reasserts the anomaly which our own contradictory readings of *Paradise Lost* nicely expose. For how is it possible that a poem whose argument Johnson and others critics regard as so blatantly, unforgivingly manifest, could produce such conflicting accounts of its purpose and significance?

Notwithstanding the lengths to which critical invention can go, the answer, I think, is twofold. On the one hand, we are variously inclined to identify the poem's predicament with its author's disappointments—loss of Eden with the demise of Cromwell, Independency, and the promise of commonwealth—given Milton's fondness for intruding his own circumstances on our notice whatever he might happen to be talking about at the time. (This is of course to overlook the fact that Milton's epic argument appears to have been in the making for twenty years or more.) On the other hand, this mutual project of justification conducted by Milton and Milton's God permits us to presume that *Paradise Lost* represents figurally what its author would have us take as the truth about particular personal and contemporary events. In other words, it tells us how we are supposed to view not only universal providence but also the specific history in which Milton took part. Encouraged by such motives as well as Milton's frequent topicality of expression, we come to expect from the poem an allegory of Milton's own position, even where as critics we may refrain from casting the allegory in those precise terms. But as literally an alternate or "other" sort of meaning from the usual sense we give words, allegory can neatly accommodate the apparent necessity of justifying Milton's own loss and failure, as it can equally fulfill our expectation that *Paradise Lost* expounds a positive and universal truth about human relations with the divine. For it is perfectly possible to speak at once figurally and exactly about the world: such is logic's own imperative, as well as the aesthetic fault which the last two hundred years of criticism have found with allegory as an expressive mode. But our readiness to detect such autobiography does not require that Milton himself adopt a transparently allegorical and supposedly inferior poetic: indeed, there is a pronounced and somewhat excessive resistance to reading more than a few sections of *Paradise Lost* in this way.

Instead, the allegory of the poet's private justification is largely kept interpretive by his critics, a significance discreetly argued off Milton's page, not on it, as though the poet had adopted a new and uncharacteristic reserve about the parallels between his own predicament and what he writes. And once dislodged or liberated from its evident sense by this allegorical potential, *Paradise Lost* can be made available to any number of exclusive and extreme constructions of Milton's argument, which it has sustained over the years no less handsomely than it does Johnson's version. Out of respect for the poem or at least its reputation, other readers than Johnson have felt compelled to edit, ignore, displace, and allegorize whatever comes between the meaning of *Paradise Lost* and their preferred understanding of it, especially if they too are made uncomfortable by what it seems to say, or what its critics claim for it. Taking Dr. Johnson as a precedent, this can result in critics addressing only as much of the poem as suits their own ideas of truth. (Johnson's refusal to follow Milton into heaven, while a decorous omission, has the interpretive advantage of leaving the supreme king and his dubious speeches unexamined and unchallenged.)[16] The "essential and intrinsick" moral of *Paradise Lost* can then freely project the widely diverging ideas and interests of its readers, with interpretation serving as a blind for the poem's real difficulties and Milton himself assuming the protean and frequently apologetic guise of Thomist, Cabbalist, aristocrat, Cartesian, sectarian, poststructuralist, Platonist, animist materialist, Ramist, Kantian, and so forth. The sheer variety and volubility of Milton's transformations again force us back upon his poem's peculiar distinction: namely, its perplexing amenability to the vagaries of interpretation, despite our presumption that it tells a positive, unequivocal truth.

But if allegory can effectively bowdlerize the sense of a text, the presumption of irony can just as easily deracinate it, since irony argues an ambivalence or instability of meaning with something like the same metamorphic effect as allegory, and very likely the same ulterior motive—our desire not to be made uneasy by the order of truth Milton is thought to assert in *Paradise Lost*. Thus the critic may undertake to reconcile or oppose the poem's ostensible argument by referring it to extrinsic forces superior to Milton's own intention and control, and for that matter, his readers'. I mean logical, psychological, historical, cultural, economic forces maneuvering subliminally or symbolically within the text to orchestrate its contradiction. Yet after Dr. Johnson's fashion, this is once more to divide the express argument of *Paradise Lost* from its "essential and intrinsick" moral, and thus to exonerate or damn Milton and whatever sense of the poem we find difficult or offensive. Given their promiscuous use, these two figural modes may seem to differ little from each other, in that they both discount the evident meaning of an expression to implicate another order entirely of significance and understanding.[17] Moreover, each trope depends upon some anomaly or incongruity attending that expression to alert us to its presence, and so resolve the seeming incoherence of meaning that initially signaled this new, unexpected sense. Yet if allegory expands the possible meanings of a text, irony tends to make us reflect upon the phenomenon of polysemia itself, not so much perplexing the significance to which we presume—the proper work of allegory—as the conditions contriving to foster any such presumption: where allegory complicates the sense of what we read, irony criticizes the very ways we are accustomed to make sense at all. As Kenneth Burke observes, such sophistications of meaning are frequently the product of highly conventional cultures, where every person can detect the slightest deviation in usage: then

equivocality is more apparent than real, a function of certitude, not its opposite.[18] Irony becomes witty antithesis—a superior conversance with what is
taken for truth, which in turn promotes a certain freedom or fluency with received ideas, as well as a special dignity of understanding for the ironist not
unlike that which the hierophantics of allegory can bestow. And Milton's critics
often assume this dignity, as allegorists disclosing the occult meanings of *Paradise Lost*, or ironists sophisticating or confounding its apparent sense.

DESCRIPTION AS SOLUTION

But it is also the case that irony and allegory can express the human difficulties
of meaning without purporting to resolve them by contradiction or hermetica.
Tragedy, for example, does this when it represents an action at once symbolic
and self-reflexive, where mimesis gets its force not from the depiction of fatal
events as such, but from how humanity conspires with the nature of things to
make them so for us. The art of tragedy lies in rightly representing a problem,
that is, how the train of contingency and misunderstanding can transform what
is humanly right, just, and true into fate, catastrophe, suffering, evil. As Vernant
and Vidal-Naquet observe:

> The tragic consciousness of responsibility appears when the human and
> divine levels are sufficiently distinct for them to be opposed while still
> appearing to be inseparable. The tragic sense of responsibility emerges
> when human action becomes the object of reflection and debate while still
> not being regarded as sufficiently autonomous to be fully self-sufficient.
> The particular domain of tragedy lies in this border zone where human
> actions hinge on divine powers and where their true meaning, unsuspected
> by even those who initiated them and take responsibility for them, is only
> revealed when it becomes a part of an order that is beyond man and es-
> capes him.[19]

Yet the very activity of this representation and its sympathetic impact on the
audience argues against the tragic dilemma as our own necessity. These narratives are enacted not because they are humanly ineluctable but because they
can be made to be, if we are not brought to a better understanding of what it
means to be human—of the actual predicament in which we collectively find
ourselves. The Delphic dictum "know yourself" does not enjoin us to individualism but to an acknowledgment of our common nature and, as Werner Jaeger
observes, how we are circumscribed and confounded by our mortality.[20] He then
comments that a delimited human being is a religious recognition even as
human suffering is a religious problem, which is to say that the understanding
commanded by the Delphic god and proffered us by tragedy delineates the extreme boundaries of rationality, where explanation and transcendence are
brought not simply to an impasse but to an insuperable conflict. But an antagonistic god is not their only conclusion: our misconceived humanity is the other.
For the hubris or outrageousness of the tragic protagonist offends not only

against a jealous deity, but against the human nature whose predicament it neglects as well. Tragic excess arises from this neglect, which Homer understands as "thoughtlessness," "recklessness"—an obliviousness to the implications of one's choices. Indeed, the person who acts out of hubris is no less mad than the one suffering from *ate*—insanity or delusion; in what they do, they both express the human paradox of pursuing the good and true only to create the most profound disorder.

Of course, just knowing the tragic myth makes possible a different fate for audience as against protagonist. It places us in an ironic relation to the choices we see enacted, kept by that single prohibitive knowledge from simply assimilating the spectacle—as we might very well do were the protagonist's predicament ours. Yet through the power of myth and mimesis, it is almost made our own, since these at once conceptual and expressive arts engage us with the action in such a way as intimately to grasp the appeal—the seemingly indubitable rightness, justice, beauty—of those choices. Thus the tragic action simultaneously immerses us in and protects us from the misunderstanding in which we ourselves participate as human beings, and tragedy itself becomes a justification not entirely unlike the legal or logical variety. For it too proposes to restore the audience to truth—to a right understanding of our world. But where logic assumes that this justification has a single, definitive, and (formally) necessary sense, and where positive law lays claim to its evidence and conclusiveness, tragedy does not do away with our difficulties. Instead, it locates justification in the acknowledgment and understanding of conflict itself. No less than philosophy in Plato's sense, tragedy is *psychagogia*, a leading of the soul by which actors and audience alike are justified, insofar as we can be brought by a certain order of representation to admit the human nature which, in all its irreducible complexity, both ennobles and condemns us. But the sense of this understanding is neither single, positive, necessary, or self-evident, since it consists in a circumstantial appreciation of the conflict we ourselves foment. This is to say nothing more than that tragic meaning is dialectical, as we all know: it does not belong to one or other of the positions—sceptical or rhapsodic— in which the action places us but in the relationship between the two, as a proper account of human being.

To that extent, right understanding in tragedy has an affinity with Wittgenstein's much-maligned statement in the *Investigations* that philosophy "leaves everything as it is" (*PI* p.124).[21] Certainly, this is Martha Nussbaum's point when she takes as an epigraph to her own discussion of tragedy the following comments from *Zettel*, which may serve to clarify this typical remark:[22] "the difficulty—I might say—is not that of finding the solution but rather that of recognizing as the solution something that looks as if it were only preliminary to it. . . . This is connected, I believe, with our wrongly expecting an explanation, whereas the solution of the difficulty is a description, if we give it the right place in our considerations. If we dwell upon it, and do not try to get beyond it. The difficulty here is to stop."[23] Rather than seeking the solution in a fix or cause, Wittgenstein would have us find it in describing the dilemma itself: this

is "solution" understood as elucidation—resolving a problem into its constit-
uents and their relations, the better to understand what the conflict entails,
with the goal as full and circumstantial a representation as possible.[24] We make
this description a solution when we use it to grasp where we actually stand—
what is "natural" to this position, by which Wittgenstein tends to mean integral
to our condition as human beings. He sees the practice of meaning as fundamental to humanity in just this way, but also peculiarly indicative of its character—an aspect of our existence exemplary of the whole. That is why, in the
Investigations, he goes on to argue that "Philosophy may in no way interfere
with the actual use of language; it can in the end only describe it. For it cannot
give it any foundation either" (*PI* p.124).

But, as he says, the rub is that our peculiar misunderstanding of language
keeps us from stopping there, because we persist in trying to regulate how words
mean in a manner wholly incongruous with the ways they actually work. Indeed, the rationality we like to cultivate effectively blinds us to our own behavior, aggravating by its solutions the crisis of meaning it has already fomented in
our usage—a compound confusion Wittgenstein calls being "entangled in our
own rules" (*PI* p.125). And as Stanley Cavell has shown, the self-imposed contradiction that inevitably arises between our "natural" practice and our "rational" theory gives scepticism its fateful impetus and tragic outcome, where we
are condemned to suffer the perpetual insufficiency not just of human meaning
but of human being to our affected notions of truth. Wittgenstein would have
it that we cannot escape this endlessly repetitive doom until we get "a clear
view" of the situation promoting it, and he argues that philosophical representation ought to supply that view in describing the modalities of human meaning. For such a description properly done would show us in turn how our analysis
is not simply inconsistent but incommensurate with our usage, thus exposing
the self-disguised entanglements of our ideas:

> A main source of our failure to understand is that we do not *command a
> clear view* of the use of our words.—Our grammar is lacking in this sort of
> perspicuity. A perspicuous representation produces just that understanding
> which consists in 'seeing connexions.' Hence the importance of finding
> and inventing *intermediate cases.*
>
> The concept of a perspicuous representation is of fundamental signifi-
> cance for us. It earmarks the form of account we give, the way we look at
> things. (Is this a 'Weltanschauung'?)
>
> A philosophical problem has the form: "I don't know my way about."
> (*PI* p.122–23)

Again, these "perspicuous representations" do not supply causes or foundations
for our verbal habits, in keeping with one sense of justification as implementing
a rigorous formal procedure or criteria for conceptual practice. Instead, "description" treats the variable activity of meaning as something precedent to our
understanding—a congenital attribute of human being ultimately groundless,

seemingly arbitrary and abhorrent to scepticism on that precise account. For philosophical scepticism argues that our expressions cannot be meaningful until they are properly rationalized, which of course it performs by adducing a set of criteria oblivious and so antipathetic to the circumstances surrounding their use. And its insistence on fulfilling these criteria succeeds only in obfuscating, to the point of paralyzing, an otherwise effectual if necessarily imperfect human practice of making sense.

Yet in analytic scepticism's obdurate refusal to accept any order of meaning but the one it imagines, Wittgenstein recognizes a profound human preference and expectation of how things *should* mean, encouraged by a symptomatic misreading of language's own myths. For the sceptic assumes that language simply and directly states what is the case with words, never suspecting that an altogether different operation of meaning obtains not only in human usage but in human grammar—in the very way language organizes its elements and idioms. To probe this entirely captivating but obtuse expectation, which is not limited to philosophical scepticism alone, the *Investigations* orchestrates a virtual anthropology of our semantic beliefs, customs, and behaviors. Or as Wittgenstein himself puts it: "What we are supplying are really remarks on the natural history of human beings; we are not contributing curiosities however, but observations which no one has doubted, but which have escaped remark *only because they are always before our eyes*" (*PI* p.415, my emphasis). So his "natural history" attends to just those familiar but unexamined circumstances of human meaning which rationalism blithely ignores, in order to gain the "clear" but equally "instrumental" view he recommends. For "What we call '*descriptions*' are instruments for particular uses": "Think," he says, "of a machine-drawing, a cross-section, an elevation with measurements, which an engineer has before him" (*PI* p.291).

Given the scope of the crisis scepticism more engenders than anticipates, jeopardizing not only the integrity but the viability of human meaning, Wittgenstein advises us first to secure this "instrumental description" of our usage before we try to proceed in any direction. Needless to say, the *Investigations* has already been engaged in representing it; for the descriptive kind of justification Wittgenstein advocates consists in such an "instrument," where right understanding refers not to any one formal protocol of meaning but to an account of the circumstances obtaining when we actually engage in that activity. Or to put the difference another way, this "description" in no way revises the vexed conditions of human meaning; it revises how we think about them. So while it may appear "preliminary" to the problem in the way Wittgenstein warns, that is because the description itself resolves the human issue, if not the human predicament of meaning which scepticism feels so acutely and so tellingly misconceives. And it does so by disclosing another coherence and viability to our practice than that expected, much less allowed by the rational paradigm scepticism assumes only to explode by its own analysis, chronically scandalized by the obstinate fact that language does not behave as it should. And the anthropology of the *Investigations* is designed precisely to effect this revelation, being comprised of an open-ended series of reluctant discoveries and astonishing encounters in which we are invited to see the oddities and incommensurables of our familiar assumptions of meaning. More particularly, Wittgenstein's speaker enacts for us the rationalist mythology our culture invents and to which it now appears strangely enthralled, in the process elucidating the human actualities of signification which we enthusiastically suppress. Thus in the ordinary-made-fantastic landscape of "intermediate cases," we discover the unexpected novelty of slabs, beetles in boxes, boiling pots and the aroma of coffee; tribes that ascribe pain solely to inanimate things and pity dolls, that only think aloud, that function entirely without the idea of a human soul; lions that recognizably yet unintelligibly talk, parrots conversing when there is a God around; simple line drawings that behave altogether eccentrically. Each event pictures an aspect of our verbal practice or our misunderstanding of it, so as to enact Wittgenstein's account of meaning and its moral entailments—especially the cost in human terms of our fond ideas.

It follows that the configuration given these conceptual events implies a certain mentality or subjectivity ("the form of account we give, the way we look at things"), self-alienated from its own expressive nature, unable to find its way about yet convinced that the confusion lies not in its own assumptions and procedures but instead in the incorrigibility of human being. For the speaker addresses his "perspicuous representation" to the sceptic's immense and recalcitrant disappointment in the world, to both dispel the confusion and alleviate the suffering attending it. As Wittgenstein observes, "The problems arising through a misinterpretation of our forms of language have the character of *depth*. They are deep disquietudes; their roots are as deep in us as the forms of our language and their significance is as great as the importance of our language" (*PI* p.111). This is not to suggest that the human predicament exemplified in language is essentially tragic in nature, but that it *can be experienced as* a tragedy—the consequence of approaching language in a particularly insistent way (the way language invites by its own self-portrait). Insofar as we persist in both denying and misprising how language practically works, so we will continue to find the world it creates a disturbing, even unconscionable, place.

So the "perspicuous representation" which the *Investigations* gives is a parabolic action involving speaker, sceptic, and reader, as well as a justification in tragedy's manner. For it also aims to dramatize the nature of our perplexities about meaning, and not to discount them—on the contrary, by profoundly imagining these confusions, to understand and express scepticism's indignant doubt. In his preface, Wittgenstein adopts (not altogether inadvertently) a Miltonic idiom to convey his dubious hopes for text and humanity together, and almost as an afterthought, his dislike of being misrepresented by any words other than his own: "It is not impossible that it should fall to the lot of this work, in its poverty and the darkness of this time, to bring light into one brain or another—but, of course, it is not likely" (*PI* vi). There is thus some relation between the occasion moving him to publish the *Investigations* in 1946 and what the text itself contains, which is not an answer or solution to those circumstances but an account of them. As he says, "I should not like my writing to spare other people the trouble of thinking. But, if possible, to stimulate someone to thoughts of his own" (*PI* vi). In this justification, we do not end in the firm possession of truth as if it were a positive and portable property; we are offered instead a picture of language that might eventually conduce to truth, that is, if we can unlearn our conceptual *habitus* and live without the appealing idea of meaning's lapidary precision and luminous simplicity.

The *Investigations* treats this philosophical conflict as a mimesis—indeed, the representation of a conceptual passage that Wittgenstein himself has made, but that he ascribes recursively to the speaker and his sceptical interlocutor, much as Milton does both with that anomalous epic voice and the Satan of *Paradise Lost*. Again I return to the point Cavell makes decisive in his own work, with both Wittgenstein and tragedy: it is these tacit protagonists who perform "long and involved journeyings" from opposed yet sympathetic positions; they who project and traverse the ideational "landscapes" comprised of the text's remarks; they who face each place's unexpected yet reorienting inhabitants (*PI* v). And in the manner of every protagonist, the vicissitudes of their travels—"over a wide field of thought criss-cross in every direction"—and their responses to what they find implicate not only the peculiar purpose of their journeying, but also the larger human predicament for which this exploration stands. As in parable, the process is therapeutic as against conclusive; surprise is the only eventuality that the text provides, for there is no end. Instead, we are simply left with the predicament the *Investigations* ingeniously engages, in the hope that the twists and turns of reading will allow us to understand it anew. I must add that Wittgenstein does not expect his allegory of thwarted assumptions and disconcerting revelations punctually to reconcile us to his version of human affairs; for the sceptic's tragedy clearly distinguishes between listening and understanding—again, like scriptural parable. On the contrary, the *Investigations* does not attempt formally to vindicate the human conditions of meaning; but it describes their difficulty in such a way that we may be enabled to say, with Wittgenstein's speaker, if not his sceptic, "Now I can go on."

Even as this expression captures the vantage of our first parents as they slowly, elegiacally descend from Eden into the open world, so I will argue that Milton provides just such an instrumental description—a justification by parable—of human meanings in *Paradise Lost*: indeed, such a description inheres in all his writings. And I make this argument not only, like Wittgenstein, to link the contradictions holding sway in the field to the way we read Milton's words. I do it because the idea of meaning and the idea of deity have always been mutual and mutually entangled, especially for scripturalists like Milton himself and the Protestant reformers, Luther and Calvin. There is something precisely perspicuous for Milton in Wittgenstein's own debt to Luther, both conceptually and in his resonant term "grammar," which is owing in no little part to the latter's

1535 lectures on Galatians.[25] There Luther talks about theology entailing a new and special kind of grammar; and Wittgenstein himself famously observes in the *Investigations* that "*Essence* is expressed by grammar," for "Grammar tells what kind of object anything is. (Theology as grammar)" (*PI* p.371, 373). Of course, the point that grammar expresses "essence" is an ironical one, since Wittgenstein holds that we are incapable of knowing anything *essentially*. Indeed, "essence" is what Thomas Hobbes would call "an idol of the brain," a figure or expression out of which we conjure an entity. He ascribes this conceptual confusion originally to the idolatrous gentiles, who "did vulgarly conceive the Imagery of the brain, for things really subsistent without them, and not dependent on the fancy; and out of them framed their opinions of *Daemons*, Good and Evill; which because they seemed to subsist really, they called *Substances*; and because they could not feel them with their hands, *Incorporeall*."[26] Afterwards, he continues, this "pagan" pathology of meaning infected the Jews in their Diaspora and, with the rise of Aristotelianism, was communicated through the distortions of scriptural commentary to the credulous modern world. Hobbes can accordingly attribute the civil and intellectual crimes of scholastic philosophy (both Catholic and Protestant) to the same hapless abuse of words that confounded the ancients: the abundant propagation of mental figments which are given a demonic because objective existence. So, at the very end of *Leviathan*, he consigns the lot to "The Kingdome of Darknesse," a conceptual miasma of course nominally inhabited by phantasms, idols, images, figures—in Hobbes's canon, things that are not.

However one regards Hobbes's version of the causes of the British civil war, the role he gives this idolatrous propensity in *Leviathan* anticipates Wittgenstein's comparable concern that we are forever wanting to treat abstract terms as though they signified substantives of the same order as bodies in space.[27] From different positions, both Hobbes and Wittgenstein argue that we habitually misconceive this species of word, and in a way detrimental to more than verbal sense. Indeed, for Hobbes, our perverse usage goes a long way toward explaining how the Presbyterians could claim England honorifically for the scriptural God, though really for themselves. In religion, Luther would say this delusive objectifying arises from the suppressed fact that "God" and "truth" or "meaning" (for him, the theological kind) are *res non apparentes*, things that do not appear as such, after Hebrews 11:1: "faith is the assurance of things hoped for, the conviction of things not seen."[28] And the difficulty peculiar to *res non apparentes* is that their inevidence surreptitiously signifies more than mere invisibility: it implicates a kind of existence ineffably distinct from those things which mediate this incommensurable life to us. For if such an alien dimension to the world can only be known and understood according to its mediations, at that same time those mediations cannot signify as they seem to do since they are invariably antipathetic to their subject. Indeed, religious language in Luther confounds us like language more largely does in the *Investigations*: we assume an easy correspondence, an evident continuity of kind between an expression's familiar and religious usages, where Luther argues there is none.

Religious *invisibilia*, he insists, must be understood in an unaccustomed fashion if they are to make any sustained sense, a circumstance we only discover when—in our world, in the scriptural text, or in the relations we argue between them—we experience deity's self-revelation as incongruous, conflicted, contradictory, unjust.

For Luther himself, such an event was fomented by a phrase of Paul's—"the righteousness of God"—which he had been taught to understand as the righteousness by which deity punishes the wicked: "For in [the gospel] the righteousness of God is revealed through faith for faith; as it is written, 'He who through faith is righteous shall live' " (Romans 1:17). Despite Luther's passionate religious commitment, these words engendered in him only an equally violent despair since he had no felt conviction that, with all his pious labors, he was adequate to this God's acceptance. What with the intensifying sensations of his own spiritual futility, Paul's words had the perverse effect of making him hate the blind and brutal God to whom, it would seem, he had all but unaccountably devoted himself:

> I did not love, yes, I hated the righteous God who punishes sinners, and secretly, if not blasphemously, certainly murmuring greatly, I was angry with God, and said, "As if, indeed, it is not enough, that miserable sinners, eternally lost through original sin, are crushed by every kind of calamity by the law of the decalogue, without having God add pain to pain by the gospel and also by the gospel threatening us with his righteousness and wrath!" Thus I raged with a fierce and troubled conscience. Nevertheless, I beat importunately upon Paul at that place, most ardently desiring to know what St. Paul wanted.[29]

Simply put, Luther's anger and despair arise from his inability to tolerate the received meaning of the phrase "righteousness of God." For he cannot reconcile with his own experience, his own sense of what is right, the sort of justice deity imposes on humanity in this understanding of Paul's words. Indeed, he finds the "truth" scripture would seem to propound humanly unintelligible, since the phrase so construed works not to assuage but to exacerbate our suffering as "miserable sinners." Implicitly, this is the consequence of pursuing a certain clarity or precision for deity's self-expressions: that is, the scholastic exegetes of scripture handle its language as though each word *meant* in a void, without any regard either for the context of statement or for their reading's human viability—an approach wholly at odds with the stated intent of the gospel, as Luther complains. Thus a conflict arises between the sense obliviously assigned Paul's phrase and the morality, the justice of that meaning, where the actual effect of the verse countermands its supposed claims: in short, the existential incoherence of Romans precipitates in Luther a crisis of faith. And just as that crisis has both grammatical and psychological symptoms, where a given reading is productive only of the most extreme mental anguish (anguish so extreme and overwhelming that it becomes a formal element of Luther's theology), so does its solution:

At last, by the mercy of God, meditating day and night, I gave heed to the context of the words, namely, "In it the righteousness of God is revealed, as it is written, 'He who through faith is righteous shall live.' " There I began to understand that the righteousness of God is that by which the righteous lives by a gift of God, namely by faith. And this is the meaning: the righteousness of God is revealed by the gospel, namely, the passive righteousness with which merciful God justifies us by faith, as it is written, "He who through faith is righteous shall live." Here I felt that I was altogether born again and had entered paradise itself through open gates. There a totally other face of the entire Scripture showed itself to me.[30]

The appalling incongruity of sense with experience moves Luther to attend to more than the phrase alone, namely, to the actual circumstances of its use, "the context of the words." And this interpretive maneuver results in a "perspicuous representation," a description which is also a solution in Wittgenstein's manner.

When Luther no longer approaches Paul's words as though their meaning were severally distinguished like the picture of bodies in space—single, discrete, and absolute—the verse has entirely another look for him. It no longer argues an unbearable antagonism between God and humanity, but an affinity achieved in the very act of reading scripture, whose newly intelligible meaning operates circumstantially, contingently, and so surprisingly. For once pervaded by this peculiarly inevident order of divine revelation, the ordinary assumes "a totally other face," which is to say that the Pauline expression gains the human viability it had catastrophically lacked. And this sensation of moving from the conflicted to the meaningful feels salvific to Luther, as if he "had entered paradise itself through open gates." The shift in his religious position is vast and almost beyond words, yet it is an interpretive creation, simultaneous with the sudden onset of the text's coherence and his own relief. For the received reading of Paul's phrase, in its semantic equation of words to things, ignores a critical contingency in the text—"He who through faith is righteous shall live"—and the force of this contingency thoroughly reorders the sense of Romans, in keeping with a certain grammatical usage, the Hebrew genitive:

Thereupon I ran through the Scriptures from memory. I also found in other terms an analogy, as, the work of God, that is, what God does in us, the power of God, with which he makes us strong, the wisdom of God, with which he makes us wise, the strength of God, the salvation of God, the glory of God.

And I extolled my sweetest word with a love as great as the hatred with which I had before hated the word "righteousness of God." Thus that place in Paul was for me truly the gate to paradise.[31]

So rather than proposing impossibly to match human to divine value, to trade human actions for God's as though these were commensurate, even fungible, scripture relates through our speech and history the groundless, redemptive movement of the divine toward humanity in a second creation, making us what we are not. Scriptural expressions thus come to signify in a new and extraordinary way a significance which Luther himself undergoes like theophany—the strange yet illuminating force of divine intent in human experience. For by their very incoherence with the usual sense we assume for ourselves and our world, these expressions implicate a meaning at once inevident and inordinate, whose reference is not the nature of God per se but the quality of God's attitude toward us. That reference Luther elsewhere distinguishes as "the will of His good pleasure" in a sense deliberately paradoxical to scholastic usage, as signifying deity's gratuitous, salvific intent in the Christ—"the one and only view of the Divinity that is available and possible in this life" (*LW* 2:49). In effect, these expressions provide an account of the relation between creature and creator, pictured as a profound distinction in the order of scriptural meaning itself. This is what Luther means by his being "born again": the shift in meaning is felt to be the virtual sensation of faith itself, and thus a palpable revolution— a conversion, that is—in our standing before God.

Moreover, in the moment the text of scripture is reconfigured, no longer terrible but sweetly reassuring to Luther, so deity itself assumes another aspect— this time as a loving God, not a hateful one. Luther's struggle with the sense of Romans, then, does not end in the seeming impasse between religious profession and human experience; for its difficulty and its authority mutually require him to seek a description resolving this incoherence—a justification. And while we might cynically assume the expedience of such justifying—that it will result in an incomplete or opportunistic reading—the opposite actually occurs. Luther's revised understanding takes more rather than less of the text into account, including the fact of its difficulty; nor is the Hebrew genitive a mere device but a real grammatical possibility foreclosed by the restrictive order of meaning on which its interpreters had previously insisted. The point fundamental to this hermeneutical episode is Luther's assumption, in the face of such soul-destroying difficulty, that God's words must be meaningful, must be true. He shares this assumption with Wittgenstein, whose sense of language as a natural and so practical, functional aspect of human being ensures his comparable reluctance either to rest in the contradiction raised by scepticism or to accept its merely arbitrary solution. For both of them, the trial of incoherence is not to be proved against language itself but against its interpreters, who are inclined to refuse any order of meaning that conflicts with their own conceptual customs, no matter the human suffering that ensues. Since human egoism automatically assigns primacy to its notions alone, we must be chastened by contradiction if we are to relinquish them.

But where the problem of meaning lies with us, the marvelous thing about its solution in Luther's account is that we are not led by this difficulty into sophistications like the epicycles of the planets—as Raphael says, building and unbuilding in order to save not so much the appearances as our preferred relation to them. Once the change in our position has taken place, we see this revision as simple in itself. It is because we are infatuated with a single idea of truth that any revolution in our assumptions feels like an arduous and fearful conflict, a challenge to our very being; that is, we want to believe in a certain immediacy, elegance, precision, and self-evidence to our perceptions of the world, because these dignify our position in it. Their quality tacitly reflects the tenor of human understanding and human being, which is why we often fail to notice that what appear to be superb explanations cannot account for the mundane facts of our experience. By exposing the discrepancy between our practice of knowledge and our representations of it, scepticism of course handily dispatches that fond idea of truth. Yet the sceptic frequently persists in the assumption that right understanding must nonetheless have the same qualities thus denied to knowledge "as we have it," in Francis Bacon's wry phrase. Indeed, the sceptical critique itself solicits just these appearances, and for the very same reason—that they commend its analysis and our megalomania. So Luther's historic break isn't with scripture or the God of that text, but with a certain interpretive egoism and conceptual infatuation which dismiss, as an abuse of meaning, whatever does not fit its preferred model. And in banishing any other possibility of significance, it banishes all the world and deity itself from human understanding.

By contrast, the different model of *res non apparentes*, in which God, truth, mind, faith, significance, and such *invisibilia* resist our expectations of meaning, requires us to rethink where we stand relative to these things as well as the way we suppose religious experience to signify. We cannot find ourselves reflected in the world in the same way as before, because understanding is no longer held captive to our own inflated demands for significance. Humanity is still the maker of meaning, if only because we must be responsible to our predicament; but that predicament implicates another relationship altogether to this practice, where our ideas are not the end but merely the beginning of understanding. That is why when Luther reads Romans effectually, meaningfully, according to what he later calls scripture's "theological grammar," he is given no transcendent version of human nature, no invisible entity, and no sublimed world. Rather, Romans reveals an unexpected coherence and value in the most familiar things—in the very words we speak. And this occurs because difficulty can lead us to abandon our fixed and ingrained ideas of the way the world or the text, deity or truth, should appear to us. For once thrown back upon our failed assumptions of meaning—as Luther was, as Wittgenstein recommends we should be in such cases—we are obliged by our condition to return again and again to the conflict until, all of a sudden, it acquires another aspect as inclusive of understanding as our previous notions were prohibitive. In apprehending the force of the Hebrew genitive, Luther's sense of "being born again and entering paradise" enacts Wittgenstein's observation that we feel as though we have discovered a new object, a new place, a new physical phenomenon. But what we have experienced is simply the "new sensation" of another grammar—a new way of speaking or looking at our world and ourselves (*PI* # 400).

In his preface to the 1545 edition of the Latin works, which recounts this crisis, Luther may be said to justify his theology by the parable of his life: we are given a mimesis of a kind, describing the now historic turn or revision in his ideas and actions peculiarly contributing to, if not solely inciting, the events of the Reformation and the establishment of Protestant doctrine. As Lutheran scholarship itself acknowledges, his justifying is retrospective and artistic inasmuch as he intends this circumstantial account of his personal and public predicament to be instrumental for himself and his reader: in effect, it is a way of making sense of the social upheaval in which he and his writings participate. For his variously strident and perplexed responses to these scandalous events surely imply that Luther knows no complacence about the European wars of religion, which last well into the next century. Rather, he feels obliged to account for the fact that the gospel rightly understood does not relieve but seemingly precipitates a conflict of such global dimensions—political, religious, economic, intellectual. In part, the solution at which he arrives is expressed in that paradoxical righteousness, where humanity is justified by no physical or material action but a conceptual and interpretive one—the living practice of *sola fides, sola gratia, sola scriptura*—which we feel in every aspect of our being, as Luther says about himself.

Yet we cannot see this justification as such, any more than Luther finds the conventional meaning of Paul's words spiritually facile or coherent: on the contrary, the statement from Romans appears incongruous, offensive to him in his malaise—a *horridum decretum*, to adopt Calvin's ironic epithet. But the existential conflict this meaning promotes moves Luther to pursue what he then profoundly experiences as the letter's proper sense and the alleviation of his suffering. It is necessary to recognize that, in the crucible of his own anguish, he remains conspicuously faithful to the text, adamantly refusing to abandon it or God but insisting on their mutual justification. And this "importuning" of the text, this insistence on its meaningfulness, conduces to the very coherence of which he despaired both in Paul's words and in his own life. That is why, in Luther, neither justification before God nor the paradoxicality of its Pauline description implicates a mystical or transcendental being. Instead, as in tragedy, as in Wittgenstein's philosophy, religious contradiction throws us back upon ourselves in such a way that we are impelled to discover not the wonders of the invisible world, but a revised meaning for the ordinary one which at some point or other we have experienced as intolerably conflicted. So although contradiction is accessory to this new meaning, it does not serve Luther as the basis for some metaphysic or counter-aesthetic. Human conflict and suffering cannot be a value or a good in themselves; nor is their painful reality to be effaced by any religious apprehension of them. That would be grossly immoral. But as its invariable effects, these misfortunes mark the occasions of our chronic misprision of the one true God, whom we want to construe as a palpable entity or transcendent analogue when he exists for us only as an alien and discomfiting sort of meaning that keeps obtruding on our unexamined lives. Since deity's hiddenness represents for Luther the limits of human understanding, we cannot expect to educe a knowledge of God directly from his expressions; we can seek to understand them only within the limits of this constraint. And the constraint places deity in the category of *res non apparentes*, things which do not appear as such, along with all religious things including the sense of scripture. So Luther insists that even in the incarnate son of God, we do not have an *analogia entis* to the divine, much less deity per se, but rather the right understanding of God expressed parabolically in the peculiar story of a human life—Jesus of Nazareth as the Christ.

Such an impassable boundary placed on religious knowledge does not allow us to say, *This* is God, or *This* is godlike; it enables us only to say, *This* is how we must go about understanding God's intent. For Luther, our knowledge does not take the form of an axiomatic doctrine of the divine nature, but a circumstantial account of our forever-vexed relations with the absolute—in the scriptural text, in history, in our present lives—whose difficulty works to revise how we take God's revelation: that is, we are brought by contradiction to acknowledge that it does not describe an order of being, one which remains beyond even our attempt at conception. Rather, what these expressions do is to introduce a new dimension and complexity of meaning into our existence; and Luther's theology of justification—"the righteousness of God"—is distinguished by that singular insight.

THE PATIENCE OF A JOB

A certain quietism has of course been ascribed to the righteousness of Job, which could be construed to have its source in a remote and arbitrary God of Aeschylean caprice, not unlike the demonic deity of Luther's religious crisis: that is, the humanly inscrutable onset of Job's affliction, and the theodicy that asserts divine prerogative over and against human expectation, could encourage and indeed enforce a posture of quietism in two senses of the word. On the one hand, Job's degradation might inhibit any effort actively to order his own or others' welfare, since such merely human efforts are subject to the arbitrary sanction of deity, in which case an insuperable abyss opens up between divine and human ideas of justice and right. On the other, his apparently causeless suffering might incline him to embrace a mystical or an implicit faith (that Protestant bugbear), which disdains all knowledge where God is concerned, so that religious action is irrational or inconsequent, motivated by either ecstatic impulse or the irresistible authority of the absolute. Either way, Job's faith seems to be vindicated by his doing nothing effectual to relieve his suffering—say, repudiating the covenant or cursing the Lord—except to endure this evil as he does the ravaging of his body, his goods, and his identity. Yet I don't think that is quite how Milton understands what he calls Job's perseverance, or what the poet brings to the seemingly impassive figure of Jesus in *Paradise Regained*, whose justification (the Father informs us) takes Job's terrible suffering as its model.

But this testimonial aside, Milton's "brief epic" has none of the scriptural story's tragic *gravitas*, since the heroic trial of his protagonist looks to involve little more than a show of sufferance. It is a problem that defies the understanding of a copiously histrionic Satan as well as many Miltonists—all of whom, after *Paradise Lost*, expect a virtue neither so fugitive nor so cloistered from the Son of God.

But if we take the encounter between Satan and the person termed "our saviour" as Milton's reading of Job, then in Wittgenstein's or Luther's sense, the difficulty comes down to a question of how we understand religious expressions—in this case, the poet's. Since very little transpires in what the angelic hosts dub the duel of wisdom between Jesus and Satan (for all that the Father smilingly adverts to this exercise in intransigence as a trial by combat or ordeal), we feel obliged to construe the narrative as a metaphysical occurrence, in which our saviour's immobility disguises an enormous symbolic activity—thus subliming the poem's imagery to offset its dramatic inertia and figural obtuseness. And like Job's patience, Jesus' passivity in the temptation scene can be read as a brief for suppressing or rejecting the impulse to do much of anything about this life except transcend it, since human thought and action appear by his responses to bear only negatively—as futile or (in Stanley Fish's always provocative reading)[32] dangerously ulterior—on the next. This is where Luther comes in: for in describing how Romans justifies not only its own meaning but also his life, faith, and theology, he shows how an interpretive maneuver can become a momentous historical event, without recourse to the transcendental paraphernalia of metaphysics. I would argue that Milton does the same with *Paradise Regained*: that is, when read as a conflict between two religious mentalities, the poem enacts how our image of God can convert not only the whole economy of our experience—as the field from which we derive sensation, selfhood, community—but also the shape of human possibility. For to rectify that religious picture is, at bottom, to readjust the world by altering what we think it expresses or how we imagine it is moved, and so by extension, to transform the way in which things can and should mean to us, and how we respond to them in turn. It is this wholesale conversion of the person that Job's suffering brings about, in which he is led to reconceive the very grounds of his existence by a transfigured vision of his God—the one maneuver or, more properly, justification that everybody but the devil's party performs in *Paradise Regained*.

Despite the fact that the Book of Job is neither single nor integral in its composition (to which formal concerns the poet is always alive), Milton seems to have read it as a whole in the fashion intended by the compositors and editors of scripture, and given his habitual use and facility with these texts, very likely in the original. This is not to say that he limits his understanding of the Job story to the scriptural version; for Barbara Lewalski has shown Milton availing himself of the whole literate—and, I should add, allegorical—tradition of Job's sufferings and its immense vitality of meaning for *Paradise Regained*.[33] Yet I think the biblical story specially explains the manner by which our saviour is justified in his encounter with Satan, and why it is that we have such difficulty in grasping, much less approving, Milton's kind of justification, inasmuch as this incarnate God is not what he, Satan, his disciples, or Milton's readers expect.[34] For having refused all the conventional and obvious ways of redeeming humanity—"victorious deeds," "heroic acts," "persuasion" (*LM* 1.196–293)—Jesus is magically transported to the temple's top, left by Satan to stand or fall in the confidence that one way or another, this person's identity must be finally decided as God or man. But the result utterly circumvents the experiment:

> There stand, if thou wilt stand; to stand upright
> Will ask thee skill; I to thy Father's house
> Have brought thee, and highest placed, highest is best,
> Now show thy progeny; if not to stand,
> Cast thyself down; safely if Son of God:
> For it is written, He will give command
> Concerning thee to his angels, in their hands
> They shall uplift thee, lest at any time
> Thou chance to dash thy foot against a stone.
>   To whom thus Jesus: Also it is written,
> Tempt not the Lord thy God, he said and stood.
> But Satan smitten with amazement fell.
>
>   (*LM* 4.551–62)

What stuns Satan is not an exhibition of godhead (which he desires and expects for his sake), but Jesus' standing where it seems humanly impossible that he should, and without any supernal machinery like those angels who shortly and allegorically help him off "his uneasy station" (*LM* 4.584). It is a religious act accompanied by a religious text equally incomprehensible to Satan, since the words—"Tempt not the Lord thy God"—here express the value of attitude over action, the implied over the demonstrable, the groundlessness of faith over mythic spectacle. This complex feat, like our saviour himself, is at once ordinary and incalculable, or as Annabel Patterson astutely comments, marvelous in another manner entirely from the theophany Satan imagines or the temptations by which he would elicit it.[35] In effect, Satan is stymied by his own ideas of the divine: beneath what he regards as the Son's human incognito, he imagines a magical god not unlike himself, one he can at once admire (or wonder at) and seduce—related ideas in *Paradise Regained* which evoke not only Satan's sensationalism, his enthrallment to the overt sense of things, but also his incorrigible expectation that revelation involves pyrotechnics. But there is no such equivalence to be had between himself and his adversary; for Satan remembers only the Son's heroic superficies in heaven, not what they meant. One might say that the crux lies in his failure rightly to conceive Jesus' hunger, which Satan understands first as a physical necessity he can satisfy, and then translates into an equally palpable ambition for earthly supremacy. Thus, in a deft allusion to *The Tempest*, he conjures up with the usual satanic excess and superlatives a banquet, replete with every delectable thing including beautiful boys and girls—an explicit eroticism that, despite his rebuke of Belial, is anticipated by Satan's newly urbane and courtly guise, and his initially avid talk of loving and adoring the "person" of God's Son as though Jesus were Charles Stuart:

> though I have lost
> Much lustre of my native brightness, lost
> To be beloved of God, I have not lost
> To love, at least contemplate and admire
> What I see excellent in good, or fair,
> Or virtuous, I should so have lost all sense.
> What can be then less in me than desire
> To see thee and approach thee, whom I know
> Declared the Son of God, to hear attent
> Thy wisdom, and behold thy godlike deeds?
>
> (*LM* 1.377–86)

The desire to gratify and be gratified which the temptations assume is simply insignificant to our saviour, who hungers for the prophetic and inevident, not the grossly apparent good with which his tempter expects to waylay him. That is why Satan's marvels of earthly power have proven empty shows to Jesus— the illusions of "glamour" (corrupt appearance), "prestige" (deceit or slight of hand), and "fascination" (the binding force of a spell), what the *Malleus Maleficarum* defines as "the tricks of the devil"[36]—all of which expediently veil the tawdriness of human violence, suffering, and vanity, as our saviour reminds Satan again and again.

It is also why the solitary Jesus, instead of coming enthroned in the heavens, trailing clouds of glory, somehow stands on his own without magical facility— effortfully, strangely, and improbably—while Satan, confounded by what he sees and hears, is struck dumb and topples into the abyss. Our saviour is then immediately proclaimed "True image of the Father"—"whatever place, / Habit, or state, or motion, still expressing / The Son of God" (*LM* 4.596–602)—which argues that, for all its peculiar vagaries, what we have seen is indeed Milton's version of theophany, the image of deity in the world as an incongruity that confounds both metaphysical and sceptical expectation. Similarly, the heavenly banquet that follows upon this queer triumph—complete with angelic transport "As on a floating couch" and "table of celestial food" (*LM* 4.585–95)—is no magical but an emblematic action, an allegory as against a supernatural apparatus, which is how Milton understands the descent of the Holy Spirit at Jesus' baptism: "*a representation of the ineffable affection of the Father for the Son*, communicated by the Holy Spirit under the appropriate image of a dove, and accompanied by a voice from heaven declaratory of that affection" (*CM* 14:366–71, my emphasis). In other words, the angelic fanfare testifies to no wondrous infusion of mana, no apotheosis of the human, but acknowledges something that is otherwise inevident—the prophetic and so world-altering significance of our saviour's posture. For if the identity of Milton's Jesus remains uncertain to Mary and his disciples who stand and wait, hungering for his presence, that is because he himself attends patiently on the disclosure of a hidden God's unexampled intent. Patience here conceals under a contrary appearance an unparalleled happening in providential history, namely, the incarnation of God in humanity, accomplished not by metaphysical engineering but by the distinctive rationality of faith. That is why the angels sing—as they do in *Paradise Lost*—to celebrate a religious *interpretation* on which Jesus acts and which ordains him messiah: "Hail Son of the Most High, heir of both worlds, / Queller of Satan, on thy glorious work / Now enter, and begin to save mankind" (*LM* 4.633–35). Our saviour does what Satan's erotically fixed and admiring mind cannot compass: in the person of us all, he expands human possibility by his preternatural poise, expressing his belief that there is another meaning potential in his predicament than his own guilt or God's abandonment. Nor does he succumb to the ascetic idea that his fast is virtuous in itself, or load it down with symbolic freight; rather, Jesus denies his hunger any necessary significance except that "Nature hath need of what she asks" (*LM* 2.253). The force of his hunger and his own circumstances remain religiously indifferent, experimental, open to whatever deity and events will make of them. And it is this posture—the way he addresses himself to his experience—which is pregnant with new meaning, rife with possibility, because it does not assume that God is like us, confined to the banalities of human invention. As Mary prophesies of her son, "some great intent / Conceals him" (*LM* 2.95–96): indeed, the whole event goes unseen, hidden in the mundane fact of Jesus' absence, who then simply departs the field of combat and "unobserved / Home to his mother's house private returned," as though nothing happened (*LM* 4.638–39). In both his absence and his return there is a meaning that does not appear as such—to Mary, Andrew, and Simon, and of course Milton's readers: faith as "the assurance of things hoped for, the conviction of things not seen." In response to Satan's perplexity, whether Jesus' kingdom is "Real or allegoric," *Paradise Regained* replies that it is simultaneously both (*LM* 4.389–90): that is, Milton's picture of the incarnation is conceptual, not hypostatic, a matter of how one envisions the experience of God; and this vision is historical, not metaphysical, accommodated to time, space, and the exigencies of human being, which is why Satan falls astonished when our saviour manages to stand.[37] As with "the righteousness of God" in Luther's reading, Jesus' preternatural attitude discloses God immanent in the ordinary, even as his estranging presence there works to explode, not to confirm our habitual understandings of the world. As Michael Fixler eloquently maintains, Milton's chiliasm is founded on our conceptual liberty, which is why, in *Paradise Regained*, Jesus must resist identifying himself with the false messiah of each temptation. But simultaneous with this restraint or refraining of our saviour, there is the more difficult restraint achieved by those who expect him in every sense, and who are ineluctably prey "to the pathetically human yearning to find somehow the assurance of divine justice in this life":

Behind the impenetrable calm of the spiritual hero, the anguish inspired by the moral obscurity of history, which in turn inspired in generations of men the unsatisfiable messianic longing, is hardly evident. A trace only of that passionate awareness momentarily flickers in him, filtered through a screen of detached retrospection, but it appears more fully in the complaint of the disciples, who remind us of the entirely human background to this symbolic action in the desert. . . . It is they, not Jesus or Satan, who must confront with their uncertainty, and withal with faith, the moral obscurity of history.[38]

It is this parable of religious movement, a conversion of understanding, that Milton finds in the story of Job's patience. Gerhard von Rad observes that the question absorbing Job himself is not the great existential crux of human suffering (*OTT* 1: 408–18): why the innocent are causelessly abused in a world that deity or mind purports to make intelligible; that is, Job does not choose to address the significance of suffering per se, as a transpersonal dilemma. On the contrary, the thing that dismays him about his condition—namely, his apparent loss of righteousness—is as particular as his own sense of self, and although variously and plausibly presented as a moral issue by his friends, it pertains to a question altogether anterior to ethics and to theodicy. The idea that appalls Job is not whether his suffering implies his sinfulness, as a magical bane inexorably following upon some evil he or his children may have committed and for which he is now penalized. Von Rad comments that, for all that Job forcibly rejects it, this idea of an unknown, redounding evil speaks to his deepest and most perverse inclination; yet it holds no more terror for him than it does for the friends who expound it. That is because the analogy argued by divine retribution—of past to present action, ordinary to religious meaning, the seen to the invisible—would circumscribe the fearful indeterminacy of human things which his suffering otherwise signals. As Job's predicament stands, there is no perceptible warrant or grounds for what occurs, any more than with Luther or Milton's Jesus.

Indeed, the brand of retributive justice to which the friends—with the exception of Elihu—variously subscribe has its appeal in just this presumption of an absolute reciprocity or satisfaction of human acts with divine effects, which operates to remove the scandal from Job's affliction by placing him ipso facto in the wrong. Retribution serves as a principle of moral but equally semantic containment, where the aggrieved party—God, from the friends' point of view—determines justice by a strict and simple ratio, if not exactly a *lex talionis*. Yet their several arguments are, I think, deceptively sophisticated, because at bottom they want to assume as Satan does, that God's intent follows however impalpably upon our own: that we suffer only for cause; that what is bad to us presupposes what is wicked to God; and consequently that there is a complete if unilateral continuity between divine and human ideas of value. Even without any intelligible warrant, Job's suffering does not disturb the friends' sense of moral order; however, the method of his complaint does, since he assumes for himself the prerogative they give solely to God, which is to justify his actions and therewith his world. For Job knows his own righteousness with such assurance that his sufferings can only strike him as incongruous and unjust; and therefore he demands redress if not from God himself, then either from some "umpire" or a future "redeemer" (Job 9:33, 19:25). And this is where he is thrown back upon himself, since he has more or less admitted into his mind and that of his friends the apparently blasphemous idea that God's justice is not amenable or coherent in any sense we can immediately understand, but must be *made* intelligible for us.

Therefore Job's distinctive question is whether the humanly, creaturely degradation that so abruptly engulfs him also indicts the relationship he thought he had with God, a relationship which Job for his part never relinquished and in which he still wants to believe himself fully, faithfully participating. His fierce self-righteousness does not pertain to the matter of his moral integrity, but instead to the very grounds of such justification: namely, the picture he sustains of God as the Lord of the ancient covenant, perpetually inclined toward human being in both wrath and loving-kindness but never oblivious to it. For it is God's apparent absence or indifference that Job suffers in the interpolated sections of poetic dialogue. Von Rad observes that the other Job, the Job of the ancient folk narrative, justifies God's word about him by serenely affirming his unconditional devotion to deity. It is this Job who may be said to reproduce the religious paradigm of seeking shelter, a covering from the incalculable in a protective faith. But while the other Job is no more perplexed by his suffering in the different, almost-irresolute colloquium this narrative frames, he undergoes a dreadful dissonance of ideas about God himself, in that he refuses to understand his state in the way it inexorably presents itself to him—as signifying the loss of that relationship's integrity as well as his own. That is why Job pursues deity with ever more impassioned urgency, because he seeks not just his own vindication but also God's, on whom his every human value depends:

> Oh, that I knew where I might find him,
>   that I might come even to his seat!
> I would lay my case before him
>   and fill my mouth with arguments.
> I would learn what he would answer me,
>   and understand what he would say to me.
> Would he contend with me in the greatness of his power?
>   No; he would give heed to me.
> There an upright man could reason with him,
>   and I should be acquitted for ever by my judge.
> Behold, I go forward, but he is not there;
>   and backward, but I cannot perceive him;
> on the left hand I seek him, but I cannot behold him;

I turn to the right hand, but I cannot see him.
But he knows the way that I take;
   when he has tried me, I shall come forth as gold.
My foot has held fast to his steps;
   I have kept his way and have not turned aside.
I have not departed from the commandment of his lips;
   I have treasured in my bosom the words of his mouth.
But he is unchangeable and who can turn him?
   What he desires, that he does.
For he will complete what he appoints for me;
   and many such things are in his mind.
Therefore I am terrified at his presence;
   when I consider, I am in dread of him.
God has made my heart faint;
   the Almighty has terrified me;
for I am hemmed in by darkness,
   and thick darkness covers my face.

(Job 23:3–17)

If Job's friends, from motives disparately practical, mystical, or necessitarian, can content themselves with the analogy of retribution to explain suffering so intuitively excessive, Job finds that analogy disabled by what he experiences as God's unaccountable withdrawal from all relationship to him. Against the friends' ready imputation of guilt, Job asserts that it is God, not his sin, that "has put me in the wrong, and closed his net about me": "Behold, I cry out 'Violence!' but I am not answered; / I call aloud, but there is no justice" (Job 19:6–7). With or without sin, he has not altered his position—God has—and therein lies the source of Job's escalating horror and vehemence. For the covenant between divine and human that he continues to cherish and this passage describes promised that his very cleaving to God would guarantee him deity's presence and thus his own meaningfulness, as the individual subject of divine solicitude whether in love or wrath. But Job is bereft of this sense of relation that also defines his understanding of divine justice, in which the righteous sheerly abide in God for good or for ill as one would a parent. And the loss of that relation and his God with it provokes Job's keenest anguish when the fidelity he assumed would ensure him recourse to deity—exemplified in the passage's figure of a lawsuit prosecuted before God—is met instead with its absence, or at other moments with what von Rad characterizes as a virtually demonic assault by the God Job perceives in his sufferings.

The darkness or impenetrability overtaking Job's picture of God threatens him where his material or moral degradation could not; because without it, he is deprived of his fundamental value as a son of God, the image of self that makes his strangely individual and now repugnant existence significant. He cannot see through his suffering to the Lord, nor can he find his wonted identity in it, so Job assumes his God either utterly to have withdrawn or horrifically transformed, thus evacuating all meaning from his world or making it ineluctably conflicted. But he has misunderstood deity's every expression but one, and from the whirlwind, the Lord tells Job as much: that he has misconceived his position in the covenant as well as the significance of his own affliction. It is not that what the friends said about a just God was true; indeed, the egregious reciprocity they assert between the appearance things have and the divine intent they signify ironically tallies with God's anger at them—"for you have not spoken of me what is right, as my servant Job has" (Job 42:7)—an anger assuaged only by Job's intercession on their behalf and an expiatory sacrifice. And this double mediation, which God also uses as the occasion for restoring Job to an abundance of earthly benefits, discloses the one actuality his friends neglected in their ostensible consolation: that neither deity nor divine justice exist in a single, much less direct or continuous line with human ideas. As the Lord himself puts it to Job, "Will you condemn me that you may be justified?" (Job 40:8).

Rather, the contingency of this world upon deity surpasses all understanding, a truth Job is moved finally to admit in rehearsing God's own indignant inquiry: "Who is this that darkens counsel by words without knowledge?" (Job 38:2, 42:3). For in the intensity of his distress (as against the self-satisfaction of his counselors), Job succumbs to an error not unlike theirs, or the one Milton ascribes to his Satan: that is, Job also simplifies the nature of his relationship to God, but by mistaking the impression of deity's absence and a disrupted understanding of their bond for the virtual abrogation of divine care, on which he depends even in the depths of suffering. This of course is the real temptation offered Jesus in *Paradise Regained*: what precipitates Job's different and despairing response is his insistence on identifying the covenantal picture with the nature and extent of deity, as though the divine were bound to human expectations and human necessities of meaning. Job's attempts at colloquy with the divine—as von Rad says, invoking this image of an assiduously attentive God against the alternately silent and ferocious deity of his affliction—only trace the dimensions of the error, which must then be rectified by a separate revelation from the whirlwind. And what this theophany declares by its litany of wonders, curiosities, and monsters is not just the strange, almost perverse impetus of divine regard, extending equally to the ostrich in its seeming absurdity and to the grand mythological evil of Leviathan as it does to Job. Theophany also describes the fragile understanding between human and divine being created by the covenant, over which looms deity in all its alien, volatile, and irresistible power. By this revised picture of the Lord or covenanting God, the vindication Job seeks in which he and deity move swiftly to reason together as equal parties at law does not legitimately elaborate the covenant's force. Indeed, it is impossible in the light of divine incommensurability. So von Rad remarks:

In answering Job's question God lifts the veil a little, just so far that Job may see how many more and—in the poet's view at any rate—greater riddles lie behind it. Thus the speech starts by countering all that human *naïveté* which fancies that immediately behind each of a man's problems there equally lies the divine solution ready for him. To this extent God's answer insists upon the absolute marvellousness of his management of the world. Behind each one of its marvels lies another greater marvel, and not one of them does God allow to be taken out of his hand. (*OTT* 1:416)

If the covenant permits neither the facile assumption of retributive justice made by the friends nor the clear exculpation Job demands (both expressing the same view of religious meaning), it does nonetheless justify but secretly, gratuitously, by ways too wonderful and too obscure to comprehend. Even as Luther experiences it in Romans, the covenantal picture circumstantially describes an inevident order of meaning that returns us to relationship with deity. And insofar as we admit and pursue that strange, unexpected significance, so we have faith and are justified all at once in Luther's theology. But the covenant does not in itself completely circumscribe or fully delineate our possible relations with God, as Job was used to think it did. What the covenant supplies is an understanding of religious things equal to our needs as participants with God, though not to our desires; and this is one significance of the theophany from the whirlwind. Job must learn the sufficiency of that knowledge—mind you, not to deity itself, but to his own affiliation with this hidden God (a harbinger of Milton's version of obedience in his last poems). Von Rad points out that the only viable response to God's picture of his own creative engagement with the world is the religious one of acceptance and adoration; for humanity is obliged to encounter divine solicitude as apparently free, groundless, and in every sense inestimable. Thus Job admits: "I had heard of thee by the hearing of the ear, / but now my eye sees thee; / therefore I despise myself, / and repent in dust and ashes" (Job 42:5–6).

With that admission, the ancient narrative and the interpolated dialogue converge so as to reassert the only appreciable grounds of Job's justification, which his anguish over his lost God and the very privilege of theophany differently implicate. His righteousness does indeed consist in adhering to the way and words of the covenant and so in fidelity to the Lord; for humanity knows no other access to God. At the same time, it requires Job's ultimate and agonistic recognition that the covenantal God is a picture accommodating deity to us as an extraordinary revelation of its care; but like Milton's image of God, the figure of our saviour in *Paradise Regained*, that picture never defines or exhausts divine possibility. And what Job understands or "sees" is this tremendous and still terrible reality—that deity as he knows it touches restrictedly and uncertainly upon an infinite, inconceivable agency. And in thus depriving him of any false security, not to mention the presumption of real parity with this being, he is left shaken to his very soul and vindicated where Satan is not. For in a most disquieting way, the Book of Job shows what it means to have the creator as one's personal God, whereby the absolutely other chooses the most familiar and vulnerable of human affinities—a loving, faithful inclination—in which to express its intent toward humanity. Every aspect of the covenantal picture consequently assumes an extraordinary vividness or intensity of meaning, since the God of Job's theophany has invested himself in it, becoming for us the person and Lord whom the covenant variously portrays: a parent, a spouse, a lover, a maker, a guardian inviting us to relationship; yet someone whose fidelity and care, jealousy and disaffection always carry with them the dreadful, inexplicable force of the divine.

The voice Job hears out of the whirlwind reproduces this conflict obtaining in deity's expression of itself, insofar as that particular theophany asserts two seemingly opposed modalities of divine intercourse with the world. For the private complaint Job makes against deity is answered ironically by a revelation of its sovereign freedom of will over and beyond the covenant to which Job individually appeals; and this is a knowledge he cannot help but find awful even as the singularity of its communication further conduces to personal intimacy with that God. Moses' dangerous sight of the divine glory in Exodus 33, to which I will return, has a certain resonance here. It illustrates the conceptual antagonism potential in even the most tender encounters we have with deity, this humanly repugnant effect accompanying its revelation. So von Rad remarks that "Even if Job suddenly and rapturously experienced the God who was his friend, he is nevertheless not able to delete the reality of the God who is his foe" (*OTT* 1:415). The dissonance of idea and emotion to which these conflicting apparitions or aspects of God contribute recurs in the grotesque extremity of suffering the Lord condones to exhibit Job's faithfulness and formally justify his own regard, exposing the gulf that separates our expectations of deity from its unfathomable reality. On this head, von Rad points out that the role of the "adversary" in the prose narrative is not satanic, which is to say, the workings of a malignant will opposed to God's (*OTT* 1:408). On the contrary, this person is a "son of God" in good standing and also an examiner or inquisitor of the sublunary, who comes to the assembly "From going to and fro on the earth, and from walking up and down on it" (Job 1:6–7). So he puts his question about Job's motives on the Lord's behalf, and proceeds with divine consent to use any degree of suffering that does not inflict death as the instrument of trial.

Difficulty is therefore presented as a condition always potential, always threatening in this relationship, with the result that Job—lacking a palpable fault in himself and ignorant of the preliminary exchange in heaven—can account for his inconceivable suffering only with the terrifying blank of divine will that theophany equally exerts. And this intent he cannot debate or resist, for "how can a man be just before God?" when it is in the power of deity to shape how things must mean: "Though I am innocent, my own mouth would condemn me; / though I am blameless, he would prove me perverse" (Job 9:2, 20). His predicament therefore appears to him as arbitrary, nonsensical, a double bind integral to human being. Yet the contradictions attending theophany in Job's experience—of the absolute freely electing to be finite and conditional; of the vast imperturbable holy experienced tensively as intimate, personated relationship; of affliction as a return for righteousness—oddly enough adumbrate the arguments made by Christianity for God's Incarnation and Atonement. The Book of Job makes quite clear that these incipient theses are not presented as an ontology of God: that is, they say nothing whatsoever about deity in itself, incarnate or otherwise. Rather, what they characterize are the pathic and noetic dimensions of our fellowship with the divine as laid down by its revelation, but which we like Job are compelled to learn and relearn in the maintenance of this unique bond.

For the propensities of our human nature as well as the manner of deity's revelation predict that the bond can be sustained only by the acutest self-consciousness, with a departure from those habits of thought which perpetually incline us to reduce God to a single evident and contradictory agency—like the friends who in the face of Job's suffering postulate an indifferent, Draconian divinity against the covenant's picture; or a thriving Job whose deity is a beloved companion, and in a profound sense household God, until affliction renders the divine an implacable nemesis. However, there is an important difference among these ways of construing God's expression of himself in human suffering. Like Luther, Job still insists on knowing deity's meaning as it can only be known—in pursuing the revelation, not the absence or abeyance of a God whom he understands to have us in unceasing if inscrutable care. And neither the framing narrative nor the poetic dialogue detract from Job's fidelity to this God, the personate image of deity expressly sensitive and accessible to humankind with whom Job insists on being allowed to plead his case. But experience amends his picture by giving him a painful sense of its constraints and its wonder: that a power so inordinate and autonomous as the deity out of the whirlwind would thus temper its expression to fulfill our peculiar demands of relationship, and that any human concept like covenant or personality could manage to sustain the enormous pressure of this strange, impending force.

Yet because Job is never shown doing anything to detract from his devotion to the covenanting God, whom he invokes ceaselessly against the deity he dreads, the way he appears to justify his righteousness (and the Lord's word about it) is once again inevident to our habitual understanding of the world; that is, justification seemingly consists in his doing nothing but, unchanged in the commitment of his faith, enduring the torment imposed by what one philosophical theist has called "a ruler of grotesque primitivity, a cosmic cave dweller, a braggart and a rumble-dumble, almost congenial in his complete ignorance about spiritual refinement."[39] Despite this ostensible quietism, Job in the end is brought to confess that he has indeed done something wrong—"uttered what I did not understand, / things too wonderful for me, which I did not know" (Job 42:3)—which suggests that the grounds for the adversary's charge against Job are in fact explicable, for all that they do not leap to the eye. From his words, it would seem that the faithful conduct which earned Job a reputation for piety in heaven and earth was somehow lacking in a certain significant attitude or understanding, which Milton's Jesus has. But this aspect of his predicament goes unexpressed until the moment of theophany, at which point Job perceptibly executes a "turn" or conversion in his attitude toward God, in order to meet the Lord's altered inflection of himself. Walter Eichrodt observes that the word *sub* or "turn" was the figure employed (mostly in prophetic writings) to capture the force, the palpable actuality, of this renovated intelligence about God that Job acquires, imbuing the religious relationship with a new meaningfulness: "The metaphor was an especially suitable one, for not only did it describe the required behaviour as a real act—'to make a turn'—and so preserve the strong personal impact, it also included both the negative element of turning away from the direction taken hitherto and the positive element of turning towards."[40] Thus Job's turn in his understanding of deity is a matter of attitude, at one and the same time a physical addressing of thought and action toward deity and also an abstinence or restraint from the ideas of God he previously entertained. The text's own discontinuous action manages inadvertently to expand this perplexing effect of engaging and refraining from something that articulates Job's conversion of ideas, since the shift in his attitude toward deity also subsides and recurs in his speeches, definitively to reappear when he confesses his error to God and intercedes for the friends.

But if Job misunderstands divine revelation, he nonetheless clings to it in his suffering despite a soul-killing sense of contradiction, from which a transfigured picture of the Lord ultimately releases him. And it is by such a conversion that Job is justified before God, because his faithfulness is meaningful in a way it wasn't before, inflected by a right understanding of the relations between deity, the world, and humankind. This revised understanding emerges phoenix-like from the remains of Job's old picture of God, ruptured both by his extravagant, groundless suffering and by the terrific intrusion upon him of the creator God out of the whirlwind; that is, it is accompanied by a sense of aberrancy or contradiction in the order of things. Moreover, their sheer somatic and subjective force alone suggests that these events should be seen as a wholesale violence perpetrated by deity upon Job's human nature, whose claims then compel him to debate (within himself and with the Lord, never really with the friends) not just what is due to his righteousness, but what sort of God would so betray his trust. Thus Job is made by suffering to reconceive the very axis of his world, which he had understood to be a kind of sensible—and in Milton's sense, satanic—analogy of character and impulse between himself and the Lord of the covenant, guaranteed by his own faithful if not necessarily impeccable life. But this good understanding between them is altogether undone by the fearfully anomalous happenings of the story, which deprive Job of both his own identity and the identity of his God.

The sundering of this dependency as Job experiences it—of divine regard on his sense of shared feeling with the Lord, of God's righteousness on his own scrupulously faithful performance—does not compromise the covenant itself, which continues intact in all its provisions for relationship between humankind and deity. Instead, his passing from utter degradation to personal theophany may be said to enlarge Job's vantage on both himself and God, so that the nature of their dependency in the covenant is newly revealed. Job is led to see that the weird propinquity of divine regard, which the theophany enacts as well as describes, isn't simply the concordant effect elicited by his personal worthiness or establishing it. Rather, this particularity of attention follows upon the creator's willing but enigmatic turn toward its creatures, which the credence Job gives to the covenantal picture enables him to see. Similarly, the picture he now has of deity cannot be contracted to one single image of the Lord and his own concerted likeness to that image: to continue the perspectival metaphor, this figure of the Lord has been foreshortened relative to theophany's endless and astounding landscape, which Job now recognizes as being also an expression of God. That landscape, it should be said, is not creation as we ordinarily know it but as religious understanding discloses to us, only erupting into human view with momentous perversities like Job's affliction that run athwart our notions of an orderly world, or with the miraculous and no less estranging onslaught of divine revelation. Job is then made to comprehend the Lord as the lone intelligible link within a vast nexus of deity's impalpable and indefinite dispositions toward the world, only one of which is given us—in the shape of the covenant—to own and observe as human knowledge of God. In other words, the original contingency in their relationship does not rest with himself as Job had once thought, whereby the devout person brings an otherwise latent or quiescent God into sensible, meaningful expression. For neither magic however defined, ritual, nor reason can compel the attendance of this deity on us; its holiness does not belong to taboo, the contagious or associative variety of the numinous, but works in exactly the opposite direction, emphatically severing as against propagating connections with the world as we receive it. Therefore any affiliation between humanity and the hidden God must begin with deity's choosing to attend to us and for its motives, not our own, with the consequence that the dispensing of divine regard may seem erratic even as its grounds—in the merit of its recipients—may appear wholly obscure. Indeed, the abrupt dislocation of Job's wonted understanding by suffering and theophany shows it to have been an egoistic device, inasmuch as he had presumed that the covenant would thoroughly account for his life if he lived it righteously. But, in fact, the covenantal God performs the inverse function, that of accommodating God to our frailty, with deity giving itself an image, a face we can apprehend and use for fellowship's sake—"use" in the sense that this God invites us to project meaning onto it, to engage with its expressions *as though* (the force of the Miltonic *as*) we would with another person. The covenantal picture is always presented as a dispensation or grace bestowed by the divine, and we are not therefore to treat our projections of the Lord as if they made manifest the whole being of deity—containing, not just conveying God, which is how Job had approached the covenant. So when the creator shows himself in theophany, revealing a divinity that unimaginably exceeds the God of Job's estimate, the neat edifice of false expectation he had built on that picture collapses like the tempter in *Paradise Regained*, forever to go unreplaced: that is to say, Job must accustom himself to a world whose meanings and possibilities are not contained or legislated by his own needs and desires, and to a picture of God that includes the idea of its distinction from the infinite reality the Lord adapts (without distorting or falsifying) to our human condition. He must approach the relationship as two disparate worlds yoked together—uneasily, incongruously, sometimes violently—by an inscrutable divine will, which the Lord makes present and knowable to us, but whose expressions will always appear potentially outrageous in our experience, as Job's suffering was.

But this turn in Job's understanding of God is not a prelude to transcendence, in which we happily repair from our incoherent experience of deity to a mental or numinous domain of perfect if not necessarily rational apprehension. Instead, the wisdom literature of which the Book of Job forms a part is distinctively pragmatical, even homely in its impetus: at different junctures and by diverse ways, the religious idea is creatively returned to the mundane fold, where it finds expression in the intractable but commonplace riddle of living rightly and well in the world as we find it. Except as this would entail relinquishing assumptions prejudicial to the ordinary, it is a religious provision designed precisely to *stop* our inveterate and misguided impulse to escape our own condition—as Wittgenstein implies, a condition we seem doomed to find disappointing, inadequate to our aspirations. Wisdom literature reproduces this limit insofar as it expresses an order reserved away from us as unknowable, with our participation in it partial and allusive, as something the world may express but never fully divulge to the mind—a knowledge that there are intervals in our understanding and that our speech to be true must be forever contingent, provisional. This is the force of our saviour as the image of God in *Paradise Regained*. Thus Eichrodt talks about the human reflex of wisdom as an understanding that effaces itself before the mystery of things,[41] and von Rad speaks of its humility in deferring to the limits placed on what can be humanly known:

> Wisdom thus consisted in knowing that at the bottom of things an order is at work, silently and often in a scarcely noticeable way, making for a balance of events. One has, however, to be able to wait for it, and also to be capable of seeing it. In such wisdom is something of the humble—it grows through having an eye for what is given, particularly through having an eye for man's limitations. It always prefers facts to theories. To be wise is therefore just not to think oneself wise. Thinking oneself wise is the hall-mark of the fool, who is no longer open to suggestion, but trusts in himself (Prov. XXVI.12, XXVIII.26). (*OTT* 1:428)

Such a knowledge is less a body of ideas than it is a distinctive rationality, a conceptual tact about knowing things of value where there is no attempt made outright to secure truth. Thus there is no immediate or necessary movement to definition, as Milton's Satan would do but not his Jesus or his Mary, who herself observes: "But I to wait with patience am inured; / My heart hath been a storehouse long of things / And sayings laid up, portending strange events" (*LM* 2.102–4). Wisdom means that the quality of knowledge we call true emerges from what lies before the mind, not beyond it. So this kind of knowing does not try to push through appearances to some other more perspicuous and truthful world. Nor does it struggle to get between the image which conveys meaning to some "thing-in-itself," since it is *our* domain of experience that we are given to see and know differently. Rather like the Lord of the covenant, our examined lives articulate the religious order of things to us at the same time that they are not analogous to that order in any facile way, acknowledging the distinction that obtains between the mind and the world, between the self and God. For representation itself—the covenantal picture of the Lord or the gospels' son of man and God—fosters their otherwise impossible engagement. Indeed, what Job discovers is that neither the world as we know it nor our faculty of understanding incorporate in themselves or transcribe the hidden, sustaining forces of our existence, whether one thinks of this as a principle of causation, an order of meaning, or an intelligence. But almost miraculously, they assimilate to us something incommensurable with human being and its self-image.

Such a recognition by no means promotes an aporia in human understanding; it stresses rather the observance of a boundary within which the knowledge we come by will make a viable sense that can content us, without growing complacent in its self-imposed restraint. By seeking after the signs of something truly other than itself, while recognizing an ineffable difference between those expressions we have of truth or deity and their consummation, wisdom describes a lifetime of religious desire—the peculiar hunger for God that afflicts Milton's Jesus but also Mary, Andrew, and Simon, and from which Satan himself suffers, if perversely (*LM* 2.245–59). The qualities of wisdom could be called largely receptive, having to do with imagining the thing sought: it involves a tolerance, even a value, for disruption and delay; a sense of pregnancy in what passes for ordinary experience and an attention or alertness about it; a scepticism about the intellectual technologies humanity invents to acquire truth and which often preempt it; and a disdain for those religious practices which do not respect the reservedness of deity and its reflexes. Yet the wisdom articulated in this biblical literature is neither esoteric nor occult, nor can it be methodically elicited in the presumptive fashion of Socratic dialectic, which it seems not a little to resemble. For there is no web of correspondences, no train of analogy here that could exult in having seen truth itself; and that is because there is no continuity however remote between our ideas and the reality of things that comes to rest in God. Rather, as Job is brought to acknowledge, the analogy that must be explored and constantly adjusted pertains to how we understand whatever knowledge deity in its expressions chooses obliquely to provide us. Luther would say that wisdom consists in our negotiating between the scriptural image of God and the picture of him we get from both our ordinary and our exceptional experience of the world. To a crucial extent, the meaning of either picture depends on the character of their inevitable intersection, which is not simple or fluent but conflicted in some fashion, like Job's two Gods or Luther's, whose opposition actually describes the irreducible contingency of divine meanings.

What wisdom tells us is that these two Gods are really two experiences of deity which we are asked ceaselessly to adjudicate, and that an appropriate positioning of our thought can reconcile them, that is, until the inevitable moment when they next conflict. The resurgent dilemma about how we think the world should mean is always being precipitated by how we choose to read either picture of God: for it was not the Lord who was in contradiction with himself but Job's ideas of him. It follows that we encounter the relation of these two pictures and, by extension, the truth about things as a brief but sudden glory which satisfies our need for conceptual clarity only for a time. So if anything, wisdom is what one means by a religious attitude toward the world as the territory of revelation, in that the hiddenness of truth requires our active reverence and a posture of suggestibility, one in which it would be possible to entertain a new idea. And the kind of meanings wisdom propounds are accordingly tentative or experimental and open-ended, waiting on the separate impetus of experience for their coherence, if not their final truth to be disclosed. This sense of pregnancy in things is evoked in the reply that the Job of the ancient narrative makes to his wife—"Shall we receive good at the hand of God, and shall we not receive evil?"—thus allowing to deity its freedom of will and expression over the world it created (Job 2:10).

As a reflex of such sovereignty, the ancient Job appears to distinguish in his response between the human sense of suffering as an evil and God's intent in inflicting it, which cannot be wrong. His faithfulness promises him relationship, not identity, understanding, not explanation, from a nature incomparable to his own. This may seem at first glance to be a mystic's excuse for historical self-subjugation; yet I would argue that the ancient Job does not so much surrender his right to understanding as he revises its direction and force. At least in their effect, his reply and his equanimity refute Job's counselors by rejecting the glib if heroic rationalism that would make God the servant of human judgment, or would equate human suffering with deity's wrongdoing. And in such a discriminate understanding, he is not threatened with despair like the poet's Job, because he is not driven by a false idea of their correlation to condemn God's actions or his own as evil. The ancient Job is left free to think about himself or God without detriment to either, and consequently without losing confidence in his own meaningfulness or the world's. But the poet's Job, our Job, knows no such equanimity or amelioration in his suffering, and indeed is susceptible to the signal error Milton ascribes to the Satan of *Paradise Lost*: namely, of mistaking the incommensurable in God for the unjust, and his inscrutable will for an eternal tyranny that aggressively holds the whole of creation in thrall—translating that which is supremely, impenetrably different from us into a monstrous hostility, a point D. Z. Phillips makes against philosophical theism.[42] For when Job interprets the covenant in such a way that it does not admit of a distinction between his righteousness and deity's, he ignores the crucial fact that its purpose is mutually to accommodate both "persons"—to place him in relationship with God despite his human nature, not because of it. He therefore treats as actual what remains only an instrumental fiction of their parity: if the question of faithfulness is put by the heavenly inquisitor to Job, on earth Job presumes to put the selfsame question to God, since the reciprocity by which he understands their relationship dictates that any compromise of his own moral worth should imperil divine integrity as well—that is, until the theophany of the creator God reproaches him unanswerably.

This estranging and impervious deity, which the more affable Lord of the covenant veils from us, impinges by its very existence on the special sense we have of our human nature as somehow being like God's, an idea implicit in Job's presumptive fellow-feeling with his maker. Thus the supposition that he can work out his status with God requires some correspondence of kind beyond shared terms and values, from which his justification would get its legitimacy as well as its persuasiveness. But the theophany discloses that Job has misunderstood the sort of resemblance to which he intuitively lays claim; that is, we resemble God in the aspect of exceptionality, yet we do not enjoy this likeness through any singular power or integrity of our nature, but in the complicated, uncertain meaning of our self-revelation—Freud's endless parapraxis of psychic expression. Like deity and truth, we have a life both hidden and revealed, in a way still mysterious to ourselves. Thus when Job acknowledges an order of dependency in religious things other than the one he had previously imagined, he must also revise his idea of human affiliation to God—how he is, as it were, the son and image of God—and what is more, how he identifies himself on that account. Since the motive for divine regard which once resided in his righteousness has now been left inscrutable—namely, as a faithful person intrinsically attractive to the Lord—he cannot pretend to an affinity that both his suffering as well as the argument of theophany in large measure deny.

Having experienced God as an assault upon his very humanity, Job must approach the covenant as expressing something other than kindredness between our ideas and the divine. And I think the poet meditates this conversion in Job's picture of his own nature as well as God's, simply by interpolating the exchange with the friends. For while the ancient narrative makes God huge with possibility, it gives Job in his very fidelity little expressive (although much conceptual) room in which to maneuver and thus to manifest his different kind of life. But that expressive latitude is what the section of dialogue supplies: a realm of enigma and potentiality at either end of this precarious relationship between divine and humankind. For the poet's Job—in his impassioned self-consequence alternating with enormous self-pity, in the ugliness of his anger against the friends, in his voracious demand that deity itself justify him—is no simple man of God like the ancient Job, even when the seemingly indomitable force of his personality abruptly attenuates to acknowledge the impact of theophany. This different sense of Job's perseverance invites us to reconsider the way we understand what Milton means by justifying God's ways, because in *Paradise Lost* that decision of the speaker arises from just those circumstances of suffering, incoherence, and seeming injustice which attend Job's encounter with his hidden God. It is our incorrigibly human predicament Milton would describe there, by way of answering the speaker's question:

> Say first, for heaven hides nothing from thy view
> Nor the deep tract of hell, say first what cause
> Moved our grand parents in that happy state,
> Favoured of heaven so highly, to fall off
> From their creator, and transgress his will
> For one restraint, lords of the world besides?
>
> (LM 1.27–32)

I too will try to describe the problem of Milton's two Gods in this instrumental sense, by way of offering a solution to our strangely kindred conflicts with the poem, a solution which begins with the peculiar hiddenness of the reformers' God and how that hiddenness informs their own ideas of the way religious things mean.

CHAPTER TWO

Milton's God

THE SENSE OF JUSTIFICATION

If Job's theophany tells us anything, it is that deity must be pictured in the manner of *façons de parler*, as a way of speaking about this world—Wittgenstein's instrumental description. We know the hidden God only by giving an account of the circumstances in which we encounter him, a representation not of deity as some invisible entity, cause, or effect but instead as an unexpected order of meaning that reconfigures our whole experience. For Job's deity is not constrained by creatural being or human thought, much less by those effects or sensations—evidence, elegance, harmony, lucidity, symmetry—which we suppose attend the truth.[1] Religious justification in this case is unlike the activity which goes by that name in logic or aesthetics, not to mention law, wherever the means of justification are identified with the *Ding-an-sich* of justice, truth, beauty, the right. The philosophical preeminence of analytic logic has encouraged this oddly primitive conflation to such an extent that, in a recent neoscholastic turn, logical forms and procedures have been enlisted to vindicate certain theological propositions like the Incarnation.[2] That maneuver not only assumes the cognation of logical and theological expressions but also in effect identifies the subject and intent of religious justification with logic's imperatives. In other words, the same analogy between formal authority and truth is thought to obtain in both kinds of knowledge, with the claims of the one susceptible of justification by the apparatus and criteria of the other.

But politics supplies the clearest instance of the form and grounds of justification being identified as justice per se, having to do with the way civic constitutions are thought to benefit the public not only materially but also subjectively, conducing to civic virtue as well as civic order.[3] These civic codes and constraints promulgate the terms in which a person or community can be made "just" in the sense of conformable but also in the sense of virtuous, and therefore as embodying that value in themselves—as "justice." When we refer to this order in the civic world, we may then say that it not merely "does justice" but "is justice." Such a view implies that there is a real, effective correspondence between legal terms and procedures and the social world subject to its representation: by a kind of formalism, justice and civic virtue are held to consist in the observance of law, while injustice and vice lie in its abrogation. So any dissent from the constituted order is wrong, immoral, even inconceivable, whether or not that formal disruption actually impairs the general welfare. One might consider in this light how a Stuart monarchy or Presbyterian theocracy imagining itself divinely ordained would approach civil dissent: when the public welfare is identified with an exclusive authority, dissent possesses no legitimacy, but as a revolt against the sovereign good, necessarily becomes a positive evil.[4]

Besides this normative or categorical idea of justification, there is the instrumental kind which conversely assumes a discrepancy between justifying and justice per se, as against an analogy or (in extreme instances) an identity: to pursue the same instance of monarchy, when a distinction is admitted between the imperatives of the king and those of truth or the common good, dissent is then legitimated and can also give impetus to civic reform. In these circumstances, another idea of the same constitutional apparatus obtains, holding it to have an instrumental function in expressing the public good as against a positive or definitive one: that is, the constitution is allowed to create conditions which either foster or do not impede the achievement of justice and civic virtue, but its offices and ordinances are not imagined to correspond to them. A constitution thus understood cannot be morally binding in the same way as the first idea of it, since its representation is supposed only to conduce to justice, as something separate and proleptic from justification. And when the constituted order is perceived not to achieve its proper purpose, then it is susceptible to revision. For dissent isn't rebelling against the good in such a case; it is reforming or revising the means by which we undertake to achieve it. This latter idea of justification as instrumental explains Milton's attitude toward the established forms of government and religion in his day, as well as his subsequent insistence on toleration and the separating of church from state. It isn't that, in Augustinian fashion, Milton supposes virtue to be antipathetic to the civic and secular realms—he is after all God's Englishman—but that his libertarianism seeks to avert any peculiar ordination of it.[5] His embrace of presbyterianism for the English church proceeds on just these grounds: he advocates that ecclesiastical model not because he imagines the rule of elders has sole divine authority, but because he thinks that a church government organized by congregation will be more cognizant and so responsive to divine and human promptings than an episcopacy insulated from the impulses of individual churches and believers and servile to the king. In short, Milton supports the presbyterium as an instrument, not the end of religious justification and church reform, to the extent that it serves to mediate God's will in the faithful; and he ceases his advocacy when Presbyterianism as a religious denomination succumbs to the same empty and arbitrary formalism as episcopacy.

What I am trying to describe is not a distinction between, say, realist and sceptical understandings of justification. It is an entirely sceptical position to argue that the particular form a thing takes fully constitutes that thing insofar as the human mind may be said to know it. The crux and the divergence in these kinds of justifying appear only in the status we choose to assign the knowledge characterized by them. If the instrumental kind of justification appears consistent with several types of pragmatism, supplying us with no absolute but a perfectly sufficient, workable, and prosaic truth, neither scepticism nor pragmatism describe Milton's sense of justifying: they lack the wonder and the anguish, the urgent desire for theophany, which motivate Job's insistence on being justified before God and, I would argue, the justification undertaken by Milton's speaker in *Paradise Lost*. If I may return once more to the theory of civic justice by way of example, this distinctiveness of the poem's justifying can be elucidated by John Rawls's "veil of ignorance" and some possible implications of that similarly instrumental fiction, which serves to exclude all particular knowledge that might keep two parties from distinterestedly and mutually pursuing justice.[6] The excluded knowledge in a case of inequity must be reciprocal, encompassing the personal or corporate circumstances of both parties at once, since the intent behind such a "veil of ignorance" is to create a position of artificial parity between disputants, and thus to remove from consideration those real differences in status and interest which might hamper even the hypothetical pursuit of justice. Perhaps more than any of the other conditions Rawls makes preliminary to social equity, not excluding the generalized assumption of a precipitating conflict between parties ("the original position" as Rawls terms it), this veiling device could be said to recognize the motive for justifying I remarked: namely, that we undertake to justify—to pursue justice in a given case—only where we first encounter some significant discrepancy between our ideas of right and our situation or the situation of others.

These disparities in condition are always present most forcibly and insistently in the particular case (which universals must ignore), specially inhering in the knowledge of individuals either as persons or as a class. It is such particular knowledge that Rawls seeks to preempt by his "veil of ignorance"—the knowledge that withstands our general assumptions of likeness and provokes a sense of our differences. But a problem can occur when the particular is eliminated even artificially and procedurally from representation; for then we tend to discount the actual differences that our fiction of parity would withstand and that moved us to justify in the first place. So although Rawls's device assumes an original injustice, I would argue that the "veil of ignorance" is nonetheless capable of expunging from our consciousness the very concern which brought it into use. For once we have effected a functional equality between two parties in a dispute, can we intellectually and psychologically sustain the disturbing, critical acknowledgment of its facticity—that this parity we assume is a fiction, not a fact? Or having as it were done justice to the idea of equality in our representation, will we stop there, with the procedural version, and not seek to rectify the far less tractable actuality? This tendency to rest in the appearance of equity articulates a political danger, arising whenever necessary fictions of equality are taken for the thing itself, with the consequence that we presume the fact of social justice when it exists only analytically or formally, and even then with difficulty. For the loss of that tensive sense of difference—not only in the conflicting circumstances motivating a dispute, but also in the distinction between our instrumental account of justice and its discordant actuality—becomes the occasion for perhaps a worse injustice still. At such a moment, the moral imperative to foster the conditions for justice can perversely place real inequity out of sight and out of mind. I'm certainly not saying this is the necessary outcome of John Rawls's "veil of ignorance"; rather, I wish merely to imagine the occasion on which it and similar representations become problematic, and thus to suggest Milton's concerns about his own justifying. Because Milton too, as a Christian of the reformed or Protestant persuasion, must argue a "veil of ignorance" that has to do simply and absolutely with the hidden God whose ways he sets out to make right with humanity. He must talk about God as though he knew deity in some sufficient shape or form, like Rawls's negotiating parties—as though there were some clear and determinate correlation between God's intent and Milton's account of it, when theologically there can be neither in his view. Indeed, the relative status of divine expressions is so profoundly, inexpressibly different from deity itself that their distinction can only sever relationship, in which case the speaker of *Paradise Lost* and humanity with him would be forced to suffer the sense of God's injustice without possibility of redress or relief—as Job fears in his own case.

Therefore, as Judeo-Christian scripture had done long ago, Milton must propose a purely functional parity in his representation between things human and divine that would allow for our experience and understanding of deity, even as this representation must somehow acknowledge the incalculable difference between what it says about God and what deity is in itself. When Calvin defines "the fear of God," he has in mind something like this predicament, where we accept deity as it expresses itself to us without claiming any clearly demonstrable grounds for doing so:[7]

> It is the mark of true religion that men submit themselves to God although he is not seen, and although he does not speak face to face, and does not openly show his hand holding the scourge. . . . Those who *fear the name* of God, do not desire to bring him out of heaven, nor do they demand obvious signs of his presence; they are content to show their faith by adoring and serving God, although they do not see him face to face, but only in a mirror or a riddle, or through his righteous and powerful judgments and the other great acts he presents to our eyes. (CC 145–46)

In other words, the "fear of God" acknowledges the abysmal difference between what deity is and what we know of it, thus restricting our ability to anticipate what its purposes are or to say how its expressions mean: the picture we have of God is thus peculiarly groundless and inutile as it applies to our knowledge of the divine nature. At the same time, it is entirely viable insofar as that picture, articulated by faith, permits and sustains a relationship between two absolutely disparate parties. As Rawls hopes for his version of the same device, a religious "veil of ignorance" is not invalidating but instead instrumental to Milton's work of justification, because it alone sets up the mutuality between divine and human worlds that must exist for any communication, much less justice to be pursued between them. But that mutuality depends on an artificial likeness or parity of persons that must constantly be exposed as such, unless we are to behave like idolaters and take God's expressions as though they said everything about God and nothing about ourselves, who are their ironical subject even as Job, not the creator God, was the subject of the Lord's theophany from the whirlwind. "The ways of God" describe deity only in its relative character as *our* God in those "acts he presents to our eyes" and in the "riddle" of our experience.

I am obviously evoking the covenant—the theological *foedus* or *pactum*—into which God as the Lord enters with humankind (an idea differently elaborated in the "federal" theology of Milton's contemporaries).[8] But the same circumstances and motives inhere in the doctrine of accommodation that theologically presupposes this covenant, whereby deity reveals itself to us in ways both historical and conceptual that we can understand and that, understood as "process of speech" and the like in *Paradise Lost,* have received considerable play from the poem's critics. But this religious accommodation as a necessary fiction of parity is susceptible to precisely the same abuses, by both theologians and Miltonists, as Rawls's functional equality among disputants in a case of injustice: under the rubric of divine accommodation, one can assume the most facile correspondence between creator and creature in the poem, especially when that doctrine is thought to promote their analogy, not to negotiate their express and signal distinction. Like the secular version but to an extreme degree, this theological "veil of ignorance" is occasioned by the experience of deity's immeasurable, unutterable difference from ourselves, an antipathy Calvin invests in the religious attitude he calls fearing God's name. But if the covenantal picture of the Lord is made to promote relationship where none would otherwise be possible, it is egregiously, sacrilegiously abused when made to argue likeness between human and divine being or ideas, given the hidden nature of this God.

So rather than acknowledge and respect the difference that always precedes analogy—the comparison of two unlike things—the correspondence theory of accommodation can result in a sort of emanation scheme, in which the divine nature can be traced up from the creature to more or less godhead itself. Accommodation taken in this sense allows human knowledge precisely that continuous access to the divine that Calvin would deny when he talks about keeping God in his heaven. Relationship according to the model of divine emanation is one pole of David Burrell's argument addressing the limits Aquinas places on his own religious analogies, in order to resist just this anthropomorphic tendency in theological method:[9] for although deity is not exactly conceived like Santa Claus, as an old man with a white beard, the unexamined and unrestricted use of analogy can lead to something little short of that position. Understood as a doctrine of likeness or correspondence as against a way of speaking or expressing the incommensurable, accommodation can dangerously

expect real continuities where there can at best be only an artificial contiguity
of ideas, as Milton famously says about our knowledge of truth in the *Areopagi-*
tica. To adopt Burrell's salient term, there is a "distinction" observed in early
Protestant theology between a creator God who is in the world but not of it,
and cannot be known even intermediately by his creatures, in spite of the overwhelming human desire for some intimate knowledge of our progenitor and of
ourselves.[10] In this theology, God is understood to be more than remote in quality and degree from human being, since the distinction effectively recognizes
that deity is alien to us and to the terms and values by which we understand it.
Yet the assumption of God's difference that both Luther and Calvin relentlessly
iterate also precludes a transcendental movement to escape incoherence in our
knowledge of the divine, whether that movement is rational (as Sanford Budick
has argued for Milton)[11] or irrational (as Stanley Fish has observed in him).[12]
The distinction not only acknowledges but also accepts the human problem of
theodicy, with the result that the "veil of ignorance" surrounding deity requires
a proportionate emphasis on the activity of justification itself—in the manner
of Wittgenstein's philosophical solution, describing the circumstances in which
we experience the divine as against describing divinity itself. For Milton, for
Luther and Calvin, that circumstantial description is the singularly availing
religious knowledge with which the sacred text supplies us—"the ways of God"
understood as an expressive order, not an ontological one.

Their theological response to the hidden God is not to sublimate or void our
categories of apprehension, but to adjust them in the necessary pursuit of what
delimited truth God allows us, which consists in our relationship to deity as
peculiarly evoked by the character of revelation itself. When Milton talks about
the force of "reason" in religious matters, revelation is its arena—the realm of
religious experience as against the mind of God, an order of expression or meaning that makes sense of scripture (because God himself employs it there) as
against a universal canon of truth. For Milton and the reformers, the epitome
of this expression is Jesus Christ, because how we understand that person and
his claims describes the affiliation of creature with creator, with religious knowledge behaving like a practice or a stance instead of a doctrine. As Paul is compelled continually to remind his irrepressible flocks, the theological virtues of
faith, hope, and charity entail both a conceptual and a moral attitude permitting us to grasp the appropriateness, the coherence, the validity of Jesus Christ
as God "for us" in the theological phrase, which is to say the God peculiar to
this world of possibility, not to some blank and irrevocable hereafter. In doing
so, they revise how we understand justification in its religious, salvific aspect,
as a condition properly belonging to human being in this life, not our death
and transcendence.

Luther gives new and disconcerting impetus to this revision by bluntly asserting that we had never understood the theological sense of that word "justification" in the first place, or the right kind of force it should have.[13] Accordingly, he devotes his theology to arguing all over again how we are justified and

the accessory meaning of faith, as these things are understood *coram Deo* or in relation to the hidden God.[14] And to Luther, that means how they are understood Christologically, through the lens of the Incarnation. He dedicates himself unremittingly to understanding this singular picture of God—deity as expressed by the person Jesus Christ—and the uses to which scripture, especially the gospels and apostolic letters, say it should be put. In doing so, Luther recognizes what others had also seen but without the tremendous, radicalizing force of his pastoral intent. For the special felicity attending this novel adjustment or justification in our "spiritual" ideas is that it can perform the very change to which it enjoins us: it can restore us to God. In Luther's account, faith in Jesus as the Christ is a conceptual revolution, which justifies by reordering how we understand the significance of our world—how we look at what is already there, or in Wittgenstein's somewhat different sense, how we perceive the world as "found." We see the same things, but they don't mean in the same way; or rather, they signify something else besides their familiar, habitual sense—the presence of the hidden God where he had seemed finally, tragically absent. Yet his presence does not allow us a symbology of the divine, since these meanings do not describe deity but instead disclose and repeat only the fact of its immanence: we return to Calvin's distinction between, on the one hand, cataloging indicative because supernatural signs of deity, and on the other, experiencing the divine in the mundane as in a mirror or a riddle, which is how Job saw God.

The mutuality between world and mind, on which Luther's theology of justification depends, does not exclude the material or the subjective nature of religious experience. For the idea of a God who is understood to create both dimensions of meaning, the world and the self, and yet is wholly other than them, defies such reductions. As the Protestant reformers conceive it, faith in the Christ operates something like Rawls's fiction of equal knowledge and so positional equality between antagonized parties, where we must imagine or postulate a condition which is not obviously the case, in order to foment the different actuality for ourselves that justification pursues. To create justice we must first imagine it. Thus the person Jesus as the Christ articulates a particularly inevident and improbable image of God which, once embraced, provides simultaneously the grounds for our belief and our justification *coram Deo*, without at the same time rendering us right and just in any absolute sense. Instead, by means of this anomalous picture, we render an unknowable God intelligible, palpable, and historical—bringing deity as it were back into the world—so that relationship with him is possible. Yet the picture's very incongruity starkly exposes the distinction between deity and the world, creating that interstitial dimension of human experience in which faith is exercised, so that God's hiddenness is never effaced or denied. In Luther's provocative sense of *facere Deum* or "making God,"[15] this artistic or postulated deity is neither fact nor figment, but what one might term a description that is also a solution to the problem posed by God's ways:

> To attribute glory to God is to believe in Him, to regard Him as truthful, wise, righteous, merciful, and almighty, in short, to acknowledge Him as the Author and Donor of every good. Reason does not do this, but faith does. It consummates the Deity; and, if I may put it this way, it is the creator of Deity, not in the substance of God but in us. For without faith God loses his glory, wisdom, righteousness, truthfulness, mercy, etc., in us; in short, God has none of His majesty or divinity where faith is absent. Nor does God require anything greater of man than that he attribute to Him His glory and His divinity; that is, that he regard Him, not as an idol but as God, who has regard for him, listens to him, shows mercy to him, helps him, etc. When He has obtained this, God retains His divinity sound and unblemished; that is, He has whatever a believing heart is able to attribute to Him. (*LW* 26:227)

To Luther, how we picture the divine not only characterizes but constitutes our relationship to God, which is why he talks about having the proper idea of deity as the one necessary condition of faith: that is, how we think about God can allow or deny us relationship with him, with the right image performing our justification *coram Deo*. So, crucially, we create deity as glorious, wise, and just against the evidence and without grounds, as Luther goes on to explain:

> Therefore faith justifies because it renders to God what is due Him; whoever does this is righteous. The laws also define what it means to be righteous in this way: to render to each what is his. For faith speaks as follows: "I believe Thee, God, when Thou dost speak." What does God say? Things that are impossible, untrue, foolish, weak, absurd, abominable, heretical, and diabolical—if you consult reason. . . . Thus when God proposes the doctrines of faith, He always proposes things that are simply impossible and absurd—if, that is, you want to follow the judgment of reason. (*LW* 26:227)

In short, God doesn't necessarily appear to us as we want to picture him; but like Job—or in Luther's reading, Abraham—our justification lies in imagining him to be otherwise than he seems from our experience. As with Rawls's instrumental fiction of equality, when we postulate a just God for a world to all appearances gone wrong, we do this precisely in order to create a renewed possibility of existential coherence or justice for ourselves. We must first create the right relationship between God and the world and then observe it in both senses of the word; for in conforming ourselves, our understanding, and our expectations to this seemingly outrageous idea, we can discover its truth. It is telling that Luther adopts the idiom of justification the better to describe the activity of "making God": conceiving God rightly in order that we may be regarded as righteous in his eyes, giving God his due in the way we think and talk so as to receive our due in return. But in the face of the distinction, what follows from this picturing, this justifying, does not directly affirm our image of the divine, at least in the form of some neat correlation between what we experience and what we suppose for deity: God does not suddenly satisfy our notions of justice and so appear conspicuously just and good himself. Rather, his apparent malfeasance indicates something profound about the way we misconceive deity, which, once understood and acknowledged, will transform our attitude toward creator and creation together. Yet the transformation itself remains something still to be defined, something to which we have yet to put the name. We are faced not with an opposition or inversion of our ideas but with an open, amorphous space, since nothing as yet fits our picture. That is why Hebrews makes hope an element of faith; for *res non apparentes* are not simply unseen as such, *invisibilia* on the model of what we can perceive, like the transcendent God we hypothesize as perfect and preeminent in every human good. Rather, these "things that do not appear" are understood to confound our expectations of the world, so that our picture of God and religious things cannot predict the shape divine justice will take, whether by positive or negative analogy.

The picture we hold of a just God expresses our attitude toward this utopian or apocalyptic possibility, which is equally the inconclusive, antipathetic position from which we must seek justice, because justification taken in the sense of *facere Deum* implies a certain antinomianism: namely, the unaccustomed fact that both our received ideas and our most novel speculations are no index of God's nature or the form of religious truth. For the incongruity we experience in our relations with the absolute describes the insurmountable barrier between creature and creator—the predicament of our mortality. This is why we cannot resolve the paradox of God's expressions by somehow pushing past the merely apparent conflict to the transcendentally, beatifically true: we experience the incongruity as impregnable because it traces the hiddenness of deity, not just in this life but the next, as something always alien and always mediated. So, in *The Bondage of the Will*, Luther will have occasion to argue against Erasmus that deity necessarily exceeds its own historical revelation as God and Lord of the covenant, and that, for all his accommodations to human understanding, God will inevitably appear to us arbitrary or wrong at some point, since as faith uniquely recognizes, deity is not amenable to our familiar assumptions of meaning and value.

Moreover, as Calvin explains the effect of fearing God, the work of faith is to acknowledge, not to overcome, this wholly human fact of the distinction between creator and creation, which we experience as the most profound existential incoherence. Reciprocally, sin in the reformers' theology consists precisely in the perverse attempt to deny God's difference and thus his deity. I would argue that Milton justifies God's ways to the same point as Luther does—not to testify to the incongruities created by human sin but to those created by the hiddenness of God, with which humanity must struggle from the moment of its creation. Sin would try to clear up the problem, to achieve an easy resolution either by denying the distinction and the hidden God with it, or by transcending this boundary between creator and creature and proposing to be like deity itself. Milton's Satan pursues both options simultaneously, in either case seeking to understand God as Satan understands himself, which is according to how he himself appears. Thus when Satan loves God, it is because he imagines unseen deity to perfect and so ratify his own sense of self as the visible form of God—a likeness and familiarity abruptly contravened by the exaltation of the Son above all the angelic hosts. Then Satan is obliged to hate God because he still supposes that deity is no different from himself, as having the same capacities and desires but now exercising them illogically, arbitrarily, unjustly, as a tyrant over his own kind. Once Satan is banished from heaven, he is bound by the absence of God to extend this argument, insisting that the fortunes of war alone made deity superior—a different chance, not a different nature, having thus disposed their fates.

Milton orders his irony in *Paradise Lost* equally to invite and to constrain the reader from Satan's sort of analogy: he asks us to read the poem within the confines of the figural and dramatic incongruities he orchestrates, climaxing in the infamous figure of God the Father, because these enable us to recognize that this person is not the one true God, but an expression of what it can be like to encounter the divine from the vantage of our humanity. Our own encounter with the Father occurs only when we have heard the plausible atheism of hell, and works ironically to explain the problem of faith as Luther plots it in his theology, which is to believe where everything conduces to disbelief, even revulsion. But irony also explains the reasons why we must attempt such an adverse belief, which is not to ratify the image of the Father—an image we do find impossible, absurd, abominable, diabolical—but to separate us from the assumptions that induce this picture and so pervert how we understand deity. For it is a particular way of thinking about God, embodied in the satanic presumption of resemblance, that secures our picture of the Father as Milton's God and dictates our suffering: every time actor and reader in *Paradise Lost* fail to distinguish between how things appear and how they are, every time we suppose a single order of significance, suffering of some kind ensues. Thus Satan comes to abhor the inescapable distinction between himself and his creator, which in his apostasy he feels as disproportion and injustice, revenging himself upon God by perpetually alienating a third of heaven's creatures, not to mention despoiling the innocence of our first parents. For their part, Adam and Eve are brought to distort the sense in which they differ from each other in creation and marriage, then grow estranged and abusive in their attempts to defy those differences, and finally reject their original condition in Eden as unjust, even as Satan had done before them.

As for the observers of these events, speaker and reader alike, we undergo a version of it: either we readily identify the picture of such disproportion—God to angel, God to man and woman, man to woman—with Milton's truth, and find his argument unjust and his deity abominable; or we are moved to resolve these incongruities by translating them into symbolic or ironical expressions, distinguishing Milton's argument and Milton's God from what they appear to

say. But unlike irony, a symbolic translation allows us to evade the felt predicament which such incongruity evokes, and leaves us with no really adequate way
of explaining why Satan, Adam, and Eve make the choices they do, which an
aversion to God the Father readily supplies. When we interpret Milton's picture
of the Fall without allowing for the existential force of its incongruities, then
we go untouched by the difficulty, the moral profundity of each character's
predicament—by what life is like on the ground of creation. We are apologetic
for their suffering in Satan's fashion, as he meditates the ruin of Adam and Eve:
accept, he says to our first parents, your maker's work, which I give to you as it
was given to me; I am compelled to do what I would otherwise abhor (*LM*
4.379–92). The reader, I must confess for myself, can be unfeeling to the extent
that we disregard whatever does not conform to the extrinsic demands of our
symbologies.

Facere Deum thus conveys the ironical relation between creation and humanity, experience and actor, scripture and reader, whose peculiar tentativeness in
Protestant thought is frequently expressed by an "invitation" or "call" which
divine grace extends to us. This call we can choose not to acknowledge in the
sense of recognizing a truth or the bestowing of a benefit upon us, and so acceding in our speech and behavior to the obligation that such things by their very
nature impose. For observance of the impalpable and inscrutable entails faith,
understood both as an imaginative leap and as a retrospection by which we
conscientiously, interpretively incorporate the hidden God into our conflicted
experience, lending coherence to a world ostensibly devoid of him. So Milton's
speaker in *Paradise Lost* exerts his faith by evoking an assistance that goes seemingly unverified, either by the sort of colloquy that occurs in Herbert's poems
of affliction, or by a clear demonstration that the story he tells absolves God
from the local injustice of his own suffering or the greater tragedy of the Fall.
It is because of the speaker's plight, his estrangement from the God he would
justify, that the proems should be understood according to the mode of "assertion" that Luther regards as indicative of Christian faith:[16] one boldly asserts
the Christian picture of deity not to affirm the apparent sense of one's experience but to controvert and change it. It is this mode of assertion in Luther's
own language that offends the irenic Erasmus, for the simple reason that the
latter wants to bring faith into conformity with experience, not experience into
conformity with faith.

THE APOCALYPSE OF THE ORDINARY

But as a species of justification (which is most usually conducted retrospectively, as Stephen Toulmin points out, to examine the validity of an act or
assertion),[17] faith is not irrational in the way we are inclined to suppose. Like
logic, it creates the grounds, the conditions, and what is more the possibilities
of its own veracity; yet in doing so, it acknowledges the difference between the
truth it postulates and what humanly appears to be the case—between deity's

presence and its seeming absence from the ordinary world—a discrepancy conveyed by the necessity of having to imagine deity at all. One of the ways Luther
expresses this pictorial aspect of faith is to speak of the "masks" or *larvae* of
God, the phenomena which convey what God intends but without any analogy
to deity as such. Accordingly, Luther comments that only "the spiritual man"
"can distinguish the position [*persona*] from the Word, the divine mask from
God himself and the work of God. Until now we have dealt only with the
veiled God, for in this life we cannot deal with God face to face. Now the
whole creation is a face or mask of God. But here we need the wisdom that
distinguishes God from his mask. The world does not have this wisdom. Therefore it cannot distinguish God from His mask" (*LW* 26:94–95). Lactantius
(whom Milton apparently read) offers an example of this sort of mutual picturing and its purposes, when he argues that we must ascribe the human affection
of anger to God in order to promote justice in our world.[18] If he doesn't put it
quite the way I have, he nonetheless points to the inscrutable reciprocity between the idea of God and the effects of God which the distinction implicates.
While this mode of meaning or postulating a different order to things may
sound like hypothesis, it isn't; or, rather, the way we usually think of hypothesis
doesn't convey the scope of the speculation involved, or the severity of its risks
and constraints. ("Speculation," by the way, is Luther's word for this kind of
looking or picturing, which of course can be not just wrong but deleterious to
faith when we mistake it for deity per se [*LW* 26:287].) A more apt comparison
would be to Columbus acting on the idea of a global earth, putting out to sea
and sailing indefinitely west, or to Einstein's equations since these managed to
make intelligible many things which didn't exist for us conceptually or factually
until quite recently. God can be a postulate along these lines, with the scriptures as the given and the distinction between deity and the world as the instrumental truth which together make him at once imponderable and available to
us, in the image of the Christ suffering on the cross. What I am describing is
the problem presented by all impalpables or *invisibilia* and which I have referred
to as the peculiarity attending *res non apparentes*: namely, how do we *know*
something which exists for us only mediately, in the promiscuously diverse
shape of a world utterly unlike it? The usual expedient is to set up some alternate, usually prior and preeminent because unseen reality on the analogy of our
own, to which these expressions sympathetically correspond, or which another
scenario has them even inhabiting, like heaven or Olympus. But for the reformers, this correspondence is foreclosed by the distinction between God and the
world: we know only what God is in the restricted domain of human history
and experience—the domain of lament and thanksgiving to which the psalms
give voice.

   This perplexity in religious knowledge moves Hebrews to claim the impalpable or inevident, not the transcendental, as Christianity's purview when it
makes *res non apparentes* the objects of religious profession. That is a more profound difference than it might seem, since the impalpable does not exceed

experience; rather, it informs our lives at every level. But we grasp the impalpable only with difficulty, because it does not behave as other aspects of our experience seem to do. Indeed, the dilemma posed by impalpables like justice or the soul has been effaced ever since Socrates raised it, by sublimating these things into perfected entities and out of this world, or confining their actuality to the demands of convention and culture, or despite their remarkable force and ubiquity in our lives, reducing them to mere words—which, no matter how you look at it, is incorrigibly to equate them with things that do in fact appear to us. No wonder, then, that we confuse the revising of an express or apparent actuality (like that implicated in Rawls's "veil of ignorance" or by the theological distinction between God and the world) with mysticism, otherworldliness, irrationalism, or the sort of transcendental philosophy assumed for the whole seventeenth century and Milton too: a rationalism hostile to all *res apparentes*, things that *are* seen and touched—the material, the sensual, and particular— and which is forever retreating into falsely asserted and privileged realities like the mental or internal. I refer to the model of Descartes, which students of this period delight in extrapolating to European intellectual culture in general, for good or ill. But not all thinkers on a topic think alike, and as their inveterate sectarianism should indicate, not all Christians understand God, the soul, or faith in the same way, or there never would have been a Protestant reformation.

When God's hiddenness is understood in the reformers' sense, there can be no stable "object," whether perceptible or metaphysical, to which our ideas of the divine can refer. For the Holy One of Israel is so actively alien from human being that, in the demonic image of Exodus 5, the Lord is moved to kill the uncircumcised Moses to whom he had just revealed his name and his will. Scripturalism is the result of this constraint upon our religious knowledge; for we are thrown back upon the sacred text as uniquely God's speech to us, even as we are prohibited from reading its expressions as though there were any analogy between human and divine things. On this head, in the *Bondage of the Will*, Luther makes an appalling remark, directed against Erasmus's propensity for hypothesizing deity's motives and capacities by analogy to the accommodated speech of scripture. Luther says simply, "Your thoughts of God are too human," especially in the context of a *Deus absconditus* whose very hiddenness signifies his resistance to all creatural understanding, even the incarnate God's.[19] Luther uses this terrific idea—of a deity so unbounded in power and so alien in will as to defy its own revelation—as a caution against the religious complacency he sees expressed in the *Diatribe*'s unexamined anthropomorphism.[20] At the same time, because he isn't sceptic or mystic, because he believes that Christianity offers an account of the human condition both intelligible and true, Luther remains unsatisfied by the temporizing sort of paradoxes which appeal to Erasmus. He wants an intelligible religion but one consistent with the expressions of this hidden God. If I may take the instance most characteristic of Jesus' utterance, we are taught to call God "*Abba*" or father, and that this picture expresses an important truth about our dealings with deity; yet we have no definite sense how deity is our father, how it has gender, or even how it is a person and capable of relationship, only that scripture tells us this is so. In Luther's view, we must not rest in the estranging sensation of this mystery, or try to trace in Jesus' usage the speculative outlines of some invisible object: we must learn the different order of meaning, another attitude toward our experience, implicated by this humane picture of the absolutely alien. To the reformers, the force of the distinction between creator and creature does not discriminate a realm of divine *arcana* or a transcendental world where we encounter deity face to face. It compels us instead to recast our ordinary experience in such a way as to admit God. As an alternative faculty of knowledge, a different kind of reasoning, the purpose of faith is not simply to separate us from the received sense of things, but to attempt an understanding of the world sufficient to its subject, as well as to the needs of a church embroiled in persecution and controversy. In the theology I am trying to evoke, faith never retreats into incoherence, since this would be to repudiate justice and truth. Rather, it revises a mentality or understanding of this world that has been found inadequate or destructive, and offers another in its place, which may perhaps be more difficult to think but also more effective in explaining our experience to us (like the idea of curved space).

In speaking about ethical activity, Hilary Putnam suggests how this understanding works to clarify that experience. Unlike Alisdair MacIntyre, who assumes a specific content for morality (as one might guess from his comment on Milton), Putnam prefers what he takes to be the approach of Kant. He defines this as doing " 'philosophical anthropology,' or providing what one might call a *moral image of the world*":

> [Kant] is not simply providing arguments for the third formulation of the Categorical Imperative, arguments for the proper ordering of the formal and material principles of morality, and so on; he is also, and most importantly, providing a moral image of the world which *inspires* these, and without which they don't make sense. A moral image, in the sense in which I am using the term, is not a declaration that this or that is a virtue, or that this or that is what one ought to do; it is rather a picture of how our virtues and ideals hang together with one another and of what they have to do with the position we are in.[21]

While the Protestant reformers are not precisely internal realists (although they are arguably Kant's progenitors), they tend to see the knowledge scripture embodies as operating along similar lines to what Putnam describes. In other words, they treat scripture as an image or picture that organizes our sense of the impalpables God, faith, and the soul, telling us how we should view these things but never what they are substantially, or even in terms of our individual experience. That last question we must answer for ourselves, by means of this picture of God that we get from the sacred text. Nor is the scriptural image an allegory to be understood as gesturing at something outside itself—charting as it were the domain of the supersensory by reference to the senses. Rather, scripture raises a problem of usage and mentality like that Luther describes for things indifferent or inessential to religious belief: "There would be no harm in carving a statue of word or stone; but to set it up for worship and to attribute divinity to the word, stone, or statue is to worship an idol instead of God. . . . For the issue is not whether wood is wood, or stone is stone, but what is attached to them, that is, how these things are used: whether this wood is God, whether divinity resides in this stone" (*LW* 26:92).

In such a theology, to assume that some religious thing has a single, constant identity or value is nothing short of idolatry. That is because the understanding which an image or practice may create in us is always distinct from the religious reality it is used to evoke. For religious signs are only made such by God, when he joins his own intention to a thing by way of expressing himself; and even then, this new significance cannot extend beyond the particular occasion in which deity is thus revealed. Certainly, there is no singular meaning to his signs that would permit us to ordain and enforce their religious use, as though deity magically inhered in the thing. Thus the sense made of the scriptural image is crucial; for if we see it as somehow containing the divine, in itself or by analogy, we become Luther's sort of idolaters. But if we understand this expression as itself an allegory of relationship—as "prattling" or "babbling," the words Calvin gives to deity's speech about itself—then we observe the unutterable difference between God and his revelation. So when Calvin reads the story of Jacob dreaming of God upon a ladder between heaven and earth, he does not imagine that deity's presence and movement were just as the text portrays them: "For God who fills heaven and earth does not change location" (CC 130–31). "He is said to come down to us when he shows us a sign of his presence suited to our littleness," by which Calvin refers not just to the manner of the theophany, but to the way in which the text pictures it. It is, he observes, a "way of speaking" that we must recognize as such, and not the actual movement of objects in space whether visionary or invisible. Similarly, if the altar Jacob erects to God looks no different to us than the altars of idols, we have not rightly apprehended the use of the sign:

> In calling the place *God of Bethel*, he may seem to be too bold; and yet the faith of the holy man is praiseworthy at this point also, and that rightly, since he kept himself within the limits set by God. The papists are stupid when they claim to honor humility by exhibiting dull moderation. Humility deserves praise truly when it does not seek to know more than the Lord permits. But when he descends to us, adapting himself to us and prattling to us, he wishes us also to prattle back to him. And true wisdom is to embrace God exactly as he adapts himself to our little measure. Thus Jacob does not dispute with learned arguments about God's essence, but ac-

cording to the oracle he has received he brings God near and makes him accessible to himself. Because he opens his mind to the revelation his prattling and his simplicity are, as I said, pleasing to God. (CC 130)

Humility in the face of the distinction between God and the world is a necessary theological virtue, since it consists here in observing the boundaries placed on human knowledge of the divine, in picturing as against profaning the presence of the hidden God. So Jacob succumbs neither to idolatry nor metaphysics because he approaches deity just as it has revealed itself to him, pictured in the incident and the name but not as bodily inhabiting the place or as an abstract entity. And this picturing is what Calvin means by the "prattle" exchanged between them, insofar as there is no greater, more exact, or more sophisticated knowledge of God than the image Jacob has of wrestling with an angel and which he acknowledges in his memorial. For the picture alone creates as well as testifies to their otherwise untenable relationship, and this is what Jacob respects in calling the place *God of Bethel*: his faith in that picture has made God present and intelligible to him, which is the significance behind setting up the altar and giving the name. The action isn't so much symbolic as it is heuristic, an idea Calvin reiterates in discussing what Moses knew of God according to Hebrews, "as seeing him who is invisible" (Hebrews 11:27). Only here he does not consider how deity is made present by revelation but how it remains concealed from us even in faith. Thus he rejects the reading that would assign Moses a mystical or ecstatic experience, "that his vision of God divested him of his bodily senses and put him beyond the peril of this world" (CC 247). God appears here as he did to Jacob:

> Strictly speaking, God gave him a sign of his presence; but he was very far from having seen God as he really is. What the apostle means to say is that Moses endured as though he were lifted to heaven and saw God alone; as though he were beyond intercourse with men, beyond the reach of this life's perils and the struggle with Pharaoh. And yet, he was certainly beset with so many difficulties that he could not but imagine sometimes that God was far away from him; or, at least, that the obstinacy of the king, supported by overwhelming arms, would be impossible to resist effectively. In short, God presented himself to Moses as living, but not so that faith became superfluous. Moses himself, beset by terrors on all sides, turned his whole mind to God. As we have said, his vision helped him to do this; but he saw more in God than was visible by the sign of the bush. (CC 247)

Calvin's "as though" is indicative of this view of revelation in more than one way: it qualifies not only Moses' sight of God ("*as though* he were lifted up to heaven and saw God alone") but equally the force of the verse from Hebrews, which he reads "*as though* seeing him who is invisible." So both the historical event and the scriptural account of it are kept pictorial or figurative in their meaning, and to that extent constrained from signifying anything more about God than the apocalyptic fact. All other meaning is the imputation of faith and not in the nature of the sign: that Moses, in recognizing this token of God's presence, was enabled to trust in the promises made him, although they had yet to be fulfilled.

Furthermore, by denying Moses any ecstatic experience of the divine, Calvin asserts not only the immanence but the peculiar mundanity of our encounters with God. Both God's medium and his domain of expression belong to this world, whose meaning religious knowledge inflects in such a way as to make God "living," which is to say, to make him actual and powerful to us. By believing God present in the sign of the burning bush, Moses is able to understand his own predicament as something besides the catastrophic exile it seems to be. But because God is not palpable in any other way than figuratively by the insight of faith, Calvin imagines that Moses in the Exodus also suffered the sensation of deity's absence and apparent injustice, which is of course the experience expressed in psalmic lament. Nonetheless, by embracing what was pictured to him, "His apprehension of God's power absorbed all fear and every peril; leaning upon God's promise, he saw his people, even while they were being oppressed under the tyranny of the Egyptians, as already lords in the Promised Land" (CC 247). This is the Lutheran kind of justification at work, inasmuch as Moses in the midst of suffering and seemingly intractable difficulties could create a different actuality for himself and Israel by means of the picture he held of his God. In such a fashion, the image of God inspires an understanding of our predicament here and now—in Putnam's phrase, "the position we are in"—and of what lies before us, not beyond our comprehension, like the Wisdom literature to which the Book of Job contributes. For the reformers' God is an immanent, indeed a very much incarnate deity, at the same time that he cannot be identified with his several orders of incarnation (a way of construing "in the world but not of the world"). And faith lies in the ongoing pursuit of an intelligible relationship with deity by means of this picture, best expressed by the Christ, the incarnate God himself. Or—viewed more pragmatically, without the possibility of the marvelous that religion entails—faith involves using scripture's image of God so that it not only renders meaningful but also permits a change in our position in the world—all of which should be reminiscent of Job's theophany but also of the gospel's parabolic language and what Jesus says about it there, as a kind of expression that specially reveals the faith of the hearer and makes the mundane extraordinary. But it would be equally appropriate to invoke picture as David Burrell uses it, which is to characterize the restricted status of analogy in Aquinan theology. Burrell argues that although Aquinas may presuppose the propriety of speech about God, he nonetheless restricts the extent to which any other person can say in what that propriety consists, given the consequent inscrutability of its major predicates (for example, how do we conceive the "unity" of God?). For there is always a gap, represented by the distinction of God from the world, that renders the theological argument a discrete, integral figure or image, with the modality it ascribes to God understood as an idea for our use, not a description of deity's hidden being.

Both Putnam's "image" and Burrell's "picture" owe something to Wittgenstein, who in the later philosophy speaks of language as a picture of things we can't get around or push through to the world as it "really" is, and yet which we must not mistake for the world, as being somehow its facsimile in words or signs. Language must be about what the world variously is for us, which is not the same as saying it is a fiction or untrue. So what all these ideas of picturing share is a sort of reciprocal constraint, first against treating the image as though it *were* the world, with its elements somehow resolvable into real things (as a naive realist might), and second against denying the image its integrity as knowledge *about* the world (as a disappointed realist, that is to say, a sceptic might). This double constraint obtains in scripture as the reformers read it: we are given a language which we believe expresses what God wants us to know about him, but how it signifies is uncertain since it cannot "refer" to God in Wittgenstein's parodic sense of "pointing to" anything, directly or by analogy. It amounts to a perpetually deflected knowledge, since we cannot even begin to plot a course presumptively parallel with deity because we can never know the dimensions of the swerve away from God qua God, only that the distinction marks the point at which it occurs.

I have refrained as far as possible from invoking the term mystery in its theological sense, a term which ought properly to go with such religious terra incognita. That is because the word is loaded down with connotations of incoherence, irrationality, and mystical transcendence, which don't convey the renewed push toward a particular kind of intelligibility in religious experience which I believe the Protestant reformation makes. In Calvin's words, "man was made not only to breathe but also to understand" (CC 131). Yet such ideas, especially as pejoratives, tend to dog nontheological accounts of Christianity, except of course when the Protestant version is accused of promoting a virtual rationalism. But this innovative picture of God, whose use justifies, suggests another understanding or attitude which, it must be said, was never meant to harmonize the vulgar opposition between knowledge and unknowledge which we too frequently impose on religion. For one thing, the culture seeking this understanding for the most part admits no such dichotomy. The theologies of Luther and Calvin evoke a rationality that defers to mystery, not just as that word applies to divine things but to the ordinary wonders with which we live, like the way we know ourselves or experience the impulse of charity toward others. These things it is required to keep sacrosanct even as theology works to make their presence or the sheer fact of them at once evident and tolerable— tolerable, since we suffer the fact of the distinction between creator and creature, of a *Deus absconditus*, often as an unsurpassed cruelty. It was Luther who recognized the source of such suffering in our habitual inferences from the creature to the creator, which is what moved him to exclude all human agency from the process of salvation and to place the power of justifying unreservedly in the hands of God. For unlike most ethical doctrines of justification, the distinction denies any actual and therefore practical continuity between our ideas and God's.

It is to underscore this critical incongruity that Luther memorably describes the righteousness of faith as "a merely passive righteousness" since "here we work nothing, render nothing to God; we only receive and permit someone else to work in us, namely God" (*LW* 26:4–5). It is, he says, "a righteousness hidden in a mystery, which the world does not understand" because we persist in thinking of the divine on the model of this world, as a physics of moral activity or a calculus manipulating imponderables. But the creator is not the creature and does not behave as it does; and when we neglect the distinction and imagine an impossible parity between them, we ineluctably confront the terrible discrepancy between the two:

> But such is human weakness and misery that in the terrors of conscience and in the danger of death we look at nothing except our own works, our worthiness, and the Law. When the Law shows us our sin, our past life immediately comes to our mind. Then the sinner, in his great anguish of mind, groans and says to himself: "Oh, how damnably I have lived! If only I could live longer! Then I would amend my life." Thus human reason cannot refrain from looking at active righteousness, that is, its own righteousness. . . . Then it is impossible for the conscience to avoid being more seriously troubled, confounded, and frightened. (*LW* 26:5)

Alister McGrath very nearly makes the argument that Luther's theology is an account of this mental anguish called *Anfechtung*—the tremendous "assault" on self which comes when we realize that there is nothing we can do (in the "active" and thus mistaken sense of "doing") to secure in ourselves a righteousness satisfactory to God.[22] One does not have to be religious to grasp the debilitation and despair that accompanies the failed attempt to be like God; for a comparable effect attends any sort of scepticism which is not merely performative or opportunistic, but so profound that it too becomes an existential holocaust, in the ancient as well as the modern meaning of that word. For as a sacrifice accepted, ancient holocaust holds out the promise of a different eventuality, even a different self than the one in jeopardy. And so Luther here attempts to bring out of mental suffering an acknowledgment of God's uniqueness, and more precisely, the exceptional and indeed unnatural sense in which humanity is justified through Jesus Christ.

We feel the suffering occasioned by the failure or inefficacy of our religious ideas as though it were an injustice, since the difference between what we desire for ourselves and what we have makes the God who disposes our world appear nothing short of hateful. It is only when we depart from our incorrigible expec-

tation of an equivalence between creature and creator—between human modalities and divine, between God's usage and our habitual ways of thinking—
that we are relieved of the impossible burden of meriting salvation by our own
means. As Luther recalls, in that moment of relinquishing, our estrangement
from deity ceases, along with the fatal sense of an irreparable human condition.
So one might say that for Luther, faith as a right understanding of God entails
a resistance to any religious order of analogy that would assume some compatibility between what we do and what deity does. This is how Luther perceived
the scholastic argument for justification by congruous merit, in which deity
rewards each person for "doing what lies within one's power" (*facere quod in se
est*)—a sort of distributive justice taken over from Aristotle and Cicero and
applied to the covenant between God and humanity.[23] Certainly, as McGrath
points out, Luther engages in "a programmatic critique of the analogical nature
of theological language," beginning with his novel reading of righteousness as
something imputed by God and never potential in bare, unassisted human
being.[24] Moreover, he denies any comparability between the classical language
of civic virtue and the scriptural language of religious justification. To Luther,
they are incommensurable, and we only discover this ironically, when we try
to understand one by the other and fail, as Luther reports of himself.

ENCOUNTERS WITH THE HIDDEN GOD

When Calvin asserts in the *Institutes* that we do not choose faith but have it
imposed irresistibly upon us, he is not so much voiding our relationship with
God of any mutuality (of our cooperative assent, say, whether rational or voli-
tional), as he is using the distinction between deity and the world to preserve
us from the very anguish Luther recalls so compellingly. For while the idea of an
irresistible faith places those limits on understanding indicative of both God's
sovereign power and the gratuitous character of the covenant we have in the
Christ, it is also the case that it permits a relationship that would be untenable
were it not in some manner arbitrarily given. (This is the force of that other
Protestant motto, *sola gratia*, by grace alone). I am referring again to the queer
reciprocity that obtains with "the veil of ignorance": while it reinforces God's
distinction from the world, the veil works equally to shield us from the knowledge of this divine incommensurability and its overwhelming subjective impact. As Calvin observes, "Hence that dread and wonder with which Scripture
commonly represents the saints as stricken and overcome whenever they felt
the presence of God": "Thus it comes about that we see men who in his absence
normally remained firm and constant, but who, when he manifests his glory,
are so shaken and struck dumb as to be laid low by the dread of death—are in
fact overwhelmed by it and almost annihilated."[25]

Rudolph Otto locates intimations of this impact in the phrase *mysterium
tremendum* (which he associates with the numinous more largely considered
than just the Judeo-Christian deity).[26] By *tremendum* is signified the oppressive

awe, the dreadful energy of the holy, causing in those persons who encounter it the acutest creaturely self-abasement or consciousness of transgression; by *mysterium*, the sense of something so "wholly other" or in Luther's preferred usage, *alienum* or strange, that every means of apprehension we have is at once confounded and fascinated.[27] What may appear irrational and arbitrary in Calvin's formulation, as a sort of brief for faith as unknowledge, is really a crucial drawing of the boundaries within which our relationship with God and our knowledge of him is viable—both capable of taking place and being sustained and understood by us. Within these subjective limits signaled by "the veil of ignorance" and upheld by the idea of an irresistible faith, our experience of deity will be coherent and creative. But if we step outside them, in a futile attempt to extract our own acceptance from a *Deus nudus absconditus*—the false because speculative God—we cannot escape confusion and ultimate despair; for unassisted, our means are incapable of reconciling the divine to the human, and we therefore confront the gulf between these two dimensions of things as abysmal and desperate.[28]

Calvin evokes this impasse in his commentaries and *Institutes* by the ubiquitous figure of a labyrinth, which he uses ironically to picture the fact that we cannot know God in any way other than through faith in the person and promises of Jesus Christ, which is to say, by the sole intervention of the incarnate God. So in speaking of the practice of blood sacrifice and aspersion, Calvin follows Hebrews in arguing that "God cannot be sought, or found, for salvation, and neither can he be worshipped truly, unless faith at all times uses the requisite blood": "It is only right that we should find the majesty of God dreadful, and the way to it a hopeless labyrinth, unless we know that he turns to us with favor through the blood of Christ" (CC 100). And again, of legal righteousness: "Since in reading the law they wander aimlessly, the law itself has become to them a complicated thing, like a labyrinth; and it will remain such until it is turned toward its fulfillment, who is Christ" (CC 112). In sum, "anyone who does not begin his way to God with Christ, must wander, as it were, in a labyrinth" (CC 135–36). But more specifically in the *Institutes*, Calvin says that unless we pursue God from the vantage of Christ, "we shall wander through endless labyrinths," which is to say that we are thrown back upon wrong semblances of God—the scholastic idea of implicit faith, the testimony of nature, the equating of worldly with religious value, the *automorphia* of rationalism—which displace and do not convey deity, since the hidden God can be known only by the singular mediation of the Christ.[29] Insofar as all these semblances of religious knowledge serve to balk humanity of its putative object, Calvin uses the figure of the labyrinth sometimes to express the idea of religious solipsism, in which we are hard put to escape the deceptive coherence of received ideas, but sometimes to suggest how it is that God exists behind or within a riddle created by the very attempt at relationship with us. Believers cannot themselves transcend the limitation described by the labyrinth, because it is about the impassable boundary between the divine and the human. And part of the experience of that boundary involves suffering and a sense of discrepancy between the divine promise and the human fact, in the poignant manner of Luther's *Anfechtung*. For if Luther's theology emerges from a psychological conflict fomented by the improper analogy between things temporal and spiritual, profane and sacred, it could be argued that Calvin's is motivated by the need to explain an experience of relentless persecution that appears wholly at odds with the claims of the faithful to deity's eternally vigilant care.

Each reformer's theology then responds to a sense of contradiction, which for Calvin as for Luther is the universal state of humankind: the wicked prosper even as they earn God's wrath, and the good must bear the cross of persecution as a trial of faith. So Calvin says that "this world is a labyrinth where no escape from evil is in sight," except insofar as we live in the knowledge of the Christ: "It is not good sense to be dreaming in the midst of tribulation of a joy which shall rid us of all trouble. But the consolations of God do temper our experience of evil so that, while we suffer, we have joy" (CC 219). Calvin uses his figure of the labyrinth not only to keep the sanctity of God inviolate even from believers, but also to underscore the reality of human suffering: for the church has no ecstatic participation with deity but only an understanding, given by faith, that allows the faithful to see the hardships they endure as meaning something more and other than we compulsively imagine. Human suffering is the intractable reality; but its mitigation and the way out of the labyrinth comes in the shape of how we take it to mean—what the sufferer makes of it. In other words, it is made remediable by a different understanding of the relationship between our experience and the religious truth about things. The force of the distinction between creator and creature also argues that nothing about life can be supposed inevitable, much less hopeless of relief. Rudolph Otto offers a further comment pertinent to this problem, which is that one of humanity's most profound impulses, in regard to the numinous, consists in a desire for "covering" or "shelter" by way of a proffered consecration or atonement like that Calvin ascribes to Christ's blood, permitting us to enter into relationship with the holy thing that extends this benefit to us. The impulse to seek shelter has its motive equally and ironically in the desire for union with the sacred and thus "a longing to transcend this sundering unworthiness, given with the self's existence as 'creature' and profane natural being."[30] Transcendence doesn't necessarily entail becoming one with the numen, the mystic's goal; instead, it can involve a kind of grateful desire that does not disdain to accept an artificial, conceptual alliance with God, as against an untenable proximity.

These possibilities may be said to represent two different ideas of religious (and I would add, discursive) accommodation: on the one hand, in mysticism, the translation or assumption of self by the numen, to the end of relinquishing any separate identity or consciousness; on the other, in the experience of covenanting, the perpetual negotiation between two entirely individual parties, mediated by some instrument like atonement—itself a species of justification—which lays the ground for relationship. In the latter, we remain unaltered in nature and identity, but our position relative to God is changed by the mutual understanding of faith. Thus atonement as covering or shelter operates some-thing like "the veil of ignorance," insofar as deity agrees to overlook the sin that separates us from it and to forego its impetus to annihilate the unholy, again, as the Lord sought to kill Moses until Zipporah provides the shelter of a symbolic circumcision. For atonement is justice or equity achieved by con-tracting a fiction in which the actual, particular state of either party is formally discounted in order to ensure their ongoing relationship. As Otto explains, the paradox of necessary protection from God so that we can have access and a kind of familiar intercourse, if not intimacy with him, conditions religious knowledge for the Protestant reformers just as it does the larger religious experi-ence he analyzes. And the form such covering takes in their theology is the mediation of Jesus, who as the Christ atones for our creaturely sin by suffering in himself the full extent of deity's alienation from the world—God's just wrath—so that we may be restored to an indefinable affinity with our creator. For both Luther and Calvin insist that we remain sinners in fact but not *coram Deo*, in the sight of God, because, in Calvin's Pauline phrase, we are clothed in the righteousness of Christ.[31] The new covenant of Jesus Christ then involves a covering or justification of us that deity chooses to create and sustain over time. So Luther develops Paul's reading of the verse about Abraham's faith— "And it was reckoned to him as righteousness"—which the apostle construes to mean faith " 'imputed as righteousness for the sake of Christ' ":

> On account of this faith in Christ God does not see the sin that still re-mains in me. For so long as I go on living in the flesh, there is certainly sin in me. But meanwhile Christ protects me under the shadow of His wings and spreads over me the wide heaven of the forgiveness of sins, under which I live in safety. This prevents God from seeing the sins that still cling to my flesh. My flesh distrusts God, is angry with Him, does not rejoice in Him, etc. But God overlooks these sins, and in His sight they are as though they were not sins. This is accomplished by imputation on account of the faith by which I begin to take hold of Christ; and on His account God reckons imperfect righteousness as perfect righteousness and sin as not sin, even though it really is sin.
>
> Thus we live under the curtain of the flesh of Christ (Heb. 10:20). He is our "pillar of cloud by day and pillar of fire by night" (Ex. 13:21), to keep God from seeing our sin. . . . On His account God overlooks all sins and wants them to be covered as though they were not sins. (*LW* 26:231–32)

Yet the Christ's mediation is at once more manifold and more mundane than this one great focal act of the kerygma, which averts God's judgment from us for a time. The justifying force of faith in the Christ is a constant in every dimension of life, with Luther declaring that we must read scripture through Christ in order to enjoy the text's wonted clarity, because this peculiar under-standing alone justifies or makes intelligible, right, and true the sense of the text.[32] Similarly, as Edward Dowey argues, Calvin organizes the *Institutes* to re-flect the order necessarily obtaining in our religious knowledge, and with it, the key to the labyrinth or maze in which we otherwise wander; for in the *Institutes*, we encounter the salvific mystery and holy terror of predestination (Book Three) solely from the retrospective vantage and shelter of faith in the promises of God the redeemer, the incarnate God and Christ (Book Two).[33]

Moreover, in rendering superfluous a degree of independent, presumptive knowledge of deity which would otherwise be mandatory for our considered assent, Calvin's definition of faith as preordained and irresistible works to as-suage the enormous pastoral and psychological fear which Luther describes: that of supplying people with some palpable assurance of their justification before this evermore hidden God, who retreats from humanity's grasp even as he gradually recedes from the scriptural landscape until the moment of Chris-tian incarnation. The occasion of faith, or what Calvin terms our "calling," marks the boundary, the event, and the assurance of our acceptance by deity; for we are not meant anxiously to anticipate our election from a standpoint we cannot comprehend—namely, that of divine fiat or eternal decree, as some-thing forever and arbitrarily to be imposed upon us from before the beginning of time (the position taken by supralapsarian Calvinists like Beza). On the contrary, Calvin's conceptual enactment of the *ordo salutis* in the argument of the *Institutes* is by way of explaining the restricted, historical character of their religious knowledge to those who already believe, and to constrain them from pursuing just those delusions of deity which circumvent the Christ's mediation and leave humanity exposed and helpless before the unknown God. So Calvin observes elsewhere: "Those who seek their or others' salvation in the labyrinth of predestination, while they move out of the way of faith set before them, are insane"; and that is because "anyone who is not content with Christ, and pries into eternal predestination, takes it upon himself to be saved apart from God's counsel"—to delve into what is forever "hidden and secret" from human under-standing (CC 303). The things of God are intelligible and tolerable only from the shared vantage of Christ's justification, as interceding between humanity and a deity whose justice must be figured in the agony of a death by crucifixion. To benefit from that intercession, however, requires participating in the para-dox demanding it—of deity's covering us from itself in order that we may know it. For "Christ is the very image of the Father, and we should fix our eyes first on him":

> Christ therefore presents himself to us as the proper object of our faith. If we direct our faith to him, it will immediately find certainty and rest. He is Immanuel, who responds within us to our inquiring faith. It is a basic article of our faith that if we do not wish to go around and around end-lessly, we must direct our faith to Christ alone. If our faith is not to waver in the midst of temptations, it must be fixed on him. And this is the evi-

dence of faith that we never allow ourselves to be torn away from Christ and the promises we have in him. The papal theologians dispute, or rather chatter a great deal, about the object of faith; but they leave Christ out, and mention only God. Those whose knowledge comes from their writings must needs waver with the least breath of a breeze. Proud men are ashamed of the lowliness of Christ; therefore they fly to the incomprehensible deity of God. But faith seeks to attain heaven only by submission to Christ, whose countenance seems to reveal a lowly God; and it finds no stability unless it find support in the weakness of Christ. (CC 134–35)

The presumptive convergence of secular and sacred affairs actually has an opposite effect from the intended one of fostering theological as well as pastoral confidence in the matter of our salvation. As Luther remarks about himself, their merely ostensible convergence only serves to emphasize the antagonism between the righteousness presumptively ours by analogy—what we are told is our position—and our lived experience of the elusiveness of justice, truth, and God. Righteousness becomes an appearance without an actuality, and a kind of hypocrisy. So Luther's theology and Calvin's are inclined practically to disallow any such specific, positive pronouncement on what spiritual righteousness amounts to in this life—pronouncements of the sort which the medieval church had made and approved by ever more ingenious orders of analogy. This reticence is in keeping with the instrumental sort of justification, where the analogy to things human and secular no longer enjoys the status of a true or even a temporal relation, but has been relegated to a way of speaking or an expressive protocol that might assist but can also obscure a better grasp of the things of God. The reformers tend to say what righteousness is not, or imagine what it might be like, but not *what it is* in any palpable or positive sense beyond the conviction of faith. They offer up no certain signs, no telling correspondences beyond this one requisite that we believe in the Christ: hence their assault on works as a means to spiritual righteousness, because to correlate human with divine action would involve endorsing the very ideas and procedures that tolerate, even incite us to, conflict with God. To the extent, then, that this justifying promotes no specific evidence of our righteousness, where divine acceptance is thought to coincide with a felt disposition for the good, the reformers presuppose the difference, not the conformity of secular to spiritual actualities. The righteousness of God is not something that we recognize as though it were an extension of civic virtue, inasmuch as its apparent perversity challenges whatever we usually suppose to be the case. Yet religious justification does not thwart our assumptions in order to put some newly definite and positive idea in its place: rather, its purpose is less formal than psychological—to suggest that with this hidden God, nothing is inevitable or necessarily what it seems to be. The contradiction in received religion, out of which the whole reformation may be said to emerge, leaves the world wide open.

Calvin succinctly puts the Protestant view of justification when he says that "we are born exiles and complete strangers to the Kingdom of God and . . . we are perpetually at war with it, until he makes us other than we are by a new birth" (CC 138). This "new birth," a phrase that anciently describes religious conversion, does not work to confirm the analogy between human and divine ideas, or to reestablish a status quo; on the contrary, it asserts their congenital hostility. Faith "makes us other than we are," transforming our assumptions so that we are not in conflict but in relationship with God, and to that extent justified by him. And we are justified because this new birth involves more than some merely apparent change in our being that sorts with our expectations; it comprises a radical shift in attitude and understanding from which real, substantive change can arise. Faith disavows the illusion of fatefulness and intransigence which the status quo—given the existential failure of its explanations—projects onto human suffering. Thus the new birth means that we need not resign ourselves to suffering or its worldly onus since we are more and other than we appear, at least as regards our position before God, our spiritual righteousness. (There is a Lutheran rub to this liberty, in the form of his conservative fear of social revolt, which, while consistent with his theology, proved incapable of warding off practical expressions of freedom like Anabaptism.) All these ideas and effects are present in the subject of faith, Jesus Christ crucified and resurrected, a figure which expresses the instrumental kind of justifying—an ordering of the world that does not secure a state of affairs but anticipates its revision. Jesus' passion graphically insists upon the reality of human suffering, the discrepancy between notional justice and our experience, and the depth of our estrangement from deity and its different valuation of the world. At the same time, this suffering is represented in order to imply its terminus in the figure of the resurrected Christ, the religious and historical picture of the new birth. The perfectly righteous man and incarnate God humiliated, scourged, and tortured to death does more than defy our assumptions of value: in that person's position we see a possibility for our own lives that resists the force of those analogies which would make our worth in God's eyes subject to human assessments.

For that reason, the shape theological justification takes—the specific conditioning of words or ideas, of facts or perceptions, actions or events—is a postulate on the order of "the veil of ignorance." Because this impenetrable veiling of the divine is not only an acknowledgment of difference and inequity but also a fiction that imagines without defining the face of change. It makes conflict humanly intelligible (as in Calvin's frequent paradox, the sorrow of affliction tempered by a joyous hope), but in the effort to create a new, potentially just or truthful actuality. And it does this by reorganizing how we think about that complex of circumstances which represents our position in the world—Putnam's moral image of things. Calvin describes such revisionary thinking this way, not to suppress the fact of injustice and suffering or to preach their acceptance, but to anticipate a change in the order of our lives as a consequence of faith: "because the children of God even now have in them the incorruptible seed of life, by which they are called and sit with Christ, by faith, in heavenly glory. . . . Even while they are besieged by death, they have peace because they know that Christ defends them adequately, and that they are safe" (CC 196).

The figure of a resurrected Christ is to be used as Calvin recommends here, again not to deny suffering but to alleviate it by a conceptual turn. In other words, we cannot simply take the predicament of Jesus' suffering at face value, which is not to say that his pain and degradation are not utterly felt and actual; on the contrary, they are so real that they enjoin us to embrace another meaning at odds with their oppressive significance—to imagine a different order of value and a different world in which suffering is at once intelligible and revocable. For Christ is not only humanity estranged from God: he is deity entering in the most intimate manner into relationship with us, by assuming our very condition in order to transform it. In Hebrews' phrase, he offers the assurance of things hoped for.

Where the categorical kind of justification presumes in some degree formally to institute justice and right, the instrumental sort variously represents in itself the circumstances that might lead to such an eventuality. And the psalmist tells us that conflict and suffering are most often the means to this revisionary knowledge, to understanding our relationship to God rightly and justifying our sense of the world. Calvin says the same thing: "The whole carnal man must be reduced to nothingness that he may be renewed by God. For how does it happen that men live, or rather think they live, and are puffed up with vain confidence in their shrewdness and power? Only because they do not know God. Before he reveals himself to us we think ourselves to be not men, but rather gods. But when the Lord appears to us, then we begin to sense and realize what sort of beings we are. Humility arises from and consists in this: that man claim nothing more for himself and depend wholly on God" (CC 124). This isn't just the humility that Calvin evokes in Isaiah's vision of the seraphim, who cover their eyes with their wings because they cannot sustain a glimpse of God's glory. Yet, insofar as he construes that gesture to picture the distinction between creator and creation, and explicitly a circumspect knowledge of deity, it also bears on the origins of human suffering in sin—our self-induced estrangement from God. It is this suffering and sin which Christ assumes with his humanity, in order to redeem us from it; but his worldly degradation makes him repugnant to us, who want to know God in glory as a vicarious proof of our own. Therefore, part of our humiliation lies in accepting the odious actuality of Jesus, the crucified felon, as a description of ourselves *coram Deo*, in the sight of God, which is also what Calvin means by the phrase "when the Lord appears to us": the very form of the incarnate God enforces the idea that we do not resemble deity but are altogether unlike him, especially in our ideas of what god should be. So in discussing the Servant passages in Isaiah, Calvin remarks that the ugliness ascribed to the messiah "ought also to be understood not only of the person of Christ who was despised by the world and condemned to a shameful death, but of his whole reign. For that reign has had, in men's eyes, neither beauty nor splendor nor magnificence. In fact, it has nothing which could by its appearance attract men or charm their eyes" (CC 152).

While hardly unprecedented, ugliness is not the usual attribute of a god; but that deity confronts us in this way argues the extent of our apostasy. Where we seek divine splendor in Jesus, the gospels give us a strange and inexplicable humanity; and while this appearance should bind us to him because it frankly depicts our own condition without illusion or fantasy, we are repelled. On the model of Jesus' sanitized comeliness in commercial icons, we prefer to see ourselves palpably perfected in God—to be charmed, flattered, and seduced by the self-regarding notions we have of him. This is to suppress the gospels' picture, on which our justification depends, but also to deny the ineluctable reality of human being. As Calvin observes: "since men claim for themselves more than is good for them, and even intoxicate themselves with self-flattery, God takes away from them their false glory" with this chastening image of himself (CC 125). In short, the repulsiveness of the incarnate God resists our inveterate and wrongful analogizing from our desires to deity. On the other hand, it also describes the violent disturbance in humanity's existing relationship with God, reflecting back to us how we appear in our transgression: where we see our beauty and power, God sees our unholiness and criminal presumption. The appearances of Christ accordingly exemplify the reciprocal barriers which hinder relationship with the divine. "Yet to know God is man's chief end, and justifies his existence," declares Calvin (CC 125); so we are still left with the question, How is that we do know deity in the Christ? To refer back to Putnam's image or Burrell's picture, Jesus' resurrection does not reduce human suffering to the temporal, bodily delusion of the unenlightened. Nor does Jesus himself in the Passion transcend agony of mind and body because he is incarnate God— the reformers having nothing to do with the sort of stoic ethic or transcendentalism that would try to deify humanity by simply effacing Christ's anguish and pain. On the contrary, in Calvin's theology, "Christ in fact put on not only our flesh but also our human feeling; and this he did voluntarily," the only choice that renders his justification or ours real and effectual (CC 164).

Besides, as Luther remarks, there never was such a human being as the Stoics imagined. The effort to efface Christ's suffering is tantamount to translating Rawls's provision of equal ignorance into an axiom of social equity or fairness, to which it is the crude preliminary—as it were, a feature of the justification but not of the just world it would create. It would be like perfecting the status quo the better to entrench its inhumanity, since human blindness and cruelty precipitated Christ's atonement. But, as Calvin reminds us, "It avails little to know who Christ is, without knowing also what his will for us was to be and to what end he was sent by the Father": "This is why the papists have but the shadow of Christ; they care only to know his bare essence, and neglect his Kingship which consists in his power to save us" (CC 176). The difference between the means and end of justifying in this theological approach is more profound than analogy will allow us to think. If the knowledge of what is truly the case depends on respecting the conditions of justification, which include suffering, we do not regard these circumstances in order to perpetuate them, since they carry in some manner the original injustice or incoherence that obliged us to doubt their rightness. Instead, we are to use the image by which faith justifies us—the figure of Jesus Christ as suffering servant—in such a way as to imagine what will supersede it, even as we admit its critical truth. The image of the Christ's suffering operates as an antidote to the analogical God if, that is, we take it to explain "the manner of revelation" according to John 14:10. Calvin offers this comment: "For, as to his secret deity, Christ is known to us no better than the Father. He is rightly called the express image of God, for the Father revealed himself totally in the Son: but in the sense that God's unbounded goodness, wisdom, and power appeared in him. . . . Still, since Christ is here speaking not of what he is in himself, but of what he is toward us, it is a question of power rather than of essence" (CC 160). In short, religious knowledge as the knowledge of God "for us" has nothing to do with essential natures, only with revealed capacities. This expressive tact is what Calvin and Luther together call Christ's hiddenness and the hiddenness of all religious things, from the election and acceptance of believers to the church to the sense of the scriptural text. Just as deity is concealed in Jesus' person, it is amply if unexpectedly conveyed in his teachings and in his life; similarly, just as deity disguises itself in Jesus' passion, so it is disclosed to the faithful in his resurrection. So when Calvin reads Hebrews 11:1, he understands it as analyzing this peculiar inevidence of the religious:

> Thus, the apostle warns us that we must exercise faith in God not for things present but for things about whose fulfillment we are in suspense. And this paradox is not without its beauty. Faith, he says, is the *hypostasis*, that is, the prop, or the place we have, on which we may plant our foot; but the prop for what? I answer, For things not in our possession, things which are not under our foot, which are in fact even beyond the grasp of our minds.
>
> The same applies to the second clause, where he speaks of *the evidence*, or demonstration, of things not seen. But demonstration has to do with things that are seen; it is used commonly with regard to things open to our senses. Thus faith and demonstration apparently do not go together. And yet they do go together very well; for the Spirit of God demonstrates to us the things hidden to us and quite beyond the kind of knowledge which depends upon the senses. We are promised eternal life, but we are dead; we are told of a blessed resurrection, but we are in a state of corruption; we are pronounced righteous, and yet we are dwelling places of sin; we hear that we are happy, and yet we are buried under countless miseries; we are promised riches of every kind of good, but are exceedingly hungry and full of thirst; God cries that he will come to us quickly, and yet to our own cry he seems to be deaf. (CC 254)

These paradoxes illustrate not only the conflicted positions of Job and the psalmist in lament, but equally the predicament of Milton's speaker in *Paradise Lost*, who in their suffering still refuse to relinquish the picture of a just God. That predicament is also Milton's—in the intransigence of his talent, in his infamy and his blindness, all precipitated by the work he undertakes for his God. For each discrepancy Calvin mentions implicates an injustice or incoherence suffered by humanity and exacerbated by the promises of deity, since in every case our actuality seemingly contravenes what we believe. And the same might be said of Jesus himself, whose life and death would appear entirely to subvert his presumptive status as the Christ. What renders each contradiction at once real and remediable is the activity of faith, which discloses a reality that would otherwise remain unseen by us. When Calvin calls faith as "the *hypostasis*, that is the prop, or the place we have, on which we may plant our foot," his etymology epitomizes religious things as the reformers understand them, insofar as hypostasis renders the conceptual real. Yet not in the patristic usage, which violates the distinction between God and the world by speculating about the nature of deity per se: this faith speculates only about our place *coram Deo*, allowing us to see our circumstances as more and other than they appear to be from the novel and revolutionary vantage of our relationship to the hidden God. As Calvin explains it here, the position of faith is dialectical, converting the immediate or apparent sense of things yet not denying its force— only its finality, its all-sufficiency as a picture of our condition. The method of this conversion is not only conceptual but temporal, insofar as faith admits a historical and interpretive delay in our understanding of experience—what Calvin calls "suspense" or what Theodor Adorno has termed "the shock of inconclusiveness" (*ND* 33). Because religious things do not appear in themselves but are expressed mediately and often contrastively, to signal the distinction between deity and us, we are obliged to uncover their presence before we can even begin to apprehend their meaning.

With regard to deity's revelation, including its disclosure in the Christ, Calvin never allows knowledge of God's nature—only of his presence and intention. This discretion or tact may be said to reinforce the distinction, because the salvific sign deflects its meaning back upon humanity's position or understanding, to the effect of criticizing our ideas of creator and creation—a critique made equally by the very fact of this mediation as by the converse significance faith imputes to our condition. Yet, as Adorno observes, "going back to what it is not must impress the subject as external and violent" (*ND* 181). For if the sign reveals the presence of God, it also instructs us in the incalculable difference between his being and our own which restricts knowledge of deity to the human and historical sphere: "For there has always been between God and man a distance too great for any communication to be possible without a mediator" (*CC* 148). That is why, in the commentaries and the *Institutes*, Calvin identifies Christ, not the hidden God, as the Lord who walked in the garden of Eden and as the angel or messenger of Genesis; and he follows Luther in doing so.

Furthermore, he reads Jesus' epithet for God, *Abba*, as expressing not only how deity inflects itself toward us, but just this abysmal distance between God and the humanity the Christ assumes: "He refers to God as his Father because he is in the lowly state of the flesh, and has concealed his divine majesty under the form of a servant" (CC 136). Such restraint in the incarnate God can only ironize our deluded sense of likeness to deity:

> Before our minds seriously approach God, our life is an empty sham. We walk in shadows in which it is hard to distinguish true from false. But when we come into light, the difference is clear and easy to know. When God comes to us, he brings light with him, and we see our emptiness. . . . But does the sight of God really bring death to men? It seems absurd that the sight or nearness of God should destroy life of which he is origin and giver. I answer that it does this contingently, since death results from our fault and not from the nature of God. For death is already in us, but we do not perceive it except when it is contrasted with the life of God. (CC 124–25)

Accordingly, we must have faith as well as the patience, the power of endurance or perseverance in suffering, that Calvin educes from Hebrews so as to "give room enough" to God's different meanings and the redemptive workings of his providence (CC 183). This "room enough" is both a conceptual space and a moral liberty that allows criticism of the evident sense of things and reveals humanity's true plight in oppression and suffering, insofar as it rejects the analogies between God and the world that disguise our condition from us.

Adorno best captures the nature of the dialectic that I would argue faith entails for the reformers, when he says that "dialectics is neither a pure method nor a reality in the naïve sense of the word":

> It is not a method, for the unreconciled matter—lacking precisely the identity surrogated by the thought—is contradictory and resists any attempt at unanimous interpretation. It is the matter, not the organizing drive of thought, that brings us to dialectics. Nor is dialectics a simple reality, for contradictoriness is a category of reflection, the cogitative confrontation of concept and thing. To proceed dialectically means to think in contradiction, for the sake of the contradiction once experienced in the thing, and against that contradiction. A contradiction in reality, it is a contradiction against reality. (*ND* 144–45)

If I may apply Adorno's discriminations to the instrumental kind of justification, which is the mode of justification implied by faith in the Christ, the picture of Jesus of Nazareth as the son of God is not a doctrine or system because it does not picture deity except as it is toward us; and what deity is toward us— the man Jesus humiliated and crucified—appears to contradict God's theological definition as well as our corrupt expectations of a *Deus gloriosus*.[34] The suffering Christ is thus the "unreconciled matter" of deity that cannot be subsumed under one or other concept, human or God, although this is what certain modes of theological analogy seek to do: by positive or inverse correlation, they de-prive the incarnate God of his humanity, which they treat as a veil or threshold through which we can speculatively or ecstatically penetrate to deity per se. But the reformers do not allow any such transparency or circumvention of the Christ's human nature; if Jesus' humanity is a veil, it is one that cannot be removed or separated from Christ's deity, because the person Jesus shelters us even as he describes in himself the appalling force of the creator's distinction from its creatures. So the meaning of the Christ always remains in excess and antagonism either to our ideas of human being or of deity, resisting any one formulation. Such paradox and instability is also why the picture of Jesus is not a reality in Adorno's sense: it does not consign this world to suffering, for the Incarnation and Passion occur precisely to provide us with an alleviating significance for our lives.

It follows that Luther and Calvin would reject the ethical model of monasticism, in which celibacy and the mortifying of the flesh are cultivated as a veritable *imago Dei*. Indeed, they regard it as a species of idolatry, since monastic practice not only asserts an equivalence between divine and human righteousness—a doctrine of works—but also assigns Christ a single, definable, and purely palpable identity as a celibate or ascetic; monasticism chooses to confine the deity of the incarnate God by analogy to what we can see of him, so that the Christ is worshipped as an image of human suffering which we at once emulate and transcend by renouncing a peccant world. But adoring Jesus' appearances is no less idolatrous than worshipping the place where God reveals himself, a delusion Jacob avoids insofar as his altar is used to signify the encounter with deity, but not to enshrine its presence. The manner of Jesus' life should be understood as comparably instrumental: it teaches us how to know the hidden God, the position of faith, not how to be like him.

In the *Institutes'* headings to Book One, "The Knowledge of God the Creator," Calvin states that "*Without knowledge of self there is no knowledge of God*" and "*Without knowledge of God there is no knowledge of self*," a reciprocity which has no point of origin, since "which one precedes and brings forth the other is not easy to discern."[35] This self-reflexive criticism is something along the lines of what Adorno says about contradiction requiring us to scrutinize our assumptions. For once confronted with the incoherence or incongruity that suffering exposes in the world, we are compelled to acknowledge a disparity between what we imagine for ourselves and our actuality, and so to rethink our position in the light of such felt discrepancy. And we do this in order to create a more viable and coherent picture of the world as we find it, which must incorporate the fact of contradiction. Yet this coherence must be speculative, conceptual, or what Adorno would call theoretical, until such utopian time as the actual causes of suffering are removed, at which point we would no longer experience contradiction. So in effect, the conflict of worlds and value embodied in our lives and pictured in the suffering Christ compels us to reflect upon and to alter our ideas even as we persist in the painful predicament this anomaly intrudes upon us. And according to the reformers, in doing this, we are justified before God.

GOD CONCEALED BENEATH HIS CONTRARY

Calvin discusses the experience and human impact of contradiction on more than one occasion, but the following passage from his commentary on Ephesians is typical:

> However, here Paul rightly enjoins us to consider the power of Christ; for, so far, its presence in us is hidden, and *God's power is perfected in our weakness* (II Cor. 12:9). How are we ahead of the children of this world, except that our situation seems to be worse than theirs? Even though sin does not reign in us, it is still there. Since death itself is working in us, the blessedness we have by hope is totally hidden from the world; for the power of the Spirit is something flesh and blood knows nothing about. Meanwhile, we are exposed to a thousand distresses, and more than all other men are become objects of derision.
>
> Hence, Christ alone is the mirror in whom we are able to see the glory which is altogether blurred in us who live in weakness under the cross we ourselves bear. Since it behooves us to raise our minds on high, to believe in righteousness, blessedness, and glory, let us learn to turn them to Christ. For we now live subject to the dominion of death; but he, having been made alive again by power from heaven, even now has life and dominion. We labor in servitude to sin; and besieged by a thousand afflictions, we are engaged in a dreadful warfare (I Tim. 1:18); he on the other hand, being seated at the right hand of God, has received all government in heaven and on earth, and triumphs wondrously over his foes as he defeats and overthrows them. We bite the dust, covered with contempt and ignominy; to him is given a name which fills men and angels with reverence, and makes devils and godless men grovel in fright. Here we are impoverished, so poor that we lack everything we need; he on the other hand has been appointed by the Father to possess all blessings and to dispense them according to his good pleasure. In view of all this, we shall be the gainers if we turn our minds to Christ, so that in him, as in a mirror, we may contemplate the wonderful treasures of divine grace and the infinite greatness of God's power, all of which we can hardly discern at present in our own lives. (CC 199–201)

Calvin thus emphasizes the hiddenness of religious things this side of the distinction, a concealment that faith and hope alone can overcome and then only to a restricted degree. Consequently, Christ's "mirroring" that religious reality for us depends on a premise also hidden in Calvin's account, in the sense of tacit or implicit. For all we can see—as against imagine—of the incarnate God is his suffering, the one analogy to our condition that if we admit its critical force in the Atonement, binds us to him and allows him to mediate for us with God. So in enumerating the miseries not just of the faithful but of humankind, Calvin underscores what we palpably share with Christ, which is our suffering humanity. That is all we can "discern at present in our lives," and all that we can immediately discern of God, inasmuch as suffering defines our experience of the world.

But by virtue of acknowledging this contradiction or injustice, both in Jesus' passion and in our lives, we are moved to imagine the possibility of its relief on the model of Christ's resurrected and translated state. That Christianity is a transcendental argument about truth has been inferred from statements just like Calvin's, where we escape the hardships and falsehoods of this world by some ecstatic or rationalized escape to the perfected reality claimed for Christ. Yet I think this is to misunderstand what Calvin is saying, or rather to neglect the image of deity he assumes, which is not a transcendent but an incarnate God whose divine essence and majesty are utterly concealed from us. So what he describes here is precisely the recognition of earthly injustice, of human paltriness and weakness when left to ourselves, without a proper idea of God and truth and so the possibility of change. But we can be redeemed from this state by a faith, or as Luther would have it, a correct picture of God, which endues our experience with altogether different meaning.

Put another way, we suffer not because God is absent or unjust; we suffer as a trial of our ability to sustain a terrible ambivalence and delay between what we are and what we desire to be—a trial of faith. And in such conflict and suspense, Calvin locates several necessities: first, that we observe the distinction by separating deity and truth from the manner of their expression, for this is the exercise of faith in which we are justified before God; that we therefore resist the world's notion of righteousness as an idol and an illusion, since it allows, even encourages, the commission of injustice and the infliction of suffering; and finally, that in resisting that idea, we imagine and pursue another reality which involves the justification or reform of this one. It is the last necessity that accounts for the impact of Calvinism on political practice from the sixteenth century onwards. For Calvin, to live according to God is to acknowledge injustice and to wish to eradicate it, although that activity may be restricted to the institution of a theocracy. In other words, the proscribed theology that drove Calvin to Geneva expresses the same impulse as his political reforms. If we do not recognize Calvin's justice as our own—although it must be remembered that he sought to save Servetus from the flames—it should not go unacknowledged that suffering and faith wrought in him an imperative desire to change *this* world, *this* actuality. Were his an ecstatic or quietistic religion, there would have been no civil war in England. Indeed, the "mirror" that Christ holds up to the faithful is not an image of transcendence, but of reform: as we are altered in our own eyes and so justified *coram Deo* by embracing that picture of deity, so we are moved to justify in the sense of revising the ideas and practices of the world in which we participate. It is precisely because of the way Calvin distinguishes between God and the world that he has no essential commitment to preserving the status quo, which he cannot regard as true or just theologically or in his own experience. Only deity and its things can claim to be such, whose pursuit then makes for an urgent, volatile faith. Despite the fact that he has seemed to some readers strangely lacking in Christology, Milton brings this dialectical, revisionary kind of justifying to the ways of his poetry, where almost every important work involves a justification on this order. And those doing the justifying, including Milton himself, are obliged by the condition of deity's hiddenness, as something incalculable and estranged, to describe how truth is expressed in this world, not what truth is per se—the argument of the *Areopagitica*. So the force of analogy or accommodation in any speaker's utterance is reflexive, comprehending how we are inclined to think about God, both the way deity would have us understand it and the way we choose to do so, which as Calvin points out, are rarely one and the same thing. Instead, these disparate understandings describe a perpetual conflict at the heart of Milton's most considerable poetry, long before he writes *Paradise Lost*.

That is because justification as an activity concerns itself with the human conditions of truth and justice, which Milton seeks at once to revise and vindicate in his writings. In their Christologies, both Calvin and Luther emphasize that Christ as the word and "express image of God" exemplifies this boundary or constraint: he is the God of the sacred text both as actor and inscription. Yet it is peculiarly Luther's contribution that, as deity become flesh and a human person, Jesus too is *absconditus sub contrario*—God hidden beneath his opposite; and this phrase or epithet describes that singular revision in the way we think about the divine, which is once again that we cannot know deity's nature by the media of its expression, including the incarnate God himself.[36] Especially as it consists in Jesus' life and teachings, we use the character of divine revelation to adjust our thinking about God, a justification that allows us to regain relationship with him. But neither revelation nor our faith in it may be said to perform our justification *coram Deo*: that lies in God's hands alone, who responds to this conversion in our religious ideas by imputing Christ's righteousness to us, not our own. The suffering Jesus as Christ and incarnate God is not deity's correlative but its instrument, which conduces in this world to justice, truth, and the right; and we know God only by repeatedly interpreting or translating our particular experience in terms of that justifying picture—a dialectical knowledge without the illusion of immediacy or the satisfaction of closure. This is one reason why even Milton's early poems—*L'Allegro* and *Il Penseroso*, the Nativity Ode, *Comus* and *Lycidas*, as well as his sonnets— do not end in any conclusive way, for they still look forward to what remains as yet inevident in the speaker's world.

Luther invokes this variously deflected or inconclusive aspect of Christian knowledge when, in the Heidelberg Disputation, he asserts that the person who seeks to understand the creator by analogy to his creation conflates the human with the divine, with the result that a theology of human glory is produced that worships the creature, not its maker:

19. The one who beholds what is invisible of God, through the perception of what is made [cf. Rom. 1:20], is not rightly called a theologian.
20. But rather the one who perceives what is visible of God, God's 'backside' [Ex. 33:23], by beholding the sufferings and the cross.
21. The 'theologian of glory' calls the bad good and the good bad. The 'theologian of the cross' says what a thing is.[37]

The true theologian is one who knows God by Jesus' torture, humiliation, and crucifixion, which taken together Luther calls deity's *visibilia et posteriora*, after the episode in Exodus where Moses asks the Lord if he may see his glory.[38] The Lord responds to Moses' request by initially speaking of the several signs through which he will express divine power and goodness so as to distinguish Israel as his people, but ends with the statement, "You cannot see my face; for man shall not see me and live" (Exodus 33:18–20). But then he admits Moses to a wondrous sight: "And the Lord said, 'Behold, there is a place where you shall stand upon the rock; and while my glory passes by I will put you in a cleft of the rock, and I will cover you my hand until I have passed by; then I will take away my hand, and you shall see my back; but my face shall not be seen'" (Exodus 33.21–23). The anthropomorphism in this episode can be read as indicative of Moses' special intimacy with God—that he knows the Lord's very "body" whereas the people know deity only by signs. At the same time, his unique knowledge of this "body" as the manifestation of God's *kavod* or "glory" is restricted both temporally and spatially, since he must view it at a distance and from behind (or in Walter Eichrodt's more faithful and exquisite phrase, "at its extreme edge and outskirts").[39] To know deity face to face is certain death, which is why Moses' theophany diverges from the apparently comparable occasion when Aias son of Oileus glimpses the legs of the disguised Poseidon, as that great god walks away from him. For in the Homeric world, Aias remarks with rare pertinence, "Gods, though gods, are conspicuous."[40] Despite or perhaps because of their propensity to conceal themselves in natural and human forms, the Olympians are always revealed by their perfected beauty and power, not by a profound estrangement of their being from the human world of value, as the different hiddenness of Moses' God implies. For however terrible its impact—a mist-shrouded Apollo looming up behind Patroklos fatally to stun him—the Homeric numinous is more or less consistent with human expectation and not absolutely inimical to us, either by sight or proximity.

By contrast, the sight Moses has of the Lord's glory articulates the paradox of the numinous in this other theology, God encountered under the covering deity itself dispenses, a picture conjoining intimacy and estrangement, enmity and dependence. The same complexity is maintained when Luther asserts that "From the day of Adam, Christ has always revealed God to mankind": "Yes, Moses himself could not behold God. When Moses desired to see God, saying: 'Show me Thy Face!' God said: 'Indeed, if you would see Me, you would have to die; however, I will show you My back and My cloak, but to behold My face means death' (Ex. 33:18–20). Thus Moses viewed God's mercy from behind, as it is seen in the divine Word" (*LW* 22:156–57). In another place, he observes:

> God also does not manifest Himself except through His works and the Word, because the meaning of these is understood in some measure. Whatever else belongs essentially to the Divinity cannot be grasped and understood, such as being outside of time, before the world, etc. Perhaps God appeared to Adam without a covering, but after the fall into sin He appeared in a gentle breeze as though enveloped in a covering. Similarly he was enveloped later on in the tabernacle by the mercy seat and in the desert by a cloud and fire. Moses, therefore, also calls these objects "faces of God," through which God manifested Himself. Cain, too, calls the place at which he had previously sacrificed "the face of God" (Gen. 4:14). This nature of ours has become so misshapen through sin, so depraved and utterly corrupted, that it cannot recognize God or comprehend His nature without a covering. It is for this reason that those coverings are necessary. (*LW* 1:11)

The "face of God" here means something other than it does in Exodus 33, where the full sight of deity kills; indeed, "face" describes the same thing as God's *visibilia et posteriora*—the creaturely and historical expressions of deity, his *larvae* or masks. The difference is positional and modal: *posteriora* evokes the recursive, interpretive, delayed, or suspended knowledge of God which we educe from the phenomenal signs of his presence and in scripture, thus expressing the distinction between God and the world. But "face" represents how we must use these signs, especially the picture of Jesus Christ, since faith requires that we regard them as the countenance of God. Given the way Luther explains the necessity of covering, the matter of religious knowledge is displaced from deity per se, which is inconceivable and unknowable in its essence, to the media of God which we encounter as his "faces"—in the theological phrase, God toward us. This is "face" in Wittgenstein's sense, when he says that "The human body is the best picture of the human soul" (*PI* p.178), or remarks parenthetically that "Meaning is a physiognomy" (*PI* p.568). It is not that the soul directly corresponds to the features of the body, or that meaning is restricted to the literal or immediate sense of words; rather, what Wittgenstein would evoke is a complex sort of expression, which involves the mastery of a figurative or pictorial idiom by which we construe such *res non apparentes* like the soul and meaning itself in relation to their appearances, but not *as* their appearances. We are gauging the sense of one thing by something altogether different on which it is contingent, or perhaps I should say, on which the knowledge of it depends— the "unseen" upon the "seen," but not, as Luther complains of the theology of glory, in the supposition that that these are analogous to each other.

We should think instead of that Protestant apothegm, best articulated by John Hales, who declares that "Scripture is the voice of God: and it is confest by all, that the sense is scripture, rather than the words."[41] The scripturalism of the reformers is of this kind, because it conceives the sacred text as implicating rather than containing a certain meaning—a memorial rather than a shrine; and for that implication to be properly understood, we should neither add nor subtract from the textual physiognomy. If we do so, we alter the terms in which deity asks to be known, the manner of its meaning, and summarily distort the knowledge of God which scripture offers us. This insistence on the integral meaning of the text, despite every obscurity and omission, explains why both Luther and Calvin reject the superadditive of tradition, as Catholicism calls its accrued history of commentary and custom: the reformers want us to encounter the relatively untrammeled text before us, without intermediaries or impositions to buffer our reading from the text's lapses and incongruities. For these play an instrumental role in organizing how we read scripture's expressions. Stanley Cavell remarks that in this kind of figurative idiom, or what Wittgenstein calls "interpretation," "secondary meaning," or "seeing something as something," there is "no antecedent agreement" about what any given expression may signify: "You could say that words used in such connections have no grammar—and that would itself be a grammatical remark" (*CR* 355). If we apply this idea to the reformers' theology of revelation, it evokes the radical contingency of theophany, by which I mean that the form assumed by God's disclosures—his tropes or signs—have only an arbitrary relationship to deity, which often incongruously joins them together to express itself. So there is no evident, much less natural, correspondence between God and his faces or coverings; there is only the relationship that he creates incidentally, in the mind and in history. In Luther's account, this contingency is conveyed by the sheer variety of deity's coverings—as a place to Cain, everything from weather to religious paraphernalia for Moses, and to Adam estranged by sin, *as if* deity were contained in a breeze.

So once again, in Luther's concept of God's faces as in his *posteriora* and *larvae*, we meet the distinction between God and the world. Such is the qualifying force of Luther's "as if": it suggests the extent to which God, or rather God's presence, is not manifest but must be detected by us—not deductively, according to what we expect, but by another faculty of apprehension altogether. Cavell makes something like the same point in elaborating Wittgenstein's remarks, since the physiognomy of meaning entails a kind of imaginative projection: "Imagination, let us say, is the capacity for making connections, seeing or realizing possibilities, but I need not accomplish this by way of forming new images, or anything we are likely to call images. . . . Vivid imagery, in fact, may defeat the purpose" (*CR* 353–54). This resistance to new or vivid imagery is like the reformers' resistance to analogy or Catholic tradition, because anything extrinsic or superimposed upon text or world has the potential to distract us from their proper meaning. To use Cavell's supple instance, imagination in this sense has to do with seeing a person's blink as a wince, and associating that wince with some occurrence elsewhere that could elicit it (CR 354). God is known in just such a fashion according to Luther and Calvin, with no more or less certainty, by a kind of intentionality which the sensitive, faithful mind brings to its experience. Cavell continues this line of thought in a direction equally pertinent to their theology, when he comments that he "would like to say that the topic of our attachment to our words is allegorical of our attachments to ourselves and to other persons" (CR 355): "The idea of the allegory of words is that human expressions, the human figure, to be grasped, must be *read*. To know another mind is to interpret a physiognomy, and . . . this is not a matter of 'mere knowing.' I have to read the physiognomy, and see the creature according to my reading, and treat it according to my seeing. The human body is the best picture of the human soul—not, I feel like adding, primarily because it represents the soul but because it expresses it. The body is the field of expression of the soul" (CR 356).

For the reformers, the world is God's physiognomy, his field of expression in Cavell's sense. It is also God's countenance, in that we are to approach deity revealed in its creation as we would a personate being, a body with a soul. This is what Luther's use of "face" means in the previous passage: that faith involves a certain attitude toward the phenomena of everyday life not only as expressive but also in a peculiar manner intelligent. But there is a further order of mediation that transforms God's signs into this animate allegory, from indices into expressions as Cavell tenders those ideas, and that is the intercession of the Christ. With the atonement, God's revelation becomes the sort of figure that Luther discovers all over scripture, catachresis or mixed metaphor, which is to say a conflating of two logically incompatible ideas as in the contradiction God-man. Cavell's "expression" resembles the kind of picturing Burrell or Putnam talk about, and the way Wittgenstein speaks of language's peculiar relation to the world, which is also as a kind of picture. If we regard allegory less as a scheme of correspondence, and more as a flexible, responsive expression in this sense—as manifesting an attitude toward what it conveys—then the world viewed from the vantage of faith in the Christ becomes an allegory of deity: our experience conveys God to us but in a way alien to his nature or mode of being, rather like the practice of impersonation. That is to say, by agreement or convention, we take a given person as though she or he were someone else, all the time conscious of the difference between them. Our awareness of this difference alters our sense of what the person says and does, giving these human behaviors an unaccustomed salience, a different intensity and inflection from the ordinary. It is as though we had to recognize our actions all over again. Certainly this is part of the pleasure of theater, as the artificer of belief.

Of course the best, most perfectly intimate impersonator of God in this sense is Jesus Christ, as he is intended to be. Since we can know God only through Christ in this theology, which is to say by observing the order of meaning he teaches and embodies, there can be no symbolic system to knowing God, no

consistent or predictable revelation. The form deity takes is arbitrary or incidental to its nature; moreover, in expressing God's desire and will and intelligence—what we think of as personality or soul—we are asked to approach these
signs in Jesus or in the world as a conversation taking place within a relationship, as the face of God to us. Because the incarnate God or God revealed in
history and in human suffering inflects deity in such a way that we experience
it as a contradiction or incongruity, neither the world nor the person Jesus
Christ (like Wittgenstein's body or physiognomy) can provide a transparent
access or simple correlative to deity. What the incongruity does instead is to
create a further deflection or swerve in our knowledge of God, even as the
incarnation brings deity into a new proximity to humankind. In the reformers'
commentary, Moses does not see God face to face, and moreover must impersonate that mediated presence of deity to Israel, which distances God even
further from his chosen people and renders our knowledge of him that much
more remote. Yet there is a purpose to such reserve, which Luther describes in
the following way, once again recalling the language of Hebrews 11:1: "faith's
object is things not seen. That there may be room for faith, therefore, all that
is believed must be hidden. Yet it is not hidden more deeply than under a
contrary appearance of sight, sense and experience. Thus, when God quickens,
He does so by killing; when He justifies, He does so by pronouncing guilty;
when He carries up to heaven, He does so by bringing down to hell. . . . Thus
God conceals His eternal mercy and loving kindness beneath eternal wrath,
His righteousness beneath unrighteousness."[42]

This passage evokes "room enough" for faith in Calvin's phrase, as well as
the deflected, interpretive experience we have of deity that Luther likes to
emphasize. To these circumstances expressive of deity's inconceivable being
and the consequent delay or suspension occurring between God's revelation
and our apprehending it, Luther adds a further aspect characteristic of his sensibility and conveyed by the image of God's "backside": we tend to experience
the divine as vulgarity—as expressed by the things we despise or neglect—so
disaffected and partial is our understanding. Again, this is not a mystical or
ascetic idea but rather the same problem posed by Christ's ugliness, which is
that we want to see God in a way that exalts, not diminishes, our sense of
ourselves. So to Luther, Moses' unparalleled sight of God represents in epitome
how deity may be intelligible to us, but also why it is that we don't acknowledge
its presence. For we desire to know and yet fail to grasp the presence of God
because of the assumptions we make about it. As theophanies go, the vision we
have of Christ is closer in kind to what Moses saw than the sight Aias had of
Poseidon, but it is one for which we are perpetually unprepared by our religious
ideas. Religion as a human practice inclines us to measure God by our own
devices and desires, only perfected and transcendent; and so we tend to lose
any sense of the holy as an ineffable departure from human value. Accordingly,
Luther locates God in the things we find repugnant or merely ordinary—in

posteriora: he wants to resist our propensity to domesticate God by making him over in our image, since in the habitual analogy we make between our ideas and the divine lie both human transgression and the cause of our apostasy from him, which Milton calls idolatry.

The rough pictorial equivalent of this propensity of ours, which Luther calls *Deus gloriosus* and Calvin attributes to the fantasies of the proud whose "intelligence is but vanity," appears in certain Romanesque crucifixions, where a dapper Jesus is shown without wounds or pain, more or less gracefully disposing himself upon the cross in his resurrected glory (CC 131). Such an image would convey to Luther no knowledge whatsoever of God, hidden or incarnate, no means of bringing us in our estrangement to the Holy One of Israel somehow present in Jesus Christ. He would regard it instead as a celebration of ourselves or more exactly, of religion's temporal power as a great affinity of humankind. But the scandalous idea that God is disclosed supremely in Jesus' suffering, which is the force of the cross for Luther and Calvin, demands that we return to the sensations of alienation and loss generated by the presence of the holy, and thus to the fact of the distinction between God and the world. What we learn from this felt discrepancy does not affirm but instead revises our ideas of deity and its relationship to its own creation. The shock of God crucified pushes us to relinquish what we think we know about God, and to set about understanding him and his things in a way less familiar and facile, yet according to the reformers, more assured. We must seek deity in the light of its resistance to our familiar ideas and revise our notions of truth accordingly.

So as an image describing what God is toward us, not to mention the manner of our own justification, the sufferings of Jesus of Nazareth have a certain unexpected complexity. Indeed, the least complicated idea attached to them is that of vicarious sacrifice, a mediation of inequivalents which possesses the profound yet simple force of myth, and the inexplicable surplus of significance that attends mystery. But Christ having performed this sacrifice on behalf of humanity, difficulties tend to accrue around the figure of Jesus for anyone wishing to know, say, how God might become human and suffer; how the hidden God without sacrilege could be imaged; how deity might be distinct persons and yet one God; how those chosen and redeemed are recognizable even to themselves. It is characteristic of the reformers that both give these questions short shrift, not so much because they are impertinent as because they are insufficiently fundamental, speculative, and at this stage of reformation, deleterious to faith. In other words, they do not bear directly on the issue of how we encounter the hidden God in Jesus. Once this encounter is understood, such questions may be susceptible of evaluation and perhaps a kind of answer (the project of Protestant scholasticism). But they can neither prove the divinity of Christ nor induce belief in an unseen God, granted "the veil of ignorance" that negotiates between humanity and God and is figured by his hiddenness.

In expounding Calvin's theology of the Eucharist, T.H.L. Parker provides a good sense of this antipathy to speculation in the reformers and how the distinction justifies it.[43] Thus for Calvin, the crucial question that theology must address is not "How is [Christ's] body eaten by us," the scholastic problem that also precipitated a great Protestant controversy. Instead, it should be "How does the body of Christ, as it was given for us, become ours? How does the blood, as it was shed for us, become ours? In other words, how do we possess the whole Christ crucified and become partakers of all his blessings?" As Parker comments, the first question, having to do with the mode of Christ's presence in the Eucharist, "is as little determined by Scripture as the primary questions: 'How did the Virgin conceive the God-man?' or 'How did the Word of God create light?' or 'How did Jesus Christ rise from the dead?' " Since deity has chosen not to answer them, all such inquiries lead away from the gospel account, the one authentic source of knowledge about God, into the realm of human speculation and fantasy. So they not only violate "the veil of ignorance" between God and the world, but also intrude upon "the room" faith should have to exercise itself, while in the process creating disunity in the church.

One need only look at the phrasing of what Calvin clearly regards as pseudo-issues to see what he would find objectionable in them, namely, that such inquiries treat the things of God as though these observed spiritual physics or biology which can be defined and detailed by us. So once again, the problem of faith devolves upon an inadequately circumspect use of theological analogy, with Calvin insisting that we cannot judge deity according to our own necessities, as though it were intelligible in such terms, much less constrained by them. Instead, we must approach divine things relationally, as expressing and not representing deity, after the way in which Calvin understands the Eucharist. Parker remarks that even as Calvin refuses to entertain the first question about eating the body of Christ, he revises the question of means or *quomodo* so that it asks instead: " 'In what way, so far as its effect upon us is concerned, is the body of Christ in the sacrament?' With the answer, *vere et efficaciter*, genuinely and effectually. Beyond this he would not go."[44]

With this refusal in the vexed issue of the Eucharist, Calvin dismisses all inquiry into deity per se, directing us to God's expressions on this side of the distinction, in the human and historical world. Similarly, the order of the *Institutes* argues that theological discussion is retrospective and justifying of Christian belief insofar as it clarifies our relationship to God. But it cannot serve as a warrant to others for faith since it is not "evidence" of that kind. In much the same way, Jesus' revelation of God in himself and in his teachings must circumscribe the kind of knowledge we claim to have of deity. On the one hand, the image of God in his humanity and passion provides us with the shelter of functional equality with the divine, admitting us into covenant with a party terrifyingly distinct from us in condition, value and being. On the other, the picture of his suffering rehearses the repugnance between deity's God and our own, in such a way as to sustain the challenge posed by divine hiddenness to our desire for a God who glorifies us. So when Luther defines Jesus Christ as God *absconditus sub contrario*, the phrase is not employed to express the union of two opposed natures or modes of agency—divine and human, the eternal with the temporal, the immaterial with the fleshly or corporeal—which in the manner of much religious paradox implicates the transcendence of all the latter and the removal of God and the believer from the ordinary world. Rather, in keeping with the reformers' repeated emphasis on faith as a matter of positional, not transcendent, knowledge (that is, knowing what God is toward us, not what he is in himself), Luther describes how God appears submerged in the mundanity of human weakness, indignity, and suffering, yet by virtue of his incalculable divinity, separate from these things. So if there is a paradox in the phrase, it is that this picture must truly be God for us, because it is the means of our justification, the instrumental truth scripture supplies us and, as something inevident in its reality, the proper subject of faith.

What Luther's phrase articulates is the paradox of atonement as a covering that shelters us from God at the same time that it places us in relationship with him. "Opposite" or "contrary" is used ironically at least in part, because Jesus' sufferings aren't so much contrary to godhead (whatever that may be) as they are contrary to our expectations of deity, constructed by analogy to what we revere in ourselves. For we share Moses' desire to know God in all in his glory, but we're given the crucifixion of an erstwhile carpenter and sectary in Roman Judea; we want a sight of godhead just like Aias had, yet God remains hidden from us in this disturbing form, on account both of his nature but even more so because of ours. It is humanity who creates the paradox and enhances the estrangement between itself and God, in the moment when the gulf between the two is being bridged, although never surpassed by the Incarnation. We can of course read "God hidden beneath his opposite" to imply a transcendent deity who in the manner of those Romanesque crucifixions discards the ignominy of the Passion as just so much scaffolding for Christ triumphant—thus solving the scandal of God's incarnation by voiding Jesus of his human and historical reality. But what Luther tells us is that this dilemma doesn't inhere in something out there but inhabits our thoughts about God, and that its resolution requires us to transcend these ideas, not our human nature, in which moment the world will be turned upside down for us. Indeed, the paradox of a deity *absconditus sub contrario* is that so long as we project ourselves onto deity, we can never know what God is toward us or how he is in the world. It is only when we recognize his ineffable difference, which the image of Jesus' sufferings pictures to us, that we can as it were see him. And that I think is what Luther intends by his paradox as well as the doctrine of justification by faith alone: in the image of Christ crucified, we are given a picture that we must construe to understand God, at the same time that we must on no account confuse it with deity per se. If we do so, we will lose all access to the truth about God and ourselves.

This is the charge Luther levels at Erasmus—that the only divinity in the *Diatribe* is its author, who promiscuously distorts the sense of scripture by super-adding "figures and implications that come out of men's heads," making its expressions mystical when incongruous and objective when familiar so that the text episodically observes two orders of meaning, one ineffable and the other rationalist.[45] This perceived license moves Luther to dub the tract "Proteus"— what with Erasmus, on the one hand, asserting the nominality of scriptural expressions about deity, but on other, claiming the indicative, unconditioned force of the text's language about humankind: "for if anyone may devise 'implications' and 'figures' in Scripture at his own pleasure, what will all Scripture be but a reed shaken with the wind, and a sort of chameleon?" The *Diatribe* is "a real Proteus for elusiveness" as well, since it evades the proper difficulties scriptural expressions pose "by tacking on inferences and devising similes," in a sort of hermeneutic extenuation for God and humankind together.[46] And needless to say, the practice of extenuation that most incenses Luther involves Erasmus's denying the very existential conflict from which Luther himself suffered: between God's commandments and human capacities. For Erasmus, operating on the assumption that a just God would never ask what humanity cannot perform, translates scripture's imperatives into human indicatives, thus importing a "novel grammar," a "new, unheard-of grammar" to the text.[47]

As Luther puts the case, the effect of this grammar is summarily to efface by paradox or rationalization the whole religious problematic that motivates his and Calvin's theologies—the felt experience of the distinction between creature and creator. And it earns Erasmus only Luther's scorn and satire, as someone who has known little intransigent perplexity, much less injustice in his life. Thus privileged and complacent in Luther's view, Erasmus can afford to relegate faith to the realm of mystery, practicing a kind of semantic apartheid in the scriptural text that separates effable from ineffable, ethical from religious, plausible from absolute meanings that no rationality can breach. So when moral or rational difficulties emerge for us, whether raised by the world or the text, our only resource in Erasmus's religion is ecstatic or eschatological transcendence. Since God and religious things are thus neither intelligible nor practical, they are humanly superfluous, functionally cloistered from the exigencies of human being. Indeed, in Erasmus's work as a whole, there are two thinkers who never quite meet—the sceptical humanist of the *Diatribe* and the ecstatic Platonist of *The Praise of Folly*: wherever the sceptical Erasmus encounters the anomalous or obscure in scripture, he temporizes or retreats, leaving the field to the mystic fool, who transcends such vagaries in what M. A. Screech calls a ludic rapture of paradox.[48] But between these two Erasmuses, what Luther and Calvin regard as the human predicament of religious knowledge—that we do not always experience God as just and good, that we know him equally from the standpoint of incoherence and suffering—is circumvented, if not elided altogether in scripture. Luther would have it that the paradox Erasmus imports to the text abstracts God, truth, and meaning from it, whereas the incongruity he and Calvin acknowledge in scripture ensures the intractable dialectic of God's meanings with our assumptions and experience.

So despite a shared emphasis on what Luther calls "the simple, natural meaning of the words, as yielded by the rules of grammar and the habits of speech that God has created among men," he and Erasmus cannot agree on what that simple sense is.[49] As Erasmus remarks, "The same Scriptures are acknowledged and venerated by either side. Our battle is about the meaning of Scripture."[50] Take, for example, the verse in Exodus which is at the heart of their controversy over free will, where God says he will harden pharaoh's heart. Erasmus reads these words as a figurative usage "by which [God] is described as the agent who merely provides an opportunity," a usage whose precedent Erasmus finds in Isaiah and for whose authority he invokes Jerome and Origen.[51] The locution becomes a paradox where God's forbearance from action is expressed figuratively as evil's direct cause. But it is paradox in a different sense than Luther understands: as against the reader's sense of an incongruity and injustice attending God's statement, a paradox describing the human experience of deity and religious meanings, Erasmus's version is not actual and existential but nominal only, whose force is fully contained by the text.

In the *Diatribe*, such anthropomorphisms as a rule do not refer to God but to us, in something like the way Dr. Johnson distributes the merits and defects of *Paradise Lost*. Tacitly, deity is the mirror in which we see our own nature reflected absolutely—what is good about human being belongs to deity by figure; what is bad belongs exclusively to us by the same means. On this principle, just as the intervention of a figure allows God to do something less distasteful than acting upon pharaoh to harden his heart, so Erasmus himself transcends the "plain" sense of scripture by relocating its significance in an entirely antithetical meaning. But Luther points out that the text says nothing about God's forbearance, only about his judgment: so he regards Erasmus's maneuver as nothing but a false extenuation, which achieves the evacuation from scripture of any religious meaning the text might have, and God with it. Tellingly, it is in this hermeneutical vacuum that Erasmus generally discovers the proofs for freedom of will, as Luther observes.[52] So when God speaks in scripture of humanity's preparing, choosing, preventing and the like, his grammar undergoes another sort of hypostasis than Calvin describes for faith, and without which Erasmus claims the words would be meaningless.[53] The conceptual is real insofar as scriptural grammar operates like a kind of divine fiat: whatever the text says is hypostasized in reference to God, whether it is expressed subjunctively, imperatively, indicatively. In this interpretation, each grammatical element has a counterpart in some invisible reality, whether metaphysical or mystical: thus "preparing" directly implicates a real human capacity to prepare, and the same goes for choosing, preventing, and so on. The invisible reality constituted by such presumptive correspondences is what Luther calls the *Diatribe*'s "Leviathan (that is, its inferential appendage)."[54] Luther will have none of this, because it is done to make scripture conformable to our ideas, not the proper way round:

"Moreover, it is a merely logical fancy that there is in man a middle term, *willing* as such; nor can those who assert it prove it. The notion sprang from ignorance of things and preoccupation with words. As though things always corresponded in fact to the very analysis of them! (The Sophists make endless errors over this.)"[55] These remarks acknowledge precisely what Erasmus would evade, the discrepancy between our ideas and our actualities, the existential conflict which the reformers explain in relation to the hidden God. By contrast, whenever Erasmus's "inferential appendage" is stymied by a contradiction of that order, which would then prohibit the hypostatic correspondence of word to real if indemonstrable thing, scripture's expressions promptly turn mystical and their intelligibility abortive. We are asked to wonder and believe instead, as though all scriptural language transubstantiates like the eucharistic elements of bread and wine.

In any case, Luther contends there isn't "room enough" left for either faith or deity in this world: as *res non apparentes*, their intelligibility is precluded, along with their historical existence. For Erasmus's hermeneutic renders positive and unconditioned the human force of scriptural language, whereas for Luther, the expressive presence of the hidden God confounds any such simple reference, compelling us instead to admit a different, contingent meaning for the text. This novel sense is argued by scripture's logical and existential incongruity, which signals to the reformers that a different order of intelligibility obtains in its expressions than the one we expect. The hypostasis Erasmus grants his "inferential appendage" is thus both qualitatively and functionally unlike that Calvin ascribes to faith: in the *Diatribe*, hypostatic reference strictly confirms the status quo, constituting a precedent, invisible reality of positive entities to which evident things either do or do not intelligibly correspond. When they don't, there are no practicable means of redressing this incoherence; one resigns oneself to the experience of contradiction and injustice, or mystically transcends the existential fact for which there is no viable remedy. By contrast, for Luther and Calvin, faith's hypostasis is instrumental, not positive: it discloses in the discrepancy between our ideas and our actualities the distinction between God and the world, and in doing so, creates "room enough" *within* our world for different possibilities of meaning and so space for change. So where contradiction in Erasmus severs the intelligible from the religious, in the reformers' theology, it occasions their rapprochement and the alleviation of incoherence.

Furthermore, by translating the force of existential conflict out of this world, Erasmus falsifies, even effaces the Incarnation as Luther and Calvin understand it: Christ becomes a gesture, a signpost, to transcendence, a mere device as against deity's investiture of this world with new because incongruous significance that relieves human suffering. Fixed as he is upon rational proprieties in religion, Erasmus commits what Luther regards as the greatest impropriety of all: he transgresses the distinction between God and the world. In other words, by his hypostatic reference, Erasmus would surpass the absolute boundary between creature and creator, violate "the veil of ignorance" Jesus Christ himself instantiates, and expose humanity to all the unspeakable horror of a hidden and unreconciled God. As Luther puts the paradox, by insisting that deity speak just like us if we are to understand it, Erasmus achieves the opposite effect, which is to make impassable the gulf in our religious understanding:

> The Diatribe is deceived by its own ignorance in that it makes no distinc-
> tion between God preached and God hidden, that is, between the Word
> of God and God Himself. God does many things He does not show us in
> His Word, and He wills many things which He does not in His Word show
> us that He wills. Thus, He does not will the death of a sinner—that is, in
> His Word; but He wills it by His inscrutable will. At present, however, we
> must keep in view His Word and leave alone His inscrutable will; for it is
> by His Word, and not by His inscrutable will, that we must be guided. In
> any case, who can direct himself according to a will that is inscrutable and
> incomprehensible? It is enough simply to know that there is in God an
> inscrutable will; what, why, and within what limits It wills, it is wholly
> unlawful to inquire, or wish to know, or be concerned about, or touch
> upon; we may only fear and adore![56]

At first glance, Luther's exhortation to "fear and adore" resembles Erasmus's mystical resignation; but he uses this terrific image of inscrutable and impervi-ous deity to return us to the word of God, God preached, which is to say the historical realm of God incarnate. As Luther sees it, the distinction does not permit us to escape contradiction, which is how Erasmus wants to employ it. Instead, the hiddenness of God throws us back upon ourselves and our world, whose incoherence is at once expressed and resolved by Jesus as God-man—the instrumental description of our predicament. This centrality of the Christ to religious knowledge is why Luther vehemently contends against Erasmus for the religious propriety of the incongruous in all religious things:

> So one of the main reasons why the words of Moses and Paul are not taken
> in their plain sense is their 'absurdity.' But against what article of faith
> does that 'absurdity' transgress? And who is offended by it? It is human
> reason that is offended; which, though it is blind, deaf, senseless, godless,
> and sacrilegious, in its dealing with all God's words and works is at this
> point brought in as judge of God's words and works! On these same
> grounds you will deny all the articles of the faith, for it is the highest
> absurdity by far—foolishness to the Gentiles and a stumbling-block to the
> Jews, as Paul says (cf. 1 Cor. I.23)—that God should be man, a virgin's
> son, crucified, sitting at the Father's right hand. It is, I repeat, *absurd* to
> believe such things! So let us invent some figures with the Manichaeans,
> and say that he is not truly man, but a phantom who passed through the
> virgin like a ray of light through glass, and then fell, and so was crucified!
> This would be a fine way for us to handle the Scriptures![57]

In short, if we disavow the salience of scriptural incongruity, especially as it applies to our condition, we disavow the Christ. That is why Luther declares that "there can be no figure" in the verse from Exodus: "the Word of God must be taken in its plain meaning, as the words stand."[58] Incongruity is not specious or superficial, a mere figure, for this kind of Christianity, as Reinhold Niebuhr observes; it is a fundamental recasting of value and meaning, which not only acknowledges the abysmal, inscrutable difference between God and the world, but attends to the reality of human suffering.[59] Thus Luther invokes the fantastic theodicy of Manichaeanism to parody Erasmus's own interpretive dualism and license, which have the effect of reducing Christ to a figment of expression, as against an historical and soteriological reality. So Luther sardonically inquires, "What became of the Arians in respect of the figure by which they made Christ to be 'God *nominally*'?"[60] His point is that reason, taken as received understanding, can be more than heretical in religion; it can eviscerate scripture of its unique significance, namely, its salvific and pastoral force. Reason, he says, "bases her judgment of things and words that are of God upon the customs and concerns of men; and what is more perverse than that, when the former are heavenly and the latter earthly? Thus in her stupidity she betrays herself as thinking of God only as of man."[61]

Luther accepts absurdity because he will not efface the reality of human suffering in a world governed by a just God. In the manner of such things, this conflicted reality that the Christ and faith together justify is expressed by a riddling order of truth, as in Luther's *larvae* or masks of God, Calvin's mazes, or for that matter, Milton's knowing good by knowing evil. Scripture's "simple sense" in this way captures God's fundamentally different kind of life: "Many things seem, and are, very good to God which seem, and are, very bad to us. Thus, afflictions, sorrows, errors, hell, and all God's best works are in the world's eyes very bad, and damnable. What is better than Christ and the gospel? But what is there that the world abominates more? How things that are bad for us are good in the sight of God is known only to God and to those who see with God's eyes, that is, who have the Spirit."[62] As against Erasmus's mystical device, the paradox does not argue the nominality of affliction: it describes instead the actual discrepancy between divine and human meanings in our experience of things. Thus Luther calls suffering *opus alienum Dei*, God's "alien work," which entails the lived experience of contradiction with which Erasmus would dispense. But Luther, arguing from his own life, recognizes in this incongruity a crucial salvific truth; for the experience especially of unwarranted suffering, of injustice, estranges us from the God of our idolatry—the deity ostensibly evident to us, either in the appearances things have for us or in their putatively transcendent perfection. As it did with Job, suffering obliges us "to flee to God against God" (*ad Deum contra Deum*), and that is what scriptural incongruity does as well: its vagaries, lapses, and absurdities presuppose and reflect the human condition of incoherence and injustice, and the need to reform our understanding so as to alleviate them.[63] Yet this alien work predicates no automatic reversal or translation of incongruity into God's proper salvific activity: evil and incoherence are not merely phenomena disguising the good from us, which the exercise of faith allows us to penetrate as just so many illusions in the manner of Erasmus's mystical usage.

In *The Bondage of the Will*, when he asserts the impervious, ineluctable hiddenness of religious things against Erasmus's rational or mystical inferences, Luther is not retreating into obfuscation or as his opponent does, invoking the obscurity of the text and deity to resist scripture's unique claim upon our understanding, as the word of God. He is describing that aspect of divine revelation which denies us unity with God but not intelligence of him. Adorno describes something like this position when he speaks of dialectics as a ruse— "the oldest means of enlightenment" (*ND* 141); by immersing itself in the rationalist version of the world, dialectics exposes that system's failure to subsume a heterogeneous experience under a single order of meaning. And Luther's ruse of revelation works comparably to controvert our claims to identify the absolute by pursuing the myth of deity's accommodation: we think that God is like his signs and so like us, only to discover by the shock of incongruity that neither they nor he can be made to fit our idea of them. Thus the ruse is doubly ironic, not only in its thrust but also in its effects—the palpable disorientation of assumed order. It engineers a collision of meanings that enacts the embeddedness of God in our experience: since we have to know deity or truth from the differential standpoint of our humanity, we chronically reencounter the incongruity that signals this distinction. In sum, Erasmean theodicy has affinities with the categorical kind of justification, at least in its rational mode, where we ratify scripture by proving it consonant with our preconceived ideas. But Luther and Calvin begin with the human actuality that our moral and religious experience is far more entangled, conflicted, and provocative than Erasmus will allow, which is why their theodicy resembles justification of the instrumental, revisionary sort. For there are some paradoxes, Luther remarks, that we don't make ourselves.

CHAPTER THREE

Milton's Text

⚬━✦━⚬

Vertiginous Speaking

One way to express the necessary quandary of the intelligible with the religious in Milton's thought would be to suggest that, in his account of the Fall, Milton believes the accusations Satan makes about God—believes them to be in a manner true, that is. At the same time, and because he believes this, he also thinks that God is right about Satan. As always, Luther puts this paradox revealingly:

> Therefore Paul is correct in calling it the evil world; for when it is at its best, then it is at its worst. The world is at its best in men who are religious, wise, and learned; yet in them it is actually evil twice over. . . . This white devil, who transforms himself into an angel of light (2. Cor. 11.14)—he is the real devil. (*LW* 26:41)

> Here let us learn to recognize the tricks and craft of the devil. A heretic does not come with the label "error" or "devil"; nor does the devil himself come in the form of a devil, especially not that "white devil." . . . where Satan emerges not black but white, in the guise of an angel or even of God himself, there he puts himself forward with very sly pretense and amazing tricks. (*LW* 26:49)

> Therefore Paul regards it as a sure sign that what is being preached is not the Gospel if the preaching goes on without its peace being disturbed. On the other hand, the world regards it as a sure sign that the Gospel is a heretical and seditious doctrine when it sees that the preaching of the Gospel is followed by great upheavals, disturbances, offenses, sects, etc. Thus God wears the mask of the devil, and the devil wears the mask of God; God wants to be recognized under the mask of the devil, and He wants the devil to be condemned under the mask of God. (*LW* 27:43)

Were this the usual sort of paradox, we could dispose of the contradiction simply by arguing that Luther, or Milton by extension, asks us to prefer a transcendent reality to the appearances of this world. These phenomena would then cease to present us with a dilemma of understanding, because all we would have to do is shift from ordinary, secular thinking to the supernal or transcendental.

But the distinction between God and the world disallows such a turn. More-over, neither Milton nor Luther wants to abstract the real and true from the quotidian or everday, since this in effect is to dismiss the claims of human being on truth. Indeed, truth matters only insofar as it elucidates our world, our humanity; when the search for truth is purely speculative, divorced from this responsibility, inevitably and effectually it is no truth at all, as Raphael reminds Adam. So both Luther and Milton want so thoroughly, so mutually to involve God's truth with the world's that we will always find ourselves obliged to speak of the one when we talk about the other. And that is because we cannot know deity any other way.

The predicament I have in mind implicates irony because, as Luther describes it, experience frequently catches us in the act of pursuing incompatible beliefs and intelligences about truth. This isn't the same as a conflicting perception that some increment of knowledge, some adjustment in understanding, will fix for good and certain. It is rather an occasion when more than one competing idea of things is intractably present, as when Luther says that the world "is at its best in men who are religious, wise and learned; yet in them it actually evil twice over." Such perplexity Paul himself represents as integral to Christian life, a perplexity which Luther in his scripturalism also extends to the sacred text. For like the hidden God it exists to proclaim, and not unlike *Paradise Lost*, scripture seems simultaneously to assert opposing truths, so that we find ourselves in the position Luther evokes here, seemingly unable to distinguish between deity and devil and yet impelled to do so. In this predicament, when we do affirm a reading of experience or text as true, we invariably confront its contradiction as well as our own jeopardy of understanding. Yet this dilemma does not permit us an aporia, a paralysis defying further movement, intellectual or moral: on the contrary, to invoke Cavell again, we are obligated to choose a reading, and then to acknowledge that reading in the way we conduct ourselves toward the world. In such a manner, we make the hidden God and truth present and practicable.

Accordingly, the mature Luther approaches the sense of scripture as though it consisted in a syntax or grammar as against a logic—by which I mean no stable but rather an irreducibly contingent order of meaning, depending on the use a particular expression is given by the persons speaking and hearing it. When he observes that Paul rightly calls the world evil, he does not intend us to take the apostle or himself as saying, like the Attendant Spirit does in *Comus*, that the things of this world have only evil as their single, constant valence, much less their essential quality. On the contrary, he is trying to articulate the notion that they are good and bad in different ways at the same time: "for when [the world] is at its best, then it is at its worst"; or more complexly, the world "*is* at its best in men who are religious, wise and learned," but it is also "*actually* evil twice over." My emphasis is there to convey the idea that, for Luther, the world is truly good and truly evil all at once, a dilemma that cannot be solved by the usual dualist approach that separates material from immaterial, phenomenal or mimetic from real, profane from sacred worlds.

For the things of this world are evil only *when they are good*, so that the force of one value is entirely conditional on the presence of its opposite, from which it derives any distinction. I see this as something on the order of Adorno's Hegelian sense of the inextricability of subject and object, which he says "constitute one another as much as—by virtue of such constitution—they depart from each other" (*ND* 174). Good and evil thus represent not so much oppositions as polarities, mutually defining fields of experience and meaning that we can know by their difference from each other, by their intelligible resistance to identity. To think religiously is to think complexly—to take into account the manifold, contiguous dimensions of human being, from the physical to the perceptual to the erotic and the moral, as we propose to describe how our world means. The mutual contingency of likeness and difference that Montaigne remarks also governs theodicy in Milton's understanding. It is what I think he has in mind when he memorably declares in the *Areopagitica* that good and evil grow up in this world together, and that we only know good by knowing evil. What Milton suggests is that we apprehend the one in the other, by an interpretive sense of their distinction which requires good and evil to be reciprocally present. In the fashion of Luther's white devil or masked God, this formulation is a recipe for irony which likewise depends for what it *does* mean on the idea of what it *does not*. That is why we simply can't separate the two senses out unless our intent is to deny the possibility of changed understandings altogether, which for Luther and Milton is tantamount to denying deity and the religious. Consider once more Luther's idea that God wears the devil's mask and the devil God's, yet God wants us to distinguish deity in the appearance of its opposite. How is such a recognition available to us when Luther in effect asserts that one cannot tell devil and deity apart by how they appear to us—that the appearance of a thing is no certain index of what it is, although its appearance is all we have to go on? Such is the implication of Milton's insistence that we rely for our knowledge of the world's goodness on the knowledge of its evil:

> Good and evil we know in the field of this World grow up together almost inseparably; and the knowledge of good is so involv'd and interwoven with the knowledge of evill, and in so many cunning resemblances hardly to be discern'd, that those confused seeds which were impos'd on *Psyche* as an incessant labour to cull out, and sort asunder, were not more intermixt. It was from out the rinde of one apple tasted, that the knowledge of good and evill as two twins cleaving together leapt forth into the World. And perhaps this is that doom which *Adam* fell into of knowing good and evil, that is to say of knowing good by evil. As therefore the state of man now is; what wisdome can there be to choose, what continence to forbeare without the knowledge of evill? He that can apprehend and consider vice with all her baits and seeming pleasures, and yet abstain, and yet distin-

guish, and yet prefer that which is truly better, he is the true wayfaring
Christian. I cannot praise a fugitive and cloister'd vertue, unexercis'd &
unbreath'd, that never sallies out and sees her adversary, but slinks out of
the race, where that immortal garland is to be run for, not without dust
and heat. Assuredly we bring not innocence into the world, we bring im-
purity rather: that which purifies us is triall, and triall is by what is contrary. . . . Suppose we could expell sin by this means; look how much we
thus expell of sin, so much we expell of vertue: for the matter of them both
is the same; remove that, and ye remove them both alike. This justifies the
high providence of God, who though he command us temperance, justice,
continence, yet powrs out before us ev'n to a profuseness all desirable
things, and gives us minds that can wander beyond all limit and satiety.
(CM 4:310–11, 320)

Even the most sterile speculation has its place in this sort of religious understanding, since it offers precisely that occasion of experience and discernment
which, for Milton, captures the peculiar vitality and moral grandeur of human
intelligence. To invoke Adorno once more as illustration, one might say that
both Luther and Milton "strive, by way of the concept, to transcend the concept" (*ND* 15): thus God and the things of God like the true and the good are
best known in the very moment when our ideas of them cease adequately to
encompass our experience.

This is vertiginous speaking. Reinhold Niebuhr shows a similar resistance to
accepting the division of faith and reason that he sees argued in Thomism,
since "this means that the finiteness of man's reason and its involvement in the
flux of the temporal world is not appreciated."[1] In short, Niebuhr regards as
irreligious any argument that would try to cut through the entanglement of our
meanings, whose intricacy is signaled by the perplexities of these passages from
Luther and Milton. Thus he evokes "the emphasis in the Christian faith upon
the unique, the contradictory, the paradoxical, and the unresolved mystery," all
of which are implicated in the belief that deity—not reason or nature—created
the world and with it, the real order of our experience.[2] And this idea itself
requires that we accept what Niebuhr calls the "final irrationality of the giv-
enness of things," which is to say, the ineluctable fact of discontinuity and
irresolution in our understanding. Attempts to alter that condition in somehow
transcending it by the faculties of "faith" or "reason," however conceived—as
when Satan and our first parents want to render Eden penetrable or exact, or
when Adam and the speaker desire fully to know Eve—are not only oblivious
but false and unjust.

Wittgenstein remarks that it is part of "the natural history of human beings"
that we encounter an ever-widening gap, a virtual abyss of difference, whenever
we try to contain our experience within a single order of things (*PI* p.415). And
that difference, he points out in another place, describes the boundary or limit
we encounter with the impalpable, whose mysteriousness occurs to us only

when we try to "*catch* hold of it" as we do other things in the world.[3] His example in this case is instructive, since it has to do with the usage "I": that is, the
difference between the sense of consciousness or selfhood we express in this
word, and how we understand the operations of the brain. For when we equate
the linguistic or experiential "I" with neurological activity, we suffer from "The
feeling of an unbridgeable gulf between consciousness and brain process," and
"This idea of a difference in kind is accompanied by slight giddiness" (*PI* p.412).
The vertigo occurs precisely because our sense of self conflicts, is not intelligible
to us, in these terms, although they pertain to the question of human consciousness. Such incongruity reveals a condition not only of our knowledge but also
of our nature, where one way of seeing or speaking about something doesn't
always neatly coincide with another.

Adorno also talks about a vertigo, consequent upon recognizing that what
we call reason does not describe the totality of our experience, only a certain
idea of things to which we exclusively subscribe at the cost of those lived meanings, those ordinary dimensions of the world and our own subjectivity, antipathetic to rationalism's canon and procedures of judgment (*ND* 31–33). Thus
Adorno's notion of vertigiousness, like Milton's, like Luther's, entails the sense
of an incommensurable difference in kind arising from the chronic disparity
between our analysis of the world and our experience. Such is the position of
human being: as we have known since Euripides at least (apparently Milton's
preferred tragedian), we are seduced by the vision of a denatured ideal, an immaculate illusion of the absolute, that comes with reflecting upon experience
in a way deliberately intolerant of the embeddedness of human thought—the
dignity and folly of a Pentheus or a Hippolytus. For Niebuhr, this ideal is faith
exercised exclusive of the world's claims upon us; for Wittgenstein, it is a realm
of reference to which all language precisely, demonstrably points; for Adorno,
it is the reality to which rationalism is identical; for Luther, Calvin, and Milton,
it is a knowledge of God as deity in itself—a *Deus nudus absconditus*. Such
intolerance, and the attendant desire to transcend or perfect the vagaries of our
condition, is what happens when the rational is mistaken for the religious—
that is, for some ultimate, univocal truth. Adorno calls this desire the "rage" of
idealism, which conveys its passion and its religiosity; he thinks of idealism as
a kind of self-hatred, or at least abhorrence of every contingency in experience
or meaning that defines human being. Yet as human beings, we are given minds
that in Milton's phrase "can wander beyond all limits and satiety" (*CM* 4:320);
and we are forever being "dazzled by the ideal," according to Wittgenstein (*PI*
p.100): "The ideal, as we think of it, is unshakeable. You can never get outside
it; you must always turn back. There is no outside; outside you cannot
breathe.—Where does this idea come from? It is like a pair of glasses on our
nose through which we see whatever we look at. It never occurs to us to take
them off" (*PI* p.103).

This perverse psychology of explanation, where the ideal decides the true,
the real, and the meaningful, is itself a source of human suffering. To the extent
that we cannot admit the fact of contingency into our knowledge without suc-

cumbing to dogma on the one hand, or scepticism and endless aporia on the other, we work to evacuate truth from the world. But even when we are faithful to our condition, truth can still be glimpsed only in that perpetual pendulation Luther describes as knowing God in the mask of the devil, and the devil in the mask of God. Religious truth especially can provoke the experience of vertiginousness, inasmuch as the whole fabric of our assumptions can seem to fall away in the face of the absolute, so that our usual understandings lose their bearings and become untenable. Thus Luther talks about "our peace being disturbed" by the preaching of the gospel, which brings with it "great upheavals, disturbances, offenses, sects, etc.," while Milton in the *Areopagitica* memorably upbraids the Presbyterian censors as "a sort of irrationall men," who insist on the strict identity of truth:

> Where there is much desire to learn, there of necessity will be much arguing, much writing, many opinions; for opinion in good men is but knowledge in the making. Under these fantastic terrors of sect and schism, we wrong the earnest and zealous thirst after knowledge and understanding which God hath stirr'd up in this City. . . . Yet these are the men cry'd out against for schismaticks and sectaries; as if, while the Temple of the Lord was building, some cutting, some squaring the marble, others hewing the cedars, there should be a sort of irrationall men who could not consider there must be many schisms and many dissections made in the quarry and in the timber, ere the house of God can be built. And when every stone is laid artfully together, it cannot be united into a continuity, it can be but contiguous in this world; neither can every peece of the building be of one form; nay rather the perfection consists in this, that out of many moderat varieties and brotherly dissimilitudes that are not vastly disproportionall arises the goodly and gracefull symmetry that commends the whole pile and structure. (CM 4:341–42)

Milton argues Luther's point with Luther's example, which is this: we respond to the good as a virtual evil not because it isn't bad—religious conflict to the point of civil war is undoubtedly bad for us—but because our ideas of good and bad serve purposes other than the right knowledge of God. His implicit irony is more paradox in the philosophical than the literary sense. For it is impossible to experience the divergence and dissimilitude of opinion Milton describes as something other than confounding, especially in a culture like his own that made "order" the paramount social and political value. Instead, what Milton exhorts his audience to do is tolerate the fact of disproportion or dissimilitude so that we can recognize, simultaneously, another kind of coherence equally present in things. Because in Milton's theology as in Luther's, essence comes "swathed in its own contradiction," for such is the way deity and truth accommodate themselves to our humanity (*ND* 167). Accordingly, this accommodated truth is revealed in the sensation of incongruence, which is what Milton expresses when he distinguishes "contiguity" from "continuity." He argues that an insistence upon continuity—on an effortless identity between the "can-

ons and precepts of men" and the things of God, transcending both time and
our human nature—is a false, divisive value that we impose on experience to
our own considerable detriment (CM 4:342). For the human world allows no
such immaculate, automatic coherence: the figure of the temple describes a
symmetry uneasily contrived in diversity, an unstable union formally exposing
not only the tension and discrepancy of its parts, but also the centrifugence of
time and matter that will inexorably dissolve their contingent bond. Proportion
even in the things of God is "timely" in Milton's usage—occasional, not absolute. Thus in the manner of Kepler's new aesthetic of the ellipse, we can only
see the symmetry, the goodly proportions of the temple, in recognizing its ki-
netic impetus; and we can only apprehend the reality of what deity is toward
us in the dynamism of its expressions.[4] As Sir Thomas Browne puts it, God
and truth are seen by *parallaxis*, through a kind of alternation or deviation of
perspective among our ideas. But then the question arises, what actually is the
case with truth in this world—symmetry or diversity? In the pamphlets as a
whole Milton is inclined to reply that both are the case, in a complex harmonic
fashion: as the revolutions in his Adam's understanding show, Milton sees
truth's appearances shifting with our position *coram Deo*, that is, with the condition of our faith. Such equivocality is the nature of truth as he expresses it in
the *Areopagitica*, where to the consternation of his recent readers, he argues
that truth of itself is one, integral and perfect, but then again, that its condition
for us is like the dismembered body of Osiris, gone all to pieces (CM 4:338):

> There be who perpetually complain of schisms and sects, and make it such
> a calamity that any man dissents from their maxims. 'Tis their own pride
> and ignorance which causes the disturbing, who neither will hear with
> meeknes, nor can convince, yet all must be supprest which is not found in
> their *Syntagma*. They are the troublers, they are the dividers of unity, who
> neglect and permit not others to unite those dissever'd peeces which are
> yet wanting to the body of Truth. To be still searching what we know not,
> by what we know, still closing up truth to truth as we find it (for all her
> body is *homogeneal*, and proportionall), this is the golden rule in *Theology*
> as well as in Arithmetick, and makes up the best harmony in a Church;
> not the forc't and outward union of cold, and neutrall, and inwardly di-
> vided minds. (CM 4:339)

At a glance, this reads like Arthur Barker's seminal argument about the tension between liberty and discipline in Milton's ideology, where truth and civil
order together consist in an achieved, not an intrinsic compatibility among
our ideas.[5] But what Milton describes is something more discomfiting, more
intractably ambivalent than testimony to the power of consensus in rightly
ordering persons and events. In the first place, the impetus of these remarks is to
uphold, not efface the fact of disorder, which takes the form of civil disturbance,
dissenters, "schisms and sects" in the polity. Milton of course is a famous tolerationist except where Catholics are concerned, and for the reason he gives here

against the Presbyterian theocrats: namely, that Catholic like Calvinist orthodoxy seeks in the form of dogma to impose a uniform appearance on our ideas
of God (thus the reference here to "syntagma" or system). With peculiar obtuseness, they would thus preclude the emergence of a viable agreement over
time, one in which God as the proper author of religious understanding is allowed to take a providential hand. For like Milton's eccentric temple, differences are entrenched in this life until that awful and inhumane moment when
deity itself becomes "all in all." Nothing could more clearly describe how he
himself diverges in his thinking from dogmatism and specifically the Calvinist
orthodoxy represented by the Presbyterian party. In Milton's theodicy, when
the true and false, good and evil, are not understood to be practically contingent meanings but instead separate and exclusive, we peremptorily render ourselves incapable of recognizing any of these values.[6] Indeed, Milton's argument
separating church government from civil magistry is made to resist just such an
arbitrary conformity, as though civic were identical with religious disorder. He
knows that the signs of truth in one dimension of experience can be anathema
in another, as the preaching of the gospel proves to Luther. And because it
acknowledges these different orders of idea and therefore the actual contingency of human judgment, Milton's separation of church from state functions
to prevent the more terrible division of civil conflict and subjective dissociation—what he calls the "outward union of cold, and neutrall, and inwardly
divided minds."

For in uniting the civil to the religious, the Presbyterian institution of censorship presumes to define and enforce a singular unity among all our ideas, discriminating true from false notions in the state as in the church by the degree to
which they apparently conform to a received canon. This practice thus asserts a
ready analogy between the two domains, contravening Milton's passionate
sense that truth, the right, the good, demand trial in order to be known, and
"triall is by what is contrary." In the *Areopagitica* and all of Milton's tracts, truth
does not rely so much upon perceived likeness as it depends on the differential
presence of its opposite. As early as the *Reason of Church Government*, he argues
this dialectical decorum of meaning:

> If sects and schismes be turbulent in the unsetl'd estate of a Church, while
> it lies under the amending hand, it best beseems our Christian courage to
> think they are but as the throes and pangs that go before the birth of
> reformation, and that the work it selfe is now in doing. For if we look but
> on the nature of elementall and mixt things, we know they cannot suffer
> any change of one kind, or quality into another, without the struggl of
> contrarieties. And in things artificall, seldome any elegance is wrought
> without a superfluous wast and refuse in the transaction. No Marble statue
> can be politely carv'd, no fair edifice built without almost as much rubbish
> and sweeping. Insomuch that even in the spirituall conflict of S. *Pauls*
> conversion there fell scales from his eyes, that were not perceav'd before.

No wonder then in the reforming of a Church which is never brought to
effect without the fierce encounter of truth and falshood together, if, as it
were the splinters and shares of so violent a jousting, there fall from between the shock many fond errors and fanatick opinions, which when
truth has the upper hand, and the reformation shall be perfeted, will easily
be rid out of the way, or kept so low, as that they shall be only the exercise
of our knowledge, not the disturbance, or interruption of our faith. (CM
3.1:223–24)

It is significant that even when, in some unknown future, reform is perfected,
Milton envisions the play of differences to be still ongoing for "the exercise of
our knowledge," although not to "the disturbance, or interruption of our faith."
He implies that deity, when it works through the creature to reform it, chooses
not to outrage but rather to accommodate the contingencies of temporal process and created distinctions.[7] Such is the variegated movement of virtue "if
any visible shape can be given to divine things . . . whereby she is not only
seene in the regular gestures and motions of her heavenly paces as she walkes,
but also makes the harmony of her voice audible to mortall eares" (CM
3.1:185). Moreover, in heaven, difference is yet observed: "Yea the Angels
themselves, in whom no disorder is fear'd, as the Apostle that saw them in his
rapture describes, are distinguisht and quaterniond into their celestiall
Princedomes, and Satrapies, according as God himselfe hath writ his imperiall
decrees through the great provinces of heav'n" (CM 3.1:185). In paradise too,
the blessed are differentiated like the New Jerusalem itself: "Yet is it not to be
conceiv'd that those eternall effluences of sanctity and love in the glorified
Saints should by this meanes be confin'd and cloy'd with repetition of that
which is prescrib'd, but that our happinesse may orbe it selfe into a thousand
vagancies of glory and delight, and with a kinde of eccentricall equation be as
it were an invariable Planet of joy and felicity" (CM 3.1:185–86).[8] Such is the
nature of the creature's condition that difference obtains even in perfection;
that truth is evinced in "the struggle of contrarieties"; that coherence is effected
in disorder and excess as well as in the sensation of conceptual violence.

Evidently, what Milton understands by the word "discipline" is not a rule
enforced or even an accomplished order: it is a dynamic, a perpetual making of
coherence, a Heraclitean flux if you will, in heaven and earth. Nor is Miltonic
discipline unchanging, always having one and the same appearance, or asserting
one and the same order of things: it is "vagant" or wandering and varying,
"eccentric" or divergent, even deviant. Yet these burgeoning and receding incongruities are not contradictions, because they show that right order consists
in the harmonic relation among disparate things on disparate occasions—a cosmic version of rhetorical *kairos* or opportune ordering. Thus when Milton addresses the problem of ostensible contradiction in the *Areopagitica*, he pictures
religious truth as he does religious discipline. "Yet is it not impossible that
[truth] may have more shapes than one," he exclaims: "What else is all that

rank of things indifferent, wherein Truth may be on this side, or on the other, without being unlike her self?" (CM 4:348). If we allow the world its "vagancy" or unsettled, voluble appearance, we will eventually discover its particular coherence; but if we enforce a single idea of truth, as censorship would do, we will achieve only implacable division.

Indeed, "that rank of things indifferent" alludes to the doctrine of adiaphorism, in which numerous matters of religious practice are left to the individual conscience to decide—and without prejudice. The possibility of choice itself acknowledges the equivocalities we encounter both in scripture and the world, where how something once appears to us does not secure its future meaning. For that reason, Milton's truth can assume more shapes than one without contradicting itself, because the conditions of meaning are not single and endogamous but emergent and fluctuating, with semblance having no single aspect. Such plurality of appearance and circumstance describes one feature of that human freedom called Christian liberty by Luther and Milton, and which is originally occasioned by God himself, insofar as he leaves humanity room to choose or deny him in its understandings and actions. Room of course is made simultaneously with the world, in the moment when creatural being is distinguished from its creator; Luther understands this room as the groundlessness of faith, and Milton as truth's contingency.[9] While these may appear to be opposed positions—Luther emphasizing the arbitrary power of God over the world, Milton arguing their intelligible affiliation—each picture is nonetheless intended to account for the discrepancy between our ideas of God on the one hand and deity as it is actually made known to us on the other. This incommensurability defines the boundary of the everyday within which faith must operate, and which humanity experiences as a crisis of coherence, when things we had assumed abruptly become disordered, inexplicable, unjust to us. The inevitable lapse of our assumptions creates faith's room for Luther, and the creative arena of moral choice for Milton: "were I the chooser," he remarks, "a dram of well-doing should be preferr'd before many times as much the forcible hindrance of evill-doing. For God sure esteems *the growth and compleating* of one vertuous person, more than *the restraint* of ten vitious" (CM 4:320, my emphasis). In both theologies, the world made by the hidden God is a place where human understanding is not so much absent or confounded as engaged, more flexible, more imaginative, more truly expressive of our condition, since here human being as "the image of God" is referred to its unfathomable creator.

The disconcerting scope of truth's appearances then implies no compromise in their value or force but rather a various, discriminate, and often novel expression that defies our attempts to master its meanings. So while "searching what we know not by what we know" could mean in theology what it often does in mathematics—educing truths on the model of the truth we have—this procedure doesn't necessarily result in a positive likeness and affirmation of what we suppose truth to be. All it does is teach us the expressive order or circumstances, the "discipline" by which we may yet find truth: that is, a means, not an end, a method, not a positive knowledge. Accordingly, where the hidden God is concerned, we must take care to be struck, to be surprised (as Wittgenstein likes to say) by how its meanings work, if we are to apprehend deity's mode of expression. This statement needn't therefore propose an endogamy of idea, but something on the order of knowing good by knowing evil, or virtue created in the trial of contraries (a version of God's *opus alienum*, which brings good out of evil). As against an axiomatic, analogous, and elegant truth, we discover a truth processive, manifold and even new to us. Certainly this construction of Milton's words seems more in keeping with the *Areopagitica's* ever expanding array of images—of unconfined spaces, cornucopias, porous vessels, and urgent to the point of explosive actions. For Milton, the present world is very like the Eden of his imagination, where nature is wantonly fanciful, always various yet not the less perfect or proportionate to its purposes; and therefore he determinedly qualifies the notion of truth by analogy that the institution of censorship may be said to assume. Milton's truth doesn't necessarily look to us like truth, even as Luther's God may not look divine. Thus he observes that "if it comes to prohibiting, there is not ought more likely to be prohibited then truth it self; whose first appearance to our eyes blear'd and dimm'd with prejudice and custom, is more unsightly and unplausible than many errors, ev'n as the person is of many a great man slight and contemptible to see to" (CM 4:350). Likening truth's effects to the unprepossessing appearance of a great man is a predictably personal choice for Milton, as someone whom writing made notorious but whose conviction of peculiar genius went unacknowledged long after he made this analogy. But the general tenor of Milton's comment, especially the obstructiveness of prejudice and custom, argues that for him, truth has a strange inevidence about it, partly by virtue of what we want and expect to see. Thus Milton castigates "the worst and newest opinion of all others"—"that none must be heard, but whom they like" (CM 4:350):

> For when God shakes a Kingdome with strong and healthfull commotions to a generall reforming, 'tis not untrue that many sectaries and false teachers are then busiest in seducing; but yet more true it is, that God then raises to his own work men of rare abilities, and more than common industry *not only to look back and revise what hath bin taught heretofore, but to gain furder and goe on, some new enlighten'd steps in the discovery of truth.* For such is the order of Gods enlightning his Church, to dispense and deal out by degrees his beam, so as our earthly eyes may best sustain it. Neither is God appointed and confin'd, where and out of what place these his chosen shall be first heard to speak; *for he sees not as man sees, chooses not as man chooses, lest we should devote our selves again to set places, and assemblies, and outward callings of men.* (CM 4:350–51; my emphasis)

Here God's reforming of the world is cast in terms of the cathartic or therapeutic kind of justification, where incoherence or contradiction instructs us to revise our ideas of truth. In this revision, we are not peremptorily to reimpose a fixed and singular order on things but rather to invent new means by which to discover what right order might be, one of which means includes suspending received judgments in a kind of sceptical *epoche*, since those judgments have been proven wrong and injurious before. And if the meanings of the God who instigates this reform aren't necessarily predictable by what we think we see and know, then obviously God's truth won't always serve our notions of that value. Those who play the role of truth's harbingers are therefore more likely to be innovators and revolutionaries than they are codifiers or systematists, much less censors. Milton's chiliasm is of the apocalyptic kind, intimated here by his anticipation of still further reform of God's England. As the imagery of the *Areopagitica* illustrates, he tends to picture the truth of things after the manner of theophany—an astounding yet always imminent disclosure of deity's will within history. It follows that the sublimity we expect from God and truth is antipathetic to their proper expression and our right understanding: like Samuel searching for God's anointed among the sons of Jesse, we look for beauty and grandeur—the atavistic impulse of idolaters in Milton's view. What we are given is none of these things, since Milton maintains that the meanings of revelation are inclined to depart from our assumptions, at the same time that he insists that they are latent and intelligible within our ordinary experience. So if Milton doesn't think that truth is simply analogous to those ideas we receive as true, he also doesn't think that the accomplishing of truth requires that we transcend history or our own mortality. Whatever transcending we do occurs in the domain of this world, if in tension with it, which is the sort of dialectic of understanding that knowing good by knowing evil exemplifies. The clash and contradiction of opposed theses or meanings, rather than canceling out one or both to form something new, describe instead a perpetual impregnation of ideas which are known and understood relative to each other, and whose force is thus oscillating and reciprocal as against stable, discrete, and exclusive.

Along these lines, Adorno argues that "expression" or the "rhetorical element" in philosophy discloses a residue or sediment in our ideas which testifies to their disparate origin from reason narrowly understood—an origin analysis itself would deny in the way Niebuhr suggests about Thomism: "It is in the rhetorical quality that culture, society, and tradition animate the thought," which is to say that in their expression lies the *raison d'être* of ideas, inimitable and distinct from their analytic identity (*ND* 56). The very particularity of human language that eludes conceptual summary also implicates a meaning and a reality antipathetic and tangential to the philosophical idea it is engaged to convey. This implication itself is an effect of what Wittgenstein calls philosophy's "logical must," or Adorno terms its *more mathematico* or *arithmetico*, which we tend to impose upon the incompatible material of our being, with humanity always falling short of the univocal truth it desires and pursues. As Adorno is moved to say elsewhere, "The distance of thought from reality is nothing other than the precipitate of history in concepts": in other words, discrepancy is the token of that entirely circumstantial reality which for Milton is elided by axiom and system.[10] Consequently, the suppressed mediations of language, culture, and motive appear in just these incorrigible moments of opacity or excess of expression, which inadvertently reveal that there is more to the text and more to the world than rationalism may choose to admit.

Indeed, mediation resists the analytical imperative precisely because it "makes no claim whatever to exhaust all things; it postulates, rather, that what it transmits is not thereby exhausted" (*ND* 172). In much the same way, rhetoric's putatively excessive expression honors "the difference that has been spirited away" by analysis—the reality inarticulate or superabundant to its descriptions that rationalism discounts and avoids (*ND* 172). And this reluctance to acknowledge the distance of thought from reality, Adorno tellingly adds, is reflected in the perpetually ambivalent reputation of Cicero, whose rhetoric denies any easy propinquity or contiguity of the two. For Luther and Milton, just such a reality exceeding our ideas, just such an incommensurable order of meaning, is implicated in the world's incongruity, equivocality, or as Adorno observes, in the intransigence of suffering—all experiences these theologians associate with the knowledge of their peculiar God and the justification of humanity. For if deity's connection to the world were understood as a strict logic, observing a necessary order of relation between the divine nature and temporal truths, then there would be no question of faith or obedience. We would simply perform the good or evil that God foresees and to which he condemns the human person from eternity; like an ornamental interlude or diversion, creatural existence would then merely adorn the metaphysical outcome on which deity had already determined. Such a notion is reminiscent of that "essential and intrinsick" moral that Dr. Johnson ascribes to *Paradise Lost*, which Milton's poetry comparably decorates. But as Milton argues in the case of censorship, such was not the character of our creation:

> Impunity and remissenes, for certain are the bane of a Commonwealth, but here the great art lyes to discern in what the law is to bid restraint and punishment, and in what things perswasion only is to work. If every action which is good, or evill in man at ripe years, were under pittance, and prescription, and compulsion, what were vertue but a name, what praise could be then due to well-doing, what grammercy to be sober, just or continent? many there be that complain of divin Providence for suffering *Adam* to transgresse, foolish tongues! when God gave him reason, he gave him freedom to choose, for reason is but choosing; he had bin else a meer artificiall *Adam*, such an *Adam* as he is in the motions. We our selves esteem not of that obedience, or love, or gift, which is of force: God therefore left him free, set before him a provoking object, ever almost in his eyes; herein consisted his merit, herein the right of his reward, the praise of his abstinence. Wherefore did he creat passions within us, pleasures round about us, but that these rightly temper'd are the very ingredients of vertu? (CM 4:318–319)

I include the remarks immediately preceding this red-letter libertarian passage, because without them, we might be inclined to overlook the nature of the compulsion Milton would have us resist, and consequently, the conditions of human choice that he evokes for Adam. It is a compulsion that Milton suggests is fomented by a particular interpretive logic instituted as law, whose effects are humanly and morally nonsensical. For were we to suppose that everything is bad or good in and of itself, like passion or pleasure in the exercise of virtue, or that the consequences attending any action would be identical in all circumstances, then we would have no need of God since we ourselves would be viewing the world *sub specie aeternitatis*. As Milton understands it, this inhuman vantage is the one to which the Presbyterian censors and religious orthodoxies in general implicitly presume. To put the case religiously, were truth always conspicuous, so would the one true God be; and the dilemma of belief moving the Presbyterians to impose censorship in the first place would be no dilemma at all. So when Milton asserts that "reason is but choosing," he doesn't intend to exalt the human faculty of understanding as a sure and exact instrument of judgment. On the contrary, its role must remain altogether experimental and suasive, and this is owing to a further aspect of our predicament. In the historical affairs of God, which Milton with irony calls the wars of truth, there is no human logic that can encompass deity's will, much less anticipate its possibilities; and so there must be no human promulgation of meaning that precludes divine judgment or preempts our own. Seen this way, neither Miltonic truth nor Miltonic reason is even remotely axiomatic: he seeks what Adorno calls "the open thought"—the sort of meaning that does not foreclose other avenues of significance (*ND* 35). And to this end, he makes truth and reason issues of particular occasion and choice, like Gorgias's *to kairon* ("the opportune") and *to prepon* ("the fitting"), or Cicero's *aptus* and *ornatus*; for these circumstances equally condition our religious predicament—the affinity in difference between creature and creator to which divine revelation addresses itself.[11]

So in bringing "sound reason" to bear on religious things in the *Christian Doctrine*—here the controversy over predestination—Milton's version of that faculty is grammatical, moral, and entirely exoteric:

> If, however, it be allowable to examine the divine decrees by the laws of human reason, since so many arguments have been maintained on this subject by controvertists on both sides with more of subtlety than of solid argument, this theory of contingent decrees may be defended on the principles of men, as most wise, and in no respect unworthy of the Deity. For if those decrees of God . . . and such others of the same class as occur perpetually, were to be understood in an absolute sense, without any implied conditions, God would contradict himself, and appear inconsistent.
>
> It is argued, however, that in such instances not only was the ultimate purpose predestinated, but even the means themselves were predestinated with a view to it. So indeed, it is asserted, but not on the authority of

Scripture; and the silence of Scripture would alone be a sufficient reason
for rejecting the doctrine. But it is also attended by this additional incon-
venience, that it would entirely take away from human affairs all liberty
of action, all endeavor and desire to do right. (CM 14:69–71)

Milton extenuates for sacred scripture in the way that I would extenuate for his
own writings. For any time we constrain a text to a single, absolute sense, it
cannot help but contradict itself if its usage is differently organized—not on
the model of logical or even symbolic coherence, but on that of deity's accommodation to the exigencies of human grammar. This expressive order is implicated here by scripture's unique position "to which we must bow, as to a paramount authority" (CM 14:69). The authority, indeed the sacredness, of the text
is the great given of Christian faith, although reasons of course can be educed
for it, even as we can rationalize existence itself. Taken this way, scripture's
sense emulates the interdiction God puts on the tree of knowledge: the seemingly arbitrary authority of scripture stands to the reader as a boundary beyond
which justification cannot reach. If we are faithful, we commit ourselves to the
terms set by the text. If we are not, we speculate without this constraint, setting
up our own ideas against scripture's expressions, and in the process giving free
rein to our own imperatives and creating God in their image. But for Milton,
the text's silence on the nature and order of the divine decrees decides the case
by default, since what God does not choose to tell us, we have no other way of
knowing—whatever is left unelucidated we cannot propose to determine for
ourselves. Milton therefore disclaims the propriety of inquiring into deity independent of scripture, before he himself inquires one step further into the implication of its language. And then he proceeds only in order to distinguish between deity's accommodating itself to our grammar, our usages, and those
inferences of our own which seek to bring the hidden God into conformity
with extra-scriptural ideas of truth and coherence.[12]

This is what I mean by the difference between a grammatical sense of the
text and a logical or metaphysical construction of its meaning. Milton's implicit
subject is that speculation Raphael deprecates as "saving the appearances,"
where reason is put to the purpose of effacing, not acknowledging, the distinction between God and the world, with humankind inventing ever greater and
more ingenious solutions to explain the seemingly inordinate motions of the
heavens, "centric and eccentric scribbled o'er, / Cycle and epicycle, orb in orb"
(LM 8.83–84). In much the same fashion, theologians also impose logical and
metaphysical necessities on the sacred text so as to rectify what they regard as its
nonsense and obscurities. Where Milton would insist that we seek to reconcile
scripture's incongruities within the terms of the sacred text, thus deferring understanding to faith, this other sort of reconciliation departs from scripture altogether in trying to rescue its "reasonableness" or "consistency": a particular "appearance" of contradiction becomes the occasion and excuse for a speculative
superstructure that ends up overwhelming and distorting even what scripture
clearly says, as here.

In this section of the *Christian Doctrine*, Milton is responding to an argument that the conditional expression of the salvific order, ascribed by scripture to God, is inconsistent with the theology of deity's absolute and unconditioned being, and therefore inactual, without force. Accordingly, the sense of scripture is circumvented by what is seen to be a prior (in the sense of logically precedent) doctrinal truth. The preeminence of the divine nature is thought to predicate another order to salvation antithetical to scripture's ostensible account, one that begins with God's "secret" as against his "revealed" will in history and presumes all unaware to penetrate into the *arcana imperium* of his eternal decrees. This may at first appear to be a version of Luther's God hidden away in majesty, except Luther refuses to do anything other than postulate a theological reality which for him is a complete blank: that is, he never says how the reality of *Deus nudus absconditus* is ordered over against the reality of *Deus crucifixus*; the boundary imposed by the distinction gets in the way. Milton observes this boundary as well, which he describes as the difference between the divine nature (deity per se) and the divine image (deity as it accommodates itself toward us). Neither theologian pretends to understand God except as he reveals himself in scripture, so neither conjures up a God against God in the manner of this argument, which in attempting to characterize the "double will" of deity achieves a peculiar affinity with tragedy.

Moreover, in the face of the distinction, they do not allow a continuity in understanding between the hypothetical absolute of deity and the revealed God of our experience: the one stands entirely outside theological discussion; the other is its only subject. In Catholic and Protestant scholasticism, this is what distinguishes "our theology" (*nostra theologica*) or the theology of the pilgrim (*theologica viatorum*) or of revelation from deity's self-knowledge and definitive theology as well as the vision of the blessed (*theologica beatorum*).[13] Yet Milton sees the textually extrinsic argument about the order of God's decrees as contravening this paramount distinction of faith, especially where scripture's account is rendered inconsequent. In his view, where deity should religiously be left alone, it is made the subject of inferences unauthorized and largely irrelevant to scripture's account of salvation. More disturbing still, deity itself is made to assume the precise shape of this interpolated necessity of logic. As the Father looks to Satan, who himself denies the force of the distinction, the God of scholastic predestination appears to Milton as a tyrant of cosmic proportions; for the decrees are terrible, unspeakable wherever they have to do with the divine nature as we infer it—its unity, immutability, infallibility, and so forth— and not with the Christ, as Calvin insists.[14] These attributes are not realities but markers, betokening the difference between human and divine being. And when they cease to be figurative and are made an end and actuality in themselves, they not only preempt the language of scripture, the sole source of religious knowledge in Protestantism, but also override all humane considerations, whether divine or theological. The propensity to impose our own necessities, our own meanings on God and the things of God, is an error against which

Milton constantly rails in the tracts, because this unself-conscious mode of interpretation tends to generate precisely those confusions and injustices which it purports to remove.

Truth for Milton is not single, self-evident, and automatic, but always impending and strange like the God of the apocalypse. Deity resists the endogamy of rationalism Adorno indicts, the self-imposed blinkering of idealism that dismays Wittgenstein: it thwarts our determination not only to reduce all things to one order, but simply to reproduce that identification again and again, without any desire to know something new and perhaps effectual about our condition. This is the gist of the charge Milton makes against episcopacy's imitative model of ecclesiology, in which the government of the church is established by correspondence to the Mosaic priesthood. Not only is such imitation irreligious in his view, since it assumes a continuity made impossible by the abrogated allegory of the ceremonial law—itself a figure of the distinction between God and the world (CM 3.1:189–90). But it does precisely as Adorno says of rationalism, insofar as religious meaning is "confin'd and cloy'd with repetition of that which is prescrib'd." For the logical imperative to clarify the world and make it neat and uniform, as Eve would clean up Eden, serves to deny the expressiveness of creation and the presence of God wherever these elude its mechanism. Then the perceived contradiction between deity's absolute nature and the terms of salvation results in a division of God into two in Job's manner and Luther's—again, a God against God: one humane, the other horrifically arbitrary, reflecting God's revealed and ostensibly secret wills. And the scriptural text is similarly divided against itself, in order to support a speculative priority outside its own argument. So where the appearance of contradiction ironically understood would compel us to reflect on our own assumptions of truth, bringing these into accordance with what the text says, the logical sort tacitly dispenses with the constraint of scripture's authority as it tries to bring the text's meaning into accordance with its own values and assumptions. In this interpretive conflict, we observe once again the divergence of revisionist from canonical kinds of justifying. In the one case, the experiential difference between our ideas and truth is made salient to any effort at making sense of scripture. In the other, truth itself consists in establishing the independent coherence of our ideas, with the evident sense of scripture not reassessed or qualified but entirely preempted.

By contrast, within the parameters of scripture's silence—that is, "If we must apply to God a phraseology borrowed from our own habits and understanding" (CM 14:81)—Milton finds God's conditional expressions, as well as the idea they seem to predicate of his contingent decrees, more than sufficiently in accord with God's scriptural image. As he sees it, "the covenant was of this kind: If thou stand, thou shalt abide in Paradise; if thou fall, thou shalt be cast out; if thou eat not the forbidden fruit, thou shalt live; if thou eat, thou shalt die" (CM 14:81). Moreover, the form of God's language observes a psychology to moral and religious practice that an unconditioned argument about God's de-

crees decisively ignores, in the process fostering a pastoral dilemma that trou-
bled the Reformed churches for many years.[15] And this psychology argues simply that the good and the true must be susceptible of our recognition and
understanding, if we are to admit their claims. It is a psychology, one might
add, that Milton sees God observing when in revelation he makes himself intelligible through the media of human categories, values, and relations. But like
the Presbyterian censors who wish to institute it, Reformed dogmatics do not
appear to honor in interpretive method the difference its theology exalts in
the phrase "God's own good pleasure"—deity absolutely considered, apart from
scripture. Instead, before the beginning of all time and without regard for any
future contingency, God's secret and absolute will would seem to dictate arbitrarily which persons will be saved and which cast out.

As Milton says, predestination must be understood in terms of God's express
and general election of humanity to salvation, which scripture clearly and repeatedly puts in terms of faith in the promises of Christ and the unseen: "in
other words . . . the privilege belongs to all who heartily believe and continue
in their belief" (CM 14:107). As against the humanly unintelligible conclave
of deity with itself, scripture pictures a meaning and a choice not only viable
but universal. This difference of interpretive position effectively renders the
idea of such a soteriology incoherent and inhumane, insofar as it prefers the
incomprehensible imperatives of divine being to the scriptural vantage—the
human condition the gospel exists to explain and alleviate. Indeed, human
existence itself is riven by the hypothesis of deity's bifurcated will. For when
the creature is elected to salvation without possibility of recognizance—that is,
experiencing the intelligible presence of God neither in the text nor the
world—then there is no way believers can *know* their own faith. And where
there is no humanly appreciable difference between the experiences of faith
and infidelity, good and evil, truth and illusion, these become indistinguishable
from the arbitrary flux of events, and God's providence feels like an indiscriminate fate. Believers are made prey to an intolerable anxiety, because they have
no way to evidence to themselves—by sensation, motive, idea, or circumstance—their faith, their sanctification, and so their salvific status. With fear-
some completeness, God alone knows what is to become of them.

In other words, because the logic of supralapsarianism (as this argument came
to be termed) can be read as an emanation scheme,[16] in which God's absolute
decrees are tantamount to creatural necessity, human events can be made to
correspond to the divine will in something like the way Milton's justification
in *Paradise Lost* becomes a cipher for his political failures. Every occurrence is
loaded with singular significance to such an oppressive yet equivocal extent
that the offer of salvation perversely intensifies the perplexities of human being,
not relieves them. And having dispensed with a role for human understanding,
deity is made the more or less transparent cause of all temporal eventualities
including sin (as Arminius and then Episcopius and Grotius maintained against
Calvinist orthodoxy). These are the complications Milton sees arising when

the medium and constraint of scriptural language, which in turn emphasizes the human conditions of salvation, is discounted in theology. As he presciently remarks, the scholastic imperative of ever more precise definition—an insistence on a logically exact mechanism for a text and a providence that evidently don't work that way—makes instead for the most profoundly incoherent, soul-destroying religion:

> Nor do we imagine anything unworthy of God, when we assert that those conditional events depend on the human will, which God himself has chosen to place at the free disposal of man; since the Deity purposely framed his own decrees with reference to particular circumstances, in order that he might permit free causes to act conformably with that liberty with which he had endued them. On the contrary, it would be much more unworthy of God, that man should nominally enjoy a liberty of which he was virtually deprived, which would be the case were that liberty to be oppressed or even obscured under the pretext of some sophistical necessity of immutability or infallibility, though not of compulsion, a notion which has led, and still continues to lead many individuals into error. (CM 14:73–75)

The meanings of divine providence and scripture consist in the particular grammar of God's expressions—natural, historical, verbal—none of which represent him as such but mediately and contingently, for the purposes of our understanding. And since all religious knowledge is comprised within the range of our creatural experience, to which the creator accommodates himself in order to be known and loved, we must reciprocate that voluntary constraint and accept deity as it chooses to reveal itself. When God applies to himself the person and condition of humanity, whether in the shape of human language or perception, scripture's anthropomorphisms or the Christ, then he should be taken in that sense even though these media cannot possibly be supposed to encompass all his meanings, never mind his nature. Gaps and incongruities, in short, are bound to arise if only to remind us of the abysmal distance between deity per se and the picture by which the divine expresses itself to the world:

> God of his wisdom determined to create men and angels reasonable beings, and therefore free agents; foreseeing at the same time which way the bias of their will would incline, in the exercise of their own uncontrolled liberty. What then? shall we say that this foresight or foreknowledge on the part of God imposed on them the necessity of acting in any definite way? No more than if the future event had been foreseen by any human being. For what any human being has foreseen as certain to happen, will not less certainly happen than what God himself has predicted. . . . [God] foresees the event of every action, because he is acquainted with their natural causes, which, in pursuance of his own decree, are left at liberty to exert

their legitimate influence. Consequently the issue does not depend on God who foresees it, but on him alone who is the object of his foresight. Since therefore, as has before been shown, there can be no absolute decree of God regarding free agents, undoubtedly the prescience of the Deity (which can no more bias free agents than the prescience of man, that is, not at all, since the action in both cases is intransitive, and has no external influence) can neither impose any necessity of itself, nor can it be considered at all as the cause of free actions. If it be so considered, the very name of liberty must be altogether abolished as an unmeaning sound; and that not only in matters of religion, but even in questions of morality and indifferent things. (CM 14:83–85)

As Milton argues the case here, the intransitive force of God's foreknowledge expresses the intransitive significance of scriptural usage and thus comparably abides by the distinction between creature and creator: precisely because God, in promulgating his revelation, constrains himself to observe human understanding and choice, so we too must observe the same tact in interpreting what he says. The theological fact of the hidden God's accommodation to creaturely appearances signals the utter discontinuity between deity and the world where our various logics presumptively obtain. We can make sense of scripture only up to the point demarcated by this distinction in usage, so that the sanctity of the divine nature is preserved from our inferences: "God is known, so far as he is pleased to make us acquainted with himself, either from his own nature, or from his efficient power. When we speak of knowing God, it must be understood with reference to the imperfect comprehension of man; for to know God as he really is, far transcends the powers of man's thought, much more of his perception. . . . God therefore has made as full a revelation of himself as our minds can conceive, or the weakness of our nature bear" (CM 14:31). Where deity accommodates the "weakness of our nature," human speculation cruelly burdens that nature with metaphysics. So Milton avers "that those who have acquired the truest apprehension of the nature of God . . . submit their understandings to his word; considering that he has accommodated his word to their understandings, and has shown what he wishes their notion of the Deity should be" (CM 14:37). Moreover, we can neither interpolate nor exclude any element of this picture, nor can we infer from our theology to deity per se: "In a word, God either is, or is not, such as he represents himself to be. If he be really such, why should we think otherwise of him? If he be not such, on what authority do we say what God has not said? If it be his will that we should thus think of him, why does our imagination wander into some other conception? Why should we hesitate to conceive of God according to what he has not hesitated to declare explicitly respecting himself? For such knowledge of the Deity as was necessary for the salvation of man, he has himself of his goodness been pleased to reveal abundantly" (CM 14:37).

The problem of faith is represented here as an impasse that occurs in our unexamined expectations of scripture and how we presume to know God; for we may want to think about deity in a fashion that scripture complicates or thoroughly resists, as Calvinism confronts in its systematic enterprise of theology. This impasse once again figures the distinction between deity and the intellectual creature; yet for all that we may find the divine image incongruous, it alone remains God for us. To that point, Luther contends in his controversy with Erasmus that despite the text's real obscurities, inconsequences, and scandals, we can still assert with complete confidence the sense of scripture, which is the knowledge of Christ as the means of our salvation. It is just these anomalous effects which are expressive of that image's divine origin and sanctity, and which should preserve us from the danger of idolatry, in the supposition that deity *ipse* is analogous in nature to God's image—that divine utterance is more than a way of speaking, more than an inference constrained and contingent upon scripture's expressions of what God is toward us. Indeed, the very incongruity with which Calvinist systematics struggles itself signals this figurative force of scriptural speech and the provisionality of our inferences. It is the effect of relating incommensurables even as the creator itself seeks to do in covenanting with its creature. But when this incongruity is extrapolated from the nature of the text to the nature of reality, by virtue of its inferential source in God's twofold will, it cannot but result in a dreadful dissociation of truth from human being. As Calvin reminds his reader repeatedly, as soon as we diverge from the scriptural image of God in Christ, who teaches us salvation, we not only lose all sense of what the text means, but find ourselves wandering in labyrinths of speculation without end.

THEOLOGY AS GRAMMAR

Given the distinction between creator and creature, deity per se as against the God of the covenant, scriptural grammar for its part must accommodate this extraordinary and estranging reference by using human language to another effect altogether. In his lectures on Galatians, Luther analyzes this "theological" force of the text, describing how in scripture the words "doing" and "working" should not be taken in their customary sense:

> These words "doing" and "working" are to be taken in three ways: the essential or natural way . . . , the moral way, and the theological way. In essences or nature and in moral matters, as I have said, these words are taken in their usual way. But in theology they become completely new words and acquire a new meaning. Therefore all the hypocrites, who want to be justified on the basis of the Law and have false ideas about God, belong to moral "doing"; against them Paul is disputing here. For they have the sort of "doing" that proceeds from amoral or human right reason

and good will. Therefore their work is merely moral or rational, not a faithful or theological work, one that includes faith. When you read in Scripture, therefore, about the patriarchs, prophets, and kings that they worked righteousness, raised the dead, conquered kingdoms, etc., you should remember that these and similar statements are to be explained according to a new and theological grammar, as the eleventh chapter of the Epistle to the Hebrews explains them: "By faith they worked righteousness, by faith they raised the dead, by faith they conquered kings and kingdoms." Thus faith embodies and informs the "doing." (*LW* 26:267)

The theological sense of "doing" and "working" does not involve what we might expect—an order of human agency or causation in religious things, or more specifically, that the patriarchs, prophets, and kings were directly, overtly made righteous before God by their own activity. Luther does not understand their historical actions as causal in any religious sense, but instead as expressing or picturing the attitude of faith that "makes God" by referring any indicative choice or event to deity's immanence in the world. Nor is God thus rendered the secondary or efficient cause behind natural or human events, which would deny the historical character of our existence, not to mention its subjective or personal dimension. Rather, Luther argues that "Once a true idea and knowledge of God is held as right reason, then the work is incarnated and incorporated into it. In this way whatever is attributed to faith is later attributed also to works, but only on account of the faith" (*LW* 26:268). Scriptural narrative then does not allegorize deity as such; it exhibits the exceptional understanding of faith which, like all *res non apparentes*, is known by its largely incongruous meanings—incongruous, that is, from the standpoint of "natural" and "moral" assumptions about the way things should signify. Indeed, Luther approaches "doing" and "working" as a case of the Hebrew genitive and "the righteousness of God" all over again; for these scriptural words refer our actions not to ourselves as their obvious subject but to the inevident deity who not only creates but redeems us:

Therefore "doing" is one thing in nature, another in philosophy, and another in theology. In nature the tree must be first, and then the fruit. In moral philosophy doing means a good will and right reason to do well; this is where the philosophers come to halt. Therefore we say in theology that moral philosophy does not have God as its object and final cause. . . . we have to rise higher in theology with the word "doing," so that it becomes altogether new. For just as it becomes something different when it is taken from the natural arena into the moral, so it becomes something much more different when it is transferred from philosophy and from the Law into theology. Thus it has a completely new meaning; it does indeed require right reason and a good will, but in a theological sense, not in a moral sense, which means that through the Word of the Gospel I know and believe that God sent His Son into the world to redeem us from sin and death. Here "doing" is a new thing, unknown to reason, to the philosophers, to the legalists, and to all men; for it is a "wisdom hidden in a mystery" (1 Cor. 2:7). (*LW* 26:262)

What Luther had read in Romans as his own righteousness effected by doing good works becomes in this "completely new meaning" another attitude or mentality taken toward the world, organized on the model of Christ's sacrifice. What the faithful see in Jesus' suffering is God acting in humanity to redeem it, in much the way that Luther sees the grammar of Romans as expressing God as "its object and final cause," not humankind. So when the scriptural text and the creature's actions are referred to God, not to our bodies or our dispositions in the way nature or morality assume, then the incongruity of meaning and experience which both Luther and Paul together call "wisdom hidden in a mystery" becomes suddenly intelligible. As I mentioned earlier, on more than one occasion in his philosophical remarks, and at length in that lecture he gives in the 1930s, Wittgenstein alludes to this uniquely Lutheran idea of theology as a grammar by which we express and know the hidden God. I mention it here to suggest an affinity between Luther's concept that our experience is susceptible of sustaining more and less compatible meanings all at once and Wittgenstein's argument that the meaning of our expressions is created by their use and cannot consist in a single continuous reference or analogy to things in the world. As Wittgenstein observes, we tend to suppose that "proposition, language, thought, world, stand in line one behind the other, each equivalent to each" in an unbroken chain of correspondences, not unlike the metaphysical and logical schemes of meaning's emanation from deity to the phenomenal world (*PI* p.96). But the supposition that words are constrained to equivalences of some kind is regularly controverted by our experience: as Wittgenstein says, language is "a labyrinth of paths," where "You approach from *one* side and know your way about; you approach the same place from another side and no longer know your way about" (*PI* p.104). Luther himself rejects the contention of the Sorbonne, which he calls "the mother of errors," that truth is the same in philosophy and theology; and he takes as his text John 1.14, "the Word was made flesh" (*LW* 38:239). In his discussion of this argument, B.A. Gerrish observes that Luther's distinction between these two orders of meaning does not represent "a theory of double truth"—again along the lines of God's secret and revealed wills in Protestant scholasticism,[17] or as Niebuhr understands it, the Aquinan exclusion of faith as an order of meaning from the phenomenal world. The distinction, Gerrish argues, is rather one of "multiple discourses," where the propositions of theology and philosophy use the same words in divergent and incompatible senses.

So while Luther allows that "the syllogism is a most excellent form," he asserts that "it is useless with regard to the matter [of theology] itself": "Therefore, in articles of faith one must have recourse to another dialectic and philosophy, which is called the word of God and faith" (*LW* 38:241). For the indiscriminate practice of syllogistic in theology has in his view fostered heresy, not contained it: "heretics, who have erred in this respect and who have rushed blindly into theology with this syllogistic form, permit themselves to reconcile all things by reasoning, and to infer everything by the syllogistic process in opposition to Scripture. For, having relied on this form and method, they have brought many difficulties and faulty inferences to Scripture even when the plain text occasionally shouts in disapprobation" (*LW* 38:259). Notwithstanding Luther's devout Trinitarianism, these could be Milton's words; the interpretive position comparably emphasizes the different criteria of theological meaning—faith, scripture, and the hidden God. Like deity, the matter of theology "is not indeed something contrary to, but is outside, within, above, below, before and beyond all logical truth" (*LW* 38:241). So, "We would act more correctly if we left dialectic and philosophy in their own area and learned to speak in a new language in the realm of faith apart from every sphere" (*LW* 38:242). But Luther is not promoting a mystical turn or irrationalism any more than Milton does. Their resistance to scholastic logic has to do with its impropriety as a means of interpreting the scriptural text. They regard logic as license not least because it refuses to respect scripture's preeminent authority, proposing to supplement the sacred text, to fill in what it has seemingly omitted and fix what is already there. And it presumes to do this because logic asserts the unity of truth, pursuing continuities among meanings disavowed by the distinction between God as unmade and everything else as made—including logic itself. One might compare Luther's and Milton's attitudes in their theology to that of William Ames, who expounds a version of Stoic synteresis—innate and axiomatic knowledge.[18] As Perry Miller argues, for theologians of this persuasion, the exercise of faith and syllogistic were distinct but functionally analogous and coordinate ways of brings scriptural meanings to bear on the world.[19] Not surprisingly, their theological affiliation played a role in inaugurating the great age of Protestant scholasticism to which Milton responds.

But his writings argue the different order of meaning and rationality that Luther acutely calls a grammar, an idea Wittgenstein recovers when he says, "How words are understood is not told by words alone. (Theology.)";[20] and again, "Grammar tells us what kind of object anything is. (Theology as grammar.)" (*PI* p.373). Wittgenstein prepares for these remarks in that lecture where he discusses our tendency to construe every concept as though it were of the same species as material things. Thus he notes how in "the grammar of ethical terms, and such terms as 'God,' 'soul,' 'mind,' 'concrete,' 'abstract,' " we want to "take a substantive to correspond to a thing."[21] By way of showing how some usages do not conform to this expectation, he comments that "Luther said that theology is the grammar of the word 'God.' I interpret this to mean that an investigation of the word would be a grammatical one. For example, people might dispute about how many arms God had, and someone might enter the dispute by denying that one could talk about arms of God. This would throw light on the use of the word. What is ridiculous or blasphemous also shows the grammar of the word."[22] Following Wittgenstein, we could say that logic talks about the number of God's arms, which appalls Luther and Milton because they do not admit an analogy between the grammar of phenomena and the grammar of God. What appears reasonable according to one model of meaning is perceived as outrageous by another (the neat irony here being that those making the charge of sacrilege could conceivably belong to that order of theologian who would deny the intelligibility, indeed the historical force, of the Incarnation, as against those who insist on the irreducible complexity of our talk about God, which Christ's nature exemplifies). Neither Luther nor Milton supposes scripture's expressions to function in the same way as those we use for the world of sensible things—the terms and relations of Aristotle's *Categories*, which Luther scorns in his disputation on John 1 (*LW* 38:240)—precisely because scriptural language has reference to *res non apparentes*, that other order of substantive embracing words like "God," "soul," and "mind." Again, in his commentary on Galatians, Luther makes a discrimination that illustrates not only God's grammar but also the peculiarly grammatical nature of our religious knowledge, which has its source in scripture's unique authority in the reformers' theology. The subject under discussion is how Paul allegorizes the conflict between Sarah and Hagar as a rejection of all ritual observance under the Mosaic law, and particularly the rite of circumcision that Genesis says began with Abraham. Significantly, Luther begins his exegesis by repudiating the interpretive method he himself once employed, especially in his early lectures on the psalms—reading the text of scripture according to the ancient fourfold sense (literal, tropological, allegorical, and anagogical).[23] His polemical purpose in so peremptorily dismissing that exegetical approach is to underscore the immanence, not the metaphysical transcendence, of the New Jerusalem that Paul chooses to personify as Sarah. For immanence is an idea at odds with the presumption of separate yet correlative realms, visible and invisible, which this venerable model of exegesis promotes, but which Luther fears would abstract faith not only from the historical but also from the moral world. So to emphasize the presence of a religious reality in this life, he asserts paradoxically that "the Jerusalem that is above, that is, the heavenly Jerusalem, is the church here in time," as against the interpretive scheme in which that phrase would severally correspond to the city of that name, conscience, the churches militant and triumphant (*LW* 26:440).

In Luther's reading, the Pauline allegory neither evades nor affirms the world through a transcendental turn, but instead undertakes to revise our present perception by departing from the meanings we usually assign these words. Thus Hagar, the old Jerusalem enslaved with her children—the law to Paul and Luther—is likewise superseded in the maternity of Sarah by "a new and heavenly Jerusalem, which is lordly and free, has been divinely established, not in heaven but on earth, to be the mother of us all, of whom we have been born and are being born every day." (*LW* 26:440) And that Jerusalem is the gospel itself:

Therefore it is necessary that this mother of ours, like the birth she gives, be on earth among men; yet she gives birth in the Spirit, by the ministry of the Word and of the sacraments, not physically.

I say this to keep us from being led astray by our thoughts into heaven. We should know that Paul is contrasting the Jerusalem that is above with the earthly Jerusalem, not spatially but spiritually. Spiritual things are distinct from physical or earthly things. Spiritual things are "above"; earthly things are "below." Thus the Jerusalem that is above is distinguished from the physical and temporal Jerusalem that is below, as I have said, not spatially but spiritually. For the spiritual Jerusalem, which began in the physical Jerusalem, has no prescribed location, as the one in Judea does; but it is scattered throughout the world and can be in Babylonia, Turkey, Tartary, Scythia, India, Italy, or Germany, on the islands of the sea, on mountains, in valleys, and everywhere in the world where there are men who have the Gospel and believe in Christ. (*LW* 26:440–41)

Luther not only describes how he thinks scriptural usage works—as a distinctive kind of allegory—but more precisely, he places the same constraints as Milton does on the aptitude and force of any scriptural expression to signify *res non apparentes*, things that do not appear as such. His exegetical allegory may make the unseen intelligible to us, but not in order to claim any real correspondence between the images it selects and the things of God. For no use of human language could possibly resemble the religious reality it is made to convey, given the distinction between deity and the world; scriptural usage remains "a veil of ignorance" that artificially permits us a relationship and knowledge of religious things otherwise impossible. Figures like Paul's provide us at best with a way to speak and think about the divine without violating its hiddenness and sanctity, speech which itself requires an act of faith since we cannot extrapolate from image to thing. Accordingly, scripture presents us with no stable or autonomous symbology of *res non apparentes*; and precisely because there can be no such discrete, single, and invisible reference for "above" and "below," what he calls "the objects of faith" can inhabit this world to the same extent that material ones do, just not in the same manner. So instead of setting up a physics of *invisibilia* in the way Wittgenstein describes, or an entire parallel universe for religion, Luther's "spiritual" sense offers a way of understanding the world with God in it. For as David Burrell observes of medieval theology, spirit "referred not in the first instance to an unfamiliar mode of existence, but to a capacity for relating on different levels and across the space-time parameters endemic to bodies," adding that Kierkegaard too "characterizes the self as spirit, that is, a *relating*."[24] It is this attitude that self takes toward the world, an interpretive posture that carries with it assumption and passion, which binds humanity to God insofar as deity too is pictured as creating by an act of "spirit," understood as "relation." Thus in Luther's own marvelous image, we in turn can find deity and truth "scattered" among our perceptions, as something actual but distinct and even estranging from our unexamined reading of experience.

The profound gap described by the divergence of theological grammar from ordinary usage evokes a conflict not unlike that taking place between Sarah and Hagar, the new Jerusalem and the old, in Paul's allegory; in both instances, injustice or human suffering precipitates a shift from old understandings to new. Thus Luther reads the passage from Galatians so that it argues the very issue of its own significance: like Hagar and the old Jerusalem, our usual assumptions of meaning are in bondage to the flesh and the world. Moreover, like the child born of Hagar's servitude, we helplessly perpetuate our suffering and, one might add, the loss of our humanity. In succumbing to this interpretation of deity and truth, we have reduced ourselves and the world to the bodies we can see and touch, the only kind of existence we recognize. However, when faith reintroduces the unknowable God and the whole order of inevident things his presence implicates, we cease to be enthralled, to suffer the gross indignities and limitations of our self-imposed servitude to the merely obvious or habituated sense we assign our experience. And as Hebrews observes, it was faith in the inevident and improbable that made a mother of Sarah: "By faith Sarah herself received power to conceive, even when she was past the age, since she considered him faithful who had promised. Therefore from one man, and him as good as dead, were born descendants as many as the stars of heaven and as the innumerable grains of sand by the seashore" (11:11–12).

When the Lord appears as three men whom Abraham feasts and whom Sarah then overhears, prophesying the birth of a son to her on their return in the spring, she laughs, saying, "After I have grown old, and my husband is old, shall I have pleasure?" (Genesis 18:9–15). It would seem that Sarah's laughter is prompted equally by the prolonged disappointment of her infertility, as it is by her consequent sense that the Lord's promise is absurd—contrary to common sense, ludicrous, incongruous with nature itself. For she is asked abruptly to put aside her notion of the settled order of things, which includes her age and her barrenness, and to see her life as taking on a meaning altogether different from the one to which she had resigned herself. In short, she is confronted with a possibility that transforms her body and herself, making her other than what she seems to be. Yet one tradition of reading Sarah's laughter, by comparison with Abraham's silent acquiescence, is as a sign of faithlessness or distrust on her part, where her seeming ridicule provokes God's query, "Is anything too hard for the Lord?" In this account, the incongruousness of the promise to which she responds with laughter reflects her alienation from deity, since a faithful person would not find the promise strange but appropriate and credible. But that would be to erase her entire intervening history and real suffering, and to suppose that Sarah should not find the sudden idea of her motherhood difficult to begin with, despite her recourse to the desperate and unjust expedient of Hagar. In short, it is to suppose that faith is a ready and easy way. But there is another meaning than derision potential in Sarah's laughter, for which the

writer of Hebrews argues: namely, an impulsive expression of surprise at the
outrageousness of deity, who would extend to her the lost sexuality and maternity for which she grieves and which in part provokes her to violence against
Hagar. The Lord sees her as neither Abraham nor Hagar do, as a lover and a
mother, and her bemusement occasions laughter at the incongruity and then
fear of the being who would bring such a tremendous alteration in her world,
and who then ruthlessly exposes her altogether human response.

This new latitude of understanding and possibility is Luther's and Milton's
concept of Christian liberty: our freedom does not consist in a further perfected
world—the heaven that anagogy stipulates as against the *saeculum* of the old
Jerusalem. Like the Christian God, Christian liberty has meaning only in relation to things here in this world, which is why our experience of either depends
upon a new use of ordinary things like language itself; yet theological grammar
has reference to no one object, time, location, or idea. Wittgenstein argues
something to the same effect when he comments that, in the expression of a
wish, we always include its satisfaction, by which I understand him to mean
that promising or expecting does not wait on "the real"—an object as against
an expression—for its sense to be complete and truthful (*PI* p.439ff.). There is
no empty space of meaning reserved for some actual if proleptic thing: the
image of incompletion is rather a picture or a figure allowing us to convey the
condition of desire, which is very much an immediate sensation. Similarly, Luther argues that religious expressions neither demand nor project transcendent
being: we don't need to "go some place" mystically or metaphysically to know
the hidden God; nor is the new Jerusalem a sort of reverse emanation from
creatural existence. In the manner of irony, this Jerusalem implicates a revised
understanding of the creatural—not abandoning but instead forcefully addressing the actualities of human being. If the spiritual sense of things does
not recognize the physical as our ultimate constraint, neither does it deny the
significance of the body. Rather, it works against the exclusions and contradictions created by physicality's unrelieved dominance of religious understanding,
which fosters an object-language in theology whose effects are both specious
and cruel.

The decidedly topical geography of Luther's new Jerusalem is indicative of
the spiritual in two ways: it places the religious not only in the *saeculum* but
also fully and frankly in the current world; moreover, it defies contemporary
prejudices about the nature of truth, since this novel *urbs* is linked to no single
people or religious institution but the civil world from Turkey to India to Italy
and Germany—an altogether improbable congregation to assemble in an age
riven by religious warfare. So where Augustine, for example, sees no insuperable
discontinuity between God's city and the institution of the church, and can
still imagine a community of celibates to be a unique extension of the divine,
Luther refuses any such exclusive and thus divisive claim to represent deity.
This refusal goes some way toward explaining the motives behind his Erastian
and (seemingly) conservative politics, since he believes the religious is so dis-

tinct that in effect it eludes all institution in this world—thus his hostility to papal jurisdiction in secular matters. There can be no reciprocity, no confluence or equation, between religious and political means or purposes: as he argues at the opening of his lectures on Galatians, "spiritual" justification cannot be identified with "political" or "ceremonial" righteousness (*LW* 26:4). It follows that Luther would see no conflict between his theology and the violent suppression by Germany's feudal overlords of the so-called Peasants' Revolt or the civil persecution of Anabaptism, both of which movements Lutheran teachings ironically encouraged. In either case, these movements sought to identity the religious with the political and ceremonial, which in Luther's view commits the same sacrilegious error instituted by Catholicism:

> We see this today in the fanatical spirits and sectarians, who neither teach nor can teach anything correctly about this righteousness of grace. They have taken the words out of our mouth and out of our writings, and these only they speak and write. But the substance itself they cannot discuss, deal with, and urge, because they neither understand it nor can understand it. They cling only to the righteousness of the Law. Therefore they are and remain disciplinarians of works; nor can they rise beyond the active righteousness. Thus they remain exactly what they were under the pope. To be sure, they invent new names and new works; but the content remains the same. So it is that the Turks perform different works from the papists, and the papists perform different works from the Jews, and so forth. But although some do works that are more splendid, great, and difficult than others, the content remains the same, and only the quality is different. That is, the works vary only in appearance and in name. For they are still works. And those who do them are not Christians; they are hirelings, whether they are called Jews, Mohammedans, papists, or sectarians. (*LW* 26:9–10)

This diatribe would appear to oppose the geography of Luther's new Jerusalem, but in fact its interpretive assumptions are exactly the same: even as the gospel lives improbably in Turkey or India, so Christians can be Turks—as Luther indeed calls them—if they conflate legal or "active righteousness" with justification before God, and thus human things with divine, natural or moral grammars with the theological. To Luther, their confusion of the religious with the political rightly places Anabaptism and the Peasants' Revolt under civil authority; and it is the civil power of the German princes to which Luther appeals in his contest with the papacy, since they are its appropriate opponents in his view.

Yet the same distinction between human and divine creates in Milton a tolerationist, even a revolutionary, because he would ensure religion's free exercise by overturning the state church, which itself is premised on the identity of political and religious orders—famously expressed in the royalist motto "No bishop, no king." Consequently, Milton practices a kind of restrictive antinomianism when it comes to civic or ecclesiastical institutions, in order to relieve what he regards as the injustice and subjective incoherence perpetrated in the name of such identities.[25] Like the demand for gentile circumcision occasioning Paul's allegory, where he believes the sign is permitted to usurp the force and preeminence of what it expresses, the Stuart insistence on conformity presumes to argue not just an identity between political and religious order, but also the supremacy of the evident over the hidden or inevident. This supremacy of "outward" signs over "inward" dispositions lies behind Milton's self-conscious use of a traditional figure: "Under the gospel we possess, as it were [*enim*], a twofold Scripture; one external, which is the written word, and the other internal, which is the Holy Spirit, written in the hearts of believers, according to the promise of God, and with the intent that it should by no means be neglected" (CM 16:273):

> Hence, although the external ground which we possess for our belief at the present day in the written word is highly important, and, in most instances at least, prior in point of reception, that which is internal, and the peculiar possession of each believer, is far superior to all, namely the Spirit itself. . . . The process of our belief in the Scriptures is . . . as follows: we set out with a general belief in their authenticity, founded on the testimony either of the visible church, or of the existing manuscripts; afterwards, by an inverse process, the authority of the church itself, and of the different books as contained in the manuscripts, is confirmed by the internal evidence implied by the uniform tenor of Scripture, considered as a whole; and, lastly, the truth of the entire volume is established by the inward persuasion of the Spirit working in the hearts of individual believers. . . . Thus, even on the authority of Scripture itself, every thing is to be finally referred to the Spirit and the unwritten word.
>
> Hence it follows, that when an acquiescence in human opinions or an obedience to human authority in matters of religion is exacted, in the name either of the church or of the Christian magistrate, from those who are themselves led individually by the Spirit of God, this is in effect to impose a yoke, not on man, but on the Holy Spirit itself. (CM 16:275–81)

No more than Paul's "above" and "below," or Luther's "outside, within, above, below, before, and beyond," should we suppose that Milton's "internal" predicates the existence of some interior or transcendent place to which scriptural images supposedly correspond: like those expressions, it distinguishes faith as a differential order of meaning that reconfigures our perceptions, a mentality or attitude we take toward the world in which the believer is said to have "the mind of Christ . . . in him," to be guided by the spirit of God or by "conscience" (CM 16:265). Moreover, like any other subjectivity, institutional constraints can obtrude, coerce, and deform this attitude, which not only is conveyed in our speech and actions but is also integral to the meaning things have for us. Indeed, Miltonic faith does not exclude our mundane experience but is inti-

mately bound up with of it. Yet even as both faith and conscience are realized
in the way we extend ourselves in the world, Milton takes pains to argue that
they are not identical with their effects. Thus faith's works "may be different
from the works of the law":

> We are justified therefore by faith, but by a living, not a dead faith, and
> that faith alone which acts is counted living. . . . Hence we are justified by
> faith without the works of the law, but not without the works of faith;
> inasmuch as a living and true faith cannot consist without works, though
> these latter may differ from the works of the written law. Such were those
> of Abraham and Rahab, the two examples cited by St. James in illustration
> of the works of faith, when the former was prepared to offer up his son,
> and the latter sheltered the spies of the Israelites. (CM 16:39)

In his account of Abraham and Rahab the harlot, Milton gives a distinctly
Lutheran twist to James's polemic about faith's works: omitting the letter's more
usual example of Abraham's faith in God's promise ("and he reckoned it to him
as righteousness" [Genesis 15:6]), Milton emphasizes the singular episode in
which the patriarch undertakes at the Lord's own insistence to violate deity's
universal commandment by killing Isaac (James 2:21–26). In Luther's theology,
this occasion offers an outstanding instance of divine *opus alienum*— an action
that appears directly to contradict God's self-revelation. While deity's obscene
demand outrages the law as well as Abraham's trust and affection, more importantly, it subverts the covenantal picture of God himself which the whole
of Genesis serves to justify. And Rahab's righteous whore functions similarly,
this time to contravene the Mosaic presumption that the unclean are the unjust, that social and spiritual anathema are one. As Milton represents them
here, faith's works share the incongruous decorum of Luther's hidden God and
therefore have the potential to disrupt any analogy between human and divine
things. Moreover, their very incongruity shifts the locus of meaning from the
evident to the inevident aspect of an event—to the mystery of divine intent
and its figural counterpart in human subjectivity. This is the domain of *res non
apparentes*, things that do not appear as such, which Milton signifies by the
topos of scripture's "external" and "internal" texts, and the inevident "workings" of the spirit, faith, and conscience which presuppose any historical action
or human choice.

As Milton uses the term in both his tracts and *Christian Doctrine*, conscience
is more or less synonymous with "right reason" (CM 14:29). It is an interpretive
faculty that faith peculiarly informs and attunes to "spiritual things," and whose
function is not so much to abstract God's meanings from creation, as to discover
and reconcile deity's expressions with human experience and understanding,
which they invariably tend to challenge and even controvert. And since Milton
supposes spiritual things to have an existence at once difficult and concealed
to the regenerate themselves, his kind of conscience differs materially from the
innate and axiomatic instrument of Stoic and Scholastic synteresis, not least

because it expresses faith as a historical, not just a conceptual, process.[26] For faith and conscience or right reason neither transcend phenomena nor are divorced from them. Indeed, Milton defines faith itself as "a frame of mind acquired and confirmed by a succession of actions, although in the first instance infused from above" (CM 16:35): "the source from which faith originally springs, and whence it proceeds onward in its progress to good, is a genuine, though possibly in the first instance imperfect, knowledge of God; so that, properly speaking, the seat of faith is not in the understanding, but in the will" (CM 15:407). For Milton then, moral praxis or *proairesis* in the form of conscience or right reason shapes and enhances the understanding of faith as it would any other, although this mentality significantly departs in motive and assumption from our ordinary notion of things:

> THE COMPREHENSION OF SPIRITUAL THINGS IS A HABIT OR CONDITION OF MIND PRODUCED BY GOD, WHEREBY THE NATURAL IGNORANCE OF THOSE WHO BELIEVE AND ARE INGRAFTED IN CHRIST IS REMOVED, AND THEIR UNDERSTANDINGS ENLIGHTENED FOR THE PERCEPTION OF HEAVENLY THINGS, SO THAT, BY THE TEACHING OF GOD, THEY KNOW ALL THAT IS NECESSARY FOR ETERNAL SALVATION AND THE TRUE HAPPINESS OF LIFE. . . . In the present life, however, we can only attain to an imperfect comprehension of spiritual things. I Cor.xiii.9. "we know in part."
>
> The other effect [of the new life] is LOVE OR CHARITY, ARISING FROM A SENSE OF THE DIVINE LOVE SHED ABROAD IN THE HEARTS OF THE REGENERATE BY THE SPIRIT, WHEREBY THOSE WHO ARE INGRAFTED IN CHRIST BEING INFLUENCED, BECOME DEAD TO SIN, AND ALIVE AGAIN UNTO GOD, AND BRING FORTH GOOD WORKS SPONTANEOUSLY AND FREELY. This is also called HOLINESS. Eph.i.4. "that we should be holy and without blame before him in love." (CM 16:7–9)

What Milton terms "holiness" and associates with a "living" because charitable faith, where the love of God "spontaneously" animates good works, he equally conceives as a signal departure from our ordinary practice of understanding and action. Yet the mentality of faith that conscience expresses in this world remains nevertheless imperfect, partial, since the regenerate are righteous only in Luther's sense—that is to say, not by works but by imputation, a position Milton also pictures as " 'clothed' with the righteousness of Christ" (CM 16:29):

> But to render to every man "according to his deeds" is one thing, to render to him "on account of his deeds" is another; nor does it follow from hence that works have any inherent justifying power, or deserve anything as of their own merit; seeing that, if we do anything right, or if God assign any recompense to our rights actions, it is altogether owing to his grace. Hence the expression in . . . the Psalm, "he delivered me, because he delighted in me"; and Psal.lxii.12. "unto thee, O Lord, belongeth mercy, for thou

renderest to every man according to his work." Finally, the same Psalmist who attributes to himself righteousness, attributes to himself inquity in the same sentence; xviii.23. "I was also upright before him, and I kept myself from mine iniquity." (CM 16:45)

If charity is the inflection of faith toward the world, then holiness manifests the distinctive predicament of the believer, who like the psalmist, remains *simul iustus et peccator*, justified and a sinner at one and the same time. As such, in Milton's theology, faith does not *essentially* separate the believer from the rest of humanity, as though justification before God entailed the invention of a whole new species—the sort of regeneracy that, in some sorts of sixteenth- and seventeenth-century Protestantism, lays claim to unique knowledge and purity, not to mention fomenting a relentless sectarianism. On the contrary, faith entails a difference in the position or attitude we take toward the world, as the realm of God's incongruous revelation, an attitude which then progressively inflects the phenomena of human subjectivity—our speech and actions. And it is that freedom and sanctity of divine expression in the human person which Milton would preserve from the yoke of dogma and law by his individual sort of antinomianism. To ensure this liberty of divine and human meanings, Milton reads the works of faith, like the text of scripture, according to Luther's "new and theological grammar": in other words, he understands them as Luther does—with reference to the hidden God, or more precisely, as picturing the presence of deity whose discontinuous and figural existence in this world supplies the conceptual latitude of faith.[27]

So although Milton derides the term "justification by faith alone," his theology nonetheless argues a decorum for revelation and exegesis not unlike Luther's: in the incommensurable relation between deity and its expressions; the radical contingency of religious meanings; the functional emphasis on the incongruous, novel, or surprising in our experience; and despite all this, the sustained conviction of their intelligibility. Equally for Milton as for Luther, imputation carries the constraining force of the distinction between creator and creature, interdicting our inveterate assumption that the spiritual observes the same *causal* order we ascribe to physical and historical actions, in which righteousness *coram Deo* is caused by, is the necessary effect of what we do ("on account of"). Milton argues to the contrary, that what we do *pictures* the position from which we understand and encounter the world, testifying to the concealed and so figural "action" or "workings" of grace and faith ("according to"). As he describes them here, works are not a cause; they are the indispensable sign or expression of a fundamentally distinct kind of life.

This divergence of spiritual from received meanings operates along the lines of Wittgenstein's "visual room," where he offers the instance of sitting in a room as against talking about the room in which one sits (*PI* p.398ff.). The difference between the two, he says, is that the latter, the "visual room," can have no owner, and this is for a number of reasons. First of all, it does not behave like a physical room, since "I can as little own it as I can walk about it, or look at it, or point to it": that is to say, as a mental image, the "visual room" does not constitute an object or place in the world, much less a property to be possessed. Instead, it evokes a (perpetually) reflexive way of speaking that observes another set of possibilities and restrictions than we immediately assume—that the image or concept functions analogously to the thing it superficially resembles; but there is no outside to the "visual room," nothing we can objectify and as it were "view." Wittgenstein then goes on to remark that "it does not belong to me *because* I want to use the same form of expression about it as about the material room in which I sit"; that is to say, conflating the image with the thing cannot bridge the gulf between their modes of existence. The "visual room" remains intractably different from the room it evokes, and the more we persist in likening them, the greater the disturbance created by their eventual conflict (the profound because self-inflicted sufferings of Wittgenstein's sceptic). Yet the contradiction of our ideas may not inspire us to recognize this conceptual misstep or confusion: "You have a new conception and interpret it as seeing a new object. You interpret a grammatical movement made by yourself as a quasi-physical phenomenon which you are observing" (*PI* p.401). Instead, what we encounter is another order of meaning or expression: "The 'visual room' seemed like a discovery, but what its discoverer really found was a new way of speaking, a new comparison; it might even be called a new sensation . . . . What you have primarily discovered is a new way of looking at things. As if you had invented a new way of painting; or, again, a new metre, or a new kind of song" (*PI* pp.400–401).

This is Luther's point about theological grammar and Milton's about scripture's "internal" text or faith's "works." Like the "visual room," spiritual things have an expressive, conceptual existence ("a new way of speaking," "a new way of looking at things") which we insist on ignoring to our subjective jeopardy, as Luther describes in his preface to the Latin works. For Milton, that jeopardy is also moral insofar as it becomes a source of injustice. Since there can be no "object," no "outside," no "view" to scripture's expressions about God, they involve a sort of catachresis, a "wrenching of words." And catachresis is the figure by which Luther understands Paul's new and old Jerusalems:[28] the apostle, he says, is deliberately distorting our sense of space and time, just as he wrenches the proper sense of person in comparing the positions of Sarah and Hagar to the physical and spiritual cities of Jerusalem. For the divine in this life is not a place any more than a person is a place; yet while we accept the initial trope or turn of meaning Paul executes, we suppress the second, which Luther then exposes in his exegesis. He knows from his own experience that we will try to live the figure out, to live the "spiritual" as though it did indeed refer to a place, thus making an abuse of sense into an abuse of deity—into idolatry, the reduction of divine to creatural being or conversely, into transcendentalism, the evacuation of God from the world.

Like Luther, Milton too pursues an exegetical program of disenthrallment to the "objective" sense of things, arguing the plurality of human usage and our freedom, even necessity, to engage in experiments of meaning as we try to make sense of scripture as well as our experience of God. Accordingly, the only kind of decorum Milton allows for scriptural expressions is a flexible one, demanded by his scrupulous respect for the distinction between deity and the world. It functions something like Wittgenstein's "propriety of vagueness": "If I tell someone 'Stand roughly here'—may not this explanation work perfectly? And cannot every other one fail too?" (*PI* p.88). By this remark, Wittgenstein pictures the efficacy of language's "continguous" senses, which, like Luther's grammars or Milton's truths, do not mean in a seamless continuity. In Milton's reading, scripture too observes a "rough," not an exact, singular, or axiomatic propriety of speech, one which requires us to negotiate the significance of each particular usage and occasion. Nor does he, any more than Wittgenstein, see this as compromising the truth or rightness of scripture's expressions ("may not this explanation work perfectly" and "cannot every other one fail too?"). Rather, as with any absolute or ideal, he believes that we suffer the totemizing of precise reference, of verbal exactitude and conformity, as inhumane and unjust. This opinion receives its most controversial application in the divorce tracts, especially *The Doctrine and Discipline of Divorce*. There he rails against the Protestant counterparts of those canon lawyers who understand the marital relation as consisting strictly in a sexual union, but he especially condemns the interpretive literalism that invents and justifies such a doctrine—those "narrow intellectuals of quotationists and common placers" (CM 3.2:375), the "obstinate *literality*" and "alphabeticall servility" which would construe Jesus' words on divorce in isolation from the contingencies of occasion, audience, and motive (CM 3.2:427). The tract thus becomes a document in the argument for meaning as usage, exemplified in Milton's chapter on the scriptural senses of fornication, "which word is found to signifie other matrimoniall transgressions of main breach to that covnant besides actuall adultery" (CM 3.2:489). These include what he regards as signs of adulterous intent ("the wilful haunting of feasts, and invitations with men not of her neer kindred, the lying forth of her house without probable cause, the frequenting of Theaters against her husbands mind, her endeavour to prevent or destroy conception"), and still more figuratively, "a continual headstrong behaviour, as tends to plain contempt of the husband" (CM 3.2:487).

Yet notwithstanding the reasonableness of this interpretive tack, Milton has been charged with willful expedience in his reading, ostensibly to suit his own thwarted desires as against the integral sense of the text. Having earlier asserted that the gospel abolishes the Mosaic law, he now appears to recant that position in the divorce tracts, making the permission of divorce under the law authorize the extension of that practice under the gospel. But were his motives as egregiously self-interested as his critics claim, or even self-justifying in his usual manner—as an attempt to reconcile scripture with what he regards as a doctrinal injustice to the man—Milton's exegesis remains entirely methodical and consistent with his idea of God and the nature of our religious knowledge. In the *Christian Doctrine*, he returns to the figure of external and internal texts to explain his position, whose seeming vagaries are arguably original to Jesus' teaching in scripture. Thus he contends "that the sum and essence of the law is not hereby abrogated [by the new dispensation of the gospel]; its purpose being attained in that love of God and our neighbor, which is born of the Spirit through faith" (CM 16:141):

> the end for which the law was instituted, namely, the love of God and our neighbor, is by no means to be considered as abolished; it is the tablet of the law, so to speak, that is alone changed, its injunctions being now written by the Spirit in the hearts of believers with this difference, that in certain precepts the Spirit appears to be at variance with the letter, namely, wherever by departing from the letter we can more effectually consult the love of God and our neighbor. Thus Christ departed from the letter of the law, Mark ii.27. "the sabbath was made for man, not man for the sabbath," if we compare his words with the fourth commandment. St. Paul did the same in declaring that a marriage with an unbeliever was not to be dissolved, contrary to the express injunction of the law; 1 Cor.vii.12. "to the rest speak I, not the Lord." In the interpretation of these two commandments, of the sabbath and marriage, a regard to the law of love is declared to be better than a compliance with the whole written law; a rule which applies equally to every other instance. . . . Hence all rational interpreters have explained the precepts of Christ, in his sermon on the mount, not according to the letter, but in the spirit of the law of love. (CM 16:144–45)

Even as charity is the distinct expression of faith in Milton's theology, binding spiritual understanding to practical action,[29] so here it serves as his great canon of interpretation; for we can claim no reading of scripture as divine intent whose consequence is human suffering and estrangement from God. In effect, Milton is simply arguing that scripture is a text for use, not just study, much less speculation, since its meanings are directed to the real exigencies of our condition, and not to be understood *in vacuo* or abstractly. He makes charity the instrument of that circumstantial order of meaning and practice to which God himself attends in his decrees, and which the systematic logic of Reformed dogmatics disguises if not disallows.

Moreover, the figure of invisibility or interiority, which Milton employs to distinguish the ostensible sense of the text from its potential meanings, has now become a figure of extension or stretching out—of temporizing in the archaic sense of gradually negotiating all the various points at issue in a given expression, not just on the page but off it. Both figures, interiority and charity, permit latitude of meaning, since they reflexively suggest an understanding "at variance" with the literal sense of the text, one that must be sought and exercised discriminately. As Milton may be said to preach it, the hermeneutic exertion of charity is to allow other possibilities of meaning whose arbitrary suppression would create greater incoherence and injustice than that inevitably arising between any account of the world and our practice: I refer to those violent divisions fomented by the dogmatic assumption that there are identical parameters of meaning operating in the world and in the text—"word for word," as one reader of Milton mockingly insists—and that a single, univocal logic can educe and characterize the truth among all the dimensions of our experience. To appropriate a remark about Descartes's metaphysics, this approach is a mathematical method applied to nonmathematical objects. And the strategy invites injustice: because even as the suppression of expressive and historical contingency in God's decrees makes them humanly intolerable, so a comparable reduction of scripture renders it unkind (once again in the archaic sense of that word), which is to say, antagonistic to human being.

As I describe him, it could be said that Milton has made just such a univocal logic out of contingency—except for the fact that the conditional relation per se, if such a thing can be imagined, would argue in all directions at once, whereas particular contingencies have their own coherence. Hence the range of meanings he educes for "fornication" from scripture: understood broadly as the deviation from legitimate expressions or practices, it can mean everything from the precise sense of "whoredom" or illicit sexual intercourse, to the allegorical sense of idolatry, as in "whoring after other gods"; and as Milton reads it after Grotius, it can mean apostasy from marriage in more than one way. Indeed, to digress somewhat, "fornication" is already a tropological creation, whose meaning is contingent upon the cumulative associations of its root word, *fornix* or vault (CM 3.2:486–90). So whatever its remotely "original" sense in engineering, the word has proven susceptible of extension without undue impropriety. For words are not only made responsive but also constrained by the peculiar occasions of their use. All this Milton assumes as he reads the sacred text, where he determines to find God's meaning in those ordinary and trivial uses which created the sense of fornication. Yet it would be untrue to say that the principle of charity cannot become extenuation in the pejorative sense, where in our efforts to excuse it, the meaning of a statement is modified beyond recognition. Milton stands accused of this because he interprets Jesus' comments on divorce to signify something in excess or even at variance with their literal sense. But the opportunistic sort of extenuation doesn't adequately account for his readings of these texts, which have a practical integrity and coherence not unlike the uses given "fornication". Milton never denies the evident sense of Christ's sayings, but complicates that meaning by referring it to other conditions of utterance than the mere words themselves. Thus the abrogation of the letter of the law in favor of the gospel spirit of charity is not the abrogation of all accountable meaning, any more than God abrogates his deity when he covenants with the mutable creature—as ultra-Calvinism was sometimes inclined to fear. Charity is rather the observance of an expanded array of concerns as against

the simple, discrete elements of language, so that a scriptural statement is rendered not only intelligible but viable, which is the claim scripture makes for
God's presence in the world.

So Milton says of scripture more largely what Jesus, reading the law, says of
the Sabbath: that it was instituted to benefit humankind and should not be
imposed in such a way that it harms those whom it was intended to help. Jesus'
principle of interpretation—that the sense is scripture, not the words—serves
to explain the transformed expression of divine law under the gospel, from
the negations of the Decalogue to the hortatory language of Christ's two great
commandments. So Milton himself attends to the shifting circumstances of
scriptural meanings, including the frequently incongruous manner of their expression, so as to allow the text its wonted moral as well as religious scope.
Again, when the sense of the religious text or the laws educed from it are taken
so strictly, their observance is rendered a practical impossibility, even injustice.
Such were the Sabbath laws to Jesus, and the divorce laws among others to
John Milton, and such are Adorno's pseudomorphs and Wittgenstein's chimeras—false necessities of meaning under which we choose to labor. But in the
Doctrine and Discipline of Divorce, there is a further issue of intelligibility that
Milton raises in the course of reconciling the letter of the text with what he
regards as its spirit, proving he is no mystic, no supernaturalist:

> we have the word of Christ himself, that he came not to alter the least
> tittle of [the law]; and signifies no small displeasure against him that shall
> teach to do so. On which relying, I shall not much waver to affirm, that
> those words which are made to intimate, as if they forbad all divorce but
> for adultery (though *Moses* have constituted otherwise,) those words tak'n
> circumscriptly, without regard to any precedent law of *Moses* or attestation
> of Christ himself, or without care to preserve those his fundamental and
> superior laws of nature and charity, to which all other ordinances give up
> their seals, are as much against plain equity and the mercy of religion, as
> those words of *Take, eat, this is my body*, elementally understood, are against
> nature and sense. (CM 3.2:476)

The interest of this theologically significant comparison lies in Milton's parameters of understanding: for although he recommends the latitude of the
spirit and charity, they do not permit of a metaphysical solution to scriptural
incongruities. To the extent that he allows himself to speak of deity's decrees
at all, he speaks of them as scripture represents them—temporally and subjunctively—not proposing to infer an order of religious *invisibilia* that would salve
the dignity of logic, while yet trespassing upon the precincts of history and
(human) nature where the sacred text properly exerts its force. Instead, he constrains interpretation to observe the modality of God's revelation in nature, in
the law, and in the gospel, making his readings conformable to the circumstances of each expression. But Milton's natural law is not nature understood
in itself, but the world construed in Niebuhr's sense as an expression of God.

Nor is reason functionally atheistic, but understanding directed by faith to see deity's immanence in things, an intelligence that exists to apprehend God's meanings, not devise its own. So far Milton's interpretive assumptions seem to coincide with the orthodox Calvinist or Catholic notion of right reason or natural law; but at this juncture—the incongruity of Jesus' words literally understood—the distinction between God and the world intervenes for him. To the extent that either Catholic or Calvinist scholasticism can be said to assert a continuity between our ideas and *res non apparentes*, God and the things of God, Milton's "nature and sense" offer a theological departure from them; he sees the incongruity as an occasion to revise our immediate impression of what these words mean, not to perpetuate the contradiction by arguing their metaphysical reality. For this, he says, is what occurs when the words of eucharistic institution are "elementally understood" in the manner proposed by the doctrine of transubstantiation: to preserve their literal sense from apparent contradiction, a metaphysical and coordinating reality must substantiate the appearances of bread and wine, in what Milton regards as a perversion of scriptural idiom. Communion, he says after the fashion of one eucharistic party (Zwingli), becomes "rather anthropophagy, for it deserves no better name" (CM 16:199).

Along these lines, Wittgenstein in a conversation remembers with distaste that, during the First World War, Krupps built a steel, bomb-proof container to transport the communion host to the German frontlines.[30] Like Milton relating the progress of the Christ's transubstantiated body as it is broken, chewed, digested, and excreted not just by humanity but by "mice and worms," to Wittgenstein the absurdity of the German effort consists first and foremost in disregarding the potential difference between divine and ordinary usage (CM 16:213, 195). Thus a grammatical peculiarity is made not only a metaphysical truth but also a magical feat, insofar as Catholic doctrine ascribes "to the outward sign the power of bestowing salvation or grace by virtue of the mere *opus operatum*" (CM 16:201). But Milton, who begins his theology from the standpoint of the distinction and scripture's accommodated speech about deity and divine things, refuses all transcendental helps. His solution to Jesus' teachings on divorce or the Eucharist works, as it were, horizontally, not vertically, grammatically, not symbolically or mystically, pertaining to the human circumstances and implications of what is said, not to a speculative order of *invisibilia*. So with some asperity he informs us that the doctrine of the real presence is tantamount to "a banquet of cannibals," commenting that this kind of conflation by analogy occurs with the sacraments more generally (CM 16:197). As objects turned signs by God, they invite the supposition of a shared nature with the divine when they signify in quite another way—"as a pledge or symbol to believers" which "can neither impart salvation nor grace of themselves" (CM 16:201):

> In speaking of sacraments, as of most other subjects between whose parts an analogy exists, a figure is frequently employed, by which whatever illustrates or signifies any particular thing is used to denote, not what it is in itself, but what it illustrates or signifies. In sacraments, on account of the

peculiarly close relation between the sign and the thing signified, this kind of identification is not uncommon; an inattention to which peculiarity has been, and continues to be, a source of error to numbers. Thus circumcision is called "a covenant," Gen.xvii.10. and "a token of the covenant," v.11. Again, a lamb is called "the passover," Exod.xii.11. which text is defended against the exceptions of objectors by the similar passages, Luke xxii.7. "the passover must be killed." v.8. "prepare us the passover." v.11 "where I shall eat the passover." v.13. "they made ready the passover". . . . The object of the sacred writers, in thus expressing themselves, was probably to denote the close affinity between the sign and the thing signified, as well as, by a bold metaphor, to intimate the certainty with which the seal is thus set to spiritual blessings; the same form of speech being used in other instances, where the certainty of a thing is to be emphatically expressed. (CM 16:199–201)

Not only does Milton insist upon the illustrative and memorial use of sacramental signs, but by his very choice of examples, he also deliberately restricts their sacral force: that is, he describes as associative and traditional the contingency of the sign on the words of promise, a meaning fostered by deity's occasional use of some one thing to signify a given religious event, like covenanting with God, or what is very similar, being shielded from his wrath. Circumcision is accordingly associated with the enactment of God's covenant with Abraham, of which it was made the palpable sign without further grounds than the aetiological assumption of cultural usage. In the same manner, lamb's blood is associated with the Passover of the angel of death before the Exodus, when it was used to distinguish the households of Israel, which were thus preserved from the angel's inimical power. Yet, Milton argues, the association does not allow us to treat these things, circumcision or the paschal lamb, as though they of themselves were somehow intrinsic to the religious significance of these events. The same qualification holds true with water, bread, and wine in the two sacraments he does recognize: these are not magical identities but figures of speech, "an expression purely metaphorical" arising from a particular religious occasion (CM 16:193). So in the case of the verse from Luke—"Then came the day of Unleavened Bread, on which the passover lamb had to be sacrificed"—which seems to assert such an identity, Milton deprecates the assumption that sacrificial "lamb" informs the significance either of the Passover observance or Christ's act of atonement, so as to give the metonymy a magical force and necessity independent of its particular use. Milton argues that the use of "lamb" in Luke was no less *occasioned* than the sign of circumcision, the gospel writer being struck by the coincidence of two great religious events—Jesus' self-sacrifice with the Passover—and expressing that circumstance with a "bold metaphor." He makes the further point that the use of figures to such a purpose is God's way of palpably guaranteeing to us the efficacy of the promises these images picture—covenant and atoning sacrifice. Yet the promises remain spiritually efficacious without the signs:

When therefore the necessity of the sacraments is under discussion, it may in like manner be urged, that it is the Spirit which quickens, and that it is faith which feeds upon the body of Christ; that on the other hand the outward feeding of the body, as it cannot always take place conveniently, so neither is it absolutely necessary. Assuredly, if a sacrament be nothing more than what it is defined to be, a seal, or rather a visible representation of God's benefits to us, he cannot be wrong, who reposes the same faith in God's promises without this confirmation as with it, in cases where it is not possible for him to receive it duly and conveniently; especially as so many opportunities are open to him through life of evincing his gratitude to God, and commemorating the death of Christ, though not in the precise mode and form which God has instituted. (CM 16:205)

The promulgation of signs as sacraments doesn't assert a likeness in kind between the events and the images accompanying their commemoration, as say, Jesus' sacrifice of himself and the wine and bread of the Eucharist. It is to signify God's accommodating his power so as to ensure the meaningfulness of the testament even as he does with the images of scripture—*as if* there were a native connection between the promise and the religious reality, but not between these things and their signs. Indeed, Luther also asserts in the *Babylonian Captivity of the Church* that the sense is not innate to the sacramental sign: it is created by faith in God's testament or promise, the meaning the sign expresses, on every new occasion in which they are rehearsed (*LW* 36:36–54). As such, there can be no continuous or intrinsic religious sense, much less metaphysical (as distinct from spiritual) reality of wine, bread, or water; meaning is made by faith in the same manner as faith makes God. Sacraments then convey what they do because of the precedent of God's positive revelation in history and the exercise of faith, not on account of the signs themselves. It is the "inattention" to this crucial difference that invites idolatry, where all religious images are "elementally understood." And such inattention begins when we ascribe the incongruous because literal sense of scripture's expressions to deity in itself. For that incongruity exists precisely to remind us of the distinction between deity and the world, God and his signs, and thus to instill a self-consciousness not only inhibiting our propensity for metaphysical speculations and magical acts, but also returning us to the historical occasion for the proper sense of a given usage.[31]

Milton has a similar reading of that other great mystery of the Christian church, the *personae* of God, which predicts that he would be no Trinitarian in the orthodox sense. For just as he disabuses his reader of the notion that Christ's physical body lies behind the appearances of bread and wine, so he denies that every expression of deity to which scripture puts the names of God must correspond to a distinct divine person (CM 14:195–97). Once again, the incongruity does not lie in deity but in scriptural grammar: like the words of eucharistic institution, to the extent that we hypostasize a grammatical appearance in theology, so we propose to know and perversely describe the unknowable God. The decorum of the distinction between creator and creature is thus breached by speculation, and speculation of the most obtuse kind in Milton's eyes, since the divine reality is represented as a strange, extravagant inversion of rational ideas. His resistance to supernaturalism has partly to do with this alleged character of God and the things of God in Catholicism, which he regards as sheerly superstitious—irrational, oppressive, grotesque. For Milton understands religious knowledge as an image or picture of God which we are given and which is intelligible up to a point, if we use it properly, and whose evident incongruities instruct us in that right use. Where scripture speaks clearly, as it does of the conditional nature of God's decrees, or in the Eucharist where communion is called remembrance, then we need impose no inexpressly figurative or speculative sense on God's words. Thus in the matter of Christ's deity dying with him, Milton does not pursue the incongruity of the two natures into the grave—he takes scripture at its word: "not a few passages of Scripture intimate that his divine nature was subjected to death conjointly with his human; passages too clear to be explained away by the supposition of idiomatic language" (CM 15:307). It is the same tact which is evinced in Milton's mortalism, that inasmuch as Jesus' whole person died and was resurrected as "God-man," so did his human soul die with his body. In sum, Milton refuses to penetrate into the religious unknown but accepts the scriptural characterization of God and God's things—the limits imposed by the distinction between deity and the world. So when we encounter an apparent anomaly in the language, then insofar as understanding is assisted by a more complete attention to the integral grammar of this speech—its motives, occasions, inflections—extrapolation is legitimate. But if we cannot resolve the difficulty within these limits, then we are not to proceed to supernaturalist explanations, for inference is interdicted by the hiddenness of this God.

As it happens, most of Milton's so-called heresies derive from his principled resistance to interpretive symbologies, whether logical, metaphysical, or magical; and he exercises this restraint most forcibly in his Christology. For Milton, the incommensurable difference of God as unmade and everything else as made is figured in the subordination of the Son to the Father: the Son does not in himself possess the attributes of deity but only as they are selectively extended to him by the one true God, in creating this being both Son and Lord (represented as simultaneous creations in *Paradise Lost*). Thus God only *metaphorically generates* the Son, in the sense of endowing this creature with the divine image and with his mediatorial office (CM 14:191), where the Son like the angels impersonates deity to the world, and therefore has ascribed to him the character and epithets properly belonging to deity alone (CM 14:245–53). So there are two orders of imputation by which the Son is made deity by God—one actual, pertaining to his character as preeminently the divine image, and the other institutional, pertaining to the Son's soteriological role in creation, atonement, and judgment (CM 14:191–357). But the Son cannot be God as such precisely because he is *created*: "The Father alone is a self-existent God . . . a being which is not self-existent cannot be God" (CM 14:209). The Son is deity by means of his Father's decree, and so as God's image, he bears in gift, figure, and deputation the divine attributes and names. For everything that is God necessarily separates deity from what it has made, even from that person with whom it participates not in essence but in affiliation—God's Son "in love, in communion, in agreement, in charity, in spirit, in glory" (CM 14:213). So even before its connotation of affinity, the figure of "begetting" signals to Milton's mind this ineradicable separateness of the Son from deity, conveyed by the language of his generation and endowment, and then enhanced by his appearances to the world—what Milton regards as his palpable agency in creation (CM 14:309), his mediation as the Lord of the covenant (CM 14:243), and his incarnation as the Christ (CM 14:229).

The Son is the face of God to the creature precisely because he is himself creatural: although he is "in the form of God" and "after God's image," to Milton the very fact that this person expresses or mediates deity implicates an altogether different mode of being from God—a distinction perpetually shrouded from understanding by our kind of existence within time and phenomena (CM 14:275). To reiterate, God's Son expresses a precedent difference of persons where their affinity requires interpretation and acknowledgment to be known—as deity makes the Son as Christ known in the words of Jesus' baptism, "This is my beloved Son, with whom I am well pleased" (Matthew 3:16–17). In the words of Matthew 11:27, with which Milton concludes his discussion of the Son's deity: "no man knoweth the Son, but the Father; neither knoweth any man the Father, save the Son, and he to whomsoever the Son will reveal him" (CM 14:349). Having argued that "God imparted to the Son as much as he pleased of the divine nature, nay of the divine substance itself," thus preserving the theological picture of deity's unity and distinction, he concludes that this encompasses all that scripture has to say on the Son's origin: "Whoever wishes to be wiser than this, becomes foiled in his pursuit after wisdom, entangled in the deceitfulness of vain philosophy, or rather of sophistry, and involved in darkness" (CM 14:193). It is at this point that Milton indicts the Trinitarian argument as a grammatical problem handled metaphysically: "Since, however, Christ not only bears the name of the only begotten Son of God, but is also several times called in Scripture God, notwithstanding the universal doctrine that there is but one God, it appeared to many, who had no mean opinion of their own acuteness, that there was an inconsistency in this; which gave rise to an hypothesis no less strange than repugnant to reason, namely, that the Son, although personally and numerically another, was yet essentially one with the Father, and that thus the unity of God was preserved" (CM 14:193–95). There is a considerable antiquity and precedent to scripture's seemingly incongruous expression, which is nothing other than the heraldic posture, where a representative of authority adopts that persona in lieu of its actual presence. Thus Milton cites the prophets' language as "showing that angels and messengers do not declare their own words, but the commands of

God who sends them, even though the speaker seem to bear the name and character of the Deity himself" (CM 14:249). As to the issue of the plural *elohim*, he understands it along the lines of the royal "we," invoking Euripides' authority for the Greek use of "Lord," which "is also used in the plural number in the sense of the singular, when extraordinary respect and honor are intended to be paid" (CM 14:247). Citing idiom may seem to contravene Milton's express injunction against importing figures to the text; yet as is the usual case with figurative speech, the literal incongruity of the usage allows its idiomatic or metaphorical sense. But the difference between integral as against extrinsic figures is a fine one, and difficult to determine nonetheless: Milton's practice suggests that, given the accommodated and so figural nature of all speech referring to God and the things of God, that we accept insofar as we can the "plain sense" of scriptural expressions, however incongruous.

Even when Milton seems most scholastic in his terms, he speaks of God's unity not so much as a logical or metaphysical predicate, but as deity's own usage for itself in the Decalogue: "But unless the terms unity and duality mean the same with God as with man, it would have been to no purpose that God had so repeatedly inculcated that first commandment, that he was the one and only God, if another could be said to exist besides" (CM 14:195). In sum, Milton begins every inference of doctrine with a grammatical analysis of scripture's language, to which he defers on the unique authority of the sacred text. And where crucial inconsistencies of statement arise, he gives priority to the text's clearest expressions: "on a subject so sublime, and so far above our reason, where the very elements and first postulates, as it were, of our faith are concerned, belief must be founded, not on mere reason, but on the word of God exclusively, where the language of the revelation is most clear and particular" (CM 14:215–17). Similarly, after pushing to its inevitably absurd conclusion the idea that scripture exactly defines the nature of divine *invisibilia*, he declares: "How much better it is for us to know merely that the Son of God, our Mediator, was made flesh, that he is called both God and Man, and is such in reality. . . . Since however God has not revealed the mode in which this union is effected, it behoves us to cease from devising subtle explanations, and to be contented with remaining wisely ignorant" (CM 15:273). Inasmuch as Milton's parody of metaphysics produces a Christ whose humanity excludes the divine or vice versa, contravening Christianity's express articles of faith, or gives Christ two mutually exclusive and simultaneous selves, which flies in the face of Jesus' historical integrity as a person, we encounter once more the peculiar result of treating scripture as though it were intended positively to characterize the hidden things of God. Nor can theological speculation propose to supplement what scripture omits, with Milton adding caustically: "I say nothing of the silence of Scripture respecting the above arcana, though they are promulgated with as much confidence, as if he who thus ventures to deliver them on his own authority, had been a witness in the womb of Mary to the mysteries which he describes" (CM 15:267). Finally, he declares on the enigma of Christ's nature:

Since then this mystery is so great, we are admonished by that very consideration not to assert anything respecting it rashly or presumptuously, on mere grounds of philosophical reasoning; not to add to it anything of our own; not even to adduce in its behalf any passage of Scripture of which the purport may be doubtful, but to be contented with the clearest texts, however few in number. If we listen to such passages, and are willing to acquiesce in the simple truth of Scripture, unincumbered by metaphysical comments, to how many prolix and preposterous arguments shall we put an end! how much occasion of heresy shall we remove! how many ponderous volumes of dabblers in theology shall we cast out, purging the temple of God from the contamination of their rubbish! Nothing would be more plain, and agreeable to reason, nothing more suitable to the understanding even of the meanest individual, than such parts of the Christian faith as are declared in Scripture to be necessary for salvation, if teachers, even of the reformed church, were as yet sufficiently impressed with the propriety of insisting on nothing but divine authority in matters relating to God, and of limiting themselves to the contents of the sacred volume. What is essential would easily appear, when freed from the perplexities of controversy; what is mysterious would be suffered to remain inviolate, and we should be fearful of overstepping the bounds of propriety in its investigation. (CM 15:265)

To Milton's way of thinking, the greater incongruity is to presume an impossible knowledge while not only contravening what the sacred text clearly says, but what is worse, excluding faith from any role in theology. Thus it remains an inadvertent irony of Milton studies that even as the author refuses to "premise a long metaphysical discussion, and advocate in all its parts the drama of the personalities of the Godhead," we still try to read his theology as a metaphysics, whether Patristic or Scholastic in character, especially in this matter of his alleged Arianism (CM 14:197). But while Milton does separate the Father, as the one true God, from the Son as electively and artificially God, he refuses to infer from scripture's expressions the nature of the Christ, as either truly divine or truly human (his use of "substance" and "hypostasis" is rigorously lexical and grammatical). Yet, arguing an ostensibly similar subordination, Arianism itself manages by a virtual emanation of inference (in the best tradition of Greek metaphysics) to end up with the incarnate God intractably divided between two ontological absolutes, the divine and the human. To save the appearances, as it were, Jesus Christ is not faithfully, grammatically allowed to be God and man, but must become a species of divine effluent contained in a human body which, however one looks at it, adds little in the way of clarity or consistency to scripture's expressions. So Milton is left to wonder "through what infatuation is it, that even Protestant divines persist in darkening the most momentous truths of religion by intricate metaphysical comments, on the plea that such explanation is necessary; stringing together all the useless technicalities and empty distinctions of scholastic barbarism, for the purpose of elucidating those Scriptures, which they are continually extolling as models of plainness?" (CM 16:261).

BOWING THE CONTRARY WAY

Milton's extrapolations from the scriptural text are accordingly of another kind altogether, having to do with the range of circumstance implicit in any utterance—the historical and subjective position from which a person speaks. In the remark Wittgenstein tellingly echoes, Luther himself argues that " 'Knowledge of meaning must be sought from the reasons for speaking,' says Hilary; it is not afforded by the terminology alone."[32] This principle guides Milton's readings in the tracts, perhaps most self-consciously in *The Doctrine and Discipline of Divorce*, where he prefaces his account of Matthew 5.31–32 with these comments on exegetical method:[33]

> First therfore let us remember as a thing not to be deny'd, that all places of Scripture wherin just reason of doubt arises from the letter, are to be expounded by considering upon what occasion everything is set down: and by comparing other Texts. The occasion which induc't our Saviour to speak of divorce, was either to convince the extravagance of the Pharises in that point, or to give a sharp and vehement answer to a tempting question. And in such cases that we are not to repose all upon the literall terms of so many words, many instances will teach us: Wherin we may plainly discover how Christ meant not to be tak'n word for word, but like a wise Physician, administering one excesse against another to reduce us to a perfect mean: Where the Pharises were strict, there Christ seems remisse; where they were too remisse, he saw it needfull to be more severe: in one place he censures an unchast look to be adultery already committed; another time he passes over actuall adultery with lesse reproof then for an unchast look; not so heavily condemning secret weaknes as open malice: So heer he may be justly thought to have giv'n this rigid sentence against divorce, not to cut off all remedy from a good man who finds himself consuming away in a disconsolate and uninjoy'd matrimony, but to lay a bridle upon the bold abuses of those over-weening *Rabbies*; which he could not more effectually doe, then by a countersway of restraint curbing their wild exorbitance almost into the other extreme; as when we bow things the contrary way, to make them come to their naturall straitnesse. (CM 3.2:429–30)

The "just reason of doubt" refers to more than a problem of obscurity: it involves those occasions when the evident sense or "literal term" of scripture seems not only incoherent but unjust as well. As believers, when we are alienated from the truth which we acknowledge as such, then both the sacred text and its God appear arbitrary and terrible. And notwithstanding his pronounced masculine

bias, Milton is acknowledging this truth when he declares that the man, suffering "a disconsolate and unenjoyed matrimony" and seemingly "cut off from
remedy" by Jesus' words, cannot tolerate them and requires "more than a literall
wisedome of equity" exercised on his behalf (CM 3.2:427). The words are intolerable not because they resist a callous inclination to divorce—to do expediently, out of "hardness of heart," what we know to be wrong—the opportunistic
reading of Milton's position that he ascribes here to the Pharisees. Rather, Jesus'
speech is intolerable because, for all that Milton does not regard the marital
bond as sacramental, he does recognize it as subjectively and theologically profound. As Milton represents the man's predicament in the divorce tracts, and
both spouses' in the *Christian Doctrine*, the motive for marriage is not economic,
familial, or sexual but "the mutual love, society, help, and comfort of the husband and wife, though with a reservation of superior rights in the husband"
(CM 15:121). When these things are not forthcoming, the unconditioned institution is "a yoke of the heaviest slavery (for such is marriage without love),"
more onerous than divorce even for "the deservedly neglected" wife (CM
15:165). Given the social and economic constraints on woman, who, in that
culture or indeed by "the consent of nations in general," stood to her spouse as
servant to master, this statement must strike us as thoroughly oblivious and
unjust (CM 15:167).[34] At the same time, we must recognize that the exegetical
dimension of his argument directly challenges his masculinism, since it assaults
the bases on which the man's claim to superiority is made: in short, the gross
imposition of meaning on text and body alike. If his marital history and idiosyncratic brand of sexism may be said to promote this proximate blindness, his
other convictions—that marriage is a moral and civil bond; that human meaning and value are contingently created; that any institution, civil or ecclesiastical, seeking to legislate the subjective should be resisted—condemn it. For good
and ill, Milton writes here as he argues Jesus speaks—out of particular circumstances which complicate the sense of his expressions; yet taken altogether, he
treats the marital relation as an intimate affinity—significantly, in the legal
sense of private—having to do with the expression of the soul and therefore as
antipathetic to positive legislation. So, with marriage, we once again encounter
an instance of Milton's restrictive antinomianism, because when Jesus is taken
to speak absolutely on divorce, his meaning does nothing short of deny the
claims of the soul, not to mention the God within whose purview it lies. Moreover, because Milton argues divorce in those cases where the man has acted in
good faith, with a consciousness of innocence and "not in compliance with the
hardness of the human heart, but on grounds of the highest equity and justice,"
he can reasonably assert that justice and morality are not upheld when doctrine
makes the man suffer to no discernible good (CM 15:161).

These are for Milton the issues and circumstances involved in suiting scripture's words to human contingencies. The apparent incongruousness, indeed
the injustice, of Jesus' dictum is the position of "doubt" from which Milton
reads, which requires him to justify its sense—that is, to make the speech con-

sistent with equity and right, remembering that the absolute interdiction of divorce, except in cases of (female) adultery, punishes both man and woman. He does this in the manner of the second order of justification, since he understands the meaning of Christ's saying as comparably circumstanced and thus mediated by the occasion in which it was uttered. In that local situation, Jesus' words speak peculiarly to the Pharisees' own hardness of heart, who ironically abuse the dispensation of divorce by their expedient judgments. The sense of the speech is therefore not just particular to Christ's hearers on this occasion, but intimately, penetratingly so; and according to Milton, this particularity creates the seeming inconsistencies in what Jesus says when he is taken "word for word," without regard for the pertinent circumstances of his speech. In thus explaining Jesus' appearance of contrariety here, Milton avers that the Christ teaches by a wholly contingent method, whose dicta taken in their local sense show just that fineness of sensitivity to the human situation, which is violated when they are handled as moral absolutes—by canon law or by Milton's sexism.

But Milton is not only underscoring the interpretive practice that properly attends the implementation of any law: if he is not a strict constructionist in this respect or with regard to scripture, neither are the reformers, all of whom practice what came to be called grammatical-historical exegesis. They advocate this procedure most vigorously against the fourfold method, whose most notorious practitioner was Origen and most expert St. Augustine—both confessed Platonists, it should be noted, unlike Luther or Milton. And as Milton expounds this method in the *Christian Doctrine*, its criteria include "knowledge of languages; inspection of the originals; examination of the context; care in distinguishing between literal and figurative expressions; consideration of cause and circumstance, of antecedents and consequents; mutual comparison of texts; and regard to the analogy of faith"—that charitable principle by which we infer nothing from scripture that contradicts the covenantal picture of the one true God's justice and mercy (CM 16:265). To put Milton's point another way, the person, idiom, teachings, and life of Jesus are the human, historical contingency that defies legal and logical absolutes: simply by evoking the concealed presence of deity, Jesus understood as the Christ pictures in himself an order of meaning and possibility for the world otherwise precluded by our habits of thought. So when Milton says that "the ultimate object of faith is not Christ the Mediator, but God the Father"—that in his soteriology, it is possible to "be saved by faith in God alone"—he is not making the Christ or his atonement irrelevant to our redemption (CM 15:403). Not at all, for these are the means by which all human relationship to God is restored and salvation made available, whether we know Christ or not: "For the same reason it ought not to appear wonderful if many, both Jews and others, who lived before Christ, and many also who have lived since his time, but to whom he has never been revealed, should be saved by faith in God alone; still however through the sole merits of Christ, inasmuch as he was given and slain from the beginning of the world, even for those to whom he was not known, provided they believed in

God the Father" (CM 15:403–5). Because the Incarnation and Atonement describe the universal crux of our justification *coram Deo*, as at once real, imputed, and contingent, they also model that kind of religious understanding we must have in order to receive and come to God (CM 15:407). Milton is arguing in a radical way the expressive contingency of God and God's things that Jesus himself teaches and embodies, namely, that we are to worship no phenomenal, no conceptual, no religious appearance including the Lord of the covenant and the Christ. We worship only what these convey to us—the hidden God who promises things which, like himself, do not appear as such: "From faith arises hope, that is, a most assured expectation through faith of those future things which are already ours in Christ. . . . Hope differs from faith, as the effect from the cause; it differs from it likewise in its object: for the object of faith is the promise; that of hope, the thing promised" (CM 15:407–9).

Milton's order of exegesis thus acknowledges and respects the mediation of spiritual things, which is the central truth of his religion—that God is present to us through the Christ and in scripture, and by extension, that the great human truths are similarly expressed in our ordinary experience. Accordingly, he adds to the standard criteria of the grammatical-historical method this further enlightening circumstance: "Attention must also be paid [in scripture] to the frequent anomalies of syntax; as for example, where the relative does not refer to the immediate antecedent, but to the principal word in the sentence, though more remote" (CM 16:265). Such anomalies regularly and significantly occur in *Paradise Lost*, where they serve to try not only our patience and attention but our faith as well; for this description of suspended reference is a little epitome of that theological grammar where, in the fashion of faith and hope, all significant appearances refer not to their most immediate agents but to God and the things of God. It follows that the sense of scripture is not fungible in the way syllogistic supposes: scriptural expressions do not permit a simple exchange or translation from the letter, because meaning exists as a complex implication, not positively or directly corresponding to the simple, unconditioned elements of the text. So rather than meaning residing discretely and singularly in each word or phrase, it lies in the many possible relations among scriptural usages, which for Milton specially includes their historical issue. As against a unitary logic, or a system of reference or analogy, one could say that Milton conceives the sense of scripture as a flexible matrix of different understandings—the moral, the spatial, the legal, the sensory, the temporal, the literate, the institutional, and so forth—which combine and recombine to new, revealing effect each time we take up the sacred text. As Milton asks rhetorically in regard to sacramental signs, "why is it necessary that things which are analogous should coincide in all points?" (CM 16:179). It is a question answered by Luther in the course of correcting Erasmus's reading of scripture: "a simile is not always applicable at every point (for otherwise it would not be a simile, nor a metaphor, but the things itself; as the proverb says, a simile halts, it does not always run on four feet!)."[35] So the "spiritual" sense works something along the lines of Montaigne's limping examples, or Wittgenstein's "family resemblance" model of meaning, as "a complicated network of similarities: overlapping and criss-crossing: sometimes overall similarities, sometimes similarities of detail" (*PI* p.66). The circumstance that motivates these likenesses is not some essential analogy, much less identity of features, but the precedent fact of their difference and thus the discontinuity among them. Moreover, there is the greater tension Wittgenstein addresses by this comparison to "family resemblance"—namely, between our ideas and the domains of experience in which they should make sense. His dismay at the objectivism pervasive in philosophical accounts of meaning comes down to just the disparity Adorno also remarks, between how we like to think meaning works and how it might actually do so. Indeed, the unacknowledged difference between the linguistic, the philosophical, and the physical universes fosters the insidious impression that language fails to mean as it should, and that, as a consequence, it is incapable of truth. Such is the sceptic's predicament in the *Philosophical Investigations*, and Adam's position in misunderstanding the mediated order of his world, so that it seems dispropor-tioned and flawed even as Christ's words do in the passage above. But God-for-us is not an absolute, but the cumulative sense of deity's historical, humanly directed expressions. Furthermore, the force of mystery expressed in God's hid-denness is not to remove deity from the world: mystery is bound to attend the human encounter with such a God, as a being only contingently and instru-mentally like us, even in the Incarnation itself. Jesus Christ as the incarnate God foregrounds the circumstances that condition our experience of the abso-lute, as when he makes the Sabbath for humanity, not the other way round. For our natural, material, and historical being, our intransigent humanity, renders religious knowledge inevitably a matter of interpretation and belief, as against rationalist or mystical transcendence. The Christ's deity-in-humanity crucially ensures the space between God and the self of each person—crucially, that is, to the exercise of choice in Milton's theology, and to anything more than an ostensible subjectivity.

It is just this space that the incongruous manner of Jesus' teaching creates and sustains. To return to *The Doctrine and Discipline of Divorce*:

> Thus at length wee see both by this and by other places, that there is scarce any one saying in the Gospel, but must bee read with limitations and distinctions, to bee rightly understood; for Christ gives no full com-ments or continued discourses, but as *Demetrius* the Rhetorician phrases it, speaks oft in Monosyllables, like a maister, scattering the heavenly grain of his doctrine like pearl heer and there, which requires a skilfull and labo-rious gatherer, who must compare the words he findes, with other precepts, with the end of every ordinance, and with the generall *analogie* of Evangel-ick doctrine: otherwise many particular sayings would bee but strange re-pugnant riddles. (CM 3.2:490–91)

Such deliberately dispersed and so conditional sense as Milton ascribes to Jesus, Luther for his part attributes to "the procedure of Moses" which "suggests by dots, as it were, situations that cannot be expressed in words" (*LW* 1:280).[36] In either case, there is no apparent meaning that is uniquely key to the whole: there are several disparate points of reference that, when combined together, make a speech or an experience not only intelligible to us, but also just and equitable. Such a discontinuous, interpretive kind of meaning is the sort of "symmetry" or coherence Milton ascribes to the temple of God, and which consists in the way various things hang together in time, space, and art. It is also the method of knowing good by knowing evil, a differential as against an antithetical relation where both possibilities have to be somehow present for us to recognize either one. Of course, this sort of meaning requires that we choose to make it, even if the option of choosing sometimes goes unseen by us.

Usually, the nature of theodicy itself ensures that we cannot avoid the choice, however indeliberate, because some particular incongruity in our experience demands that we make an interpretive decision simply to understand what we see—as, for example, when deity conspicuously clothes itself in all those things we most dislike about the world, from civil disturbances to offensive opinions and "strange repugnant riddles." Thus, on the model of irony, the manifold incongruities of scriptural expression serve as a threshold to another significance, which can strike us as "surprising" or "queer" in the manner Wittgenstein associates with the "dawning of an aspect," "noticing an aspect," "seeing *as*," or "regarding *as*." In much the same fashion, when this peculiar phenomenon occurs, we find ourselves suddenly provoked into acknowledging a perfectly integral circumstance that decisively alters the meaning something has for us; and Wittgenstein illustrates this experience by a number of optical examples like his celebrated "duck-rabbit" drawing, the picture of a three-dimensional rectangular box, a "picture-face," all of which simultaneously offer more than one way to make sense of their lines and shapes. In the case of the duck-rabbit drawing, he mentions a similar sense of surprise to Luther's and Milton's—in excess or distinct from the intellectual recognition that the lines can appear differently to us at different times. When they are perceived to undergo a transformation, we too undergo a revolution of sorts—a sensation of being "struck" that doesn't so much pertain to the image as to the psychological event attending a change in meaning. It is something on the order of what we mean when we say something "has the force of truth," or what the reformers and Milton all distinguish as the "living" as against the "dead" letter of scripture (Wittgenstein himself remarking that "a picture does not always *live* for me while I am seeing it" [*PI* p.205]). In all these instances, what was perfectly obvious to us seems to *materialize*, as Wittgenstein puts it, into something else altogether (*PI* p.199). In that moment, we like Luther feel as though we were encountering a new, unexpected reality:

> we can also *see* the illustration now as one thing now as another.—So we interpret it, and *see* it as we *interpret* it. . . .

But how is it possible to *see* an object according to an *interpretation?*—
The question represents it as a queer fact; as if something were being forced
into a form it did not really fit. But no squeezing, no forcing took place
here.

When it looks as if there were no room for such a form between other
ones you have to look for it in another dimension. If there is no room
here, there *is* room in another dimension. (*PI* pp.193, 200–201)

Wittgenstein is talking here about the experience of meaningfulness and interpretation more largely, which argues that our words are capable of more than
one sense because their significance is created by the circumstances of their
use—on the play of expressive "aspect" that allows them to mean first one way,
then another. The sensation of dimensionality that this range of possible signi-
ficances creates, especially his instance of imaginary numbers that are seemingly
precluded by "the continuum of real numbers," suggests just how it is that the
illusion of linguistic "objects" conspires to restrict the way we think about
meaning (*PI* p.201). For like Milton's "irrational men" in the building of the
temple, we suppose that truth consists in this exact continuity of reference, as
it were a plenum with no space in between. But given a change of circumstance
or use, when the possibilities of meaning expand in another direction altogether—or as Wittgenstein remarks after Luther, "find room in another dimension"—then we learn something conceptually new. In *The Reason of Church
Government*, Milton demonstrates this contingency of meaning and value with
particular vividness when he interprets Ezekiel's prophetic vision of the temple
against episcopal ecclesiology:

In the Prophecie of *Ezekiel* from the 40 Chapt. onward, after the destruction of the Temple, God by his Prophet seeking to weane the hearts of
the Jewes from their old law to expect a new and more perfect reformation
under Christ, sets out before their eyes the stately fabrick & constitution
of his Church, with al the ecclesiasticall functions appertaining; indeed
the description is as sorted best to the apprehension of those times, typi-
call and shadowie, but in such a manner as never yet came to passe, nor
never must literally, unlesse we mean to annihilat the Gospel. But so ex-
quisit and lively the description is in portraying the new state of the
Church, and especially in those points where government seemes to be
most active, that both Jewes and Gentiles might have good cause to be
assur'd, that God when ever he meant to reforme his Church, never intended to leave the governement thereof delineated here in such curious
architecture, to be patch't afterwards, and varnish't over with the devices
and imbellishings of mans imagination. Did God take such delight in mea-
suring out the pillars, arches, and doores of a materiall Temple, was he so
punctuall and circumspect in lavers, altars, and sacrifices soone after to be
abrogated, lest any of these should have beene made contrary to his minde?
is not a farre more perfect worke more agreeable to his perfection in the

most perfect state of the Church militant, the new alliance of God to man? should not he rather now by his owne prescribed discipline have cast his line and levell upon the soule of man which is his rationall temple, and by the divine square and compasse thereof forme and regenerate in us the lovely shapes of vertues and graces, the sooner to edifie and accomplish that immortall stature of Christs body which is his Church in all her glorious lineaments and proportions. And that this indeed God hath done for us in the Gospel we shall see with open eyes, not under a vaile. We may passe over the history of the Acts and other places, turning only to those Epistles of S. *Paul* to *Timothy* and *Titus*: where the spirituall eye may discerne more goodly and gracefully erected then all the magnificence of Temple or Tabernacle, such a heavenly structure of evangelick discipline so diffusive of knowledge and charity to the prosperous increase and growth of the Church, that it cannot be wonder'd if that elegant and artfull symmetry of the promised new temple in *Ezechiel*, and all those sumptuous things under the Law, were made to signifie the inward beauty and splendor of the Christian Church thus govern'd. (CM 3.1:190–91)

Milton does with Ezekiel's image what Luther does with Paul's: he resists reading scripture merely analogically, once again as though the imagery of the text "imitated" or "patterned" the divine, with the figure of the temple providing a manual for church practice.[37] The distinction of deity from the world contravenes any such claim to resemblance or continuity of meaning; and that is why Milton declares that Ezekiel's temple "never yet came to pass, nor never must literally, unless we mean to annihilate the gospel." For their accommodated status necessarily circumscribes their sense. Scriptural images cannot be simply transposed from the text to the world without losing their religious character, which includes the significant sensation of an image's incongruity. And to the extent that the image thus transposed and reduced can then only mirror our own ideas, it is idolatrous in Milton's view.

The only occasion on which Milton properly discusses expressive decorum or propriety is in the *Apology for Smectymnuus*, where his ridicule is directed against the rule of convention and specifically "that specious antiquity" or classicism invoked by his opponents against him, whose originals he claims better to understand and observe (CM 3.1:285). Significantly, like "the Scarlet Prelats, and such as are insolent to maintain traditions" and over whose heads Zeal as spiritual propriety must drive, this classicism would reduce decorum not only to a single argument in the church but to a single expression in the text (CM 3.1:314). Milton accordingly advocates an expressive order dedicated to the proposition that truth when it appears can be incongruous, even offensive to our familiar tastes and ideas. Although he propounds this "unseemly" decorum to justify his own satirical language—"a tart rhetorick" and "a vehement vein throwing out indignation, and scorn upon an object that merits it"—in doing so, he argues a general inclusiveness and particularity of speech, on the authority of scripture itself (CM 3.1:315, 312): "Doth not Christ himselfe teach the highest things by the similitude of *old bottles and patcht cloaths?* Doth he not illustrate best things by things most evill? his own *comming* to be *as a thiefe in the night,* and the righteous mans *wisdome to that of an unjust Steward?*" (CM 3.1:311–12). But perhaps Milton's most sensational precedent is the word of Yahweh: "Turne then to the first of Kings where God himselfe uses the phrase; *I will cut off from Jereboam him that pisseth against the wall*" (CM 3.1:316). Since deity speaks to the whole human being in its passions, functions, and occasions, as does scripture and Jesus, then those who would censor this decorum are "Fools who would teach men to read more decently then God thought good to write" (CM 3.1:316). Yet Milton offers one more authority, who exemplifies his own impetus:

> Thus did the true Prophets of old combat with the false; thus Christ him-
> selfe the fountaine of meeknesse found acrimony anough to be stil galling
> and vexing the Prelaticall Pharisees. But ye will say these had immediat
> warrant from God to be thus bitter, and I say, so much the plainlier is it
> prov'd, that there may be a sanctifi'd bitternesse against the enemies of
> truth. Yet that ye may not think inspiration only the warrant thereof, but
> that it is as any other vertue, of moral and general observation, the exam-
> ple of *Luther* may stand for all: whom God made choice of before others
> to be of highest eminence and power in reforming the Church; who not
> of revelation, but of judgement writ so vehemently against the chiefe de-
> fenders of old untruths in the Romish Church, that his own friends and
> favourers were many times offended with the fierceness of his spirit. (CM
> 3.1:314)

In distinguishing Luther from the prophets, judgment from inspiration, the religious from the noumenal, Milton would seem to be describing his own posi-tion, inasmuch as he makes the reformer's predicament of expression his own.[38] Theodicy can appear perverse, even odious, and acts of conscience are no more prepossessing or better received than acts of God: the repugnance Luther's audi-ence felt for civil disorder, though it accompanies the preaching of the gospel, Milton would argue obtains in our aversion to other kinds of indecorum, espe-cially in speech. So Luther is hauled before the Holy Roman emperor and Mil-ton slandered by bishops and primates; yet religious indecorum in a world gov-erned by a hidden God is finally the truest propriety, because once again it has reference to deity's fundamentally different kind of life. As Luther observes: "Many things seem, and are, very good to God which seem, and are, very bad to us. Thus, afflictions, sorrows, errors, hell, and all God's best works are in the world's eyes very bad, and damnable. What is better than Christ and the gospel? But what is there that the world abominates more? How things that are bad for us are good in the sight of God is known only to God and to those who see with God's eyes, that is, who have the Spirit."[39] Those "who see with God's eyes, who have the spirit" are those who see with "open eyes" in the case of Ezekiel's temple; they do not mistake the image for its meaning, the "veil" for the truth, the law for the gospel. For religious expressions often participate in a riddling order of truth—Luther's *larvae* or masks of God, his notion of deity's "alien" as against "proper" works, Calvin's mazes and labyrinths, or Milton's knowing good by evil. The ruse of revelation is comparably dialectical, since it too controverts our claim to identify truth: we think that the hidden God is like his signs and so like us, only to discover by incongruity that neither they nor he can be made to mean that way. In either case, the ruse is doubly ironic, not only in its thrust but also in its effects—the palpable disorientation of assumed order. It thus engineers a collision of ideas, an incongruity characterizing the embeddedness of God's meanings in our condition: in other words, we have to know deity from the differential standpoint of our humanity, and that distinction is perpetual and abysmal—a chronic reencounter with incongruity, which we evade at our spiritual peril. Yet this is what the Laudian reading of Ezekiel's image would do.

If Milton offers us, with dramatic hesitation, the "elegant and artful symmetry" of the prophetic temple as an image of the "inward beauty and splendor" of the church that faith will perfect, he does not suppose these things to be anything like analogous. If I may take issue here with Northrop Frye's terms, while yet retaining his considerable insight that divine things in Milton are not transferable in themselves: "inward" here means like Luther's adverbs of mediated presence—an index of spiritual or religious actualities, not some discrete interior space insusceptible of general knowledge or expression.[40] Milton is talking about the current and actual reformation of the British church, which begins but does not end with the living souls of God's Englishmen. So although he rejects the naive imitation of Ezekiel's image—a reading that supports the tradition of liturgy and bishops—neither does he confine its force to sublime or psychological esoterica. Nor does he imagine, like the ancients, that such *invisibilia* are structured like the natural and social worlds, which become a source of virtually organic analogy to the things we cannot see. Rather, he asserts their reference at once evident and profound to *res non apparentes*; when deity abrogates the law, it simultaneously abolishes the "veiling" of salvific knowledge by its "typical, and shadowy" understanding. Because each assumes the essential analogy of seen to unseen, the tacit symbology of the ritual law veils in the sense of shrouds and obscures the order of God's meanings, even as the moral law veils with works the nature of our justification *coram Deo*. Thus Milton links the abrogation of the law with the abrogation of a particular approach or grasp of religious things that he calls "typical, and shadowy" here. This "veiling" is not to be confused with a moral and mystical symbology of the divine, articulated by ethical dicta, religious paraphernalia, ceremonies, and texts like Ezekiel's, which purport to characterize the hidden things of God. On the contrary, "veiling" here implies human estrangement, not affinity with the divine, to the extent that we compound our original distance from God by our recourse to this interpretive tack, suppressing the incongruity that attends the distinction between deity and the world. When we try to transfer Ezekiel's temple lock, stock, and barrel to the church here and now, we are not simultaneously translating its religious significance: we are setting up as God's meaning what Milton calls "the devices and imbellishings of mans imagination"—where scripture is ironically made to mirror human assumptions and values, while effacing deity and *res non apparentes* together from the text.

By reinstituting a mode of interpretation that deity has itself abolished— what Luther, Calvin, and Milton understand by "the law"—the episcopal party idolizes the false God of that obsolete reading. To the extent that the law is construed as a prelude or anticipation of the gospel, a "fleshly" and visible representation of a "spiritual" or invisible righteousness, then the law is not only misprised but that very misprision expresses and induces sin by disfiguring their relation. And although law and gospel describe two different orders of religious understanding which should not be collapsed, when the "old testament" is understood by the "new," it assumes an altogether different "look" and force than its received or ostensible sense. Seen with "open eyes" or "the spiritual eye," or what Adam calls his "eyes true opening" once he grasps Abraham's faith, the law signifies very much as the gospel does—not as the virtual identity of religious things but a picture of how they can be known and understood, and through them, the unknowable God (*LM* 12.274). Thus Samuel reproaches Saul: "Has the Lord as great delight in burnt offerings and sacrifices, / as in obeying the voice of the Lord?" (1 Samuel 15:22). By "such light as I have receav'd," Milton will disclose in response "what danger there is against the very life of the Gospell to make in anything the typical law her pattern":

> This very word of patterning or imitating excludes Episcopacy from the solid and grave Ethicall law, and betraies it to be a meere childe of ceremony, or likelier some misbegotten thing, that having pluckt the gay feathers of her obsolet bravery to hide her own deformed barenesse, now vaunts and glories in her stolne plumes. . . . It cannot be unknowne by what expressions the holy Apostle S. *Paul* spares not to explane to us the nature and condition of the law, calling those ordinances which were the chiefe and essentiall offices of the Priests, the elements and rudiments of the world both weake and beggarly. Now to breed, and bring up the children of the promise, the heirs of liberty and grace, under such a kinde of government as is profest to be but an imitation of that ministery which engender'd to bondage the sons of *Agar*, how can this be but a foul injury and derogation, if not a cancelling of that birth-right and immunity, which Christ hath purchas'd for us with his blood? (CM 3.1:198–99)

Milton alludes here to the same allegorical passage in Galatians on which Luther comments, and to the same point of Christian liberty: namely, that from the vantage of the gospel, the law enthralls us with the deceptive splendor, the mere appearance of ceremony, thus "evaporating and exhaling the internall worship into empty conformities, and gay shewes" (CM 3.1:199). And to the extent that the Laudian argument from tradition also mistakes Mosaic ceremony for the "solid and grave Ethicall law," still preferring the sign to its sense, so it exalts religion grossly understood at the expense of God's proper knowledge. As Milton represents it, episcopal ceremony not only conceals a spiritual void and inefficacy with its "obsolet bravery," but further disfigures the law's proper expressions by making them the overt "pattern" and strangely atavistic fulfillment of the gospel. For Christ's image of the church is not "glorious prelaty," as Milton likes to call episcopal order: it is the "form of a servant," "a mean, laborious and vulgar life aptest to teach," by which he understands "pure simplicity of doctrine, accounted the foolishnes of this world, yet crossing and confounding the pride and wisdom of the flesh" (CM 3.1.243–45). In this ironical difference, Milton says, consists "the deep mystery of the gospel":

> Albeit I must confesse to be half in doubt whether I should bring it forth or no, it being so contrary to the eye of the world, and the world so potent in most mens hearts, that I shall endanger either not to be regarded, nor not to be understood. For who is ther almost that measures wisdom by simplicity, strength by suffering, dignity by lowlinesse, who is there that counts it first, to be last, somthing to be nothing, and reckons himself of great command in that he is a servant? yet God when he meant to subdue the world and hell at once, part of that to salvation, and this wholy to perdition, made chois of no other weapons, or auxiliaries then these whether to save, or to destroy. It had bin a small maistery for him, to have drawn out his Legions into array, and flankt them with his thunder; therefore he sent Foolishnes to confute Wisdom, Weaknes to bind Strength, Despisednes to vanquish Pride. And this is the great mistery of the Gospel made good in Christ himself, who as he testifies came not to be minister'd to, but to minister; and must be fulfil'd in all his ministers till his second comming. To goe against these principles S. *Paul* so fear'd, that if he should but affect the wisdom of words in his preaching, he thought it would be laid to his charge, that he had made the crosse of Christ to be of none effect. Whether then Prelaty do not make of none effect the crosse of Christ by the principles it hath so contrary to these, nullifying the power and end of the Gospel, it shall not want due proof, if it want not due belief. Neither shal I stand to trifle with one that will tell me of quiddities and formalities, whether Prelaty or Prelateity in abstract notion be this or that, it suffices me that I find it in his skin, so I find it inseparable, or not oftner otherwise then a Phenix hath bin seen. (CM 3.1:243–44)

Milton's use of Christian paradox doesn't apply in the Erasmean fashion to mystical things but instead to urgent human actualities—as it were, to the *skin* of God's ministers and the practice of church government here and now, *before* the second coming of Christ and the millennial reformation of this world. In doing so, he repudiates all continuities, all likenesses, with the typical expressions and practices of the law. These paradoxes evoke no idealities, no transcendent worlds for him, but descriptions of Christian life—wisdom by simplicity, strength by suffering, dignity by lowliness. They not only overturn the "carnal" assumptions of the ritual law and its imitators, but they also argue the expressive contingency of God's signs, which are incongruous precisely because they mean more and other than they appear to do—the lesson embodied in Christ as messiah and suffering servant, which episcopacy has yet to learn in Milton's view.

As Niebuhr observes, no logic is sufficient to account for our condition.[41] The inability of our ideas to encompass our experience, the incoherence and suffering which occurs when they don't, throws us back upon ourselves, to reflect on our assumptions and to revise our notions of truth. So instead of a transcendental turn, there is an ironical and critical maneuver to which we are constrained by scripture's incongruity. Here Luther locates the room of faith, and Milton the space in which to choose God; it is also the reason Milton says that Ezekiel's temple "never yet came to passe, nor never must literally, unlesse we mean to annihilat the Gospel." He argues throughout *The Reason of Church Government* that perfection in spiritual things does not depend upon so copious, exact and material an order as Ezekiel's temple represents, but instead on the more or less untrammeled impulse of the faithful, when they are left free to receive the motions of God. In this contingency, he comprehends the difference of "a heavenly structure of evangelick discipline" from human modes of ordering; for it requires faith and hope to discern another meaning in the flux of our experience than may at first appear: true "discipline" derives from recognizing, not preempting, the connection between religious things and faith in the hidden God, as their author and the proper source of their meaning. But religious conformity, like the enforced imitation of scriptural images, presumes to orchestrate the manner of deity's engagement with the world, in effect rescinding the operations of grace and providence, so that the practice of religion is wrested away from spirit and life, only to devolve upon the dead letter of the text. It is to stress this critical divergence in the ordering of religion that Milton reads Ezekiel in the first place, against any effort to make that prophet an avatar of ritual and hierarchy, "patterning" and symbology. For that is not how the hidden God works: *were* we, say, to understand Ezekiel's temple as the image of the church perfected, it does not express this unseen and much anticipated perfection in its own images and ordinance. Milton advises us to go instead to another text entirely—the pseudo-Pauline epistles of Timothy and Titus—for the means by which God promotes the renovation of his church. And these letters recommend not a hieratic person or sacerdotal object, but a common practice; not a single building or set form, but a pastoral ethic that orders the church in another, less ostentatious fashion—the difference distinguishing Milton's hell from his heaven in *Paradise Lost*, and separating sacrifice from hearkening to the voice of the Lord in Samuel's rebuke to Saul.

It could be said that Milton executes a kind of catachresis—that comparison of manifest incompatibles—when he wrenches the sense of Ezekiel's image to picture an otherwise inevident ecclesiastical order. Although Milton's reading retains the same putative and actual reference, namely, to the church perfected by God, Ezekiel's temple is disallowed its episcopal meaning and any symbolic equivalence between the ordering of the scriptural image and religious practice, between divine and human ideas of the good. The prophetic temple expresses the sense of a different, if not unrelated, text and the effect of an opposed religious observance. Following the grammatical-historical method, what *looks* priestly and liturgical is *understood* to signify the presbyterian and congregational. Moreover, as the idea of an ethical order suggests, the perfecting of the church that Ezekiel newly envisions is both contingent and proleptic, something that depends on the choices we as individuals make in our lives, none of which have been prejudged. Perfection cannot then be defined by the text, the immediate result of its correct interpretation, but is left elective and suspenseful, as the outcome of all our potential understandings and actions. This inveterate tendency to make the religious sense defer to our self-image, to force the analogy of divine and human things, is what elicits Milton's own figure likening the building of the temple to God's applying "line and level" to the human soul—a figure no less outrageous than Donne's twin compasses, and intentionally so. It is a subtle satire, since his reading of Ezekiel disallows precisely this manipulation—spatializing, gauging, quantifying—of religious meanings, as though they were one or other sort of object. Thus his fantastic image serves to make us see how casually we abuse the sense of scripture with our "carnal" assumptions of analogy, and to teach us that the operations of the spirit are inimitable. By these ironical maneuvers, Milton not only converts a hostile text to the service of church "discipline" as he conceives it—a proof for the contingency of religious meanings in his theology—but also uses them to argue the abolition of those usages, the devices and embellishings of man's imagination, which do not sort with deity as a truth altogether unlike the ones we have invented, pursued, and calculated. And he does this to the conjoint purposes of personal and public justification.

CHAPTER FOUR

Milton's Speaker

ECCE HOMO

When Deutero-Isaiah declares, "Truly, thou art a God who hidest thyself, / O God of Israel, the Savior," he speaks of deity's hiddenness from the standpoint of the creature, to whom divine providence can appear altogether blasphemous, as it does here in God's choice of the Persian Cyrus to be Israel's messiah and redeemer (Isaiah 45:15). Yet the real scandal of this election is not deity's judgment, but Israel's presumption that the savior would match its national idea of a messiah. For that reason alone, God's anointed appears doubly alien to Israel, since Cyrus does not even acknowledge the deity he serves—"I surname you," says the Lord, "though you do not know me" (Isaiah 45:4). Once again human events raise the vexed issue of divine impropriety, to which the Lord responds not by justifying his action, but by repudiating the very suggestion that he must give grounds for anything he does:

> Woe to him who strives with his
>   Maker,
>   an earthen vessel with the potter!
> Does the clay say to him who
>   fashions it, "What are you
>   making"?
>   or "Your work has no handles"?
>
> (Isaiah 45:9)

In rehearsing the abysmal difference between creator and creature, the Lord expounds by indirection the predicament in which humanity finds itself, viewing the work of God's hands. And that predicament demands a singular exertion of faith, since deity's expressions tend to appear senseless and arbitrary from this side of the distinction. With the psalmist too, the predicament of faith begins with a God who acts toward his people like amoral necessity, imposing suffering on the righteous and innocent while bolstering the wicked. The late prophets recount the further outrage of a God against God, when deity induces Israel incorrigibly to resist its defining identity as God's chosen, promoting the people's impulse to do evil and thus to compromise Israel's tenuous status *coram Deo* and before the world. In all the biblical literature written at this time (the final years of the monarchy, the conquest of Israel and exile), Gerard von Rad finds a common recognition that the elect nation had failed to fulfill its part of the covenant and shown itself incapable of living with its peculiar God (*OTT* 2:266–77). Indeed, it is the national covenant with deity that renders Israel's sufferings peculiarly mysterious and harrowing, inasmuch as the relationship that should have sustained the people has become instead the instrument of their affliction.

The Lord's choice of Cyrus exactly describes this gulf in religious understanding: from Israel's vantage, God not only inflicts faction, implacable foes, and their own expropriation upon his people, but he also humiliates them by electing their messiah from among the godless who are their enemies. By contrast, as the Lord pronounces deity's position in the prophets, affliction is the effect of Israel's chronic apostasy, its refusal to obey and trust the one true God—in short, to take shelter in the covenant deity proffers. Events have fully exposed Israel's scepticism about the divine ordinance of things, as a murmuring people who demand that deity suit their notions of the good and just, denying to very God the inconceivable difference and prerogative of the world's maker. Thus the distinction between creator and creature, which the Mosaic covenant at once acknowledges and mediates, occasions the rupture in Israel's covenant with the Lord. The nation cannot recognize apostasy in its criticism and avoidance of God's inhuman ways; it sees only that deity perversely afflicts the people whom the Lord had chosen before all other nations to be a light to the world. So although each party acknowledge the same covenant, the pact between divine and human is understood from hopelessly incompatible positions. Israel thinks enacting the covenant should mean a similar observance by God and his people—that God will behave in kind, will be readily intelligible in human terms, which is one way to understand the activity of divine accommodation. But the Lord intends the covenant to give his people knowledge and relationship with their maker, a being incommensurable to human nature in every way, which is accommodation taken in an entirely different sense. It is this second understanding that the apostle Paul evokes in Romans, when he adopts Isaiah's analogy of potter and clay to argue the divergence of divine from human meanings, and thus God's freedom to elect gentiles as well as Jews to relationship with him:

> You will say to me then, "Why does he still find fault? For who can resist his will?" But who are you, a man, to answer back to God? Will what is molded say to its molder, "Why have you made me thus?" Has the potter no right over the clay, to make out of the same lump one vessel for beauty and another for menial use? (Romans 9:19–21).

Once again this simile addresses human difficulties with divine judgments: as in Cyrus's case, alien nations are inexplicably embraced while the chosen are hardened without cause. Paul must moreover meet the related objection that a just God cannot hold the wicked responsible for the evil to which he has now seemingly reserved them. For where the Lord of the covenant damned pharaoh for not acknowledging him, he abuses the faithful precisely because they do so, with those who understood themselves uniquely elected to divine protection now consigned to suffer its indifference and neglect (Romans 9:14–18). But to this appearance of divine injustice, Paul responds, "By no means!" Instead, he argues by analogy to the potter's clay that what the historical contradiction properly expresses is the distinction between God and the world: "Will what is molded say to its molder, 'Why have you made me thus?' " That is to say, God's choices for the creature are just and right from the standpoint of the creator, and not arbitrarily so, because the simile in Paul's hands makes an argument not only for deity's power over the world but also for its care and design. As Milton might read the figure, the potter and the clay do not picture God's indifference but his acutely intimate and decisive regard for the individual person. But this regard is disguised by an incalculable disparity in knowledge that makes the Lord's choices appear scandalous and arbitrary—"one vessel for beauty and another for menial use"—where they are ultimately apt and just. Paul conceives this divine regard similarly, as intelligible but discriminate in ways God's people would prefer to ignore:

> What shall we say, then? That Gentiles who did not pursue righteousness have attained it, that is, righteousness through faith; but that Israel who pursued the righteousness which is based on law did not succeed in fulfilling that law. Why? Because they did not pursue it through faith, but as if it were based on works. They have stumbled over the stumbling stone. (Romans 9:30–32)

The apostle emphasizes here the same divergence in understanding that Deutero-Isaiah ascribes to the covenantal relationship between God and Israel. Insofar as the law presumptively taught that suffering was guilty suffering only, and righteousness a statutory innocence, a difficulty arose when the innocent thus understood suffered as well, or what is virtually the same, when God's chosen people lost the righteousness that was theirs by divine ordination. This is the enigma that confronts the psalmist and the prophets, inexplicable suffering or incorrigible, helpless evil in Israel, which equally look and feel like necessity imposed by an unjust God. But Paul replies that righteousness *coram Deo* is not ours to adjudicate but God's, as the potter with the clay. Nor can it be caused or evinced in the same manner as natural or moral phenomena, since religious justification belongs to that category of things which do not appear as such, observing another order of existence altogether. Precisely because we insist that religious righteousness is something humanity works and effects, we find ourselves unable to perform what God seemingly demands, condemned by a failure of human understanding that we conceive as a failure of divine justice. Once again, this is the force of Samuel's reproach to Saul, who observes human imperatives over divine, familiar ritual over the Lord's estranging word of holocaust: "Behold, to obey is better than sacrifice, / and to hearken than the fat of rams"

(1 Samuel 15:22). For justification does not involve what we obviously perform or omit, but the attitude our speech and actions far more subtly express—what Wittgenstein would call "the echo of a thought in sight" (*PI* p.212).

In other words, sin and righteousness describe deity's response to the inevident condition of human understanding and cannot be simply correlated with a person's outward flourishing or outward affliction, in the manner predicated of the blind man that Jesus cures in John's gospel. In keeping with their choric role as the voice of conventional wisdom, the disciples put the question: " 'Rabbi, who sinned, this man or his parents, that he was born blind?' Jesus answered, 'It was not that this man sinned, or his parents, but that the works of God might be made manifest in him' " (John 9:2–3). The man born blind did not work, in the sense of merit, his own affliction, as though it were a sign of sin, a bane brought upon him by his own guilt or his parents'. His suffering has religious value exclusively in the moment when *God himself works it as a sign*: that is, when Jesus justifies the blind man to his disciples, and by curing him, transfigures a random natural cruelty into the pointed expression of divine love and grace. For only in suffering—in the catastrophic experience of a human finitude we otherwise disavow—can room be found for deity and the miraculous in our lives, which is why the blind man calls Jesus a prophet. Only then do we learn that we cannot master our condition, much less our fate, and that we are not sufficient to ourselves, a knowledge that begins in the intolerable sensation of being enthralled to necessity. Thus our mortality moves us to seek a further meaning than the one that immediately, fearfully presents itself in affliction, creating the occasion for us to believe against "the appearances" and for God to bring good out of a creaturely evil. But a doctrine of works contains no place for this untoward possibility: to the Pharisees of John's gospel, Jesus is not a prophet but a sinner who violates the Sabbath with miracles. Yet this wonderful transgression of their canon equally compels some to ask, "How can a man who is a sinner do such signs?" (John 9:16). They do not see the creator acting in and through the creature, only acting upon it in a promiscuous indictment of human nature. This is how Israel is obliged by interpretation to view its own devastation and Diaspora; and this is how, in Paul's theology and the reformers', the law is said to humiliate and condemn humanity, not redeem it.

By contrast, in those theologies, faith shows the world disclosing deity in the same way that the human body expresses the human soul; for humanity itself offers possibilities of significance beyond its evident condition. This expressive potential of creatural being—the world's capacity to mean more than it says—is "the stumbling stone" to which Paul and the gospels refer. We casually suppose that deity operates in the world as we see ourselves doing: that its meaning and intent is the sum of its appearances; that prosperity *is* righteousness and suffering *is* sin—until we too suffer unjustly or inexplicably, like the man born blind. This idea of suffering as the singular predicament of faith predictably becomes the stumbling block when Luther and Erasmus read Paul's argument in Romans 9.[1] As is his wont, Erasmus denies the sense of conflict and necessity that deity's distinction from the world presupposes for Luther; he simply avers once more that the simile of potter and clay is meant to rebuke a wicked people for murmuring against God, without any reference to issues of human suffering or divine injustice. Indeed, Erasmus remains oblivious to the dilemma of religious understanding that suffering itself reveals, where in the manner of psalmic lament, the faithful cannot discover a viable reason for their affliction, or in the prophets, where God's chosen people cannot do what the Lord himself demands of them. Certainly from the *nunc stans* of eternity, the vantage from which the Lord speaks to his prophets, the people do indeed murmur because they doubt; but from the human position, their doubting has real grounds. So Israel responds uncomprehendingly to its affliction—" 'Eli, Eli, lama sabachthani?' that is, 'My God, my God, why hast thou forsaken me?' "—even as Jesus did on the cross (Matthew 27:46).

Why the good suffer and the wicked prosper is the enigma Erasmus's reading refuses even to consider: that those who murmur against God might do so because they are innocent in any terms they can recognize. When such issues of theodicy are inescapably raised by Paul's version of the potter's clay, Erasmus adduces what he sees as a comparable vessel and comparison in 2 Timothy 2:20–21, proposing this further analogy to deflect, if not refute any reading of Romans which grants the aspect of necessity to our experience of God: "In a great house there are not only vessels of gold and silver but also of wood and earthenware, and some for noble use, some for ignoble. If any one purifies himself from what is ignoble, then he will be a vessel for noble use, consecrated and useful to the master of the house, ready for any good work."[2] Without preface, Luther replies that there is more than just a pot in Isaiah and Romans—there is a maker of the pot, who has a distinctive relation to the clay that it molds. He charges his opponent with eliding the active engagement of deity with its creature, even as Erasmus disregards the potter acting upon the clay, as well as the decision of the householder in determining a vessel's purpose; for it is "their master, who prepares them for their intended use."[3] And this prerogative of judgment, Luther observes, "is what offended so many men of outstanding ability, men who have won acceptance down so many ages":

> At this point, they demand that God should act according to man's idea of right, and do what seems proper to themselves—or else that He should cease to be God! 'The secrets of His majesty,' they say, 'shall not profit Him; let Him render a reason why He is God, or why He wills and does that which has no appearance of justice in it. It is like asking a cobbler or a belt-maker to take the seat of judgement.' Flesh does not deign to give God glory to the extent of believing Him to be just and good when He speaks and acts above and beyond the definitions of Justinian's Code, or the fifth book of Aristotle's Ethics! No, let the Majesty that created all things give way before a worthless fragment of His own creation! . . . He must be brought to order! Rules must be laid down for Him, and He is not

to damn any but those who have deserved it by *our* reckoning! . . . But if God works in such a way as to regard merit, why do objectors grumble and complain? Why do they say: 'Why doth He find fault? Who resists His will?' Why need Paul restrain them? For who is surprised, let alone shocked or inclined to object, if one is damned who deserved it? Moreover, what becomes of the power of the Potter to make what vessel He will, if He is controlled by merits and rules, and is not allowed to make as He would, but is required to make as He should?[4]

Luther interprets the resistance to Pauline necessity as an effacement of deity's distinction from the world, which leaves religious things to be assessed by human orders of meaning and value, with suffering inexorably read as the sign of metaphysical crime and punishment. While this scenario betrays Luther's barely suppressed anxiety about his own position in debating someone of Erasmus's reputation, he nonetheless asserts the predicament of faith with brutal irony, demanding to know "who is surprised, let alone shocked or inclined to object, if one is damned who deserved it?" For we quarrel with God only when the world contradicts our judgments or thwarts our expectations; yet it is on these occasions, in the experience of injustice or suffering, that Luther believes deity is most fully expressed—as Jesus says to his disciples in the case of the man born blind. It follows that Luther would tacitly identify the murmurers against divine prerogative as those persons of rank and status like Erasmus himself, who have yet to know suffering or its terrible onus in human eyes. These can afford a complacent rationalism in religion that would reduce deity to a universal mechanic or artisan, subject to human patronage and constraint. But necessity describes the very passion of suffering—in the original sense of affliction, of being cast down by a force wholly outside oneself, left dejected without grounds or warrant. In short, the theological predicate that Erasmus calls unreasonable, "stupid," or "absurd," Luther understands as true to the human experience of suffering. And in placing crucial boundaries on our knowledge and agency in religious things, this absolute freedom of deity reasserts the distinction between creator and creature, refutes the conflation of divine with human proprieties, and opens up new horizons of meaning which Luther calls "the room" of faith.

For Luther, unlike Erasmus, intimately knows that the analogical scheme organizing any doctrine of works can conduce to the gravest despair, not least because the drawing of metaphysical correlations inevitably devolves upon God as the point to which all human evils refer. Indeed, it is his unique pastoral insight that incoherence, necessity, and suffering attend the analogy of divine to human things but not the observance of their distinction, as Erasmus and "the men of outstanding ability" contend against him. He likens this aspect of religious experience to fate in the poets of antiquity, especially Virgil, whom Luther cites as arguing the immutable and irrevocable law of existence to which even the gods are bound.[5] He wonders why Erasmus, the educated man, would proscribe the religious discussion of necessity when it is "on the lips of heathen poets and ordinary people so frequently?": "Those wise men knew, what experience of life proves, that no man's purposes ever go forward as planned, but events overtake all men contrary to their expectations."[6] To Luther, the inevitable frustration of our designs implicates other forces at work in the world than human agency alone, even as the perpetual discrepancy between our purposes and outcomes counters the claim of human knowledge to master human experience. In actuality, we enjoy nothing like the rational autonomy we assume, a delusion that ensures we will be caught unawares in the web of contingency, seemingly acted upon and moved against our will like the Agamemnon of Aeschylus. This tragic metamorphosis from glory to suffering describes one experience of necessity, which the Greeks analyzed as the human obligation to honor the incoherent demands of deity. As Martha Nussbaum explains, the result "for a typical Greek agent [was] a sense of the binding force and inevitability of the conflicting requirements, even in a conflict situation."[7] Such an intractable dilemma is peculiarly religious since only religious meanings, in their character as expressions of the absolute, have the power to bind us so; and tragedy, a religious art, puts this dilemma at the center of its dramatic action, making it the source of the most radical human suffering.

Outside of theology, the same tragic predicament is rarely extended to Christianity, which is supposed—however illusorily—to transcend such purely existential difficulties, as Jesus did the grave. But this exclusion not only suppresses the primacy of the Passion in the gospels and in the Christian liturgy, but equally the predicament of faith on which Luther and Calvin together insist, that is to say, the indelible reality of human suffering. It is the suffering that accompanies conceptual or psychological incoherence, the suffering created by persecution and injustice, which provides the reformers with their motive for doing theology in the first place, as well as the original position from which they interpret scripture. And this is where Luther parts company with Erasmus, because he understands his religion as both an account and an alleviation of human suffering, not unlike tragedy for the Greeks. I have mentioned more than once Luther's recollection of how he came to understand Paul's phrase "the righteousness of God," the reading on which depends his theology of justification. He feels the impact of Paul's words as utterly personal and existential, in part because these are words which (unlike Erasmus) he not merely believes but believes to be absolutely binding upon him. And when his understanding of the text becomes untenable, incongruous, or antagonistic, Luther finds himself in an impossible situation, since he cannot simply leave off his conviction of their truth any more than he can leave off using language. So Luther in his anguish and hatred of an unjust God pounds away at Romans, loathing but never altering Paul's words until the text abruptly, absurdly changes before his eyes and takes on a new significance.

This interpretive conversion Milton associates with the misunderstanding of Christ's "strange, repugnant riddles" in the *Doctrine and Discipline*. For when

Jesus' sayings are "elementally understood," they appear not only incongruous and absurd to us, but like the "righteousness of God," as terrible, disproportionate, and humanly deleterious meanings of the kind Adam hears in the Lord's curse. And like Adam's exclamation of *felix culpa* at the end of *Paradise Lost*, release from the sheer oppressiveness, the virtual bondage of these interpretations is tantamount to theophany: this is the sweetness that Luther finds in his newly circumstantial understanding of the text. If I may enlist Wittgenstein here: "what I perceive in the dawning of an aspect is not a property of the object, but an internal relation between it and other objects" (*PI* p.212). In Milton too, meaning by relation gives deity's idiom its coherence, a result justifying in his mind the method of grammatical-historical exegesis. But this is to render merely procedural and prosaic what appears rather as an effortless act of recognition; and such profound discovery of coherence in the seemingly arbitrary *feels* to Adam, to Luther, to Milton, like a sudden access of grace and the liberation of self from necessity. So the chorus in Aeschylus's *Agamemnon* should remind us that "grace comes somehow violent," "wisdom / comes alone through suffering."[8] Nussbaum puts this idea of *pathei mathos* felicitously for Luther, since she says that the tragedians uniquely "notice that often it takes the shock of such suffering to make us look and see":[9]

> So far we have spoken as if the experience of grief is a means to a knowledge of self that is by and in the intellect alone. We have, that is, spoken as if we took *pathei mathos* to mean 'through the means of suffering (experience) comes (intellectual) understanding.' A full and correct understanding of our human practical situation is available in principle to unaided intellect; these people require passional response only because of their deficiencies and blind spots. This reading, which in effect makes the whole experience of tragedy (both in drama and in life) of merely instrumental worth, seems to me to trivialize the poets' claim against the (anti-poetic) philosophers and to skew the debate in a way that is advantageous to the latter. We would do more justice to the Aeschylean claim if we considered another possibility. Here we would see the passional reaction, the suffering, as itself a piece of practical recognition or perception, as at least a partial constituent of the character's correct understanding of his situation as a human being. . . . the Chorus' sleepless agonies, are not means to a grasp that is in the intellect by itself; they are pieces of recognition or acknowledgement of difficult human realities. There is a kind of knowing that works by suffering because suffering is the appropriate acknowledgement of the way human life, in these cases, is. And in general: to grasp either a love or a tragedy by intellect is not sufficient for having real human knowledge of it.[10]

In effect, Nussbaum explains by her own considerable act of imagination the distinct interpretive positions of Erasmus and Luther: namely, the difference between an intellectual recognition and what she calls a "passional" under-

standing that engages the whole human person. Once again to recall Wittgenstein, he distinguishes between our merely remarking upon the contingency
of human meaning and our actually undergoing it, in the interpretive crisis or
separation of "noticing an aspect." He sees this separation not as a procedure
or even a process in the sense of something initiated and progressive: it is rather
a "*state* of seeing"—a condition of human being itself (*PI* p.212). Thus he talks
about "seeing" in this way: "That is what I treat it as; this is my *attitude* towards
the figure. This is one meaning in calling it a case of 'seeing' " (*PI* p.205). Cavell
also understands the experience of "seeing *as*" to be a shift in attitude at once
existential and moral, because it elicits this fundamental level of human engagement—of taking a viable approach, of decisively inflecting oneself toward
others and the world. For "seeing *as*" is not only to understand something, but
particularly to orient one's behavior in the light of that understanding, to make
it a world-altering event. Nussbaum also suggests that, in tragedy, suffering itself
can constitute such an event and can express such an understanding—a transfiguring of our entire relation with the world.

For Luther and Milton then, both of whom approach faith from the passional
predicament of tragedy, divine incongruity explains the human crisis which
suffering at once precipitates and embodies. Yet to Erasmus, who does not share
this understanding, the argument from divine incongruity is a rational scandal,
an offense against God; and it prohibits him from penetrating past this idea's
repugnant expression—Luther's verbal violence and vulgarity, his apparent intransigence—to the depth and power of his opponent's theology. To this extent,
Luther is a better reader of Erasmus. The same impasse obtains in Milton's case,
and not just with his editors; for the polemical or "satiric" speech that peculiarly
signifies his gross turpitude to the Remonstrant and Modest Confuter, Milton
himself conceives as holy zeal for the one true God (CM 3.1:312–15). In either
instance, the most profound conceptual commitment is felt to be incompatible
with the decorum of disinterestedness that signals reasoned debate; and this
disinterestedness is not just an intellectual decorum but the reflex of social and
political proprieties that their theologies, however inadvertently, violate with
aplomb. That is because religious meaning for each involves a "conversion" in
the fundamental sense of that word—a charged intimacy with our condition
that is more than ideological, since it begins by acknowledging the almost intractable difficulty of human suffering. And when understanding derives from
the lived experience of injustice and contradiction, ideas cease to be concepts
only: on the model of Luther's "assertions" in *The Bondage of the Will*, they
become urgent, passionate imperatives to reform the conduct of human life. As
a religious account of necessity, the whole thrust of Luther's argument in that
tract is directed toward the passional understanding of God and religious things
which, here at least, thoroughly eludes Erasmus.

This impasse may explain their disparate appeal as Christian theologians and
apologists, as John Bunyan's experience of Luther suggests:

129. But before I had got thus far out of these my temptations, I did greatly long to see some ancient Godly man's Experience, who had writ some hundred of years before I was born; for, for those who had writ in our days, I thought (but I desire them now to pardon me) that they had Writ only that which others felt, or else had, thorow the strength of their Wits and Parts, studied to answer such Objections as they perceived others were perplexed with, without going down themselves into the deep. Well, after many such longings in my mind, the God in whose hands are all our days and ways, did cast into my hand, one day, a book of *Martin Luther*, his comment on the *Galathians*, so old that it was ready to fall piece from piece, if I did but turn it over. Now I was pleased much that such an old book had fallen into my hand; the which, when I had but a little way perused, I found my condition in his experience, so largely and profoundly handled, as if his Book had been written out of my heart; this made me marvel: for thus thought I, this man could not know anything of the state of Christians now, but must needs write and speak of the Experience of former days.

130. Besides, he doth most gravely also, in that book debate of the rise of these temptations, namly, Blasphemy, Desperation, and the like, shewing that the law of *Moses*, as well as the Devil, Death, and Hell, hath a very great hand therein; the which at first was very strange to me, but considering and watching, I found it so indeed. But of Particulars here I intend nothing, only this methinks I must let fall before all men, I do prefer this book of Mr. *Luther* upon the *Galathians*, (excepting the Holy Bible) before all the books that ever I have seen, as most fit for a wounded Conscience.[11]

Bunyan yearns for a passional understanding of his predicament—one that is more than intellectual, more than clinical, that acknowledges how suffering puts both self and God in utter jeopardy. And such a felt and genuinely reflexive theology, whose meaning lives off the page, is what Luther's lectures on Galatians provide him: "my condition in his experience, so largely and profoundly handled, as if his Book had been written out of my heart." Significantly, Bunyan finds his mental anguish at once explained and prophesied by the Pauline paradox of the law—"the which at first was very strange to me"—which obtains when scripture is mistakenly read with reference to human, not divine agency. Then the sacred text imposes the double bind of necessity, humiliating and condemning even as it claims to justify, which is why Bunyan ranks the law—as figuring this kind of interpretation—with the devil, death, and hell as temptations to blasphemy and despair. For the religious crisis engendered by his continued imprisonment—and this because he refused to stop preaching, to cease asserting in Luther's sense—instructs Bunyan that deity and religious things mean differently than they appear to do, and that a failure to draw this interpretive distinction produces the relentless travails of conscience recounted in his autobiography.

On this head, Roger Sharrock acutely observes that "the mental conflicts depicted in *Grace Abounding* . . . though they are real states of the soul, grow out of quibbling misunderstandings about texts."[12] He makes the point to suggest both Bunyan's febrile sensibility and his theological confusion; but the interpretive source of Bunyan's suffering implies more than a sensitive temperament, or the ignorance alleged equally against tinkers and nonconformists. It reprises the conversion Luther undergoes, as Bunyan also seeks to reconcile the truth of scripture with its lived contradiction, his own ordeal with the Christian promise. Moreover, the "marvel" of finding himself in Luther's account exemplifies the power of interpretation to act upon the whole person, shaping and affecting an entire response to the world. It is for that very reason that Milton, in *Paradise Lost*, makes the speaker's recounting and reinterpreting the Fall the means to redeem this alter ego. Needless to say, the experience and the idea of such power derive from the scripturalism in which the reformers' theology is founded: Bunyan's urgent need for a viable reading of both scripture and himself, pursued in the form of an old book that might contain "some ancient Godly man's Experience," itself expresses a truth of evangelical practice—namely, the astonishing interpenetration of mind and text. His inability to find relief or consolation in the writings of his contemporaries, his sense of confronting an impasse not only in his own understanding but also in those who profess to represent his condition, produces a religious incoherence that describes and intensifies Bunyan's suffering. The orthodox account of scripture simply will not satisfy him, any more than it does Martin Luther; and it is precisely this inadequacy of received readings to human actualities, and the injustice done by enforcing such readings, which move both Luther and Bunyan to dissent from institutional religion.

And their dissent entails a strange, seemingly incongruous or eccentric, interpretation, provoked by the failure of orthodoxy to reconcile human suffering with scripture's expressions. The received sense of the text not only alienates Luther and Bunyan from the God they seek, but also condemns them to suffer for their very desire to know and be approved by him. Such is the position of the psalmist in lamenting the plight of Israel, abandoned to its foes; and such is the position of the prophets, who like Bunyan with his conscience struggle to lead an incorrigible nation to truth. Milton also refers to this predicament in his anti-prelatical tracts, because it pictures his own experience in writing. Thus he opens the second book of *The Reason of Church Government* by arguing the distinction between divine and human valuations: for "all earthly things which have the name of good and convenient in our daily use, are withall so cumbersome and full of trouble"; whereas the right understanding "of God, and of his true worship, and what is infallibly good and happy in the state of mans life, what in it selfe evil and miserable, though vulgarly not so esteem'd" can alone allay what he calls the perturbations of the soul (CM 3.1:229). But because this truly effectual understanding opposes the human status quo, worldly interest requires the silencing of anyone who would spread its imperative truth, a suppression that creates in God's evangelists "a sorer burden of mind, and more pressing then any supportable toil, or waight, which the body can labour under":

> And that which aggravats the burden more, is, that having receiv'd amongst his allotted parcels certain pretious truths of such an orient lustre as no Diamond can equall, which never the lesse he has in charge to put off at any cheap rate, yea for nothing to them that will, the great Marchants of this world fearing that this cours would soon discover, and disgrace the fals glitter of their deceitfull wares wherewith they abuse the people, like poor Indians with beads and glasses, practize by all means how they may suppresse the venting of such rarities and such a cheapnes as would undoe them, and turn their trash upon their hands. Therefore by gratifying the corrupt desires of men in fleshly doctrines, they stirre them up to persecute with hatred and contempt all those that seek to bear themselves uprightly in this their spiritual factory. (CM 3.1:229–30)

To the extent that Milton associates episcopacy with the maintenance of prerogative—of "great pleasure and commodity" in church and state (CM 3.1:231)—this entails a religion that not only panders to the gross sensuality of its own purveyors, but also traffics in "fleshly doctrines" to the world. And these doctrines dispense glamour instead of truth, which is to say, the bewitchment or enchanting of the senses by glorified appearance. In a typical reworking of his texts—the mercantile parables of the talents and the pearl of great price—Milton's "spiritual factors" would dispense a product of real if unprepossessing benefit for little or nothing, while episcopacy exploits the meretricious to ensure its own power and position, passing off "trash" as "rarities" like the traders who bought Manhattan. And in promoting this purely specious sense of truth and the good, they pervert the people's valuation of God's own meanings and those freely communicating them, who are then repudiated as charlatans and provocateurs. As Milton would have it, then, the pomp and ceremony of episcopacy is an idol that deludes and maddens, spreading internecine violence to sustain the ostentatious, superficial religion it promulgates, and by that means the institution of an ecclesiastical nobility. Truth is thus silenced for its appearance alone, its incongruity with received values, to the anguish of the dissenter who wishes to "dispose and employ those summes of knowledge and illumination, which God hath sent him into this world to trade with" (CM 3.1:229).

But it is deity, not the merchants of episcopacy, who foments their anguish by endowing God's apostles with an imperative knowledge—a knowledge that, when unexpressed, becomes terrible and onerous to the possessor because God "even to a strictnesse requires the improvment of these his entrusted gifts" (CM 3.1:229). The incongruous understanding of faith in this way doubly jeopardizes all those who wield it. So Jesus in the gospels observes that the simple novelty or idiosyncrasy of another truth, never mind its criticism of the familiar and approved, is bound to offend the world in which it is revealed and provoke its persecution.[13] This contrary effect defines the predicament of the converted, the sectarian, the schismatic, and the dissenter, all of whom suffer ostracism, even persecution for the scandal of faith. That is why the recognition of religious truth can feel like an impending fate—like necessity, in short:

> yet needs must it sit heavily upon their spirits, that being in Gods prime intention and their own, selected heralds of peace, and dispensers of treasure inestimable without price to them that have no pence, they finde in the discharge of their commission that they are made the greatest variance and offence, a very sword and fire both in house and City over the whole earth. This is that which the sad prophet *Jeremiah* laments, *Wo is me my mother, that thou hast born me a man of strife, and contention.* And although divine inspiration must certainly have been sweet to those ancient profets, yet the irksomenesse of that truth which they brought was so unpleasant to them, that every where they call it a burden. Yea, that mysterious book of Revelation which the great Evangelist was bid to eat, as it had been some eye-brightning electuary of knowledge, and foresight, though it were sweet in his mouth, and in the learning, it was bitter in his belly; bitter in the denouncing. Nor was this hid from the wise Poet *Sophocles*, who in that place of his Tragedy where *Tiresias* is call'd to resolve K. *Edipus* in a matter which he knew would be grievous, brings him in bemoaning his lot, that he knew more than other men. For surely to every good and peaceable man it must in nature needs be a hatefull thing to be the displeaser, and molester of thousands; much better would it like him doubtlesse to be the messenger of gladnes and contentment, which is his chief intended busines, to all mankind, but that they resist and oppose their own true happinesse. But when God commands to take the trumpet and blow a dolorous or a jarring blast, it lies not in mans will what he shall say or what he shall conceal. If he shall think to be silent as *Jeremiah* did, because of the reproach and derision he met with daily, and *all his familiar friends watcht for his halting* to be reveng'd on him for speaking the truth, he would be forc't to confesse as he confest, *his word was in my heart as a burning fire shut up in my bones, I was weary with forbearing, and could not stay.* (CM 3.1:230–31)

This account of the prophet's position speaks exactly to Bunyan, since he too is compelled to preach by the very nature of the truth he expounds.[14] And because authority and custom find this truth obnoxious, it does more than land John Bunyan in jail: his refusal *not* to preach, consequent upon receiving and acknowledging God's call, secures his imprisonment—deprived for more than a decade of wife, children, church, and freedom. That actuality verifies Milton's decision to invoke Sophoclean tragedy and the myth of Tiresias in illustrating the predicament of faith, where "it lies not in man's will what he shall say, or what he shall conceal." This is the necessity that, in Aeschylus, the god Apollo imposes upon Cassandra; for Milton's apostle too is almost somatically constrained to speak or do the thing that excites intractable resentment, obloquy, and suffering. But the further comparison Milton draws, to the position of the prophets and especially Jeremiah, while perhaps more expected is still more profound; for Jeremiah, in von Rad's view, specially exemplifies the religious problem posed by suffering. For this prophet's increasingly dire situation places in almost unparalleled relief the distinction between God and the world—between deity's holy imperatives and human desire, between truth and custom, enigma and understanding. Thus in the so-called confessions or colloquies, Jeremiah attests to the sensation of being enthralled by necessity, in the form of a God whom suffering has rendered vicious and unjust:

> O Lord, thou hast deceived me,
>   and I was deceived;
> thou art stronger than I,
>   and thou hast prevailed.
> I have become a laughingstock all
>   the day;
>   everyone mocks me.
> For whenever I speak, I cry out,
>   I shout, "Violence and
>   destruction!"
> For the word of the Lord has
>   become for me
>   a reproach and derision all day
>   long.
> If I say, "I will not mention him,
>   or speak any more in his name,"
> there is in my heart as it were a
>   burning fire
>   shut up in my bones.
> and I am weary with holding it in,
>   and I cannot.
> For I hear many whispering.
>   Terror is on every side!
> "Denounce him! Let us denounce
>   him!"
>   say all my familiar friends,
>   watching for my fall.
>
> (Jeremiah 20:7–10)

Jeremiah's account of his prophetic call consummately expresses the ambivalence of dissent. For he himself fears and distrusts the source of his authority, finding the "violence" and "destruction" of the Lord's word as terrible as Israel does. Von Rad comments that the sense of "deceived" here has to do with erotic entrapment—"the act of enticing and seducing a young girl" (*OTT* 2:204)—

with Jeremiah picturing himself in his creaturely innocence and vulnerability unable to withstand deity's cynical ravishment. Yet the Lord's word is nonetheless true to him: against the resistance of his mind and the hostility with which his speech is met, his very body demands that he acknowledge its truth. Thus creatural nature itself bows to the creator's will, with the appalling result that even those who had loved Jeremiah now eagerly await his destruction. The calamitous dissociation of the Lord from Israel is worked out in the individual person of the prophet, a man agonistically divided against himself and his God. And although the image of divine seduction connotes no mystical rapture, only an intimate and calculated betrayal, this betrayal does not bear on the truth Jeremiah must inexorably speak to Israel. It refers to his being seduced and abandoned by God to the cruel predicament of prophecy itself:

> I sat alone, because thy hand was
>   upon me,
>   for thou hadst filled me with
>   indignation.
> Why is my pain unceasing,
>   my wound incurable,
>   refusing to be healed?
> Wilt thou be to me like a deceitful
>   brook,
>   like waters that fail?
>
> (Jeremiah 15:17–18)

If Jeremiah's relentless agony and overmastering indignation accompany his conviction of truth, it is an acknowledgment forced upon him by deity, just as prophecy is his almost involuntary vocation. For God's calling has effected a fearful discordance, with the prophet himself inhabiting both sides of the question of divine justice. Even though Jeremiah is convinced of the truth he pronounces upon his people, he still shares their revulsion at that word, their sense of deity's betrayal: his self-understanding is their familiar one, not the estranging conviction of the Lord's. Unlike Isaiah, Jeremiah cannot view his world *sub specie aeternitatis*, which is to say prophetically; he sees it from the standpoint of his own human complicity, and for that reason, the God of his lamentations is deity at its most terrible and demonic, like the God of Job's affliction.

As von Rad concludes, "With Jeremiah, the man and the prophetic task part company; indeed serious tensions threaten the whole of his calling as a prophet" (*OTT* 2:205). And this separation or crisis is evinced in the very form of Jeremiah's confessions, which while participating in the genre of cultic lament, are more vehement and extreme than psalmic speech, more poetically and even gratuitously personal than prophetic complaint (*OTT* 2:201). Indeed, it would seem as if the pressure of Jeremiah's dilemma induces a cognate estrangement from liturgical and prophetic convention: in his hands, the form loses the assurance and seeming universality of tradition, becoming more pointed, expressive, and novel—so novel, von Rad comments, that Jeremiah is sometimes thought to introduce single-handedly the lyric *ego* and its liberty of personal conception to cultic literature. This formal aspect of the prophet's confessions coincides suggestively with what Dr. Johnson says about Milton's "uniform peculiarity of speech" and his incorrigible lack of decorum in *Paradise Lost.* It also evokes Bunyan's equally eccentric utterance (if not by the standards of pamphlet literature in his day), inasmuch as the narrative of *Grace Abounding* is pushed and pulled almost out of recognition by its author's intense efforts to grasp the valence of deity's expressions as they apply to his torment. And here, as in Jeremiah, the attempt is paralleled by impressive deviations in form. Yet von Rad maintains that to argue a kind of individualism for this effect is to mistake the prophetic impetus of Jeremiah's speech, because the whole nation of Israel is implicitly asked to find its sufferings in those of its prophet, as Bunyan does in Luther and Luther in Paul.

Not Altogether a Nullity

It may seem too much to claim this predicament for John Milton, whose personal sense of injustice hasn't anything like the tragic scope of Jeremiah's, and whose injuries consist largely in their imaginative apprehension, unlike Bunyan locked in the Bedford county jail. Yet it is significant that, in his early tracts, Milton himself conceives his own position to have that kind, if not that degree, of ambivalent intensity. This is not the outcome of his political disappointments, since they have really yet to occur. It is habitual to his outlook from as early as the sonnet "How soon hath time," where he complains about his appearances to the world—that he does not seem to others as he knows himself. For Milton even at twenty-three worries about being misunderstood and unacknowledged, not because he wants the world or God to pass judgment on him, but because he is acutely conscious of the difference, that in his subsequent experience becomes a yawning gap, between the idea and the fact of self. He knows that subjectivity is tenuous and even dangerous to the person when it is rendered inaccessible to others, that private conviction is nonsensical until it is tried against public actualities, and that the world's understanding very often and grievously departs from one's own. These are the reasons Milton writes his tracts—to assess himself against his own reception in a vexed, ever anxious activity of self-prophecy, with his argument compulsively if indirectly interpreting John Milton to the world, to himself, and to God. And this is where his situation verges imaginatively on the predicaments of Jeremiah and Bunyan. Milton's original and all-absorbing concern is the relation of the whole person to God, of humanity to the absolute, which takes this issue of acknowledgment to its unanswerable extreme—unanswerable, that is, in familiar human terms, because God sees not as we see, chooses not as we choose. Acknowledgment is equally at the heart of Bunyan's despair because suffering moves him to wonder, as Jeremiah does, whether the God whose truth he proclaims is a deceit, an illusion that has betrayed him. And contrary to his reputation in some quarters,

Milton wonders the same thing—because what we are to deity cannot be known in this life except by the groundless assurance of faith, which tells us not what we are in ourselves but what we are imputed to be, as creatures *simul iustus et peccator.*

However, as Nussbaum argues, the religious position requires us to be the person to which we lay claim—to assert this self by expressing it outwardly, publicly, for all the world to see, but also intimately, personally, so as to grasp the crucial assurance of relationship with God. All religion is proclamation of truth, and to be religious is to be obligated in that sense, to be under the necessity of one's convictions. As Luther insists, the religious person cannot subside into sceptical *epoche*, or escape the problem of self by mystical ecstasis, as Erasmus prefers. Insofar as our experience somehow manifests our position *coram Deo*, it must be actively engaged and understood, for deity holds us accountable to living out our belief. This is what Milton means when he says that God strictly requires the betterment of his gifts; but that demand becomes the most grievous necessity when a conflict arises, as it invariably does, between how we understand ourselves and how others see us, as Milton acknowledges in everything he writes. To make the case more vividly, this is how Mrs. Sadleir, daughter of Edward Coke the jurist, rejects the unsolicited and amazingly obtuse proposal of Roger Williams that she read *Eikonoklastes*:

> For Melton's book, that you desire I should read, if I be not mistaken, that is he that has wrote a book of the Lawfulness of Divorce: and, if report says true, he had, at that time, two or three wives living. This perhaps were good doctrine in New England: but it is most abominable in Old England. For his book that he wrote against the late King that you would have me read, you should have taken notice of God's judgment upon him, who stroke him with blindness; and, as I have heard, he was fain to have the help of one Andrew Marvell, or else he could not have finished that most accursed libel. God has begun his judgment upon him here; his punishment will be hereafter in Hell.[15]

Mrs. Sadleir's response manages marvelously to realize every worst fear about his own situation and that of his poem, to which Milton himself gives no less passionate but more artistic utterance in the tracts and in the persona of the speaker of *Paradise Lost*. In her eyes, he is made infamous by his positions for divorce and against the king, a notoriety rendered even more sensational by the allegation of his bigamy, and the very popular and current notion that his blindness was God's condign punishment for abetting regicide or, as the royalists liked to call it, parricide. But although Milton throughout his life is extravagantly tender of his reputation, what I think would disturb him most about Mrs. Sadleir's reply to Williams is that she dismisses him out of hand. His infamy is so enormous that she will readily espouse the cause of his opponents, while refusing to countenance even the request that she read Milton's work. And his blindness deprives him of that much credit with her, since Mrs. Sadleir—

with no attention paid to time or logic—repeats with obvious relish the rumor attributing his odious writings to Andrew Marvell (as author or amanuensis), hating Milton by reputation alone. In sum, she refuses to acknowledge the slightest possibility that he could be other than he appears to her, a prospect Milton regularly finds so daunting that he feels compelled to devote space and eloquence in the tracts to presenting himself as someone impossible for Mrs. Sadleir to ignore.

As it happens, Milton addresses something very like these charges in his *Second Defense of the English People* (more or less contemporary with Mrs. Sadleir's letter), particularly the notion that his blindness was a judgment visited upon him by God. And the manner in which he vindicates himself is as pertinent to Mrs. Sadleir's peremptory refusal to know him better, as it is to his opponent's inevitably more elaborate attack. For both their accusations are informed by a mentality, or more exactly, a way of levying meaning that he must for his own sake strenuously resist. This mentality or interpretation operates in the fashion of Mrs. Sadleir's "common report": because Milton advocates more liberal divorce laws, he must himself be a libertine; because he wrote justifying the legality of executing the king, that mortal god, his blindness must be divine retribution. In other words, a position regarded as immoral predicates the immorality of the person holding it, just as an evil suffered discloses a sin committed. Thus Milton too encounters the injustice this supernatural order of analogy perpetrates in human affairs: a correspondence is drawn between the evident sense of something and its nature, between the symbolic valuation put on a fact and its ultimate cause, establishing an implacable logic and metaphysical continuity among things more charitably and more properly understood in a discriminate, circumstantial fashion.

This is how Milton rebuts his detractors in the *Second Defense*, invoking the judgment of Jesus "that the man whom he had healed had been blind even from the womb, for no sin either of himself or of his parents" (CM 8:67). In doing so, Milton emphasizes Jesus' decent reticence before the sufferer, but equally his reluctance to plumb the unfathomable depths of divine intent. For this assertion of such an obvious and exact ratio between our fate and our virtue, our condition on earth and our standing before God, is no less presumptuous than it is cruel and unjust. These are, he suggests, distinct orders of things whose intersection is not in our power to determine but in God's, and as such, mysterious. Neither do our bodies so unambiguously reveal, much less dictate, our nature or capacities, with Milton remarking by way of proof that no one would take him for forty, much less the desiccated, effete monster that his current opponent (presumably Alexander More) portrays him to be (CM 8:61). He then uses this fallacy to scorn it, by satirically forbearing to mention that More's own appearance is reputed to be "most contemptible, and the living image of the wickedness and malice which dwell within you" (CM 8:63). Like rumor itself or the decorum of polemic, mere appearance is no secure index in

Milton's case or More's, which is why his blindness can apply only uncertainly, if at all, to his own worth or the rightness of his actions: "But why should I be unable to bear that which it behoves every one to be prepared to bear, should the accident happen to himself, without repining? Why should I be unable to bear what I know may happen to any mortal being,—what I know has actually happened to some of the most eminent and the best of men, on the records of memory?" (CM 8:63). In other words, his blindness is an ordinary and indifferent consequence of human mortality, occurring without regard for person or merit, and therefore pitiable but unremarkable—except in the manner such suffering is received; to Milton, how we conduct ourselves in affliction is a surer sign of character than the brute fact of suffering.

At this distance, and upon mature reflection, it seems perfectly obvious that the victims of misfortune need not have incurred their own fate; but in practice we remain intuitively receptive to the notion. For the interpretation and mentality Milton battles here, which transforms coincidence into fate and appearance into fact, is more enduring and pervasive than the single question of his blindness suggests. Indeed, the real subject of Milton's apologetics is theodicy itself—the expression of truth and the obligations we have to it in a world of controversy. Because Mrs. Sadleir's truth has the clarity, confidence, and force of the damnation she visits upon Milton, she is likely to regard the civil and religious conflict to which he is party as decisively engaging a manifest good and evil, and not as a crisis of assumptions about the nature of church and state. But his own exigencies aside, truth for Milton has a polymorphous aspect, with none of the self-evidence Mrs. Sadleir expects, which is why it must be discerned, read, and adjudicated on each occasion when controversy arises. In support of this argument, he offers the contradiction (to Mrs. Sadleir's way of thinking) of blinded virtue, citing once again the example of Tiresias—not of course Tiresias the voyeur and hermaphrodite—but also Phineus, the Promethean man of Apollonius, whom jealous deity renders blind and deathless for the sin of bringing truth to an oppressed humanity. But Milton does not stop with a simple counterexample: he uses the myth to assault the whole interpretive scheme that enables More to read Milton's blindness as a certain sign of turpitude in himself and the Good Old Cause. Thus, in a characteristic maneuver dating from the first Prolusion (in the new genealogies he invents for Night and Day), Milton freely revises Phineus's legend so that it becomes a tacit fable about the false Helenas of truth and the nature of his own justification:[16] "But God himself is truth; and the more closely any one adheres to truth, in teaching it to mankind, the more nearly he must resemble God, the more acceptable must he be to him. It is impious to believe God to be jealous of truth, or to be an enemy to the utmost freedom of its communication to men. It does not appear, therefore, that it was for any crime, that this ancient sage, who was so zealous to enlighten human kind, and that many among the philosophers, were deprived of light" (CM 8:65).

It would appear that Apollonius and ancient tradition misrepresent the blinding of Phineus in much the same way Mrs. Sadleir and More depict Milton's loss of sight. Depending on the attitude taken toward the sufferer, a just or unjust God is the cause of their affliction, on the grounds that what seems good or evil to us signifies the same way to deity. To Milton's way of thinking, this would mean that deity and truth, whose identity he asserts here, must fluctuate like opinion in every wind and weather and so contradict themselves, in which case they would cease to be what they claim. But while it is the case, in the language of the *Areopagitica*, that truth may have more shapes than one, now on one side, now on another, this is the function of its expressive contingency, not its incoherence. For unlike the superficial continuities between things that analogy generates in religion, whose speciousness our experience chronically exposes, divine intent lends new integrity to the world's appearances even as it is expressed by them. Milton's God would uphold the complexity of religious experience and not punish Phineus for the false sacrilege of truth telling, just as he does those ancient and modern worthies, their sight lost in the course of exemplary lives, whom Milton enlists in his own defense. Milton's God would do so, that is, if the precedent operations of providence in such cases are allowed to be a guide (CM 8:65–67). This proviso is on the same order as Milton's earlier insistence in the *Apology* (the one point on which he and the Modest Confuter agree) that martyrdom itself is no index of truth, since a person can always suffer courageously in a wrong cause (CM 3.1:325–26). The vicissitudes of human understanding only underscore the role played by prejudice and custom in how we decide the truth, since we eagerly invest mere opinion with supernatural authority and thus a heightened appeal—a point Milton makes simply by disputing Apollonius's account of an already protean myth.

So when he denies that God is unjust or a censor of truth, summarily removing deity as the source of Phineus's blindness and human suffering generally, Milton goes a step beyond revision of the myth to deplete its metaphysical force entirely. With Phineus and all those blind notables, he carefully omits any speculative cause even as Jesus did with the man born blind. Instead, he describes the particular circumstances of their misfortune to set the parameters within which an understanding of their predicament and his own may be sought. He says, first of all, that he can discern no guilt in himself that might arouse God's anger and signal that his blindness is a punishment: "Whatever I have written, yea, at any time (since the royalists in their exultation imagine I am now suffering for it, by way of atonement, as they will have it) I call the same God to witness, that I have written nothing, which I was not persuaded at the time, and am still persuaded, was right, and true, and pleasing to God" (CM 8:67). Nor were his motives for writing ulterior, out of a desire for personal profit or fame; rather, he chose deliberately to lose what remained of his sight in order to write on behalf of the republican cause (CM 8:67). These reflections presuppose the idea that, in the matter of both human and divine justice, our guilt should be somehow intelligible to us, as otherwise judgment would be at once meaningless and without moral force. For the same reason that Milton resists the implication of supralapsarianism—that we are arbitrarily elect or reprobate, without recognizance—he refuses to believe that his guilt would be hidden from his own inquiry. Indeed, his very identification of deity with truth asserts the ultimate and fundamental intelligibility of good and evil, even or perhaps especially when they seem most obscure.

In a peculiarly salient analogy, Milton proceeds to compare his choice between writing and retaining his sight to the decision Achilles must make between glory and long life. And once again, as he did with Phineus, he revises the story, keeping as the point of comparison a dilemma between two desirables but transfiguring the "look" we assign the right and true:

> above all, I have done this, with a view not only to the deliverance of the commonwealth, but likewise of the church. Hence, when that office against the royal defence was publicly assigned me, and at a time when not only my health was unfavorable, but when I had nearly lost the sight of my other eye; and my physicians expressly foretold, that if I undertook the task, I should in a short time lose both. . . . I thought with myself, that there were many who purchased a less good with a greater evil; for example—glory, with death. On the contrary, I proposed to purchase a greater good with a less evil; namely, at the price of blindness only, to perform one of the noblest acts of duty; and duty, being a thing in its own nature more substantial even than glory, ought on that account to be more desired and venerated. I decided, therefore, that, as the use of light would be allowed me for so short a time, it ought to be enjoyed with the greatest possible utility to the public. These are the reasons of my choice; these the causes of my loss. (CM 8:67–71)

In distinguishing the object of his sacrifice, the common good as against personal glory, Milton meditates on the liabilities of his less prepossessing pursuit. An act of glory compels our acclaim, being something that is intensely apparent, that makes its appeal inescapably to the mind as grand, vivid, beautiful, splendid; this is the way sheer celebrity can create the impression of a positive, unequivocal significance. Duty and the common good, on the other hand, are never so fine, so popular, or so distinct as ideas, and for those reasons more subject to cavil and debate. Hence the force here of Milton's "ought": it is as though, in going blind, he has chosen not one but two kinds of obscurity, besides "the dimness which is produced by a stain" on his character (CM 8:117); and the seductive ephemera or superficies of things which he has foregone now more completely define his sense of lost glamour and reputation (CM 8:71):

> As to blindness, I would rather at last have mine, if it must be so, than either theirs, More, or yours. Yours, immersed in the lowest sense, so blinds your minds, that you can see nothing sound or solid; mine, with which you reproach me, deprives things merely of their colour and surface; but

takes not from the mind's contemplation whatever is real and permanent in them. . . . Neither am I concerned at being classed, though you think this a miserable thing, with the blind, with the afflicted, with the sorrowful, with the weak; since there is a hope, that, on this account, I have a nearer claim to the mercy and protection of the sovereign father. There is a way . . . through weakness to the greatest strength. May I be one of the weakest, provided only in my weakness that immortal and better vigour be put forth with greater effect; provided only in my darkness the light of the divine countenance does but the more brightly shine: for then I shall at once be the weakest and the most mighty; shall be at once blind, and of the most piercing sight. Thus, through this infirmity should I be consummated, perfected; thus, through this darkness should I be enrobed in light. (CM 8:71–73)

As Luther does with Erasmus, Milton links interpretive to existential complacency: like the great merchants of the world, who prefer to define value by "colour and surface" as against choice and action, his opponents are blind to the more profound reality of *res non apparentes*—the inevident value of things which expresses itself in the religious dilemma of suffering. So he implies that More's sight is more fragile and delusive than his own, caught by that same entrancing, glamorous veneer that episcopacy exalts and over whose seeming value angel and humankind alike come to grief in *Paradise Lost*. At the same time, the Pauline fugue of paradox succeeding this point does not argue Milton's transcendence of his suffering: on the contrary, it has the same subjunctive, proleptic character as the psalms and prophets, an assertion of his faith against the gross constructions royalism places on his blindness. In that moment when deity and the world seem most inimical to self, when belief itself has grown "simply impossible and absurd," Milton makes God in Luther's sense (*LW* 26:227). His paradox is therefore therapeutic: it offers a picture of his blindness that addresses the mere fact not arbitrarily but judiciously, discriminately, according to the variable circumstances attending it which include his faith in a God that does not appear as such:

The divine law, the divine favour, has made us not merely secure, but, as it were, sacred, from the injuries of men; nor would seem to have brought this darkness upon us so much by inducing a dimness of the eyes, as by the overshadowing of heavenly wings; and not unfrequently is wont to illumine it again, when produced, by an inward and far surpassing light. To this I attribute the more than ordinary civilities, attentions, and visits of friends. . . . For they do not suppose that by this misfortune I am rendered altogether a nullity; they do not suppose that all which belongs to a man of sense and integrity is situated in his eyes. Besides, as I am not grown torpid by indolence, since my eyes have deserted me, but am still active, still ready to advance among the foremost to the most arduous struggles for liberty; I am not therefore deserted even by men of the first rank in the state. On the contrary, such men, considering the condition of humanity, show me favour and indulgence, as to one who has completed his services; and readily grant me exemption and retirement. (CM 8:73–75)

If royalism in the persons of Mrs. Sadleir and More reduces the whole person to its distasteful affliction, the impalpables of Milton's mind to his physical incapacity, deity itself expands the significance of his blindness through the exceptional regard his friends and associates show him. What may appear to others as a slighting and degradation by providence, experience itself endows with an opposed meaning, just as Milton claims that his most salient feature in the view of his opponents—his eyes—tells us the least about him. Notwithstanding this principle, Milton's endless vanity moves him to report that his eyes do not *look* impaired, that his face does not reveal his disability, so that "In this respect only am I a dissembler; and here, it is against my will": whatever deception is practiced in the case of his blindness is not his but his interpreters', who impute to this affliction the sign of divine anathema (CM 8:61). By contrast, Milton experiences the loss of sight as a grace extended to him in this life; because far from shunning him, his immediate community has treated him with such generosity and consideration of his dignity as a person, that their human kindness leads him to imagine that God may have lit him "by an inward and far surpassing light" than the one now obscured.

Moreover, as this image of illumination inevitably suggests, he continues to perform at least some of the duties of his office and, as the *Second Defense* itself proves, to write. And since it was this activity to which his blindness should have put a stop, as the price divinely exacted for traducing the king, he implicitly contravenes the royalist slander by still writing. His unspoken fears have thus gone unrealized, or at least impressively resisted in the process of composing his own apology here—namely, that he might be cut off from all possibility of making himself known and understood, betrayed by his body and vocation into seeming other than himself, and so helpless to prevent a worse transformation than blindness itself. But his writing preserves him from this fate. He is not silenced, although denied a hearing by Mrs. Sadleir and those who share her opinion of him (a shunning which, despite his protestations of forbearance, always troubles him). The profound relief and pleasure at being allowed to defeat the predictions of his enemies and make his own sense of his affliction (as against accepting the one thrust upon him) is such that his blindness has for him the quality of a special dispensation from God, to which the publication of the *Second Defense* palpably testifies. It is crucial to note that Milton does not admit the meaning of his blindness to be supernatural in the sense of a mark and fate magically, ineluctably imposed upon him—what he calls the "dreamy forgeries" of his enemies, who in the process of reviling him vilify deity's judgments (CM 8:71). To his own discomfiture, deity does not pander thus egregiously to human prejudice and desire, but like the God of his new mythology tends largely to defy them, creating a perpetual gap between the supernatural deity we project for ourselves and the preternatural one incongruously expressed in this world. We cannot read our human fate into the nature and intent of God—the sum of the argument from glory—unless we wish to suffer a terrible disenchantment; yet the religious world is not the less marvelous for being merely preternatural, that is, more and other than we suppose. As Milton reads his predicament, it is an ongoing disclosure of the unknown that observes the manner of revelation itself, where God answers prophecy in new, surprising, and still more pregnant terms.

His concatenation of paradox enacts this difference by bringing good out of the evil of his own misfortune, as Joseph declares God to have done with his enslavement. I mention Joseph again because Milton does not assert by his version of paradox some transcendent or supersensible reality (a symbolic force we too readily ascribe to figures of "light," "the spiritual," or "the internal," whose meaning varies with their use). Paradox bears instead on how humanity elucidates, as it were, the world expressive of deity, because the sense we give to our experience is the tie that binds us to an unseen God. As the *Areopagitica* argues, we are more likely to experience what is significant and valuable in the form of a difficult, perhaps ungainly, choice, whose conditions appear as hard as its satisfactions seem obscure—a strange, inevident good that may go unrecognized by others, even derided and reviled, and therefore functionally invisible. Milton does not suggest his blindness will provide him an immediate redemption from suffering or for that matter, a mystical rapture; instead, he prophesies a "consummation" that will emerge over course of time and sustained affliction, as an exertion of faith. He is talking about a meaning elective, evolving, and historical, not a meaning decreed by the overt facts of our lives, which avoids or suppresses their human reality. Rather, his use of paradox embeds meaning in the circumstances surrounding his affliction, which is evidence understood not from the vantage of glory or reputation, but in a forensic manner. Its significance consists in Milton's disposition toward his infirmity and the disposition of others toward him, all of which—as humanly mysterious—have yet to be fully revealed, much less rightly understood.

Milton's truth, like his predicament, is therefore something moral and judicatory as against transcendent, precisely because it presents itself to him as a dilemma of understanding. Because his affliction is incompatible with what he knows to be his motives in writing, which sought truth and the general welfare, it cannot mean to him what it does to More and Mrs. Sadleir—a graphic retribution for his particular brand of wrongdoing. But since deity does not allow martyrdom to be an index of truth, it cannot have the traditional import of Phineus's story—either saintly suffering in a just cause, or as the sacral blindness of those who penetrate divine mysteries. His affliction remains at once ordinary, as the unsurprising consequence of his intellectual habits, and a sudden and anomalous jeopardy, because it threatens to deny him the one identity and recognition he has never ceased to crave—as an eminent English and Protestant poet. He must therefore struggle to understand and vindicate its occurrence in relation to a good and truth-loving God; and he does this by attending to the circumstances, both immediate and potential, which might give him a better idea what to make of it. Thus, somewhat later in this excursus, when Milton returns to the example of Achilles, he pointedly disclaims the hero's arms, so as to emphasize what he has chosen to relinquish along with his sight:

> for though I could most ardently wish that I were Ulysses, that is, that I had deserved the most highly of all my country; yet, I covet not the arms of Achilles; I seek not to carry before me the heavens painted on my shield, which others may look to in a contest, though I do not; it is my endeavour to bear on my shoulders, a real not a painted burden, to be felt by myself, rather than by others. Indeed, as I have no private malice or enmity against any man, nor, as far as I know, has any man against me, I am the less concerned at the torrent of abuse which is cast upon me, at the numberless reproaches which are hurled against me, as I bear all this not for myself, but for the sake of the commonwealth. (CM 8:85)

In effect, Milton declares that he does not seek the false paradise that glory might have won him, preferring to endure his sufferings—both of blindness and ignominy—with what he earlier calls his "consciousness of what I have done" to preserve him, in the hope of gaining a truer and more substantial bliss (CM 8:71). But there is more than one aspect to the figure of Achilles' shield: seen one way, the imperceptible weight that he alone feels is his devotion to the public good. Seen another, it is the cost of carrying this burden in the world, in that he is made to appear other than he is, and is thus misunderstood and unknown. And in yet another, it is the imperative of conscience pursuing a different standard and a different heaven as its reward—those of an inevident God and truth. By contrast, the arms of Achilles, that emblem of glory and reputation but also of thwarted, internecine desire, is no actual but merely an ostensible defense—like the glittering trash of episcopacy, an ornament not worth the contest. The shield is a device for brandishing, for self-aggrandizement, but not for use in guarding against the assault of afflictions like those presently plaguing Milton. Faith alone provides such shelter, as "the assurance of things hoped for, the conviction of things not seen."

Extrinsic Paragraphs

In Milton's reading of the Genesis myth, heroism begins with the loss or countermanding of this ostensible identity between glory and truth (we should remember Eve's chivalrous reasons for separating from Adam), which is the occasion that usually elicits the second sort of justifying from him. We may think of heroism as fortitude in affliction and thus as imitating Christ and still not think of it as Milton does, since the issue to him isn't bearing up stoically under pain and misfortune so much as it is enduring the trial of insignificance or misunderstanding. Almost all of Milton's sonnets speak to this perplexity in one way or another: insofar as their complaints arise from a crisis of desire, the crisis is engendered by issues of identification or, as Cavell would put it, of acknowledgment—of recognizing or being recognized according to one's claims. For there always seems to be a barrier against such recognition that must be confronted by Milton's speakers or their subjects. It happens with the "virgin wise and pure" in "Lady, that in the prime," to Cromwell and, strangely enough, to the massacred Waldensians who regularly serve as Milton's example of an indomitably faithful people. Milton recounts his own experience of this impasse, in the sonnet deploring the reception of his divorce tracts, "On the Detraction which followed upon my Writing Certain Treatises," or still more intimately, in the confessional sonnets "How soon hath time," "When I consider how my light is spent," or "Methought I saw my late espoused saint." Or else he calls for a similar barrier of prejudice and custom, this time to the public good, to be lifted by the likes of Fairfax, Cromwell, Vane, and of course deity itself.

The sonnets thus depart from the conventional topics of erotic or political praise and blame to meditate on the precedent problem of theodicy—this chronic order of injustice and failure of acknowledgment committed by a world resistant to the truth more largely, if not to the speaker himself. And if the world is adversarial, there is always the implication that the providence governing it permits and may even foster the injustice humanity commits. In other words, a discrepancy between human and divine ideas of right is implicit in the sonnets, whether the speaker locates this gap between the world and himself, the world and God, or more terribly, between God and himself. Like the proems of *Paradise Lost*, Milton's sonnets of this temper make something very like psalmic lament, which of course includes in its protocols the related ideas of supplication and prophetic or promised redemption, even as lament also implicates a God who is accessory to this injustice, this contradiction of truth and right. However, in his sonnet to Skinner on his blindness, written about the time of the *Second Defense*, Milton's speaker singularly and expressly refuses to recriminate with deity; so there is no complaint as such motivating his utterance or organizing the sonnet's argument, only a description of how he sustains his loss:

> Cyriack, this three years' day these eyes, though clear
>   To outward view, of blemish or of spot;
>   Bereft of light their seeing have forgot,
>   Nor to their idle orbs doth sight appear
> Of sun or moon or star throughout the year,
>   Or man or woman. Yet I argue not
>   Against heaven's hand or will, nor bate a jot
>   Of heart or hope; but still bear up and steer
> Right onward. What supports me dost thou ask?
>   The conscience, friend, to have lost them overplied
>   In liberty's defence, my noble task,

> Of which all Europe talks from side to side.
>   This thought might lead me through the world's vain mask
>   Content though blind, had I no better guide.
>   (LM 1–14)

The consolation of conscience—that "consciousness of rectitude" to which Milton refers in his own defense—does not efface but rather underscores the problem of injustice posed by the speaker's blindness and captured in the figure of "the world's vain mask." This last phrase evokes a manifold sightlessness and works ironically to define the significance of his own blindness: on the one hand, masking implies an aversion to recognizing or being recognized truly; on the other, it describes an obliviousness to the actual condition of human being—that is to say, its mortality whose echo is the speaker's own sufferings—which renders any such masquerade both self-deluding and futile. He escapes this futility and delusion through his "noble task," that act of conscience in defense of human liberty whose only certain result is his lost sight. But unlike the larger world, the speaker believes that he and his nation have defended the truth, even though it has won them both (so his choice of words suggests) more infamy than recognition, like the regicide itself. But the various permutations of blindness and acknowledgment here do not expunge the speaker's loss by any means, since otherwise he would not linger on the idea of the things he can no longer see. Nor does he represent himself as redeemed from his predicament by conscience, which tells him only that it was a sacrifice well worth making. He is still blind and still requires a guide, despite the palliating conviction of his rectitude.

The real token of the speaker's suffering, as well as the general disorder and injustice of the world that his predicament evokes, is the sonnet's own dislocated form, which is a tactic frequently adopted by Milton, although it never seems to mean quite the same thing. While the proper rhyme scheme is meticulously observed, I would argue that the disruption of the Petrarchan syntax to the point of breakdown expresses the speaker's sense of lost sympathy or attunement with the world, with its logic if not its timing. In effect, his thoughts and his articulation no longer coincide with what is understood or expected; and *that* disunity is the dramatic occasion of Milton's writing the sonnet to Skinner as much as the anniversary of his blindness. The speaker's sense of alienation—of being set apart from "sun or moon or star throughout the year, / Or man or woman"—demands an acknowledgment that circumstance and the indifference of the world confines to a personal confession. So Milton composes a sonnet to his friend Skinner, which at once captures and fulfills this need for understanding and recognition in the way Wittgenstein argues for all our expressions of hope or expectation. However submerged the motive may be in the speaker's expression, his very enlisting of a witness challenges the justice of this compound oblivion he must endure. It could even suggest that by suppressing the sonnet complaint, Milton further pursues the poem's estrangement from received understandings, aggravating the havoc that suffering has already wrought in its formal logic. Given the speaker's alienation, the tortured sonnet form as well as the unerring and almost habitual ambiguity of Milton's final reference, the question remains whether conscience is indeed the speaker's "better guide," or whether it is the locus of his confusion, which is what happens to Jeremiah and Job. Like the cognate language of paradox in Milton's apologetics or the proems of *Paradise Lost*, the peculiar objects of faith inevitably raise this moral and forensic dilemma. I refer to the predicament in which suffering is not admirable but difficult, offensive, and misunderstood, an agony as much or more of mind than body. For the psychology in Milton's case and his speaker's involves protesting their certainty of God and truth, since the very adherence to these things has rendered their position in the world profoundly ambiguous and insecure.

Such is the predicament of psalmic lament. Beyond his copious citations of the psalter in the tracts and *Christian Doctrine*, and its more subtle and pervasive presence which Mary Anne Radzinowicz has shown in his poetry,[17] Milton translated two sets of nine psalms (1–8 and 80–88) within five years of each other (1648 and 1653), on both occasions most obviously as prosodic experiments. Their further significance is less clear, although Marian Studley has made a persuasive case for the relationship between the second series of translations and the onset of Milton's blindness.[18] Yet despite the arbitrary inclusions of a given sequence and the bare fact that lament dominates the psalter, Milton's selection has evident affinities with the sonnets and proems in that they share a common language of suffering. God is usually experienced as remote or hostile where once he had been familiar and kind; the speaker's friends have turned against him, and he is surrounded by enemies; he suffers in spirit and in body. And from these circumstances emerges speech of both complaint and petition, pleading with the Lord to relieve the distress of the people he had once redeemed and cherished—as the psalmist reminds himself and deity—but also to punish the wicked who are their foes. Of the psalms Milton translates, the one that most completely incorporates the motifs of lament we find in the proems is the last of the 1648 sequence, Psalm 88, whose final lines he renders this way:

> But I to thee O Lord do cry
>   *Ere yet my life be spent,*
> And *up to thee* my prayer *doth hie*
>   Each morn, and thee prevent.
> Why wilt thou Lord my soul forsake,
>   And hide thy face from me,
> That am already bruised, and shake
>   With terror sent from thee;
> Bruised, and afflicted and *so low*
>   As ready to expire,

> While I thy terrors undergo
>   Astonished with thine ire.
> Thy fierce wrath over me doth flow
>   Thy threat'nings cut me through.
> All day they round about me go,
>   Like waves they me pursue.
> Lover and friend thou hast removed
>   And severed from me far.
> They *fly me now* whom I have loved,
>   And as in darkness are.

(LM 53–72)

The psalmist's contemplation of his oblivion, which is imaged as death, Sheol or the pit, the grave and utter darkness, precedes this accusation against God. And whatever the occasion or nature of suffering here (understood as conventional to cultic lament at least in part), his predicament remains that of Jeremiah and Milton's speaker, in which affliction contravenes identity because it seems to alter the nature of relationship to God, thus jeopardizing our place in the order of things. So here not only does the psalmist's affliction assert the displeasure of deity, but that displeasure is also read into the ostracism he faces within his community ("Thou does my friends from me estrange, / And mak'st me odious, / Me to them odious, *for they change*" [Psalm 88:8; LM 33–55]). Like Milton's blindness, there is a strong intimation that the psalmist's suffering is understood to be a judgment upon him, and for that ostensible cause his friends abandon him. Such shunning by God and humanity at once deprives his world of meaning and himself of value and identity. So when the psalmist says that "I am a man, but weak alas / And for that name unfit" and that he is "From life discharged and parted quite / Among the dead *to sleep*" (Psalm 88:4–5; LM 15–17), he laments not just the extinguishing of vitality but his erstwhile significance among the living. And behind the notion of so aberrant a death and his own activity of premature mourning lies his "astonishment" at God's treatment of him—at anger where there had been mercy, silence where there should be reassurance and the promise of redemption. Yet this is the context within which the psalm initially proclaims, "Lord God that does me save and keep" (Psalm 88:1), and which virtually models those seemingly confident expressions that the speaker makes in the proems of *Paradise Lost*. It is important to note that nowhere does the psalmist admit to sin or wrongdoing, to some specific culpability that would deserve his sufferings. On the contrary, deity's outrageousness takes him by surprise, so he complains and wonders at this inexplicable turn of events. Once again, God is the rebel against the right, not he; and although this psalm is unusual in the persistence of its complaint, even in petition, the dilemma of the supplicant is repeated in almost every case of psalmic lament, including those that praise and remember God's salvific acts with thanksgiving.

If we turn to Milton's version of Psalm 86, whose expressions overtly appear more secure and even exuberant, the fact remains that this assurance is almost wholly proleptic in nature, as the psalmist looks toward his redemption from a position of great anxiety: proud and violent men rise up against him, men who do not fear God as he does (Psalm 86:14; LM 49–52); he is poor in spirit and needy (Psalm 86:1; LM 3–4); by implication, God's face is turned from him (Psalm 86:16; LM 57–58); and he sees himself, for all his lauding and thanking of the Lord, requiring instruction in God's ways (Psalm 86:11; LM 37–40). The implication of these last verses is clear: the psalmist is uncertain of where he stands and lacks understanding of the very thing he requests (Psalm 86:11; LM 37–40). That doubt intrudes upon his petition because his implicit predicament is entirely at odds with his felt conviction of faith. His professions of trusting deity are then made despite an actuality altogether subversive of such trust: "Preserve my soul, for I have trod / Thy ways, and love the just, / Save thou thy servant O my God / Who *still* in thee doth trust" (Psalm 86:2; LM 5–8). "Still" is Milton's small and telling interpolation, not just a metrical filler, and I think more indicative of the speaker's predicament in *Paradise Lost* than may at first appear. Its position here suggests what Milton takes to be the psalmist's exemplary position in lament: against what he understands to be his fidelity and righteousness *coram Deo*, he suffers; so the faith he professes is jeopardized by his unaccountable affliction. Yet Radzinowicz, who is fully alive to the negative elements of the proems, sees these primarily as the occasion for the speaker's transcendence.[19] And certainly, projecting the event of theophany in the shape of an inner voice mitigates the force of suffering not just for the speaker but for Milton's reader as well. Such interventions do occur in Milton's sonnets ("When I consider" immediately comes to mind); and they are, as Radzinowicz points out, composed on the model of certain psalms of lament which picture not only the crisis into which Israel and the individual are precipitated, but also their expected deliverance by God, or a renewed sense of assurance taking the form of praise.[20]

Claus Westermann also argues that renewed assurance is the case with Psalm 86, but he understands the significance of this renewal rather differently than Radzinowicz, precisely because it transpires within the context of lament. He doesn't regard it as a moment in which God summarily relieves the psalmist of his own dilemma, allowing him to transcend its dreadful contradiction in more than one sense. Instead, Westermann sees renewal as the opposite movement, an expression of the experience of human finitude and the problem of faith. For humanity in the Judaic scriptures is not "idealized or spiritualized," since these acknowledge "man only within the limitations related in the stories of his creation in Genesis 2–3, the limitations of transitoriness and failure" in which the psalmist's predicament consists.[21] The boundaries of understanding within which any viable transcendence must take place are thus historical or existential, inclusive of the ordinary conditions in which we live. That is why lament alternates with thanksgiving in the psalter: it is time-bound and idea-bound speech even as its picture of God implies another order of existential possibility. Perhaps the most salient sign of these limitations appears in what Westermann terms the lament of the individual (which best describes the speech of Milton's sonnets and proems). There the perceived peril or antagonism comes from within the psalmist's own community, not from without; like Jeremiah's, his crisis arises from the experience of personal, familiar betrayal, exposing the dissolution of communal understandings already in process.[22]

This is typically the position of the prophets in lament, a circumstance that Jeremiah's confessions take to an intolerable extreme. By its very nature, their office makes them uncomfortably exceptional, setting them against the community to which they belong and to whom they speak. But while such a rupture in shared understandings might account for the psalmist's sense of lost value and identity, the antagonism from which he suffers is not just human. His loss is compounded by the unavoidable idea that God has betrayed him too, engulfing his entire world in disorder. And it is this fearful implication which governs the psalter's tonalities of praise and petition: as Westermann observes, the essential impetus of lament is conveyed by the psalmist's question, "how long O Lord" and "why?" Only deity can resolve that issue of understanding, because it is a matter of theodicy—how the wicked are punished and the good rewarded.[23] But in lament, divine justice itself is challenged by the psalmist's senseless sufferings, which Westermann identifies as an "absurdity" impelling him to protest.[24] Indeed, in Westermann's view, one of the psalmic laments most damning of the covenantal God is uttered by that reluctant prophet, Jeremiah, who in spiritual extremis requires the Lord to justify his suffering: "Why did I come forth from the womb / to see toil and sorrow, / and spend my days in shame?" (Jeremiah 20:18). Yet even as they are savaged by experience, neither Jeremiah nor Job, the psalmist nor Milton's speakers, cease to call upon the Lord; for lament is a movement toward petition, if not revelation, as Westermann remarks. Their urgent pursuit of colloquy is the expression of their embattled faith, and the heart of the contradiction they endure, seemingly abused by the God in whom they still valiantly put their hope of justice and redemption. In biblical literature as in Greek tragedy, humanity suffers not only for its apostasy but also because of its devout adherence to the demands of deity and truth; and this absurdity is what drives the faithful to justify God's ways, in the process transfiguring how they understand the covenant between divine and human being and the character of their experience.[25] Something very like that revisionary event is recounted here:

> When I consider how my light is spent,
>   Ere half my days, in this dark world and wide,
>   And that one talent which is death to hide,
>   Lodged with me useless, though my soul more bent
> To serve therewith my maker, and present
>   My true account, lest he returning chide,

>   Doth God exact day-labour, light denied,
>   I fondly ask; but Patience to prevent
> That murmur, soon replies, God doth not need
>   Either man's work or his own gifts, who best
>   Bear his mild yoke, they serve him best, his state
> Is kingly. Thousands at his bidding speed
>   And post o'er land and ocean without rest:
>   They also serve who only stand and wait.
>
>   (*LM* 1–14)

In this, perhaps Milton's most experimental sonnet, the speaker introduces the circumstance fomenting his sensations of personal and universal incoherence: the simultaneous loss of physical and conceptual light or capacity. His blindness exposes a contradiction in the speaker's relationship to deity and truth which the octave laments, concluding with the question about divine injustice that abruptly inaugurates the sestet: "Doth God exact day-labour, light denied." For Milton's speaker murmurs against God because he cannot do the one thing he believes deity demands of him—to use "that one talent which is death to hide," but which in his blindness remains "Lodged with me useless, though my soul more bent / To serve therewith my maker." And while this frustration and its ensuing anxiety move him to urgent colloquy with God and perhaps renewed intelligence, his sufferings like Job's and Luther's are intensified by the conviction of his own rectitude—his "true account." Divine injustice, experienced as the awful discrepancy between his self-knowledge and his predicament, thus obscures within "this dark world and wide" what the speaker feels is his proper and rightful identity. Indeed, the necessity under which he labors entails something still crueler than being deprived of sight and intelligence in one fell swoop. By simply acknowledging deity as his "maker," faith itself catches the speaker in a double bind; for then he sees himself as created by God to do the one thing deity pointedly denies him. So he confronts a dilemma in which one identity excludes the other, with either God or the speaker not as he should be. Yet as Luther would predict, the existential problem is an interpretive one, created by the way the speaker construes the expressions of scripture—in this case, Matthew's parable of the talents whose figurative terms govern the octave.

For while the question "Doth God exact day-labour, light denied" reads as the speaker's reproach to deity and the anguished climax of the octave's heaped up and enjambed clauses, it also expresses with precise equivocality the complaint of the covenanting God against the speaker, who perceives deity as tyrannical and unjust. And this irony extends to the parable's figures of talents and accounting, which Jesus uses to expound the paradox of faith but which the speaker understands as a doctrine of works. Accordingly, in the octave he assigns *res non apparentes* the character not just of symbolic objects like number, but substantial or corporeal ones on the order of Wittgenstein's "arms of God," treating the human soul and the righteousness of God as calculable things he can manipulate and measure by the standards of time and his own judgment. There is even in the speaker's lament a suggestion that peremptory deity has miscalculated the return on its investment, and that it owes him the chance to recoup his talent and balance his religious accounts. This implicit criticism assumes two things about God which Isaiah, Paul, and Luther all emphatically deny: that deity must justify its acts to humankind because—and this tacitly—such glaring anomalies prove God to be fallible ("Does the clay say to him who / fashions it, 'What are you making'? / or 'Your work has no handles'?"). Since the speaker not only anticipates deity's false judgment of his soul but also reads his blindness as divine impunity, he expects a comparable act of God to redress his wrongs—a miraculous restoration of sight, identity, and righteousness all at once, allowing him then to "present my true account." These ideas of course presuppose a likeness and continuity between divine and human, religious and phenonomenal being, an assumption which deludes the speaker into thinking that his religious predicament can be solved simply by curing his bodily suffering. It also explains why he conflates a worldly righteousness with the righteousness of God, expecting providence to secure and ratify his self-estimation, as someone possessed of a talent incipient but incontrovertible because it is God's own gift. By virtue of his talent alone, deity owes him not just vindication but glory.

When this epiphany fails to occur—when blindness intrudes between the speaker and his hopes—he finds himself abandoned to the bind his own theology creates, of being held accountable by God for the one thing God himself has seemingly excluded by his affliction. The speaker's experience of this necessity, in the shape of "that one talent which is death to hide," renders him desolate of identity and understanding yet frantic to reclaim them both, giving the octave a virtually satanic momentum and syntactical confusion (along the lines of Satan's cherubic speech to Uriel). But the workings of providence refuse to conform to his solution and agenda—refuse, that is, to indulge the human penchant for glory—and, in the sudden access of that patience he so manifestly lacks, engage in a further act of divine impropriety. In the sort of formal pun Milton savors, patience "comes before" the Petrarchan volte, thus preventing the speaker's murmur by a sudden rupture in expressive continuity within the eighth and ninth lines.[26] Moreover, although patience supplies an answer to his question, that answer is not the one the speaker looked for and required, since it dismisses every preceding assumption and especially the octave's reigning hypothesis that we can "do" and "work" righteousness *coram Deo*. Instead of performance, patience counsels obedience, as befits its name: "who best / Bear his mild yoke, they serve him best." And the conceptual echo of Samuel's apothegm (and Isaiah's development of that idea in its initial chapters) is matched by a syntactical incongruity as well, with a full stop placed in the middle of the four subsequent lines. Dislocating the sonnet's pattern of closure, patience's speech concurs only to deviate from convention, effectively rebuking the conceptual complacency of reader and speaker alike.

By its very nature, patience is not a deus ex machina or even a voice out of the whirlwind, but in the best sense a mundane human virtue whose force is "not of revelation but of judgement," as Milton distinguishes in Luther's case. It offers neither miracles nor transcendence to console the speaker, but an interpretation of his predicament which admits the inevident and paradoxical: "They also serve who only stand and wait."[27] As the substance of the sonnet's resolution, this statement is not neat and summary but proleptic and equivocal, an account of the speaker's position that is suspended by time and knowledge in the manner of all *res non apparentes*. That is why righteousness in the sestet no longer consists in the quid pro quo, the specious symmetries and objectifications, to which the octave reduces covenant with the creator. Since "God doth not need / Either man's work or his own gifts," we cannot infinitely sustain the delusion of congruence between our doing and deity's; nor does God's "mild yoke" resemble the exacting burden of proof under which the speaker places himself, in supposing that his own actions can determine, in the sense of causing his status *coram Deo*. According to the grammar Luther calls theological, human action is never a transitive force when it refers to God, but an intransitive sign of mutual attitude that faith alone apprehends and expresses, as that posture or inflection of the person toward God which is figured by the sestet's final image of standing and waiting. Even when patience allocates universal activity to God's "kingly" state, the posting of those thousands says little about the sender but everything about his message, after the fashion of Ezekiel's temple in *The Reason of Church Government*. For these multitudes and their immense movements don't accomplish in themselves anything more than Milton's lone speaker does in his blindness. Their single purpose is to picture God's omnipresent engagement with the world, to convey his universal disposition toward us, which is something we know only mediately through such manifold expressions.

But then, theologically speaking, human existence is all about the incalculable intent of our creator toward us, and not a supernatural account of ourselves—a fact thoroughly obscured by the speaker's morbid self-absorption. To convey this idea, his justification before God becomes a trial of understanding in the face of physical disability and worldly failure, battling his own appearances, as it were. For patience never tells the speaker how he stands in God's eyes, or confirms that now onerous, unnamed talent (arguably the same one vexing Milton for most of his life). In other words, it doesn't assert or promise him a particular identity, much less fame (any more than the early "How soon hath time"). Rather, like the grace shown Milton in his blindness, patience obliquely answers the speaker's complaint, responding not so much to what he says about himself but how he thinks about God. After the perfect inconsequence of the octave's frenetic movement, this shift in understanding and attitude transfigures his forced inaction, which now becomes both effectual and momentous in Luther's sense of faith as passive righteousness—the position from which the speaker relates this entire religious event. Lament itself then occasions the speaker's "turn" or conversion of ideas, as it does with Job and the psalmist: his benighted understanding obliges him to "make God" in the midst of conflict and suffering, and in the process reconceive that fundamental relationship and his own valuation of things. This adjustment implicates a possibility of human significance he himself had foreclosed, revealed by the access of patience and enacted by the sonnet's disfigured expression: the octave's perpetual motion, that simultaneous reproach of creature and creator, the sestet's premature volte and eccentric practice of resolution. After all, the poem is a study in the chronic assault that Luther calls *Anfechtung*, a recurrent crisis the speaker relates in his own case to an exemplary purpose: he wants to show how faith understands the God and truth we habitually conceal from ourselves, that is, until they are revealed in suffering by a tremendous act of imagination and expression—the peculiar aptitude of poets.[28]

THE MEANING, NOT THE NAME

This account of the speaker's position tends to fit with the odd combination of tentative and inordinate statement obtaining in Milton's proems or "invocations" to *Paradise Lost*. It is easy to see these poetic occasions as demonstrating the divine afflatus they request, following Jonathan Richardson's report on the way Milton wrote his poem: "that he frequently Compos'd lying in Bed in a Morning ('twas Winter Sure Then) I have been Well inform'd, that when he could not Sleep, but lay Awake whole Nights, he Try'd; not One Verse could he make; at Other times flow'd *Easy his Unpremeditated Verse*, with a certain *Impetus* and *Aestro*, as Himself seem'd to Believe. Then, at what Hour soever, he rung for his Daughter to Secure what Came."[29] Despite the fact that Richardson unabashedly patterns his account on what the speaker says in *Paradise Lost*, the story conjures up just the sort of marvelous enabling, whether expressive or encyclopedic, one would like an invocation to produce. His enthusiastic reading of Milton's device could even supply some insight into the sensations of genius, which has its own peculiar fascination as Richardson himself could attest—a victim of Milton's posthumous celebrity if ever there was one. More cynically, Richardson's account argues that Milton surpassed his predecessors in the epic, if only in this one regard: that where their invocations were largely ritual or figural, his were real after a fashion, depicting his own fervent belief in John Milton the latter-day oracle. The speaker's hesitance in locating and naming different supernal agencies would thus respect their superseding power and authority (and by extension his own), in keeping with the vaunted superiority of Milton's epic subject and argument. But one needn't accept a supernaturalist reading of this convention or Milton's language to argue the invocations' transcendental force, especially if deity or the spiritual are made a proxy for other equally inevident but more naturalized principles like the poet's mind, reason, imagination, ideology, history, or a range of psychological projections. Then the proems are seen to objectify a universal and normative as well as personal faculty, to which Milton ascribes a degree of godlike power no less consonant with our notion of his egotism than the direct inspiration of the absolute. Either way, Milton's use of this convention is thought to authorize his justification—his version of the truth—so that each time the narrative of *Paradise Lost* reconvenes, despite those obstacles on which the speaker dwells, Milton confirms his own transcendent if insufferable talent.

But one can also understand the proems to say something similar to Milton's apology for himself in *The Second Defense*, as detailing what he wants us to see as the special predicament of his poem. So when, in the opening lines of *Paradise Lost*, Milton memorably proposes to "assert eternal providence, / And justify the ways of God to men" (LM 1.25–26), and to do this by recalling the universal calamity of Adam and Eve's fall, the argument assumes an obvious affinity with the intractable problem of knowing what his blindness means: for both poet and speaker share an impulse to vindicate divine justice in a case of human misfortune. And if, as subsequent proems encourage us to do, we extend the valence of the poem to its speaker's tenuous position in a restored and selectively punitive monarchy (Milton himself was the subject of a royal proclamation in 1660 and briefly in custody, although never incapacitated for office), then the parallel with his own life becomes sustained and involved.[30] Yet the misfortune Milton confronts now is proportionately greater than the loss of his sight, because he has seen the overthrow of his republican, ecclesiastical, and millenarian hopes. These of course were things that consoled him for his blindness in *The Second Defense* and extenuated his sense of what that loss meant, enabling him to resist the notion that his infirmity was punishment by God for the sin of upholding the wrong cause. Because in spite of his blindness, the world still appeared to be going his reformist and republican way: the community that comforted him was not itself dispersed or persecuted; nor had the truth he forwarded at the cost of his blindness been discarded by the public it was meant to benefit. But with the restoration of Stuart monarchy, the problem of glory has returned yet once more to discomfit John Milton, who finds himself solitary, diminished in resources and status, much vilified and fearing for his life. The sole circumstance remaining to mitigate this voluble disaster is of course his poetry, given that his career in controversy and policy is for the moment utterly defunct.

As everyone knows who reads him, *Paradise Lost* embodies a lifetime's desire to express the poet Milton always thought he had in him. It is intimately connected with his sense of self and capacity, and moreover, with the predicament I've described, where identity doesn't take the form we want or assume for it— "knowing my self inferior to my self," as Milton puts the case in *The Reason of Church Government* (CM 3.1:235). If, at this juncture, Milton's blindness does not manifest his grand villainy, so neither regretfully does he look like the oracular artist, the great man, he once claimed to be (a position with which he was all too familiar, since his opponents were always fond of amplifying his insignificance, not to say his turpitude). But with the poem he had so often and so publicly imagined virtually in his hands, and this despite the seemingly insuperable obstacles of blindness and infamy, Milton has had world enough and time to reflect upon that human frailty we call reputation. It is one reason why the topic of a fit audience reappears in the proems, although that idea is more properly the furniture of satire and his own polemics, where in Deutero-Isaiah's phrase, he continually justifies "those sharp, but saving words which would be a terror, and a torment in him to keep back" (CM 3.1:232). Yet if Milton bestows upon his speaker not only the facts of his life but also his own twin fears of odium and insignificance, this is done after the fashion of all art. That is to say, the proems are an ironic expression of their author's self-under-standing, with the speaker of *Paradise Lost* a persona, an actor in the individual drama of creature and creator no less than his counterparts in Milton's previous poetry (from *L'Allegro* and *Il Penseroso* and the Nativity Ode to *Samson Agonistes*), who almost initially and invariably address the problem of theodicy—the vicissitudes of human relationship with a hidden God and truth.

And if report may be trusted in this instance, Milton was right to anticipate the perfectly ordinary oblivion of himself and his masterwork (legend aside, Masson calculates that *Paradise Lost* sold reasonably well)[31]—that is, until the Earl of Dorset went book hunting in Little Britain, as Richardson's story goes, picked up the poem, and gave it to John Dryden: then, sometimes around 1669, a full two years after its first publication, Mr. Milton became a celebrity.[32] Appraising his nephew's account of the event, Masson puts this latest but certainly not final vindication of the poet felicitously: "His uncle had again, at the age of sixty, become a mentionable person. The blind Republican and Regicide had redeemed himself, so far as his redemption was possible, by the atonement of a great poem."[33] Or in Dryden's less ambivalent phrase:

> Three poets, in three distant ages born,
> Greece, Italy, and England did adorn.
> The first in loftiness of thought surpass'd,
> The next in majesty, in both the last:
> The force of Nature could no farther go;
> To make a third, she join'd the former two.
>
> (*Epitaph on Milton*, frontispiece to the
> fourth edition of *Paradise Lost*, 1688)[34]

The remarkable artistry of *Paradise Lost* was bound to secure Milton's reputation, in the sense of a literary eminence that took effect almost immediately. Indeed, the acclaim bestowed on the author was enough to promote a traffic in Miltoniana after his death, with the public sifting his widow for anecdotes and much later, in the person of Addison, relieving the poverty of his elderly daughter Deborah—out of sympathy for her or respect for her father, it is hard to tell.[35] But fame aside, whether Milton managed in *Paradise Lost* to vindicate

more than himself—to justify the ways of deity and truth—remains another
question altogether. Part of this justification necessarily required his showing
that the human condition as well as his own predicament were not simply
divine retribution for an obscure and irresistible sin.[36] Yet, as the tracts more
and less directly anticipate, I think Milton still saw his poem as an occasion for
deity somehow to bring a good yet unknown out of evil, and reconcile his own
ardent idea of the truth with his experience. But to do this would not entail
glory but irony, in keeping with the hiddenness of Milton's God.

The irony of course appears in the fact that it is completely possible to admire
Paradise Lost without allowing it to vindicate Milton's career or his ideas. And
the poet must have found that out for himself in the midst of his sudden glory,
if Milton's reported dismay at being lionized signifies anything more than that
he disliked the interruption of his routine by a different kind of eminence:
persons of rank and repute in the new order.[37] Dryden perhaps excepted, few of
these appear to have grasped the full import of *Paradise Lost* any more than Dr.
Johnson did. It is thus thoroughly appropriate that Johnson in the *Life* would
capture, however inadvertently, the sensation of this impasse in Milton's recognition. He has been relating the blind poet's infamous expedient of having two
of his daughters, most likely the middle one, Mary, read to him in languages
which he taught them to pronounce but not to understand. Johnson's comment
on "the scene of misery which this mode of intellectual labour sets before our
eyes" is as always remarkable in its sensitivity: "It is hard to determine whether
the daughters or the father are most to be lamented," since "A language not
understood can never be so read as to give pleasure, and very seldom so as to
convey meaning."[38] Required to speak what remained unintelligible to them,
while their father listened to a language estranged from its sense, this mutual
suffering has an ironic resonance in the character of Milton's celebrity, since
his admirers may well have read his poem without understanding it in the way
he did. Then his fame, like his past afflictions, would have felt comparably
inexplicable, comparably obtuse, and comparably a form of durance to him,
which it appears he nevertheless handled with a certain sceptical equanimity.
But Johnson's "scene of misery" would also make a suitable epigraph to the long
tradition of controversy surrounding Milton, and the remarkable gap between
the argument of *Paradise Lost* and what its critics have read there—a predicament not unlike that posed by Luther's masked God or Milton's good swathed
in its own contradiction.

This predicament the poet himself recuperates in the fictional circumstances
of his speaker, whom an impervious world drives to justify himself and the God
who seemingly abandons him. Like the sonnets and the *Second Defense*, here
again the implacable controversy of self-understanding preoccupies Milton's
speaker. If self and deity, as Calvin observes, are best known in their relation,
the reverse is equally true; because when the experience of injustice renders
God dubious and incoherent, identity itself suffers a shock more considerable
and pervasive than the catalog of adventitious error and contradiction we fac-

ilely ascribe to the speaker's "postlapsarian" corruption. That is to say, when we do not obliviously assume that the proems glorify Milton or his God, the speaker's narrative gains a new coherence and the suffering he describes a new force that inflects each word and, I would argue, thoroughly reorients the meaning of a myth whose very familiarity has become an obstacle to its understanding. This effect is ironical, for neither sonnets nor proems are mere recitals of the poet's wrongs: they argue from inside, ruthlessly and intimately in character, the provocation to apostasy or conversion that suffering ambivalently offers us. For we tend to forget that suffering is why the speaker of *Paradise Lost* is moved to justify in the first place—that his ideas of the good, the right, or the true have proven desperately inadequate to his experience. In this predicament the only recourse that allows him human dignity—the dignity of intelligence—is to wrench a new understanding from the outraging of the ordinary, one which may surprise both him and his reader even as patience surprises the speaker in Milton's sonnet.

Something to this effect occurs with Jeremiah and the new covenant he prophesies, a covenant von Rad claims is unusual precisely in its stated departure from the old: "the old covenant is broken, and in Jeremiah's view Israel is altogether without one. What is all important is that there is no attempt here—as there was, for example, in Deuteronomy—to re-establish Israel on the old bases. The covenant is entirely new, and in one essential feature it is to surpass the old" (*OTT* 2:212). This covenant is and must be a new thing, because Israel has proven itself incapable of keeping its relationship with God under the Mosaic order; as Jeremiah caustically remarks: "Can the Ethiopian change his skin / Or the leopard his spots? / Then also you can do good / who are accustomed to do evil" (Jeremiah 13:23). And yet the Torah, God's revelation, nevertheless remains the foundation of the new order: what has changed is not the sacred text but Israel's apprehension of it, for God promises his people a new heart to understand and obey him. Recalling yet once more his preface to the Latin works, Luther experiences a conflict like Jeremiah's, forced by private agony to dissent from a canonical text—in this case, Paul's letter to the Romans, which like the Torah for Judaism defines in his mind what it means to be Christian. Without Romans, Luther believes himself unable to have identity or relationship *coram Deo*; therefore he must scrupulously, exactly conserve the text even as every aspect of his being protests against what it appears implacably to argue. That is why the interpretive reconciliation of self with text brings Luther such unutterable pleasure and relief, with scripture assuming a loving face where it had been nothing but inimical to him, even as the old covenant had proven to Israel.

As a conceptual trope or "turn," irony can perform a similar transfiguration of the necessary and familiar, which under its expressive sway abruptly gains an expanded, innovative coherence complicating our ideas of the way things are. On this head, Kenneth Burke comments that, for irony to be felt at all, it first requires a strong decorum, a sense of proprieties well established or clearly recollected, against which to work the peculiar effect he terms perspective "by planned incongruity."[39] Thus a propensity for the incongruous—"*the realm of 'gargoyles'* " as Burke puts it—often appears in cultures where custom or convention exerts the most powerful hold on human understanding.[40] Confining this phenomenon to poets, the Athens of Euripides and Aristophanes comes to mind, as well as imperial Rome and its satirists, or the Italy of Dante and Boccaccio, from whose separate cultural proprieties the ironic takes its departure as an aberrant, excessive, or recalcitrant expression. But irony of the comprehensive, assumption-altering sort that informs any encounter with the hidden God can do something besides conserving through extravagant negation our received patterns of value and significance—satire's casual strategy. And it can disclose a more profound crisis and threshold of meaning than the ever shifting play of human expression: as Burke goes on to remark, the incongruous can be revolutionary—not in its elements, which must be received ideas and forms, but in its conceptual implications.

Similarly, Cavell observes that an acute consciousness of the ordinary itself has something *inherently* "uncanny," absurd, or grotesque about it, precisely because the act of reflecting upon our familiar assumptions estranges us from them—relieves them of their perfunctory, repetitive status in order to recreate their wonted force—to give them renewed vitality: "Sharing the intuition that human existence stands in need not of reform but of reformation, of a change that has the structure of a transfiguration, Wittgenstein's insight is that the ordinary has, and alone has, the power to move the ordinary, to leave the human habitat habitable, the same transfigured."[41] The conventional—exegetical, institutional, artistic—stands to Milton's intellectual and expressive practice in this way, as the improbable, antipathetic medium of a transfigured understanding. And it does so for the reasons Cavell locates in Wittgenstein, because Milton apprehends no revolution or utopia that evades the ordinary, the mundane condition of human being. Although occasioned, not designed, the second order of justifying shares this revisionary role with Burke's "planned incongruity" and Cavell's "uncanny," because injustice and the conceptual disorder ensuing from that event warrant our reimagining the world *as we have it*—not as we would have it be. And in that world incorrigibly riven by injustice, we cannot tell what shape truth will take, any more than Jeremiah can picture the new covenant he prophesies; the revolution, if there is one, lies rather in how we approach these things.

With Milton, this innovative approach cannot be divorced from his brand of neoclassicism, which is experimental and even avant-garde like Ben Jonson's, especially when viewed from the vantage of prevailing taste. Not unusually for a rhetorical culture, he handles *traditio* and *imitatio* as expressive principles equally as conducive to present deviation as they are to the enterprise of perfection. An obvious instance would be Milton's prefatory note announcing and defending the blank verse of *Paradise Lost*, in which he counterposes rhyme to the metrical syntax of the ancients and presumably Shakespeare: "This neglect then of rhyme so little is to be taken for a defect, though it may seem so perhaps to vulgar readers, that it rather is to be esteemed an example set, the first in English, of ancient liberty recovered to heroic poem from the troublesome and modern bondage of rhyming" (*LM* 456–57). His paradoxical associations here of decorum with neglect, the exemplary with the defective, the customary with the modern, classicism with freedom, militate against any categorical or generalized explanation for his art—the demise of the medieval synthesis; the eclipse of Christian humanism; the rise of capitalism or science; the onset of the baroque, enlightenment, or modernity. It also obliges us fully to admit Milton's exceptionality within convention, his particular revision of the cultural materials at hand; and this admission in turn requires an effort to grasp the position and motive behind a species of expression which invites, even insists, upon the acknowledgment of its eccentricity, indecorum, and sheer difficulty. It so happens that one of Cavell's earliest projects has been to describe this formative dissenter—an intelligence that both engages and breaks our familiar understandings, as he argues here for Luther, Rousseau, Thoreau, and Wittgenstein himself:

> The rhetoric of humanity as a form of life, or a level of life, standing in need of something like transfiguration—some radical change, but as it were from inside, not *by* anything; some say in another birth, symbolizing a different order of natural reactions—is typical of a line of apparently contradictory sensibilities, ones that may appear as radically innovative (in action or feeling) or radically conservative: Luther was such a sensibility; so were Rousseau and Thoreau. Thoreau calls himself disobedient, but what he means is not that he refuses to listen but that he insists on listening differently while still comprehensibly. He calls what he does revising (mythology). Sensibilities in this line seem better called revisors than reformers or revolutionaries.
> They can seem to make themselves willfully difficult to understand.[42]

The difficulty Cavell raises is peculiarly the one he himself confronts in describing such minds, which is that they are virtually impossible to appreciate— Milton no less than Thoreau, who inscribes the former in his own writings.[43] If these persons differ from other thinkers, they differ in often deceptive and sometimes inexpressive ways, which can be entirely misconstrued or entirely overlooked in the effort to understand them. That is because we are inclined to pursue what seems obvious or readily legible about their work, in both admiring and dismissing it; for novelty itself has a certain recognizable order and shape to it, a tacit convention as it were, which may mislead us into assertions about these writers' radical or conservative impetus. But the kind of revisionary activity Cavell has in mind cannot be so easily defined or contained by its critics: one need only think of Dr. Johnson's travails in his *Life* of the poet, or for that matter Eliot's response or Empson's, to admit the aptitude of Cavell's picture for Milton. His virtuosic use of convention, taken in its broadest sense, tends rather to efface what he actually does with it; and even when we suppose him radical, it is just this appearance of conventionalism that moves critics (from Blake and Shelley through Kerrigan) to insist upon the author's unconsciousness of his own impulses and effects in writing. But that argument misconceives the nature of dissent like Milton's, which still participates in a community of meaning, a "form of life," even as it proposes to transfigure that community from within. The assiduous attention Milton gives to making himself intelligible in the tracts or poetry expresses this complex engagement of his ideas with his historical moment. So does the formal difficulty of his work—that novel, often notorious use of language that disturbs Johnson and Eliot, not to mention Milton's editors. In another place but on the same topic, Cavell observes:

> It is worth saying that conventions can be changed because it is essential to a convention that it be in service of some project, and you do not know a priori which set of procedures is better than others for that project. That is, it is internal to a convention that it be open to change *in convention*, in the convening of those subject to it, in whose behavior it lives. . . . Only masters of a game, perfect slaves to that project, are in a position to establish conventions which better serve its essence. That is why deep revolutionary changes can result from attempts to conserve a project, to take it back to its idea, keep it in touch with its history. To demand that the law be fulfilled, every jot and tittle, will destroy the law as it stands, if it has moved too far from its origins. Only a priest could have confronted his set of practices with its origins so deeply as to set the terms of Reformation. (CR 120–21)

This last reference to Luther tells everything about Milton's lifelong project of justification—always seeking to bring his understanding, his art, his world into accordance with the expressions of a hidden God. The proems not only exhibit the enormous pressure of this informing conviction; they also carry the burden of its intelligibility, in the shape of an authorial "mythology" not unlike Thoreau's, with which Milton endows the *ego* of *Paradise Lost*. This automorphic figure pictures the poet quite differently than does *The Reason of Church Government*, where Milton projects an image of himself as the future dispenser of untrammeled truth to a waiting nation. Yet even here, he imagines this prophetic Milton in order "to disswade the intelligent and equal auditor" from reducing the tract's author to a hack mired in "distastfull and disquietous" controversy, "lest it should be still imputed to me, as I have found it hath bin, that some self-pleasing humor of vain-glory hath incited me to contest with men of high estimation, now while green yeers are upon my head" (CM 3.1:233, 234). If the pamphlet anticipates a perennial, incontrovertible recognition for Milton and his sometime-masterpiece—famously, that "I might perhaps leave something so written to aftertimes, as they should not willingly let it die"—once again, an image of glory arises from the opposed predicament, in which he

appears to his audience vulgar, presumptuous, incompetent: that is, other than
how he appears to himself (CM 3.1.236). The proems of *Paradise Lost* work this
situation into their own mythology of the speaker, but not uncritically. Like
Adam's picture of an Eve "so absolute . . . And in her self complete," Milton's
youthful dream of a splendid, unsullied achievement becomes the speaker's
frailty, the furniture of both a humanly needful illusion and the crisis leading
to his near-apostasy (LM 8.547–48). For by the time Milton writes his great
work, he recognizes no truth unimplicated in its circumstances, no good without the knowledge of evil, no mortal God; and he observes this principle of
theodicy by having his speaker impersonate himself—an irony too often eluding Milton's readers even as it does Thoreau's.

And that irony organizes the whole poem. Just as there is no magical resolution of difficulty in Milton's sonnets or in the *Second Defense*, so there is no
direct or unambiguous response to the speaker's petitions that might perfectly
secure the authority of his narrative, which remains messianic, as John Guillory
has argued for Milton himself.[44] The speaker too has only the ordinary consolation of his own perseverance in telling the story, with the result that speech
here is the locus of revelation in a transfigured but not a supernatural sense. If
the speaker's narrative, no less than Milton's, responds to the mysterious economy of suffering in a world governed by a good and just God, his initial purpose
in retelling the Fall is not the poet's. Because it is the speaker, not Milton, who
wants to trace an impossible origin, to lay blame on some first cause for "man's
first disobedience" and his own affliction, thus alleviating the morbid sense of
a discrepant fate which haunts the proems:

> Say first, for heaven hides nothing from thy view
> Nor the deep tract of hell, say first what cause
> Moved our grand parents in that happy state,
> Favoured of heaven so highly, to fall off
> From their creator, and transgress his will
> For one restraint, lords of the world besides?
> Who first seduced them to that foul revolt?
>
> (LM 1.27–33)

And in urgently pursuing that first cause, the speaker himself violates the "one
restraint" Milton peculiarly pictures in the interdiction the Lord places on the
tree of the knowledge of good and evil: namely, the distinction between creator
and creature, the hiddenness of a God whose expressions are inexplicable in
causal terms. It is only in the course of Milton's poem that the speaker comes to
understand his narrative, however equivocally, as an exemplary case differently
describing his own predicament. Indeed, this is the thrust of the final proem.
But like his predecessors in lamentation—Job, Jeremiah, the psalmist, the Jesus
of Mark and Matthew—the speaker suffers the sensation of being utterly forsaken and betrayed by the God to whom he has dedicated himself, and whose
providence now feels like the most intractable necessity. So he tells the story

of humanity's fall to understand and relieve his sufferings; but he must do this without recourse to an expedient admission of guilt, which he knows is subjectively false, or to the explanations of other people not so afflicted, since his position is not theirs. Thus it isn't sufficient to say, as the speaker may be said to do, that *Paradise Lost* describes how sin first came into the world, or how the disobedience of our first parents brought about the perpetual apostasy of humankind, or the British nation, much less that renegade John Milton whom Dr. Johnson abhors. Milton doesn't leave his argument there, with human degradation, but places it within the larger context of our redemption by "one greater man." At the same time, if the speaker's prayers are answered, they are answered in no definitive way since we leave him, as we leave Adam and Eve, in the position to which events and his own actions have brought him and where he began his narrative—choosing how he will understand his own suffering, his own humanity.

Like that of Adam and Eve, the shape of the speaker's redemption does not appear as such in *Paradise Lost*; instead, it is expressed in the quality of his understanding as it is our first parents'—how they conceive their common, creatural predicament. In the tracts Milton himself handles his own or others' figurative blindness as a strange, surprising good that demands paradox: strength in weakness, light in darkness, good in evil. His use of this idiom evidently shares something with the language of the proems, which depict the effects of the speaker's recounting—that is, the operation of grace upon his speech—as somehow elucidating but not remedying his situation. For the speaker's justification does not end his suffering: his blindness (the second proem), his ostracism (the third), the tyranny of a received literature that improperly idealizes humanity, mistaking glory for truth (the final excursus in Book Nine). Despite the impact of revelation, these remain for him, as for Adam and Eve, one aspect of their joint humanity. So even as the speaker claims to compose his narrative more or less rhapsodically, his litany of tribulation qualifies that presumptive marvel to dissuade us from supposing (which we have anyway) that, in his case at least, God is in his heaven and all's right with the world. For the proems do not present the speaker agonistically to suggest some mystical overcoming of the flesh and all it is heir to, freeing him up to deliver a sublime truth like the poet-prophet Milton once imagined himself. Instead, in the speaker's figure they enact the superb insight of Luther, that faith in the hidden God represents a chronic crisis or dilemma in our understanding, not only of deity but also of human being and ourselves. As the appalling devastation of his present experience separates the speaker from the self he knew, the people around him, and the established order of things, his very sense of identity requires that he understand and not void by cynicism or ecstasy the world of affliction and injustice he now inhabits. That is the reason he undertakes a justification, and why Milton in a similar position does the same: by telling the story of humanity, they tutor our understanding as well as their own in the ways of a hidden God.

Besides, if the proems served merely to confirm the narrative "truth" of *Paradise Lost*, however grandiosely, Dr. Johnson would not have found it necessary to dismiss such "extrinsick paragraphs" as meaningless to the epic.[45] For these eloquent "superfluities," as he calls them, position the narrative in a way that compromises Johnson's account of *Paradise Lost* as an unheralded palinode, since Milton does not represent his speaker's sufferings as condign punishment for sin, which is how Johnson would like to take them.[46] So Johnson surreptitiously censors the text by confining the force of the proems to Milton's own incorrigible character, methodically and caustically rebutting the speaker's lamentations precisely because the suffering they relate is felt as an injustice and expressed as a complaint. To vindicate God's providence in a case of causeless suffering, which is how the proems ask us to understand the speaker's justification, is an enterprise very different from upholding deity when it duly inflicts punishment for transgression. The latter argument makes a rebel against God out of Milton, which is how Dr. Johnson wants to read the poem; but the former makes a rebel out of God, and this is the problem *Paradise Lost* must somehow resolve, since such a scenario isn't so much false as it is unbearable, as William Empson argues on Satan's behalf. Like Job and Jeremiah, Milton's speaker is not condemned in a religious sense by the way he conceives his predicament; but his attitude does intensify the anguish he suffers in confronting a world made incoherent, deprived of its motive and proportion by a God suddenly unrecognizable.

Of course, it could be the case that the speaker's sufferings manifest an underlying dishonesty in himself or in deity, in which case his affliction would then be explicable along the same lines as Tiresias's was to Apollonius. But given the Jobean "consciousness of rectitude" premising his lament, an attitude enabling the speaker to petition deity in the first place, and given Milton's theological axiom that God as truth cannot contradict himself, both these explanations become less rather than more tenable. The only one left is the precedent example of Milton's sonnet: that the speaker, acting in good faith, has somehow misconceived deity's expressions and consequently what God it is that he believes in, so that his sufferings appear meaningless and unjust to him. It can accordingly be argued that the proems exhibit this imaginative failure as a formally skewed and disjointed understanding that begs justification, which is to say, a conversion in religious attitude. And because this attitude consists in interpreting God's ways as they bear on his predicament, the venue of the speaker's revelation would naturally be the narrative of *Paradise Lost*. So rather than see the proems as summarily authorizing his (and by association, Milton's) account of the Fall—either through the speaker's transcendence of his mere humanity, or as Dr. Johnson fears, by expediently defending the career of poet and regicide—it is reasonable to regard them as a sort of prologue to the action. Like the introduction preceding Job's narrative, or the one Goethe in emulation composes for *Faust*, or which Genesis provides for the whole Judaic bible,

Milton's dispersed and episodic prologue establishes a critical scenario within which speaker and reader together must make sense of the Fall.

Prologue-like, the speaker's first address to his muse begins in disparity, not unanimity with God, asserting the reality of human disobedience even as that idea is made almost necessarily to implicate our redemption by "one greater man." This foreshadows the order of human things at his narrative's end, when moments before the expulsion from the garden, Michael announces the gospel to Adam, who in turn declares the Pauline paradox of *felix culpa*:

> Full of doubt I stand,
> Whether I should repent me now of sin
> By me done and occasioned, or rejoice
> Much more, that much more good thereof shall spring,
> To God more glory, more good will to men
> From God, and over wrath grace shall abound.
>
> (LM 12.473–78)

It is not that Adam no longer feels guilt or remorse for his transgression, or that he is less conscious of what he has lost by it, or even that he has properly understood everything Michael relates to him. Rather, he is allowed to *conceive* the suffering into which humanity has fallen as a prospective good, in excess of the human evil he has witnessed speculatively with the angel, and which he has already himself begun to undergo. And that idea alters his sense of his predicament, since the gospel message makes divine justice discriminate and transfiguring as against retributive and promiscuous—the universal calamity consequent upon his single sin—which is how it appears to Adam in his despair. The paradox of *felix culpa* in effect transfigures human history, which had seemed little more than cycle upon violent cycle of apostasy in the eleventh book, but which becomes more fully purposive and salvific in the twelfth, as Michael prophesies God's covenant with Abraham.

And just as Abraham takes God at his word, so does Adam to whom providential history is now presented as a word and a promise—figured as Michael's reciting instead of envisioning these new events—in which he chooses to put his faith. Yet the fulfillment of the promise begins with its impact upon our general ancestor, who now faces the prospect of expulsion differently, as possessed of something besides its immediate and tragic force. In this way, Adam's position imitates Milton's in the *Second Defense*; for he has also been given grounds by faith to think of suffering in a manner that revises its overt significance. Even Adam's use of paradox (good in evil, light in darkness), inevitable to any expression of *felix culpa*, retains Milton's emphasis on the ordinary as the realm of marvels. Moreover, because this wonder exists for him by faith alone—choosing to believe in God's promise of human actors and actions which have yet to be born—Adam's paradox revises his present world without transcending it, as a new order of meaning thoroughly contingent and embedded in the tragic history of the Fall and defying all his expectations, which is why Adam abruptly shouts for joy. For God has surprised him with the story of the second Adam, just as God enables Milton, despite his blindness, to surprise his detractors with a great poem and the resurrection of the republican apologist. In the way that they picture the speaker, Milton's proems also prepare toward such a surprise; for speech is this sufferer's defiance of his circumstances and, more crucially, the means by which those afflictions almost compulsively described in the second and third proems are made intelligible and purposive.

The proems themselves are typical of the way Milton re-creates convention in *Paradise Lost*: exchanging the ritual of poetic invocation for the tremendous drama of Lutheran *Anfechtung*, converting the magical, virtually automatic access of knowledge into a situation from which all outward assurance—even petition itself—is evacuated by injustice and suffering. Thus to introduce the vehicle of his God's justification, the narrative of humanity's fall from grace, the speaker requests for himself a new proximity to deity and truth that, in the instance of the brooding Spirit, links natural tenderness with the most awful profundity. As this traditionally ambivalent figure suggests, the speaker's desire for intimacy with the divine arises precisely from his sense of God's remoteness, of being abandoned in the plight to which he helplessly alludes—blindness, ostracism, the extinction of identity and hope.[47] In the psalmic manner, each time the speaker petitions for an understanding and assurance he manifestly lacks, each time he slides irresistibly into lamentation. And this aggravated sense of an antagonism between himself and God is what compels him to compound his solicitation, both in its locales ("that on the secret top / Of Oreb, or of Sinai . . . or if Sion hill / Delight thee more, and Siloa's brook" [*LM* 1.6–12]), in its agencies (the muse, the Spirit, light or the Logos, and by association, Wisdom), and in its epithets ("The meaning, not the name I call" [*LM* 7.5] and "Or hear'st thou rather" [*LM* 3.7]). But despite his supernaturalism—a propensity he shares with Satan and Adam—the speaker cannot simply identify what he seeks, much less perceptibly grasp it; and his efforts to bring this uncertain agency nearer results only in the fecklessness of his speech. The paradox that Milton and Adam each make an explicit feature of their position has then a dramatic resonance here, expressed by the tension between what the speaker requests and how he requests it. Thus the second proem evokes every sort of figural and physical light in order to anticipate the subject of deity and heaven, and to celebrate the speaker's freedom from one exigency of his story—to tell about Satan, sin, and hell, and in the process to exercise those feelings of alienation and loss which move him incontinently to sympathize with his subject.[48] For that "obscure sojourn" evokes more darkness than hell, his own lost sight or human corruption; it figures the capital error of which supernaturalism itself is a symptom and evil an invariable consequence in the reformers' theology and Milton's experience—namely, glory (*LM* 3.15).

Understood as humanity's self-deification, glory is one reason why the speaker talks in the first proem of his "adventurous song" superseding both ancient and modern exponents of the epic convention—"That with no middle flight intends to soar / Above the Aonian mount, while it pursues / Things unattempted yet in prose or rhyme" (*LM* 1.13–16). Yet as the narrative proceeds, another aspect presents itself to this seemingly shameless avowal that the speaker's art will outdo his poetic rivals (the sort of artistic manifesto to which epic speakers, Dante's pilgrim for example, are inclined).[49] But the novel aspect of this claim is fully manifest only in the final proem, where the speaker anticipates the impending estrangement of divine and human being, "That brought into this world a world of woe, / Sin and her shadow Death, and Misery, / Death's harbinger" (*LM* 9.11–13). At this juncture the speaker himself confesses the sublime unpleasantness Dr. Johnson imputes to *Paradise Lost*— "sad task, yet argument / Not less but more heroic"—and this acknowledgment of his subject's difficulty leads him to address the problem of glory in an artistic sense (*LM* 9.13–15). Thus he juxtaposes his own unprepossessing and painful subject with the moral and dramatic wasteland of epic, the trivial plotting and glittering superfluities of chivalric romance:

> Wars, hitherto the only argument
> Heroic deemed, chief mastery to dissect
> With long and tedious havoc fabled knights
> In battles feigned; the better fortitude
> Of patience and heroic martyrdom
> Unsung; or to describe races and games,
> Or tilting furniture, emblazoned shields,
> Impreses quaint, caparisons and steeds;
> Bases and tinsel trappings, gorgeous knights
> At joust and tournament; then marshalled feast
> Served up in hall with sewers, and seneschals.
>
> (*LM* 9.28–38)

We meet here the same issue of Achilles' choice and arms that Milton ponders in the *Second Defense*, namely, the distinction between glory and truth but applied this time to the conventions of heroism as well as epic and romance. If the speaker's claim for "the better fortitude / Of patience and heroic martyrdom" is hardly original, he makes new use of it here, in effect to explode the aristocratic conflation of beauty and honor with the good, which underlies the convention's literally fabulous picture of a splendid, consummate virtue. But Milton doesn't just have in mind the immediate fate of our first parents or Satan's swift degradation of himself in Book Nine: instead, the speaker is acknowledging the same inadvertent disparity of appearance in his art which he suffers in his person. That disparity, however, is designed by the poet, who chooses epic for his great poem equally to criticize those assumptions of meaning and value that, in the form of glory, collapse the human with the divine, the evident with the real, the pleasurable with the good.

This is the way in which Milton's art surpasses convention while observing it: from *Comus* to *Samson Agonistes*, *Lycidas* to the late sonnets, his avid experimentation with "set forms" entails a philosophical disturbance in their plot, a reorienting of their presumptive meaning. And yet, because that revision preserves even as it transfigures the sense of convention, there is an intractable ambiguity to Milton's poetry. On this head, Cavell remarks that it is our attitude in speaking that gives any utterance its interest, its meaningfulness to others and ourselves. Accordingly, he conceives "valuing"—understood as the inflection and implication we give our words, the desire and history they evoke—as "the other face of asserting" which defines the possibilities of meaning in any circumstance: "So that what can be communicated, say a fact, depends upon agreement in valuing rather than the other way around" (CR 94). Thus, in *Paradise Lost*, Milton retains intact the cultural thesis of epic, namely, the grandeur of a heroic humanity descended from the gods yet in itself manifestly ennobling and perfecting deity. But like Dante, he invests that thesis in a world and a predicament repugnant to its valuation, where God and humanity are incommensurables, and the divine antipathetic, to the point of subverting the dignity and significance of human culture. The result of this juxtaposition is a convention fully, acutely understood but to another purpose. I am not referring here to the ostensible practice of Christian humanism, as professing to adapt Greco-Roman forms to Judeo-Christian ideas. For one thing, that practice argues a tacit analogy between these cultural understandings—in their notions of meaning, value, and order—permitting a seemingly unproblematic translation. For another, we tend to assume that ideology shapes convention (a prejudice engendered by the ornamental fallacy of artistic form); but as Cavell suggests, the relation tends to work historically in the opposite direction, with convention by its very precedence determining how any adventitious ideology can be expressed—what it can or cannot say.

Accordingly, Milton does not alter convention in *Paradise Lost* but repositions it: "listening differently while still comprehensibly," he allows epic to figure a human belief about the world profoundly felt and approved, as well as incorrigibly hostile to any relationship with the hidden God of Job, Isaiah, and the psalmist. This is what I mean by saying that, in the poem, Satan is right about God even as God on that very account is right about Satan. For Satan's tragedy is the Father's satire not least because they value the entire order of events—from the Son's exaltation to the fall of humanity—in entirely incompatible ways; and this impasse between creator and creature in the poem's fundamental criteria of meaning appears in how the speaker or his surrogates relate the actions of these antagonists. To invoke Cavell again: "Criteria are the terms in which I *relate what's happening*, make sense of it by giving it its history, say what 'goes before and after.' What I call something, what I *count* as something, is a function of how I *recount* it, tell it" (CR 94). And as Cavell observes in Thoreau's case, one might also say of Milton that he too determines "to tell all and to say nothing" in *Paradise Lost*—to make the speaker's story evince the mutual scandal of Satan's fall from God's grace, which each figure conceives as a categorical betrayal (CR 95). The difficulty confronting the reader of Milton's poetry lies in appreciating that difference, since it involves a peculiar nuance, a certain subtle angle of expression—irony, in other words. So however removed in time and practice, Milton does not suppose that the reformed subject of his epic or the novel identity of the speaker's muse purge invocation ipso facto of its ritualism, the word-magic compelling deity's attendance with a name. It is an index of the speaker's religious extremity that he succumbs to this appealing device and the idea implicit in its use—that if he could just discover the right epithet, or locate the right place for deity, he could master his own predicament. But to presume the efficacy of invocation is to suppose some real likeness and continuity between the divine and its expressions, to transgress the distinction between creator and creation, to argue humanity's supercession of God—in short, as Milton argues in the *Christian Doctrine*, to commit idolatry of the same order as the Catholic mass.

So despite the speaker's bald claims, his invocations are not formally answered in the way Richardson records for the oracular Milton—with a sort of sudden Sibylline ecstasy or rapture modeled on these lines:

> If answerable style I can obtain
> Of my celestial patroness, who deigns
> Her nightly visitation unimplored,
> And dictates to me slumbering, or inspires
> Easy my unpremeditated verse.
>
> (LM 9.20–24)

Nothing magical or extraordinary happens here except the simple sensation of fluency; for the speaker's enabling impetus is thoroughly naturalized by his circumstantial account of it—that he continues freely to recount the story against all odds, not to mention all appearances. Indeed, as his subjunctive phrase signals, it is this mundane liberty of expression that the figure of the muse explicitly *interprets* as a supernatural dispensation or grace. And that is miracle enough to a Protestant for whom oracles never spoke before or after the birth of Christ. It is interesting to note that when Milton discusses invocation, specifically the invocation of the Spirit of God, he resists its magical sense, preferring to understand it as a request made of deity for benediction: "If the Spirit were ever to be invoked personally, it would be then especially, when we pray for him; yet we are commanded not to ask him of himself, but only of the Father. Why do we not call upon the Spirit himself, if he be God, to give himself to us? He who is sought from the Father, and given by him, not by himself, can neither be God, nor an object of invocation" (CM 14:393–95). It's not just that Milton's irony would empty invocation of false objects in *Paradise Lost* but that, on the model of his exegesis, he appraises this convention according to the human circumstances of its use. And he sees that use as implicating a world demonic and oppressive, where calling upon ambivalent deity offers the same fragile illusion of security for Milton's speaker as it does for Job, "though fallen on evil days, / On evil days though fallen, and evil tongues; / In darkness, and with dangers compassed round, / And solitude" (*LM* 7.25–28). The very presence of antimetabole here—the tautological inversions preferred by the satanic—marks a confusion in the speaker that is more than perceptual. For the speaker's invocation affords Milton a picture of religious error and its causes, an approach that dissents from the convention's banal meaning in order to deepen its significance—or in Cavell's phrase, "to take it back to its idea, to keep it in touch with its history." So while the speaker returns his thoughts "that voluntary move / Harmonious numbers" to the figural light he makes the source of their volition, still that light "Revisit'st not these eyes, that roll in vain / To find thy piercing ray, and find no dawn" (*LM* 3.22–24). His attempt to elicit supernatural illumination only ramifies the opposed ideas of darkness and obscurity, encompassing the speaker's manifold blindness and a life rendered so solitary and impoverished of sensation that its only other stimulus is merely residual—the memory of what he has read and seen. Milton conveys the poignancy of this recollection in a scheme of words almost identical to the speaker's expression of lost sight, in the sonnet to Skinner on his blindness:

> not to me returns
> Day, or the sweet approach of even or morn,
> Or sight of vernal bloom, or summer's rose,
> Or flocks, or herds, or human face divine;
> But cloud in stead, and ever-during dark
> Surrounds me.
>
> (*LM* 3.41–46)

These last lines are reminiscent of the double obscurity figured by paradox in the *Second Defense*; for the speaker's second proem also expresses a passionate desire to be recognized and embraced by the world from which something besides blindness has excluded him. In other words, the speaker is deprived not just of sight and knowledge, but as his elegiac language implies, of significance and community. It is this issue of acknowledgment that, exaggerated as "fate" and "renown," governs the speaker's ambiguous allusions to blind bards and prophets[50]—Thamyris, Homer, Phineus, and Tiresias; and the same loss of recognition frames the third proem's lament, with its sensational image of a second Orpheus struggling to fend off demonic deity by invocation (*LM* 3.33–36):

> the barbarous dissonance
> Of Bacchus and his revellers, the race
> Of that wild rout that tore the Thracian bard
> In Rhodope, where woods and rocks had ears
> To rapture, till the savage clamour drowned
> Both harp and voice.
>
> (*LM* 7.32–37)

Given their patent source in Milton's apologetics, it is perhaps predictable that the proems would show the speaker complaining that he is made at once negligible and notorious to others by his truth-telling. Nor is it surprising that when the speaker anticipates the change in humanity's condition after the Fall, he thinks of it in the same way that Adam does, as a loss of familiar communion with God, or more properly, with God's mediations (*LM* 9.1–5). But in the ninth book, that sense of human isolation and religious crisis overwhelms any attempt at invocation, as Adam and Eve choose their now separate ways to catastrophe. The speaker here relates a situation which he says is wholly within his mortal precinct, requiring neither extraordinary assistance nor exertion to depict, only to understand: namely, the creature's apostasy from its creator, which is what Milton calls tragedy. For the one thing humankind intimately knows is this sense of separateness or alienation which the speaker's lament underscores, and which destroys that intricate web of dependencies binding mind to mind, and the soul to God in paradise—the truly salient attribute of the Edenic world as Joseph Summers has taught us.[51] Where contingency then was seen as affiliation, even affinity between disparate things, after the Fall this connection feels random and arbitrary, the source of oppression and anxiety. So in the face of his expulsion from paradise, Adam desires to worship every spot in Eden where he had seen or spoken to the Lord, as if to secure by idolatry something of the relationship he once enjoyed; for "In yonder nether world where shall I seek / His bright appearances, or footsteps trace?" (*LM* 11.328– 29). And although Michael promises him God's loving and intelligible presence, the fact that any knowledge of that presence depends on interpretation— on deciphering signs remote from deity—puts Adam in the speaker's room, desperate for the consolation of what seems to be God's rapidly receding presence from the landscape. Adam too has lost any clear or constant sensation of divine proximity, and so yearns to encounter God palpably, not merely to construe the effects concealing him. The contingency that had exemplified the human connection to deity before the Fall, when seen from the other side of apostasy, looks and feels like abandonment and divorce.

Christopher Ricks compassionately observes that this is the force of the speaker's wordplay on the prefix *dis-*, meaning both separation and reversal or negation (*LM* 9.6–9): "distrust," "disloyalty," and "disobedience" in humanity, the speaker says in this final exursus, creates "distance" and "distaste" in God.[52] The creature's alienation from its condition of dependence on the creator is the circumstance that at once begets faith and contravenes it, and moves Milton's speaker to tell again how paradise was lost to us. Moreover, this sense of estrangement from God is what makes his confidence in invocation no statement of fact but instead an exertion of faith, a heroic act of imagination in the manner of Luther's Christian assertion. Thus, in the second proem, we are told distinctly that there is no vision or visionary event attached to the speaker's account except what is imaged by memory and text. And the other proems argue only a figurative dictation (the force of that "or" in the ninth book's excursus), taking the form of an impetus or celerity of speech which works both to advance the story from scene to scene, and to overcome perforce whatever obstacles of composition the speaker apprehends. In short, the proems' symbology of mount and light and muse are not claims, but rather professions of belief in things that do not appear as such, as the speaker himself distinguishes when he says, "The meaning, not the name I call" (*LM* 7.5). The dramatic hesitation attending this invocatory language magnifies its negative contingency, by which I mean the doubtfulness of the speaker's attempts to secure the epithet or locale for the agency that might invest his speech with truth, and vindicate both his God and himself (*LM* 7.5). So what the proems make marvelous—the expressiveness bestowed by a "voice divine" which the speaker apprehends only by its mediate effects upon imagination—isn't supernatural but interpretive (*LM* 7.2). And this interpretation is motivated by an impossible if inveterate human desire to recover the rapport of Eden's mythic intimacy with God, who has seemingly absconded from the speaker's life until he begins his story. The idea of divine visitation is taken up explicitly in the third proem where he laments his "solitude; yet not alone, while thou / Visit'st my slumbers nightly, or when morn / Purples the east" (*LM* 7.28–30). But the preceding image of Bellerophon's presumption and fate implies that this supernal presence may also be an illusion, even transgression of human desire (again, an idol or superstition), in which case the adventure of the speaker's epic enterprise would leave him simply as he is—blind, forsaken and erring—shrouded in the disgrace, the shame of suffering, which Westermann regards as a steady element in biblical lamentation (*LM* 7.15–20). Like Jeremiah, then, he fears deception and delusion or madness, living and speaking estranged from God and therefore with a real sense of his personal jeopardy—fearful of a providence that has bereft him of his sight, of community, of significance, and what is perhaps worst of all, of any conviction that what he believes or pictures about God and the world is true.

Thus, in the same breath that the speaker proposes to assert what "justly gives heroic name / To person or to poem," he admits that what he describes may be his invention alone, an epic tale that portrays the extent of his egoism and alienation:

> higher argument
> Remains, sufficient of it self to raise
> That name, unless an age too late, or cold
> Climate, or years damp my intended wing
> Depressed, and much they may, if all be mine,
> Not hers who brings it nightly to my ear.
>
> (*LM* 9.40–47)

This proviso—"and much they may, if all be mine"—signals the speaker's fear of deception, not only by desire and mortality, but also by his God; for the act of invocation itself represents a trial of his faith. To adopt the idiom of Wittgenstein and Cavell: although suffering has rendered the speaker blind to that aspect of his world expressive of deity—has left him incapable of making the right connections in the picture he describes of heaven, hell, and Eden—he perseveres in soliciting the understanding he manifestly lacks so as to justify the God whom he still refuses to deny. Were there no crisis of faith, Milton would not have supplied us with this image of an afflicted and embattled speaker, since his predicament is never represented as a punishment for sin. It is the speaker's experience that explains why God's interdiction of the tree of knowledge could appear inexplicable and needless to humanity long before the Fall. For such is the nature of faith's objects that the perplexity of *res non apparentes* cannot but begin with creation, in that primal moment when the creature recognizes its distinction from the creator. And this distinction is what makes Satan's notion—that the ban on the tree is unjust and tyrannical—both plausible and profound to Eve, because even in a state of grace without sin, deity's ordinances can appear outrageous to us. So the logic behind the speaker's account of the Fall is also at stake: besides the personal liabilities he names, every circumstance introduced by the proems constitutes a boundary or limit within which his narrative is obliged to make its meaning. The vindication of divine justice requires that he discover not merely coherence—which can prove specious and forced—but equity in his own predicament as well as our first parents'. For it is one thing to justify God's ways from a (false) position of certainty, as those readers who subscribe to the notion of Milton's rationalism suppose for him. But it is something else altogether to attempt this from the position of felt injustice and suffering in which Milton's proems place his speaker.

So although Stanley Fish has memorably and wittily argued that human sin ensures the disparity of meanings in *Paradise Lost*, such disparity is not—as Fish inevitably implies—susceptible of being transcended by human regeneracy and right thinking about God.[53] In Milton's view, the force of human suffering neither can nor should be denied, nor does he suppose God can be found by crossing over to the other side of the distinction. Rather, the sense of disparity represents an intractable constraint upon our understanding of deity and truth both before and after the fall of humanity, and this constraint the proems may be said to dramatize. It comes down to the question of what attitude one adopts toward the fact of a hidden God: whether, on the one hand, the constraint figured by deity's hiddenness is seen as something to be circumvented and effaced, or on the other, admitted and incorporated into our ideas of the divine. For the things of God aren't invisible or absent but mediated to us by phenomena which we insist on treating as a concealment of some sort, in the way that the body is thought to hide the soul, while what it really does is picture self with a different and incomparable appropriateness. We encounter here the now-familiar problem of Eve's hair, where the need for interpretation is felt by Satan and the speaker to be a veiling, an obstruction between them and what they insist on knowing fully and of course erotically. Thus Cavell observes that "The soul may be invisible to us the way something absolutely present may be invisible to us," because "The block to my vision of the other is not the other's body but my incapacity or unwillingness to interpret or judge it accurately, to draw the right connections" (CR 368–69). Since we desire another sort of experience or meaning for ourselves—the absolute legibility of glory, say—we choose to be oblivious to what we *can* know, we choose *not* to interpret (or so we think), and this is what Wittgenstein calls aspect-blindness. But as Cavell points out in exploring the motives for scepticism in the *Investigations*, we may also use this "hiddenness" or lack of immediacy in such a way as to deny any knowledge of what is pictured or told, which among other consequences can then promote the false necessity and language of penetration or transcendence, not only in the case of Milton's God but also in his poem. A sense of disparity is true to those religious realities that don't appear as such, whose dilemma of expression sin does not foment, much less "cause," but to which it responds by reading that disparity as a crisis, an antagonism, a fundamental contradiction in deity itself. So even as suffering may engender religious conflict, it may also promote a knowledge of what has gone unseen or remained inevident to us, and consequently invite that revisionary species of justification that I would argue the speaker performs in *Paradise Lost*. As Michael explains to a disconsolate Adam, only a new regard for the inevident will reveal the creator's regard for us:

> Yet doubt not but in valley and in plain
> God is as here, and will be found alike
> Present, and of his presence many a sign
> Still following thee, still compassing thee round
> With goodness and paternal love, his face
> Express, and of his steps the track divine.
>
> (LM 11.349–54)

CHAPTER FIVE

Milton's Devil

∘━✦━∘

DARKNESS VISIBLE

It is one of the many anomalies of *Paradise Lost* that Milton opens his justification of God's ways in hell, with Satan only now discovering this newfound land:

> At once as far as angels' ken he views
> The dismal situation waste and wild,
> A dungeon horrible, on all sides round
> As one great furnace flamed, yet from those flames
> No light, but rather darkness visible
> Served only to discover sights of woe,
> Regions of sorrows, doleful shades, where peace
> And rest can never dwell, hope never comes
> That comes to all; but torture without end
> Still urges, and a fiery deluge, fed
> With ever-burning sulphur unconsumed:
> Such place eternal justice had prepared
> For these rebellious, here their prison ordained
> In utter darkness, and their portion set
> As far removed from God and light of heaven
> As from the centre thrice to the utmost pole.
> O how unlike the place from whence they fell!
>
> (LM 1.59–75)

The peculiar way in which physical and conceptual horror exist on the same plane of representation—Satan seeing at once an endlessly conflagrant landscape that is also a place palpably without hope or rest—is typical of Milton's epic decorum even as it is Dante's and Virgil's. For this coextension is the effect created when we imagine *invisibilia*, as then the ordinary distinction between ideas and objects, the psychological and the physical worlds, no longer obtains. Poetry can do this precisely because figuration, as a way of speaking, needn't observe such constraints—except insofar as they may predict the reader's response to what is shown. As it happens, the "darkness visible" Satan perceives here becomes symptomatic not only of his predicament, but also that of Milton's critics, unable to decide whether this sort of figure is evocative (Christopher Ricks and David Daiches) or failed (T. S. Eliot). Because what Eliot wants thoroughly envisioned, Ricks and Daiches would prefer only remotely to see, inasmuch as each has a different idea of how religious *invisibilia* should be depicted—Eliot desiring to see a certain graphic complexity, a palpable trial of poetic articulation, while Daiches and Ricks want a tactful abstraction or generalized image that leaves the reader imaginative room in which to maneuver. So if Eliot can deplore Milton's famed attenuation of the visual in this oxymoron, Daiches can relish a poetic discretion he feels is only fitfully exercised in hell as well as in heaven, where we are given what Ricks, for his part, describes as godhead given to histrionics.[1]

Needless to say, difficulty with evoking the religious—as Daiches puts it, "Sometimes we almost feel that Milton had too little a sense of the numinous"—is a liability in a poet whose putative subject is God.[2] Moreover, this apparent inadequacy tends to coincide with what is, for the reader at least, the central issue of Milton's great argument—the question of where the poet's own allegiance lies: whether it is with heaven's supreme king as Dr. Johnson insists, or with the devil's party in Blake's phrase. For the persuasiveness of Milton's images ought to say something about the pull his own argument has for him; and inasmuch as their success seems equivocal, so does Milton's attitude toward what we are shown. The case is still more complicated by his having Satan appear first upon the scene in somber, elegiac splendor. In doing this, as any rhetorician knows, Milton allows the devil to make an uncontested claim upon our sympathies even as he does the hapless speaker's, who quickly finds his own necessity and suffering mirrored in Satan's: thus their psychological convergence in that sudden, incontinent exclamation of loss, "O how unlike the place from whence they fall!" Even his imprecations against the devil tend to sound conventional and hollow in hell, suggesting to the reader that Satan is being condemned without a hearing, which the speaker then fully if obliviously proceeds to give him. So by the time we meet his God, Milton has given us every reason to accept his devil's account of religious things. And to the extent that we endorse the devil's position, we also embrace a particular characterization of *invisibilia*—as conspicuously, abundantly detailed in the manner of Satan himself, who is described

> talking to his nearest mate
> With head uplift above the wave, and eyes
> That sparkling blazed, his other parts besides
> Prone on the flood, extending long and large
> Lay floating many a rood.
>
> (*LM* 1.192–96)

Like his graphically buoyant and extended angelic body, sooner or later the sights caught in Satan's despairing glance are made distinct, even methodically exact, as tends frequently to occur in Milton's landscapes. The oxymoron of "darkness visible" itself becomes a pattern of antithetical figures in the speech and experience of the fallen angels, conveying their sense of the situation's unexampled strangeness, its irresolvable contradiction. Yet this order of poetic apprehension does not seem to translate well to heaven, where Milton's fondness for imagistic engineering, if not Eliotic intensity, earns him mostly reproach for what Pope calls a "God turned school-divine," a deity that has been made to *argue*, as both Ricks and Daiches complain.[3] In short, the grand spectacle of hell looks tawdry in heaven. What we find persuasive about the figure of Satan—the very explicitness of his perceptions, speech, movement, and gestures—hangs awkwardly, improbably, disturbingly on Milton's God, both Father and Son. The reader's latent prejudices against the divine thus being realized in Book Three, the justification of God's ways would seem to be jeopardized by Milton's utter disregard for the effect his poetic choices have on the reader; for if a secular age is less likely to be disturbed by the notion of Satan as hero, it is also more inclined to resist an anthropomorphic deity.

Certainly, Ricks and Daiches are disappointed, although they are too wise to allow themselves to be altogether put off by the figure God cuts: they just go elsewhere for the beauties of Milton's language—to Eden where, in their eyes, the poet handles his material with more tact and real eloquence. Perhaps they are right in supposing that *invisibilia* like God and the devil, heaven and hell, require a different decorum than other things do, an insight of which John Milton is presumed to be unaware because of the very religiosity, the iconographic crudeness, with which they see his God depicted. But he is after all the poet of *Paradise Lost*, the author and disposer of its effects, so it is also possible that Daiches and Ricks, and of course T. S. Eliot, have misunderstood the nature of what is being represented and what Milton intends by it. Because what they are really reluctant to admit is that this poem is allegorical, and that Milton's decision not only to open with Satan, but to have God argue as well, arises from the things being allegorized: namely, *res non apparentes*, that different order of human experience pertaining to faith and apostasy. For the sense we have of Satan as a fully formed person is actually a concomitant of his apostate condition: that is, inasmuch as Satan conceives self and deity as the plausible sum of their appearances, then the greater particularity and exactitude of those appearances, the more verisimilar the representation. In this fashion, Satan impersonates in himself that idea of religious truth which argues an analogy between what we see and what is actually the case with *invisibilia*—God, the soul, truth, justice. Of course, he does this because he is rapidly becoming a consummate hypocrite, whose own stock-in-trade is plausible appearances. But such is the sophistication of the allegory that we ourselves are taken in, not so much by Satan's performance as by his assumptions of identity and value, which are expressed in that tortured yet utterly credible view of experience, to which we are made privy by Milton's equally susceptible speaker. It is only when Sin and Death appear abruptly in the same landscape with him that the reader is made to notice that Satan may not be quite all he seems—that his figure may impersonate a religious idea too.[4]

Moreover, the entrance of such extravagantly, irreducibly figurative actors right before the scene in heaven ought to alert us to the possibility that the Father, whom we are inclined to identify as Milton's God, is no less an impersonation than Sin and Death, or in a different way, the Son and those angels whose explicit purpose it is to image deity to the rest of its creatures. Yet the parts of *Paradise Lost* that have provoked in its readers the greatest unease, to the point of distaste, are just these occasions when the figurative may be said to intrude upon the myth, and allegory is made inescapable.[5] Whenever Milton gives us this order of graphic figuration, as he does, for example, in the war in heaven, the poetry itself is thought to suffer—to be degraded as language as well as mimesis by what seems to many readers an unaccountable breach of decorum. But the decisive presence of allegory in the poem isn't just felt as a fatal lapse in taste, but as though it were an eruption of the grotesque, something in excess of Sin's divided and self-consuming body, or the wounds sustained by Satan's literally engrossing legions. That is to say, allegory is experienced as a kind of violence done to the poem's more thoroughly naturalized and plausible expression. As Wolfgang Kayser observes, the grotesque alienates us from the world on which it encroaches, inasmuch as things no longer behave in the way we expect them to do: like allegory, the distinction between animate and inanimate, object and idea, the very order of space and time break down.[6] We cannot recognize our surroundings; we are put off balance; we are repelled. Abstract personification in *Paradise Lost* has just this ironical, vertiginous species of effect, since it also involves a crucial reordering of the way we had supposed things to mean in the world of the text—from mimetic to allegorical.

It is an effect similar to that Milton and Luther associate with the hidden God, whose revelation also operates by a species of allegory, while Wittgenstein and Adorno link it to the disclosure of meaning's contingency—the fact that in our words and ideas we do not deal with reality per se but with variable pictures of it. But we have only rather recently in Milton studies, with the work of Joseph Summers and Stanley Fish, come to see the disturbance of our assumptions as ironical—as a calculated criticism by the poet of our habits in reading, as against Milton's imaginative and poetic failure. I refer to the contradictory sense that the poet's expression is relentlessly programmatic and yet somehow out of control, a notion at least as venerable as Dr. Johnson and as current as Ricks and Daiches. Partly it results from the ignorance or obtuseness that would see Milton's enterprise of justification as an exercise in religiosity, as against a challenge to that very mentality. But the impression is mostly owing to the baldness of these allegorical episodes—their flagrant resistance to the kinds of figural transparency critics have been idealizing for years. Because while we may allow the greatness of the poem, like Dr. Johnson, we are still uncomfortable with its achievement and inclined to think as these readers do, that it succeeds in spite of its peculiarities, not by virtue of them. But the tracts suggest that Milton himself would locate the success of *Paradise Lost* precisely in this order of response to its allegory. And that is because our aversion exposes a particular prejudice of which he vehemently disapproves, and in which his fig-uration handily catches us out, not least by letting Satan put his own case first.

In interpreting Paul's allegory in Galatians, Luther takes a moment to digress somewhat on the nature of allegorizing itself, which may serve as an explana-tion for what Milton intends by his own use of that trope in *Paradise Lost*. To begin with, Luther says that in Galatians, allegory is not a proof but an illustra-tion or picture, such that Paul has recourse to it only when "he has already fortified his case with more solid arguments—based on experience, on the case of Abraham, on the evidence of Scripture, and on analogy—now, at the end of the argument, he adds an allegory as a kind of ornament" (*LW* 26:436). In effect, Luther is simply acknowledging the tendentiousness of Paul's picture, the fact that it is devised to underscore a specific theological point already substantiated by methodical exegesis. But then he talks about the allegory's achievement, which somewhat unexpectedly he calls "marvelous" for this rea-son: where Paul, on the model of the law as Mt. Sinai or Hagar (the Arabic name for that place), might have completed his comparison by making Jerusa-lem stand for the gospel and Sarah, he does not. Indeed, "he neither dares nor is able to do so," according to Luther (*LW* 26:438). For Paul does not *locate* the gospel at all; he does not compare one place with another in his analogy. And he doesn't because his theology excludes just this option:

> I for my part would not have had the courage to handle this allegory in this manner. I would rather have said that Jerusalem is Sarah, or the new covenant, especially since it was there that the preaching of the Gospel began, the Holy Spirit was granted, and the people of the New Testament came into being. And I would have thought that I had constructed a very apt allegory. Therefore not everyone has the skill to play around with alle-gories. For a pretty external appearance will impress a person in such a way that he will go astray, as here all of us would have thought it appropriate to say that Sinai is Hagar and Jerusalem is Sarah. Now Paul does indeed make Sarah into Jerusalem—yet not the physical Jerusalem, which he simply attaches to Hagar, but the spiritual and heavenly Jerusalem, where the Law does not rule and the physical people are not enslaved with their children, as they are in Jerusalem, but where the promise rules and the spiritual people are free.
>
> To bring about the complete abolition of the Law and of the reign estab-lished on Hagar, the earthly Jerusalem with all its ornaments, the temple, its form of worship, etc., was horribly laid waste, with the permission of God. Although the new covenant began there and went out from there into the whole world, it still pertains to Hagar; that is, it is the common-wealth of the Law, of the form of worship, and of the priesthood established by Moses. In other words, it was born of Hagar the slave, and therefore it

is in slavery together with its children. That is, it remains in the works of the Law and never attains to the freedom of the Spirit; it remains forever under the Law, under sin and an evil conscience, under the wrath and judgement of God, under the sentence of death and of hell. Of course, it does have the freedom of the flesh; it has a physical realm, magistrates, wealth, possessions, etc. But we are speaking about the freedom of the Spirit, where we are dead to the Law, sin, and death, and where we live and reign as free men in grace, the forgiveness of sins, righteousness, and eternal life. The earthly Jerusalem cannot achieve these things; therefore it remains with Hagar. (*LW* 26:438–39)

Luther understands the figurative economy of Paul's allegory to argue, against the assumptions of the law, that righteousness before God and indeed all religious *invisibilia* are not places, practices, or persons. In his view, that is why Paul abstains from associating the gospel with a precise location or entity like the holy city Jerusalem, since there is no one thing, natural or supernatural, that corresponds to the position of faith—it is not "heaven" any more than it is "the earthly Jerusalem." Thus the image of the gospel as the new city of God is a figure that, unlike the law as Jerusalem proper, hasn't a particular object against which to try the suitability of Paul's comparison. What is appropriate or decorous about the analogy lies in its acknowledgment by omission—its telling refusal to supply a single, discrete correlative.

This theological decorum—an attention paid to a particular meaning as against a symmetrical appearance—gives the allegory its exceptional felicity in Luther's view. For the comparison Paul draws is to an entirely different order of phenomenon, the conceptual or psychological position imaged in Sarah's story. Paul's allegory is thus Luther's sort of catachresis—a yoking together of incompatible ideas but not in the simple sense of material to immaterial, visible to invisible worlds, which is the relation we tend to expect from allegory. Rather, it is catachresis in that the figure compares two incompatible orders of religious meaning and experience which obtain and conflict in human history, even as Hagar and Sarah were said to do. For Luther, the whole scriptural text is in this way catachresis. That is because deity's peculiar usages, with their reference to *res non apparentes*, defy the ordinary sense of words and things, and reciprocally, because the world viewed from the vantage of faith has an entirely transfigured "look" to it. So although the gospel, Sarah, and the New Jerusalem express an aspect of human experience even as the law, Hagar, and the old Jerusalem do, this peculiar dimension of meaning cannot be tied to one spot any more than God or his promises can. By contrast, the allegory gives the law an exact location in the place Jerusalem and a definite form and appeal—"a physical realm, magistrates, wealth, possessions, etc."—and this because of the kind of religious meaning it expounds, affiliating God idolatrously with the particular places and things in which at one time or other he has been revealed. But this analogical mentality provides our existence with only an ephemeral coherence, which disintegrates under the pressure of the human need for a viable truth—a description of the world that can account for our conflicted experience, which the law itself evokes and aggravates.

In short, it is his idolatrous understanding that makes Satan's hell a place devoid of rest or hope. And for the same reason that the inexorable consummation of the law is necessity and suffering to Luther, with the devastation of the old Jerusalem figuring the integral sensation of divine wrath consequent upon observance of the law. But where the law subscribes to "sight and visibility," as Milton puts it, in keeping with the idolatrous propensity of our ideas, the gospel sense of the world is inevident precisely because it diverges from that pervasive, deleterious assumption of meaning and value (CM 3.1:209). The conceptual catachresis or linking of incompatibles in the allegory of Sarah and Hagar is therefore perfectly right and necessary, given the distinction between God and the world, the gospel and the law, spirit and flesh. Indeed, for Luther, its impropriety is the source of the figure's "marvelousness," since this effect indicates the religious origin of Paul's meaning: for here there can be no easy equivalence of expression, as there is no equivalence in kind, between the meanings of faith and the received or apparent understanding of things we thoughtlessly cultivate. Paul's allegory thus discloses a different, unexpected, even astonishing decorum from the one Luther confesses he himself would have pursued, in demanding for the gospel a correlative place to the law. What is apt in the sense of a symmetrical and plausible comparison would be wrong in this case, for "a pretty external appearance will impress a person in such a way that he will go astray." To the extent that Luther's hypothetical allegory would rely upon and confirm the merely evident sense of religious things, so its overtly felicitous appearance would grievously mislead the reader about the experience of faith and the hidden God.

Paul's actual figure, by contrast, is disconcerting and difficult insofar as it discriminates between these opposed orders of religious meaning. So even as Milton does in the tracts, Luther distinguishes here an anomalous expression for God and religious things, on account of their accommodation to human grammar and human ideas. While deity makes itself intelligible in scripture and our experience, it doesn't do so in the fashion we like to suppose: it accommodates its meanings to our humanity, but it never proposes to accustom us to them. From this aspect of religious expression, there emerges a further argument of Luther's, having to do with the abrogation of the law. It is that the giving of the gospel coincides with the destruction of Israel, the second Temple, and the Diaspora of God's chosen people: "the earthly Jerusalem with all its ornaments, the temple, its form of worship, etc., was horribly laid waste, with the permission of God." The law by its physicalism does not just invite actual violence against the site of its religious and political institution. But even as that violence deprives the law of its own peculiar place and expression, so the order of religious meaning constituting the law is bereft of its ostensible objects—literally, its point of reference. In an act of conceptual as well as physical devastation, the Mosaic covenant is abrogated by the giving of the gospel. But psychologically and religiously, Luther argues that it does not end, because the order of meaning promulgated by the law still continues to exert its atavistic, seemingly incorrigible, hold over the human mind.

This is the whole point of Paul's allegory as Luther reads it: because the law locates religious meaning in Jerusalem, truth in the apparent sense of things, it inevitably courts incoherence because the Lord of the covenant is a God who hides himself in his appearances—indeed, he is a God antithetical to the condition of appearance. The destruction of Jerusalem then ironically figures for Luther the existential incoherence resulting when deity and truth are identified with the merely evident sense of things, which, like all idols, eventually betrays the trust we put in it. So God separates his people from what they regard as their peculiar appearances—"the earthly Jerusalem with all its ornaments, the temple, its form of worship"—in which they had mistakenly invested him. And insofar as Israel refuses to relinquish this mode of religious significance, so the people suffer the world and their God as necessity and wrath—the arbitrary and unjust *cause* of their ruination. I am describing the predicament of the psalmist or Jeremiah in lament, the position of Milton's speaker as well as Luther before his conversion—each laboring under the sense of necessity and injustice that attends the failure of this presumptive order. For necessity is the experience Paul's allegory pictures in the customary bondage of Hagar as Abraham's slave and concubine, a figure used to evoke a state of mind fearfully enthralled to the "fleshly" world, like Israel to the old Jerusalem, and in Luther's view, to a false and detrimental idea of religious things tending only to sin, judgment, death, and hell.[7]

When Milton invokes Paul's allegory, this time in his *Treatise of Civil Power*, he understands it similarly. He argues that the intrusion of civil magistracy into religion, as a means of ensuring orthodoxy, transforms the gospel back into the law because magistracy precludes the free exercise of conscience in trying to legislate and enforce the right expression of religious truth. It can do this only by compelling conformity to a given *appearance*, by reducing religion to a particular configuration of outward profession, practice, and place. So as Milton sees it, what the gospel leaves to individual choice as things indifferent, magistracy would be obliged by its own assumptions to determine and regulate, right down to chapter and verse. Yet he resists the civil ordering of religion not only because he regards the attempt as doomed to failure, since souls are "to outward force not lyable," as the case of Bunyan himself proves: that is, they are not identical with the bodies that express them, which magistracy would restrict and confine even as it seeks to do with religious meaning (CM 6:20). He does so because "conscience or religion" is not an institution, an object, a time, or a place, but instead "that full perswasion, whereby we are assur'd that our beleef and practise, as far as we are able to apprehend and probably make appeer, is according to the will of God & his Holy Spirit within us" (CM 6:5). The gospel is thus a human condition finally incapable of being regulated, even as the attempt to order other minds does terrible violence to them and to God's truth:

Gal.4.3, &c. *even so we, when we were children, were in bondage under the* *rudiments of the world: but when the fullness of time was come, God sent forth* *his son &c. to redeem them that were under the law, that we might receive the* *adoption of sons &c. Wherfore thou art no more a servant, but a son &c. But* *now &c. how turn ye again to the weak and beggarly rudiments, whereunto ye* *desire again to be in bondage? Ye observe dayes &c.* Hence it planely appeers, that if we be not free we are not sons, but still servants unadopted; and if we turn again to those weak and beggarly rudiments, we are not free; yea though willingly and with a misguided conscience we desire to be in bondage to them; how much more than if unwillingly and against our conscience? Ill was our condition chang'd from legal to evangelical, and small advantage gotten by the gospel, if for the spirit of adoption to freedom, promisd us, we receive again the spirit of bondage to fear; if our fear which was then servile towards God only, must be now servile in religion towards men: strange also and preposterous fear, if when and wherin it hath attain by the redemption of our Saviour to be filial only towards God, it must be now servile towards the magistrate. Who by subjecting us to his punishment in these things, brings back into religion that law of terror and satisfaction, belonging now only to civil crimes; and thereby in effect abolishes the gospel by establishing again the law to a far worse yoke of servitude upon us than before. It will therfore not misbecome the meanest Christian to put in minde Christian magistrates . . . that they meddle not rashly with Christian libertie, the birthright and outward testimonie of our adoption: least while they little think it, nay think they do God service, they themselves like the sons of that bondwoman be found persecuting them who are freeborne of the spirit; and by a sacrilege of not the least aggravation bereaving them of that sacred libertie which our Saviour with his own blood purchas'd for them. (CM 6:31–32)

Contrary to the received sense of heresy as a sign of the apostate, for Milton, it is rather a sign of true religion—of faith demonstrably "free not only from the bondage of those ceremonies, but also from the forcible imposition of those circumstances, place and time, in the worship of God" (CM 6:28). Citing Galatians, Milton calls this dependence upon set forms and fixed places "weak and beggarly rudiments," by which he understands that order of religious meaning founded in the ostensible appearance of things, and which he associates with the law's "veiling"—its banal, infantalizing disfigurement—of God's truth. His epithet for the law itself involves a bit of interpretive latitude: Paul uses "elements" to talk about the nature deities of the gentiles and their worship, idols which Milton chooses to translate as "rudiments" in the sense of a crude, undeveloped religious understanding. Yet he does so because the apostle portrays the legal requirements of the Jewish party as a comparable idolatry to pagan religion, upholding the truth of icon and ritual which proves inadequate and contradictory in its observance.

It is the "bondage" to mere appearance, the "servile" or oppressive fear of jealous, implacable deity, the "terror" of retribution, which Paul and Luther equally associate with the supernaturalism Milton indicts. And to the extent that we claim the interpretive freedom of scripture he himself displays, which consists in choosing how to understand and enact the gospel, so we escape the psychological and religious enslavement of the law's magical mentality—what he regards as its primitive presumption that human things determine divine ones. But Milton doesn't stop there; for in practicing this very interpretive liberty, we manifest all at once the presence of the spirit of God, the attitude of faith, and in the idea of "adoption," our justification *coram Deo*—virtually a whole *ordo salutis* (CM 16:51–55). So religion is not conceived in terms of a doctrine but as a state or condition integral to the person, along the lines of Wittgenstein's "seeing something *as* something," which is expressed in the imaginative scope of interpretation itself. It follows that when we seek conformity or adherence over choice in religious things, we not only disclaim the liberty of conscience that Milton cherishes in the wielding, and which to his way of thinking signals the true believer, but also disavow the gospel whose nature is itself interpretive and imaginative, whose purpose is to restore humanity to the right knowledge of a God always concealed from our view. This is a knowledge that Milton believes can be discovered only in the contingency, not the uniformity, of our lives: the exercise of Christian liberty thus requires of us an expanded notion of the possible, a belief in the meaningfulness of what cannot be seen as such; and these are the values Luther and Milton both associate with Paul's figure of Sarah as the gospel. For Sarah made the hidden God in Luther's sense, by believing "him faithful who had promised" her the impossible (Hebrews 11:11).

Like Luther, Milton understands Paul's figure of Hagar to express the perverse, self-alienating mentality that attends willful servitude to evident or received ideas of religion. As an attitude taken toward God and the things of God, it is at once a sacrilege and a pathology: a sacrilege to the extent that what Milton regards as an obsolete, deleterious idea of the divine is imposed upon the gospel and God's people; and a pathology insofar as we willingly and persistently impose it upon ourselves to our own detriment. So Milton also reads Paul's allegory of Abrahamic birthright as distinguishing between mentalities as well as meanings, "legal" as against "evangelical," which for him (unlike Luther) extend to every sphere of human life, including the civil. Since the "legal" mind is enthralled by the accoutrements and performance as against the meaning of religion, its knowledge of God becomes a conversance with superficies—a purely formal understanding. Moreover, because this subservience to forms is a religious mentality, and thus absolutely binding in its obligations, we cannot help but experience it as an Aeschylean "yoke of servitude": we enact these forms out of a purely arbitrary idea of their significance, with the consequence that we live in perpetual fear of the retribution which will ensue when they aren't observed. This is to live under necessity, in the kind of psychological bondage Milton sees revived by the legal governance of religious expressions. When we relinquish the exercise of religious choice to the magistrate, we relinquish the possibility of our recognizance as well as subjective integrity, becoming "the sons of the bondwoman" and thus persecutors of ourselves.

The "evangelical" position, on the other hand, enfranchises us to emulate Christ, to be "filial towards God" in the sense that we know and obey him voluntarily, by understanding and choice as against necessity and coercion. Indeed, the hallmark of faith is its liberality or charity, which is equally the sign of divine grace for Luther and Milton, here understood in the kindly, clement sense of a dispensation or exemption from established requirements. "What evangelic religion is, is told in two words, faith and charitie; or beleef and practise": "both these flow either the one from the understanding, the other from the will, or both jointly from both, once indeed naturally free, but now only as they are regenerat and wrought on by divine grace" (CM 6:21). Conceptual and practical liberty then distinguishes the "evangelical" mind. It is the untrammeled exercise of an intelligence about God which expresses the divine, not in one place or practice, but omnipresently in our ordinary lives. "Evangelical" religion is accordingly the opposite of the law's hieratic sequestering of deity into set sacral occasions and forms, in that this mentality allows the individual person both initiative as well as responsibility for securing right knowledge and so relationship with God. In the *Apology*, where Milton defends worship without the prayer book, he gives informality just such a role in religious maturation. For a set form of service or liturgy, he argues, "hinders piety rather than sets it forward, being more apt to weaken the spirituall faculties, if the people be not wean'd from it in due time. . . . For not only the body, & the mind, but also the improvement of Gods Spirit is quickn'd by using. Whereas they who will ever adhere to liturgy, bring themselves in the end to such a passe by overmuch leaning, as to loose even the legs of their devotion" (CM 3.1:351). The "evangelical" then entails a spontaneous, catholic, and independent discipline—"independent" in the sense that there are no singular, palpable objects on which this religious understanding is fixed, nothing to which it corresponds as such, not even the text of scripture. There is only a special aptitude in seeking the true propriety of things, because God's order in the world is the canon by which the "evangelical" mind governs itself: "obedience to the Spirit of God, rather then to the faire seeming pretences of men," Milton asserts, "is the best and most dutifull order that a Christian can observe" (CM 3.1:350). And as he says in the *Treatise*, this mentality characterizes not only the primal state of humanity in Eden, but the very sensation of abundant, surprising possibility that is the experience of Christian liberty, unconstrained by customary assumptions of religious meaning and value, which are all civil law is fit to recognize and judge.

A *Treatise of Civil Power* is itself peculiar for the very reason that Milton is not so much arguing the orthodoxy of particular doctrines as he is trying to evoke an altogether different idea of religion as knowledge, namely, as something neither axiomatic nor preceptive but existential and heuristic. He understands religion as the most intimate expression of the soul, manifest in the range of possibilities we embrace for ourselves and our world. And like the soul, this religion belongs to the order of *res non apparentes*, things that are made known mediately and contingently in an almost unprecedented variety of ways, like deity itself. With the sole exception of scripture's unique authority, there is no one dogma with which Milton chooses to identify the Christian religion, even including the gospel, since it is possible in his theology to be justified by faith in the scriptural deity without knowledge of Jesus Christ as such: faith is not a content but a mode of religious understanding, an attitude taken toward God and the things of God (CM 15:403–5). Thus like Paul's figures in Galatians, the *Treatise*'s argument is an allegory without an object because the attitude is the religion, not the "rudiments" of doctrine. And its elaboration of Paul's images as different kinds of religious mentalities, evoking what it feels like to experience God from the positions of the law and the gospel, owes much to Luther's commentary: namely, that Sarah and Hagar, like the old and new Jerusalems, picture meanings and attitudes, not places and persons. For as Luther explains them, Paul's figures stand in relation to each other not as separate and contrasting religious institutions or doctrines, but as two ways of looking at one and the same divine revelation. So in the manner of irony, the images of the "spiritual" city and the "earthly" one describe and interpret a single reality, in this case, our historical relations with the one true God. One image of Jerusalem argues that the sacred is restricted in its expressions to a people, a place, a building, a ritual, a priesthood; it refers to these things in the sense that religious value consists in them. But the other image, the "spiritual" city, argues an opposed relation to the sacred—that insofar as any place, person or thing participates in the mentality or meaning which is the gospel, so they are all holy and "Jerusalem."

But Paul's figures not only evoke opposed readings of divine revelation. They also comprise in themselves two distinct but related orders of allegory, which in turn reflect these two contiguous religious mentalities. The law interprets scripture as an allegory of God according to the evident sense of its images, with the result that religion takes on the shape of the things described there. And since deity is understood by analogy or correspondence to its palpable signs, religious knowledge becomes an observance or reenactment of the restricted terms of revelation, reiterating the sum and form of God's appearances. By contrast, the gospel interprets the allegory of God not as a singular order of appearance, but as an order of interpretation which distinguishes between God's meaning and the evident sense of the scriptural image. Deity per se is not identified with the terms of its revelation; rather, it is understood to be distinct from these, of another nature altogether, so that what revelation pictures for us is not God's nature but an understanding of God's expressions. Here religious knowledge isn't conning over an imagery or doctrine but learning a particular way of thinking. Where these two allegories depart from each other is in their account of *invisibilia*: under the law, religion proposes to emulate deity itself; under the "gospel," religion emulates the manner of deity's revelation.

The Jerusalem of the gospel is accordingly "new" in Wittgenstein's sense; for we are discovering not a new religious entity—a new God or a new revelation—but a new way of understanding what we already know, along the lines of Jeremiah's new covenant. Similarly, as Milton reads them, Paul's figures do not refer to particular polities and churches, but to meanings that defy national and sectarian boundaries, in much the same ecumenical fashion as Luther argues.

Milton's thesis is that we profoundly misunderstand the gospel when we read it as enforcing conformity to a particular form of religious appearance, as against freeing us from such speciousness.[8] On the model of God's incongruous expression as sufferer both in the prophets and the gospels, Milton emphasizes the defining tension between deity's valuations and our own, even as the gospel can only be understood in agonistic reference to the law, or in Paul's allegory, the enfranchisement of Sarah's children against the bondage suffered by Hagar's. For the possession of freedom as a birthright is fully meaningful only within the memory of enslavement, understood in the *Treatise* as that mentality which reads and esteems religious things according to their merely ostensible significance. This is the dialectical relation to which Paul recalls the Galatians—that, in Luther's phrase, they had fled *ad Deum contra Deum*, against God to the one true God, from the law to the gospel, that the gospel gets its force and vitality from their past and present idolatry of the law, namely, in the difference between a life led in bondage and a life led in promise. Paul is obliged to remind his congregation of this relation because, under the gospel, the allegory of the hidden God implicates no objects, places, or entities, only difficult and seemingly repugnant meanings which we refuse to sustain because they do not gratify a narcissism as old as our humanity. Preferring an immediate ease and satisfaction to a prospective joy, we habitually succumb to the allure of the ostensible despite the injustice and suffering this lapse invariably foments, which is why the gospel must be understood in relation to the law, like Luther's masked God and devil, or Milton's knowledge of good and evil. For once we lose sight of this human consequence—when we reduce religious expressions to a single, irrevocable form, as the Jewish party sought to do in Paul's view or the Presbyterian party in Milton's *Treatise*—then all unconsciously we adore not God but the devices and embellishings of human imagination and in effect will our own ruin. So, in Milton's masque, those weary travelers drink Comus's "orient liquor in a crystal glass" impulsively, recklessly, out of sheer physical appetite, expecting pleasure only, not delusion and abjection (LM 65):

> Soon as the potion works, their human countenance,
> The express resemblance of the gods, is changed
> Into some brutish form . . .
> And they, so perfect is their misery,
> Not once perceive their foul disfigurement,
> But boast themselves more comely than before.

> (LM 68–75)

Divine Similitude

The dialectical relation between law and gospel explains why the allegory in *Paradise Lost* cannot represent invisible entities—persons, places, or things— nor the Father monopolize Milton's idea of God. His figure can picture only a certain aspect of religious experience, just as Satan does another; and this de-limited and dislocated reference readily resolves the problem created by their formal parity, that is to say, the impression we are given by the narrative that the Father and Satan are comparable beings, if not agencies. This impression is itself fostered by the mentality of the law, which assumes correspondences— between apparent and real likeness, between seen and unseen—where there are none. And it is the presumption of correspondence that deludes Satan, first into comparing and likening himself to God, and then into defying and competing with this figure. But Milton understands deity's expressions in scrip-ture and history always as a way of speaking, an impersonation of deity per-formed by those media which severally convey God's will to humanity: the sacred text, the angels whose singular role is to personate deity to the world, and preeminently the Son as divine word—the agent of creation, the Lord of the covenant, the Christ and incarnate God (CM 14:277–303). So personified evil has the status of a trope in Milton's religious thought as well as his poem, with the devil's promiscuous exfoliation in the demonology of *Paradise Lost* observing the ironic decorum that Milton ascribes to *res non apparentes*. We can know religious things properly only as our experience presents them to us, which is to say figuratively, by the mediating signs of their presence; and it is to make just this point that Milton introduces Sin and Death into the landscape of hell, exposing as allegorical what Satan and Milton's readers are inclined to regard as a natural and positive order of meaning.

But he underscores the allegory with a further maneuver largely lost on the naive imagination, which is to place the figures of the Father and Satan on what appears to be the same plane of representation, giving us that impression of their equality for which Satan himself contends. Deity's accommodated ex-pressions in scripture or in history have this ambivalent effect: on the one hand, they provide in Rawls's sense a "veil of ignorance," an instrumental picture or figure like the Lord of the covenant which enables human relationship with the incommensurable; but on the other, their ambiguous because tropological character permits the fundamental misunderstanding which Paul, Luther, and Milton ascribe to the law, in which we expect a correspondence between the nature of *invisibilia* and the things that represent them. This ostensible equality is what makes all religious imagery so dangerous, obliging not only these theolo-gians but also, significantly, the archangel Raphael in *Paradise Lost* regularly to separate how God's things appear from how they must be understood. And it is just this ironical grammar to which Milton's speaker remains oblivious for a great part of his own narrative, until he discovers its redemptive force along with Adam, Eve, and notionally at least, Milton's reader. The distinction be-tween creator and creature sets a mimetic limit to deity's expression that sin

effaces until it abruptly, violently, devastatingly obtrudes upon our experience
in the shape of perceived injustice or incoherence. But sin itself is not the cause
but the psychology of affliction under the law, fomented by the assumption of
a correspondence between divine and creaturely being, between religious and
received orders of meaning: idolatry, in brief. It is the law that supposes that
the creature can orchestrate, even compel, the creator's response in invocation,
that human actions can justify us *coram Deo*, that divine order and value are
congruent with human ideas of these things. It is the law that shapes the speaker's question, "say first what cause / Moved our grand parents . . . to fall off"
(*LM* 1.28–30), and that mistakes narrative for causal order in *Paradise Lost*,
transforming God into tragic necessity and implicating him in evil. And it is
the law which thus objectifies religious expressions and thus promotes the illusion of parity between Milton's devil and his God, allowing Satan the equal
stature to which he lays claim as "Antagonist of heaven's almighty king," holding creation in divided reign (*LM* 10.386–87).

But as the story progresses, it becomes less and less possible to extend to
Satan that bad eminence the speaker gives him as the cause of human apostasy,
or to recapture the power of those manifest attractions and compelling grievances which seemed to displace his guilt onto God. For what seems most heroic
about Milton's devil gradually transforms itself into an almost comic ignominy:
his principled resistance to tyranny becomes an act of spite, callously inflicted
upon our grand parents as God's proxies; his grand design for the overthrow of
good involves, as someone has said, the equivalent of hiding behind doors and
listening in at keyholes; the residual glory of his angelic nature is increasingly
debased by his schemes at self-promotion and the shapes he expediently assumes to effect his bad ends. Having fashioned the devil's inordinate appeal,
Milton seems unaccountably to withdraw it, methodically orchestrating the
eventual and final banality of his evil. As any number of critics have observed
since Dryden, it is as though neither the poet nor his speaker could decide
where to place their allegiance, so that Milton's great argument seems inexplicably to exchange its objects of derision. Notwithstanding the theological confusion this perplexing of value creates, it raises the very dramaturgical problem
that the poem appeared already to have solved. For if good and evil are compellingly to contend with each other, their representatives must somehow share
each other's status, even when one of them is putatively the inconceivable
God: otherwise, the disproportioning of significance between the two would
completely incapacitate the drama, as well as make Milton's justification into
an excuse for God's tyranny, just as Satan claims. But as it happens, the fall of
Satan in our esteem is balanced by the other singularity of *Paradise Lost*, which
is the distasteful and, it would appear, artistically inept person of the Father.

Empson of course devotes his entire book to the critical tradition of complaint about what passes for Milton's God and the difficulties this character
creates for the poem as whole.[9] Northrop Frye too finds the Father "disastrous,"
Milton's having inexplicably entrusted his entire case to the "one character

who is conspicuously no good at argument," who comes across not as imponderable deity but as "a smirking hypocrite."[10] "There is nothing to be done with this objectionable creature except swallow him," Frye reluctantly concludes;[11] and this is pretty much the opinion of Christopher Hill, for whom the Father is a mere cipher for the injustice of history—an unpleasant, ineluctable fate for England, the poet, and needless to say, Milton's unfortunate reader.[12] So if Satan degenerates, it seems he only lowers himself to the ignoble level of Milton's God, where their shared mediocrity restores them to a dismal kind of parity. Given that Milton's theology allows evil as such no comparable agency or stature to the role given Satan in the poem, we are bound to infer that the devil's eventual denigration baldly and simplistically confirms a doctrinal point more than evident in the *Christian Doctrine*—that appearances aside, the poem does not present us with a Manichaean universe. However, it does make Milton's great argument into a deck stacked against Satan, Adam, Eve, and the reader, with the Father having been dealt all the cards: for despite the human catastrophe involved, what looks to be a contest between good and evil turns out otherwise, because God so effortlessly proves Satan the dupe of sacred history and no angel of light. But while this view of Milton's justification is not uncommon, the figure of the Father cannot sustain it, since we find Milton's God at least as culpable and—for a time certainly—far less credible than we do Milton's devil.[13] And once the contest of good and evil degenerates into a battle of competing mediocrities, moral and artistic, we are also at a loss to account for the stature of *Paradise Lost*.

But to identify Milton's truth with either figure, the Father or Satan, would be to commit the very fallacy of reifying religious meanings that Paul avoids in his allegory and Luther professes to make in his hypothetical version. It is an error on the same order as supposing that God's adversary is some metaphysical counterpart to deity, or that the accommodation of idea to figure in *Paradise Lost* entails a discrete correspondence between theological and poetic persons, places, and things, or that the sense of the poem is equivalent to what it appears to say. These assumptions are themselves idolatrous, since they contravene Milton's insistence on the expressive contingency of religious meanings, where no one thing can perpetually express deity's presence, much less divine being. Perhaps if the poet named his actors as Bunyan did—Save-all, By-Ends, Faithful, Mr. Legality—we would be less inclined to fall into this error, or to assume that Satan and the Father represent real entities as against personified concepts. But then we could not intimately learn the consequences of our religious ideas, since it is the justification of our understanding that Milton attempts here. We do succumb because the poem's argument is conducted by means of these apparent vagaries of figuration: Satan's graphic splendor and graphic degeneracy, the Father's alternately prosaic and despicable figure, the erratic and grotesque intrusion of allegory on the profundities of the Genesis myth, the religious obtuseness of the speaker and the erratic play of his perceptions and sympathies, not least the apostasy lurking in his epic similes. Indeed, as Milton remarks about the doctrine of the Trinity, "the drama of the personalities in the God-head" in *Paradise Lost* is a drama about our ideas of God and truth (CM 14:197).[14] He no more wants us to believe in the mimetic integrity of his figures than he wants us to suppose that heaven and hell are as he describes them. Yet that is just what we do when, with Ricks and Daiches, we propose to see deity or "the numinous" imaged in the Father, as against one aspect of our delimited, mediated, ironical knowledge of the divine, which the figuration of *Paradise Lost* expresses.

The appearance the poem has for us thus betrays our own religious affections, not in Fish's sense of directly manifesting sin or righteousness, as though a certain rhetorical power like Satan's was tantamount to apostasy and the Fa-ther's legal logic the formal equivalent of faith. On the contrary, Luther shows us that the same image or form of expression can be productive of profoundly different meanings, in a kind of figural adiaphorism. Thus, seen one way, Paul's New Jerusalem becomes the transcendent habitation of the saints; seen an-other, it expresses the actual ubiquity of the gospel in this world. Simply because they describe *invisibilia*, these readings can appear comparably "spiritual" or "transcendental" to the indifferent reader, yet they aren't to the theological mind. One translates God and value out of the world, while the other embeds them in it; one makes religion the perfection of the phenomenal or rational, while the other sets it against all such presumptive truths; one structures *invisi-bilia* after what can be seen, while the other entirely distinguishes them from it. Milton's figuration not merely discriminates between these different orders of religious value and understanding, but does so by making them simultaneously present and available to us in the same image, which is the figural work of irony. For we err in *Paradise Lost*, as we do in scripture, when we assume that a given image singularly and completely embodies the religious meaning it conveys, or that the most reverent expression is also the most poetic or the most plausible.

For Luther and Milton interpret the Pauline discrimination between law and gospel as posing a problem along the lines of body and soul in Wittgenstein's remark, and as arguing the difference Cavell discerns between representing and expressing as kinds of intelligence about the world. If we suppose that the body directly represents the soul, as visible to invisible, sooner or later we will find ourselves at an impasse, unable to account for the discrepancy between our reading and our experience of a person. Then we may do one of three things: we can decide that the body conceals the soul in the sense of hiding or disguising it, which leads us to expect deception and betrayal in every human encounter, at which point we will very likely repudiate any intelligible speech, gesture, countenance as false, deny all means of access to other minds, and live in para-noia and contradiction. Or we can persist in applying the same obsolete under-standing to people and live in perfect obliviousness, without reflection, adoring the body as the equivalent of the soul while rejecting every indication that it belongs to another order of phenomenon. Or we can recognize that the body conveys the soul contingently, not systematically, which requires us to work out the particular meaning of its expressions with each new encounter (which, as Wittgenstein reminds us, is what most of us do when we are not doing metaphysics, when experience goes on holiday). If we substitute here either scripture's expressions or Milton's, we reproduce the predicament of law and gospel where the law leads us to assume, if not an identity, then an analogy between deity and the things which convey it. When this putative analogy breaks down, as it invariably does in the face of human experience, then the logic of the law compels us to deny that there is a God, or to suppose that this God is demonic and hostile to human being, or to imagine that God has forsaken us on account of some unknown or unacknowledged guilt on our part. This is a version of the sceptic's crisis of meaning in Wittgenstein and Cavell, where the interlocutor insists that language signify in one way only—by reference to single, discrete, and palpable things—since he believes the world's very intelligibility is threatened when it does not. In Adorno, the crisis of the law appears as a rupture in the isomorphic universe of rationalism, a rupture taking the form of suffering's intractable reality; in Jeremiah, the psalmist, Job, the autobiographical excurses of Martin Luther, John Milton, and the speaker of *Paradise Lost*, it shows as injustice or religious incoherence compelling a tormented humanity to revise its knowledge of self and God together.

The same ironic disruption is why apostasy in *Paradise Lost* is expressed as a lapse or disjunction in meaningfulness—as failed intimacy between Adam and Eve, as the speaker's inability to locate or name his muse, and as the reader's sensations of aesthetic and logical incongruity—making these deprivations of coherence an allegory without an object in Paul's fashion. This experience emulates the operations of Lutheran *Anfechtung*, where the apparently seamless continuities of rationalism are exploded by existential incoherence, in the form of an intolerable discrepancy between our understandings and our actualities, precipitating the dilemma of faith—whether to believe and hope against deity's appearances or to resign oneself to tragedy's conflicted universe and the force of necessity. The assault upon faith is made by those assumptions of meaning— of patency, self-evidence, elegance, symmetry, and so on—to which humanity is ever susceptible, even when we acknowledge the hiddenness of God. Then deity's concealment becomes an excuse for supernaturalism and analogical speculation, a pleasant fiction of human transcendence to which the experience of injustice puts a catastrophic stop. And this crisis is what Milton would achieve when he places Sin and Death on the same plane of figurative reality as Satan and the Father, drastically qualifying the fatal impression (for his argument at least) that his devil and his God are persons in the naturalized sense. The figural vagaries, the dramatic inconsequence, the exposed artifice—in sum, the "bad" poetry of *Paradise Lost*—is then no inadvertency, no lack of skill or consciousness on the author's part. Because with this apparent disruption of religious myth and literate mimesis, we are forced back upon our assumptions of meaning; and unless we want to rest in the facile presumption that Milton nods in contradicting himself so baldly, we are obliged to rethink how the poem means. What his critics regard as Milton's artistic lapses or perversity thus challenges the reader to perform the interpretive revision of our criteria of meaningfulness that faith in the hidden God entails. But this justification entails the experience of expressive incongruity—"the rhetorical element," as Adorno calls it—intruding between us and our infinite capacity for idolatry, that is to say, our desire to believe adamantly, without reflection, in whatever pretty image takes us.

Like Paul's allegory in Galatians, *Paradise Lost* pictures mentalities, not entities. That ironic effect is ancient and usual to epic, inasmuch as it represents the discrepancy between what a character believes and what narrator and audience know to be the case. But when the effect itself becomes the subject of poetic expression, when the meaning of an image lies in the very way we determine to construe it, then the reflexive aspect of irony verges on the phenomenological. Yet because our interpretations are religious in nature, having to do with the binding force of truth itself, the phenomena of meaning cannot be subjective or ideal: as with any ideology, we inevitably re-create its assumptions in our engagements with others. On the ironic model of *facere Deum*, they express the truth we choose to live by and inevitably foist upon the world beyond the mind; and it is this pregnant relation, not God or truth, that Milton depicts in *Paradise Lost*. So when Satan suddenly and, it would seem, incongruously encounters Sin and Death in the mythic landscape of hell, his surprise and ours at this allegorical intrusion is the effect of those flawed assumptions of meaning engendering Satan's monstrous daughter and son in the first place. Milton's readers have pondered this propensity for objectification ever since it was observed that the artificial behavior of soliloquy is a convention among the fallen. The estrangement that soliloquy expresses in *Paradise Lost*—most obviously in relationship to other persons but also from any value or meaning not originating in the self—explains why fabling and allegorizing more generally predominate in the perceptions of Satan, the speaker, and our first parents when they move to discount the reality of God.[15] It is a tendency evinced in those remarkable epic similes describing the fallen angels in hell, which take on a narrative and psychological life all their own; in the speaker's obsessive, desirous likening of Eve as he anticipates her seduction by that old serpent; and in the curious fact that the figure of *prosopopoeia* or apostrophe, itself an objectifying of meaning or perception, accompanies Satan wherever he goes.[16] So it is inevitable that Satan would encounter the person of his own sin as he passes through hell toward the newly created world, and that he would not recognize her as his own:

> Thus roving on
> In confused march forlorn, the adventurous bands
> With shuddering horror pale, and eyes aghast
> Viewed first their lamentable lot, and found
> No rest: through many a dark and dreary vale
> They passed, and many a region dolorous,

O'er many a frozen, many a fiery alp,
Rocks, caves, lakes, fens, bogs, dens, and shades of death,
A universe of death, which God by curse
Created evil, for evil only good,
Where all life dies, death lives, and nature breeds,
Perverse, all monstrous, all prodigious things,
Abominable, inutterable, and worse
Than fables yet have feigned, or fear conceived,
Gorgons and Hydras, and Chimeras dire.
   Mean while the adversary of God and man,
Satan with thoughts inflamed of highest design,
Puts on swift wings, and towards the gates of hell
Explores his solitary flight; some times
He scours the right hand coast, some times the left,
Now shaves with level wing the deep, then soars
Up to the fiery concave towering high.
As when far off at sea, a fleet descried
Hangs in the clouds, by equinoctial winds
Close sailing from Bengala, or the isles
Of Ternate and Tidore, whence merchants bring
Their spicy drugs; they on the trading flood
Through the wide Ethiopian to the Cape
Ply stemming nightly toward the pole. So seemed
Far off the flying fiend: at last appear
Hell bounds high reaching to the horrid roof,
And thrice threefold the gates; three folds were brass,
Three iron, three of adamantine rock,
Impenetrable, impaled with circling fire,
Yet unconsummed. Before the gates there sat
On either side a formidable shape;
The one seemed woman to the waist, and fair,
But ended foul in many a scaly fold
Voluminous and vast, a serpent armed
With mortal sting: about her middle round
A cry of hell hounds never ceasing barked
With wide Cerberian mouths full loud, and rung
A hideous peal: yet, when they list, would creep,
If aught disturbed their noise, into her womb,
And kennel there, yet there still barked and howled,
Within unseen.

                                (*LM* 2.614–59)

This concatenation of infernal sights is symptomatic of the same religious pathology that comes to order the human debacle of the earthly fall, where an insistence on the superficial aspect of creation effaces its expressiveness, its dependence upon God's informing goodness. The result is a world disintegrated into random, grotesque, and distinctly allegorical effects—allegorical in that each image is made to carry an unaccustomed burden of significance by some flagrant incongruity in its use. Indeed, allegory of one kind is the peculiar, inescapable mode of existence in hell, a fitting *contrapasso* for those who idolize mere appearance, which is why the fallen angels in their survey confront a blighted, ominous landscape where nature is now alienated from its own principles of order, operating against all expectation, unnaturally, monstrously. For that very reason, the image of hell's gate expresses a manifold shielding of the outside world against hell itself—a venerable piece of heroic iconography from Homer and Horace, aptly turned inside out like the place it guards. Everything familiar has given way to this inverted species of operation and meaning. There is the absurdist image applied to Satan, "puts on swift wings," where figuration itself has become strangely oblivious to its subject and so redundant, tautologous. The same unconstrained and incoherent fancy also allows for the licentious animation of the epic simile, which begins by comparing the "flying fiend" to the pendant sight of a merchant fleet between sea and sky—an optical illusion significant of the speaker's now casual misperception of the satanic. But abruptly, in the approved manner of such infernal similes, it telescopes and shifts imaginative emphasis to recount the journey and drug-laden cargo of the ships themselves, with Satan's appearance exerting a comparably narcotic effect on the speaker and, at his journey's end, our first parents. Fittingly, after this fugue of figuration, we are shown the all-encompassing allegory of Sin's divided and dissociated body, whose iconographical precedents are of course legion and whose mode of existence encapsulates all the images that have preceded it. For they too have been denaturalized in such a way that they no longer describe sympathetic but estranged, distorted perceptions of the world.

In effect, then, the sequence of the speaker's imagery works out the implications of the law, present here in the horrified vision of the apostate angels, whose religious precipitate and token is hell's extravagant allegorizing. For the infernal landscape enacts a whole psychology that looks like a place and appears to be inhabited; yet its "Gorgons, Hydras, and Chimeras dire" describe creatural experience divorced from all ordinary meaning by satanic fancy and fear. Milton's hell is decidedly an invented, artificial realm: it exists not because, in Dante's fashion, deity has consigned the operation of the otherworld over to the ineluctable perfection of each person's sin, as the speaker in yet another causal fallacy suggests when he says that "God by curse created evil." There is no entelechy, no absolute or extrinsic necessity to sin that orders the hell through which, it seems, Satan makes his way. Rather, its horrors are contingent on how Satan, and on this occasion the speaker with him, *choose* to understand the world God has made. When Satan "breaks union" with creation's ordained significance, he is obliged perforce to construct for himself and his companions another meaning that will explain their experience (*LM* 5.611–15). But what he and they first see, "Cast out from God and blessed vision," is the utter decimation of meaning that denying their creator entails. To reiterate, Milton himself does not argue a phenomenology here: that is Satan's idealizing account of his own position, not the poet's. Rather, in the perceptions of the fallen angels, Milton shows what the world becomes when we exclude the expressive reality of *res non apparentes*. And it looks like Satan's first glance around him from the burning lake, or his cohorts' survey of hell's disjointed, repetitive features— "rocks, caves, lakes, fens, bogs, dens, and shades of death"—a landscape devoid of creative purpose, and thus light and hope, peace and rest.[17]

In the *Christian Doctrine*, Milton describes a state of affairs not unlike the position in which the devil and his crew find themselves, having fallen the distance of their alienation from God. The subject at hand is how we know that there is a God, to which Milton responds with these proofs of deity's existence:

> Though there be not a few who deny the existence of God, "for the fool hath said in his heart, There is no God," Psal.xiv.I. yet the Deity has imprinted upon the human mind so many unquestionable tokens of himself, and so many traces of him are apparent throughout the whole of nature, that no one in his senses can remain ignorant of the truth. . . . There can be no doubt that every thing in the world, by the beauty of its order, and the evidence of a determinate and beneficial purpose which pervades it, testifies that some supreme efficient Power must have pre-existed, by which the whole was ordained for a specific end.
>
> There are some who pretend that nature or fate is this supreme Power: but the very name of nature implies that it must owe its birth to some prior agent, or, to speak properly, signifies in itself nothing; but means either the essence of a thing, or that general law which is the origin of every thing, and under which every thing acts; on the other hand, fate can be nothing but a divine decree emanating from some almighty power.
>
> Further, those who attribute the creation of every thing to nature, must necessarily associate chance with nature as a joint divinity; so that they gain nothing by this theory, except that in the place of that one God, whom they cannot tolerate, they are obliged, however reluctantly, to substitute two sovereign rulers of affairs, who must almost always be in opposition to each other. In short, many visible proofs, the verification of numberless predictions, a multitude of wonderful works have compelled all nations to believe, either that God, or that some evil power whose name was unknown, presided over the affairs of the world. Now that evil should prevail over good, and be the true supreme power, is as unmeet as it is incredible. Hence it follows as a necessary consequence, that God exists.
>
> Again: the existence of God is further proved by that feeling, whether we term it conscience, or right reason, which even in the worst of characters is not altogether extinguished. If there were no God, there would be no distinction between right and wrong; the estimate of virtue and vice would entirely depend upon the blind opinion of men; none would follow

virtue, none would be restrained from vice and by any sense of shame, or fear of the laws, unless conscience or right reason did from time to time convince every one, however unwilling, of the existence of God, the Lord and ruler of all things, to whom, sooner or later, each must give an account of his actions, whether good or bad. (CM 14:25–29)

Milton is not asserting a natural theology here: instead, like Wittgenstein, his naturalism consists in the lived, practical coherence sustaining human existence; and while it can never be absolute or even continuous, he sees providence in a world ordinarily intelligible and viable. But precisely because the world is not automatic, because the miraculous is yet possible, he rejects nature as the origin of nature since, as he says, to make it such would be tautologous, as well as a sublimation that translates the objective dimension of human experience into universal necessity. The impinging of both fate and chance on natural regularity denies such necessity, even as these arbitrary forces express nothing more than our thwarted expectations—one made seemingly intelligent, the other inadvertent, both of which describe the human experience of contingency. At the same time, this opposition of nature and fate creates the perpetually conflicted universe of tragedy, the double bind of "two sovereign rulers of affairs" who behave like Nussbaum's implacable gods, tyrannizing over humanity with their contradictory demands. But Milton argues that a Manichaean universe of known good and unknown evil, which holds out the possibility of evil triumphant, is actually inconsistent with ordinary experience; for this picture is itself contradicted by the preeminent and enduring sense we have of the world's beauty, in which the universal idea of deity originates. The supremacy of evil cannot account for the mundane if partial prevalence of good, which is the force behind Milton's "unmeet" and "incredible": it contradicts natural and subjective realities, especially the indomitable human sense of conscience.[18]

Despite the reference to a final judgment, Milton isn't talking here about conscience as a canon of absolute value. He understands it as that forcible impression we have of a more-than-physical order and meaningfulness to the world, whereby deity is made present to us. Yet the divine is not present in the shape of any one interpretation we devise for things, but consists in the world's very capacity for moral significance—its potential for meaning in this principled way. As Milton understands these values here and in the tracts, "right" and "virtue" lie in the recurrent event of such meaningfulness—in nature and history, in the worship of God, in marriage—too often concealed by the flux and vehemence of human opinion. In this way, the feeling of moral coherence Milton calls conscience is a proof of God; for it allows us to distinguish a meaning, an order, to our lives that is not hopelessly circular or ad hoc. It is also why the peculiar intelligence of right reason is not simply eclipsed where evil is most complete, since, as Milton remarks, the fact of such latent meaning to things is still acknowledged by the vicious—by Satan himself even as one of his originals does, Shakespeare's Richard III. Only for them, it no longer discloses a manifold possibility of coherence: instead they suppress and efface the moral aspect of being—the goodness and appropriateness of the world—as a residue of intelligibility that has long since vanished from the landscape, along with deity and truth. This evacuation occurs whenever our expectations are betrayed by the appearance things have for us—something that happens to Satan, as well as the speaker and our first parents—because, in that moment, the familiar world seems violently eviscerated of its wonted significance.

Yet contrary to the appearance lent things by the speaker's own suffering, creation after the fall of angel and human being retains its original beauty and integrity, for neither creator nor creature has wrought its fundamental ruin; what changes is the creature's attitude toward its own congenital condition, its very life. As the Son observes, deity does not unmake what it has created, nor does it permit the triumph of evil (LM 3.150–66). In loving inflection, the creator continues to exert the ordering power of good that is its modus vivendi in history, ensuring by its expressive presence the restoration of the world that evil would fix forever in devastation. This is the point Milton makes by the Son's ready and imperturbable willingness to sacrifice himself for humanity, in which "Love hath abounded more than glory abounds" (LM 3.312), and by the display of heaven's imperviousness to the great upheaval transpiring there, when Messiah rides over a landscape that angelic warfare had left (so we are told) disrupted and desolate: "At his command the uprooted hills retired / Each to his place, they heard his voice and went / Obsequious, heaven his wonted face renewed, / And with fresh flowerets hill and valley smiled" (LM 6.781–84). The face heaven shows to deity is always the same, a reality expressed here in both its sentience and its almost seamless renewal, with no sign of devastation left upon the landscape. By contrast, the apostate have themselves unconsciously, catastrophically changed toward the world God made, and specifically in the way they perceive the force of deity's distinction. If the creator's awful difference is figured in the latency of the world's meaningfulness, to which Milton argues conscience is specially alive, that circumstance becomes curiously aggravated in hell, where the nature of creation, its character as *expression*, has been almost skeletally exposed. And that is because the fallen mind understands such inevident coherence as a grievous withholding of what rightfully belongs to it, its natural prerogative of likeness to God. Accordingly, the signs of deity's distinction are felt not only as injustice by those who have refused or somehow perverted the sense of personal dependence on God, but also as a summary and inexplicable evacuation of significance from self and world. Because with the cessation of this religious relationship goes the experience of an infinitely meaningful and possible creation, pictured here in the image of heaven's vital response to the advent of the Son. So the apostate angels are left with what amounts to the carcass of creaturely appearance, which humanity experiences both as the removal of deity from the landscape of creation and, as Milton argues in The Reason of Church Government, as the veiling of divine meaning by the law. For evil is nothing other than the intelligible loss of that coherence, that living presence of the creator in creation, which faith reveals and conscience recalls to our uncertain understanding.

We are shown the event that precipitates the hell of the apostate only indirectly, and it would appear, much belatedly by Raphael, when he tells the story of Lucifer and the war in heaven to Adam and Eve, an account testing how we as readers understand the accommodation of divine to human things. For in the course of one heavenly day, the Father declares to the assembled angelic hosts:

> Hear all ye angels, progeny of light,
> Thrones, dominations, princedoms, virtues, powers,
> Hear my decree, which unrevoked shall stand.
> This day I have begot whom I declare
> My only Son, and on this holy hill
> Him have anointed, whom ye now behold
> At my right hand; your head I him appoint;
> And by my self have sworn to him shall bow
> All knees in heaven, and shall confess him Lord.
>
> (LM 5.600–608)

The absurdity of the exaltation, with the Son begotten and anointed in the same eternal duration, not only signals the distinction of God from the world, in the form of deity's freedom from logical and phenomenal constraint, but also translates this historical event from physical and temporal action into *façons de parler*, a way of speaking about the Father's relation to the Son, which now appears allegorical or emblematic.[19] At the same time, begetting and anointing are distinguished as two separate actions by the Father, for lineal or dynastic rule has no more place in *Paradise Lost* than it does in *The Tenure of Kings and Magistrates* (CM 5:10–14). Begetting is expressed here as an act of formal adoption, to distinguish it from creation proper since the Son's being, as first-born creature and deity's singular agent, presupposes this moment as it does the very existence of heaven and the angelic hosts. So we have the impression that this person is peculiarly present and active in creation, but that deity has paused before uniquely distinguishing him: the Father marks the interlude not because the Son was unmade or absent, but because no created thing can claim continuity or nature with the hidden God. Creation does not descend from deity in the manner of an emanation scheme: it is made by divine fiat, not metaphysical or material engendering, just as the Son is here; and like the Son, its affinity to God is comparably a matter of imputation and acknowledgment. The same holds true of the Son's lordship, his status as messiah; for where there is no descent, there is no hereditary right, only ordination.

It is precisely this seeming arbitrariness in the Father's decree that tries angelic fidelity, in much the same manner as God's interdiction of the tree tries the understanding of our first parents. Where the exaltation's temporal illogic may strike the reader, what strikes Satan in the virtual eternity of heaven is its groundlessness, its injustice. The Father declares what is seemingly inevident to the creatural world of the angels, namely, the special relation of this person to him. So to the extent that the exaltation obliges Satan to watch the Son "created" before his eyes, in the sense of both being "engendered" and "ennobled," he is forced to confront his own creatureliness and the unbridgeable gulf between himself and God. His response is to deny both actualities, which he does by immediately refusing to admit the divine claim and authority of the person thus exalted, and so to exclude from his world the creator who exists in the very implication of creatural being, as Milton suggests above. And when Abdiel challenges this willful defacement of creation, Satan argues idolatrously that the world is nothing more than the sum of the creature's perceptions, and that there was no intervention, no mediation between nonexistence and angelic being—no "work / Of secondary hands" (*LM* 5.854):

> who saw
> When this creation was? Remember'st thou
> Thy making, while the maker gave thee being?
> We know no time when we were not as now;
> Know none before us, self-begot, self-raised
> By our own quickening power.
>
> (*LM* 5.856–61)

Satan's account of creation as circumscribed by angelic memory explains how the title "gods," which the angels bear in their impersonation of deity to the world, becomes self-definition and identity for the apostate. The reality of *res non apparentes* is summarily excluded from existence, since Satan makes all being coextensive not just with mental images but with things that can be *seen*, demanding a graphic memory of his creation as the only valid proof of a creator. The "tokens" and "traces" that deity leaves upon human and natural being— the allegory of divine presence to which Milton alludes in his proofs of God— are refused and discarded as insufficient evidence: proof must be direct and visual, in keeping with Satan's assumption that appearances supply an absolute canon of what is real and true.[20] All sense of creatural expressiveness is thus extinguished, with Satan demanding of Abdiel, "That we were formed then say'st thou?" (*LM* 5.853). In other words, he rejects the idea that he was created a "form," figure, or sign expressive of something unlike himself, here the unseen agency that made him. Not only does he suppose that his being is autonomous, without relation to anything other than himself, but that it is effectively self-evident. In Satan's understanding, self is an integral, discrete, and immutable entity, which is pretty much the theological definition of God. So before he decrees the godhead of the angels, Satan first denies deity's ineradicable difference from himself as well as the contingency and expressiveness of his own being—the force of the distinction between creator and creature. And the occasion of this denial, although not the cause as Satan contends, is the Son's exaltation, when Satan imagines himself at once betrayed in his presumption of significance and (as Raphael puts it) "impaired" or diminished in identity (*LM* 5.665). For Satan's as yet tacit atheism had allowed him to suppose that his likeness to God, his divine semblance, consisted in the correspondence of his being to the supposedly manifest nature of deity, and that he was by glorious kind and degree the image of God to the world—God in all but name.

Consequently, when he denies his creator, he succumbs simultaneously to the illusion of a nature absolutely of, by, and for itself, a subjective autarchy or solipsism whose effects he proceeds to implement in rebellion. Moreover, by rejecting self as an order of relation to God, Satan has become in his now-exilic mind (in the archaic sense of devastated or ruined) an object displaced, an entity whose proper nature and position in the world has been usurped by the Son. Thus his way of describing the exaltation to the conspirators: "Another now hath to himself engrossed / All power, and us eclipsed under the name / Of king anointed" (*LM* 5.775–77). The emblematic character of the Son's creation is read as a material, forcible, and adversarial action by God, inaugurating the "engrossment" and estrangement of religious meaning and value that Sin's simultaneous birth and personification allegorize. But this reifying of religious value is discovered by the satanic angels only when they suffer bodily pain in battle with the unfallen forces of God. Since his sense of psychological deprivation has now become a calculable injury—physical, martial, and political— Satan ironically realizes self as the sum of his appearances, which once physicalized can be measured and depleted. Indeed, the notional and rhetorical claim that God has diminished him becomes palpably the case in heaven's war, not because deity does this but because Satan has performed a reduction on himself when he denies his expressive or figural being. The whole heavenly world, once eloquent of relationship with God, is fragmented by Satan into objects or particles of singular, autonomous, self-evident meaning and agency like himself: this is what the battle signifies, when the fallen angels lose sight of the landscape's sentient being, objectifying, ravaging, and eviscerating its living body in search of material with which to make a new and adverse creation that will be deployed against heaven itself. Such is the dissociating force of Satan's reinterpretation of the creature, and the devastation that it wreaks.[21]

But if his own self-induced estrangement thus palpably diminishes and injures the world around him, Satan feels this manifold loss as a deprivation *caused* by the Father's arbitrary preferral of the Son over himself. He reads the exaltation as an injustice, an attempt to deprive him of his congenital and conspicuous claim on the divine semblance, since the Son's ordination in effect decrees that Satan is no longer the person he had thought himself to be, God's exclusive image. For in Satan's ontological hierarchy, physical position in heaven—relative height or proximity to God's holy hill—reflects degree of personal perfection and so likeness to the best; and in thus conceiving himself in his sheer superficies—priority, power, prerogative, and insignia—to be the apex of creatural existence, he ranks as god on the model of divine right monarchy.

Accordingly, Satan understands the Son's preferment as an act of *lèse majesté*, the arbitrary usurpation of his rightful place as God's lieutenant and treason against his person, which creates a sudden, terrible disproportion and incoherence in heaven. And although he professes to see the exaltation as an assault on the status and privilege of all the angelic hosts, in which divine illogic and injustice leaves creation desolate of its evident meaning, the reality is that Satan apprehends in the Father's act the ruin of his most dearly held assumptions about himself. That is why Satan not just dissents from the new order under the Son but organizes a rebellion against God, ostensibly acting in defense of angelic liberty and against divine tyranny, but really to preserve the delusion that the identity and value of created things is manifest, irrevocable, and absolute. And Abdiel says as much to Satan's face—that both before the Son's exaltation and after, his self-appointed supremacy had distorted his understanding of the relationship between creature and creator:

> Shalt thou give law to God, shalt thou dispute
> With him the points of liberty, who made
> Thee what thou art, and formed the powers of heaven
> Such as he pleased, and circumscribed their being?
> Yet by experience taught we know how good,
> And of our good, and of our dignity
> How provident he is, how far from thought
> To make us less, bent rather to exalt
> Our happy state under one head more near
> United. But to grant it thee unjust,
> That equal over equals monarch reign:
> Thy self though great and glorious dost thou count,
> Of all angelic nature joined in one,
> Equal to him begotten Son, by whom
> As by his Word the mighty Father made
> All things, even thee . . . ?
>
> (*LM* 5.822–37)

This is Milton's version of the potter with his clay: by underscoring the absurdity of what is made giving law to its maker, of Satan disputing with the being "who made / Thee what thou art" in no creatural sense, Abdiel makes Isaiah's point that an acknowledgment of deity's incomparable status completely reorganizes our experience of God. The insurpassable difference between potter and clay, conscious and inanimate existence, intellectual and material being, agency and passivity, is suppressed when the idolatrous deify the work of their own hands. Like Satan with Sin, they incontinently project their own subjectivity onto things, deluded by this false creation into supposing that they can control the world through images. But such magical mastery merely disguises the oppressiveness of the demonic world these practices predicate; for as long as we imagine that deity is invested in its appearances or images, that there is a continuity of being and power between them, we are bound to hate God. In the same conversation where he talks about the bombproof container Krupps made to carry the Eucharist, Wittgenstein comments on the alienation that inexorably attends our assuming that the divine is analogous to human being, only perfect and transcendent. Thus he observes that Catholicism had made a dogma of the thesis that "the existence of God can be proved by natural reason," which is to imagine not only a likeness but a complete continuity between deity and the world.[22] He then goes on to say that such a dogma would prohibit his becoming Catholic, because "If I thought of God as another being like myself, only infinitely more powerful, then I would regard it as my duty to defy him."

On the same grounds, Milton refuses to see scriptural anthropomorphism as even remotely analogous to the divine nature, rather than a picture deity composes to express and accomplish relationship with us insofar as we believe it; it is also why he makes human experience the proof of God, as against nature somehow independent of our lives and perception. The truly salient analogy Milton's religion admits is between the impalpables of faith and charity, that is, the conceptual and the moral expressions of God in human life: there can be no such thing as an analogous appearance, much less a correlation of nature or essence to the divine as Satan imagines in his own case. So having idolatrously circumscribed in his mind what deity is—restricting its nature to his creatural one—he must defy the God he patterned after his own being, who has violated outright Satan's standard of similitude and equality. Having suppressed God's incommensurable difference, Satan has also forgotten himself. And without acknowledging the distinction between deity and the world, he cannot find in the exaltation what Abdiel sees: namely, the creature's far more profound affinity with the creator through the Son's intimate mediation of God, "by whom / As by his Word the mighty Father made / All things, even thee." With his idolatrous emphasis on the divine image as against the divine word, on sacramental sign over testamental promise in his very creation, Satan experiences only a further disproportioning, a veiling and removal of God from himself—the apostate's experience of mediation—since the Son now stands between Satan and God, obstructing what was notionally his free and rightful access, his liberty of communion.

Angelic apostasy thus observes a similar order of conceptual effect to that Wittgenstein calls "noticing an aspect": when we see something *as* something, it has that character for us; and in *Paradise Lost*, the world as found exhibits just this volubility of appearance, articulating each person's understanding and experience of God and self. But when we refuse to acknowledge the play of aspect itself—expressiveness implicating something besides the superficial sense an appearance has for us—then our whole world is spontaneously depleted of meaning. One might see this as a version of Luther's distinction between the scriptural word experienced *vocaliter*, as the mere letter, and *vitaliter*, as profoundly, spontaneously meaningful.[23] Bereft of God, it becomes alien, inconsequent, and perverse, like the landscape Satan views on waking and through which the fallen pass in horror. Yet hell, Sin, and Death are no less real because they have their origin, as Sin herself parodically professes, in Satan as their author and disposer: "Thou art my father, thou my author, thou / My being gavest me; whom should I obey / But thee, whom follow?" (*LM* 2. 864–66). On the contrary, they are more so because they entirely embody the experience of his suffering, even as they and the demonic deity of Satan's speeches are the picture of it. It is this effect expressive of Satan's disaffection, and, through him, the speaker's predicament, which Daiches and Ricks rightly find appalling; yet it is dreadful not because Milton's imagery is false to the "numinous," but because it is true to the ravages of a peculiar religious mentality Satan exemplifies, which Luther and Milton both combat in their theologies, and in which we all inveterately participate in some degree or other. But religious psychology is not confined to religion alone: as Wittgenstein, Adorno, and Cavell each observe in secular culture, how we think the world means informs our expectations of truth and equally the kind of life to which we believe truth enjoins us.

It is because any ideology or system of ideas, regardless of its motives, will prove inhumane when pursued for its own sake, that Milton invokes charity in scriptural exegesis: when religious interpretation ceases to enfranchise human experience, out of a desire to sustain some impertinent idea of logical or doctrinal integrity, then God's word becomes a source of the worst injustice—as he says, a "strange, repugnant riddle." And Satan's infamous fixity of mind is all about detaching meaning from its circumstances, so that the enterprise of knowing the world ironically becomes involuted, a species of solipsism—a Cartesian *cogito* without God to bear out its ideas, but also a false Stoic imperturbability that denies the claim of suffering (*LM* 1.97). And this transcendent because intransigent intelligence that Satan celebrates in himself is nothing short of that raging idealism which in Wittgenstein and Adorno so deforms human subjectivity and human life. As a poet, Milton's distinctive contribution to the analysis of our religious mentalities lies in giving them an aesthetic or figural expression consistent with their presuppositions of meaning. He attends to that aspect of the problem not only because idolatry raises an issue of expression; but also because, as *Lycidas* argues, poetry itself raises an issue of idolatry and has at least since Plato.

All Monstrous, All Prodigious Things

Walter Benjamin makes this recognition about the *Trauerspiel* or German "mourning-play," in which he also takes issue with the uncircumstanced kind of aesthetic judgment critics have pronounced on Milton's hell, heaven, and God.[24] Indeed, Benjamin regards the extravagances and ineptitudes of these baroque dramas as in some measure vindicating allegory, which becomes its own subject of reflection. He argues that the *Trauerspiel*'s elaborate badness, located for the most part in its manner of allegorizing, is not a flaw but a significant aspect of its dramatic argument, having to do with the way we imagine access to the absolute or true. What in this theatrical form seems like an incorrigible propensity for defective drama enacts instead the disfiguring of our humanity and the world when, against all indications to the contrary, we insist on idealizing the conditions of human meaning. Then the whole creation becomes "ruins" or "fragments," a grotesque, blasted landscape where the significance of things is almost entirely arbitrary, where "Any person, any object, any relationship can mean absolutely anything else."[25] There are no integral constraints in this ravaged domain, no functional logic or order among things that might keep the projection of meaning by author or actor within plausible bounds. So, unsurprisingly, Benjamin reports that the *Trauerspiel* is deprecated for the sheer prodigality of its depictions—for being bombastic, violent, repetitive, overly elaborate, and trivial even in excess of its obviously Senecan models. "Never," observes Benjamin, "has poetry been less winged."[26] Nor, he concedes in a comment reminiscent of Daiches on Milton, do these professedly religious plays about the downfall of tyrants, or princely and womanly virtue martyred, offer us anything approaching a sublime account of their material. "And they lack any feeling for the intimate, the mysterious," for all that they "attempt extravagantly and vainly, to replace it with the enigmatic and concealed."[27] Their recourse is to allegory, conceived as a sort of occult knowledge of the meanings behind the awful, licentious spectacle of courtly intrigues, incest, patricide, wars, assassinations, suicides, and so on, which this drama favors along with the Tudor and Stuart stage in England. And its tabloid relish for histrionic extremes, manifest as an invasive visualism which extends to the picturing of dreams, tortures, fits of insanity, and ghosts, renders the *Trauerspiel* not just sensational but stagey. That is because its preferred mode of occurrence isn't action but discontinuous tableaux, made up of figures who are rendered "expressive statuary" as against dramatic persons.[28] So rather than a depiction which we can believe into virtual transparency, allegory here obtrudes to astonish and amaze us, like Sin and Death or angelic warfare in *Paradise Lost*.

If this is allegory's impact in the *Trauerspiel*, it is also an expressive purpose according to Benjamin. The plays' self-indulgent artifice describes a terrible alienation of truth from the world, dramatized at one level by the cruelty and injustice in which this drama exults, but at another by its own conspicuous efforts to extract some sense from arbitrary plotting—efforts which produce a dramatic argument impressively overwrought and overburdened in every way. This I gather to be the ground of Benjamin's redemption of German Baroque drama: in a proper antinomy, the success of these plays lies in detailing the sources of their own pathology, the studied mourning or lamentation for the human state their writers cultivate, or as Benjamin refines its many ambivalent and literate symptoms in the sixteenth century, with melancholy. For Benjamin doesn't see the presumptively "bad" art of the *Trauerspiel* as attenuated or abortive mimesis, but as a response to the disorder of a particular historical moment and as a contemporary analysis of the mentality accompanying this disorder:

namely, the ideological and civil upheaval of the Reformation and the Thirty Years War. For the reality the drama describes is the perpetually mediated one of human experience, an account both profound and true within these limits. Melancholy in the *Trauerspiel* serves not only as the response to catastrophe but equally as its motivation, so that tyranny is understood to result from the melancholic's simultaneous despair of and desire for a viable, creaturely truth in the face of injustice and evil. Yet the prodigious evil these dramas depict does not pertain to God's creation itself, which remains whole and entire. They belong to melancholy's shattered fantasy of the ideal and its enforced illusion of injustice and disaster which afflicts both author and actor, whose simultaneous allegorizing of experience betrays a mutual despair of regaining its significance.

In such a way, the perceived disaffection of meaning from the world is an occasion for the melancholic's subjectivism, where everything that occurs is made to rely on this estranged, anomic observer for its value, as the world's and the drama's real sovereign agency. The melancholic willfully and promiscuously reimposes meaning in the form of allegory—promiscuously, because the drama's grotesquerie and artifice arise not so much from the ostensible encounter with injustice as they do from the abjection of the person meditating that possibility. So if melancholy mourns the wreck of once substantial beauty and order, it is also complicitous in their destruction, licensed by the fact of injustice to treat the world as a place of abstruse, arbitrary, and demonic significance, and thus to engulf it in sheer subjectivism. Its loss is then largely a self-induced, self-reflexive disaster, the effect of overweening despair. And despair also governs the way this oddly literate drama uses various kinds of pictorialism at once to assert and expose its own erratic and grotesque idea of things. In Benjamin's view, the "mourning-plays" criticize by their very excesses the mentality they enact and express, and to that extent they share Milton's understanding of religious pathology. But their special similarity appears in the link Benjamin discerns between a certain order and quality of figuration and Baroque culture's obsessive interest in melancholy itself as the mania of the imagination. This is the connection Satan's speeches inadvertently and ironically evoke for the reader, in expressing "that fixed mind / And high disdain, from sense of injured merit, / That with the mightiest raised me to contend" (*LM* 1.97–99). For hell originates in the very sense of devastation and injustice to which Satan testifies in his first great manifesto to the fallen, where he shows himself enthralled to the idolatrous mentality which would equate deity with its appearances, making God a being no different from himself, except in the extrinsic attribute of power:

> Is this the region, this the soil, the clime,
> Said then the lost archangel, this the seat
> That we must change for heaven, this mournful gloom
> For that celestial light? Be it so, since he
> Who now is sovereign can dispose and bid

What shall be right: furthest from him is best
Whom reason hath equalled, force hath made supreme
Above his equals. Farewell happy fields
Where joy for ever dwells: hail horrors, hail
Infernal world, and thou profoundest hell
Receive thy new possessor: one who brings
A mind not to be changed by place or time.
The mind is its own place, and in itself
Can make a heaven of hell, a hell of heaven.
What matter where, if I be still the same,
And what should I be, all but less than he
Whom thunder hath made greater? Here at least
We shall be free; the almighty hath not built
Here for his envy, will not drive us hence:
Here we may reign secure, and in my choice
To reign is worth ambition though in hell:
Better to reign in hell, than serve in heaven.

(*LM* 1.242–63)

The noble temper of this speech is deceptive, if only because the stoicism it exemplifies is usually suspect in Milton's eyes and for the very reason that Satan gives in advocating the posture of imperturbability here: that is, Stoicism's ideal of self-sufficiency, its refusal to acknowledge dependence on anything but the individual mind, so that God and the world are effectively denied their proper claim upon the self. Accordingly, God is Satan's equal by right of nature or "reason," and "sovereign" over him only forcibly and arbitrarily, by chance possession of "thunder." The "right" held by deity appears unjust, since Satan conceives it to be right by conquest as against nature or law.[29] As I remarked earlier, because Milton's narrative order appears to give the devil figural equality, even primacy, over God—an idea enforced by the exactly calculated yet deficient correspondences between hell and heaven—and because we have been told by Satan and the apostate angels that there is no God, only the person "almighty styled," the circumstances in which we meet Milton's God promote a certain incredulity, if not disdain (*LM* 9.137). In short, there is no God like the one theologians, Milton included, define by a litany of inconceivables (infinitude, immutability, omniscience, omnipresence, omnipotence, and so forth): the Father is merely heaven's tyrant, whose supremacy is not real or essential but titular and enforced by accidental power. In every other respect, he is like Satan, possessed of Satan's own desires and imperatives—for place, dominion, power, in sum, for absolute and incontrovertible significance. But it is the freedom that power grants to "dispose and bid what shall be right," and thus to legislate meaning for others, in which Satan locates the Father's actual sovereignty and which he determines to exercise himself in hell.[30] Lacking deity, there is no obvious constraint on how he may order his world; yet his mind is not free but fixed, and, absorbed by the memory of his loss, it reduces existence to a competition between himself and God about how the rest of creation will mean. For Satan's so-called "conquest" of the new world involves disseminating his mentality among its inhabitants, so that they see God as he does, choose as Satan chose to do; and this conquest begins with his claiming physical and political dominion over that religious estate in which he now finds himself: "and thou profoundest hell, receive thy new possessor."

Thus Satan errs even as Luther claims to do in supposing that Paul's New Jerusalem would be a place like the city of that name, or one perfected by transcendence like "heaven." For the pathology of the mind as "its own place" consists only partly in the subjective order this statement would predicate in preference to God's. It also appears in Satan's idolatrous conflation of mind *with* place and hell *with* property and dominion, which is no more figurative for him than those "sights of woe, regions of sorrow, doleful shades" upon which he first claps eyes. These *invisibilia* are made objects in the sense of entities and agents like Sin, precisely because that is how Satan chooses to see and represent the hidden God—as no different from himself or his angelic compeers in discrete, autonomous, and material being. The invisibility of the divine is understood not as a fundamental departure in being but as mere optical effect, the impression created when an object is placed at a distance or concealed from view. Deity simply looks to the fallen angels as heaven looks to earth, invisible because distant and distant because precedent in the hierarchy of things that Satan maps onto all creation. Indeed, to Satan's way of thinking, deity's hiddenness is a matter of the Father ceremonially staging his preeminent rank, as though God were as shrewd and theatrical a politician as the Sun King, and his glory equally engineered by the mysteries of court etiquette or the smoke and mirrors of royalist spectacle.[31] In Raphael's accommodated and so—for its audience—dangerously ambiguous picture, Satan entertains the image of "the almighty Father where he sits / Shrined in his sanctuary of heaven secure"; deity itself thus becomes a citadel liable to siege, invasion, conquest, not to mention the reifying vision of the apostate mind (*LM* 6.671–72). The same propensity is evinced in those correspondences I mentioned, which consist in the automatic efforts of the fallen to recapture by palpable imitation the heaven they remember, and in Satan's strenuous determination to simulate the appearances of deity. In pursuing this episcopal fallacy, he makes a shrine to himself wherever he goes—a *sanctum sanctorum* or Holy of Holies on the model of Jewish, pagan, and of course Roman Catholic ritual—because he conceives God's inevidence as a place of physical withdrawal, to which the Son has privileged, hieratic access where he does not. All the civic or martial works of the fallen angels pattern themselves after deity's expressions, because the religious is not understood as a distinctive meaning to experience but, in the shape of *invisibilia*, as an elite order of entity and location.

Accordingly, "In imitation of that mount whereon / Messiah was declared in sight of heaven," (*LM* 5.764–65) Satan devises "his royal seat / High on a hill, far blazing, as a mount / Raised on a mount, with pyramids and towers / From diamond quarries hewn, and rocks of gold" (*LM* 5.756–59). This interpretation of the divine glory—an artificial illumination created by gold and jewels, and thus expressive of burgeoning satanic materialism—provides the setting for that false theophany which occurs when the apostate literally declare themselves gods. Moreover, to keep up the appearance of godhead, the place is subsequently sacralized by Satan as the very locus of satanic divinity, which is how he understands the anointing of the Son—as a cult of place, or the enthronement of a god in the manner of Roman imperial apotheosis. And when consigned to hell, the apostate in their usual mania for lost significance manufacture Pandaemonium as a trompe l'oeil heaven of golden pavements and starry vaults—the staged effect of heaven's great horizon and the perfect harmony of its spaces, its celebrations and entertainments, and of course in Satan's privy cabal, the occult hiddenness of divine power. But these effects and Pandaemonium's hugely if incoherently ornate facade succeed only in exaggerating the fair outside, the mere appearance of heavenly things, a reflection far less flattering to the apostate than they suppose; that is, to the extent that satanic creation is entirely derivative and superficial, it is also felt as decadent, perverse. For the effort to structure hell after heaven reveals a constraint obtaining among God's things, which is that they cannot be imitated without falsehood or injustice (a point Northrop Frye makes from another angle).[32] The palace's grandeur haphazardly elaborated in every type of ornament, including Satan himself opulently and exclusively enthroned, feels neurotic, compulsive, wrong—because this gorgeousness is dead, a splendid relic emptied of any purpose but self-display. Pandaemonium is what the fallen mind remembers of heaven; and the seeming immediacy of satanic invention that the speaker admires is not ease but suddenness, the violence of magic exemplified in Sin's demonic birth.

In this perversion of God's things lies the essence of idolatry for Milton, leading Satan to assert that the mind is its own place, and can make a heaven of hell, a hell of heaven. Like his subjectivism, hell is Satan's artifact, his own creation, the place his fixed mind has reserved for him; and he can no more transform or escape it than he can repent. By rejecting the reality of dependence upon God as the source of life, Satan has deprived himself of vitality—all natural movement, change, growth, the very condition of possibility itself—in perverse favor of self-animation, making his existence grotesque and parodic. Moreover, in consciously separating themselves from the order of expressiveness which is their very being as creatures, divine providence itself becomes unintelligible to the apostate except as an arbitrary, punitive imposition of order upon God's enemies. So creation to the fallen mind feels like necessity, not providence; and Satan must lay claim to autarchic will and significance in this speech if he is to secure any sense of dignity. For the loss of good that defines the satanic experience of evil—that "celestial light" exchanged for "this mournful gloom," those "happy fields / Where joy forever dwells" for these "horrors" of hell—isn't seen as the consequence of voluntary dissociation from God and the world he has made. With the solitary exception of Satan himself, the angels in hell perceive themselves to be cast out of heaven by "thunder"—their proper place, their possession of heavenly rank and privilege forcibly wrested from them by heaven's king.

Moreover, the futile idolizing of their erstwhile creaturely appearances, their literal and so promiscuous sense that they in themselves are gods, simply compounds their anguish. In Benjamin's reading of the *Trauerspiel*, such ambitious striving for the absolute itself signals the catastrophic loss of meaning—the force of the speaker's allusion to all those "towered structures" Mulciber builds in heaven for the apostate, who in imitation of deity fancy themselves enthroned "as princes, whom the supreme king / Exalted to such power, and gave to rule, / Each in his hierarchy, the orders bright" (*LM* 1.734–37). Memorializing is the means by which melancholy transfigures the beautiful, the whole and the orderly into ruins and fragments of value, so as to regret them. And the fallen angels indulge in just this reciprocal action, where the false apotheosis of self leads to a Wagnerian immolation of the world. So when Satan catches sight of the "equal ruin" of his beloved companion, Beelzebub, whose appearance should mirror his own back to him, he too speaks a hyperbolic language of loss, exclusion, and exile: "If thou beest he; but O how fallen! how changed / From him, who in the happy realms of light / Clothed with transcendent brightness didst outshine / Myriads though bright" (*LM* 1.84–87). There is a revealing relationship between these lines and his previous speeches, where Satan asserts not just equality of nature but essential likeness to God. For without his anguished remembrance of lost beauty ("changed in outward lustre") and status ("injured merit"), he couldn't still think himself on a par with deity. Loss then does not make him quiescent: rather, the idealizing memory of former good drives him furiously to recuperate the past at all costs. This motive and effect confirms Benjamin's insight that one way of responding to a world abruptly bereft of real meaning is the determination to reimpose significance by an all-out exertion of will—the activity of the melancholic and the despot. Both in heaven and hell, the denial of God results in this frenetic push for personal, autarchic significance, inasmuch as the satanic now confronts a great void at the heart of things. With God, meaningfulness is no issue; but without him, in Milton's view, we lose our bearings in the world and so feel compelled somehow to orchestrate its significance in order to secure our own. Pandaemonium and its ceremonies, as well as the devils' efforts at diversion in hell, thus represent more than a desire to approximate past glory—to be like God and heaven still are. They are a futile attempt to reassert failed certainties:

> Thence more at ease their minds and somewhat raised
> By false presumptuous hope, the ranged powers
> Disband, and wandering, each his several way

Pursues, as inclination or sad choice
Leads him perplexed, where he may likeliest find
Truce to his restless thoughts, and entertain
The irksome hours, till this great chief return.

(LM 2.521–27)

This endless, confused, and inconsequent movement of body and mind describes the labyrinth of despair to which their own apostasy has abandoned the fallen, a condition they seek to dignify with every sort of feat—martial, physical, poetic, and philosophical—all celebrating creatural culture as a sort of Panhellenism and thus a cult of individual genius. It is also the religious state which occasions Satan's great soliloquy in Book Four, where he seems to express some vestige of what Milton calls conscience or right reason, that is, a sense of the world as God created it to be. Yet that residual idea is juxtaposed with Satan's present apostrophe of the sun, disfiguring deity's new creation just as he had the old:

O thou that with surpassing glory crowned,
Look'st from thy sole dominion like the God
Of this new world; at whose sight all the the stars
Hide their diminished heads; to thee I call,
But with no friendly voice, and add thy name
O sun, to tell thee how I hate thy beams
That bring to my remembrance from what state
I fell, how glorious once above thy sphere;
Till pride and worse ambition threw me down
Warring in heaven against heaven's matchless king;
Ah wherefore! He deserved no such return
From me, whom he created what I was
In that bright eminence, and with his good
Upbraided none; nor was his service hard.
What could be less than to afford him praise,
The easiest recompense, and pay him thanks,
How due! Yet all his good proved ill in me,
And wrought but malice; lifted up so high
I sdeigned subjection, and thought one step higher
Would set me highest, and in a moment quit
The debt immense of endless gratitude,
So burdensome still paying, still to owe;
Forgetful what from him I still received,
And understood not that a grateful mind
By owing owes not, but still pays, at once
Indebted and discharged; what burden then?

(LM 4.32–57)

In the egoistic allegory of the sun's diminishing the stars, apostrophe and personification at once betoken and illustrate Satan's estrangement from his creator as well as creation itself. These figures betray his already habitual projection of self onto everything he sees, his urgent impulse to make the whole world conform to his privative experience of it. If it is usual to interpret these figures as creating the illusion of presence for someone or something desired, then Satan's recourse to them expresses a much greater, more pervasive absence. For he says that in heaven, he experienced the creator's difference from himself as a terrible obligation—as guilt and necessity—and it is from this single perversion of ideas that all of Satan's woe and his peculiar allegory stem. Where gratitude would freely affiliate him with God as that which is absolutely other than himself, his resentment of deity's distinction and his ensuing guilt simply widens the breach, rendering him incapable of the lived affinity with the divine whose complacence in the Miltonic sense is the created order. Gratitude would have sheltered Satan from the terrible force of deity's difference from himself, which he feels as perpetual indebtedness and as servitude; and it would do this by making him sensible of God's grace freely extended to the creature in the gift of life. This religious departure in meaning is expressed by the paradox of faith that Milton ascribes in the *Second Defense* to the operations of divine grace: the psychological reality that gratitude can relieve the sense of obligation, that the acknowledgment of indebtedness can itself satisfy a debt, exemplifies a fluency of meaning and relationship unfettered by the endless calculus of objectification. But for all that he recognizes this dimension of creatural experience, Satan still construes gratitude very much as Hobbesian obligation—a material disproportioning and depletion of power and status. As a result, his subsequent apostasy resembles Hobbes's state of nature—a human condition from which all actual, recognizable value has been subtracted away.

Moreover, after his fall he can no more allow God's creatures their distinction, their individuality, then he can acknowledge deity's. His hatred of God is hatred of the creator's difference from himself not in circumstance—his defeat as against God's triumph—but in mode of life. This is one source of hell's conformism, that unrelieved, compulsive unity of the apostate angels which the speaker so admires, yet which renders all their activity hopelessly identical—a constant reiteration of the fate they have chosen for themselves (*LM* 1.546–59).[33] But it is also Satan's explicit desire, as he gazes upon the human pair, to make them live his own predicament, conform to his mentality, tellingly expressed in the liturgical terms of the doxology: "league with you I seek, / And mutual amity so strait, so close, / That I with you must dwell, or you with me / Henceforth" (*LM* 4.375–78). Identity must be achieved precisely because Satan feels the incommensurability of the numinous as a disproportion or flaw in the divine order, at least as regards his own place in it. Since there is now no veil of grateful affiliation between him and deity, only the unbearable reality of their difference and the anguish it creates in him, he seeks a world of endless likeness as compensation, ironically conceived as individuality. Instead of faith, he con-

verts this antipathetic sense of disproportion into guilt—guilt for his own inability to render the world exact and symmetrical by reciprocating deity for the
benefits it bestows on him: "Ah, wherefore! He deserved no such return / From
me, whom he created what I was." Satan's burden of unfulfilled obligation is
like that creaturely guilt Rudolph Otto makes an aspect of our experience of
the holy, calling it "*numinous unworthiness* or *disvalue*"; because in confronting
deity, we confront the finitude of our own nature.[34] But Satan incorrigibly refuses to recognize angelic creatureliness, because to admit his own limitations
is to acknowledge God's distinction, and with it, the reality that he will always
be separate, other, and (painfully to his mind) less than the being with whom
he desires the impossible communion of identity.

    This is the real significance of his allegorizing and his jealousy of the Son: at
that psychological juncture in his history, Satan didn't want to be as God but
wanted to be with God—the possession of the good being the creature's ultimate desire—yet he wants this in a manner only deity can enjoy in itself, as
"perfect" with "no deficience found" in Adam's phrase (*LM* 8.415–16). This is
Satan's hyperbolic misreading of the Son's exaltation, for the position of God's
vice-gerent and lordship of heaven describes more than the Son's mediatorial
office to the rest of the world. It exemplifies the Son's unique affinity with God,
the source of his obedience, which Satan passionately desires for himself while
publishing it to the fallen as the magical identity of shared godhead, a shamanis-
tic power over life and death since "our quickening power is our own." He
obliviously believed this position was his until the moment of the Father's decree, when, all of a sudden, the meaning of heaven itself undergoes a revolution
before his eyes. Then Satan distorts desire for deity's perfect good into a desire
to surmount the distinction between creator and created, to *be* God in order to
reciprocate God in kind. And he feels thus impossibly obligated, feels relationship with God as a fate and necessity imposed upon him, because he has already
lost faith—that religious attunement with which, Milton argues, their creation
endows all creatures. Satan's predicament is just what the reformers describe
when they argue the coincidence between right knowledge of self and right
knowledge of God: without the one, we cannot have the other, and by his
ingratitude Satan refuses both. Once he has realized this breach between himself and deity in outright revolt, Satan cannot rid himself by desire or force of
God's ineluctable difference; the guilt he suffers then becomes a magical bane
imposed upon him (a bane he himself assumes in order to inflict it, as Sin and
Death, upon the new world), with deity depicted as his "punisher" (*LM* 4.103).

    Such is the imputed subjugation of stars to sun, but actually the incipient
subjugation of every living thing to Satan's own obsession with the calamitous
divide between his creator and himself. Indeed, Satan's aggravated sense of the
distinction between God and himself evokes Adorno's comment that "going
back to what it is not must impress the subject as external and violent": having
separated himself from the holy and disdained the shelter of understanding and
mutuality that gratitude provides, any relation to the divine would feel to Satan

as though God sought to annihilate him. In effect, he confronts the same demonic being from whom Job, Jeremiah, and the psalmist flee; but Satan has no
faith and therefore no God other than self with whom to seek protection. Unable to close the gap between them, Satan must reinterpret this discrepancy,
and not just by making deity his foe but his betrayer, his seducer. For he speculates that his susceptibility to sin was the effect of extraordinary "highth" in
heaven, which argues that the very eminence of Satan as archangel was itself
temptation. As Adam will do both before and after the event of the Fall, he
blames God for sin, in that the allegedly disproportionate conditions of his
being conspired to make him disobey his creator.

If Satan's erstwhile "proximity" to the divine—in Raphael's words, "he of
the first / If not the first archangel, great in power, / In favour and pre-eminence"
(*LM* 5.659–61)—ironically served to enlarge the gulf between creator and creature, that is because it signified to the apostate angel not only his supremacy
over his peers, but also his perfect likeness to God, which, at the Son's exaltation, he translates into specious equality. So he "sdeigned subjection, and
thought one step higher / Would set me highest, and in a moment quit / The
debt immense of endless gratitude." As Satan recalls the progress of his apostasy,
the sensation of being diminished or condemned by deity, that creatural humiliation Otto describes, does not precede but follows upon the denial of difference,
the ensuing experience of ingratitude and then guilt. It is only in response to
such diminishment that Satan then conceives pride and ambition, since he
must somehow recapture the illusion of self voided by his unprotected encounter with deity's appalling distinction. In short, Satan aspires to God's place only
when he has suppressed his creatural nature, effectively depriving himself of
any proper sense of the person he would resemble. But if hatred of God and
satanic aspiration proceed from guilt and the sensation of necessity it foments,
the first fruit of guilt is not self-aggrandizement of meaning but rather, in the
thwarting of his desire for intimacy, the conviction of meaning's catastrophic
loss. For Satan, the awful reality of the creator is a fatal disproportion or inequity of desire, transforming the world into a horror—the desiccated, fragmented, fantastic relic of creatural meaning which is the landscape of hell. We
return here to Luther's and Milton's analysis of law and gospel, inasmuch as
these positions represent two different ways of understanding the same religious
relation, one of which results in estrangement and convulsive loss of meaning.
Truth seems evacuated to Satan only because it was never present in the ideal
manner he wanted and assumed, that is, in the idolatrous sense of immediate
and self-evident. But truth must be expressed ironically in a world governed by
a hidden God; and irony seen by the law, the mind that mistakenly invests God
in mere appearance or works, looks like paradise lost:

> Hadst thou the same free will and power to stand?
> Thou hadst: whom hast thou then or what to accuse,
> But heaven's free love dealt equally to all?

Be then his love accursed, since love or hate,
To me alike, it deals eternal woe.
Nay cursed be thou; since against his thy will
Chose freely what it now so justly rues.
Me miserable! Which way shall I fly
Infinite wrath, and infinite despair?
Which way I fly is hell; my self am hell.

(*LM* 4.66–75)

Satan's self-allegorizing here—'Which way I fly is hell; my self am hell'—is at once a confession and a display of the most profound dissociation, no doubt modeled upon Richard III's strange colloquy with himself in the last act of Shakespeare's play: both speeches are the work of melancholy; both use stichomythia to express the moral conflict of the antagonist; and both play upon the fantastic theatricalism of evil—its capacity to objectify self. For in the midst of his torment, Satan yet recognizes that other possibility of meaning to which conscience painfully and fitfully recalls him. And like Sin and Death, that possibility is objectified, so that his soliloquy gives us two conflicting Satans, one remorseful and the other defiant. But the stichomythia dramatizes more than the polarizing effect of Satan's denaturing himself: along with the hidden God, it exhibits the regression of meaningfulness from his experience. Without deity, the sense of things appears fearfully volatile, chancy, undecidable; and theodicy itself feels to Satan like a labyrinth and contradiction from which he cannot escape, in which divine goodness is intelligible yet irresistibly works an opposed effect in him, "since love or hate / To me alike, it deals eternal woe." And this dreadful confusion of meaning, consequent upon his despairing and so denying God, is what moves Satan, the theologian of glory, to declare, "Evil be thou my good" (*LM* 4.110).

When the illusion of his likeness to God catastrophically breaks down in the face of the Son's exaltation, so the visible order which was once thought to represent the absolute appears inverted and deformed by this exposure of its mediating role. And creation includes self, which is not only the locus of misperception but the intransigent experience of it as well: "Which way I fly is hell; my self am hell." Subjectivity has also lost its coherence, since that effect was the expression of the creator, figured in the beneficent, provident ordering of the creatural world—in the orison of our first parents, a creation that declares "goodness beyond thought, and power divine" (*LM* 5.159). As a result of Satan's refusing relationship with the divine, subjectivity itself feels forced and artificial, since it is now seemingly self-animated—an imitation of life and an allegory of the soul in the vulgar sense. Moreover, because divine providence is now experienced as necessity and wrath, the fallen feel themselves to be acted upon, like the newly inert and forsaken landscape the apostate exploit; and that passive posture is confessed in Satan's locution "me miserable"—the objectifying of self as the victim and recipient, not the agent of events and meanings. While this peculiarly anguished and suffering "me" alternates with the imperial ego of Satan's vaunted subjectivism, the same locution is adopted by the Son as well, because it captures both the passional as well as the alienated experience of deity in *Paradise Lost*.

In the manner of hell itself, Satan then is a relic of what he once was, because the false identity that he idolized has been disenchanted, deprived of its glamour by apostasy. Again, in dissociating from God, self seems emptied of that full and fluent expressiveness which is the creature's proper life; consequently, any attempt to restore one's identity and significance in hell is arduous and distorting, memory itself grotesquely exaggerating the wonted semblance of self. Of course, the epitome of this effect is the appearance Sin herself has for Satan, which is why he refuses to recognize her at the gates of hell—declaring, "I know thee not, nor ever saw till now / Sight more detestable than him and thee," a greeting to which she replies:

> Hast thou forget me then, and do I seem
> Now in thine eye so foul, once deemed so fair
> In heaven, when at the assembly, and in sight
> Of all the seraphim with thee combined
> In bold conspiracy against heaven's king,
> All on a sudden miserable pain
> Surprised thee, dim thine eyes, and dizzy swum
> In darkness, while thy head flames thick and fast
> Threw forth, till on the left side opening wide,
> Likest to thee in shape and countenance bright,
> Then shining heavenly fair, a goddess armed
> Out of thy head I sprung: amazement seized
> All the host of heaven; back they recoiled afraid
> At first, and called me Sin, and for a sign
> Portentous held me; but familiar grown,
> I pleased, and with attractive graces won
> The most averse, thee chiefly, who full oft
> Thy self in me thy perfect image viewing
> Becamest enamoured, and such joy thou took'st
> With me in secret, that my womb conceived
> A growing burden.

> (LM 2.744–67)

Here Milton uses the iconography of Zeus's promiscuity and Athena's parthenogenesis as a figure of false creation as well as idolatry; but Sin is not only the self-deluding, self-deifying image Satan entertains. Indeed, she exemplifies in herself the problem of meaning when it is made unaccountable to the actuality of things: her birth and this crisis are simultaneous with Satan's separation of himself from his creator, whose acknowledgment keeps the creature's experience of contingency from spiraling out of control into sheer whimsy and randomness. But having dissociated himself from deity and divine order in that moment of "bold conspiracy against heaven's king," Satan suffers a sudden vertigo as his thought becomes unmoored from any meaning but his own. Indeed, he has a brainstorm which results not only in the ambivalently armed allegory of Sin but also in unconstrained figuration generally. For idolatry in Milton is nothing other than the devices and embellishments of human imagination—our indiscriminate projection of self onto the world, in the shape of our ideas of God and truth. This is what generates all those centrifugal similes of the speaker's, whose imagery always turns self-reflexive, enacting not only the dangers of comparison but also the religious problem of human perception as an investment in mere appearance.[35] It is also why the speaker's description of Sin herself devolves upon one storied image after another:

> Far less abhorred than these
> Vexed Scylla bathing in the sea that parts
> Calabria from the hoarse Trinacrian shore:
> Nor uglier follow the Night-hag, when called
> In secret, riding through the air she comes
> Lured with the smell of infant blood, to dance
> With Lapland witches, while the labouring moon
> Eclipses at their charms.
>
> (LM 2.659–66)

This propensity to elaborate endlessly explains why the fallen angels are themselves the gods of fabling and shape-shifting, why epic similes are specially in vogue with the apostate, and why the most crass and unabashed allegorizing always dogs Satan's tracks: first in the invention of Sin as his self-image; then in the begetting of that nebulous goblin Death; then in the "double form" or reallegorizing of Sin by the hellhounds to which she gives birth; then in the creation of that whole host of incipient idols—the fallen angels reinterpreted as pagan gods. Such spontaneous, demonic figuration originates in the narcissism motivating Satan's denial of his creator; for narcissism—Lucifer's adoration of his own appearances as God—leads to his self-seduction and then to incest with Sin, whose consequence is the ultimate sterility of Death. And Death finally and completely disrupts all natural relation by coupling with his parent, violently disfiguring and in a shocking manner exposing her speciousness. Sin is thus further deformed and demonized by reinterpretation, her body becoming a mere palimpsest of meanings—the work of idolatry's uncontrolled, endogamous engendering of significance. If we admit the validity of Benjamin's analysis for *Paradise Lost*, then Satan's frenzied allegorizing has an ulterior purpose and psychology behind it. For while the authors and personages of *Trauerspiel* obsessively contemplate the remnants of departed meaning, the loss they mourn is also self-perpetuated and indulgent. On the one hand, fascination with the ruin of things is the behavior of a person whom injustice and suffering have left transfixed, without a viable way to conceive the once-familiar. On the other, despair of meaning can also be a license to subject this seeming relic of existence to copious allegorizing, as a field of inert, concealed significance susceptible to the most arbitrary interpretation.

Such behavior then becomes an assertion of the interpreter's occult knowledge and power over things, inasmuch as the perceived devastation of the world gives the melancholy an authority by default to rename whatever comes within their purview, including themselves in the case of the satanic. Yet the reinscription of things is always felt as deficient, fantastic, and corrupt, when measured against the illusory remembrance of heaven's simplicity and self-evidence. Finally, prelapsarian meaning is a myth fostered by the same elegiac malady—the longing for an illusion, a figment of imagination which the melancholy use almost voluptuously to intensify their sense of loss, even as the apostate angels recall a heaven that was never theirs. A comparable imaginative aberrancy produces the demonology of Book One that parodies divine variety even as it elicits the memory of past beauty and order. It is a telling slip that Sin, in remembering her erstwhile glory, also recalls how Satan's fellow conspirators perceived her sudden appearance—as unnatural, ominous, and allegorical. She herself is utterly oblivious to the disparity, and familiarity or custom eventually reconciles the apostate to the estranged quality of her being—its artificial animation and self-regarding splendor. Her history recounts the narrative of Satan's personal delusion, which, like the fictions proleptically accumulating around the fallen angels, generates an egregious nostalgia for a false past. The myth of prelapsarian glory, as a world of indubitable meaning and value, is of course a blind to disguise God's distinction from the creature (a blind which misleads many of Milton's readers); for deity's hiddenness creates the existential condition of irony that this fiction of self-evidence would make the cruel device of a punitive God. So taken altogether, the Fall and its ramifications really express the satanic aversion to divine difference, the fundamental reality that would separate them from the creaturely being they idolize, in which they locate their own godhead: as Satan declares to Abdiel, "Our puissance is our own" (*LM* 5.864). That is why Satan fails to recognize his sin, because it doesn't resemble the self-aggrandizing image to which his lapsed memory subscribes.

In sum, the prelapsarian whether in heaven or paradise, understood as an intrinsically different world than that inhabited by the fallen, is an extravagance of estranged imagination and memory. The same aberrant cast of mind informs Satan's hypocritical shows, as well as the configuring of his duplicitous appearance as both fawning cherub to Uriel and obsequious serpent to Eve. All unconsciously, his posturing parodies the natural decorum of praise and thanksgiving among unfallen things, which he reenacts to Uriel and Eve as a sort of specious enthusiasm or cheerleading, a hyperbolical celebration of the good. Thus if allegory is supposed to be doubly histrionical, parading the artifice of figuration by the theatrical extremes to which it is taken, then Satan himself is always allegorical in this fashion—whether rage gigantically distends his body, or pride transforms him into the grand Turk. The same histrionics, the same automorphia, the same compounded allegorizing govern the productions of the apostate more largely. These repeatedly imitate and reinterpret God's works since, even in the birth of Sin, the satanic is incapable of any original idea, inventing only novel and of course degenerate uses of the world it mourns and misremembers, as in the unrelieved if predictably ersatz imitation of antiquity in hell. As Satan all unconsciously confesses, "New laws from him who reigns, new minds may raise / In us who serve, new counsels"—the reactionary imagining himself as innovator (*LM* 5.680–81). Because the fallen angels have chosen to understand deity as the apotheosis of self and consequently as the utmost magnitude of creaturely perfection as against divine distinction, their works are splendid clichés, not to say fabulous architectural pastiche.

To Satan especially, the creatural condition of allegory is now experienced as adverse, like the antagonistic use he makes of it. And it is this self-adversity that Uriel discerns when he watches Satan grow "disfigured" in soliloquy (*LM* 4.127): "Thus while he spake, each passion dimmed his face / Thrice changed with pale, ire, envy and despair, / Which marred his borrowed visage, and betrayed / Him counterfeit, if any eye beheld" (*LM* 4.114–17). Still in his cherubic guise, Satan appears to Uriel very like Milton's "bad" allegories do to Daiches and Ricks, or *Lycidas* to Dr. Johnson, whose elegy he said was "not to be considered as the effusion of real passion; for passion runs not after remote allusions and obscure opinions":[36] because his appearance is distorted by the force of inappropriate emotion, his "counterfeit" is discovered; that is, his disaffection from the thing he imitates exposes his imposture, as allegory is thought to compromise its own enterprise of expression. So it is not only hypocrisy that Milton would seem to make simultaneous with Satan's advent in this world, but hyperbole too. Yet notwithstanding the devil's sensations, Milton's conception of allegory is equally a matter of what Uriel sees as what Satan enacts. Does Uriel see Satan's falsehood, his deficient claim? Or does he rather see Satan's unprecedented alienation—a face distorted by anger, envy, and despair, indicative of that all-consuming sense of disproportion the soliloquy meditates? According to the speaker, the archangel "Saw him disfigured, more than could befall / Spirit of happy sort: his gestures fierce / He marked and mad demeanor" (*LM* 4.127–29). The very idea of "visage" or "demeanor" becoming disfigurement argues the allegory of the subjective, since Uriel now sees an appearance made incoherent by its strange inflection. The inference of insanity that the angel draws from Satan's expressions is key, since madness is the other sense of the brainstorm accompanying Sin's eruption from his head: it is a virtual icon of the psychotic, ever compounding dissociation of mental images from the world.[37]

For what Uriel beholds is an affect, a disposition of soul wholly incompatible with being a cherub or with the purpose Satan gives for viewing the new creation—to celebrate the glory and goodness of God. He sees "looks / Alien from heaven, with passions foul obscured" (*LM* 5.570–71). And to the extent that madness is that condition where speech and behavior are somehow skewed from the ordinary, where they depart from our assumptions of how people act, then Satan is insane—incapable of the very meaning he purports to represent. His manner is no longer that of the heavenly society of which Uriel is still part, which has its life in each creature's grateful attunement to God. Having lost that sympathy in the same moment that he misconceived relationship to his creator, Satan's entire being if not his mere appearance sets him apart, including the kind of meaning he makes. It is the predicament Wittgenstein evokes when he observes that if a lion could talk, we could not understand him. Satan may evince the image of the heavenly, but he no longer gives it a familiar inflection—no longer observes the same usage. As Abdiel exclaims at the sight of his ruined glory in battle: "O heaven! That such resemblance of the highest / Should yet remain, where faith and realty / Remain not" (*LM* 6.114–16). The discrepancy between Satan's semblance and his "faith and realty" describes this altered inflection. For sin dissociates him from himself: since deity does not destroy what it has made, permissively he retains the nature given him at his creation, that image of God or divine semblance to which Abdiel refers. What occurs is rather an expressive difference or deviation in the image accessible to right understanding, as it is to Abdiel here; or to Adam in the shape of that "addition strange" that he discerns in Eve's account of her dream; or to our general mother when she confronts the duly ornate and labyrinthine sight of a serpent who can talk both volubly and unctuously.

The latter disguise is the epitome of every other apostate production, most of which tend to superfluous, intricate, and of course towering splendor; and to that extent, it defines the peculiar character of fallen allegory as a palpably excessive because incoherent significance. As Abdiel implies, Satan's apostasy appears in the discrepancy between the original, expressive sense of his beauty and goodness, and its present aggrandizement to self; for self is not a sufficient explanation of what we see. Yet the vestige of divine goodness is what makes Satan so dangerous and so influential with the credulous, those who like the fallen angels or our first parents cannot or will not see beyond the mere fact of his appearance. It isn't that Satan seems unchanged to his peers, but that, admiring him so outrageously, they misconstrue the nature and meaning of the change, even as their leader does when he first catches sight of Beelzebub after their fall. For what his companions see in Satan is the ravages of injustice and suffering, his melancholy affliction, while what Abdiel sees are the degenerative effects of apostasy. Thus we hear from Raphael of that countenance with which Satan "as the morning star that guides / The starry flock, allured them" (*LM* 5.708–9); we are given the speaker's perversely seductive because elegiac image of Satan's "excess of glory obscured" in hell (*LM* 1.593–94); we are told of that remnant of (conformist) virtue the damned manifest even to this day (*LM* 2.482–83); with Gabriel, we see Satan's "regal port / But faded splendour wan" (*LM* 4.869–70), and later that "permissive glory" and "false glitter" with which he triumphantly and momentarily astounds the satanic masses after the fall of humankind (*LM* 10.451–52). And "power no less he seemed / Above the rest still to retain" even at the moment when Satan's sin recoils back upon himself (*LM* 10.531–32). Then at last he is given his heart's desire, to be just what he seems; for his sin finally collapses all distinction between self and image, and Satan becomes the emblem of his vengeance against God, the greatest serpent of them all.

Process of Speech

As a nature alienated from its proper being, Satan's very presence evinces a degree of estrangement so profound that, in the new world, the unfallen and inalienate angels can only negatively distinguish his difference in kind from the heavenly, not that wonted, positive individuality to which the speaker and Raphael testify. Thus Zephon replies to Satan's indignant demand, "Know ye not me?" (*LM* 4.827):

> Think not, revolted spirit, thy shape the same,
> Or undiminished brightness, to be known
> As when thou stood'st in heaven upright and pure;
> That glory then, when thou no more wast good,
> Departed from thee, and thou resemblest now
> Thy sin and place of doom obscure and foul.
>
> (LM 4.835–40)

If the apostate angel assumes the fixity and evidence of his own identity, Zephon's response argues the opposite—the contingency of creatural being and value on the creator, whose goodness it manifests. So although Satan admits some diminishment of his glory, on earth he is as yet unprepared to discover his nature, like his name and appearance, utterly defaced in heavenly eyes. This transfiguration of course is not absolute but relative to who perceives him: his tragic grandeur in hell, so resonant of their history and identity to the fallen, is experienced by the faithful as a semantic void—an impenetrable opacity of meaning that communicates little more than its dreadful failure of expressiveness. For having repudiated deity, Satan conveys a negation only—the absence of that divine inflection whose creaturely aspects include variety and individuality, not to mention orderly, intelligible change. To this defacement he and his followers are oblivious, fondly supposing that even their residual greatness would provoke the jealousy of heaven's tyrant; for the popular notion of God's active hostility allows them to believe in their continued importance. But to the unfallen angels, the ravages of sin reduce the apostate almost to an impassive blank—simply put, evil as the absence of good. Thus each party perceives the same incoherence wrought by apostasy, but they experience and understand it differently, with the angelic locating that incoherence in a nature divided against itself, and the satanic projecting their self-contradiction onto a newly demonic and capricious cosmos. There is of course no little irony in Satan declaring, "Not to know me argues your selves unknown," since it is his own catastrophic failure of self-knowledge, as creature to creator, that precipitates his ruin (*LM* 4.830). But it is precisely the cherubs' recognizance of deity's distinction, both here and by implication in heaven, that permits them to identify Satan's evil, if not his person (*LM* 4.830). And despite the false hierarchy of angelic being fixedly preserved in Satan's memory, "abashed the devil stood" in the presence of the faithful, "And felt how awful goodness is, and saw / Virtue in her shape how lovely, saw, and pined / His loss; but chiefly to find here observed / His lustre visibly impaired" (*LM* 4.846–50).

Without Satan's stunned dismay at going unrecognized by his putative inferiors, as archangel to cherub, neither he nor Milton's reader would have a real sense of the tragic dimensions of his loss. His predicament gains a new and terrible clarity in confrontation with the unfallen, who respond to him with distaste, not the reverence or fear his mere presence commands among the apostate. At the same time, in his ineluctable egotism, he cannot appreciate the anomaly of that unexampled and degraded imposture which discovers him to Ithuriel and Zephon: "Why sat'st thou like an enemy in wait / Here watching at the head of these that sleep?" (*LM* 4.825–26). He has shown himself altogether alien by his attitude, crouching secretly and disguised beside humanity at its most vulnerable; for with Satan's apostasy, the covert or inevident has itself become a new and ominous sign of evil, implying the possibility of deceit where it had once meant only the shelter of divine mediation. And once unmasked, Satan expects to be known by his familiar appearances, which he regards as the indelible mark of his superiority, only to suffer the disdain of the cherubim, and in himself the very sensation of envy he would impute to them. But in his self-induced melancholy, it is their insensibility that most affronts Satan, whom mania has conversely rendered irritable, febrile in imagination where he himself is concerned: he is thus confounded by his own expectations of significance—by the mentality of the law. In sum, each party is aberrant and unjust in the other's terms, but the apparent equivocality of good is resolved by the different quality and outcome of their interest in the human pair—their inclination toward an innocent world. The cherubs' errand to Eden and our first parents is to assert just this freedom of the creature to distinguish meaning and value, while Satan's is to destroy it; and in Milton's eyes, that is evil.

The same dubious valuation and the same quandary of liberty and conformity attend the act of dissent itself in *Paradise Lost*. Given the arbitrary impression the Son's preferment is bound to make upon any disaffected mind, the revolt against heaven's incumbent order is perfectly plausible, an effect enhanced by Satan's own archangelic splendor and prestige, his talk of equity and equality, and his theatrical appeal at least among those who gather to witness the spectacle in heaven's north. By contrast, Abdiel's dissent from this rebellion has an altogether inglorious look to it, neither politic nor consonant with the conspirators' notion of their angelic dignity. Yet the behavior that Northrop Frye would call priggish (both in the proper and contemporary senses of precisian and nonconformist) expresses that selfless zeal for the holy which also made John Milton appear so "out of season," so "singular and rash" to his opponent (*LM* 5.850–51). For rather than saving appearances, or pandering to a selfish desire for glory and power, Abdiel in his dissent exposes both religious errors, abjuring Satan to "tempt not these" to embrace his own delusion and impending disaster (*LM* 5.846). As Abdiel observes, "thy hapless crew involved / In this perfidious fraud, contagion spread / Both of thy crime and punishment"; for like the magical contagion of taboo, sin compulsively, infectiously makes everything the same, erasing all individual difference in pursuit of a compulsive, fatal identity (*LM* 5.879–81). But although his companions eagerly succumb to Satan's blandishments, Abdiel scorns to adopt the likeness of the apostate. His indecorum at such an unctuous meeting of like minds; his unshakeable conviction of God's goodness and justice despite the plausibility of Satan's complaint against Father and Son; the social onus, the threats, and the opprobrium his stand incurs: all ensue from Abdiel's adherence to the distinction between creator and creature, which makes him appear obtuse, rigid, and fanatical to his peers. But it is they who are won to suffering by dissent, not he, and this by their own self-punishing decorum—by the way they conceive and observe the good under the law, which entails conformity to "the fair seeming pretences" of the creature, not obedience to the creator.

So when Satan and Michael meet on heaven's plains, they speak each other's language only in the most superficial sense, with one referring all significance to the abundantly manifest, and the other to things that do not appear as such. To begin with, Satan does not understand that Michael, as God's angelic champion, addresses him from that position of surrogacy, out of a consciousness of divine incommensurability to every combatant there. Michael knows what Satan refuses to see—the inevident power convening the forces of the unfallen long before Abdiel's return from the apostate throng. Their exchange in its very inconsequence (like that between Comus and the Lady) thus exemplifies the distinction between creator and creature, to whose peculiar effects Michael gives expression:

> think not here
> To trouble holy rest; heaven casts thee out
> From all her confines. Heaven the seat of bliss
> Brooks not the works of violence and war.
> Hence then, and evil go with thee along
> Thy offspring, to the place of evil, hell,
> Thou and thy wicked crew; there mingle broils,
> Ere this avenging sword begin thy doom,
> Or some more sudden vengeance winged from God
> Precipitate thee with augmented pain.
>   So spake the prince of angels; to whom thus
> The adversary. Nor think thou with wind
> Of airy threats to awe whom yet with deeds

Thou canst not. Hast thou turned the least of these
To flight, or if to fall, but that they rise
Unvanquished, easier to transact with me
That thou shouldst hope, imperious, and with threats
To chase me hence? Err not that so shall end
The strife which thou call'st evil, but we style
The strife of glory: which we mean to win,
Or turn this heaven it self into the hell
Thou fablest.

(LM 6.271–92)

The sober certainty with which Michael assumes Satan's defeat appears absurd, since, as Satan himself remarks, the battle between the angels is so far a draw. But this impasse is not because the apostate party has matched heaven's king, as Satan prefers to suppose; it happens because deity has, in Raphael's phrase, "overruled / And limited" the power of both sides, so that heaven might not be disturbed and the battle allow for a different meaning and resolution than the one Satan would seem reasonably to expect (LM 6.228–29). For the war in heaven is not a combat of creatural powers, where force and strategy determine the outcome. It is a war of truth, an allegory of divine omnipotence illustrating to fallen and unfallen alike the abysmal difference between creature and creator. Angelic combat simply prepares toward that meaning, as Michael prophesies when he says that his sword will only begin Satan's doom, anticipating in faith the singular and irresistible terror of the Son's presence, whose divine agency never touches the apostate, only confounds it. But from the position of apostasy, Michael is being equally obtuse, nonsensical, threatening without sufficient grounds. For Satan has excluded from consideration everything that is not evident as such—God is but a word, "him named Almighty," and hell but a fable as it is to Marlowe's Faustus (LM 6.294)—acknowledging no reality but the forces palpably, measurably drawn up upon the field. It is a progressive materialism that ironically spreads to his own angelic body when Michael's sword, lent from God's armory, sheers through that newly engrossing substance (LM 6.320–34). In sum, Satan's assumptions of meaning and value presage his grotesque undoing, distorting his entire being even as his "ambiguous words" of diplomacy promise instead the new graphically corporeal ordnance of satanic war, perverting the purpose of colloquy to deceit (LM 6.568).

Satan's stated motive for conflict is comparably superficial and absolute, a matter of achieving "Honour, dominion, glory, and renown" in heaven or the mutually assured destruction of all parties (LM 6.422); but the ostensible signs of his superiority, such as his splendor, power, eloquence, and courage, prove nothing but his creatural finitude and frailty—his benighted trust in only what he can see and touch. This ironic dimension of Satan's war with God has its reflex in the Father's joke about fearing to lose his throne and dominion by force of arms. "Let us advise," he smilingly directs the Son, "and to this hazard draw / With speed what force is left, and all employ / In our defense, lest un-awares we lose / This our high place, our sanctuary, our hill" (LM 5.729–32). Were this the Almighty in Aeschylean fashion amusing himself with the futile spectacle of his creatures, then there would be nothing more horrible than Milton's God. But however ruthless, the joke tells us something important and true about Satan and his endeavors: namely, his own decision to behave ab-surdly, which is to say nonsensically, ineffectually, in a world governed by a hidden God. For the Father speaks of God not as deity, but as Satan would have it be—as though God's reign were circumscribed by time and space; as though creatural intelligence and force would decide the legitimacy of that reign; as though God and his regime were not only to be located but fixed upon a high place—like a Canaanite idol physically to be overthrown, or Dr. Johnson's su-preme king to be usurped and martyred. The three-day war is simply an ex-tended satire on Satan's delusion of analogy between himself and God, revealed in the anticlimax of the Son's almost entirely emblematic victory. The supposed discrepancy of power between deity and angel, in the form of the extrinsic and accidental possession of thunder, is actually a divergence in kind so profound that it requires all of Milton's extravagant vulgarity to emphasize a point his readers are still inclined to ignore: that what deity does in *Paradise Lost* is simply not comparable to what its creatures do. God's attributes, which the angels praise in Book Three, do not define him in the satanic sense as an infinite magnitude of creatural knowledge, power, goodness, and so forth; they are meant instead to express his incommensurability. Nor is the outcome of the war finally about the awesome scope of divine power: it describes an unbridge-able gulf in understanding between the faithful and the apostate—omnipotence conceived in antipathetic ways, as either force and causation or meaning and coherence.

In this antipathy, we encounter the two models of divine accommodation, law and gospel, whose relation explains what we see and, more importantly, what we don't see transpire upon the plains of heaven. The incongruities of the heavenly war are there to argue its departure from our expectations, rather than its likeness: if the insuperable artifice of Raphael's picture—its variously crass and ostentatious figuration—describes the satanic mind and its hyperbolic ef-fects, then the war's strange inconsequence pertains to its instrumentality as a religious sign, in the way Jesus distinguishes for the man born blind, not a supernatural action. Just this theological distinction ensures that creatural works decide nothing in the poem, while religious attitude or position is piv-otal—the point made by the Son's allegorical discomfiture of his foes, a finale devoted far more to arming and proclaiming than routing. His virtual inactivity is thus both ironical and emblematic: on the one hand, it satirizes the apostate belief in action's efficacy; on the other, it allegorizes divine omnipotence no less than the chariot of God in which the Son rides and on which eagle-winged Victory perches. Indeed, the difference in weaponry between the two angelic parties distinguishes their religious positions, not their supernatural capacities,

with the faithful wielding the heavenly world without fundamentally transforming its elements, and the apostate perverting and disfiguring its fabric beyond recognition, in token of their estrangement from the created order of
things. Raphael may proclaim the duel between Michael and Satan inconceivably, ineffably heroic—"for who, though with the tongue / Of angels, can relate,
or to what things / Liken on earth conspicuous, that may lift / Human imagination to such highth / Of Godlike power" (*LM* 6.297–301)—yet the action is
oddly anticlimactic, lasting only the space of Michael's single, decisive stroke.
Finally, the crude and antic comedy of the battling angels itself discredits Satan's claim to transcendent power and glory, because it subverts the very glamour or corrupt illusion of supernatural heroism on which that expectation depends. For efficacy and value in heaven's war is expressed by the way the
antagonists levy meaning, not force.

On the subject of creatural inconsequence, it is appropriate to address the
general distaste for Raphael's whimsical errand to hell's gate, at the very moment when humanity is in the making:

> For I that day was absent, as befell,
> Bound on a voyage uncouth and obscure,
> Far on excursion toward the gates of hell;
> Squared in full legion (such command we had)
> To see that none thence issued forth a spy,
> Or enemy, while God was in his work,
> Lest he incensed at such eruption bold,
> Destruction with creation might have mixed.
> Not that they durst without his leave attempt.
> (*LM* 8.229–36)

On what appears to be the feeblest of pretexts, he is obliged by God to miss an
event that holds extraordinary interest for the angelic hosts, since it entails the
creation of another intellectual creature like themselves, which Raphael learns
about only secondhand. For similar reasons, Empson finds the guard details to
Eden absurd, inasmuch as God knows the angels cannot perform the thing they
are seemingly asked to do, which is to keep Satan out by force.[38] As Empson
sees it, God degrades them by their own ineffectual motions, in what looks like
a galling insensitivity to the dignity of the creature. But the angelic hosts are
not sent to do or work any effect, as they well know: as Raphael explains in his
own case, "us he sends upon his high behests / For state, as sovereign king, and
to inure / Our prompt obedience" (*LM* 8.238–40). In other words, they are
sent to signify God's governance over events, as bearers of divine presence and
meaning, not as a causal force in themselves. At the same time, angelic obedience serves as an expression of creatural faith against the appearances, as it
were, of divine malfeasance ("Destruction with creation . . . mixed") or caprice
("Not that they durst without his leave attempt"). Their purpose is always illustrative of religious things, of *res non apparentes* like faith and divine grace, in

the manner of Raphael's mission to our first parents and Michael's at their exile. For whatever effects attend the angels on such religious occasions pertain to God, not themselves, in the fashion of Luther's new and theological grammar.

Yet because he furiously struggles to deny his creator's difference from himself, Satan ignores the conceptual catachresis or wrenching of meaning that occurs when deity is being expressed, which is why—as Northrop Frye inimitably puts it—everything rational in the poem is so profoundly unreasonable.[39] If Luther's catachreses tend to allegorize what scripture recounts into a case of conscience, translating its expressions from their proper to their pastoral or personal sense—in short, to the predicament of faith—so do Milton's: every narrative occurrence reflexively depicts a conceptual event, every description manifests a religious attitude. This ironical turn and ambiguity obtain equally in the speaker's account of the angels' duties or Raphael's extenuation of his errand: what in Milton's God appears incongruous and worse, abusive or tyrannical, reflects our religious condition, just as it does Satan's, the speaker's, or our first parents'. Indeed, to a great extent, the persistent power of Empson's argument is that, in his determined attempt to naturalize the narrative of *Paradise Lost*, he manages better than anyone before or since to describe what it would be like to experience deity without faith.[40] In Luther's phrase, this is to suffer deity as *Deus nudus* or God naked, "not dressed and clothed in His Word and promises" as the Christ, and so the ineluctable source of human despair— a theological fallacy that Luther condemns in his commentary on Psalm 51:

> The people of Israel did not have a God who was viewed "absolutely," to use the expression, the way the inexperienced monks rise into heaven with their speculations and think about God as He is in Himself. From this absolute God everyone should flee who does not want to perish, because human nature and the absolute God—for the sake of teaching we use this familiar term—are the bitterest of enemies. Human weakness cannot help being crushed by such majesty, as Scripture reminds us over and over. . . . The absolute God . . . is like an iron wall, against which we cannot bump without destroying ourselves. (*LW* 12:312)

Together, Empson, the speaker, and Satan confront Luther's *Deus nudus* in *Paradise Lost*, simply because they insist on identifying the Father with Milton's God, "the absolute God" or "God as He is in Himself," which is not the way the unfallen conceive that figure nor how they experience deity. That is, the apostate mind "does not take hold of the God [the psalmist] names as He is veiled in the sort of mask or face that is suited to us; but he takes hold of God and invades Him in His absolute power, where despair, and Lucifer's fall from heaven into hell, must necessarily follow" (*LW* 12:313). For that reason, the problem posed by the distinction of creator from creature is addressed by Raphael and the speaker, with each admitting the predicament of expression involved in recounting divine or heavenly things. The point is made explicitly by Raphael in his scrupulous disclaimers to Adam, where he specifies that he cannot represent either heavenly things or the acts of God as they really are, whether he has recourse in the former case to "likening spiritual to corporeal forms, / As may express them best" (*LM* 5.573–74), or in the latter, to "process of speech"—"So told as earthly notion can receive" (*LM* 7.178–79). The same problem of accommodation is taken up in the proem to Book Three, where the speaker declares the difficulty of ascending to heaven from hell, a circumstance significant of not only Christ's harrowing but also his own estrangement from God and the intractability of his subject to ordinary expression, as "things invisible to mortal sight" (*LM* 3.55). For either narrator, the difficulty of finding apt expression signals the fact of accommodation, and with it, the ambiguous idiom by which deity reveals itself in history and scripture. And this contingency of religious meanings organizes the narrative of Milton's poem, whose strategy creates the dilemma of faith that Paul and Luther cast in terms of law and gospel: whether, in finding the God of *Paradise Lost* repugnant and contradictory, we recognize our failure rightly to construe Milton's religious expressions; or whether we refuse to entertain the possibility that Milton's God could mean other than it appears to do, and make our indignation definitive of its nature.

Yet as a revised reading of divine revelation, the gospel has its force only in relation to the alienating, dispiriting experience of the law; and the revulsion we feel at Milton's God is instrumental to his argument in much the same way as the law, where our notions of significance and value promote what we experience as an intolerable contradiction in the poem. It is Raphael's peculiar task to instruct our first parents in this contingency of religious understandings, by way of preparing them for Satan's conceptual assault. Accordingly, he makes the disproportion or opacity of the cosmos, as our general ancestor is inclined to view it, a lesson in the allegory of creation, where neither the force of appearance nor analogy can satisfactorily account for the divine disposition of things. Rather, in their copious reconfiguring and empty ingenuity, humanity's vulgar or speculative explanations at once preempt and obscure God's design, thus evolving into the apostate fascination with the occult significance of things, whose invariable outcome is sceptical despair of meaning itself. To constrain this speculative propensity in Adam, Raphael prefaces his own explanation of such ostensible disproportions or flaws in creation with the qualifying phrase, "let it speak," referring the overt appearance of the world to the expression of deity's care even as Milton does with Ezekiel's temple (*LM* 8.101). Indeed, the archangel conducts his whole interpretive exercise in the subjunctive mood, inaugurating each account of things with the words "what if," so as to emphasize the provisional force of creatural understandings and the hiddenness of God's (*LM* 8.122, 140).

By comparison, the experience of equivocality receives no such self-conscious or methodical expression in the speaker's narrative, where the religious position of the observer promiscuously shapes the meaning something has, as when Empson imputes to Raphael the faithless sense of divine caprice in his errand. Perhaps the most instructive of these ambiguous episodes involves

Satan's vision of the ladder Jacob saw, let down from heaven with angels passing to and fro upon it. To reiterate, Calvin reads Jacob's vision, and his naming the place "house" or "gate of God," as the patriarch speaking to deity in the accommodated manner he had been spoken to; that is, Jacob pictures God even as God pictured himself in Jacob's dream of the ladder, as an allegory of the relation between human and divine being, but, Calvin stipulates, without the patriarch supposing that deity inhabited or was in any way correspondent to that place. In Jacob's usage, the sanctuary of Bethel is not an idol in the fashion of the Canaanite high places it apparently imitates. It is a way of speaking, a memorial of a religious event that allows Jacob to express affiliation with his God, just as Milton argues for the sacraments. And when the speaker describes Satan's disaffected view of the same ladder in Book Three, he begins by introducing its allegorical status—that "Each stair mysteriously was meant, nor stood / There always"—thus discriminating the religious significance of that image (*LM* 3.510–25). What the speaker shows is not access in the physical but in the religious sense, not an object but a meaning—an emblem like God's gold scales in Book Four or his compasses in Book Seven, which picture the state of relations between divine and humankind. Cavell remarks that "I do not enter another's mind the way I enter a place," and the same is true of Milton's allegorical heaven; yet that is what both the speaker and Satan assume here (*CR* 368). A similar contingency obtains with the tree of life, "what well used had been the pledge / Of immortality," but which to Satan is merely another high place, suitable both to his occult dignity and desire for prospect, leading the speaker on this occasion to editorialize: "So little knows / Any, but God alone, to value right / The good before him, but perverts best things / To worst abuse, or to their meanest use" (*LM* 4.200–204).

Like the tree of life, Jacob's ladder is a device not in Satan's objectifying fashion but in God's allegorical one: that is, a "pledge" or token of promised salvation, an emblematic figure which shows itself open in our fidelity and drawn up with our apostasy, so that Elijah and Lazarus must be carried over the figural gulf the ladder now spans but that will then separate heaven from an estranged world. By way of confirming this emblematic and ironical sense of religious things, Satan suffers the sight as a deliberate condemnation of himself, his ambition, overthrow, and loss. Indeed, the speaker's description of the ladder evokes the satanic memory of heaven—of hierarchy and towering structures, of rank and aspiration—whose portal exhibits the material gorgeousness to which the apostate reduce every natural thing they lay eyes on, as an expression of their insatiable interest in acquisition:

> far distant he descries,
> Ascending by degrees magnificent
> Up to the wall of heaven a structure high,
> At top whereof, but far more rich appeared

> The work as of a kingly palace gate
> With frontispiece of diamond and gold
> Embellished, thick with sparkling orient gems.
>   (LM 3.501–7)

Of course, the ladder does not directly address Satan's predicament at all but the new world, whose uncompromised affiliation with God it pictures. Yet when the apostate angel accidentally comes across it, the device abruptly becomes pointed and ulterior in its meaning, assuming the character that all of creation has for Satan, as the domain of divine injustice, deprivation, and struggle. That this effect is owing to Satan's melancholy is obvious; that it is also the consequence of his idolatry is less clear, until we recognize that it is only when he construes the ladder as proffering actual entry to those celestial fields he mourns, that it seems designed to spite him. For when the expressive or illustrative use of the ladder is ignored, when it is objectified and made instrumental in the physical sense, then it cannot but goad Satan to undertake the impossible yet once more. Tellingly, it is the speaker who complacently alleges the sadism of heaven, moved by his own suffering to endorse Satan's contradictory sense of the ladder as both a calculated temptation and access denied: "The stairs were then let down, whether to dare / The fiend by easy ascent, or aggravate / His sad exclusion from the doors of bliss" (LM 3.523–25). His account thus reflects the interpretive pathology Luther and Milton call the law, whose propensity to read God by analogy to the creature ensures that religious signs like Jacob's ladder will appear only "to accuse, condemn, sting, sadden, disquiet the heart, show a wrathful God, hell, and the like" (LW 12:328). All this Satan and the speaker undergo because they do not admit the catachresis that distinguishes divine from human, religious from rational expressions: where they see incongruity, they find conflict and compulsion, not the liberty of a different order of meaning and value.

A similar ambivalence of meaning shadows Raphael's narrative. Although the archangel is not himself governed at this moment by any special trial of faith, nevertheless, in relating the angelic fall, he confronts a comparable trial of expression to the speaker's. For now his real and fictional audiences are in the position of choosing how to understand the events he depicts, since evil is always potential in Eden. This is not only because Milton's speaker and reader have engaged the apostate mind in hell, while Adam and Eve have newly encountered it in Eve's dream, but because the distinction between creator and creature, deity and its expressions, obtains in the human paradise as it does everywhere else. And this contingency of divine meaning ensures that the signs of God are susceptible of being misread in Eden even as they were in heaven: human liberty lies in the interpretive choice. Indeed, by the time Raphael offers the analogy of "the bright consummate flower" to explain how God's creation is ordered, this emblem is capable of widely divergent appearances and interpretations (*LM* 5.468–503). Seen one way, the ascension to spirit illustrates the coherent, gradual movement of all creatures toward their origin and the source of all good; seen another, it is a strict ordering of the world according to degree, an ontological hierarchy of fixed ranks where the higher the creature is placed, the more refined and superior its nature. Seen yet another way, the analogy describes a causal order, which locates reason pregnantly as the necessary consequence of eating fruit; or conversely, it is an anticipation of the Fall in Francis Bacon's sense of a figure or allegory presciently conveying future knowledge. It follows that when the flower is understood to represent the world as a hierarchy and a causal relationship, like Satan's first sight of the human pair, then it expresses the mentality of the law in its character as both entity and fate or necessity. But when the flower is read as illustrative and allegorical, an emblem of faith and obedience, then it expresses the perspective of the gospel, where creation exemplifies the relationship between God and the world, in both faith and apostasy like Jacob's ladder.

Unsurprisingly, the beatific vision in *Paradise Lost* itself exhibits a comparable oscillation of significance. What we see of God in his heaven, as the speaker describes it, is what the angels celebrate here—a spectacle reproducing the sight Isaiah has of the Lord seated in the temple, which Satan typically imitates when he enthrones himself on the plains of heaven and then in hell:

> Thee Father first they sung omnipotent,
> Immutable, immortal, infinite,
> Eternal king; thee author of all being,
> Fountain of light, thy self invisible
> Amidst the glorious brightness where thou sit'st
> Throned inaccessible, but when thou shadest
> The full blaze of thy beams, and through a cloud
> Drawn round about thee like a radiant shrine,
> Dark with excessive bright thy skirts appear,
> Yet dazzle heaven, that brightest seraphim
> Approach not, but with both wings veil their eyes.
> Thee next they sang of all creation first,
> Begotten Son, divine similitude,
> In whose conspicuous countenance, without cloud
> Made visible, the almighty Father shines,
> Whom else no creature can behold.
>
> (*LM* 3.372–87)

It is helpful here to rehearse again how Calvin reads Isaiah's vision. He argues that even as the seraphim hide their eyes from the sight of the Lord in glory, so they themselves are concealed from the prophet's view and by extension our own. The concatenation of averted sight thus signals a compounded distance—of humanity from the angels, and heavenly from divine things. "Let men learn that since they cannot even look at the angels, they are very far from the perfect knowledge of God," Calvin advises, since the seraphim themselves cannot gaze directly upon the effects of the divine glory (CC 122–23). With regard to the figure Isaiah calls the Lord, Calvin follows the gospel of John in asserting that "Isaiah saw the glory of Christ," not deity itself, "because Christ was the image of the invisible God": "Since men crawl on the ground, or at least dwell far below the heavens, there is no absurdity in the statement that God descends to them in order to turn upon them, as though he used a mirror, some reflected rays of his glory. Therefore Isaiah was shown a form of a kind that enabled him with his own understanding to taste the inconceivable majesty of God. This is the reason that he attributes a throne, a robe, and a bodily appearance to God" (CC 120–21). Calvin is giving here an account of divine accommodation, in the person and anthropomorphic shape of the Lord sitting in judgment, whose throne, robe, and body are understood to signify the creature's mediated experience of the divine, not deity per se. Like the sense of human finitude and humiliation that theophany impresses upon Job, Isaiah also suffers a bout of abjection as he envisions the Lord enthroned on high, with his *extrema* or "skirts" filling the temple, and the thunderous calling of the seraphim: "Holy, holy, holy is the Lord of hosts; / the whole earth is full of his glory" (Isaiah 6:3). This holiness, inducing in the prophet a deep conviction of his sin, is what Calvin calls a "taste [of] the inconceivable majesty of God." Its awfulness is signified by the seraphs' averted gaze, but primarily by the preexistent Christ himself, as Lord of the covenant between God and his people. Yet Calvin does not treat the Lord's figure as the correspondence of visible to invisible, phenomenal to religious being, which is the idea of divine accommodation under the law. Rather, in distinguishing the glory of the Lord from the glory of God, the brightness of the Lord's skirts from what illuminates them, Calvin asserts the impassable boundary between deity and its expressions, of which this is one. What we see of God in the Lord's figure is a sight doubly diverted, to the extent that this person, however glorious and terrible to the creature, is yet entirely different from the deity whose penumbral effect he expresses. For Calvin's analogy of the vision to a mirror image—"the reflected rays of his glory"—defines two removes of mediation, distinguishing both in nature and appearance the source from its image, the image mirrored from its reflection.

This formidable yet parallactic view of the divine is what Luther and Milton both understand by the *posteriora* of God—the sight Moses has not of deity itself but God's glory, seen obliquely from his place of concealment as the Lord moves off into the distance. As I have already remarked, the *Christian Doctrine* concurs in Calvin's reading of Isaiah, with Milton arguing that "it was not God himself that he saw, but perhaps one of the angels clothed in some modification of the divine glory, or the Son of God himself, the image of the glory of his Father" (CM 14:251). Inasmuch as the Son is not deity's glory but the image of it, Milton thus sustains the degree of mediation on which Calvin and Luther equally insist. This shared understanding of the prophetic image describes something very like the spectacle of Father and Son, except that a less terrible

awe seems to attend the angelic vision of deity in *Paradise Lost* than it does
Isaiah's, who is separated from God both by his humanity and by the apostasy
of his people. But then Milton's heaven always fails to suffer the same revulsion
of feeling we do at the Father. In the always canny assessment of Northrop
Frye, whenever the Father "opens his ambrosial mouth, the sensitive reader
shudders,"[41] while Empson has devoted an entire book to this one peculiarity.
And that shudder makes Milton's whole point: just as Zephon and Ithuriel are
unmoved by Satan's glamour, so what the angels see in theophany isn't necessarily what we or the speaker find there:

> Thus while God spake, ambrosial fragrance filled
> All heaven, and in the blessed spirits elect
> Sense of new joy ineffable diffused:
> Beyond compare the Son of God was seen
> Most glorious, in him all his Father shone
> Substantially expressed, and in his face
> Divine compassion visibly appeared,
> Love without end, and without measure grace.
>
> (LM 3.135–42)

The Son "substantially expresses" the Father in the sense that his is the intelligible face that deity as God turns toward its creatures. And while the divine
countenance shows "love without end, and without measure grace," it also communicates in heaven's war the awfulness of the *mysterium tremendum*: thus the
Son acknowledges to the Father, "whom thou hatest, I hate, and can put on /
Thy terrors, as I put thy mildness on, / Image of thee in all things" (LM 6.734–
36). He is the inflection of God toward the world as creatural personality and
condition, the conversable figure Adam meets and talks with on his birthday,
and to whom Eve listens on hers, the sovereign presence. Under the prophetic
epithet of messiah, he is the preexistent Christ who acts for the Father in the
creation of heaven and earth and in the war against Satan, where each time he
ascends "The chariot of paternal deity," he emblematically assumes godhead
(LM 6.750–67)—"Girt with omnipotence, with radiance crowned / Of majesty
divine, sapience and love / Immense, and all his Father in him shown" (LM
7.194–96). This allegory of deity's expression, as both divine word and spirit,
is definitive for the spectacle of God in Milton's heaven, which again is understood variously. Thus in making their unholy pact, Satan, Sin, and Death together imitate what Satan remembers of heaven, ostensibly a triune God—
Father, Son, and Holy Spirit. But there is a problem with that Trinitarian parallel of persons, since there is in fact no heavenly correlate to hell's triad, any
more than there is to Paul's allegory of gospel and law. Like the Lord when he
appears as three men to Abraham by the oaks of Mamre, Milton's God is manifest in an array of figures, including such obvious devices as the living chariot
of deity. Indeed, the only triumvirate we see as such is hell's, because Milton
refuses to put the devil on a par with God, as evinced in the negligible role

demonology plays in the *Christian Doctrine*. Hell's translation of God into a trinity of discrete persons objectifies divine expressions in the same way that episcopacy does with Ezekiel's prophetic temple, reducing meaning to singular entities even as Satan elaborates in the persons of Sin and Death his own self-professed agency as adversary of God.

But hell's reification of heaven is but one peculiarity attending Milton's image of God; the way the speaker and the angels convey the sight of deity suggests a comparable indirection to that Calvin assigns Isaiah's vision of the Lord. For it is quite easy to overlook the fact that although both human and angelic narratives refer to two individuals, they show only the person Calvin sees—the Lord enthroned in glory, that is, the Son exalted.[42] Furthermore, there is no occasion in *Paradise Lost* on which the Father is heard and the Son not visibly present: even in the eternal moment of the Son's begetting and anointing, that figure is there to be seen and recognized by the angelic hosts. Indeed, he is always already there, as they say, because there is yet another sense to the exaltation than the Son's affiliation and lordship: that is to say, the Father does not create the Son in the fashion that Satan bodily produces his daughter out of himself, like the incestuous creator in Vedic myth. What the Father does is reinterpret his own revelation or image, which no longer refers to God in the rudimentary sense of the law, as the "typical and shadowy" form of the divine nature. That provisional understanding is abrogated with the exaltation, when God's image is referred to the Son as divine word and similitude. In Book Three, Heaven no longer apprehends the figure of the Lord as God but as Christ, not as the Father's glory but as the Son's—a radical revision in the modality of God's expression: as Milton puts the paradox of spiritual sight in *The Reason of Church Government*, God is no longer "under a veil," the concealed being to which the Lord's figure ostensibly corresponds; instead, deity is "openly" revealed in the Son as Lord and God for the creature. Thus the Father enacts the distinction between God and his appearances, which are of an absolutely different order from deity itself. For Milton's heaven has always seen the person the Father now designates as his son, but in the manner of the law; since this figure was enthroned on God's holy hill, it appeared as the Lord of the covenant in the law's sense—that is, as the figure of God himself. But the poem's continued anthropomorphisms, which describe the Father as turning, beholding, smiling, speaking, follow Calvin in referring not to deity per se but to the image of God, the preexistent Christ.[43] In this way, the decree of exaltation anticipates the giving of the gospel, since it abrogates the precedent understanding of divine accommodation in which Satan is forever fixed—the law as an order of representation in Cavell's sense, predicating invisible entities to which the visible correspond.

It follows that the figure of God in *Paradise Lost* is ambiguous in the same way that the divine image is ambiguous in scripture, since it can be argued that Isaiah saw the person of the Lord either as God, or as Christ where "God is meant." And once Milton's version of that image is understood in this way, the course of Satan's idolatry becomes obvious, as does his terrible disappointment and alienation. For his conviction of likeness to God arose from self-comparison to the palpable because invested glory of the Son as the divine image, whom he took to be God until the moment of the Father's decree. Then abruptly, incongruously, in the usual manner of revelation, that image is ironized, and he himself placed at an unsuspected and seemingly disproportionate remove from deity. Satan's disaffection from God—his ingratitude, his guilt, his denial, pride, envy, and ambition—proceeds inexorably from the hiatus or interval of media-tion thus disclosed between himself and his creator. Yet that perceived break in deity's expression does not alter what the faithful angels understand by the Lord: unlike the apostate or the adventitious reader, the host of the unfallen knows that the figure of God in heaven is a *persona*, an impersonation. The Son's enthroned figure is what Luther calls the "face," "mask," or "veil" of deity in another sense than the law's—God by a historical act of affiliation and inves-titure they themselves witness in Book Five. And their song articulates this intelligence in Book Three when it addresses the Son as "of all creation first" and "divine similitude."

The distinction of creator from creature, deity from its expressions, is thus made explicit by Milton, since the Son is God by the Father's creation and institution while the Father is God precisely by implication of these very acts. Father and Son in this way describe the diverse aspects of scripture's image of deity, while their relationship allegorizes the history of divine revelation, and their speech the theological distinction between law and gospel. Yet Father and Son are not therefore the simple polarities of divine justice and mercy, wrath and love, the God of the old dispensation as against the new, Jehovah and Christ. They picture instead the experience of deity as mediated or unmediated by faith. In Milton's view, the meaning of divine revelation is not changed from law to gospel, only the way we understand it. And the exaltation of the Son enacts this equivocal sense of theophany, since it introduces a revisionist ac-count of the creatural world as the "work of secondary hands," in Satan's dis-dainful phrase. The exaltation serves not only to remove the illusion of the Father's distinct and integral figure, since all divine gestures are now referred to the Son as God's only intelligible form, but also to completely disembody and disintegrate him. The one true God can neither be seen nor heard according to Milton, so when he speaks or appears in scripture, any such effects must pertain to the *nature of his expression*—to the character of deity's image, not its hidden being: "For the Word is both Son and Christ, that is, as I say, 'the anointed'; and as he is the image, as it were, by which we see God, so is he the word by which we hear him" (CM 14:401). That scriptural image of God is of course variously configured—as fire or thunder, as one or more persons, as a still small voice—in such a way as to complicate, if not discard, any simple anthropomor-phic idea of deity. In *Paradise Lost*, all these divine manifestations congregate around heaven's sacred hill and the person who is ambiguously seated there, as a sort of numinous array signifying God's presence. And when the Father beholds or speaks to the Son, or the Son replies to the Father, this figure changes inflection and aspect to reflect their different positions, along the lines of a Mexican *retablo* or icon that I own. There the three persons of the Trinity are all Christ, distinguished only by their position, the color and draping of their gowns, and the emblems they bear—the Father a scepter, the Son the stigmata of the Passion, the Holy Spirit the blazon of a dove. But they share one and the same exquisite face. In other words, the Father is an aspect of the Lord, the person the angels see and hear, and the Son another; they alter in speech and manner, but not in figure, and together they both impersonate the hidden God and inflect his similitude. Thus von Rad comments that Yahweh, in surrounding himself with a heavenly court and in enlarging his self-reference to it, in effect "hides himself in their plurality" (OTT 1:145); and something like this occurs with the God of *Paradise Lost*.

Besides his moral and artistic failure, most critical discussion of the Father centers on what Milton means by this figure: for example, does the Father signify pure Being as Irene Samuel has suggested,[44] or very differently, the consummate logical principle and rational authority proposed by Stanley Fish?[45] Since neither Fish nor Samuel acknowledge the force of deity's hiddenness—the divine concealed in the very form of its own revelation, which is all humanity can know or the poet represent—they tend to read the Father in the manner of the law, as though he singularly expressed Milton's idea of deity, uncircumscribed by the religious problem this identity poses. But given his theology, Milton is unlikely thus to deify the devices and embellishings of man's imagination, even if they are his own: he would hardly presume to depict God *as* anything, since he consistently argues that this is deity's unique prerogative in scripture and history, as its own revelation; nor would he propose to define God by any one order of image, since he himself condemns and avoids promulgating just such singularity of religious expression in the tracts. On that account, the God of *Paradise Lost* is perforce scriptural and exegetical, not simply in image but in mode of signification; for the poem seeks to justify not God but God's ways, which finally all come down to the issue of how deity manifests itself to us. Hobbes has occasion to remark on perhaps the most salient aspect of theophany when he observes in *Leviathan* that "The true God may be Personated," which he was by Moses, Jesus, and the Apostles.[46] In history as in scripture, the revealed God is what Hobbes calls "a *Feigned* or *Artificiall person*": "*Persona* in latine signifies the *disguise*, or *outward appearance* of a man, counterfeited on the Stage; and somtimes more particularly that part of it, which disguiseth the face, as a Mask or Visard: And from the Stage, hath been translated to any Representer of speech and action, as well in Tribunalls, as Theaters."[47]

In effect, Hobbes is arguing Luther's point, which is that we know deity by counterfeit only, in the various impersonations or masks of the scriptural God, which deity authorizes contingently, instrumentally, in no way defined by their expression, much less constrained to observe their nature. So although God is personified as speaking and acting, he is not an invisible person in the law's sense; again, for Luther and Milton, the scriptural God is himself a *persona* of the absolute God—of unknowable, inconceivable deity. That is why the singular, preeminent godhead which we habitually bestow on the Father—as a sublime disembodied voice or grand Masonic eye—is not borne out by the collective experience of Milton's heaven, in the shape of what Satan assumes about God, what the Father and the Son say, what the angels sing, or what Raphael or the speaker describe. For Satan could not misunderstand his relation to God so grievously if he had recognized that the figure seated on heaven's holy hill, to whom he refers his own godlike appearance and nature, was not the *ipse* of deity but its personation—its mask in Luther's sense. If he had understood the ironic, properly dramatic existence of God in Milton's heaven, Satan would not conceive himself as the divine semblance, he would not define deity by the sum of its appearances, and the Son's preferment would not so utterly devastate his world. But he does all these things because Milton's God is not incontrovertibly figural until the event of the exaltation. Yet even when Satan acknowledges the Son's mediation, he still tacitly anthropomorphizes the *Sturm und Drang* of heaven's holy hill into an invisible personate being, his version of a God beyond God, even as he expects that deity is confined to this place and susceptible of being thrown down and removed. It is not only the Son exalted but also this figment he imagines—the concealed yet proper person of God—which Satan would imitate when enthroned as "Idol of majesty divine, enclosed / With flaming cherubim, and golden shields" in heaven's war (*LM* 6.101–2), or elevated "High on a throne of a royal state" in hell (*LM* 2.1). Thus he refuses to grasp the peculiar hiddenness of God in the Son which the exaltation describes, adoring as it were the form of divine revelation itself—not deity but its image; and strangely enough, so do we as Milton's readers, insofar as we assume the Father somehow exists independently of the Son as divine image. Then we too make an idol out of Milton's God.

But if the Son's position in the poem is made intelligible by the gospel, so the Mosaic covenant elucidates the Father's, who does not represent absolute being or reason because he articulates a particular, circumstantial understanding of God. He signifies neither a timeless natural law in Samuel's sense nor the rational principle Fish argues, but deity's historical covenants with humankind which the Son as Lord performs and elucidates by his acts of intercession in the poem. Indeed, the relationship between these aspects of God's image in *Paradise Lost* is temporal, in that the Father's speech always precedes the Son's, but also theological. For what the Father does is to represent deity's *pactum* with its creatures, beginning with the ordinance that accompanies the Son's exaltation and extending through all of providential history—from the creation of humanity and the interdicted tree, to the curse and promise made to Adam and Eve, to all the succeeding covenants between God and humanity that Michael recounts, until the promise of salvation in Christ. All of these the Father must expound, which is why he seems to argue. For he voices deity's federation with the world even as the Son embodies it; and that is why the Father is always engaged in convening, devising, implementing, altering, and enforcing. He is the adjudicating aspect of the scriptural God, the Lord and preexistent Christ as judge, establishing the terms and regulating the performance of each party to the contract inaugurated whenever deity engages with its creation. His speech is accordingly judicial, insofar as he is perpetually fashioning and refashioning the covenantal means, which include the vicarious suffering of the Son, by which humanity is enabled freely to participate with the divine.

Either we can understand the Father as this integral aspect of the scriptural *persona* of God, or we can experience him as Satan does after the exaltation, exploded into a plethora of superstitious fragments—voice, light, cloud, thunder, hill—that Satan reanimates as an invisible entity, a body, not a meaning. For in the moment of the Father's decree and the Son's exaltation, Satan's original refusal to construe heaven's sights as an allegory results in a catastrophic loss of coherence extending to the Father's figure as well. Satan sees what we think we see—God as an assortment of magical images or signs which attend a person concealed from our view, like the God of Sinai to an idolatrous Israel. And if we approach the Father's speech as Satan does his person, according to its most conspicuous sense, then his meanings will go the way of his figure: they will appear irrational and grotesque, like the Father's seemingly random effects. However, the revulsion we feel at this figure is not the result of its religious disenchantment but the consequence of our having supernaturalized Milton's poetic expressions and made the Father uniquely Milton's God. And as Wittgenstein predicts, when God is taken to be a person like us, only infinitely greater and more powerful, his every speech and act appalls us, which is what happens when the Father observes Satan from the *nunc stans* of eternity, having allowed him off the lake and thereby his freedom to indulge the twin delusions of autonomy and action:

> Only begotten Son, seest thou what rage
> Transports our adversary, whom no bounds
> Prescribed, no bars of hell, nor all the chains
> Heaped on him there, nor yet the main abyss
> Wide interrupt can hold; so bent he seems
> On desperate revenge, that shall redound
> Upon his own rebellious head. And now
> Through all restraint broke loose he wings his way
> Not far off heaven, in the precincts of light,
> Directly towards the new created world,
> And man there placed, with purpose to assay
> If him by force he can destroy, or worse,
> By some false guile pervert; and shall pervert
> For man will hearken to his glozing lies,

> And easily transgress the sole command,
> Sole pledge of his obedience; so will fall,
> He and his faithless progeny: whose fault?
> Whose but his own? Ingrate, he had of me
> All he could have; I made him just and right,
> Sufficient to have stood, though free to fall.

(LM 3.80–99)

The Father's punning parodies the way Satan reanimates his world by objectifying his own notions of it: the play on "transports" is directed precisely at this idolatrous habit of mind, which inclines Satan to experience his journey out of hell as though it were the heroic physical trial he represents to his adoring public. But from heaven's vantage, all the barriers he so graphically surpasses are markers, not constraints: that is, the boundaries, bars, chains, and abysmal gulf are there not to impede Satan but to illustrate him and the ironical operation of his rage against God, which renders the whole undertaking absurd. Because as intent as Satan is bent on revenge, so in the reflexive way of all religious things, he does even greater evil to himself. Each barrier he overleaps brings him closer to self-degradation and bondage, as well as endless torment. And this fact is what the word "transports" signifies—that Satan in the rage and ecstasy of his delusion goes nowhere even as he battles his way "directly towards the new created world." "Directly" is the Father's sardonic emphasis, because despite his cosmic wanderings, heaven's adversary is incapable of swerving from his own destruction since he brings a mind never to be changed. Thus he cannot convert, he cannot turn in the prophetic sense from the ostensible understanding of things in which he is fixed, where meaning is either evident and singular or occult. The figure of the Father serves as the litmus of these interpretive propensities, whether Satan makes him an idol or a demon.

"The Almighty" ("God, the one of the mountains," a cult name the Judaic deity appropriates for itself in Genesis) has much the same function for Milton's reader. When we take him in the law's sense, as the singular form of deity, then his expressions assume its punitive because analogical character, as an impossible demand that binds humankind to a fate it cannot therefore avoid; thus the Father becomes as hateful as the God of Romans was to Luther. And like Luther's demonic God, what this figure articulates and enacts here is the doctrine of predestination, which is itself susceptible of more than one meaning; that is, if we read this theological argument from the vantage of faith in Christ's atonement—"dressed and clothed in His Word and promises"—then predestination appears a marvelous expression of divine clemency, the way Paul describes it in Romans: "We know that in everything God works for good with those who love him, who are called according to his purpose. For those whom he foreknew he also predestined to be conformed to the image of his Son, in order that he might be the first-born among many brethren. And those whom he predestined he also called, and those whom he called he also justified; and those whom he justified he also glorified" (Romans 8:28–30). But if we take predestination in the indicative, causal sense that Paul's figure of climax or progression may be said to invite, then it is nothing but the double bind of tragedy, which extracts from humankind a meaningless obedience, since God has irrationally decided the issue of election in advance of human choice. Then the divine dispensation Paul celebrates has exactly that aspect for us that Satan projects on the Father—an absolute and capricious tyranny exerted over the world. This tyranny is what we hear when the Father in Book Three declares the terms by which divine grace will redeem humanity from sin, only to add a catch which apparently contradicts that offer. For our redemption depends upon humanity's first expiating the sin of disobedience, couched here in Satan's sense as *lèse majesté* or treason against a feudal God:

> This my long sufferance and my day of grace
> They who neglect and scorn, shall never taste;
> But hard be hardened, blind be blinded more,
> That they may stumble on, and deeper fall;
> And none but such from mercy I exclude.
> But yet all is not done; man disobeying,
> Disloyal breaks his fealty, and sins
> Against the high supremacy of heaven,
> Affecting Godhead, and so losing all,
> To expiate his treason hath nought left,
> But to destruction sacred and devote,
> He with his whole posterity must die,
> Die he or justice must.
>
> (*LM* 3.198–210)

When we allocate exclusive deity and authority to the Father, making him "the absolute God," then his dispensation converts into the rule of necessity and retribution: that is to say, his figure and speech are no longer dramatically or poetically conditioned, as one historical and theological personation of deity—the Lord of the covenant whose terms are always being adapted to meet the emergencies of human motive, understanding, and action. After the manner of the law, we arbitrarily constitute the Father as the autonomous and positive form of truth, which leads of course to contradiction, since we are giving absolute force to a contingent meaning. And when placed in the mouth of what is notionally the one true God, the concatenation of religious effects by which Paul expounds election looks like sheer determinism, especially in the case of the reprobate: "They who neglect and scorn, shall never taste; / But hard be hardened, blind be blinded more, / That they may stumble on, and deeper fall." Yet the Father here does not actually picture himself as imposing evil, since his locution is impersonal and descriptive. The effect of necessity, as an inexorable movement toward evil, is the sensation of sin itself which, insofar as it excludes all meanings but the seemingly self-evident, simply consigns us to more of the same—a prognosis Satan in himself works assiduously to confirm. But because we do not recognize, any more than Satan does, that it is not the person of the Father but the *relation* between the speeches of Father and Son which pictures deity in *Paradise Lost*—as a word expressed to a word interpreted—divine justice appears like necessity, with Milton's God subservient to the principle of condign punishment in a strict ratio of satisfaction to penalty.

Daiches makes a similar point, while remarking that the Father's formulation of justice is "very far from the Christian doctrine of the atonement": indeed, he is moved to conclude from the seeming inhumanity and illogic of the Father's speech that "Milton's heart was not fully in this sort of justification, whatever he might consciously have thought," and as a result of such evident confusion of ideas, that "his poetic instinct was better than his logical powers."[48] Once again, the appearance of contradiction in the poem is rendered as a judgment on Milton's religious and intellectual integrity, when it is an effect the poet carefully orchestrates to challenge the very conflation of religious with rational, overt with authorial meanings that Daiches so instructively achieves: in assuming that the figure of the Father is Milton's God, not only does Daiches make deity a person like us, only invisible and infinitely more powerful, but he also assigns this figure's expressions the entire burden of the poem's argument, of justifying God's ways. He has thus taken the contingent and ironic as univocal, with the result that the Father's speech assumes the arbitrary force and metaphysical causality of fate; and Milton's justification becomes the dreadful, repellant necessity under which Satan and Dr. Johnson both labor, and which we too feel compelled to defy.

But the character of the Father's decree is no more accidental than is the reader's response to it, since Milton has undertaken to stage our experience of deity in Book Three *as* predestination, and to the point that Luther argues in interpreting the psalmist's lamentation:

> But let us answer the argument: "Why are these things attributed to God when He does not do them Himself but uses His means? Satan kills, the Law accuses; and yet the Scriptures attribute both of these to God." This is the reason: so that we might be preserved in the article of our Creed that there is only one God, lest with the Manichaeans we make more gods. They established two principles, of which one was good and the other evil. In good things they ran to the good god, in evil things to the evil god. But God wants us, whether in pleasant or adverse circumstances, to have confidence in him alone. He does not want us to be among those of whom Isaiah says (Is.9:13): "The people did not turn to Him who smote them." This is what our nature usually does; in sudden terrors and dangers it is turned from the true God because it believes He is wrathful, as Job did (Job 30:21): "Thou hast turned cruel to me." But this is to imagine another god and not to remain in the simplicity of the faith that there is one God. Nor is God cruel, but He is "the Father of comfort" (2 Cor.1:3). Because

He delays His help, our hearts make a wrathful idol of God, who is always like Himself and constant. . . . So God is good, righteous, and merciful even when He strikes. Whoever does not believe this departs from the unity of the faith that God is one, and he imagines another god for himself, who is inconstant, sometimes good and sometimes bad. But it is an outstanding gift of the Holy Spirit to believe that when God sends evil, He is still gracious and merciful. (*LW* 12:374)

In entering heaven from the mimetic delusion of Satan's hell, we immediately find ourselves caught in the predicament of faith: like the speaker of Psalm 51, we are faced with a world that seems wrong and nonsensical even as it is divinely ordained, and so we too imagine another god for ourselves, "inconstant, sometimes good and sometimes bad." Since we believe heaven and deity observe the same overt, objective existence and meaning as Satan assumes for himself, having denied his own expressive or allegorical character, we construe the two figures of Father and Son ostensibly, discretely, as distinct entities, only one of which bears the name of God. And when that supreme figure proceeds to condemn humanity before we have even set eyes on our first parents, we find ourselves presented with a fait accompli which seems not only unwarranted but unjustified by the evidence of Milton's narrative. For if we have a theoretical knowledge of the Fall when we enter *Paradise Lost*, we have no poetic experience of it; and the significance deity attaches to events that are eternally present to it, we can understand only after they have happened, which is to say retrospectively, in the manner of all such forensic justifications. Moreover, humanity conceives judgments of value as it conceives moral responsibility, as a matter of sufficient cause, having to do with the grounds that warrant a consequence and a valuation, which is why we immediately ascribe a causal order to the speaker's narrative. On that basis, the Father's presumption of human sin and his assessment of our guilt appear both pat and circular, a judgment that determines the narrative's outcome and secures human sin and suffering—divine foreknowledge as the cause of evil, at least as Milton organizes the speaker's account of events. So when the Father infamously and brutally declares of the man, "Die he or justice must," we are scandalized and confounded by that sentence, which seems cruel and inordinate punishment. But all of these ideas depend on our first naturalizing the speaker's picture of religious things, which is to do as Luther describes: namely, to read Milton's expressions like deity's, according to their merely evident sense, with the result that the God of *Paradise Lost* assumes the person of the Father alone, a "wrathful idol" and the source of evil, with the Son the inferior and sometime dispenser of good. Then, as Milton himself observes, the religious decorum of the poem must appear "unmeet" and "incredible," because evil is made supreme over good.

But the contradiction—the appearance of a double bind—in the Father's proffered redemption of humanity is rhetorical and figurative. Since it looks like a logical and so metaphysical necessity, his either/or is bound to strike us as Draconian, an impression enhanced by the speech's idiom of vassalage and its primitive formulation of retributive justice, as like for like. But that necessity is specious, created by the physicalism and singularity of signification that Paul associates with the law, which assumes the continuity of human and divine, rational and religious meanings. It is this understanding of the Father's expressions which Satan and the speaker reinforce, suppressing other possibilities of significance which the Son will shortly articulate as the paradox of the gospel. In that moment, deity breaks the illusion of equivalence and, surrogating for humanity in order to redeem it, freely atones by perfect obedience for the crime committed against it, which is something only deity itself can do. But first, the Father's speech must inaugurate the legal institution and prophetic revision of the covenant between divine and human being, enacted in the dialogue between Father and Son. It is Moses whose laws make a nation of Israel, to whom the Father refers when he says, "Some I have chosen of peculiar grace / Elect above the rest; so is my will" (*LM* 3.183–84). And it is the prophets, faced with an incorrigible nation, who translate Davidic kingship into messiah and apocalypse, as the Father proceeds to do when he asks the messianic question: "Say heavenly powers, where shall we find such love, / Which of ye will be mortal to redeem / Man's mortal crime, and just the unjust to save?" (*LM* 3.213–15). This occasions a figural as well as historical interval, captured in heaven's silence preceding the Son's announcement of the gospel, which is represented not so much as a new dispensation but as the anticipated culmination of the old, whose frankly allegorical language expresses a shift in interpretive mode.

However much we may neglect its effect, when the Son declares, "Account me man," and the Father responds, "be thou in Adam's room / The head of all mankind, though Adam's son," they both argue an artificial identity, a *persona* in Hobbes's sense of a "Representer of speech and action, as well in Tribunalls, as Theaters" (*LM* 3.238, 285–86). All religious identities are impersonations in this fashion, created by the device of divine imputation to permit the relationship of incommensurables. Thus, in faith, we take deity as it presents itself to us in scripture, in the manner of a dramatic *persona*, as "good, righteous and merciful," while deity in its turn accepts the juridical *persona* of the Son's humanity, so that in heaven's tribunal, his perfect obedience can atone for human sin, as the only righteousness sufficient to satisfy divine justice. In both cases, personality is artificial and ironic, with incarnate God and humankind *simul iustus et peccator*, at once just and sinful; and this paradox abrogates the illusion of natural, discrete identity under the law, and with it, the rule of analogy and necessity, action and causality in religious things. If we observe the force of their incongruity, then the scenes in Milton's heaven perform the same sort of abrogation for the poem, in which the seeming mimesis of Book One is reconceived as allegory after the introduction of Sin and Death in Book Two, with Milton's God understood not as a person but a personation, not as a single, discrete figure but the historical and theological relation organizing the speeches of Father and Son—not as an entity but a mode of meaning.

In short, Milton invites us to do with God in *Paradise Lost* what he himself recommends when interpreting the plural *elohim* or Lord in scripture, which is to attend to the particular grammar of its use rather than inventing a metaphysical analogy and with it, a plurality of invisible persons (CM 14:247). If Trinitarianism is a grammatical misunderstanding, the Father is a poetic one insofar as we mistake his impersonation for the one true God, with the result that we deify an image and render salvation a *horridum decretum*. As Northrop Frye, a theologian, remarks:

> The fact that the Father in Book Three claims foreknowledge but disclaims foreordination is to be related to our earlier principle that liberty, for Milton, arrests the current of habit and of the cause-effect mechanism. We are not to read the great cycle of events in *Paradise Lost* cyclically: if we do so, we shall be reading it fatalistically. . . . If we think of human life in time as a horizontal line, the Father is telling us that he is not to be found at the end of that line, as a First Cause from which everything inevitably proceeds. He is above the line, travelling along with human life like the moon on a journey. The great events of *Paradise Lost* should be read rather as a discontinuous series of crises, in each of which there is an opportunity to break the whole chain.[49]

Not only in argument but also in the manner of his expressions, the Father's incongruous figure exists to "arrest the current of habit and of the cause-effect mechanism," and thus to argue the distinction between creator and created as the possibility of human freedom, both conceptual and practical, in *Paradise Lost*. There is no entelechy of the creature and no necessity, no emanation scheme from deity, who exists "above the line" of human orders of meaning like the causal and anthropomorphic. As a justification of the revisionist sort, the poem's repeated crises of religious expression and understanding work to separate us from our assumptions about the way the action means, and, as Frye says, provide us with "an opportunity to break the whole chain" of narrative necessity, which is a consequence of the way we read.

In other words, insofar as we persist in identifying the Father's figure with Milton's God, thus saving the mimetic appearances of the poem, so we experience *Paradise Lost* in the way Milton argues for the law—as injustice and tragedy. But if we allow the poem's incongruities their proper role in exposing the dialectic between Father and Son, law and gospel, mimesis and allegory, the ostensible and ironic, they work like deity's *opus alienum* to bring good out of evil: as Milton puts the Pauline paradox, the law exists "that it might call forth and develop our natural depravity; that by this means it might work wrath; that it might impress us with a slavish fear through consciousness of divine enmity, and of the handwriting of accusation that was against us; that it might be a schoolmaster to bring us to the righteousness of Christ" (CM 16:131). Then Milton's narrative converts from myth into parable; for parabolic language operates like Lutheran catachresis, using one conceptual idiom to express another

utterly distinct from it, where the estrangement in usage describes a fundamental divergence in understanding. That is why Jesus' parables are neither "true
similes" in the sense of drawing palpable or sustained likenesses, nor rational
myth in the Platonic fashion. As Robert Funk remarks, "the introductory
phrase, in its simplest form the bare dative, should not be translated 'It is like
. . .' but 'It is the case with . . . as with . . .' "[50] This is not analogy but analysis,
for the parables are "not meant to *be* interpret*ed* but to interpret."[51] To that
end, they do not argue a correspondence in appearance or nature, but present
a religious problem whose variable description reconfigures ordinary meanings,
attitudes, experiences in such a way that the familiar world gains new significance in the telling, itself revealed by the conceptual crisis that the effect of
incongruity promotes.

The room of faith and *res non apparentes* exists in this novel implication of
the ordinary, so that parable saturates verisimilitude or mimesis with an antipathetic valence. Moreover, by locating humanity's formative encounter with
God in the world before us, where deity remains concealed beneath its contrary,
the decisive mundanity of Jesus' images constrains us equally from any attempt
to transcend our condition or the self-complacency custom and habit induce. In
the gospels, Funk comments, "Man's destiny is at stake *in his everyday creaturely
existence*";[52] and for that reason, "the parables as pieces of everydayness have an
unexpected 'turn' in them which looks through the commonplace to a new
view of reality":[53]

> Like the cleverly distorted picture puzzles children used to work, the para-
> ble is a picture puzzle which prompts the question, What's wrong with
> this picture? Distortions of everydayness, exaggerated realism, distended
> concreteness, incompatible elements—often subtly drawn—are what pro-
> hibit the parable from coming to rest in the literal sense; yet these very
> factors call attention to the literal all the more. Just as the literary imagery
> is not simply credible, so the parable points to a world where things run
> backward or counter to the mundane world. Yet that other world, like the
> literal sense, has a certain plausibility, a strange familiarity.[54]

The world of parable is not absurd in any absolute sense; it is rather differently
coherent, differently intelligible—"a world where things run backward," where
the "familiar" and "plausible" are transfigured by the estranging use to which
these values are put. Accordingly, its strategy involves propagating distinctions
instead of likenesses, in the discreet conversion of ordinary expression to an
unexpected reference, dislocating the habitual sense we have of things so that
parabolic speech can seem inconsequential and revelatory all at once: "Everydayness is framed by the ultimate. The commonplace is penetrated so that it
becomes uncommonly significant. . . . Vividness of this order, as Barfield notes,
requires that the strangeness produced by the superimposition shall have *interior*
significance. . . . 'It must be felt as arising from a different plane or mode of

consciousness. . . . It must be a strangeness of *meaning*.' "[55] The religious precedent for this order of expression is prophetic speech, whose peculiar conceptual
difficulties enact the interpretive problem of theodicy, namely, the hiddenness
of this God in his revelation. And Jesus acknowledges as much when he answers
his disciples with the paradox of the Lord's commission to Isaiah: "This is why
I speak to them in parables, because seeing they do not see, and hearing they
do not hear, nor do they understand" (Matthew 13:13–17). If the Lord intends
that Isaiah's prophecy should not only argue but also exhibit the spiritual insensibility of an apostate nation, so Jesus' parables diagnose a comparable obtuseness in those who acknowledge only the rudiments of what he says, refusing
in this way to know an otherwise unknowable God.

It is to resist such intransigence of understanding that both wisdom literature
and prophetic religion address the human capacity to perceive the otherwise
inevident, to break the stranglehold of received and customary ideas on our
experience, since conceptual liberty is what allows us more adroitly to apprehend the world, but also to engage our predicament as intellectual creatures
anew. As von Rad explains, it is this critical impulse that motivates writings
like Proverbs and the Book of Job: for a "conflict arises only when insights
which were at one stage correct become 'dogmatically' hardened; when, that
is, experience no longer continues to liberate that which is known and where
that which is known is not being constantly reexamined, but where knowledge
itself is kept firmly under control and where a twisted, and therefore inauthen-
tic, knowledge comes into conflict with the evidence of reality."[56] In other
words, scriptural wisdom emerges from the discordant reality of lived contradiction, injustice, and causeless suffering, where we too are betrayed by our own
expectations of meaning—an eventuality which again has its theological source
in God's hiddenness.[57] By invoking Isaiah and the reflexive significance of
prophecy for its audience, Jesus responds to this endemic condition of human
being, asserting not only our need but also our religious obligation of attention
and intelligence about the world, which parable demands in its seemingly perverse apprehension of the ordinary. So von Rad observes that "There is no
knowledge which does not, before long, throw the one who seeks the knowledge back upon the question of his self-knowledge and his self-understanding,"
which is why in his view Israel "made intellect itself the object of her knowledge."[58] For the wisdom literature recognizes that the one truly fundamental
understanding we must have is this consciousness of our conceptual disposition.
Like parable, then, wisdom takes as its religious problem the daily scandal of
the way we conceive and practice truth, which the Judaic scriptures precisely
refer to our engagement with God, whose appearances are not supernatural
or transcendent but rather preternatural—different, queer, contradictory, even
illegible in the usual sense. These disconcerting effects attend the expression
of deity, whose mundane presence invests human experience with possibilities
only a critical intelligence can discern, much less appreciate. "There are," says

von Rad, "not only depths of the abyss and of the dark; there are also depths of light"; and parabolic language plumbs those depths by its transfiguration of the ordinary and expected.[59]

Like Satan with the figure of God, or our first parents and the interdicted tree, Milton's expressions demand a similar discernment from his reader and to the same ironic purpose of testing the adequacy of interpretation to our experience of *Paradise Lost*. Nor are we, any more than Adam and Eve, left without a guide, because it is as parable that the Father intends Raphael's narrative, not mimesis.[60] The archangel's stated constraints on expression should prepare us for those incongruities—the Son's exaltation, the Father's jokes, or the war in heaven—which withstand our desire to read supernal history as inspired reportage or vulgar allegory of the eternal and infinite. But the same order of incongruity that disrupts the literal or mimetic force of parable—"distortions of everydayness, exaggerated realism, distended concreteness, incompatible elements"—should also restrain our propensity to supernaturalize what Raphael depicts: that is, our desire to take his images as the mythography of Milton's God, not an allegory of religious understanding like Jesus tells his hearers. In the same way, it is our inveterate supernaturalism in religion that moves us to scorn Milton's picture of angelic warfare—because it is strange and inglorious even at its most "godlike," in the oddly perfunctory character of the combat between Michael and Satan or the narrative terseness of the Son's rampage (as against his arming). But the divine does not perfect our desires, it confounds them: in the parables of the talents, the laborers in the vineyard, the marriage feast, or the dishonest steward, the ordinary is made extraordinary not by the sublimation but by the seeming perversion of received values, daring us to find justice in the outrageous, meaning in the inconsequent. And as Funk argues, the same perversity governs parabolic expression, where mimesis is challenged by its deliberate distortion.

It is this distortion we hear in the Father's repellant phrasing of his commission to Raphael, since it looks very much as if God were engineering his own blamelessness for sin, neither defending the human pair in their innocence, nor in their guilt "fulfilling all justice":

> Go therefore, half this day as friend with friend
> Converse with Adam, in what bower or shade
> Thou finds't him from the heat of noon retired,
> To respite his day-labour with repast,
> Or with repose; and such discourse bring on,
> As may advise him of his happy state,
> Happiness in his power left free to will,
> Left to his own free will, his will though free,
> Yet mutable; whence warn him to beware
> He swerve not too secure: tell him withal
> His danger, and from whom, what enemy

Late fallen himself from heaven, is plotting now
The fall of others from like state of bliss;
By violence, no, for that shall be withstood,
But by deceit and lies; this let him know,
Lest wilfully transgressing he pretend
Surprisal, unadmonished, unforewarned.
 So spake the eternal Father, and fulfilled
All justice.

(LM 5.229–47)

Like the speaker who cries, "O for that warning voice," in the moment that Satan bends his flight toward the new world, we want the Father to do something forcible and immediate to prevent the Fall, since he himself is eternally prescient (LM 4.1). We want divine foreknowledge to avert, not predict, the outcome—in short, to preclude what transpires in Genesis. But as Lord of the covenant, the Father cannot transgress God's part of the pact between divine and human being, which is simultaneous with our creation. Justice under the covenant means giving what is due to Adam and Eve, namely, full knowledge of their predicament and their foe. Yet as Milton argues in the case of predestination, knowledge whether divine or human must not compel, must not coerce, the creature, since its liberty is what makes its experience meaningful. Thus there is another aspect to doing justice on this occasion, which is adherence to equity—something more profound than the merely formal compliance we attribute to the Father here. Although the parity of human and divine is an instrumental fiction, the covenant binds God from intruding upon the creature's primal freedom to understand and choose, which the Father regularly reiterates and exemplifies in his own self-delimitation and observance of the law. As von Rad remarks of the creation accounts more generally, deity forms stability within instability; and this providential poise of all things is extended to human being, when the Father speaks of our first parents' sufficiency to stand. Yet it is because our liberty includes the possibility of confusion, error, and suffering, giving the human condition its ambivalent as well as mutable character, that we would surrender it out of hand. We would have God choose for us, even as we want Raphael conclusively to identify Satan and his machinations to our first parents, so that there is no chance of their mistaking him, no leeway for misinterpretation. In the manner of the law, we want his speech to be unequivocal, imperative, and compulsory, acting upon Adam and Eve like virtual necessity. We never reflect that this is what we find odious about every ambrosial utterance of the Father.

But that desire, captured in the speaker's exclamation, is neither equitable nor just, nor is it consistent with the distinction between God and the world, all of which entail the contingency of creatural meanings. In casting his counsel to the human pair not as law but as narrative, and a narrative whose incongruities defy any simple sense it might appear to have, Raphael tacitly respects this circumstance and the conceptual liberty it implicates. If his tale of angelic apostasy and the new world's creation seems to imitate an action, that action has coherence only when it is understood parabolically—not as mimesis of the supernal but as a way of speaking about religious things. Then the world's prehistory describes the clash of religious mentalities, not rival forces, which is how Adam and Eve must construe it if they are to gain a wisdom sufficient to repulse Satan's fraud. In Milton's phrase, that wisdom is to know God aright, because the unprecedented possibility of fraudulence, of "deceit and lies" in Eden, requires that they understand creation's equivocality—the consequence not so much of evil but of deity's distinction from the world. Since it is fostered by the predicament of faith itself, such an intelligence would enable them not just to conceive the as yet unknown operations of hypocrisy or deceit, but to distinguish and prefer truth over mere plausibility, deity over its expressions. For this issue is what our first parents must address and decide as Raphael speaks the incongruous language of revelation; and like Isaiah's prophecies and Jesus' parables, how they understand his account will implicate their faith or apostasy.

For Adam and Eve can bring to the story a mind alive to those religious things which do not appear as such; or they can enthrall themselves to sheer semblance and contradiction, grasping what Raphael says only in its most specious sense. So at the end of their conversation in Book Eight, it is not a little ominous that the archangel finds himself obliged once more to warn Adam against his penchant for saving the appearances, leading our general ancestor inevitably to exalt the creature at its creator's expense as he confesses his inordinate passion for Eve. Raphael responds to this disturbing insensibility by demanding that Adam exercise the same attention and intelligence about the world which wisdom, prophecy and parable inculcate, and which Milton also requires from the reader of *Paradise Lost*:

> Accuse not nature, she hath done her part;
> Do thou but thine, and be not diffident
> Of wisdom, she deserts thee not, if thou
> Dismiss not her, when most thou need'st her nigh,
> By attributing overmuch to things
> Less excellent, as thou thy self perceiv'st.
>
> (LM 8.561–66)

It is not Eve or her beauty whose excellence is really challenged here, but the play of superficies in which Adam invests both truth and preeminence, exposing his obliviousness to Raphael's parable of faith and to his own burgeoning idolatry.

CHAPTER SIX

Milton's Eden

❦

CREATURES OF OTHER MOLD

The predicament of faith in Milton's theology ensures that, with *Paradise Lost* as with Genesis, controversy would surround the *selem elohim* or image of God, since the intransigent hiddenness of this deity cannot but confound the divine semblance to which human beings congenitally, relentlessly aspire. Indeed, it is because the *selem elohim* must implicate some aspect of our appearance—some perceptible correspondence between the creature we can see and the creator we neither see nor understand—that we find ourselves in a quandary about its meaning. For how can humanity claim, much less evince, any likeness to a being from whom we are made irrevocably different at least in this one respect? Moreover, in Milton's poem, where the image of God nevertheless is somehow in evidence, such palpable likeness raises the fraught issues of power and gender as well as quality of being, inasmuch as the speaker famously declares, "He for God only, she for God in him," at just that point where humanity's resemblance to God is introduced (LM 4.299):

> wide remote
> From this Assyrian garden, where the fiend
> Saw undelighted all delight, all kind
> Of living creatures new to sight and strange:
> Two of far nobler shape erect and tall,
> Godlike erect, with native honour clad
> In naked majesty seemed lords of all,
> And worthy seemed, for in their looks divine
> The image of their glorious maker shone,
> Truth, wisdom, sanctitude severe and pure,
> Severe but in true filial freedom placed;
> Whence true authority in men; though both
> Not equal, as their sex not equal seemed;
> For contemplation he and valour formed,
> For softness she and sweet attractive grace.
>
> (LM 4.284–98)

The "unequal" or disproportioned appearances of our first parents would seem to warrant the speaker's pronouncement that Adam in his nature corresponds directly to God, while Eve's being addresses God only mediately, as derived from Adam. Humanity's resemblance to the divine is then visibly qualified by sexual difference: because he is a man, Adam seems to enjoy some greater likeness to deity on that account. His gendered distinction from Eve—his "masculine" valor and intellect, and the way these qualities are somehow manifest in his body—is what makes him behave and be more like God, or so it appears to Satan, whose initial view of our first parents the speaker relays here. Eve's likeness to her maker is then attenuated according to the degree of her difference from Adam, since she does not share the same body and cast of mind and so presumably the same extent of resemblance. Their "unequal" appearances thus translate into a primal inequality of nature or being, with the divine image observing the sex of the bearer, as an attribute eclipsed in the woman and preeminent in the man, and so significant of their unequal status in creation and before God.

Like Satan or Milton's speaker, what we find in the world of *Paradise Lost* tends to reflect how we understand this divine image. For when we suppose that Milton makes likeness to God contingent on male sex and what is conceived to be masculinity, we understand the *selem elohim* as a particular, exclusive sort of appearance which corresponds to some attribute in deity itself. Moreover, we see it as an endowment one can have more or less of, while others may have none at all: that is, like the blind speaker of "When I consider how my light is spent," we tend to think about this identity as some sort of objective, measurable property possessed by Adam, and susceptible of being diminished in Eve and of course denied the animals altogether. This is how Adam himself comes to conceive the divine image, when he impulsively complains to Raphael about the beauty of his spouse:

> For well I understand in the prime end
> Of nature her the inferior, in the mind
> And inward faculties, which most excel,
> In outward also her resembling less
> His image who made both, and less expressing
> The character of that dominion given
> O'er other creatures.
>
> (LM 8.540–46)

If we think in Adam's fashion about God's image, as a calculable and so positive appearance where the "inward" and "outward" are neatly reciprocal, we are likely to suppose that Milton's expressions observe a similar order of meaning and value. The quality of an image will thus define the nature of the thing it signifies, as Adam's sex is thought by the speaker to imitate some aspect of God; and value will be assessed by the same canon of gendered appearance—Eve's value is proportioned to her perceptible difference from Adam and therefore her departure or deviation from the supposedly commensurable nature of God. The Edenic world will accordingly enjoy a certain self-evidence that we like to associate with the "prelapsarian"—the erstwhile purity and innocence of creation and our first parents—and the poet's expressions will share that original naiveté or (viewed from another angle) dogmatism of meaning. But when we read his imagery in this way, assuming an unproblematic equivalence between what the speaker recounts and the poet means, we get the usual Miltonic discrepancy between script and spectacle: creatural "freedom" and "equity" are figured as an absolute, impenetrable hierarchy of being, with deity or its surrogates at the top and everything else demoted to the degree that it departs in appearance and nature from Milton's God or, on earth, from his image in Adam. However, we will elicit another world, another God, and another argument altogether from the poem if we recognize that the divine image, as Milton cagily introduces it, needn't propose an essential likeness between deity and the man, as against the woman—that is to say, a single, restrictive appearance and cast of mind; if we admit as well that what the speaker of *Paradise Lost* is inclined to show us may convey something besides what he intends, especially in Eve's case, for whom he has a thoroughly vexed, erotic regard; and finally, if we allow more largely that the ultimate force of Milton's images—like the expressions of Luther's *Deus absconditus sub contrario*—is not dictated by their most immediate or obvious sense.

More exactly, if we understand Milton's imagery along the lines of the *selem elohim*, as proposing a complex negotiation between divine idiom and human understanding, then *Paradise Lost* cannot offer the monument to received ideas (including the ideology of the feminine) which many of its critics have sought to document and explain. Rather than some simple, sensuous, and passionate correlative to Milton's notion of truth, his poetic language becomes a methodically intransparent expression and so a differential term on the model of irony and the revisionist sort of justification. Moreover, with this change in interpretive protocol, Milton's poetic design gains a newly subjective reference, delineating how he conceives the affections of the mind, not things in the world. For the cumulative, limitary circumstances which *Paradise Lost* intrudes between any image and its evident sense—those divergent accounts of the creature's predicament whose partiality the narrative sequence itself aggravates—shift the locus of the poem's argument from the world described to the still greater drama of that world's apprehension. Von Rad remarks that in the Judaic scriptures, "Israel was obviously not in the position of conceiving the world as an entity thus philosophically objectified which man sees as set over against himself":

> We have to seek the reasons for this in the fact that for Israel the 'world' was much less Being than Event. It was for man something continually new and experienced in many different ways, and was therefore much more difficult to comprehend conceptually—least of all by reducing it to a principle. Israel did not see the world as an ordered organism in repose,

for on the one hand she saw Jahweh as much more directly at work in all that goes on in the world, and on the other, man on his side recognised that he had a share in this, because he too continually determined the reactions of the world about him by his actions, whether good or bad. (OTT 1:152)

The world of *Paradise Lost* is self-consciously a religious event, not an entity, as something that happens profoundly not just within time but within human history, and which occasions our self-conception; accordingly, its landscapes are not places but pliant and occasionally precipitous fields of meaning and experience. In this way, *Paradise Lost* enacts the Arminian realm of liberty and election from which deity witholds its active will, even as the Father announces at creation that "uncircumscribed my self retire, / And put not forth my good-ness, which is free / To act or not, necessity and chance / Approach not me, and what I will is fate" (LM 7.170–73). And this is especially true of Milton's Eden, which evinces that disconcertingly fluid range of significance obtaining in both his heaven and hell, yet even more so because Eden carries the burden of the poem's argument, with all the narrative strands converging on the cru-cially human event of the Fall. Yet despite this ironical turn that *Paradise Lost* shares with parable, we have shown ourselves no more disposed than Satan to doubt the adequacy of our interpretive assumptions, preferring difficulties of our own invention to the dilemma the poem at once crafts and explains. Thus we enact unawares the scriptural irony of those who seeing do not see, hearing do not hear or understand: that is, like the *selem elohim* itself, which cannot mean what it simply says unless we would become idolaters on Milton's model, these manifold constraints re-create in *Paradise Lost* the modality of divine revela-tion, converting the ordinary or apparent sense of things to a meaning that is necessarily reflexive, since it relates in parabolic fashion how our own expecta-tions of God and truth conspire to hide deity and self from view.

For Milton's dramatis personae, their inability to acknowledge the different order of divine existence and expression reflects the obstacles which also im-pede recognizing the dignity of other persons, especially when their sort of life seemingly conflicts with a character's self-understanding or identity—as the Son's existence conflicts with Satan's, or Eve's confounds Adam and the speaker. This perplexing of mutual apprehension hinges on the way we choose to conceive the image of God, inasmuch as it constitutes an expression of the good and thus the way human identity and value are manifest, in both the Genesis narratives and Milton's understanding of them. And insofar as his justi-fication intends us to reflect upon and revise the way we approach the problem of God's ways, so imaging in *Paradise Lost* will emulate the *selem elohim*, obliging us to exercise that critical attention about his fictional world which addresses the daily intersection of the intelligible and the incommensurable, history and the absolute, the familiar and the estranging, and which the Judaic scriptures call wisdom.

Our alter ego in this regard is specially Adam, who incorrigibly persists in inferring excellence from great and bright despite Raphael's explicit instruction to the contrary. On that account, he finds himself more than erotically disturbed by his spouse, who would seem to outrage this nice propriety of meaning, in which the significance and value of everything is neatly proportionate to its palpable appeal. As he sees it, she has too much beauty and grace and adroitness of mind for the subordinate position in which she is placed, as only secondarily and contingently God's image. Therefore—and ironically—this sheerly prepossessing quality of Eve becomes for him a kind of obscurity or incongruity in the design of creation, inasmuch as the man is supposed more directly to image God than the woman and thus to manifest the divine glory. Why, then, he asks Raphael, does he admire and prefer Eve's every movement and word before all others, given her stated inferiority to himself: shouldn't she *appear* less to him because she *is* less? Yet Adam doesn't want to see Eve's loveliness diminished, since he takes such exceeding pleasure in it; nor does he want an adjustment in her status as against his own. Instead, as the course of his whole inquiry in Book Eight predicts, he makes an issue of Eve because she represents a strangeness or confusion in his world—an incongruity that inspires "something yet of doubt," not about his spouse so much as about the intent and wisdom of her maker (*LM* 8.13). In sum, his problem lies in understanding what God and Eve together express by her appearances. For Adam is disturbingly inclined to insist upon clarity and exactitude of meaning as an index of the truth or rightness of something, such that while he delights in being overmastered by Eve's beauty, exulting in its sensuous immediacy and seeming excess, he nonetheless wants her appearance to make an obvious sort of sense. If her image has an irresistible power over him, he also finds it curiously indistinct, opaque, resistant to his assumptions of meaning and value—not unlike, one might add, the signs of the hidden God.

And this is Milton's point to his reader: that Adam's attempt to clarify or resolve Eve's appearance by calling it wrong, improper, inordinate entails a misunderstanding of his God and so a kind of faithlessness to spouse and creator alike. As Arnold Stein remarks, "The very confidence of Adam's pronouncements makes his behavior in the disclosure of passion all the more threatening; being able to define wisdom does not, it is plain, guarantee its possession. Nothing in the nature of innocence prevents an excessive trust in one's command of issues, however authoritative the language of their exposition."[1] Tacitly, the order of analogy Adam assumes will not allow any latitude of expression for God or subjectivity for Eve, and no mystery to either one of them. Each must be, as it were, fully penetrable, fully intelligible to him. In Adam's version of the *selem elohim*, the divine image should articulate the real correspondence of properties manifest and esoteric: were a man invisible, he would be like God, and God would be like a man if we could but see him. This is also what Raphael would seem to do when he likens "spiritual" to "corporeal" forms to express the unseen vicissitudes of angelic warfare, adding—"though what if earth / Be but the shadow of heaven, and things therein / Each to other like, more than on earth is thought?" (*LM* 5.575–76). But Raphael is not trying to represent God here but his angels, as well as the marvelously sentient being of Milton's heaven, itself enlivened by faith; and in comparing the entirety of God's creation to "the bright consummate flower," he has just suggested that there is some real continuity between earthly and supernal creation. Certainly, if we see Milton as laying out a sort of emanation scheme like that David Burrell describes (Raphael himself using the equivocal words "proceeds" and "returns"), we could argue that human being more or less corresponds with divine;[2] and that this is how we should understand the image of God in humanity: namely, as signifying that we are higher up the scale of being than any other earthly nature, and so more completely resembling deity, especially if we happen to be a man. But again, that is to ignore the character of creation itself which explodes into life with the divine Word—"So spake the almighty, and to what he spake / His Word, the filial Godhead, gave effect" (*LM* 7.174–75)—imaging what von Rad calls "the absolute effortlessness of the divine creative action" (*OTT* 1:142). Adam's very request that Raphael attempt to express this action simply brings on another disclaimer, for "to recount almighty works / What words or tongue of seraph can suffice, / Or heart of man suffice to comprehend" (*LM* 7.112–14). In short, there is no commensurability between deity and creatural things, including language and mind; and this is the whole point: "It only needed the brief pronouncement of the will of Jahweh to call the world into being. But if the world is the product of the creative word, it is therefore, for one thing, sharply separated in its nature from God himself—it is neither an emanation nor a mythically understood manifestation of the divine nature and its power. The only continuity between God and his work is his word" (*OTT* 1:142). A propensity to read Milton's creation account as though it were myth, not allegory—to suppose that its supernal machinery expresses anything other than the informing and sovereign power of deity over the world—is to imagine such continuity, and prelatically, satanically, to treat poetic figure as entity and Book Seven as pre-Socratic ontology. It is also to ignore the sheer incongruity of what Raphael describes, seduced by the temporal illusion attending "process of speech" to see divine fiat as somehow naturalized.[3] Then the Spirit becomes a biological agency on a par with water, light, air, earth, and the word itself a person standing upon heaven's verge, who then returns through space and time to "heaven's high-seated top, the imperial throne / Of Godhead, fixed for ever firm and sure":

> The filial power arrived, and sat him down
> With his great Father (for he also went
> Invisible, yet stayed [:] such privilege
> Hath omnipresence), and the work ordained,
> Author and end of all things, and from work
> Now resting, blessed and hallowed the seventh day,
> As resting on that day from all his work.
>
> (*LM* 7.585–93)

As always at such points of ostensible transparency of image, verisimilitude is exploded by divine illogic to reveal an allegory of omnipresence: like Lycidas, whom the uncouth swain pictures as bodily inhabiting heaven and earth at once in a virtual parody of transubstantiation (*LM* 175, 183), the Son both invisibly departs and visibly inhabits the throne of heaven's hill, seemingly in the fashion of a false Helena. But the only deception potential here is the superstitious enthrallment to image which would deny the figural force of deity's distinction and argue some magical because objective actuality for what Raphael describes. In *Paradise Lost*, Milton's word mediates the significance of what we see even as the Son does Milton's God; and what the poem's scandalous imagery reveals here is the form and substance, as it were, of our religious attitudes.

For the *selem elohim* in Milton could also be understood in terms of the distinction—the infinite dimension of difference between divine and human being, the creator and the creature, which obliges us to speak figuratively in the first place—to talk about one world or one order of thing *as if* it were another. And this expressive decorum emphasizes the force of difference as against likeness: because deity is his subject, Raphael must now confess the limits of analogy in conveying what is utterly and finally distinct from the created world, including himself. So although Raphael witnesses God's supernal acts, they remain temporalized for him just as they do for Adam and Eve; and Milton himself argues in the *Christian Doctrine* that motion and time obtained before the creation of this world, equally an aspect of angelic existence as they are human being (CM 15:35). Properly speaking, then, the poet reserves the standpoint of eternity for deity alone, in its infinite and inconceivable nature. And even though Raphael's disclaimer circumscribes his description to the angelic *sense* of what occurred in the moment of the new world's creation, he still cannot supply the same order of image he uses for heaven—of visible to describe invisible because heavenly things—not least because Miltonic angels are themselves still recognizably material or substantial beings, though "more refined" and "spirituous" than humanity (*LM* 5.475).

So where Raphael's picture of the supernal explicitly argues an affinity of kind between the seen and the unseen, heaven and earth, this new attempt at analogy must cope with the creator's different sort of invisibility, where the ineluctable distinction of deity from everything else results not in "likening" but in "process of speech." To reiterate, "likening" as he uses it may be said to entail an appreciable continuity among things that allows us not only to assert an analogy, but also to find it significant and effectual in elucidating our experience. To that end, Raphael's admittedly figurative account must promote our first parents' understanding of what took place in heaven when the angels sinned against God, since its sole purpose is to prepare them for Satan's assault. But the invisible actions of deity there and in creation, as against the unseen actions of the angels, are not scrutable to anyone in this way. The intervention of "process of speech" between God's acting and creatural understanding implicates a separate meaning or reality which language can picture for us, without that picture signifying anything more than an intelligible response to an otherwise unintelligible subject. As Calvin would have it, the creature's ideas can evoke only the creator's presence, the sensations of God acting in time; they cannot encompass the actions themselves, much less the divine actor, since "God's judgment shows him certainly to be of a mind quite different from our own" (CC 295). So although Raphael conveys to Adam how the angels experienced the world's creation, the sense of simultaneity he mentions isn't the effect of their intuitive (as against discursive) intellects, moving as it were in tandem with the divine mind. As in the case of the Son's exaltation, the episodic collapse of temporal and natural frames is the incongruous symptom of deity's expressions in the world, deviating from expectation and, moreover, rational possibility in such a way as to describe the departure of divine from creatural being. What we are shown, then, implicates something in itself exempt from the conditions of space, time, and appearance to which the human and angelic are more and less bound in the poem; for God has none of these qualities in himself but only by virtue of his image, his covenant with the creature.

Because it epitomizes the relation between things human and divine, the sexual distinction we see drawn by the *selem elohim* also tends to reflect what we think Milton is arguing more largely—his grand theory of eternal providence and the justice of God's ways with his creatures. On the one hand, we can suppose with Satan and the speaker that Adam is the image of God because in his palpable and impalpable being, he more directly and exactly resembles the nature of his creator, in which case we can judge his choices as excusable or inexcusable on that account. In the same way, we can assume that Eve is less like God because of her evident difference from Adam, both in the manner of her creation and in her sex, and thus terribly condemned to fall by her very inferiority. But it is also possible that deity could be expressed by them both in some way that does not efface those real differences of sex and gender on which Milton indefatigably insists, yet still ensures that what separates Adam and Eve in appearance binds them equally to God and to each other, in their innocence and their guilt. If I may enlist him as support for the latter approach, Walter Eichrodt suggests that in imagining the *selem elohim*, the priestly writer of Genesis "is certainly not thinking primarily, or even at all, of the difference between human and animal bodies, but of the psychophysical totality of human existence, which bears the stamp of a fundamentally different kind of life, and thus has reference to its creator."[4] As Eichrodt understands it, the divine image is not equivalent to a specific appearance like maleness or a propensity of character like masculinity. Nor, when he speaks of "a fundamentally different kind of life," does he mean the wholly subjective or internal, the immaterial or transcendental, since he is talking about an image or semblance that must somehow be evident and intelligible in us—a "psychophysical" expression. "Kind of life" would therefore seem to describe how the human person in its entire being evokes the difference, the singularity of this God, by the peculiar manner in which our palpable existence elaborates a still mysterious self.

It is this personal inflection or modality of human appearance that Milton also understands by the image of God. Thus, in discussing "the visible creation" in the *Christian Doctrine*, he comments that Genesis extends "soul" to all living things, each of which is equally "body-and-soul," and that when the Lord made humanity, "it was not the body alone that was then made, but the soul of man also (in which our likeness to God principally consists)" (CM 15:37–39). Yet this peculiar aspect of our being has no unique, autonomous, and metaphysical existence which allows its separation from the body; rather, it is a phenomenon of nature, observing what Milton calls "the laws of generation" or reproduction just as the body does (CM 15:49). For even in its primal creation, at the beginning of the world, humanity being "formed after the image of God [was] endued with *natural* wisdom, holiness, and righteousness" (CM 15:53, my emphasis). By ascribing to the human soul the same natural life shared by the body, not to mention other creatures, Milton denies the divorce of soul from body which grants us the spurious dignity of a transcendental or supernatural generation, which he allows only to the Christ as Jesus (CM 15:53). And he makes this denial because a transcendental soul suppresses both the historical actuality and moral obligations of our humanity, thus falsifying the peculiar exceptionality of human being in the pursuit of likeness to God:

> we learn that every living thing receives animation from one and the same source of life and breath; inasmuch as when God takes back to himself that spirit or breath of life, they cease to exist. Eccles.iii.19. "they have all one breath." Nor has the word "spirit" any other meaning in the sacred writings, but that breath of life which we inspire, or the vital, or sensitive, or rational faculty, or some action or affection belonging to those faculties.
>
> Man having been created after this manner, it is said, as a consequence, that "man became a living soul"; whence it may be inferred (unless we had rather take the heathen writers for our teachers respecting the nature of the soul) that man is a living being, intrinsically and properly one and individual, not compound or separable, not, according to the common opinion, made up and framed of two distinct and different natures, as of soul and body, but that the whole man is soul, and the soul man, that is to say, a body, or substance individual, animated, sensitive, and rational; and that the breath of life was neither a part of the divine essence, nor the soul itself, but as it were an inspiration of some divine virtue fitted for the exercise of life and reason, and infused into the organic body; for man himself, the whole man, when finally created, is called in express terms "a living soul." (CM 15:39–41)

"Soul" describes no independent, supernatural existence of the human person but the opposite condition—the profound intimacy of life with what lives in the world. Hans Wolff points out that the word usually translated as "soul" in the Septuagint and Vulgate, *nepes*, expresses this inextricability since its initial etymology refers to the vital functions of throat and neck: "we see above all man marked out as the individual living being who has neither acquired, nor can preserve, life by himself, but who is eager for life, spurned on by vital desire, as the throat (the organ for receiving nourishment and for breath) and the neck (as part of the body which is especially at risk) makes clear."[5] And as Milton remarks in the instance of Adam's creation, the epithet *nepes hayya* indicates that deity by its breath makes the inanimate body of the man "a living being, a living person, a living individual," as against *nepes met*, a corpse.[6] Indeed, *nepes* "is never given the meaning of an indestructible core of being, in contra-distinction to the physical life, and even capable of living when cut off from that life."[7] And the same is true of the divine "wind" or *ruah* which quickens the human body: this wind is itself what Wolff calls a "theo-anthropological term," since it signifies both human breath and more usually the irresistible power or energy by which deity moves the world, including human emotion and will, and which it elects to bestow or withhold.[8] Thus, like *nepes*, *ruah* evokes no incorporeal thing like spirit, but gathers its meanings from a cumula-tive association of ideas which extends the sense of a perceived phenomenon (the way Milton understands and uses etymologies in his exegesis).[9] At the same time, what Wolff calls the empowering force of divine breath implicates the dependency of all things on God, in the manner expressed by *nepes*: for in the Judaic scriptures, life is neither automatic to matter nor self-willed and autogenous, as Satan professes to believe. Instead, *ruah* and *nepes* together im-plicate the human relation to God, since life is in his gift alone.[10]

Milton clearly recognizes this aspect of scriptural usage and as his definition should suggest, "soul" is a creature of human language too, something which accordingly has an expressive or grammatical existence for us even as God does. In scripture, he remarks that "the attributes of body are assigned in common to the soul," such as touch and hunger, that the soul is called by Paul an "animal" even as the body is, and that an emphasis on the body as "a mere senseless stock" should be taken as an occasional usage allowing us to express by contrast the wonder of the body's action, its vitality or its intelligence, which we our-selves characterize as "spirit" or "soul" (CM 15:41–43). Thus, in Milton's ac-count, "soul" does not belong to the order of entities putatively set apart from language, but to the order of *façons de parler* or ways of speaking about things that do not appear as such. And indicatively, Milton remarks the same usage with regard to the religious idiom of "spirit and flesh," which he says should "be understood in a theological, not in a physical sense," as a way of speaking about the condition of the whole, historical person (CM 15:51).[11]

For this reading Milton has Luther's good authority, who in his commentary on Romans argues that "flesh and spirit" is a Pauline expression evoking the "dialectic [*utrunque*]" of experience and understanding to which a person is bound by faith:[12] "Moreover, we must note that the apostle does not wish to be understood as saying that the flesh and spirit are two separate entities, as it were, but one whole, just as a wound and the flesh are one. For although the wound is something by itself and the flesh is another thing, yet because the wound and the flesh are one, and because the wound is nothing else than wounded or weakened flesh, we can attribute to the flesh the properties of the wound. In the same way man is at the same time both flesh and spirit" (*LW* 25:339). Luther here expounds in different terms the sense in which the faithful are *simul iustus et peccator*, righteous and sinners at the same; for "flesh" and "spirit" do not describe modes of being but simultaneous attitudes that the whole person takes toward the world, attitudes which are inseparable to the extent that they express the contingency of religious upon ordinary meanings. As Luther elaborates this "twofold idea," the religious speaks to the "wound"— the injustice and subjective incoherence—created by the received idea we have of things, which denies the reality or efficacy of the religious argument (*LW* 25:340). The language of "spirit" and "flesh" is thus a way of distinguishing this intractable because existential conflict, this perplexity of living which would of course be obviated by "spiritual" transcendence whether metaphysical—as defining a separate world—or analogical—as simple and discrete entities to which Paul's then facile usage would refer. Such, however, are the deleterious fictions which false theologians build on the apostle's words:

> In the light of these points it is obvious that the idea of the metaphysical theologians is silly and ridiculous, when they argue whether opposing appetites can exist in the same subject, and when they invent the fiction that the spirit, namely, our reason, is something all by itself and absolute and in its own kind and integral and perfectly whole, and similarly that our sensuality, or our flesh, on the opposite end likewise constitutes a complete and absolute whole. Because of these stupid fantasies they are driven to forget that the flesh is itself an infirmity or wound of the whole man who by grace is beginning to be healed in both mind and spirit. (*LW* 25:340–41)

In Luther and Milton, there is the same resistance to segregating God and the things of God from the human condition more largely. For to argue, as Luther's metaphysicians or Milton's philosophers do, that spirituality or the inevident dimension of human being can be isolated from the body, from the world, and, most instrumentally, from scriptural usage is to denature religion, which each sees as a mundane practice of the whole person. When Milton associates the *selem elohim* with the expressly natural wisdom, holiness, and righteousness of primitive humanity, he makes that image integral to our condition, not its transcendence. And by his choice of attributes, Milton also describes it as a quality to human life that peculiarly emulates the hidden God—the sense in which Eichrodt says the divine image "has reference" to deity as expressing a "fundamentally different" order of existence. For this difference describes a marvelous, virtually inimitable intelligence, animation, or expressiveness to human being, the peculiar meaningfulness or "soul" of the human person in which Milton asserts the *selem elohim* "principally consists."[13]

What human being shares with the divine is not the "soul" or "spirit" as some separable entity or domain but as an order of self-expression, the way in which we convey ourselves, our subjectivity, to one another, in the proportioning of what can be seen of a person to what can't. For our expressions always signify more and other than they seem to do—thus their affinity to deity, which historically discloses itself in such a "disproportioned" fashion. As Charles Taylor has observed, "the self's interpretations can never be fully explicit. Full articulacy is an impossibility."[14] No less than the hidden God, then, human subjectivity at bottom is profound and mysterious (a quality of scripture's description remarked by Auerbach and Richard Alter): our appearances reveal us to each other and to ourselves without exhausting the possible meanings of self, giving the personal a depth or dimensionality which resembles God's revelation in its expressive scope. To that extent, the manner of divine and subjective revelation is incongruous, not because it is supernatural but because these *invisibilia* are simply incommensurable with what conveys them, even as they are inseparable. In his writings, Milton consistently respects this differential sort of imaging, where likeness to God does not consist in a specific, positive feature of body or mind but in a general quality of expressiveness that nonetheless distinguishes between what is shown and what is meant, as Calvin argues about Isaiah's vision of the Lord enthroned in the temple. The intricate dialectic of "body and soul," "spirit and flesh," exemplifies for them all the difference between religious or "theological" usage and other modes of figuration, a difference predicating a turn in hermeneutical emphasis and ethic: for where the interpolation of metaphysical entities for idiomatic speech voids the existential force of scripture, these theologians would handle its expressions in the manner of parable— to interpret the always surprising and dynamic phenomenon of religious things.

In *Paradise Lost*, where this distinctively religious idiom stymies Satan, it also tends to elude the speaker as well as Adam, all of whom are chronically dismayed by the resurgence of incongruity in the world. As we do with Milton's text, they always expect some more perfect, more facile access and claim on God and other people than the human condition will allow us. They too want to confine deity and the truth of things by ready analogy to what they see and know; but such continuities are disallowed by the image of God, the epitome of Edenic decorum. For the *selem elohim* may be said to argue that an image can evoke simultaneously something quite different from its immediate or its directly symbolic valence, just as the dialectic of body and soul permits our affinities with others to be elective as against compulsory, and the disproportion between theophany and "process of speech" works to preserve us from idolatry. Moreover, the *selem elohim* neither translates humanity out of history and beyond phenomena nor enthralls it to the arbitrary reign of appearance. Its dialectical expression offers instead a salutary separation—a break or lacuna in the illusion of necessity under which we place ourselves in this world—which, in disclosing other possibilities of meaning to our lives, enables the present exertion of hope and the exercise of freedom. But the image of God returns us to the mundane in perhaps a more important sense, since it argues that human identity is itself neither discrete nor autonomous, but a relation of mutual acknowledgment, along the lines of the covenant between the creator and his intellectual creature:

> If God be said "to have made man in his own image, after his likeness," Gen. i.26. and that too not only as to his soul, but also as to his outward form (unless the same words have different significations here and in chap. v.3. "Adam begat a son in his own likeness, after his image") and if God habitually assign to himself the members and form of man, why should we be afraid of attributing to him what he attributes to himself, so long as what is imperfection and weakness when viewed in reference to ourselves be considered as most complete and excellent when *imputed* to God . . . . In arguing thus, we do not say that God is in fashion like unto man in all his parts and members, but that as far as we are concerned to know, he is of that form which he attributes to himself in the sacred writings. (CM 14:35–37, my emphasis)[15]

With regard to the *selem elohim*, Milton argues this reciprocity: just as deity assumes to itself a creatural image in order that it might be known and understood by the creature, so God may be said to author humanity by endowing it not with the divine nature but with this figural resemblance—"in his image, after his likeness." For we cannot imitate deity in its being, which, to recall the fundamental principle of Milton's theology, is "impossible to comprehend accurately under any form of definition" (CM 14:39). As Anthony Yu has observed, this is "the paradox central to the Christian affirmation that man who bears the image of God must also live by the realization that he is not like God."[16] Rather, we are like deity as it expresses itself to the creature, and to that extent we resemble God insofar as we are both more and other than the sum of our appearances—Eichrodt's "stamp of a fundamentally different kind of life." That is to say, we are like God in this abiding difference between the person and its expressions—in the manner of our subjective revelation, which, however impoverished or banal, never exhausts the potential of self. When he discusses what it means "To be in the form of God," as that Pauline phrase applies to the Son or preexistent Christ, Milton says that it "seems to be synonymous with being in the image of God; which is often predicated of Christ, even as man is also said, though in a much lower sense, to be the image of God, and to be in the image of God, that is, by creation" (CM 14:275). While the Son does not possess deity in his own right, since he cannot share God's inimitable "form" or nature, he is nevertheless that intelligible image deity assumes to itself—the perfect and entire realization of that instrumental truth, the Lord of the covenant. Milton's further point is that the Son evinces this divine resemblance "by creation" even as we do, which is to say that it distinguishes his sort of being—a condition uniquely signifying deity's imprimatur—as the image of God.

So the *selem elohim* as Milton explains it is figural in more than one way: in the sense that it describes the divine image, God's expressions, and not God's nature; in the sense that it betokens the artistic or "created" status of the bearer, on the model of the *persona* deity fashions for itself in revelation; and in the sense that, like any *persona* or identity, it requires acknowledgment to be evinced, as the Father in *Paradise Lost* acknowledges the Son in the exaltation.[17] As Wolff remarks, God's determination to "make man in our image, after our likeness" (Genesis 1:26) expresses the idea that "man proceeds from God's *address*"—"that man, in hearing and then also in obeying and in answering, corresponds to the word of God's address": "The unique nature of man in creation is to be understood in the light of his special relationship to God. In the context it would be still better to speak of God's relationship to man as the presupposition for man's self-understanding."[18] If scripture employs the same language to speak of this connection between God and humankind as it uses to describe Adam's generation of a child who resembles him (whether in its humanity, its sex, or some other quality, it is hard to say), the concept of "attribution" limits the force of likeness, since a figural quality or trait is being ascribed that the person does not self-evidently possess:[19] Milton handles Adam's image in his child, like God's image in his Son, as not only creative but also elective—an acknowledgment of affinity between two different persons made intelligible by a shared, even public, picture of their relation. To be "made in the image" accordingly signifies a bond, a relation, something on the order of creator to creation, in both heaven and on earth. While the creation evidences its creator, the manner of that evidencing is profoundly and irreducibly mediated: like paternity in most patrilineal cultures, it is a resemblance that must be discerned and recognized to be known, inasmuch as father and child are more obviously two different persons than mother and child.

That is why the Father addresses his consummate image and humanity's intercessor as "accepted Son" (*LM* 11.46): he does so not only to anticipate the latter's self-sacrifice, but also to indicate just that acknowledgment of relationship permitting and inaugurating the atonement for humanity's sin—as divine and human "son" at once, made so by an act of God's imputation or "acceptance." Cavell's analysis of the body-soul relation in Wittgenstein again holds true of the *selem elohim*, inasmuch as deity's expression in us entails a particular appearance from which it can never be divorced. But for the resemblance to be evident requires that we must first interpret that appearance and then acknowledge it, as the Father acknowledges a unique affiliation with the Son as image and sacrifice, and as Adam recognizes his child. The *selem elohim* thus signals in the creature deity's eternal acknowledgment of its own creation—its relatedness. On this head, we should recall that, in Satan's apostasy, God still sustains in him that residual image of divine affinity as well as goodness which moves Abdiel to exclaim upon the discrepancy. For even as the image of God represents no single overt appearance but rather a distinctive expressiveness, an order of self-manifestation, what it evidences is not a private essence but a peculiar bond or relationship—the covenant God upholds with creation de-spite Satan's failed "faith and realty." On this head, Charles Taylor remarks that "One is a self only among other selves": "A self can never be described without reference to those who surround it."[20] To the same point, the *selem elohim* argues that, in the case of human identity, deity is the reference, the relationship, which uniquely describes us, an idea borne out by the usage of *nepes* and *ruah*. And it describes us, as Taylor observes, according to our attitude or orientation toward the good—"Truth, wisdom, sanctitude severe and pure / Severe but in true filial freedom placed"—understood by Milton as our congenital affinity for our creator, whose self-revelation is thus figured in us.

Again, that resemblance must first be disclosed by interpretation, since it is not immediately intelligible in the manner of a positive likeness. Moreover, interpretation in the ironic world of Milton's poem always manifests self, in the sense that it implicates those motives, values, attitudes, and understandings which distinguish the individual person. The way Taylor pictures the self as existing within "webs of interlocution," as an open and evolving narrative of identity, is pertinent here:

> What I am as a self, my identity, is essentially defined by the way things have significance for me. And as has been widely discussed, these things have significance for me, and the issue of my identity is worked out, only through a language of interpretation which I have come to accept as a valid articulation of these issues. To ask what a person is, in abstraction from his or her self-interpretations, is to ask a fundamentally misguided question, one to which there couldn't in principle be an answer.
>
> So one crucial fact about a self or person that emerges from all this is that it is not like an object in the usually understood sense. We are not selves in the way that we are organisms, or we don't have selves in the way we have hearts and livers. We are living beings with these organs quite independently of our self-understandings or -interpretations, or the meanings things have for us. But we are only selves insofar as we move in a certain space of questions, as we seek and find an orientation to the good.[21]

The self that Taylor evokes belongs to the order of things that do not appear as such, that are mediated to us not only by personate expressions such as speech and choice, but also by the responses these expressions elicit from others, and specifically the way they attest to agreement or disagreement about the good. Such responses do not legislate the self but describe its parameters, the bound-aries within which it makes its particular sort of sense, since each of us—as Taylor points out—is engaged in perpetual discussion with the community whose expectations and values we either assume or address. As parable predicts, the "language of interpretation" pictures the self in terms of its ideas, passions, and experiences, a relation among impalpables captured through each person's imperative need to articulate in both speech and action the vicissitudes of identity, and so to understand the psychophysical phenomenon of self which always remains mysterious at its core. There is an enduring and irreducible reciprocity between these human dimensions on which Taylor comments, after Wittgenstein; for even as articulation in this way traces the limits of self-consciousness, so human consciousness defines the limits of articulation as well. Where issues of subjectivity are raised, we cannot escape interpretation, we cannot get past the language of self, because human expressions no more represent a separable entity or object than soul and spirit do in Milton's theology (as Wittgenstein observes, there is no thing to which the idiom "I" refers). Since it shares this inevident and therefore interpretive status—because, like deity and all *res non apparentes*, it confounds our predilection for the objective—how we understand the image of God reflects not only our valuations but our self-conceptions, as here, when Satan exclaims "still in gaze, as first he stood" on beholding the human pair:

> O hell! What do mine eyes with grief behold,
> Into our room of bliss thus high advanced
> Creatures of other mould, earth-born perhaps,
> Not spirits, yet to heavenly spirits bright
> Little inferior; whom my thoughts pursue
> With wonder, and could love, so lively shines
> In them divine resemblance.
>
> (*LM* 4.356–64)

Not unexpectedly, Satan still conceives the *selem elohim* as a rightful place or status ("room") that he and the angelic hosts once owned, but which humanity has now usurped. In other words, he understands God's image as personal property, an attribute and ranking ("little inferior") to be possessed, calculated, and compared, for all that this likeness can only be conveyed to the reader by amorphous abstractions ("Truth, wisdom, sanctitude severe and pure"). There is accordingly a significant difference between Satan's usage here and the Father's in Book Three, when the latter refers to the Son as inhabiting Adam's "room"—"be thou in Adam's room / The head of all mankind, though Adam's son":

> As in him perish all men, so in thee
> As from a second root shall be restored,
> As many as are restored, without thee none.
> His crime makes guilty all his sons, thy merit
> Imputed shall absolve them who renounce
> Their own both righteous and unrighteous deeds,
> And live in thee transplanted, and from thee
> Receive new life.
>
> (*LM* 3.285–94)

"Room" in Satan's sense can be altered only by an arbitrary and implicitly unjust act, taking away the possession of identity as it were from its rightful owner; in his hierarchical mind, place is congenital and absolute, something altogether integral to the person. But "room" in God's usage is not a property but a position *coram Deo*, a relation to God that deity allows to be voluntarily assumed even as the Son assumes the headship of humanity. And the paradox of this identity—that the son of Adam is converted into his head—at once contravenes Satan's assumption of irrevocable, substantive identity. Deity's imputing headship to the Christ and merit to humanity disrupts the original, supposedly ineluctable progress of sin, even as the children of Adam, in renouncing "their own both righteous and unrighteous deeds"—which is to say, their claim to perform and image their righteousness in God's eyes—in effect repudiate the reign of mere appearance. And by this manifold act of imputation, in which each party radically reinterprets the other, humanity is no longer made captive to a congenital guilt nor confined to its evident capacities. Our position or "room" has been "transplanted" in a manner Satan refuses even to imagine, since it challenges the very bases of his self-understanding.

For the likeness to God that Satan recognizes in Adam and Eve he associates with his own erstwhile self, as supreme among that species of "heavenly spirits bright" whose nature supposedly matches the unseen being of deity. So the resemblance he sees here and could love—love as he loved his own sin—is first to himself as godlike, as the visible form of God. His admiration of Adam and Eve thus betrays his inveterate egotism, because the analogy he draws is to his own remembered beauty and power as God's putative semblance, and then by extrapolation to the divine nature itself—a train of inference to which his usual assumptions of self-evidence, autonomy, and hierarchy of being conduce. For Satan conceives God's image in the singular aspect of dominion, as ruler of creation yet not as the *persona* of divine rule, but a dominion he as autarch possesses exclusively for himself.[22] The result of Satan's self-conception, of *his* perverse notions of identity and value, is that Adam and Eve are made to bear the divine image with such strange precision and particularity, since Satan has always assigned the inevident a specific body or appearance, to which readily accrue the epiphenomena of this religious misunderstanding—beauty, gender, and power. Yet intruding upon the picture of our first parents is the repeated use of the word "seemed" and the activity of interpretation it implies. In other words, at every juncture of valuation, the inaugural sight of Adam and Eve raises the problem of perception or mere appearance: the speaker says, "*seemed* lords of all, / And worthy *seemed*," "though both / Not equal, as their sex not equal *seemed*." And while Genesis's creation accounts are invested with these ideas of dominion, merit, and gender, in *Paradise Lost*, they tend to be the peculiar and duly infectious concerns of the apostate: it is Adam at his most deluded who speaks of God's semblance as the sheer exercise of "dominion" even as he complains about Eve's "absolute" appearance; and it is Eve, flushed with the illusion of godhead, who discusses the relative advantages of mastering Adam as against deifying him. The presence of such ideas in Eden well before the Fall signals the ironic function of the *selem elohim* in *Paradise Lost*, an image which reveals as much or more about the beholder as it does the bearer, since its significance always consists in a *relation*.

This compounded semblance, describing both perceiver and perceived, would then suggest that the gender of Adam and Eve as well as their disproportioned value are equally an interpretation of what it means to be in the image of God. That interpretation is imposed upon what Milton regards as the incontrovertible fact of sexual difference by Satan and the speaker together, who choose to understand the individuation of human being in this way. For the specific "look" ascribed to the *selem elohim* is not intrinsic to God's image, never mind the proper spirituality of the angels, who are amorphous in themselves: although these are erotic, they are distinctly sexed and gendered only as they are described or appear to humanity, including the speaker. Moreover, when Milton talks about God as "spirit" in the *Christian Doctrine*, he doesn't take that attribution in the way Satan does here, namely, "spirit" as characterizing deity's own mode of being. He expounds *nostra theologica*, what God is for us; or as Richard Muller describes this departure in interpretive approach, "The issue is to understand the 'mode' or 'manner' by which 'we have a knowledge of God in this life.' "[23] Thus before he even turns to the subject of material creation, Milton carefully frames the litany of divine attributes with the principle of God's inconceivable nature, so that "spirit" is strictly understood to be an attribute of the scriptural image, as a radically qualified inference or speculation about the picture deity provides of itself. Moreover, spirit as applied to God is unlike creatural existence, either angelic or human, because it is imagined to be absolutely simple: it is "that most perfect essence by which God subsists by himself, in himself, and through himself" (CM 14:43). Theologically, then, only the creator God has this single autonomous being, while everything else exists contingently and temporally—or as Sir Thomas Browne puts it, by a distinction—including the Son and angels, not to mention the matter of creation itself (CM 15:22–29).

But the distinction is not all that separates Milton's image of God from Satan's, when the latter condescends to find our first parents "to heavenly spirits bright / Little inferior" and so to resemble the divine. If "spirit" does not describe the mode of being observed by deity in itself but instead pertains to the divine image, the Son, which is the likeness to God that Satan infers from his own invisible nature, it follows that the angels are no less an image of God than the sacred text or humanity, since all picture or express deity as spirit, which is to say something that we cannot see as such. If I may put it this way, the very shape-shifting of the angels which renders their appearances indeterminate—Raphael appearing in winged or seraphic form to Adam and Eve before the Fall, Michael coming after it in the form of a man to banish them—enacts just that idea. We see them according to our position, not their nature, so that their appearance remains figurative, reflexive, relational, implicating our experience of them (so Milton argues that their wings *image* angelic swiftness [CM 15:35], and implicitly, that angelic celerity is not *caused* by those wings—a distinction in modality of meaning like that Michael expresses in heaven's war [CM 15:35]). Thus, in attacking the notion of creation ex nihilo, Milton distinguishes between orders of imperceptibility—the nonexistent, and the modal or perceptual—characterizing *res non apparentes* in this way: "Again, what we are required 'to understand through faith,' respecting 'the worlds,' is merely this, that 'the things which were seen were not made of things which do appear.' Heb.xi.3. Now 'the things which do not appear' are not to be considered as synonymous with nothing, for nothing does not admit of a plural, nor can a thing be made and compacted together out of nothing, as out of a number of things, but the meaning is, that they do not appear as they now are" (CM 15:17–19). Since he takes Hebrews' "things that do not appear" as expressing what lies beyond human ken and so belongs to the realm of faith, Milton is making a positional distinction of time and appearance, not a categorical, much less an ontological, one. That we do not experience *res non apparentes* as such doesn't necessarily mean they do not now exist, or were not already in being then—rather like the person ordained God's Son. Indeed, these things share the condition of existence but "do not appear as they now are": Milton is distinguishing here between some original state of created things (as undifferentiated matter) and things as they were subsequently made and known, not between being and nonbeing. He is also tacitly denying our ability to penetrate the boundary of time and appearance—as it were, the domain of history—into the realm of the metaphysical.

Res non apparentes thus describe for Milton an expressive and epistemological, not a metaphysical existence. As with Luther, their present appearance to humanity does not delimit or define their nature; for the mystery of religious things in Milton's sense—those things "we are required to understand through faith"—has to do with God's defying and so extending the bounds of human possibility. In short, the phrase *res non apparentes* refers not so much to *invisibilia* in themselves as to our relationship with them. Their inevidence describes the point at which human experience and understanding cease to make sense of the world, implicating a different order of *meaning* as against being. Take the creation as an example: Satan sees it is an ontological hierarchy in which each creature's nature dictates its rightful and unalterable place or "room," and which archangelic being accordingly surmounts as most proximate and most like God. The unfallen angels, by contrast, see creation organized into a gradual, limited disclosure of deity, and in that way an activity of expressing God in which all things participate. We encounter this reading when Raphael is faced with Adam's hyperbolic assumption of a vast, unapproachable difference between himself and his angel guest, "whose excellence he saw / Transcend his own so far, whose radiant forms / Divine effulgence, whose high power so far / Exceeded human" (LM 5.456–59). Adam is therefore not a little surprised to

see the angel, as God's supposedly transcendent extension ("divine effulgence"), eat earthly food with a certain gusto. And this incongruity elicits a
favorite question and perspective he increasingly shares with Satan—"yet what
compare?" (*LM* 5.467). That is, with his notions of the heavenly upended,
Adam wants to know how he should think about the relation between the
angelic appearances he so extravagantly admires and his own capacities, between heavenly and earthly being. Raphael answers him this way:

> O Adam, one almighty is, from whom
> All things proceed, and up to him return,
> If not depraved from good, created all
> Such to perfection, one first matter all,
> Indued with various forms, various degrees
> Of substance, and in things that live, of life;
> But more refined, more spirituous, and pure,
> As nearer to him placed or nearer tending.
>
> (*LM* 5.469–76)

It is easy to find Satan's absolute hierarchy of being in this speech, in which
a thing is simply better ("more refined, more spirituous, and pure") the closer
it approaches to God, in the presumption that deity itself is spirit. This would
seem to be Adam's notion too, and why he is disconcerted to learn that angels
can eat his own food with unfeigned relish: were the hierarchy exclusive in
Satan's sense and heavenly being absolutely distinct from earthly, this would
be merely a polite gesture—the angels would not eat, nor would they digest,
excrete, and copulate, as Raphael blushingly describes. But since everything
derives from "one first matter," nothing within creation differs except by degrees
of materiality and modes of intelligence. The great divide is not between
heaven and earth, but between the creature as made and its creator as unmade—that is, between a comparable life and an incomparable one, a life that
Milton says "must be styled by us WONDERFUL and INCOMPREHENSIBLE" (CM
14:61). Raphael's speech then expresses something other than a pyramid of
being: it argues precisely the contingency of everything upon God as creator as
well as the perfection of all creatures in their kind, who are thus different without prejudice, given that one cannot be more or less dependent on its maker
than another. And it suggests that such an intricate web of dependence and
difference is rather a picture (in Wittgenstein's sense) or an expression (in Cavell's) of God—resonant of deity's goodness, where creaturely being may be
said to figure this loving inflection of its unknowable author toward the world—
spirit understood in the medieval sense as inevident and conceptual "relation."

Indeed, it is in the nature of all God's creatures to picture God's glory, power,
and goodness, with their expressions varying according to the manner of deity's
acknowledgment. Sometimes that acknowledgment is conveyed by the idea of
proximity, as it is with the worlds of heaven and earth; sometimes it is expressed

by investiture, as with humanity, the angels, and the Son of God, who image
not only the intent of the creator but the diverse order of his historical revelation as well; for the most part, acknowledgment consists in the very fact of
creation itself. In any case, what is good about the divine image derives from
the intellectual creature's contingency on God, its status as deity's expression,
not from some material, much less essential, continuity between its nature and
God's. Accordingly, Milton says that even though the angels are called sons of
God, and even gods themselves, "they are not to be compared with God" (CM
15:37). Rather, those legions of "thrones, dominations, princedoms, virtues,
powers" which the Father and Satan intone at various points, are not signs of
angelic quality but angelic variety: angelic "offices and degrees" merely distinguish the range of deity's goodly expression in them. So when Milton talks
about the superior status of things invisible, "if not in respect of origin, at least
of dignity," the unseen world does not possess this superiority in itself, but only
on account of its figurative as against essential proximity to the divine: "For the
highest heaven is as it were the supreme citadel and habitation of God," whose
presence the angelic hosts may be said differently to manifest to each other
(CM 15:29). The highest heaven is that invisible state where "God permits
himself to be seen by the angels and saints (as far as they are capable of enduring
his glory,) and will unfold himself still more fully to their view at the end of
the world" (CM 15:31–33). In other words, the invisibility of heaven doesn't
picture deity's supremacy so much as its unutterable difference from us, its remoteness or inaccessibility as an element of our experience, which is always in
process of being "unfolded," disclosed, or revealed by a perpetual apocalypse
even to the angelic hosts. So we should not conflate the sight of heaven with a
sight of God himself—Milton speaks here only of the divine glory or *conspicien-
dum*—nor mistake its aspect of majesty and eternity for the divine essence. Like
the rest of creation, heaven is instead a creature that we are to regard as part
of God's self-expression, but by no means a vision of deity in itself:

> It is improbable that God should have formed to himself such an abode
> for his majesty only at so recent a period as at the beginning of the world.
> For if there be any one habitation of God, where he diffuses in an eminent
> manner the glory of his majesty, why should it be thought that its founda-
> tions are only coeval with the fabric of this world, and not of much more
> ancient origin? At the same time it does not follow that heaven should be
> eternal, nor, if eternal, that it should be God; for it was always in the power
> of God to produce any effect he pleased at whatever time and in whatever
> manner seemed good to him. We cannot form any conception of light
> independent of a luminary; but we do not therefore infer that a luminary
> is the same as light, or equal in dignity. In the same manner we do not
> think that what are called "the back parts" [*posteriora*] of God, Exod.xxxiii.
> are, properly speaking, God; though we nevertheless consider them to be
> eternal. (CM 15:29–31)

Like the relation of light to luminary, Milton constructs his heaven as an endless revelation of God, but not as deity per se. The analogy as he explains it is particularly instructive. That which illuminates is palpably distinguished from the light it conveys, as distinct in nature and yet wholly necessary to its communication, since "we cannot form any conception of light independent of a luminary." This, says Milton, is the contingency of things heavenly on God, and for the purposes of understanding, expressive of God's intent that his creation more largely communicate him to us—although as deity he can arbitrarily select any effect he desires to express himself. Here Milton argues a similar relation to that between body and soul in Wittgenstein's remark, where the body is an entirely different order of manifestation from the soul it communicates, even as the soul is unknowable without the body. So while heaven is an image that never ceases picturing God, it also never ceases to be distinguished from him until the end of things, when all creatural distinctions—Son, angels, heaven, humanity, earth—collapse, and God somehow becomes "all in all" in the Father's Pauline phrase (*LM* 3.341).

In this case, then, inference does not implicate a correspondence, a point made still more forcibly by Milton's reference to the *posteriora* of Exodus 33, where deity's "back parts"—the *kabod* or glory of God seen from cover and at a distance—are as much of God as Moses can safely view. Milton conceives heaven as *posteriora* in the sense that it too is a vestigial or deflected effect of God's presence, a vehicle of deity's revelation and so light rather than luminary. That is also why heaven doesn't enjoy the same imputation of eternity as the *posteriora*. So the comparison Milton draws between heaven and what Moses glimpses argues that the Lord's care to shelter humanity from his face is an allegory of deity's limited disclosure in its creation, even in the highest heaven. It is therefore telling that when Milton concludes his discussion of the angelic and the invisible more largely, he remarks: "To push our speculations further on this subject, is to incur the apostle's reprehension, Col.ii.18. 'intruding into those things which he hath not seen, vainly puffed up by his fleshly mind' " (CM 15:37). It is a principle that we, as readers of *Paradise Lost*, should observe.

Their Looks Divine

Since the *selem elohim* in humanity, which *Tetrachordon* defines as "Wisdom, Purity, Justice, and rule over all creatures," does not refer to deity in itself but its scriptural image, that image may be said to exemplify the expressive, historical existence of all things that do not appear as such, including this litany of abstract qualities (CM 4:74). For God's expressions specially share that modality with those of its intellectual creatures, a circumstance that gives the speaker's pronouncement of "he for God only, she for God in him" a novel significance. The sexual distinction becomes simultaneously a model of divine but also subjective mediation, in which our first parents' "unequal" or individual appearances articulate not so much a disparity of nature and value as a kind of expressive relation or contingency along the lines of divine revelation: that Eve stands to Adam as the *posteriora*, heaven, and the angels stand to God. So the difference Milton assumes between the sexes characterizes less an order of birth and priority than an order of expression, where the image of God itself lies in the *relation* between the human pair and God, not in any one (gendered) attribute. Thus in *Tetrachordon*, Milton effectively translates Paul's remarks about the polity of marriage (largely from 1 Corinthians 11 and Ephesians 5) into a model of theophany:

> But St. *Paul* ends the controversie by explaining that the woman is not primarily and immediatly the image of God but in reference to the man. . . . Neverthelesse man is not to hold her as a servant, but receives her into a part of that empire which God proclaims him to, though not equally, yet largely, as his own image and glory: for it is no small glory to him, that a creature so like him, should be made subject to him. . . . Moreover, if man be the image of God, which consists in holines, and woman ought in the same respect to be the image and companion of man, in such wise to be lov'd, as the Church is belov'd of Christ, and if, as God is the head of Christ, and Christ the head of man, so man is the head of woman; I cannot see by this golden dependance of headship and subjection, but that Piety and Religion is the main tye of Christian Matrimony. (CM 4:76–79)

At one level, these discriminations appear all too depressingly familiar; but if we look carefully at the terms of his argument, Milton is putting marriage to the more or less original purpose of explaining how the hidden God is made intelligible to the world by an order of imaging. What one might call the sexual protocol of revelation works something like this: deity is itself expressed by the historical manifestation of God, whose image is the Son and Christ, expressed in turn by the man, as the man is imaged in the woman, the woman in the church, the man in Christ, and so on. In each of these instances, the image is understood to be not only distinct from what it pictures, but so palpably different that it requires interpretation and acknowledgment, even as the man acknowledges the image of God in the woman by finding himself in her—implicitly for Milton the force of the pun, *'is* and *'issa*, when the man says in Genesis: "This at last is bone of my bones / and flesh of my flesh; / she shall be called Woman, / because she was taken out of Man" (Genesis 2:23). Needless to say, crediting the force of the image is a matter of faith, inasmuch as believers must discern and then profess a series of relations which, strictly speaking, are otherwise inevident because they are imputed and interpretive, not intrinsic or self-evident. Hence the significance of marriage as an account of deity's connection with the world: God has an interpretive reality and presence in the relationship between man and woman in much the same manner that Luther characterizes by the phrase *facere Deum*; that is, if the woman refuses to see God in the man, if the man cannot love the woman as Christ loves the church, if neither can see deity imaged in Jesus as the Christ, then God's presence is altogether lost to them.

The importance of this acknowledgment argues the role of faith and choice not only in the religious but in the marital relation as well, as an affinity that must be elected and constantly reasserted in Luther's fashion, if it is to have its proper significance and effect. Returning to his account of the creature's natural ascension, Raphael stipulates, "if not depraved from good"; and the very occasion for such depravity signals the conditional value of all created things, which are good only insofar as they continue to express deity as their author. But once that dependence is refused, as the serpent is dispossessed of this relation by Satan's alien occupancy, or as Satan denies it in assuming a cherub's godliness, then the goodness of the creature is perceptibly and existentially attenuated. For a convention or agreement here evoked by the idea of imaging has been broken—the covenant of creator with created. And when Milton uses the *selem elohim* to articulate the order of the marital relation both in the divorce tracts and *Christian Doctrine*, he naturally supposes it to have just this contingency, this responsiveness to the vicissitudes of faith and love:

> For man, therefore, in his state of innocence in Paradise, previously to the entrance of sin into the world, God ordained that marriage should be indissoluble; after the fall, in compliance with the alteration of circumstances, and to prevent the innocent from being exposed to perpetual injury from the wicked, he permitted its dissolution; and this permission forms part of the law of nature and of Moses, and is not disallowed by Christ. Thus every covenant, when originally concluded, is intended to be perpetual and indissoluble, however soon it may be broken by the bad faith of one of the parties; nor has any good reason been given why marriage should differ in this respect from all other compacts; especially since the apostle has pronounced that "a brother or a sister is not under bondage," not merely in a case of desertion, but "in such cases," that is, in all cases that produce an unworthy bondage. (CM 15:173–75)

Not only is marriage a covenant whose force is subject to the fidelity of the parties thus engaged, but that force is also historically circumscribed by the event of humanity's breaking faith with God. But then, marriage is always contingent for Milton on humanity's covenant with the hidden God, which it expresses as a separable bond by which two distinct parties are voluntarily conjoined. So although Milton firmly believes in the principle of the woman's subjection to the man as her superior, he does not think of this sexual subordination as an essential constant in marriage or in nature. For immediately following his remark about how splendid it is for the man to have the woman subject to him, Milton introduces this proviso: "Not but that particular exceptions may have place, if she exceed her husband in prudence and dexterity, and he contentedly yeeld, for then a superior and more naturall law comes in, that the wiser should govern the lesse wise, whether male or female" (CM 4:76–77).[24] By invoking natural law, both here and in the passage above, Milton emphasizes the conditionality of subjective value and relation. In marriage, either person's "room" or position cannot but alter with the character of the individuals who covenant, since this relation figures the priorities—wisdom among them—of an unseen God who is himself unbound by the received sense of things. That is why both Satan and our first parents can fall *or* stand; however much we are inclined to overlook this circumstance, the image of God depends on the mutual acknowledgment of both parties—a covenanting, an act of good faith, like that the believer performs in the case of scripture's anthropomorphizing language, or that which Milton says obtains in the making of a marriage. And we have that choice because the distinction between God and the world renders every sign of truth an image we must interpret and elect to see as such.

Indeed, Milton's indubitable sexism simply underscores the extent of this expressive contingency, as when he says that "the woman is not primarily and immediatly the image of God but in reference to the man." The woman's difference from the man describes the limits of analogy or likeness, not only within humanity but also between divine and creatural being: even as the woman knows God as expressed in the man, so the man knows God only as he is expressed in the Son and Christ as God's preeminent image, both Lord of the covenant and Jesus of Nazareth. At each step of the way, an act of faith and imagination must occur to disclose what is as yet unapparent, because the *selem elohim* begins with a precedent, unsurpassable difference between the image and what it is understood to convey, where interpretation must discover their coherence.[25] When Cavell says that human expressions to be understood "must be *read*," he has this species of elective experience in mind: "I have to read the physiognomy, and see the creature according to my reading, and treat it according to my seeing." Again, in the manner of Luther's *facere Deum*, interpretation renders an expression significant, even as acknowledgment gives it force and actuality; and that protocol of meaning is reflected in Milton's concept of the marriage bond. In the first place, he celebrates the woman as uniquely the expression of the man, not because of her likeness to him but because of her difference: as Milton observes in *Tetrachordon*, "heer *alone* is meant alone without woman; otherwise *Adam* had the company of God himself, and Angels to convers with; all creatures to delight him seriously, or to make him sport . . . yet for all this till *Eve* was giv'n him, God reckn'd him to be alone" (CM 4:83). He was alone, that is, because he lacked the means of man's expression—the company of woman as his glory and image; for "the different sexe in most resembling unlikenes, and most unlike resemblance cannot but please best and be pleas'd in the aptitude of that variety" (CM 4:86).

Without its distinct expression by the woman, masculine subjectivity—like the divine in the creatural—would be frustrated, indeed catastrophically silenced; and the same reciprocity holds true in the woman's case, although it must be emphasized that the divorce tracts in their polemical character never attend to her predicament as they do the man's (an imbalance only partially rectified in the *Christian Doctrine*). Yet it is significant that Milton here raises in order to refute Augustine's "crabbed opinion" that the only truly appropriate companion for Adam would have been a member of the same sex: that is, "manly friendship" as preferable to spending "so many secret years in an empty world with one woman"—"secret" in this sense of being silenced, without any avenue of expression for himself (CM 4:85). But that is precisely what marriage prevents in Milton's view, since in woman it offers to the man "a minde answerable," not just (in Donne's ironic phrase) "mummy possessed" with which to procreate (CM 4:87). Indeed, one could say that their respective positions on marriage equally describe their different understandings of allegory: for Augustine, in likeness consists our access to truth—the apparent as a luminous corollary to the unseen; conversely for Milton, difference—the image as a way of speaking about the incommensurable—creates the very possibility of inevident realities like self, affinity, truth, and God. Thus it is indicative that Adam is Augustine's ventriloquist at the Fall, when the former utters the *summa* of antifeminism:

> O why did God,
> Creator wise, that peopled highest heaven
> With spirits masculine, create at last
> This novelty on earth, this fair defect
> Of nature, and not fill the world at once
> With men as angels without feminine,
> Or find some other way to generate
> Mankind? This mischief had not then befallen.
>   (LM 10.888–95)

Adam's faithless logic begins with the idea that the angels are in heaven exactly as they appear to him on earth—"masculine," "without feminine"— from which it follows that the perfect because transcendent order of heaven argues the "superior" propriety of the male sex companioning itself on earth; that by comparison with heaven, God must therefore have created imperfectly when he created woman; and finally, that Adam did not willingly deviate from divine ordinance, but deity itself erred temptingly in that second creation. In just the same way, he supposes that Eve is the sole cause and culprit behind the Fall because she offered the fruit to him, drastically inferring from his own failure that man by nature is weakened, even resistless in the presence of woman, that "fair defect." But as Raphael predicts and this speech shows, it is Adam, not God or Eve, who turns the right order of things upside down by incoherently insisting that appearance is identity: that outward sex dictates inward affinity; that the assumed gender of angels evinces their religious value; that heavenly being is different and better because unseen; that because he himself succumbed to Eve's blandishments, all women will tempt and all men be found susceptible. But appearance has long been the god of Adam's idolatry, as here where he describes Eve in another mood, yet one still pregnant with misunderstanding:

> when I approach
> Her loveliness, so absolute she seems
> And in her self complete, so well to know
> Her own, that what she wills to do or say,
> Seems wisest, virtuousest, and discreetest, best;
> All higher wisdom in her presence falls
> Degraded, wisdom in discourse with her
> Looses discountenanced, and like folly shows;
> Authority and reason on her wait,
> As one intended first, not after made
> Occasionally; and to consummate all,
> Greatness of mind and nobleness their seat
> Build in her loveliest, and create an awe
> About her, as a guard angelic placed.

(LM 8.546–59)

This romantic dithyramb obliges Raphael "with contracted brow" to remind Adam once again that he must beware attributing overmuch to the sheerly palpable or apparent: "For what admir'st thou, what transports thee so, / An outside? Fair no doubt, and worthy well / Thy cherishing, thy honouring, and thy love, / Not thy subjection" (*LM* 8.560, 567–70). Not unlike Milton in the divorce tracts, where the archangel may here deprecate the woman, his real disdain is reserved for the man's obtuse and improper reading of her beauty— the erotic effigy, the idol Adam has fashioned for himself from Eve. Since Adam in the satanic manner ascribes the significance of her beauty exclusively to Eve, he perversely renders it at once "absolute" and superlative, in the sense not merely of supreme, but of excessive, incongruous, disproportioned. Moreover, since such beauty graces a nature he believes to be less perfect than his own, he implicitly evacuates the inevident reality which the *selem elohim* itself substantiates: thus wisdom in Adam's speech is refused both expression and credit, appearing "discountenanced" before the voluptuous abundance of Eve's fair outside. But Eve is not imperfect, any more than she is self-consummated; nor is her beauty insular and self-regarding in the way that Adam supposes. It expresses her relation to her spouse as his glory—the unique image or manifestation of his own being as well as divine goodness. Eve's identity is entwined with his own, and Adam's with hers, as a relation: that is why, arguing an act of judgment and distinction rather than comparison, Raphael requires Adam to "weigh with her thy self; / Then value," because marriage cannot exist without the mutual understanding and esteem of self and spouse together, like the reciprocal knowledge of self and God (*LM* 8.570–71). But blind to this deeper, less ostentatious mutuality, abject in that sensual admiration to which the satanic succumbs whenever it encounters a splendid object (hence the train of superlatives, itself echoing the hyperbolic praise of Eve's dream), Adam cannot see her expressiveness. He cannot discover himself or Eve in her appearances, much less the good and judicious providence of his God. Having lost what Milton in *The Reason of Church Government* calls "the spiritual eye" of faith, as the conviction of things not seen, the man mistakes the "veil," the "shadow" or *figura* for the woman.[26]

The peculiarity of Miltonic marriage is therefore not its putative transcendental emphasis on *invisibilia*—on the mental or psychological bond over the united bodies of canon law, or for that matter, latitude and contingency of meaning over the strict letter of the scriptural text. Nor does its distinction lie in Milton's subordination of the woman to the man—hardly an eccentric notion in his society. Rather, what distinguishes marriage as Milton describes it is the extent to which the man has no proper self, is unable to render himself to the world, without the "meet and happy conversation" of the woman; for "the chiefest and noblest end of mariage" consists in "this prevention of lonelines to the mind and spirit of man" (CM 3.2:391):

> And with all generous persons maried thus it is, that where the mind and person pleases aptly, there some unaccomplishment of the bodies delight may be better borne with, then when the mind hangs off in an unclosing disproportion, though the body be as it ought; for there all corporall delight will soon become unsavoury and contemptible. And the solitarines of man, which God had namely and principally order'd to prevent by mariage, hath no remedy, but lies under a worse condition then the loneliest single life; for in single life the absence and remotenes of a helper might inure him to expect his own comforts out of himselfe or to seek with hope; but here the continuall sight of his deluded thoughts without cure, must needs be to him, if especially his complexion incline him to melancholy, a daily trouble and pain of losse, in som degree like that which Reprobats feel. (CM 3.2:391)

Milton's picture of the unconversable marriage as self enthralled to the empty illusion, the mere appearance of affinity—with the mind "hung off in an unclosing disproportion" like some unsightly appendage—underscores the extent to which the marital relation in his view subserves personal expression and knowledge. For the "meet help" saves the man from a degree of alienation only slightly less catastrophic than that final, irrevocable apostasy of the soul from God, which ends any real movement and expressiveness of the creature. So what Milton discusses under the rubric of divorce is not what a man *is* over against a woman, but how a man is made known to himself and others through relationship with the woman—a problem of knowledge, not an ontology. The man's loneliness consists in the absence of this benefit, or perhaps one should say, the denial of this prerogative since, in Milton's view, God created woman to receive and honor his self-disclosure. So the man peculiarly gains identity and impetus through the presence of "an intimate and speaking help, a ready and reviving associate in marriage," moved by what Milton celebrates as "this pure and more inbred desire of joyning to it selfe in conjugall fellowship a fit conversing soul (which desire is properly call'd love)," "that rationall burning," that "unfained love and peace," that "coequal & *homogeneal* fire" (CM 3.2:396–401).

As Raphael represents this expressive relation to Adam, woman as the man's image "yields" her "shows" to his "realities" when he performs the masculine part of their compact; and predictably, that part is wisdom—a critical intelligence that can "yet distinguish, and yet prefer that which is truly better," in the *Areopagitica*'s always salient phrase. But if the woman's part, as the speaker originally and salaciously implies, lies in "yielding" or subjecting herself to the man, Raphael gives this idea its proper and active sense here. For Eve won't automatically, arbitrarily, submit to Adam to assuage his desire for personal recognition: the woman must exert her own judgment in freely choosing to exchange her autonomy for his good governance, discerning, acknowledging, and assenting to the man's different and putatively superior understanding before she subjects herself to it. Choice inevitably alters the proportioning of value and power among the sexes from absolute to conditional, since Milton pretty much argues that neither man nor woman can be fully themselves without the other voluntarily conducing and ratifying that identity. So while we must in no way seek to mitigate Milton's insistence on the woman's subjection, subjection here entails something more subtle and complicated than the unilateral act of domination. It describes the creatural paradox of freedom in dependency, where subjection is not coerced and policed (in the sense of subjugation), but rather observed on both sides as an acknowledgment of identity and its attendant obligations.

For although he may assiduously rationalize the Protectorate, Milton is perfectly well aware that subjection, whether private or public, is unjust in principle whenever it is compelled, since no partial creature can forcibly dominate another without committing both bodily tyranny and subjective violence.[27] Even his God, whose absolute goodness might arguably justify such coercion, utterly disdains it. Accordingly, Milton gives marital subjection a contractual aspect like that which obtains in his own and others' republican theory, where the members of a polity at least notionally agree to subject themselves to law and rule in order to secure their well-being. Moreover, because Miltonic marriage is still a polity in the traditional Aristotelian sense—a "civil knot" and legal institution as against a religious one (CM 4:116)—it inevitably participates in the assumptions and values of the community sanctioning that practice, as the *Doctrine and Discipline* doubly proves. And the ideas endemic to Milton's own society include the conservative, customary ones of personal and masculine rule as well as the dependency and subordination of inferiors, to which the divorce tracts appeal in pursuit of Milton's entirely controversial ends.[28] But precisely because it has this civil character, as a means to social welfare no less than other civic institutions, Milton renders the binding force of marriage conditional, not absolute—contingent, that is, upon "the mutual consent of the parties themselves" as "the first and most important requisite; for there can be no love or good will, and consequently no marriage, without mutual consent" (CM 15:153). If subjection to the marital bond is not mutual—if marriage does not express a real affinity—then this human institution (from Milton's effortlessly masculine perspective) will become abusive like any other, and the source of human suffering. It is therefore qualified, as the observance of a voluntary and reciprocal esteem recognizing the other person's excellence—and in the man's case, presumptive superiority—which, when it ceases on either side, simultaneously abrogates both the personal and legal bond. Thus, in addressing Adam as "My author and disposer," Eve unprompted acknowledges his primacy and subjects herself to his government:

> what thou bid'st
> Unargued I obey; so God ordains,
> God is thy law, thou mine: to know no more
> Is woman's happiest knowledge and her praise.
> With thee conversing I forget all time,
> All seasons and their change, all please alike.
>
> (LM 4.635–40)

For us, there is a certain perversity attending the superlative pleasure Eve takes in Adam's conversation, given her submission to him as the "law" of her being. Yet in this, she follows the political model most familiar and intelligible to Milton's age—the ideal of aristocracy as "the rule of the best," in which a people acknowledge the natural merit (as against customary or enforced privilege) of its governors and agree to subject themselves to that intelligible and approved authority, for the sake of the general welfare and the cause of civic virtue. And civic virtue itself consists in the emulation of these sovereign paragons, variously performed by all the members of the community in their several spheres.[29] On the aristocratic model—whose canon of merit also justifies the exceptions Milton admits to masculine rule—Eve's submission secures her own virtue, since she is subjecting herself to Adam's distinctive excellence: namely, that wisdom she experiences in their conversations as both imaginative transcendence and domestic sympathy. Her virtue in turn ensures Adam's, since his love at once inspires and obligates him rightly to exercise the authority Eve perceives and willingly grants him. As he says moments before they separate in Book Nine, "tender love enjoins, / That I should mind thee oft, and mind thou me. / Firm we subsist" (LM 9.357–59). So while the erotic affinity of our first parents is as much political as sexual, it is also moral but not in any sterile, denatured fashion: in keeping with the pronounced sensuality of Miltonic marriage, what Eve finds so intensely pleasurable here is *relation*—a mutual understanding embedded in the satisfactions of human presence, accomplished by that intimate conversation distinguishing yet uniting one spouse to the other. This is relation in Taylor's sense and Cavell's, because it entails a specifically expressive act, in which an individual gains identity in *relating* or recounting the full range of its personal, historical connections, as Eve and Adam each do in the course of *Paradise Lost*. And without relation of the kind they jointly profess—in Pauline fashion, she calls him "O sole in whom my thoughts find all repose, / My glory, my perfection" (*LM* 5.28–29), while he names her "Best image of my self and dearer half" (*LM* 5.95)—they would be bereft not only of each other but of self as well.

Again, woman peculiarly provides this benefit to the man not by degree of likeness (since then another man would do as well), but by what is conceived to be her unique difference—the original contingency of her creation upon the man's need, which the speaker of *Paradise Lost* calls our first parents' inequality. As Eve declares to Adam, her identity is fully expressed, indeed consummated by his, "for whom / And from whom I was formed flesh of thy flesh, / And without whom am to no end, my guide / And head" (*LM* 4.440–43). That is what Milton means when he reads the words of marital institution as giving to Adam "*another self, a second self, a very self it self*"—not, as Augustine would prefer, an identical but instead a truly distinct person with a mind "answerable" to his own (*CM* 4:90). Conversing in the old sense means "living with another," and marriage accomplishes this viable bond not by likeness but by unlikeness: the woman expresses the man by the different, contingent order of her life and, in doing so, figures in their relation the unique dependency of the creation upon the creator, whom the world comparably manifests. Once again, the woman's difference does not implicate an ontogeny as such, but exemplifies the fundamental expressiveness of creatural existence, as disclosing a presence which is not only inevident but distinct and unlike itself.

This further inflection and deepened meaningfulness of the creature can be denied in the unconversable marriage even as it is in apostasy, since it requires an imaginative, desiring mind to perceive, one yet unbound by the obvious or expected. Thus Adam's yearning for "Collateral love, and dearest amity" (*LM* 8.426), and specially "By conversation with his like to help, / Or solace his defects" (*LM* 8.418–19), expresses the sociable necessity and moral obligation of intelligence, which he exercises in God's trial of his discernment, "To see how thou couldst judge of fit and meet" (*LM* 8.448). Understood in the parabolic sense as a capacity to conceive more than is merely apparent, to imagine something other than the same, it is intelligence that renders Adam discontented and restless in what Milton regards as the man's inhuman solitude, consumed by an eroticism of the whole person which only woman's different yet responsive being can satisfy. The animals, who "know / And reason not contemptibly," cannot meet his need because they are "unequal" to conversation with him; and conversation is the hallmark of humanity's reflective consciousness, which requires its own distinctive mutuality "in proportion due / Given and received" (*LM* 8.374, 385–86). Indeed, as God observes, they cannot satisfy Adam because "My image [was] not imparted to the brute" (*LM* 8.441):[30] that is, to bear the image of God is to be self-conscious in Adam's fashion and discriminate on that account, knowing the limits to likeness even as he seeks to find himself in another. It is also to allow more than appears as such—to conceive as Adam does of something still potential, even extraordinary in his experience, the creation of a life "in most resembling unlikeness, and most unlike resemblance." It follows that the Lord would find God's image in the man, praising Adam for proper knowledge "of thy self, / Expressing well the spirit within thee free, / My image" (*LM* 8.439–41). Paradoxically, then, it is Adam's drawing of right distinctions, not correspondences or analogies, that gains him Eve as his image: "Thy likeness, thy fit help, thy other self, / Thy wish exactly to thy heart's desire" (*LM* 8.450–51).

This puts a perhaps novel light on Eve's "unequal" because different and emphatically contingent being, to which Raphael's myth of creation gives peculiar salience inasmuch as the plants and animals each seem to have their own independent raison d'être regardless of sex. Thus the archangel characterizes their genesis with epithets that virtually epitomize each species, rather in the manner of an incipient poetic diction: "the tender grass," "the clustering vine," and "swelling gourd" (*LM* 7.315–21); "the prudent crane" and "solemn nightingale" (*LM* 7.430–35); the "tawny lion" and "swift stag," the "river horse and scaly crocodile" (*LM* 7.464–74). But unlike these, humanity is first made mankind in dignity and power, and then woman on what looks like a technicality— "for race" or offspring. Or as Raphael relates (although he wasn't there at the time), Eve would appear to be given a dependent function—as mate and as consort, literally, the person with whom the man shares his lot—while everything else gets its own integral life. Thus Raphael represents the Father as saying to his Son, in familiar language yet in a curiously disrupted order that accentuates the distinction the angel consistently emphasizes between the sexes:

> Let us make now man in our image, man
> In our similitude, and let them rule
> Over the fish and fowl of sea and air,
> Beast of the field, and over all the earth,
> And every creeping thing that creeps the ground.
> This said, he formed thee, Adam, thee O man
> Dust of the ground, and in thy nostrils he breathed
> The breath of life; in his own image he
> Created thee, in the image of God
> Express, and thou becamest a living soul.
> Male he created thee, but thy consort
> Female for race; then blessed mankind.
>
> (*LM* 7.519–30)

Raphael uses "man" in the collective manner of Genesis where, as Phyllis Trible observes, the creature God forms from the dust is called by one word ('*adam* from '*ha-dama* or "earth"), although plural in number ("them"), and not primarily but latterly distinguished as male and female.[31] That is to say, humanity is *'adam* in the same sense that the angels appear as men, or deity itself assumes an anthropomorphic character and the pronoun "he": "man" is an expression, a way of speaking, which can be understood variously. On the one hand, the collective "man" can signify the priority and supremacy of the man, who gives "his" name to the woman (a usage that puts one in mind of the legal joke that *foemina item non proprie est homo*, "woman properly speaking is not a human being").[32] On the other hand, "man" in the sense of humankind can express the equal claim of male and female to human being, and by extension, to the divine image which the previous reading gives exclusively, intimately to the man.[33]

Raphael's syntax leans toward the prejudicial reading, as Milton himself stipulates in the divorce tracts, but with an important proviso. After Genesis 1, he does frame the sexual difference of our first parents with the ambiguous fact of their common humanity ("let them rule"; "then blessed mankind"), so that they are one if not the same. And the locution of this difference—*pace* Genesis 1, the angel's insistent appropriation of making and imaging for "thee," for Adam alone, while using a delegating phrase for Eve—implies that woman is not a simultaneous but a contingent creation in more than one sense. While Raphael's account of creation, sexuality, and divine image is variously amplified by Eve and Adam, they all agree in making the woman subsequent to the man in that timeless day of their creation, with first Eve and then Adam emphasizing the dependence of woman's being, born to assuage the man's virtual solipsism. This dependence is underscored in their birth narratives by "the gracious voice divine," which describes her as Adam's "likeness" and "other self," (*LM* 8.450) and identifies Adam to Eve as "he / Whose image thou art" (*LM* 4.471–72). On this head, Wolff comments that, in Genesis, the act of sexual differentiation expresses "the fact that men can only fulfill the commission as the image of God given to them in their creation by turning towards one another and by complementing one another, like man and wife."[34] And on their meeting, in both accounts of our first parents' creation, Adam pronounces scripture's words of marital institution with the usual Miltonic embellishment:

> I now see
> Bone of my bone, flesh of my flesh, my self
> Before me; woman is her name, of man
> Extracted; for this cause he shall forego
> Father and mother, and to his wife adhere;
> And they shall be one flesh, one heart, one soul.
>
> (*LM* 8.494–99)

In Adam's addition of "my self before me," Milton once again brings the activity of imaging to bear on the sexual distinction of our first parents, even as this expressiveness is explained in terms of the mutuality of marriage, in which they cleave to each other as "one flesh, one heart, one soul." As Trible observes, in Genesis, their difference in amity is signified by a new order of parallel naming (*'is* for man, *'issa* for woman).[35] So in the moment when "man" becomes "man" and "woman," which is to say in the moment of Eve's presentation to Adam and their mutual acknowledgment, they are made each other's expression even as Adam in the moment of his creation is made deity's. And image understood as self-expression entails the acknowledgment of difference, as Adam argues with his perfectly autonomous God (as against the Lord to whom he speaks); for man, he says, is to "beget / Like of his like, his image multiplied, / In unity defective," propagating as it were the individual as against the unitary (*LM* 8.423–25). Again, the decorum that Adam's phrase implicates is not one of identity or continuity: it is an order of relation in which the image is evidently differentiated from the thing it expresses, as our first parents are distinguished from each other by their sexual appearances, or as deity is distinguished from its creatural revelation. Eve's birth thus discloses a meaning to the world and the images of *Paradise Lost* crucial to their right understanding, where the creature is connected to the creator as the veritable picture of divine love; for that is what Milton means when he says that the woman is the image and glory of the man, even as the man is the image of God. Without Eve's distinctive presence, not only Milton's reader but Adam as well would surely refuse this peculiar expressiveness of things. We would read the Edenic world, that is, in the fashion of Luther's theologian of glory, as "one who beholds what is invisible of God, through the perception of what is made, calling the bad good and the good bad," even as Adam shortly does when he describes his spouse to Raphael. This is why woman's creation—so tenderly described by Adam from the indicative remove or departure of "fancy" (*LM* 8.460–61)—is given a divine crafting as well as a poetic prominence comparable to Raphael's recounting of the man's emergence from the dust of the ground. Indeed, Trible argues that the woman's creation in effect *makes* man all over again, this time in terms of the sexual distinction conveyed by *'ha-adam*'s punning names.[36] Milton suggests something to the same effect when Adam recounts to Raphael the delectable change wrought in his world by Eve's new life, although it is a memory now shadowed by his gross infatuation with her "fair outside":

> The rib he formed and fashioned with his hands;
> Under his forming hands a creature grew,
> Manlike, but different sex, so lovely fair,
> That what seemed fair in all the world, seemed now
> Mean, or in her summed up, in her contained
> And in her looks, which from that time infused
> Sweetness into my heart, unfelt before,
> And into all things from her air inspired
> The spirit of love and amorous delight.
>
> (LM 8.469–77)

Notwithstanding her contingency on the man's need and the man's body, Eve's making has a unique dignity since she is formed by God, not from the dust of the ground like all other creatures, but from Adam's own flesh. This is

Trible's point in her reading of Genesis, and I think it is Milton's too in his poem, since Eve as it were unites whole worlds in herself, because her existence expresses just that distinction in elective affinity describing deity's relationship to its creatures, as well as the mysterious accommodation of the divine image to human ways of speaking and understanding. In our general mother, Milton evokes the love for what is different, for what is outside oneself, which enables the bond between the sexes, even as it captures the force of an otherwise impossible affiliation between divine and human being. As David Burrell observes, the action of divine desire is itself the means by which deity may be said to exist for us. So the Lord calls as he walks in the garden on the evening after humanity's fall: "Where art thou, Adam, wont with joy to meet / My coming seen far off? I miss thee here, / Not pleased, thus entertained with solitude" (*LM* 10.103–5). Moreover, if creation pictures deity's loving movement out of itself toward a life from which its own differs inconceivably, absolutely, so Eve has traced a similar movement from the very day of her birth. Then the divine presence—invisible to her, who always sees deity mediated in the man—spoke and separated her from that pleasing "shape within the watery gleam," (*LM* 4.461) her own reflection and the inhumane and empty passion for the self-identical:

> what could I do,
> But follow straight, invisibly thus led?
> Til I espied thee, fair indeed and tall,
> Under a platan, yet methought less fair,
> Less winning soft, less amiably mild,
> Than that smooth watery image; back I turned,
> Thou following cried'st aloud, Return fair Eve,
> Whom fly'st thou? Whom thou fly'st, of him thou art,
> His flesh, his bone; to give thee being I lent
> Out of my side to thee, nearest my heart
> Substantial life, to have thee by my side
> Henceforth an individual solace dear;
> Part of my soul I seek thee, and thee claim
> My other half; with that thy gentle hand
> Seized mine, I yielded, and from that time see
> How beauty is excelled by manly grace
> And wisdom, which alone is truly fair.

> (*LM* 4:475–91)

Here Eve acknowledges Adam as her perfected self and glory—the "truly fair" which immediately seems less appealing because different from her own mirrored shape, the form that so exactly mimics her as yet "unexperienced" affections and desires (*LM* 4.457). This episode has received much insightful discussion,[37] to which I would add only that Milton once again casts subjectivity as an expressive relation: in encountering Adam, Eve peculiarly recognizes self in another distinct person, whose difference she initially dismisses not only as unlikeness but also as inferiority—"less fair, / Less winning soft, less amiably mild." Her preference for familiar self precludes the creation of human society, as she returns to the facile but inconsequent pleasures of her own reflection, until Adam speaks; and on the model of marital conversation, his speaking, his articulation of their bond, introduces her to a new understanding, a new valuation of her predicament. In effect, Eve is led by God to distinguish between self as a simple reflex of appearance (identity understood in Satan's fashion) and self as a differential relation in which subjectivity, in the moment Adam speaks, is revealed to be more and other than it seems (identity in the manner of the hidden God). So the strange countenance of Adam, manifest to Eve newly and suddenly in the landscape, has the quality of a Cavellian expression. In claiming her as "part of my soul," "my other half," Adam confronts Eve with an allegory of self which his speech and gesture move her to reconsider, interpret, and acknowledge—yet not without suffering a sense of incongruity, a certain shock or violence.

Yet when she describes her response to God's leading—"what could I do, / But follow straight?"—Eve does not thereby signal compulsion or constraint in acceding to deity and then Adam (unless we take divine ordination for necessity where Milton does not). While the phrase shortly recurs in Eve's relation of her bad dream—"I, methought, / Could not but taste"—its appearance there is owing to Satan's perverse refashioning of the birth narrative he overhears, in which it testifies to the supposedly irresistible force of that corrupt illusion (*LM* 5.85–86). But although deity may break the erotic spell of Eve's own image, precipitating by its own speech the conceptual crisis, the consciousness of self-delusion which is parabolic wisdom, it does not compel her acceptance: it offers prophecy instead, which places a different order of demand on Eve—that she believe in the divine promise of human society, of sociable difference, as a possibility she hasn't imagined or anticipated. For that very reason, Adam's estranging appearance and passionate, even vehement, expression free Eve to distinguish and choose where the sensuous magic of Satan's dreamwork does not. To rehearse Adorno's remark, we tend to feel objectivity as an incursion made upon the self—Eve "seized" by Adam's "gentle hand"—yet this sense of violation does not mean that we should therefore avoid the knowledge it conveys. For were Eve unable to separate herself from "that smooth watery image," as she herself says, "there I had fixed / Mine eyes till now, and pined with vain desire," in a life consumed by idolatry (*LM* 4.465–66). The same is true for Adam, who, exhausted by an inquiry where "answer none returned," would have lost himself in the inexorable quiescence of solitude (*LM* 8.285). But God timely intervenes before the dissolution of either life, uniting Eve and Adam with each other and with their proper selves: that is, until the Fall, when in a new and disturbing sense, "Her hand he seized, and to a shady bank, / Thick overhead with verdant roof embowered / He led her nothing loth" (*LM* 9.1037–39). Then a different, newly "oppressive" sleep of dissolution descends upon them, this time anticipating not union but shame as well as mutual revulsion, and a contagious estrangement from their world. As Wolff comments, "In unbridled lust desire and revulsion lie directly side by side. The revulsion lays bare

the false desire for what it is. This is what happens when love lacks completeness, when only something in the man and something in the woman become
one, and not the man himself and the woman herself—when there is lack of
the complete partnership which is in its very nature always exclusive. 'Coitus
without co-existence is daemonic.' "[38] Satan's relations with his own sin perfectly picture this erotic dynamic, even as that fatal physical separation of our
first parents engenders an isolation from God and themselves that no simple
proximity can assuage.

The primal histories of our first parents suggest that the possibility of self-
consciousness, as the intelligence peculiar to human beings, presupposes theophany—God's revelation in history—since neither Adam nor Eve can by
themselves desist from the solipsism of their initial, unaccompanied lives. As
their creator, the Lord is the first companion of each but in a telling and difficult
fashion. For the figure who appears to Adam from among the trees, like the
voice Eve hears, has no unambiguous identity: it is Adam who conceives it as
divine—God expressed prophetically in vision ("lively shadowed") and only
then fulfilled as it were in Adam's hearing with the Mosaic words, "Whom thou
sought'st I am" (*LM* 8.311, 316). This interlude of interpretation is crucial in
two ways: on the one hand, although Adam experiences his very being as marvelous, it initially promotes in him a species of natural theology, moving him
to extrapolate the character of his creator from the wonder and goodness of this
new world, whose individual features he predictably if ingenuously apostro-
phizes in what he significantly calls his "wandering" pursuit of an original to
whom he can trace his life (*LM* 8.273–82, 312). But the sudden incongruity of
miracle, when he finds himself transported to the paradise of his dream and
confronting his maker, disrupts Adam's naive expectation of a person like himself or creation more largely. This effect is compounded by the dream, which in
the manner of prophecy at once mediates and imagines his encounter with God:

> one came, methought, of shape divine,
> And said, Thy mansion wants thee, Adam, rise
> First man, of men innumerable ordained
> First father, called by thee I come thy guide
> To the garden of bliss, thy seat prepared.
> So saying, by the hand he took me raised,
> And over fields and waters, as in air
> Smooth sliding without step, last led me up
> A woody mountain; whose high top was plain,
> A circuit wide, enclosed, with goodliest trees
> Planted, with walks, and bowers, that what I saw
> Of earth before scarce pleasant seemed. Each tree
> Loaden with fairest fruit that hung to the eye
> Tempting, stirred in me sudden appetite
> To pluck and eat.
>
> (*LM* 8.295–309)

When Adam awakes, paradise remains but the "shape divine" is gone, only to reappear. But that discontinuity—like the personified dream—is crucial to Adam's understanding of what he sees, because it expresses the distinction between creator and creature, divine and human, the image and what it pictures, which Adam's fancy seemingly confounds. For the landscape he envisions is attended by all the sensory vividness of Eve's dream, and it too moves him "with sudden appetite to pluck and eat," even as it proves no corrupt illusion but truly anticipates that Edenic plenitude and pleasure to which he wakens. No local genius, God must vanish and then return as Eve does, so that Adam is compelled to separate the imagining from the actuality—a decorum observed on every such occasion in *Paradise Lost*, including Adam's vision and Eve's dream of providential history, not to mention Michael's account of the Christ, where image is placed at the further remove of narrative, and then allegory. Since fancy has the power of virtual reality, in the sense of putting a face to belief and desire, so it serves at once as an antagonist and, as here, an auxiliary of faith: in sacramental fashion, it makes the divine promise palpable. Thus Adam says, echoing the words of Milton's most anguished and personal sonnet, "methought I saw, / Though sleeping, where I lay, and saw the shape / Still glorious" forming Eve (*LM* 8.462–64): "She disappeared, and left me dark, I waked / To find her, or for ever to deplore / Her loss, and other pleasures all abjure: / When out of hope, behold her, not far off" (*LM* 8.478–81). It is indicative that Adam's vision, first of the divine presence, then of Eve, begins as a promise of things inevident, a promise which is fulfilled only after a marked delay. In Milton's memorable discrimination, continuity of experience between the fancied sight and the actuality is thus disallowed even when God, as truth itself, deploys images; this is the force of that pregnant qualification, "methought I saw," even as it is in Milton's sonnet where, poignantly, "I waked, she fled, and day brought back my night" (*LM* 14). There must be a disjunction between experience and understanding, and so contiguity only, in order to secure the room of faith in which affinity with others is freely chosen and observed. So in Adam's dream, the Lord creates the same prophetic suspension between the promise and its fulfillment, an interlude that in Eden as in scripture amplifies the contingency of any image. Whether that image pertains to the course of events, to human personality or the will of God, its interpreter must nevertheless reckon with this crisis or separation of the appearance from what it might signify; and the same holds true of Miltonic marriage.

For in arguing the contingent creation of the woman, as well as the man's dependence upon her for recognition and identity, Milton makes the sexual relation uniquely evocative of the one he asserts between deity and the creature, beginning with its firstborn—the Son and Christ. If the difference between the sexes, especially the woman's idiosyncratic creation, is figured as the distance between any image and its meaning, that difference also implicates the unutterable distinction of creator from created, which gives to human being its inherent tension and fragility, as a life forever poised between acknowledgment and revulsion at its own contingency upon the hidden God. As Trible observes of Genesis, "Human life, then, is God's gift; it is not possession. Playful creation is precarious existence."[39] That is why Milton locates the causes of the Fall itself in the understanding and practice of this expressive relation by Adam and Eve—not because our first parents violate a hierarchy of place and property (the satanic version of God's image and their sin), but because how they understand each other and themselves in marriage reflects their religious attitude, their tolerance for the incongruent and things that do not appear as such. In Hosea, the prophet is commanded by the Lord to seek out, marry, and sustain relationship with the harlot Gomer, thus becoming a living parable of Israel's apostasy from its God, in which the very names of Gomer's children carry the figural burden of this religious alienation—"Not pitied" and "Not my people" (Hosea 1:6–8). The perverse singularity of God's command is itself significant of the groundlessness of divine love—Eichrodt emphasizes, in the context of a patriarchal culture, this "wooing of a wanton" is "an absolutely grotesque proceeding, flying in the face equally of morality and of justice"—even as the prophet's patient durance evokes the inexhaustible depths, the perpetual resilience, of that love.[40] Moreover, as Eichrodt explains, the erotic figure is the peculiar invention of prophecy itself, exemplified in deity's seduction and betrayal of Jeremiah who knew and palpably understood Hosea:[41]

> It was the prophets who first dared to transcend these hitherto absolute limitations [on erotic comparison] under the impact of direct divine self-revelation. It is, moreover, a remarkable fact that the first man to take this step, *Hosea*, was also the one to attain the richest and most profoundly developed understanding of the idea of love in the whole Old Testament. The transition from the idea of the covenant to the conception of the marriage between Yahweh and Israel was made easier by the element of contractual obligation common to both, but it needed the shattering experience of the prophet, whose whole being was committed to Yahweh's service, to make the marriage-bond the supreme demonstration of Yahweh's attitude to Israel. However, the application of this parable, which the prophet acquired the right to use only at the price of his own heart's blood, brought out overwhelmingly *the quite irrational power of love as the ultimate basis of the covenant relationship*, and by means of the unique dialectic of the concept of love illuminated the whole complex of the nation's history. . . . The prophet's use of the imagery of marriage means that for him the relationship of law is largely displaced by a living fellowship of love, which demands the total allegiance of man as the object of that love, and can never be satisfied with the formal fulfillment of obligations.[42]

Addition Strange

The *selem elohim*, then, has no single or self-evident but rather a positional and interpretive character: even as deity by the loving acts of creation and covenant renders itself intelligible to humanity, thus revealing its image in us, so humanity acknowledges this image of God in order that we might rightly know and understand self and each other. Deity makes us and we make deity known. And this same reciprocity obtains in Miltonic marriage, where the difference between the sexes emulates the distinction between God and the world, so that identity is evident only through a differential relation—the man in the woman, and the woman in the man. That is why Raphael makes marital love of the same order as heavenly, refining thought and enlarging the heart to encompass what is unlike oneself but in a discriminate, "judicious" manner (*LM* 8.589–92). And this refinement does not abstract the marital relation from sensual pleasure, but rather resists that unthinking engrossment with the merely apparent, which leads Adam to ignore the proper expressiveness of Eve's beauty and the speaker to mistake its meaning.[43] For in *Paradise Lost*, not to mention the whole tradition of biblical commentary, she poses a dilemma of understanding comparable to deity, in that her figure excites promiscuous interpretation and a Spenserian sort of misprision in those who view her:

> She as a veil down to the slender waist
> Her unadorned golden tresses wore
> Dishevelled, but in wanton ringlets waved
> As the vine curls her tendrils, which implied
> Subjection, but required with gentle sway,
> And by her yielded, by him best received,
> Yielded with coy submission, modest pride,
> And sweet reluctant amorous delay.
>
> (*LM* 4.304–11)

"Veiling" describes the sensation of the speaker and Satan, each of whom finds Eve somehow intransparent and tantalizingly so, although both our first parents are not only unashamedly but emphatically naked. But Eve seems always more or less enclosed in her hair, or disappearing semantically into oddly postlapsarian shrubbery, or keeping her own counsel when Adam is talking, or going away when the speaker wishes her stay. But this seeming purdah and her elusiveness are bestowed upon Eve (it is the speaker who projects his own desire on Raphael, whose focus is consistently Adam): the erotic intensity attending her description is engendered by the masculine sense that she is somehow both concealed and concealing, and to that extent frustrating the observer's manifest desire. So where Adam is said to "declare" his significance outright—albeit distorted by the twin satanic desiderata of autonomy and domination, Eve's nature is tellingly "implied." And that frank intrusion of the interpretive into this initial sight of the human pair accounts for the "feminine" paradox—that is to say, the strangely charged, ambivalent quality of Eve's "yielding" or "subjection" to her spouse. For the manifold contradictions which introduce our first mother—wantonness and modesty, pride and submission, coyness and reluctance counterposed to yielding and desire—do not describe what is shown but what is understood. The curious particulars of the speaker's account betray his own inordinate, demonic passion, not least because he chooses to see in her hiddenness impulses of seduction and shame as yet unknown in Eden, himself caught like Paul in the tempting morass of woman's hair.

For the speaker's sort of wordplay regularly implicates the presence of the apostate, whose incorrigible antagonism it captures. It is the apostate who demand and project clarity and exactitude upon their world, like the arrangement of Adam's hair decisively to frame his face and body, leading us to believe that he is precisely as he appears—a completely composed and secure character. And such falsifying of creatural experience typically generates antithesis or contradiction: while the sight of Eve entails a richness of effect, to the extent that it is met with passion and an insistence on the compulsive, "ravishing" power of her beauty, as well as the knowledge of her impending fall and what the world has become, we are given to believe that this density signifies her inscrutability and moral ambivalence. But what the speaker's view of Eve manifests is the apostate preoccupation with superficies—its delusion of self-evidence, which precipitates yet another new creation of woman by the speaker's febrile fancy and Satan's insatiable desire—now as Pomona, now as Prosperine, each ravishing and ravished. It is indicative that Eve shares this distinctive inevidence or incongruity with Eden itself, a landscape that not only expresses deity as its maker but is also intimately affiliated with the mother of us all, who tends it as though it were her first child. Accordingly, when Raphael enters the garden on his errand to our first parents, he passes

> through groves of myrrh,
> And flower odours, cassia, nard, and balm;
> A wilderness of sweets: for nature here
> Wantoned as in her prime, and played at will
> Her virgin fancies, pouring forth more sweet,
> Wild above rule or art; enormous bliss.
>
> (*LM* 5.292–97)

The garden is not neat but "wanton" in appearance, not symmetrical but "wild above rule or art." Thus the speaker finds himself, or rather his art, incapable of doing more than rehearsing the sights of paradise—unable "to tell how, if art could tell" the nature of its maker's design (*LM* 4.236). This incapacity is more than the usual disclaimer: we are given the impression that the Edenic landscape is perfectly wrought but inexplicably so, presenting in its sheer abundance of effects an informal and negligent, almost gothic appearance. Thus the tiers of variegated verdure which first meet Satan and the reader's eye comprise the view of a "steep savage hill," within which "To all delight of human sense exposed / In narrow room nature's whole wealth, yea more, / A heaven on earth" (*LM* 4.172, 206–8). Waters flow "diverse, wandering," "With mazy error under pendant shades" (*LM* 4.234–39), "dispersed" in rivulet and gathered in lakes (*LM* 4.260–63). Flowers unconfined to knots and beds "nature boon / Poured forth profuse on hill and dale and plain" (*LM* 4.241–43); there are "umbrageous grots and caves," where "the mantling vine . . . gently creeps / Luxuriant" (*LM* 4.258–60). It is, quite intentionally, a cornucopia of things seen, smelt, heard, tasted, and touched.

But the suggestion of disorder, of a certain extravagance at work, isn't just the effect of divine plenitude. For Milton is making the point that the beauty of creation is qualified to the disaffected eye, because it has yet to be reduced to the exacting artifice of sin—an aesthetic characterizing the fallen angels and their works in hell, where "nice art" mimics and so distorts heaven's altogether different composition (*LM* 4.241). Nor do Adam and Eve pursue any improvement in their domestic design, working only to contain the "wanton growth" of Eden (*LM* 4.628–29)—"wanton growth . . . / Tending to wild," says Eve just before she falls (*LM* 9.211–12). That is to say, they do not propose to transform outright what God has made until the moment when they sin, and Adam observes to his spouse that she is "exact of taste, / And elegant" (*LM* 9.1017–18). In thus distinguishing the appearance of paradise as seemingly confused and indecorous, Milton fashions (as he does throughout *Paradise Lost*) an allegory of gardening. Yet his allegory is not so much the classical topos of a primitive or authentic nature as yet uncorrupted by human sophistications, as it is a meditation on the way difference or incongruity excites prejudice as well as violence in the pursuit of a clear, masterful order. So when that erstwhile archangel, Satan, ventures toward paradise, he

> to the border comes
> Of Eden, where delicious Paradise,
> Now nearer, crowns with her enclosure green,
> As with a rural mound the champaign head
> Of a steep wilderness, whose hairy sides
> With thicket overgrown, grotesque and wild
> Access denied.
>
> (*LM* 4.131–36)

Like Eve's veiling or Jacob's ladder, the "access denied" here is not physical or even perceptual, although "so thick entwined, / As one continued brake, the undergrowth / Of shrubs and tangling bushes had perplexed / All path of man or beast that passed that way" (*LM* 4.174–77). For Satan immediately overleaps the bounds of Eden, and the new world is otherwise empty of those intruders the speaker readily supplies, being one himself. Rather, inaccess in Satan's case is rather conceptual and ironic: after the fashion of Eve's tresses, the "hairy sides grotesque and wild" are there to evoke just that inevidence of religious things, including the *selem elohim*, which regularly confounds God's adversary both in heaven and on earth. For the sense of a barrier is doubly emblematic: it is the sign of a sacred space set apart and defended in a manner other than material, which Satan proceeds to ignore with impunity, thus illustrating both the ruthlessness of his intent and his intensifying indifference to any life and any meaning not his own. But his choice of entry also raises an issue of religious apprehension—how we decide what is meant by this overtly difficult approach to Eden. In penetrating paradise, Satan doesn't simultaneously penetrate the *arcana imperium* of deity, as he had imagined he would do in hell ("what strength, what art can then / Suffice, or what evasion bear him safe / Through the strict sentries and stations thick / Of angels watching round?" [*LM* 2.410–13]): once there, his knowledge remains restricted to eavesdropping and speculation. Instead, the palpable obscure of Eden places a boundary on understanding as against movement, so that Satan once again mistakes a conceptual limit for a spatial, with his intrusion here a false attempt made at clarity as well as control of his predicament. As in heaven, he cannot tolerate even the suggestion of mystery—of a limit placed on apprehension, taken in its most tangible sense as grasp, either with regard to deity or its creation.

Later, an apostasizing Adam will exactly imitate this conceptual intolerance and profligate drive to penetrate the mind of God; and Raphael will respond by teaching the virtue of noetic restraint just as Milton does with his reader in the *Christian Doctrine*: "Solicit not thy thoughts with matters hid, / Leave them to God above, him serve and fear . . . joy thou / In what he gives to thee, this Paradise / And thy fair Eve" (*LM* 8.167–72). To "be lowly wise," in Raphael's phrase, is to find deity and the marvelous in the world before us, which is that reflective wisdom of the ordinary Job learns from his sufferings and the theophany from the whirlwind and which the parables equally advocate (*LM* 8.173). This is the sense in which the Judaic wisdom literature also speaks of fearing God, as von Rad explains:

> Even Israel did not give herself uncritically to her drive for knowledge, but went on to ask the question about the possibility of and the authority for knowledge. . . . One becomes competent and expert as far as the orders of life are concerned only if one begins from knowledge about God. To this extent, Israel attributes to the fear of God, to belief in God, a highly important function in respect of human knowledge. She was, in all seriousness, of the opinion that effective knowledge about God is the only thing that puts a man into a right relationship with the objects of his perception, that it enables him to ask questions more pertinently, to take stock of relationships more effectively and generally to have a better awareness of circumstances. . . . Faith does not—as is popularly believed today—hinder knowledge; on the contrary, it is what liberates knowledge, enables it really to come to the point and indicates to it its proper place in the sphere of varied, human activity.[44]

As the ethic of faith, "the fear of God" recognizes the reality and force of the inevident in the world, that religious and conceptual principle Satan violates in overleaping Eden's bounds, and which the speaker struggles similarly to disregard in his lubricious picture of Eve: namely, the different existence of those things that do not appear as such, like God and the soul. It is this intellectual transgression against which Raphael warns Adam, exhorting him to "Think

only what concerns thee and thy being," a deference or humility in the face of
the unknown that Adam affirms as the wisdom of knowing "That which before
us lies in daily life" (*LM* 8.174, 193). When we refuse to admit and revere the
presence of the religious in the ordinary world, then we are doomed to suffer
contradiction, and what is worse, to commit the sort of injustice that the
speaker does against Eve, when he makes her figure bear the burden of his own
ambivalence toward the hidden God. For the mystery she poses to her masculine audience is of the same order as deity's, since both God and other minds
have an expressive existence resistant to speculation, as Raphael reminds
Adam.[45] Von Rad remarks on the quality this recognition gives to wisdom in
Israel's practice, observing how the culture was disinclined in Egyptian or even
Hellenic fashion "to objectivize certain entities mythically or speculatively":

> There was never a special domain in which [Israel] was alone with her
> understanding and the objects of her knowledge, and therefore she found
> herself—if one dares such a comparison at all—with her search for knowl-
> edge in an essentially difficult starting position. With no possibility of an-
> ticipating what was not known or experienced, she was forced to hold fast
> only to what could be discerned from time to time on the basis of individ-
> ual questions, at the same time always fixing the boundary which was
> drawn to prevent her from gaining a total picture. This means that Israel
> was obliged to remain open, in a much more intensive way, to the category
> of the mysterious. When she spoke of mystery—again the language lacks
> the term but not the object—she did not mean something vague and inex-
> pressible which defied being put into words. In wisdom and didactic con-
> texts it refers rather to something perceived by the understanding than by
> the feelings. The term is precise in so far as it refers to God's activity in
> the world, in which very special domain the wise men dared to look for
> rules.[46]

In keeping with Calvin's reading of that idea, "the fear of God" asserts the
force of mystery in ordinary life, as the predicament of faith and the difficult
position from which Israel inaugurates its special kind of knowledge, within the
boundary drawn by the distinction between creator and creature, divine and
human. This idea accounts for the self-consciously interpretive and reflexive
character of Judaic wisdom, which predicts no future outcomes but instead in-
culcates a certain understanding or expectation of the mundane as the realm
of divine revelation. Yet "the fear of God" does not advance a species of know-
nothingness and a concomitant quietism both religious and political, which is
sometimes how Raphael's speech is taken—as though human innocence were
a calculated policy of ignorance devised by God to keep our first parents down
(Satan's account of the divine interdiction). Rather, from "things remote / From
use, obscure and subtle," it returns our attention to the dilemma of human being
indubitably manifest in suffering, which goes some way toward explaining why
Israel's wisdom is not a metaphysics, nor a mythology of supernal entities, but

a profoundly circumstantial knowledge attentive to the human person, temporally episodic, disjunct, open-ended, and hortatorical (*LM* 8.191–92). Its subject is Milton's perennial concern, namely, the tremendous significance and
painful vicissitudes of our self-understanding, which the relation with deity reveals as accessory to the creation of human suffering.

On that account, Milton introduces God's interdiction of the tree of knowledge before he discusses Edenic marriage in the *Christian Doctrine*, because how
Adam and Eve understand that constraint—"The only sign of our obedience
left"—anticipates how they know deity, themselves, and each other (*LM*
4.428). And in this self-reflexive wisdom, as against a metaphysics or occult
science, consists the knowledge of good and evil: "It was called the tree of
knowledge of good and evil from the event; for since Adam tasted it, we not
only know evil, but we know good only by means of evil" (*CM* 15:115). The
tree is nothing in itself—it possesses no intrinsic power or even religious meaning; instead, its significance like its name derives from its use, first by God, then
Satan and the human pair, a contingency that discloses their religious affections
or attitude and the good or evil which ensue from these.[47] Thus, in the eyes of
the speaker and our first parents, the fruit of the tree becomes not just a magical
entity or substance that will deify them, but implicitly the key that will open a
secret knowledge of *invisibilia*, like the mind concealed from view by Eve's body.
But "the force of that fallacious fruit" is an illusion, manufactured by the apostate propensity to supernaturalize the signs of God—to invest deity in its appearances and mythologize the world (*LM* 9.1046). It is a false surmise to which
the speaker also succumbs at the Fall, when he describes how the fruit "with
exhilarating vapours bland / About their spirits had played, and inmost powers /
Made err" (*LM* 9.1047–49). Yet even before that moment, when Adam recalls
the language of the Lord's injunction for Raphael, the divine expression has
assumed a different equivocality:

> But of the tree whose operation brings
> Knowledge of good and ill, which I have set
> The pledge of thy obedience and thy faith,
> Amid the garden by the tree of life,
> Remember what I warn thee, shun to taste,
> And shun the bitter consequence; for know,
> That day thou eat'st thereof, my sole command
> Transgressed, inevitably thou shalt die;
> From that day mortal, and this happy state
> Shalt loose, expelled from hence into a world
> Of woe and sorrow.
>
> (*LM* 8.323–33)

Under satanic influence and the compulsion apostasy itself foments, first Eve
and then Adam will conceive the tree's "operation" as magical causality, having
a material power to transfigure their condition: "As with new wine intoxicated

both / They swim in mirth, and fancy that they feel / Divinity within them breeding wings / Wherewith to scorn the earth" (*LM* 9.1008–11). At the same time, however, God refers to the tree as a "pledge" or token of faith and obedience, which gives the idea of "operation" an opposed significance. Indeed, to Milton, the tree and its fruit don't even have the force of a sacramental sign like circumcision or the Eucharist, although their meaning too derives from the use to which deity puts them on this occasion. Here they are again called "a pledge, as it were, and memorial of obedience [*sed erat veluti pignus et monumentum quoddam obedientiae*]," which is to say, not so much a guarantee or security of performance but an exemplum of fidelity (CM 15:115):

> This is sometimes called "the covenant of works," though it does not appear from any passage of Scripture to have been either a covenant, or of works. No works were required of Adam; a particular act only was forbidden. It was necessary that something should be forbidden or commanded as a test of fidelity, and that an act in its own nature indifferent, in order that man's obedience might be thereby manifested. For since it was the disposition of man to do what was right, as a being naturally good and holy, it was not necessary that he should be bound by the obligation of a covenant to perform that to which he was of himself inclined; nor would he have given any proof of obedience by the performance of works to which he was led by a natural impulse, independently of the divine command. (CM 15:113–15)

Insofar as relationship with the hidden God involves an assurance about what is promised, not what is in hand, and a conviction that the unseen is as actual and immanent as the seen, so the proof of this relationship consists in an activity as peculiar as its objects—equally a matter of implication, equally inevident, equally something that does not appear as such. For humanity shows its faith and manifests its affiliation with this God by abstaining from the one thing deity prohibits—a palpable negation, as it were, because the only way this abstinence or omitting of action becomes intelligible, not to say significant, is by virtue of its being prohibited. In other words, obedience to God does not take the form of any ordinary "doing" or "working"; it appears only as an attitude taken toward the world, in the manner of Luther's passive righteousness.

By virtue of its ordinary "indifference," or rather its seemingly incongruous and arbitrary importance on this occasion, the command against eating from the tree of knowledge enunciates the distinction between creature and creator, like all religious expressions. It implicates a conceptual limit within which humanity is asked to conduct its life and understandings, exemplifying in effect how our first parents are to interpret the whole creation—not as self-evident and autonomous in meaning and value, but as the expression of something profoundly, unimaginably different from themselves. God's ordinance in paradise thus "operates" like the sexual distinction in Edenic marriage, where a perceived incongruity signifies neither disproportion nor injustice in the created order of things, but instead the peculiar existence and meaning of the religious in this life, as a differential relation between what appears and what is meant. As God's image is Adam, and Adam's is Eve, so the divine interdiction and its sign in Milton's account incongruously manifest human faith: that is, until the appearance of incongruity is itself objectified as injustice—as Satan would have it, "Envious commands, invented with design / To keep them low whom knowledge might exalt / Equal with gods"—in which case divine expressions become doubly ironic, the revelation of deity's ineffable difference as well as each person's disposition toward the hidden God (*LM* 4.524–26). But unlike its observance, the transgressing of this religious boundary is an ostentatious enactment of meaning, not least because the apostate mentality is itself fixed upon the immediate and superficial sense of things—Eve upon Satan's articulate serpent, the tree's fruit, and the delusion of her own gain; Adam upon Eve's superlative beauty, the letter of God's interdiction, and his own presumptive loss—an appearance which goes unexamined and misunderstood. The result is a veritable *show* of disobedience, on the model of that gorgeous spectacle Satan orchestrates for himself in heaven's north.

For evil does not create but follows upon that estranged state of mind moving the human pair to dislike and doubt God and then to disobey him, even as good is the consequence God brings out of this evil when, by the Son's sacrifice, he restores their posterity to relationship with him. Although Adam in apostasy refuses to understand this religious conversion of meaning, the event of sin reveals God's redemptive love, not his hatred, with evil made the foil of good in providential history. Or to put the case conceptually, we are brought to the recognition of good by its loss and absence; at the same time, evil consists for us not only in present suffering but in the memory of lost happiness, as the story of Job or the prophetic history of Israel describes. Genesis of course is an aetiological myth of this loss, picturing humanity's congenital belief that we have been bereft of an existence we somehow know and desire without experiencing as such. So it is also a primal echo of human repletion and contentment to which Milton alludes when he says that, ever since the Fall, "we not only know evil, but we know good only by means of evil." Moreover, when the speaker evokes the end of humanity's innocence, "that as a veil, / Had shadowed them from knowing ill," he introduces ideas of abjection—nakedness, uncovering, destitution, bareness: the human pair, he says, are like Samson "Shorn of his strength" (*LM* 9.1054–63). For unveiling here not only expresses their unprecedented sense of shame, but also conceives their new exposure as guilt and estrangement from God and each other, a loss of affiliation and shelter, vulnerability succeeding isolation, a sense of withdrawal and lack. But our first parents' conviction that they and their world are tremendously altered is not a physical reality—it is a religious and interpretive one: Adam and Eve are to all *appearances* the same, but to the "spiritual" eye, the eye of faith, they are morbidly changed since now they understand

> Both good and evil, good lost, and evil got,
> Bad fruit of knowledge, if this be to know,
> Which leaves us naked thus, of honour void,
> Of innocence, of faith, of purity,
> Our wonted ornaments now soiled and stained,
> And in our faces evident the signs
> Of foul concupiscence.
>
> (LM 9.1072–78)

As a religious state, the depredations of sin involve the loss of those inevident qualities Adam mourns here—honor, innocence, faith, purity—which had dignified and accommodated primal humanity in the form of the *selem elohim*, the sign of our first parents' relationship to the divine. Revulsion and mere carnality have taken their place, expressed in the inflection of self toward the world and God. Indeed, the abstract diction Eliot deplores in Milton here figures the force of intuition itself—of knowing something that eludes the very tokens of its presence. What Adam describes as humanity's "nakedness" is the loss of the sacral connection, that loving bond among things more profound than mere appearance, which is suffered as a crisis or separation from the created order, and imaged as the abeyance of divine likeness.

Following the expressive order of Edenic marriage, this catastrophe is experienced by Eve as a vicious estrangement from Adam, while Adam becomes utterly unlike his wonted self, undergoing a decisive break in intimacy with his spouse and the God who made her—the persons upon whom the right knowledge of himself depends. He attributes his infatuation with Eve's beauty to a calculated policy of deceit on her part, and a temptation devised by deity to torment and seduce him away from his proper happiness. Indeed, it is in the context of erotic relation that Hosea defines sin against God as ingratitude, which Eichrodt connects with "an antipathy to God's very nature and will."[48] And even as Satan makes it the centrifugal motive of his own apostasy, so Adam echoes the devil's extenuations here, newly justifying the Father's proleptic epithet of "Ingrate":

> Out of my sight, thou serpent, that name best
> Befits thee with him leagued, thy self as false
> And hateful; nothing wants, but thy shape,
> Like his, and colour serpentine may show
> Thy inward fraud, to warn all creatures from thee
> Henceforth; lest that too heavenly form, pretended
> To hellish falsehood, snare them. But for thee
> I had persisted happy.
>
> (LM 10.867–74)

Eve's beauty is now "but a show / Rather than solid virtue," and she herself "but a rib / Crooked by nature, bent, as now appears, / More to the part sinister" (LM 10.883–86). With these clichés of clerical antifeminism, Adam proves himself yet under the sway of spectacle: if evil to his mind consists in illusion, duplicity, the subversion of the ostensible sense of things, Adam upholds mere appearance by arguing a vulgar correspondence between the visible (his own "crooked" rib) and the invisible (Eve's "bent" and "sinister" nature).⁴⁹ More subtly but on the same principle of palpable, magical sympathy to which his own delusion has consigned him, our general ancestor is moved to hide from God because he can no longer participate, except vestigially by guilt and remorse, in the holy: he now fears that the "dazzle," the "blaze insufferably bright" of heavenly things will actively injure him (*LM* 9.1083–84). And since Milton makes the sacred encompass the whole creation, informing every element of the new world, Adam renders himself nothing short of denatured, dissociated from his own well-being. This self-perversion is reflected in his implicitly abdicating all responsibility for the Fall, whose corrupting effects he pictures as ineluctably infecting his own posterity, cast as they are in the sinful and impotent image of their father: "But from me what can proceed, / But all corrupt, both mind and will depraved, / Not to do only, but to will the same / With me?" (*LM* 10.824–27). Thus Adam, speaking the language of emanation, denies the special contingency and transfiguring power of human intelligence and choice; and he acknowledges as much in his own case by a bestial impulse "In solitude [to] live savage," not just concealed but fenced off from the terrible, injurious goodness of God and angels: "in some glade / Obscured, where highest woods impenetrable / To star or sunlight, spread their umbrage broad / And brown as evening" (*LM* 9.1085–88).

His desire literally to "take umbrage"—to anticipate punishment and pain by seeking the illusion of shelter in the garden—manifests humanity's estrangement from its proper condition, while the resistance to communion with their creator epitomizes how the human pair have lost any real sense of divine and human possibility. In their sin, deity's presence however mediated has become intolerable and infinitely desirable all at once: "How shall I behold the face / Henceforth of God or angel, erst with joy / And rapture so oft beheld?" (*LM* 9.1080–82). So where the speaker would show us evil as a physiology almost narcotically induced by the tree and its fruit, if formally by human sin, Adam unconsciously confesses to another order of meaning to the event, which observes Milton's idea of the tree as an emblem, not an agency. For the betokening of evil does not correspond to a substantial or material loss of good, like the banishment of Adam and Eve from paradise: such mensurable deprivation occurs only after an interlude in heaven, during which the Father brings the cosmic and natural worlds into conformity with human disaffection, so as to express the altered religious state of his creatures.

But the interdicted tree does not cause these things to occur, in a sort of irresistible, sympathetic effect that rages through all creation. Such a magical order of transformation is instead reserved for Satan, the fallen angels, Death, and Sin, who testifies to a "sympathy, or some connatural force / Powerful at greatest distance to unite / With secret amity things of like kind / By secretest conveyance," in an ironic counterpoint to the estrangement between Adam and Eve, humanity and God (*LM* 10.245–49). Indeed, her notion of an imperial prompting among fallen things is made immediately to conflict with the heavenly account of this change, which is represented as lawful and expressive, not causal and necessary. For the dependence of the world's well-being upon human obedience to God is not a physical order of contingency: on the contrary, the Father decrees the alteration even as he permits Sin and Death to follow their fatal instincts out of hell toward earth. The suspension that takes places between the religious event and its phenomenal consequences, the human choice and the divine decree, deliberately marked by the interlude in heaven, refutes any impression of necessity in a universe governed by the one true God. Indeed, the divine decree ironically deprives Satan and his minions of any claim independently to determine the course of human history. The supreme agency of God supervises every occurrence, but once again, not in the sense of causing—"doing" or "working"—evil: instead, "as sorted best with present things," the Father simply upholds and illustrates the sensations of estrangement our first parents already project upon deity and each other, which the primal "curse" describes but does not enact.

So although the speaker pictures the heavenly bodies moved by the angels to "noxious efficacy," "synod unbenign," and "influence malignant" (*LM* 10.660–62), we are nevertheless given to understand that earthly evils do not originate in the Father's decree, with human being placed under the sway of what Alistair Fowler calls "astrological determinism" (*LM* 960n.). For the relation between the heavens and earth in *Paradise Lost* has always been ingeniously, architectonically pictorial, as when Satan's character and intent as well as his ostensible movements are mapped across the sky. No less than the tree of knowledge or the war in heaven, the motion of planets and stars are emblematic—signs that manifest the attitude of the creature toward its creator. So while the astronomical order generates physical atmosphere, it does not make, only image, humanity's religious and moral miasma: superstition as such exerts no real power over the world, except in the shape of creatural delusion like that fatalism which consumes the minds of the human pair, as it had Satan and his legions. Thus, in exhibiting to the reader a universe of meteoric evils—darkness, heat, cold, tumultuous wind, thunder, ice—all at war with terrestrial life, the speaker persists in arguing something more than a figurative meaning for these phenomena, just as he had the forbidden fruit:

> At that tasted fruit
> The sun, as from Thyestean banquet, turned
> His course intended; else how had the world
> Inhabited, though sinless, more than now,
> Avoided pinching cold and scorching heat?
>
> (*LM* 10.687–92)

The question "else how?" is part of an entire explanatory apparatus that gets out of hand, as the speaker prefaces his descriptions of new and more intricately detrimental operations and effects of the stars with "Some say" (*LM* 10.668,

671). His activity is very like the aetiological fabling that takes place in hell, not only in the cataloging of idolatrous names and locales, but in the speeches and appearance of the apostate angels which he elaborates in detail. What we see in the speaker's penchant for an ever more exploding cosmology *is* "hell"—the phenomena attending that revulsion from the good which our first parents suffer. But here this effect is original to Milton's speaker, whose tragic position they now have come to share, as he himself implies in the proem of the ninth book, where his subject by its dreadful familiarity can be expressed without invocation. Yet the new creation has not become perforce the insolubly conflicted universe of tragedy: it is precisely tragic insofar as each person experiences the world God has made and governs as driven by implacable necessity—hostile, incoherent, arbitrary, and unjust. Now Adam and Eve, not just the speaker and Satan, are alienated by the nature of their religious understanding from the gracious contingency of all things upon their divine maker, sustaining through the poem's final books that oscillation between faith and apostasy, which is a considerable source of its ambiguity. For in disobeying God's injunction, our first parents have taken offense at the very order of creation itself, a shift in attitude that Adam's remarks about Eve, the universe, and everything anticipate. The result is a world grown fearfully antagonistic, animated in the most disturbing way—grotesque, demonic, and flagrantly allegorical, a war of all against all:

> thus began
> Outrage from lifeless things; but Discord first
> Daughter of Sin, among the irrational,
> Death introduced through fierce antipathy;
> Beast now with beast gan war, and fowl with fowl,
> And fish with fish; to graze the herb all leaving,
> Devoured each other; nor stood much in awe
> Of man, but fled him, or with countenance grim
> Glared on him passing.
>
> (LM 10.707–14)

Until this moment, paradise was a living because expressive thing; but perceived by Adam and the speaker in their simultaneous disaffection from the source of that life, its animation has another quality than the expressiveness of the natural creature. It is a vivification, not a vivacity, since to this point there were really no "lifeless things" in the new world, nor were the animals "irrational" creatures. But the entrance of abstract personification in the form of Discord, "first daughter of Sin," is only the most conspicuous sign that the easy mutuality attending creation and giving it its proper vitality—the shared dependence of all creatures upon their creator—has vanished from sight. That commonweal disintegrates as mortality takes hold, to be replaced by a grotesque objectification of meaning, manifest in the figure of Discord, who is not a quality or relation but an entity, and an image of hell on earth. It is also present in the hierarchy of being the speaker implicitly expounds—the new ranking of "lifeless" and "irrational" which utterly contravenes the fluent movement of all things toward God. As a consequence of this objectifying, the grand and subtle play of difference in affinity among creatures appears as indiscriminate antagonism, a failed kindliness not only of animals but among elements, all of which are shown succumbing to fratricide. And humankind, the erstwhile lord of this world, is no less an object of hostility than anything else, seemingly without soul or affiliation to the life that surrounds and engages it. Having chosen ungratefully to dispense with the divine order in which it, as the image of God, enjoyed singular value, human being is bound to undergo the loss of its own charisma.

So what with ideas made persons and living things mere objects, the world is rendered demonic in Wolfgang Kayser's sense, when he emphasizes that the grotesque is not a foreign country but the familiar made strange and ominous by a sudden alteration in the way things look and behave. They seem possessed by an artificial life or false animation, with the consummate image of the grotesque that of human beings reduced to automata, puppets, mannequins, and the like. In Milton's hands, this perception is the artifact of idolatry, that worship of appearances whose failed efficacy as a description of human experience engenders the terrors and absurdities, the depleted and despairing meanings of sceptical reaction. For the transformation expresses a perceived loss of human agency—of understanding and choice: we are prey not only to the world around us, but to subjective necessities as well, like the lust in which the human pair abruptly and incontinently indulge and the mutual disgust which follows. But the world as such hasn't changed, only we have changed toward it; as Kayser observes, "the grotesque is experienced only in the act of reception."[50] If creation after the Fall appears dissonant, skewed, chaotic, as though God had withdrawn himself and taken with him all coherence and clemency along with Eden's eternal spring, humanity has engineered the effect but in no magical sense.

Instead, this disproportioning and dissolution of created order raises the role of fancy once again, as it did when Adam first found fault with God's design. In excusing himself to Raphael on that occasion, Adam suggests that "apt the human mind or fancy is to rove / Unchecked, and of her roving is no end": speculation is thought on holiday, with the mind relinquishing judgment to the play of imagination, whose activity quickly grows futile and desperate as "we our selves / Seek [anxious cares] with wandering thoughts, and notions vain" (LM 8.186–89). Thus Adam disclaims his dubious inquiry into creation even as he will extenuate the same ideas when he projects them onto Eve, ascribing the mentality that disturbs Raphael to the implicit, irresistible power of sensuous appearances. However, the circumstances under which Adam derides fancy here significantly distinguish this account from the seemingly comparable version by which he explains Eve's dream. If fancy now takes the mind captive, then he described it as a faculty of mental imaging amenable to reason's government, discreetly running riot not in our waking life but only in sleep where "misjoining shapes / Wild work produces oft, and most in dreams, / Ill matching words and deeds long past or late" (*LM* 5.11–13). What is significant about this austere, unduly mechanical picture of faculty psychology is its perfect inadequacy as explanation here: for even as Adam supposes that Eve's fanciful mismatching of ideas is the source of that "addition strange" to their remembered conversation, he fails to grasp the imaginative power, the real seductiveness of that new aspect to things which he calls evil. Eve may not, in Adam's phrase, "approve" what she dreamed, but it hardly leaves her or himself untouched, "No spot or blame behind" (*LM* 5.118–19). Not only in the dreaming but also in the telling, the familiar images which Satan lends a heightened, "magical" appeal—a glamour—exert a recurrent hold over the human pair. This effect is evinced almost immediately in the way Adam misconceives angelic being as absolute, and of course preeminently in his subsequent conversation with Raphael and then in Eve's novel pursuit of self-glorification. For all of these conceptual events turn upon the admiration of mere appearance, a human propensity originating in that vile dream:

>   methought
> Close at mine ear one called me forth to walk
> With gentle voice, I thought it thine; it said,
> Why sleep'st thou Eve? Now is the pleasant time,
> The cool, the silent, save where silence yields
> To the night-warbling bird, that now awake
> Tunes sweetest his love-laboured song; now reigns
> Full-orbed the moon, and with more pleasing light
> Shadowy sets off the face of things; in vain,
> If none regard, heaven wakes with all his eyes,
> Whom to behold but thee, nature's desire,
> In whose sight all things joy, with ravishment
> Attracted by thy beauty still to gaze.
> I rose as at thy call, but found thee not;
> To find thee I directed then my walk;
> And on, methought, alone I passed through ways
> That brought me on a sudden to the tree
> Of interdicted knowledge: fair it seemed,
> Much fairer to my fancy than by day.
>   (*LM* 5.35–53)

It is no coincidence that moonlight here emphasizes superficies, "the face of things," or that this landscape, like Eve's beauty, would exist "in vain" without someone to admire it—to look with wonder on its sights as that feigned divinity gazes upon the tree. The inutile, unconsumed sight of either appearance rehearses with a difference Eve's earlier question about the stars—"But wherefore all night long shine these, for whom / This glorious sight, when sleep hath shut all eyes" (*LM* 4.657–58). On that occasion, Adam replies that their light is more than ornamental but efficacious in a manner unseen by humanity, working at once to nurture life as well as to express deity's dominion by "enlightenment." But his second explanation is more ambiguous, since he then asserts the sight never goes unobserved or unappreciated—"That heaven would want spectators, God want praise"—inasmuch as "Millions of spiritual creatures walk the earth / Unseen [who] with ceaseless praise his works behold" (LM 4.676–79). If every creaturely spectacle is witnessed, there is nonetheless a difference between praise and admiration: one activity sees the sight as expressive of something besides itself, while the other is absorbed in just looking. And needless to say, the unreflective absorption in the sheer appearance of a thing is idolatry, enacted first in Eve's dream and then realized when she abases herself before the tree, "as to the power / That dwelt within, whose presence had infused / Into the plant sciental sap, derived / From nectar, drink of gods" (LM 9.835–38).

Spectacle becomes an end in itself, a sensation divorced from any other meaning or purpose, granting any object or image a magical aura—the effect to which Adam succumbs when he confesses that Eve's loveliness renders her not only supreme in virtue but autonomous in being ("so absolute she seems / And in her self complete"). Needless to say, Eve is more and other than the fetish made of her beauty; yet when Satan in her dream and in the guise of the serpent claims to be "ravished" by her appearance, he simply exaggerates the tendency evinced by Adam and the speaker, each of whom objectifies his distorted desire so that Eve is made to solicit it—animating the idol, as it were:

> With goddess-like demeanour forth she went;
> Not unattended, for on her as queen
> A pomp of winning graces waited still,
> And from about her shot darts of desire
> Into all eyes to wish her still in sight.
>
> (LM 8.59–63)

Next to the apostate angels themselves, no figure in *Paradise Lost* receives such abundant analogy as the speaker bestows on our first mother; and as with Satan and his hordes, this copia of images expresses an absorption in the sheer spectacle of her beauty, onto which the speaker projects the same range of ambivalent emotion that Adam himself feels for his spouse after the Fall—passion, resentment, condescension, and anxiety. Masculine ambivalence obscures the fact that Eve herself does nothing to invite these responses, even as her admirers present themselves as constrained and then beguiled by her beauty to do so. Like the magical image, beauty appears to exert the force of erotic compulsion on anyone who beholds it, with Satan on a variety of occasions insinuating that Eden, Eve, the tree all ask to be violated precisely because of the way they appear—in effect, the rationale for their rape. It is they who ravish him with sheer spectacle ("still to gaze"), declares Satan, not the other way round; but it is he who in Eve's dream concocts a vision of herself and Eden which possesses its own tyrannical necessity, driving her not only to eat but then also abruptly, astonishingly, to fly, with the tempter's image of the whole earth spread out below her:

> So saying, he drew nigh, and to me held,
> Even to my mouth of that same fruit held part
> Which he had plucked; the pleasant savoury smell
> So quickened appetite, that I, methought,
> Could not but taste. Forthwith up to the clouds
> With him I flew, and underneath beheld
> The earth outstretched immense, a prospect wide
> And various.
>
> (LM 5.82–89)

Just as the dream Eve succumbs involuntarily to the fruit's fragrant lure, so its immediate effect of physical exaltation creates the illusion that she too has a supernatural and autonomous power, a notion that will inform Eve's waking and similarly impetuous drive to independence from Adam. And the same subjection to her speciously "absolute" appearances will move him to accede to it. Given the religious significance of the sexual distinction, Eden is turned upside down when the expressive relation between Adam and Eve is collapsed: self is reduced to its image, so that in the moment of their physical divorce, Eve becomes Adam's specious semblance—the author and disposer of their marriage, and in the likeness of her maker, the judge of who will do what and when. And having granting his spouse a false liberty, Adam in turn becomes yielding, compliant, submissive to the idol of Eve's self-sufficiency. He adopts not so much passivity as the role of willing recipient that was Eve's, since initiative to this point—erotic, ritual, and intellectual—had largely been his own. Thus he weaves the elegiac garland for her hair in a fashion more like those wives in antique literature who fatefully await the return of their hero-husbands, than the harvest homecoming the speaker ironically imagines: "Great joy he promised to his thoughts, and new / Solace in her return, so long delayed" (LM 9.843–44). Since subjectivity and so gender is expressive and relative, not essential in Milton, the human pair in their mutual alienation now unconsciously parody each other's role. Indeed, at this juncture, Eve is described and describes herself as an actor assuming a *persona*: she is self-made in the same way that the fallen angels are self-created—by repudiating her contingency upon Adam and so God. I refer not only to her sudden chivalry—as one who quests in order that her virtue or rather prowess be evinced, with self-glorification substituting for theodicy in a spurious rehearsal of the *Areopagitica*'s argument. But like Beelzebub in hell and Satan in serpent guise, Eve displays a certain theatricalism shortly before the Fall—"As one who loves, and some unkindness meets" (LM 9.271)—and after it: "to Adam in what sort / Shall I appear," she muses (LM

9.816–17); and then, on meeting him, "in her face excuse / Came prologue, and apology to prompt," with a flood of emotional violence that bears no accidental likeness to the language of satanic seduction (*LM* 9.853–54). The estrangement these histrionics imply has already occurred in Eve's relinquishing dependence on her spouse; but the artifice of her animation intensifies up to the moment when, as the speaker puts it, "they their fill of love and love's disport / Took largely, of their mutual guilt, the seal, / The solace of their sin" (*LM* 9.1042–44):

> Carnal desire inflaming, he on Eve
> Began to cast lascivious eyes, she him
> As wantonly repaid; in lust they burn:
> Til Adam thus gan Eve to dalliance move.
>
> . . .
>
> But come, so well refreshed, now let us play,
> As meet is, after such delicious fare;
> For never did thy beauty since the day
> I saw thee first and wedded thee, adorned
> With all perfections, so inflame my sense
> With ardour to enjoy thee, fairer now
> Than ever, bounty of this virtuous tree.
>   So said he, and forbore not glance or toy
> Of amorous intent, well understood
> Of Eve, whose eye darted contagious fire.
>
> (*LM* 9.1013–36)

In its utter visualism or specularity, transforming each person into a libidinal object, and its complete abstraction from the decorum of Edenic marriage, fallen eros has a pornographic quality to it. Like the fruit itself, Adam and Eve have become each other's fetish, not only in the sexual but also in the magical sense, where their exclusive fixation on each other's body behaves like a charm, moving them irresistibly to lubricious excess. They are wholly without relation, mere bodies to "enjoy"; and this illusion of autonomy is what gives the visual its compulsive power for those so enraptured, as when the fallen angels in Dantean fashion look upon the metamorphosed Satan and "the dire form / Catched by contagion, like in punishment, / As in their crime" (*LM* 10.543–45). By that "horrid sympathy; for what they saw, / They felt themselves now changing," hell is made over in the degraded image of its great chief, in a virtual parody of the *selem elohim* (10.540–41). The apostate become the thing on which they gaze, since Milton makes absorption in the appearance tantamount to absorption by it. For idolaters relinquish subjectivity—mind, volition, individuality—to the delusion of absolute and self-evident meaning, inasmuch as they willfully refuse intelligence about what they see.

But Eve's dream does something more besides estrange the familiar elements of human life: it offers a vividly, enticingly plausible account of the interdicted tree and our first parents' position in Eden, to stand against God's forbidding

word. Ambiguity—an ineluctable consequence of the distinction between creature and creator—has long preceded Satan and the speaker into paradise, with
its "wild" and "wanton" plantation, its waters flowing in "mazy error," its very
pregnancy with allusion, especially whenever Eve is seen. It is a world susceptible of being misunderstood because its ordering of things is both immensely
pleasurable and, like all deity's expressions, disconcertingly (to the apostate
mind) oblique and incongruous. Like Eve herself, Eden is the field of desire and
imagination; and this is where Adam's abstract explanation of the dream comes
crucially short of the reality. He neglects, even trivializes, the extent to which
theodicy has an imaginative, mediated existence for us, in which the predicament of faith consists long before the Fall. For fancy does much more than
supply the conveyance of evil to humanity. It brings Adam to his God, Eden,
and Eve; and nature's fancy, wild above rule or art, amplifies the enormous bliss
of paradise. In other words, imagination is not all "wild work," nor is it confined
to the model of "ill matched" meaning: it is equally the stuff of faith, as the
assurance of things hoped for and the conviction of things not seen.

For making God in Luther's sense is rightly to imagine him: so when Adam
disregards Eve's dream as more strange than true—like Shakespeare's Theseus,
dismissing imagination as that faculty which, "if it would but apprehend some
joy, / It comprehends some bringer of that joy"—he slights the revelation of
the good as well as the power of evil.[51] To know evil is to know its ability to
captivate us by a single, exclusive, and apparent idea of things, deluding us into
thinking we grasp the absolute in the image. But this is also to know good, in
the exercise of that critical intelligence which acknowledges the reality of *res
non apparentes* and the ordinary fact of a mediated, deflected truth inextricable
yet distinct from the things conveying it, which does not confuse the image
with its significance and so can "yet abstain, and yet distinguish, and yet prefer
that which is truly better." For that reason, in Milton's view, Spenser is a better
teacher than Aquinas or Scotus, because as a moralist, Spenser does not discount the enchantment of sensuous appearances; nor as a poet, does he refuse
to enlist its conceptual power, in supposing that either truth or deity can be
known apart from the essential phenomena of human experience (CM
4.1:311). The same can be said of Raphael, whose narrative addresses this predicament of religious understanding at every level. If imagination is the element
of the poet, poetry is the gift of God that Milton anticipates throughout his
life, famously in *The Reason of Church Government* where he declares it has that
reforming power

> beside the office of a pulpit, to inbreed and cherish in a great people the
> seeds of vertu, and publick civility, to allay the perturbations of the mind,
> and set the affections in right tune. . . . Teaching over the whole book of
> sanctity and vertu through all the instances of example with such delight
> to those especially of soft and delicious temper who will not so much as
> look upon Truth herselfe, unless they see her elegantly drest, that whereas

the paths of honesty and good life appear now rugged and difficult, though
they be indeed easy and pleasant, they would then appear to all men
both easy and pleasant though they were rugged and difficult indeed. (CM
3.1:238–39)

Like scriptural revelation, poetic images have the capacity to find the truth in
human difficulty, and through that incongruous and unexpected meaning, to
justify, to adjust, to rectify the mind.[52] So by putting his own callow words
about fancy in Adam's mouth—the words of the seventh Prolusion—Milton
introduces the special danger to innocence in *Paradise Lost*, which lies in its
failing to respect the ineluctable complexity of a world governed by the hidden
God. Innocence without the self-consciousness inculcated by Jesus' parables, or
Raphael's for that matter, is no virtue but "an excrementall whitenesse" in the
Areopagitica's phrase—a natural affinity for the good which can become not
only self-regarding but, in its sensations of moral ease and simplicity, also self-
deluding (CM 4:311). It can confuse facility with truth, inferring excellence
from great and bright, and so slide imperceptibly into idolatry as Adam does
and then Eve. The way Milton describes it, human being was never made static
or inert but dynamic, forever seeking a poise between possibilities whose mutable achievement demands an active, discerning intelligence. Again, this precar-
iousness that attends human life is expressed in the Father's creation of our first
parents as "Sufficient to have stood, though free to fall"—evoking not fixity but
a vital equilibrium that implies the constant trial of choice, and more importantly, the liberty to choose (LM 3.99). And trial, as Milton says, is by what is
contrary: for the great contrariety innocence faces in Eden is not evil but instead the distinction of God from the world, exemplified by his interdiction of
the tree of the knowledge of good and evil.

It is a difficulty compounded, moreover, by the primordial problem of self—
the egoism Adam epitomizes at the Fall, succumbing at once to self-pity and
Satan's autarchic "me" at the thought of his own diminishment: "O miserable
of happy! Is this the end / Of this new glorious world, and me so late / The
glory of that glory, who now become / Accurst of blessed" (LM 10.720–23). His
anguish concerns himself alone and the deprivation of what now appears as
hyperbolic preeminence and pleasure—a loss which, despite his gestures at culpability, Adam implicitly presents not as his own doing but as violently exacted
from him. This is the force of that perversely passionate "me" which dominates
the rest of his speech, culminating in the denial of all volition and responsibility
for his own being as mere "clay," since "God / Made thee without thy leave"
(LM 10.743, 759–60). That Adam, debating in satanic dissociation with his
own soul, has now objectified himself as something acted upon, not acting,
perfectly manifests the narcissism of apostasy which would answer guilt with
anomy and grotesque passivity, rejecting the obligation of intelligence in which
the *selem elohim* consists. In the mind of our general ancestor, the decree of
humanity's creation has become cruel necessity, his life intolerable, and his

creator oppressive, from whose newly "dreadful voice" he regresses to "my mother's lap"—the "earth / Insensible" out of which he was formed—in an utter renunciation of human being (*LM* 10.776–79).

This petulant relinquishing of agency is the cognate of Adam's latter-day explanation of fancy, because both speeches picture him as manipulated by iconic powers—deity's creation and his own imagination—which he is unable to withstand, even as Eve's beauty subjugates him at the Fall, having "erred in overmuch admiring / What seemed in thee so perfect" (*LM* 9.1178–80). To excuse himself, he renders the image absolute and arbitrary whose meaning is contingent and elective, and no more crucially than in Eve's case, where Adam claims that "Her doing seemed to justify the deed"—idolatry for which the Lord rebukes him (*LM* 10.142–46). In effect, the sovereign presence declares that Adam, in transgressing the distinction between man and woman—"to her / Thou didst resign thy manhood"—simultaneously transgressed the distinction it figures, that between God and the world (*LM* 10.147–48). And in doing so, he also failed to distinguish religious expressions from what they signify: Eve's beauty from what it implicates—his own glory as the image of God; deity's interdiction of the tree from what it pictures—faith in divine goodness and justice; the *selem elohim* from what it manifests—not godlike identity but the unique "look" or manner of the intellectual creature. For bearing the image of God enforces no such compulsive identification as the fallen angels suffer, since the faithful choose to acknowledge deity's expressive order of existence in this life, an observance that then enables them to see the divine as something other than self.

While Milton's version of the ensuing judgment upon our first parents doesn't specially depart from Genesis, he does not have his God say that the woman's desire will be for her spouse, so that Eve would be compelled to pursue her own sorrow in childbirth. It is a doom too closely resembling reprobation in the way argued by high Calvinism, where the necessity of suffering is imposed upon humanity by divine decree, and there is no "room" left for choice, faith, and redemption. And that is because Milton reads the Lord's account of our first parents as more predictive than punitive, an image diagnosing not so much their sin as the state to which apostasy has brought them. The connection with God and each other, articulated by the *selem elohim*, becomes to the human pair either enmity or bondage, which they replace with anomy. Thus Eve, standing before the interdicted tree, understands her dependence upon the man as a deprivation and injustice for which its forbidden fruit will duly compensate her. Faced with his estranged yet glittering spouse, Adam sees the condition of his obedience as condemning him to perpetual loneliness; and once he has followed Eve's licentious example, he presents himself as a veritable Oedipus, the prey of necessity whose guilt is supernaturally enjoined and contagious or polluting, with the once-divine benefit of the woman transformed into the fated cause of human suffering. But tellingly, it is the woman who first discloses another aspect to the Lord's judgment and their predicament than the man has chosen to see. Thus Eve, contrite with "tresses all disordered, at his feet" (*LM* 10.911):

> Forsake me not thus, Adam, witness heaven
> What love sincere, and reverence in my heart
> I bear thee, and unweeting have offended,
> Unhappily deceived; thy suppliant
> I beg, and clasp thy knees; bereave me not,
> Whereon I live, thy gentle looks, thy aid,
> Thy counsel in this uttermost distress,
> My only strength and stay: forlorn of thee,
> Whither shall I betake me, where subsist?
>
> (*LM* 10.914–22)

However excessive her speech and posture, Eve acknowledges the relation Adam has just summarily repudiated, which she intimately understands from the position of her own unexampled contingency: she discovers the "headship" lost to his present view—his looks, his aid and counsel, his strength—in which he completes and sustains his spouse. Moreover, by the novel initiative of her repentance, which in the fallen world is the truest grace, she allows him that proper deliberating self he lost in submission to her beauty and to the merely evident sense of things. Thus Eve assists Adam in observing the peculiar decorum of his God, since her violence of gesture and "vehement despair" occasions and inspires in him a responsive restraint sufficient now to abhor the suicide he himself had contemplated. This dialectical shift in attitude is represented by a gradual readdressing of their postures, from the very matter of their being, to each other and then their maker: from Adam the earth creature "on the ground / Outstretched," cursing his creation (*LM* 10.851–52), to Adam spurning the solitary Eve's timid movement toward him (*LM* 10.863–66), to the weeping Eve as anguished supplicant embracing her spouse's feet and meditating self-murder (*LM* 10.910–13), to Eve upraised by Adam in forgiveness (*LM* 10.946), to their mutual prostration before God in penance, whose only seemliness for Milton lies in its expression of faith and reliance upon the divine (*LM* 10.1099–1104). And the alteration is owing to Eve, who, echoing in her mea culpa the speaker's phrase, "He for God only, she for God in him," invokes the right order of things—that expressive contingency to which her own creation is specially the key, enabling Adam to know himself aright and then his God.

Milton elects Eve, whom Adam calls the frailer, infirmer sex, to redeem her spouse and humanity not by a false heroism but by that incongruous virtue of obedience: as in the Christ, God is revealed in Eve's admission of weakness and dependence, in her humility, in that patience with which she persists in seeking Adam's reluctant forgiveness. In such fortitude, it can be said that the woman more truly bears the *selem elohim*, the image of God, than the man, who continues to neglect the significance of their "unequal" marriage until Eve reminds him of it. To the extent that the sexual distinction figures the difference between creator and created, so the marital relation describes the peculiar way in which human being affiliates itself with God and truth, even as Eve pursues reunion with her estranged and abusive consort. And in restoring this bond by her own repentance and gratuitous love, Eve restores God to his creation from which Adam's idolatry and her own had effectually removed him. Now Adam can confess his fault to the spouse he first abandoned, "To me committed and by me exposed," becoming more and more like himself in pondering "some safer resolution," which of course begins with revising his sense of the Lord's speech (*LM* 10.957, 1029). The delusion apostasy fosters of a magical curse—immediate, absolute, and irresistible judgment executed upon themselves and proleptically upon their children—gives way to a different understanding, more attentive to the character of deity's expressions and more thoroughly circumstanced and subtle. Adam recognizes first that the curse upon the serpent is an allegory and not literally to be realized; that Satan, "our grand foe," is the subject of the Lord's words, the unseen "addition strange" which animated the serpent's appearances as well as the images of Eve's dream; and that the action the Lord pronounces is prophetic, extending beyond their own time into the human future. In short, Adam acknowledges the proper significance of divine revelation, whose force is rarely automatic but inevident and suspended, contingent upon the exercise of human understanding and choice in history, which is the domain of Michael's subsequent "speculation" and promise. But before he attains to that prophetic understanding, Adam here perceives a condition to the Lord's decree at once historical, justifying, and redemptive: that as they and their progeny make their way in the world, so their faith will imperceptibly exact retribution from their foe. Hope for humanity thus lies in the suspension or delay between deity's promise and its fulfillment, the delay that Adam a moment since found so cruel, but which now opens up to him a realm of possibility and justice he himself had foreclosed. Indicatively, in emulation of this idea, he imagines their own attitude in prayer and God's responsive mercy, which in a significant variation on the iterative style of Homeric sacrifice, our first parents and then God, both Father and Son, elect to fulfill: "Undoubtedly he will relent and turn / From his displeasure; in whose look serene, / When angry most he seemed and most severe, / What else but favour, grace, and mercy shone" (*LM* 10.1093–96).

Adam now begins to understand the motions of eternal providence; for even as the Lord is serene in wrath, merciful in severity, so he with "timely care / Hath unbesought provided" for human being in the exigencies of its fallen state (*LM* 10.1057–58). Grasping the difference between deity's ways and the world's, as bringing good out of evil, he makes his creator anew: not the absent or demonic God fashioned by his own apostasy, but the Lord who "Clothed us unworthy, pitying while he judged," whose prophecy leavens suffering with the promise of redemption in the psalmic manner (*LM* 10.1059). This deity has no single, exclusive expression, but, in the image of the *Areopagitica*'s truth, is as manifold and individual in its dispositions as the humanity to whom it responds. So when Michael concludes the story of salvation, Adam can exclaim:

> O goodness infinite, goodness immense!
> That all this good of evil shall produce,
> And evil turn to good; more wonderful
> Than that which by creation first brought forth
> Light out of darkness!
>
> (*LM* 12.469–73)

It is the paradox of the creator's affinity in distinction from the creature that imbues the *saeculum* with wonder and irony, teaching Adam the incommensurability of divine with human things and thus to expect the impossible from his God, who

> Merciful over all his works, with good
> Still overcoming evil, and by small
> Accomplishing great things, by things deemed weak
> Subverting worldly strong, and worldly wise
> By simply meek; that suffering for truth's sake
> Is fortitude to highest victory,
> And to the faithful death the gate of life.
>
> (*LM* 12.565–71)

In speaking this credo, which describes how deity will appear to the world in the figures of Israel and Jesus as the Christ, Adam also evokes the manner in which humankind will bear the *selem elohim*—not conspicuously or splendidly, but as our first mother exemplifies, incongruously in the negligible, the weak, the humiliated, and the suffering. For Eve's position, not Adam's, is our own at the end of *Paradise Lost*, because she observes in herself that seemingly inglorious action, that unprepossessing kind of speech in which God's image consists. At the same time, Adam fully, not superficially, recognizes that these things encompass true knowledge, for "beyond is all abyss, / Eternity, whose end no eye can reach" (*LM* 12.555–56).

This "abyss" is the boundary drawn between creature and creator, describing the utmost limits of human understanding—"Beyond which," Adam confesses, "was my folly to aspire" (*LM* 12.560). Now the order and venue of his knowledge is obedience: that is, to "love with fear the only God, to walk / As in his presence, ever to observe / His providence, and on him sole depend" (*LM* 12.562–64). Understood in wisdom's sense as "the fear of God," faith then as now preserves that expressive contingency by which we know the truth of things in a world governed by a hidden God. For the creature has always walked *as in* God's presence, imaginatively but also ironically, and the experience of deity has never been continuous, much less immediate or absolute for humankind. Even in paradise, humanity apprehended God from afar like Moses, at a distance in time, space, and appearance, deflected in the most surprising ways because Milton understands the position of faith not as occasioned by the Fall, but rather made self-conscious through that event and so deliberate and disciplined. In admitting deity's distinction from us, we are justified *coram Deo*, creating the domain of the divine, the soul, and the imagination; the arena of history, interpretation, choice, virtue; and the proper power of poetry. So when Michael abjures Adam to add "Deeds to thy knowledge answerable, add faith, / Add virtue, patience, temperance, add love, / By name to be called Charity, the soul / Of all the rest," he describes how humanity by these means is *creatrix divinitatis* and itself regains the image of God (*LM* 12.582–85). The prospect confronting our first parents at the eastern gate of paradise, as they stand looking out upon creation, thus holds out as yet unsuspected possibilities:

> Some natural tears they dropped, but wiped them soon;
> The world was all before them, where to choose
> Their place of rest, and providence their guide:
> They hand in hand with wandering steps and slow,
> Through Eden took their solitary way.
>
> (*LM* 12.645–49)

For there can be no endings in Milton's poetry, where understanding is always imminent.

NOTES

PREFACE

1. *Milton's God* (Norfolk, Conn.: New Directions, 1961), 7.

2. Michel de Montaigne, *The Essays: A Selection*, tr. and ed. M. A. Screech (Harmondsworth: Penguin, 1993), 370.

3. *On Poetry and Poets* (London: Faber and Faber, 1957), 154.

4. After commenting on the seemingly unsystematic order of his remarks—he calls them "really only an album"—Wittgenstein observes in the preface to the *Philosophical Investigations*: "I should not like my writing to spare other people the trouble of thinking. But, if possible, to stimulate someone to thoughts of his own" (*PI* vi). Again by way of preface, Cavell recounts how his need to liberate himself from the very sound of the *Investigations*, which had so consumed his own inquiries, "meant discovering ways of writing which I could regard as philosophical and could recognize as sometimes extensions—hence sometimes denials—of Wittgenstein's, and of course also of those of any other writer from whom I make my way" (*CR* xv). And in yet another preface, to the *Minima Moralia*, Adorno justifies his use of extended aphorism—"The disconnected and non-binding character of the form, the renunciation of explicit theoretical cohesion"—as an expression of both conceptual and circumstantial injustice, the melancholy inequity of life with thought (tr. E. F. N. Jephcott [London: Verso, 1974], 18). Whatever one thinks about its self-conscious difficulty, a profound moral compunction drives Adorno's language: "A writer will find that the more precisely, conscientiously, appropriately he expresses himself, the more obscure the literary result is thought, whereas a loose and irresponsible formulation is at once rewarded with certain understanding. . . . Regard for the object, rather than for communication, is suspect in any expression: anything specific, not taken from pre-existent patterns, appears inconsiderate, a symptom of eccentricity, almost of confusion" (101). Inasmuch as Adorno simultaneously indicts here "The logic of the day, which makes so much of its clarity," the commonality of purpose among these writers is hardly specious, for in their own fashion, they each challenge the moral sterility of analytic philosophy.

5. Walter Burkert, *Greek Religion*, tr. John Raffan (Cambridge, Mass.: Harvard U P, 1985), 148.

6. Notwithstanding the tacit polemic directed at critics like Saurat, who do not share his regard for the historical and specifically theological sources of Milton's poetry, I do think that Maurice Kelley has compellingly shown (*pace* W. B. Hunter) the intellectual integrity as well as pertinence of the *Christian Doctrine* to our understanding of the later poetry (in *This Great Argument* [Princeton: Princeton U P, 1941]). That pertinence must not preclude other interpretive frameworks; but neither should we indulge a resistance to theology by ignoring this considerable resource, the conceptual vehicle regularly chosen by Milton and his contemporaries to address what we may regard as nontheological problems. For in neglecting it, we betray our own religious attitudes. At the same time, the tract is itself susceptible to misreading, insofar as we fail to bring Milton's other pamphlets to bear on its argument, as well as a hundred and fifty years of Protestant theology.

CHAPTER ONE

1. *Milton's God*; but there is also his chapter on Milton and Bentley in *Some Versions of Pastoral* ([Norfolk, Conn.: New Directions Books, 1960], 141–83), in which Satan's grievances and Bentley's opinions are simultaneously vindicated, while "Milton's appalling God" is quite put down (160).

2. These and the following remarks are Richard Strier's, made at the 1995 MLA Convention in Chicago, on the occasion of Empson's belated induction into the Milton Society.

3. *Mimesis*, tr. Willard Trask (Princeton: Princeton U P, 1953), 14.

4. Ibid., 15.

5. John Shawcross, ed., *Milton 1732–1801: The Critical Heritage* (London: Routledge & Kegan Paul, 1972), 241.

6. *Milton* (1900; reprint, New York: Benjamin Bloom, 1967), xx.

7. Eliot is particularly acute about Johnson's Milton: see *On Poetry and Poets*, 153–59.

8. See Masson, *The Life of John Milton*, 6 vols. (1880; reprint, Gloucester, Mass.: Peter Smith, 1965), 6:751–54.

9. *Lives of the English Poets*, 2 vols. (London: Oxford U P, The World's Classics, 1906), 1:118.

10. Ibid., 1:125.

11. Ibid., 1:127.

12. Ibid., 1:124.

13. Ibid., 1:131.

14. Ibid., 1:109.

15. To be fair, MacIntyre makes this remark parenthetically, as he reviews Lucien Goldmann's *The Hidden God*: he observes how political dispossession in Goldmann's account of the *noblesse de robe*, who are betrayed by the monarchy they serve, contributes to Pascal's "tragic vision." See his *Against the Self-images of the Age* (1971; reprint, Notre Dame, Ind.: Notre Dame U P, 1978), 76–87, esp. 82. I would obviously resist the comparison (see below n.17), if only because Milton methodically refuses to admit the absolute claims of Stuart monarchy, and indeed most any institution, including parliament and the church, and so undergoes nothing like the tragic contradiction Pascal suffers. Milton was not an ironist in that style, but a satirist, Independent, and Cromwellian whom politics and controversy continued to engage, right up to his final pamphlet, *Of True Religion, Heresy, Schism, Toleration*, published the year before he died, and who ceased attending worship in his later life, not out of despair but (Aubrey's comments suggest) from a certain witty scepticism, as Toland recounts in his *Life* (see Helen Darbishire, ed., *Early Lives of Milton* [1932; reprint, St. Clair Shores, Mich.: Scholarly Press, 1972], 195; and Masson, *Life*, 6:682–83). There is Richardson's story of his impartially tormenting one of his servants, a nonconformist, to this effect (Darbishire, *Early Lives*, 237–38).

16. "Dr. Johnson, with a fearful and sincere piety, refused to follow Milton into Heaven," although "Milton himself would have been the last to claim sanctuary in Heaven for the imagination on which the whole fabric of the poem depends" (Raleigh, *Milton*, 127).

17. As Angus Fletcher remarks:

Irony we often equate with paradox, that is, with seemingly self-contradictory utterances where tenets normally in polar contradiction to each other are collapsed together into one single ambivalent statement. In irony and paradox extremes meet, while the tension of ambivalence increases proportionately. Because irony seems to collapse the multileveled segregations of allegory (e.g., a fourfold schema would collapse), it has been called "antiallegorical." This seems to me an unfortunate usage, since irony still involves an otherness of meaning, however tenuous and shifty may be our means of decoding that other (*allos*) meaning. Rather, I think we might call ironies "collapsed allegories," or perhaps, "condensed allegories." They show no diminishing, only a confusion of the semantic and syntactic processes of double or multiple-leveled polysemy. Where they do differ from an allegorical norm might instead be in the degree of emotive tension they manifest; anxiety increases in European literary works as they approach what Frye calls their "ironic" phase. (*Allegory* [Ithaca: Cornell U P, 1964], 229–30)

On this relation between irony and allegory, see also Gordon Teskey's "Irony, Allegory, and Metaphysical Decay," *PMLA* 109/3 (1994): 397–408, as well as the expanded version of his argument in *Allegory and Violence* (Ithaca: Cornell U P, 1996). For the problem as it pertains to Milton, see Catherine Gimelli Martin's ingenious and productive *The Ruins of Allegory* (Durham: Duke U P, 1998), with whose idea of ironic or meta-allegory in *Paradise Lost* I have felicitous sympathy. Tellingly, both Teskey and Martin are indebted to Benjamin's account of allegory in the German *Trauerspiel*, which each reads toward a more sceptical (because poststructural) version of Fletcher's ironically expanded polysemy. Coming myself from Wittgenstein, who conceives the fundamental condition of human meaning as in a manner allegorical, and from Cavell, who argues that the sceptic's crisis constitutes and magnifies this very insight (an argument not unallied in predicament or effect to Benjamin's melancholy allegorist), I am inclined to see the poststructural account of figuration as a performance of polysemy ironically predicated on the analyst's tacit anxiety, even despair of that condition (this is how I am inclined to read De Man's essay "Pascal's Allegory of Persuasion" [in Stephen Greenblatt, ed., *Allegory and Representation* (Baltimore: Johns Hopkins U P, 1981), 1–25]). In other words, like scepticism in the *Investigations*, here allegory is equally the response of a disappointed metaphysics, a discountenanced idealism, to the contingency of human meanings. The better to analyze what he describes, after Macaulay, as "a strategic wavering, or oscillation, between idealism and materialism" in Milton's writings, Herman Rapaport brings Derrida's different idea of the undecidable to bear, rightly arguing the methodical, iconoclastic intent of their putative "inconsistency" (*Milton and the Postmodern* [Lincoln: U Nebraska P, 1983], 3). And with Teskey and Martin, Rapaport recognizes the significance of an integral equivocality or dialectic to Milton's conceptual idiom, which he regards as resisting and indeed incapable of any authentic resolution, calling it *thanatopraxie*: "With *thanatopraxie* there is no rest and no equilibrium; there is no peace or home . . . only the loss of stabilizing antinomies, of decidable certainties, of definite points of reference" (9).

While this model of meaning leads to some important recognitions, especially about the figure of Eve, I don't think the poet embraces it, since what Rapaport describes is Milton's hell—the very image of satanic existence, which finds "no end, in wandering mazes lost" (*LM* 2.561). Cavell puts the case in a fashion instructive for Milton, remarking that "today's advanced literary use of the idea of the undecidable is produced by the same distortion or prejudice as yesterday's advanced philosophical use of the decidable" (*In Quest of the Ordinary* [Chicago: U Chicago P, 1988], 136). He goes on to distinguish his analytic practice as only ostensibly similar to Derrida's, since it inquires instead into the *possible* conditions of human meaning, one of which is sceptical aporia—this telling preclusion of significance sometimes anguished and austere, sometimes facile and self-regarding. Cavell speaks in effect for the reformers and Milton when he says that "to me such courses seem to give up the game; they do not achieve what freedom, what useful idea of myself, there may be for me, but seem as self-imposed as the grandest philosophy" (135). Mourning the contingency of our knowledge is a kind of faithlessness, an illusion of loss, which the allegory of *Paradise Lost* seeks to understand and describe even as it does the predicament of faith more largely. Cavell would do the same philosophically, after Wittgenstein. I will just add that, *pace* Martin (whose argument on this head is appropriately qualified), I believe there is little shared religious because moral or political ground between the Arminian Milton and the Jansenist Pascal, an Augustinian Catholic whose great and somber paradox of the hidden God exerts a Draconian hold on the believer, as irrationalism rationalized. Although both effectively resist the Cartesian juggernaut, Milton has an antipathy for rationalist accounts of religious things, however ironic, in the manner of Luther's response to Erasmus. Moreover, his scriptural theology would find the exclusionary logic of Pascal's melancholy science foreign, especially in its tacit intellectual formalism; for the same reason he would have no use for Pascal's wager, since Milton admits no more than the delusion of *aporia*, in which consists the anguish and tragedy of the sceptic. Perhaps most importantly, their bourgeois politics distinguishes them, as Lucien Goldmann's incomparable study shows (*The Hidden God* [London: Routledge & Kegan Paul, 1964]): although it has been argued otherwise, Milton's restrictive antinomianism does not lead to quietism or withdrawal. Both Christopher Hill (*Milton and the English Revolution* [Harmondsworth: Penguin, 1977]) and Joan Bennet (*Reviving Liberty* [Cambridge, Mass.: Harvard U P, 1989]) have made compelling arguments on this head (see below n.37).

18. *Permanence and Change*, 2nd rev. ed. (Indianapolis: Bobbs Merrill, 1965), 32.

19. Jean-Pierre Vernant and Pierre Vidal-Naquet, *Myth and Tragedy in Ancient Greece*, tr. Janet Lloyd (New York: Zone Books, 1990), 27.

20. Werner Jaeger, *Paideia: The Ideals of Greek Culture*, vol. 1, *Archaic Greece: The Mind of Athens*, tr. Gilbert Highet, 2nd. ed. (New York: Oxford U P, 1945), 167–68.

21. Although I discovered it belatedly, Thomas Merrill, in his astute *Epic God-Talk: "Paradise Lost" and the Grammar of Religious Language* (Jefferson, N.C.: McFarland, 1986), has already brought Wittgenstein methodically to bear on Milton's model of meaning, in the form of religious language studies where the later philosophy especially has been influential (Ebeling, Funk, and Phillips figure in his account). Merrill argues—among other things—the distinction between deity per se and the scriptural God that Milton makes the object of religious knowledge, with the latter a "fictitious God" whose peculiar logical status transforms religious expression into encounters between conflicting language games, which comprise the parabolic action of *Paradise Lost*: " 'Stretched' also expresses how God-talk overextends its base to effect its characteristic double vision, for ideally, God-talk is a linguistic double exposure of sacred and profane truths. . . . This is the very essence of God-talk and the moment it is lost, either through authorial or interpretive failure, the blight of literalism sets in" (12).

If our ways of reading and applying Wittgenstein's argument differ (Merrill tends to think ontologically), we converge on this critical point, which Northrop Frye anticipates in his account of *Paradise Regained*; for there are rarely new ideas, only new ways of putting them. In my case, the difference is owing to the connection Stanley Cavell draws between scepticism and tragedy: while its confusions are all my own, whatever insights my argument offers belong to Cavell's ongoing dialogue with the *Investigations* and his peculiar vantage on that text: "It was some years before I understood it as what I came to think of as a discovery for philosophy of the problem of the other" (*CR* xiii). But I have also benefited particularly from the work of P. M. S. Hacker (especially *Insight and Illusion*, rev. ed. [Oxford: Clarendon, 1986]); in a critical fashion, David Pears (*Ludwig Wittgenstein* [Cambridge, Mass.: Harvard U P, 1986]; and *The False Prison*, 2 vols. [Oxford: Clarendon, 1988]); Paul Johnston (*Wittgenstein and Moral Philosophy* [London: Routledge, 1989]); Charles Taylor's moral philosophy (for Wittgenstein specifically, *Philosophical Arguments* [Cambridge, Mass.: Harvard U P, 1995]); D. Z. Phillips (*Wittgenstein and Religion* [New York: St. Martin's, 1993] and *Faith after Foundationalism* [London: Routledge, 1988]); and for my initial understanding of Wittgenstein, Henry LeRoy Finch (his wonderfully lucid *Wittgenstein: The Later Philosophy* [Atlantic Highlands, N.J.: Humanities Press, 1977]). Needless to say, this thorough indebtedness to Cavell means that I present a different Wittgenstein than the one understood by most analytic philosophers.

22. *The Fragility of Goodness* (Cambridge: Cambridge U P, 1986), 23.

23. *Zettel*, ed. G. E. M. Anscombe and G. H. von Wright, tr. G. E. M. Anscombe (1967; reprint, Berkeley: U California P, 1970), #314.

24. See D. Z. Phillips's account of these remarks as representing the difference Wittgenstein argues between elucidation and explanation, and Phillips's comments on the inability of philosophical inquiry to "stop" where Wittgenstein says it should, especially when God and religious belief are its subject (*Wittgenstein and Religion*, 79–102). It is almost superfluous to observe that the philosophical misunderstanding of Wittgenstein not coincidentally resembles the sceptic's misunderstanding of human language, since the *Investigations* is diagnosing a conceptual pathology.

25. Since Luther's commentary on Galatians dominates my theological analogues, I should just mention that its pertinence and conceptual aptitude for sixteenth- and seventeenth-century British literature has already been established, more or less simultaneously, by Richard Strier (*Love Unknown: Theology and Experience in George Herbert's Poetry* [Chicago: U Chicago P, 1983], esp. xiii n.9), and Georgia Christopher (*Milton and the Science of the Saints* [Princeton: Princeton U P, 1982], esp. 37 n.9). For some reason, Calvin's relevance is generally presumed for Milton, yet often without the understanding that (as has been frequently remarked) he is Luther's greatest disciple, and that Calvin's theology sufficiently differs from the arguments of high, scholastic Calvinism that Arminius can regard his alleged heterodoxy as consistent with Calvin's views. Although Milton is not a scholastic—a scripturalist, he admits no extrinsic logic that would require him to posit a device like God's "middle knowledge"—his approach to the divine decrees and his view of creatural freedom are consonant with Arminius's.

26. *Leviathan*, ed. C. B. Macpherson (Harmondsworth: Pelican Books, 1968), 435.

27. *Wittgenstein's Lectures: Cambridge 1932–35*, ed. Alice Ambrose (Chicago: U Chicago P, 1979), 31–32.

28. On Luther's concept of *res non apparentes*, see David C. Steinmetz, *Luther in Context* (Bloomington: Indiana U P, 1986), 12–46.

29. *Martin Luther: Selections from His Writings*, ed. John Dillenberger (Garden City, N.Y.: Doubleday, Anchor Books, 1961), 11. My account largely relies on Alister McGrath's discussion of the preface in *Luther's Theology of the Cross* (Oxford: Basil Blackwell, 1985), 95–147; but see also Walther von Loewenich, *Luther's Theology of the Cross*, tr. Lawrence W. Denef (Minneapolis: Augsburg, 1986), 83–91.

30. Dillenberger, *Martin Luther*, 11.

31. Ibid., 11–12.

32. "Things and Actions Indifferent: The Temptation of Plot in *Paradise Regained*," *Milton Studies* 17 (1983): 163–85. Stanley Fish understands the status of "things indifferent" as expressing neither possibility nor latitude of action, but instead a crucial temptation to preempt deity and falsely resolve his predicament which Satan cunningly offers our saviour, whose refusal then thrusts the poem's meaning into an interior and functionally transcendent realm. I would argue conversely that, from Milton's vantage, *adiaphora* and the perpetual choice they present do not have the oppressive, contradictory effect of over-determining human choice—an effect exacerbating the alleged interiority and inexpressiveness of Milton's faith, which Fish opposes to the overt and "objective" character of idolatry. This is to mistake the inevident for the transcendent, and by conceptual dichotomy to remove God from the world, as Luther argues. What Fish calls "the intentional disposition" of our saviour is neither negative nor hypostatic in expression; rather, his identity is unexpectedly, emergently, incrementally manifest. For Milton as for Shakespeare, the discovery of self is a public event, which is one reason why he himself writes.

33. *Milton's Brief Epic* (Providence: Brown U P, 1966).

34. In his remarkable essay "The Typology of *Paradise Regained*" (in Arthur Barker, ed., *Milton: Modern Essays in Criticism* [Oxford: Oxford U P, 1965]), Northrop Frye comments that, *dramatically*, our saviour is "an increasingly unsympathetic figure, a pusillanimous quietest in the temptation of Parthia, an inhuman snob in the temptation of Rome, a peevish obscurantist in the temptation of Athens," and altogether a fitting offspring for his comparably repulsive God (439). Nevertheless, Frye maintains with perfect equanimity that "the real source of life and freedom and energy is in the frigid figure at the center" of Satan's more pleasingly antic behavior (439–40):

> It is quite possible for a poem to be, as *Paradise Regained* may be, a magnificent success in its structure and yet often tired and perfunctory in its execution. In structure, however, *Paradise Regained* is not only a success but a technical experiment that is practically *sui generis*. None of the ordinary literary categories apply to it; its poetic predecessors are nothing like it, and it has left no descendents. . . . Its closest affinities are with the debate and the dialectical colloquy of Plato and Boethius, to which most of the Book of Job also belongs. But these forms usually either incorporate one argument into another dialectically or build up two different cases rhetorically; Milton's feat of constructing a double argument on the same words, each highly plausible and yet as different as light from darkness, is, so far as I know, unique in English literature. (440)

I would only add to this unprecedented insight that *Paradise Regained* is not singular in its dialectical meaning, as Frye contends: *Paradise Lost* is also a "double-argument on the same words," an idea to which Fish has given a formidable expression.

35. "*Paradise Regained*: A Last Chance at True Romance," *Milton Studies* 17 (1983): 187–207, esp. 206. In the same issue, Stuart Curran makes a comparable point about the trial endured by our saviour: "Like other epic heroes, Jesus has a divine patron and a mission, but uniquely he is left to his own devices without recourse to intervention or miracle" ("*Paradise Regained*: Implications of Epic," 209–33, esp. 222). Milton is no supernaturalist, a remark I will have cause to repeat.

36. *The Malleus Maleficarum of Henrich Kramer and James Sprenger*, tr. Montague Summers (1948; reprint, New York: Dover, 1971), 17–20, 58–60.

37. Against Andrew Milner's Cartesian Milton (*John Milton and the English Revolution* [London: Macmillan, 1981]) and Rapaport's Derridean version, both of whom assert the ultimate quietism of *Paradise Regained*, Joan Bennet argues powerfully that Milton understood "the paradise within" to be no retreat from the world: on the contrary, it expresses the conceptual disposition of Christian liberty, whose proper domain is history and whose proper action is political, as all his writings maintain. See her discriminate and informed account of Milton's "radical Christian humanism" in *Reviving Liberty*, esp. 161–202.

38. *Milton and the Kingdoms of God* (Evanston, Ill.: Northwestern U P, 1964), 270–71.

39. This is Hermann Tennessen's description, quoted by D. Z. Phillips, *Wittgenstein and Religion*, 158.

40. *Theology of the Old Testament*, tr. J. A. Baker, 2 vols. (Philadelphia: Westminster, 1961–67), 2:465–69.

41. Ibid., 2:88–89.

42. *Wittgenstein and Religion*, 153–70. Taking Tennessen as his example, Phillips observes:

> That we have to appeal to our language in order to understand what might be meant by 'the ways of God' is not in dispute. What can be disputed is Tennessen's further claim that *human language only speaks of human standards*. Evidently, that is not so, since *in our language* there *is* talk of the ways of God, ways said to be beyond human understanding. Nothing Tennessen has said shows why the philosopher cannot explore the grammar of this talk. The exploration will not be successful, however, if *prior* to looking at the use of language in question, we come to it with our minds already made up about what it *must* mean. Tennessen comes to that language armed with conceptions of 'the norms of the deity' and an 'image of God as an optimum.' God is located on a human continuum of wisdom and hence is answerable to it. Inevitably, he fails the test of answerability. God fails, however, given Tennessen's preconceptions about what religious language must mean. To free himself from these preconceptions, Tennessen must be prepared to do something he explicitly warns us against, namely, derive the concept of deity from 'the given God.' (163)

As Phillips describes it, philosophical theism is the position of Milton's Satan, lost in the delusion of commensurability between divine and human meanings, and so translating the contingent expressions of deity into a horrifying absolute. As Tennessen's description of that figure makes entirely clear, he finds the God of Job and theodicies generally an affront to human value and understanding, since these refuse to conform to philosophical standards of intelligibility. Thus Phillips on the consequence of this species of religious analysis: "The god we believe in, the god who still lords it over our experience, is a god of blind caprice. Further, for Tennessen, the only decent response to such a god is in terms of what he calls 'weapons of the spirit': heroic martyrdom or hidden despair in the heart" (162). It is a brief and immaculate diagnosis of Satan's ambivalence in *Paradise Lost*.

CHAPTER TWO

1. For a contrasting aesthetic, see Umberto Eco's *The Aesthetics of Thomas Aquinas*, tr. Hugh Bredin (Cambridge, Mass.: Harvard U P, 1988), in which Eco imaginatively celebrates the ontological or transcendental force of beauty in Aquinan theology.

2. The reference is to Thomas V. Morris's *The Logic of God Incarnate* (Ithaca: Cornell U P, 1986); but I am thinking of William P. Alston's *Divine Nature and Human Language* (Ithaca: Cornell U P, 1989), and in a different sense Alvin Plantinga's *God and Other*

Minds (Ithaca: Cornell U P, 1967). Contrasting philosophical tacks would be D. Z. Phillips's Wittgensteinian approach, or the speech-act model of Nicholas Wolterstorff's *Divine Discourse* (Cambridge: Cambridge U P, 1995).

3. A version of the following distinction between normative and instrumental order is argued by Carl J. Friedrich in his *Transcendent Justice* (Durham: Duke U P, 1964), 3–20.

4. See William Haller for the classic account of the "puritan" debate on dissent (*Liberty and Reformation* [New York: Columbia U P, 1955], 143–287).

5. Milton's republicanism is instrumental in this sense, as a mutual contract occasioning the exercise of individual agency, choice, and virtue, not determining or precluding them, a view he shares with Algernon Sidney, that other Whig worthy. On English republicanism more generally, besides Hill and Walzer, see J. G. A. Pocock, *The Machiavellian Moment* (Princeton: Princeton UP, 1975), 333–422. For Milton's version, among others, see Don C. Wolfe, *Milton in the Puritan Revolution* (1941; reprint, New York: Humanities Press, 1963); Arthur E. Barker, *Milton and the Puritan Dilemma 1641–1660* (Toronto: U Toronto P, 1942); Haller, *Liberty and Reformation*; Fixler, *Milton and the Kingdoms of God*; Hill, *Milton and the English Revolution*; Bennet, *Reviving Liberty*; David Loewenstein, *Milton and the Drama of History* (Cambridge: Cambridge U P, 1990); Robert Thomas Fallon, *Milton in Government* (University Park, Penn.: Pennsylvania State U P, 1993); David Quint, *Epic and Empire* (Princeton: Princeton U P, 1993); Victoria Kahn, *Machiavellian Rhetoric* (Princeton: Princeton U P, 1994), esp. 169–235; David Armitage, Armand Hiny, and Quentin Skinner, eds., *Milton and Republicanism* (Cambridge: Cambridge U P, 1995).

6. *A Theory of Justice* (Cambridge, Mass.: Belknap P, 1971), 136–42.

7. For my purposes, the salient work on Calvin has been Edward A. Dowey, Jr., *The Knowledge of God in Calvin's Theology* (New York: Columbia U P, 1952), and Richard A. Muller's writings on post-reformed doctrine (see below). But I have also drawn variously on Francois Wendel, *Calvin*, tr. Philip Mairet (New York: Harper and Row, 1963); John T. McNeil, *The History and Character of Calvinism* (Oxford: Oxford U P, 1954); Wilhelm Niesel, *The Theology of Calvin*, tr. Harold Knight (1956; reprint, Grand Rapids, Mich.: Baker Book House, 1980); T. H. L. Parker, *John Calvin* (1975; reprint, Tring, Herts.: Lion, 1987) and *Calvin's Old Testament Commentaries* (Edinburgh: T. & T. Clark, 1986); William J. Bousma, *John Calvin* (New York: Oxford U P, 1988); Brian Armstrong, *Calvinism and the Amyraut Heresy* (Madison: U Wisconsin P, 1969); David Little, *Religion, Order, and Law* (Chicago: U Chicago P, 1984); R. T. Kendall, *Calvin and English Calvinism to 1649* (Oxford: Oxford U P, 1979); Donald K. McKim, ed., *Readings in Calvin's Theology* (Grand Rapids, Mich.: Baker Book House, 1984); and Alister E. McGrath, *A Life of John Calvin* (Oxford: Basil Blackwell, 1990).

8. On this "federal" theology, see Perry Miller, *The New England Mind: The Seventeenth Century* (Boston: Beacon, 1961), 365–462; Miller, *Errand into the Wilderness* (Cambridge, Mass.: Harvard U P, 1956), 48–98; Richard A. Muller, "Covenant and Conscience in English Reformed Theology," *Westminster Theological Journal* 42/2 (1980): 308–34; Muller, "The Federal Motif in Seventeenth-Century Arminian Theology," *Nederlands Archief voor Kerkgeschiedenis* 62/1 (1982): 102–22. Although Miller would appear to argue otherwise, it is important to remember that the concept of *pactum* or *foedus* is neither original nor exclusive to high Calvinism: as Richard Muller points out, it is a feature of Arminianism, but it also plays a significant role in Luther's thought, whose source was the theology of the *via moderna*. See McGrath, *Luther's Theology*, 58–62, 86–90.

9. *Knowing the Unknowable God* (Notre Dame, Ind.: Notre Dame U P, 1986), 8–11. Needless to say, in using Burrell's illuminating concept of "the distinction" for the reform-

ers' theology, I am departing from his specific discussion of that idea as it applies to Aquinas and two further points of comparison, the arguments made by Ibn-Sina and Maimonides about the relationship between creator and creation. But as he remarks, quoting another theologian, this emphasis on the status of analogy where talk about God is concerned gives us an "Aquinas who looks more like Wittgenstein than Avicenna": "In fact, the reflections of the later Wittgenstein on the multiple uses to which *we* put language will appear as serendipitous confirmation of the role Aquinas' distinction plays in our attentiveness to language and the ways we use language" (37).

10. Ibid., 14–34.

11. *The Dividing Muse* (New Haven: Yale U P, 1985).

12. I am referring particularly to Fish's "Spectacle and Evidence in *Samson Agonistes*," *Critical Inquiry* 15 (1989), 556–86.

13. Besides the studies already mentioned, my most considerable resource for his theology has been Gerhard Ebeling's matchless *Luther*, tr. R. A. Wilson (Philadelphia: Fortress, 1970). I have also fruitfully drawn on Paul Althaus, *The Theology of Martin Luther*, tr. Robert C. Schultz (Philadelphia: Fortress, 1966); John Dillenberger, *God Hidden and Revealed* (Philadelphia: Muhlenberg, 1953); B. A. Gerrish, *Grace and Reason* (Oxford: Clarendon, 1962); Heiko A. Oberman, *Luther*, tr. Eileen Walliser-Schwarzbart (1989; reprint, New York: Doubleday, 1992); and Jaroslav Pelikan, *Luther the Expositor* (Saint Louis: Concordia, 1959).

14. For the crucial concept of *coram Deo*, see Ebeling, *Luther*, 192–202.

15. For the significance of this idea in Luther's theology—faith as *creatrix divinitatis* in the following passage from his commentary on Galatians—see ibid., 257.

16. Martin Luther, *On the Bondage of the Will*, tr. J. I. Packer and O. R. Johnston (London: James Clarke, 1957), 66–70. See also Ebeling, *Luther*, 244–48.

17. *The Uses of Argument* (Cambridge: Cambridge U P, 1958), 1–10, 211–17.

18. "A Treatise on the Anger of God," in *The Ante-Nicene Fathers*, vol. 7, *Fathers of the Third and Fourth Centuries*, ed. Alexander Roberts and James Donaldson (n.d.; reprint, Grand Rapids, Mich.: Eerdmans, 1989), 259–80, esp. 269. Lactantius puts his syllogistic to the service of theodicy here: "It is therefore the fear of God alone which guards the mutual society of men, by which life is sustained, protected, and governed. But that fear is taken away if man is persuaded that God is without anger." For possible traces of Lactantius's influence on Milton, especially in the way they picture the word or son of God, see Kathleen Ellen Hartwell, *Lactantius and Milton* (New York: Haskell, 1974). For the affinities between Lactantius's God and Luther's, see Rudolph Otto, *The Idea of the Holy*, tr. John W. Harvey (New York: Oxford U P, 1958), 96–97.

19. *Bondage of the Will*, 87, 170.

20. On the potential opposition of will between Luther's *Deus revelatus* or *incarnatus* and this *Deus absconditus*, "God hidden in Majesty" (ibid., 169–77), see McGrath, *Luther's Theology*, 165–69.

21. *The Many Faces of Realism* (La Salle, Ill.: Open Court, 1987), 51.

22. McGrath, *Luther's Theology*, 169–75. On this head, it is significant that Luther again and again returned in his commentaries to the psalms.

23. Ibid., 107–13.

24. Ibid., 159.

25. *Calvin: Institutes of the Christian Religion*, ed. John T. McNeill, tr. Ford Lewis Battles, 2 vols. (Philadelphia: Westminster, 1960), 1:38–39.

26. Otto provides an extended discussion of the *mysterium tremendum* in *Idea of the Holy*, 12–71.

27. For Luther's understanding of *opus proprium Dei* and *opus alienum Dei*—God's "proper" and "alien" works—see McGrath, *Luther's Theology*, 151–58, 167–73. The *opus alienum* has the quality of paradox, as "Luther's term for actions performed by God which apparently contradict his nature, and yet which ultimately lead to a conclusion in keeping with that nature" (192).

28. I believe the phrase is Luther's; but Richard Muller equally observes that, given his Christological emphasis, "there can be no *Deus nudus absconditus*, no God abstractly considered apart from his work, in Calvin's system" (*Christ and the Decree* (Durham, N.C.: Labyrinth, 1986), 17–38. The *ordo salutis* itself delimits the force of that natural theology Bousma ascribes to Calvin (*John Calvin*, 98–109). As Calvin himself concludes, "Consequently, we know the most perfect way of seeking God, and the most suitable order, is not for us to attempt with bold curiosity to penetrate to the investigation of his essence, which we ought more to adore than meticulously to search out, but for us to contemplate him in his works whereby he renders himself near and familiar to us, and in some manner communicates himself" (*Calvin: Institutes*, 1:62). "Works" here refers not just to nature but to history, with Calvin conceiving the contemplation of God in nature as a devotional activity of the faithful, a consoling display of divine goodness; and I would emphasize his insistence in the *Institutes* on the human incapacity to benefit from these natural evidences unassisted by grace and faith. "For each man's mind is like a labyrinth," he writes; so "although the Lord represents both himself and his everlasting Kingdom in the mirror of his works with very great clarity, such is our stupidity that we grow increasingly dull toward so manifest testimonies, and they flow away without profiting us" (*Calvin: Institutes*, 1:63–65). As Dowey observes, "The revelation in creation, then serves the formal purpose of preserving responsibility before God, which is one of the essential characteristics of man, endued as he is with an internal sense of divinity, a conscience, and the ability to see the revelation God has given of himself in nature and history. . . . It is only from the standpoint of special revelation that one can judge properly the revelation in creation, since the fall of man" (*Knowledge of God*, 82–83). In its soteriological role, as natural law, the evidence of deity in creation serves only to condemn the mind that rejects it; there is no human possibility of ascending by a train of inference from creation to the positive knowledge of God, much less the nature of deity per se (for further discussion, see Dowey, *Knowledge of God*, 3–86).

29. *Calvin: Institutes*, 1:544.

30. Otto, *The Idea of the Holy*, 54–55.

31. *Calvin: Institutes*, 1:499.

32. *Bondage of the Will*, 70–74.

33. Dowey, *Knowledge of God*, 184–88.

34. As Ebeling remarks: "Luther contrasts this *theologia crucis* with the knowledge of God obtained by the Gentiles, which is also described by allusion to Paul (Rom. 1:20), and which was an attempt to perceive the invisible nature of God from the works of creation, through reason. By this method, the ascent from the visible to the invisible, one can only know the glorious God, the *Deus gloriosus*, in his metaphysical attributes as omnipresent and omnipotent, as the highest good and the highest object of *eros*. . . . For

the invisibility of the *Deus gloriosus* as perceived by reason is a glorification of the world. To know him in this way is a pretentious and deceiving wisdom, and the affirmation of man's endeavour to realize himself in his works in a way analogous to the divine principle of creation" (*Luther*, 227–28).

35. *Calvin: Institutes*, 1:35, 37.

36. On Luther's concept of Christ as "God concealed beneath his contrary," see Ebeling, *Luther*, 234–41; and McGrath, *Luther's Theology*, 155–68.

37. Dillenberger, *Luther: Selections*, 500–503.

38. On Luther's understanding of the *posteriora*, see McGrath, *Luther's Theology*, 149–50.

39. Eichrodt, *Theology*, 2:31. John Rumrich, in his *Matter of Glory: A New Preface to "Paradise Lost"* (Pittsburgh: U Pittsburgh P, 1987), gives an important and extended discussion of this scriptural usage for Milton's poem, allying it simultaneously with Homeric ideas such as *time, kudos, arete,* and *kleos*.

40. Richmond Lattimore, tr., *The Iliad of Homer* (Chicago: Chicago U P, 1951), 273.

41. *The Works . . . of John Hales*, 3 vols. (Glasgow, 1765), 2:27.

42. *Bondage of the Will*, 101.

43. *John Calvin*, 52.

44. Ibid., 52–53.

45. *Bondage of the Will*, 192.

46. Ibid., 191.

47. Ibid., 166, 195.

48. *Erasmus* (Harmondsworth: Penguin, 1980). It is not insignificant that Erasmus is a thorough Platonist, as Screech demonstrates, while Luther is not. See von Loewenich (*Theology of the Cross*, 149–66), who argues the antipathy between Luther's thought and mysticism, especially the Neoplatonism of Johannes Tauler and the German theology. Referring to the work of Heiko Oberman, McGrath also observes: "The results of this approach suggest that Luther appropriates ideas from mysticism, and reshapes them to suit the purposes of his own theology of justification" (*Luther's Theology*, 171). In short, the similarities are more ostensible than real.

49. *Bondage of the Will*, 192.

50. E. Gordon Rupp and Philip S. Watson, eds. and trs., *Luther and Erasmus: Free Will and Salvation* (Philadelphia: Westminster, 1969), 43. Rupp translates Erasmus's *De Libero Arbitrio*, to which Luther refers as the *Diatribe* of Erasmus's full title.

51. Ibid., 65.

52. *Bondage of the Will*, 191.

53. Rupp and Watson, *Luther and Erasmus*, 55–58.

54. *Bondage of the Will*, 164.

55. Ibid., 147.

56. Ibid., 170–71.

57. Ibid., 201.

58. Ibid., 194.

59. See his essay "Coherence, Incoherence, and Christian Faith," in Robert McAfee Brown, ed., *The Essential Reinhold Niebuhr* (New Haven: Yale U P, 1986), 218–36.

60. *Bondage of the Will*, 192.

61. Ibid., 152.
62. Ibid., 203.
63. McGrath, *Luther's Theology*, 172–73.

CHAPTER THREE

1. Brown, *Essential Niebuhr*, 226.
2. Ibid., 222.
3. *Zettel*, #126.
4. See Fernand Hallyn, *The Poetic Structure of the World*, tr. Donald M. Leslie (New York: Zone, 1990), for the divergent aesthetics of Copernicus and Kepler, with the latter's cosmology characterized as "mannerist." See also Erwin Panofsky's *Albrecht Dürer* (4th ed. [Princeton: Princeton U P, 1955]), for the suggestive relations between Dürer's theory of proportions and Kepler's as Hallyn describes them, and by the way, for the impact of Luther—"the Christian man who has helped me out of great anxieties"—upon the late Dürer (198).
5. Barker, *Puritan Dilemma*, esp. 19–120.
6. As he remarks in the *Areopagitica*: "To sequester out of the world into *Atlantick* and *Eutopian* polities, which never can be drawn into use, will not mend our condition; but to ordain wisely as in this world of evil, in the midd'st whereof God hath plac't us unavoidably. . . . Suppose we could expell sin by this means; look how much we thus expell of sin, so much we expell of vertue: for the matter of them both is the same; remove that, and ye remove them both alike" (CM 4:318–20).
7. This accommodation is what Molinist and Arminian scholasticism argue by the doctrine of God's *media scientia* or "middle knowledge." See Richard A. Muller, *God, Creation, and Providence in the Thought of Jacob Arminius* (Grand Rapids, Mich.: Baker Book House, 1991), 235–68.
8. It is telling that Milton draws his figure from astronomy, suggesting the expanded contingencies of planetary movement argued by Kepler. See Hallyn, *Poetic Structure*, 163–252, on what he calls the "eurythmy" of Kepler's ellipse: "Insofar as it represent the union of contraries, the curve and the straight line, and it is interpreted by consulting two different geometries, [the ellipse] is more like the *oxymoron*—an oxymoron based, of course, on the metaphor of the curve and straight line" (215). Moreover, Kepler himself associates these contraries of curve and straight line with creator and creature, respectively, leading him to remark: "To attempt to establish an equivalence between the Creator and his Creation, God and man, divine judgment and human judgment, is almost as vain as attempting to make the curved line equal to the straight line and the circle to the square" (175).
9. Milton's version of "room" has distinct if not exact resemblances to the Arminian and Molinist doctrine of God's middle knowledge, in which deity by delimiting its active and determining goodness through covenant creates a domain of contingent order—that is, the realm of human choice to which it is responsive. Muller argues that, in Arminius's antispeculative scholasticism, "God's power over creation is bounded by the limitation of the communication of his goodness to finite things. God is, to be sure, transcendent, absolutely good, the ultimate standard of justice—but he is no longer conceived as operating at the same time within the world order and beyond its laws. The temporal order itself now measures and defines the ways of God, and the practical, morally goal-directed character of theology discerns this truth both for this life and the next" (*Jacob Arminius*, 282).

10. *Minima Moralia*, 127.

11. For Gorgias's rhetorical values, see G. M. A. Grube, *The Greek and Roman Critics* (London: Methuen, 1965), 16–19; Mario Untersteiner, *The Sophists*, tr. Kathleen Freeman (Oxford: Basil Blackwell, 1954), 196–201; George Kennedy, *The Art of Persuasion in Ancient Greece* (Princeton: Princeton U P, 1963), 66–67. For Cicero, his own *De Oratore*, *Brutus*, and *Orator* remain the best resources on his theory of expressive decorum; but see also Kennedy, *The Art of Rhetoric in the Roman World, 300 B.C.–A.D. 300* (Princeton: Princeton U P, 1972), esp. 244–52.

12. At this juncture, it is appropriate to address Milton's alleged monism, an argument William Kolbrener—himself an "epistemological monist"—excavates in Toland (*Milton's Warring Angels* [Cambridge: Cambridge U P, 1997], 114–18), but whose recent currency I believe is owing to Barker (*Puritan Dilemma*, 318ff.) and William Kerrigan (*The Sacred Complex* [Cambridge, Mass: Harvard U P, 1983], 193–262). It has received some imaginative and various restatements, most recently by Christopher Kendrick, *Milton: A Study in Ideology and Form* (London: Methuen, 1986), Stephen Fallon in *Milton among the Philosophers* (Ithaca: Cornell U P, 1991), and John Rogers in *The Matter of Revolution* (Ithaca: Cornell U P, 1996); and Stanley Fish embraces the idea in his preface to the second edition of *Surprised by Sin* (London: Macmillan, 1998). Yet like the related argument for his animist materialism, Milton's monism is premised on a surprisingly selective reading of discontinuous passages in the prose (especially the *Christian Doctrine*)—more on what one might call the logic of his apparent positions, especially his so-called heresies, as against the logic of his actual arguments. Indeed, the appealing thing about the whole trend lies in its Brunonian fascination with what we now call occult science (or theosophy), an interest shared by the seventeenth century which yet may appear more considerable than it was, since that culture did not restrict intellectual inquiry to our frequently falsifying division of knowledge by exclusive discipline—Newton of course being a fan of Joseph Mede, and Boyle's experimentalism including the practice of alchemy. But occultism did not shape the assumptions of scientific practice; on the contrary, scientific practice determined the uses of the occult. The new science recognized that nature was distinctly different from our experience of it, as against the science of the preceding centuries, which assumed a physical coordination and objective analogy between how things appear to us and what they actually are. This is the shared assumption behind magic, occult knowledge, and animistic universes, as well as their symbologies: as Freud remarks, such interpretations of our experience are instances of "the omnipotence of thought," which with the usual megalomania of human being compulsively assimilates the world to self very much as Satan does in *Paradise Lost*, without acknowledging any different order or explanation for what we see.

This acknowledgment is seminal to science's emphasis on method, which is devised specifically to negotiate between human perception and natural phenomena. Thus, in the seventeenth-century controversy over Aristotelian "occult" as against "manifest" qualities, two trends emerged: first, a scepticism or repudiation of 'manifest' qualities like color and taste, since the increasingly mathematical practice of science from Galileo on recognized a distinction between our perceptions and the structure of phenomena, or as A. R. Hall puts it, between "visual experience" and "mathematical rationality" (*The Revolution in Science 1500–1750*, 2nd ed. [London: Longman, 1983], 128). Second, what had been called "occult" qualities underwent a revolution of meaning from "unintelligible" to "imperceptible": that is, those qualities whose presence and operation are known only by their palpable effects, from which we infer their existence (see Keith Hutchison's "What Happened to Occult Qualities in the Scientific Revolution?" *Isis* 73 [1982]: 233–53). Thus the perceptual transcendence of "occult" qualities was no longer held to preclude our understanding them in some degree. Simon Shaffer has described this peculiar transition or threshold in contemporary understanding of the "occult," showing how "spirit" and mechanism coincided philosophically in any number of variations ("Occultism and Reason," in A. J. Holland, ed., *Philosophy, Its History and Historiography* [Dordrecht: Reidel, 1985], 117–43). But the shift in the word's meaning also signaled a movement away from the notion of the imperceptible as spiritual or supernatural agency, and toward the idea of its calculable and so potentially intelligible force—in other words, away from the occult as an ontological or metaphysical category, and toward its status as a formal concept with a methodological and not necessarily causal function. Newton, for example, generally regarded the force of gravity as occult in the second sense, not in the first. So Hutchinson distinguishes this new approach as markedly methodological, observing that where the Aristotelians avoided supernaturalism by arguing for an inherent "soporific virtue" or property to a drug (as against spiritual agency),

> To the moderns, by contrast, the seating of the cause of drowsiness *within* the drug was not the only alternative to supernatural causation. The action of the drug, to them, represented some special relationship between the mechanical properties of the drug and the frame of the human body, so that to locate it in the drug itself was mere nominalism, *an acceptable way of speaking, but no causal explanation.* Furthermore, even if it were true that the action of the drug was supernatural in origin, as Newton at times thought gravity might be, such nominalism allowed one to continue to speak of the action as attached to the drug, and one could study its effects exactly as one would study the effects of nonsupernatural actions, so long as they were regular.
>
> ("Occult Qualities," 252 my emphasis)

My point here is simply that seventeenth-century material or mechanistic physics resisted in their concept of impalpable agencies not only supernaturalism, as in the case of animist materialism, but also the immediate and gross ascription of physical status to secondary qualities, as in monism: "occult" properties were treated *as if* they were actual, mensurable, and physical, but theoretically at least, they were understood to have a nominal or formal existence. It is significant that, in this context, Hutchinson comments that both Luther and Calvin denied that occult qualities in the traditional understanding inhered in the sacrament, as a supernatural "virtue" or property, although they still argued the efficacy of the sacrament but not in a material or physical sense (234 n.1). I would extend that observation to Milton's heresies, which taken out of the context of his theology and poetry are the source of more than one sort of category mistake by literary critics: like the physicists, Milton understands the imperceptible as the inevident; as a scripturalist, he also argues the imperceptible to have a nominal or expressive existence, as a *way of speaking* that is peculiar to religious things; he also regards the imperceptible as a potentially intelligible reality, "occult" only in the second sense. But unlike the physicists and like the reformers, he dismisses even the tacit analogy of the imperceptible to the physical or mensurable: religious realities are of another order altogether, at the same time that they have a temporal existence and palpable effects. Such is the force of the distinction between creator and creature in Milton's theology and the force of irony in his poetry: our religious knowledge—of God, the soul, the action of providence—consists of a preeminent picture, an all-pervasive figure of speech, which is meaningful and effectual when understood in its own terms, and false and abusive when handled analogically, never mind substantively.

In everything he writes, Milton is concerned about interpretive and expressive *method*, and to that extent perfectly attuned to the epistemological concerns of the emerging sciences, which have their origin in the sceptical crisis of the sixteenth and seventeenth centuries (salutary here are Steve Shapin's and Simon Schaffer's *Leviathan and the Air-Pump: Hobbes, Boyle, and the Experience* [Princeton: Princeton U P, 1985]; Richard Kroll's *The Material Word: Literature Culture in the Restoration and Early Eighteenth Century* [Baltimore: Johns Hopkins U P, 1991]; and Shapin's *The Social History of Truth: Civility and Science in Seventeenth-Century England* [Chicago: U Chicago P, 1994]). Given the sceptical tenor of the age (in which Milton thoroughly participates), I am less sure about ontology in a British intellectual culture devoted to understanding the conditions that shape human knowledge than, say, John Rogers, who dismisses the difficult mediations of interpretive method, both in Milton's case and his own, and who does a swift injustice to historians of science who are more than conscious of the political valence of physicalist arguments (see, for example, Shapin's essay above, where he addresses the political ramifications and dangers involved in denying the existence of spiritual or supernatural entities). And without method, Rogers is unable to discriminate between what something appears to say and what it may actually mean, for all that his stated object of study is "the ideologically resonant language constitutive of physical theory itself" (x). Indeed, he proceeds to do precisely what Milton rejects when discussing the death of the body, which is to embrace "the opinion of those, who think that truth is to be sought in the schools of philosophy, rather than in the sacred writings," while Milton himself chooses to "declare freely what seems to me the true doctrine, as collected from numberless passages of Scripture" (CM 15:219). And this doctrine does not consist in an ontological but instead in a philological, largely grammatical, argument about the relation between scriptural usage and religious things like the soul, which are occult in the sense of inevident and imperceptible. It is important to recognize the obvious here: namely, that on the model of his scriptural sources, the prophets especially, Milton's so-called mortalism is intended to demythologize death—to deny death its supernatural capacity or aura and so extinguish the cult of the dead, as the realm of ghosts, demonic forces, conjurations, and the like, all of which are implicitly retained in the Roman Catholic doctrine of purgatory. Indeed, his grammatical arguments invariably work to disenchant the spirit-driven world insofar as they describe an order of *meaning* as against an order of *being*, and their sceptical and iconoclastic thrust in this regard is a far more manifest tendency in the prose writings than either monism or animist materialism. Perhaps that is why he finds his heresies much less exciting than his readers do, since he knows their origins to be literally prosaic.

But as Kolbrener makes clear in his timely and acute account of the Miltonic wars of truth, since both parties are responding in one way or other to the Whig myth and Milton as a Whig worthy, the argument for monism is inseparable from the argument for Milton's dualism (see the very different arguments of R. A. Shoaf's *Milton, Poet of Duality*, which resists dualism as such [New Haven: Yale U P, 1985]; or Regina Schwartz's "*continual struggle between oppositions*" in *Remembering and Repeating* [Cambridge: Cambridge U P, 1988], 7; or the strained negotiation between the two argued in Jason Rosenblatt's *Torah and Law in "Paradise Lost"* [Princeton: Princeton U P, 1994]). Although it is of course good suasion, a principle I myself am trying to observe, each party emphasizes a significant aspect of Milton's expression but in such a way that it tends to preclude other dimensions of meaning. Moreover, each understands these expressions in either sceptical or metaphysical terms, which get their impetus from the expectation that Milton's argument is at least ontological. That is to say, in much the manner of current theory, he is either denying or justifying human claims to truth—to the real, to being itself however understood—where truth shares the peculiar nature of Milton's God. And as Milton's God goes, so goes Milton's truth, either transcending the humanly intelligible or being thoroughly assimilated into it—to take two extremes of reconciling what appear to be conceptual contradictions in the prose (there is the middle ground of the poetry to which both sides productively gravitate). As usual in Milton studies, the interpretive conflict has produced some considerable intelligence, especially as regards the status of "the contingent" in his arguments, on which the question of Milton's "monism" or "dualism" eventually devolves: an example would be Edward Tayler's *Milton's Poetry: Its Development in Time* (Pittsburgh: Duquesne U P, 1979). Yet this conflict persists because, as Luther or Wittgenstein likes to remark, we are in the habit of importing categories and relations to a subject that does not recognize, much less satisfy, them. Whether one understands metaphysics in the Platonic or Aristotelian, Patristic or Scholastic manner, as Spinozan ontology or Cartesian epistemology, Milton declares himself uninterested in pursuing or refuting that speculative order of inquiry—the truth of the philosophical schools—which he dismisses as both impertinent to scripture and irrelevant to religion. In short, the ontological presumption is our own: along with the reformers and Arminius, Milton's concern is exegetical and moral in the best sense, having to do with the insistent perplexity of being human, a condition he believes the scriptural God uniquely elucidates and relieves. Indeed, Empson—himself thoroughly intrigued by the idea of God being "all in all"—invokes against Saurat's mystical ontologies the enduring authority of G. N. Conklin's *Biblical Criticism and Heresy in Milton*:

> [Conklin] says that Milton could not have been influenced by the *Zohar*, or by the mystics around him in the Commonwealth such as Fludd either, because he was "a Puritan, a logician, and, whatever else, assuredly no theosophist," and furthermore that it is mere justice to admit that Milton extracted his beliefs from the ancient texts of Holy Writ by scientific philological techniques, as he steadily claimed to do. Thus his crucial decision that matter was not created from nothing turned simply on an analysis of the Biblical words for *create*, chiefly but not only in Hebrew. Admittedly, this is what Milton claims in Chapter VII of *De Doctrina*, but he was accustomed to defend a position rhetorically, so as to convince other people, after arriving at it himself by a more conscientious assessment of the evidence. The philological argument here is only, and could only be, that previous uses of the word had not meant this unique concept before the attempt at expressing it was allegedly made; thus the word in the Bible does not have to mean what theologians say, and is never redefined by the Bible in a phrase or sentence as meaning that. (*Milton's God*, 141)

The philological and grammatical as against metaphysical nature of Milton's arguments is part and parcel of his very Protestant scripturalism; and we err when we approach his own text in Cabbalistic fashion, as though (in Gershom Scholem's description) its significance lay not in the discursive relations among words, but in the occulted essences or arbitrary *leitmotiven* of a palpably adversive meaning that—however marvelous—makes "no contribution to concrete exegesis" (see Scholem's *On the Kabbalah and Its Symbolism*, tr. Ralph Manheim [1965; reprint, New York: Schocken Books, 1996], 32–77, esp. 42–44). If we wish to elucidate as against manipulate them, we should do with Milton's texts as Milton does with scripture, which is simply to address the discursive and historical circumstances of what he says. For Milton's scripturalism or what she calls his " 'literary' theology," see Georgia Christopher's, *Science of the Saints*, which in my view remains the best account of that fundamental aspect of his thought, especially in its use of the reformers. But Christopher Hill's magisterial *Milton and the English Revolution* is very astute about the theology and its larger implications, as is Hugh MacCallum's *Milton and the Sons of God* (Toronto: U Toronto P, 1986), which in a single chapter gives a virtually definitive account of Milton's position in the intellectual culture of his times, separating him from precisely the presumptive proofs of his notional ontology.

Moreover, as Hill points out, "Milton's thought is dialectical: he prefers seeing unity rather than dualism. . . . [He] is always stressing the dialectical interrelation of apparent opposites" (*English Revolution*, 258). If Hill's is a Hegelian dialectic, it nonetheless seems a better fit for Milton than monism or dualism if only because it argues the nature of human history and knowledge, not being in itself. This is equally the thrust of dialectic in Marshall Grossman's insightful reading of *Paradise Lost*, expressed in terms of the religious tension between experience and truth, contingency and significance, action and character (*"Authors to Themselves": Milton and the Revelation of History* [Cambridge: Cambridge U P, 1987]). We would do well to remember, since that model of education dominated the age, that Milton like Dryden was brought up a rhetorician to whom the dialectic of expression *in utramque partem* was second nature—witness his Prolusions—and whose exegesis always enlists rhetorical criteria, as does the reformers' (for his early education, see D. L. Clarke, *Milton at St. Paul's School* [New York: Columbia U P, 1948]). Virtually every intellectual at that time knew Cicero's *De Oratore* by heart, including Bacon, Hobbes, and Boyle; and the sceptical and political impetus of Cicero's rhetorical theory militates precisely against metaphysics of the sort Milton derides in the third Prolusion's Baconian assault on Scholasticism and in the *Christian Doctrine*. In *Of Education*, Plato comes under *proairesis* and moral philosophy, and with Aristotle under rhetoric; metaphysics makes only a negative appearance, along with Scholastic logic. Indeed, the *Apology* is devoted to displaying Milton's formal or academic facility in argument as well as defending his "tart rhetoric," which significantly he justifies from the examples of Jesus, the prophets, Luther, not to mention the one true God, all of whose speech he understands rhetorically, according to the circumstances of its use. If Milton does not divorce rhetoric from theology, neither should we, as a source for his contingent or dialectical model of revelation; for Milton's God is a maker insofar as he is a speaker. Moreover, adducing proofs of Milton's monism or animist materialism from the poetry invariably results in a new sort of idolatry, treating imagery as if it were an objective, not figural, description. In chapter 6, I will discuss the passage on body and soul that Barker reads rather too easily as monism and against his own thesis, since in Milton it is the dialectic of revelation itself which allows human being its liberty: were religious and natural meanings correspondent, much less identical, we would be in the thrall of necessity, the pawns of divine determinism. I will only add here that Victoria Kahn is especially good on the conceptual significance of rhetoric for Milton's politics and poetics (*Machiavellian Rhetoric*, 169–235).

13. See Muller, *Jacob Arminius*, 60–61, in which he duly complicates the ascendant account of supralapsarianism and Reformed theology more generally, namely, as a metaphysical order of causation (although this is how Milton would seem to have taken it). Indeed, Muller argues against Brian Armstrong that recourse to the terms of Aristotelian

logic or system in Protestant scholasticism does not mean that they are used in Aristotelian fashion or to an Aristotelian purpose, not least because Augustine's innovations crucially intervene for Calvin. It is a salutary argument for those who tend to abstract such references, in the assumption that they always mean the same way, regardless of the circumstances of their use. This issue of usage would be the crux of my disagreement with the application of Patristics and especially Origen's Platonizing formulations to Milton's theology, *pace* W. B. Hunter, C. A. Patrides, and J. H. Adamson, *Bright Essence* (Salt Lake City: U Utah P, 1973): in an odd way, the very question they address—Milton's putative Arianism, as raised by Maurice Kelley—encourages them to import the terms and relations of that Patristic controversy to the *Christian Doctrine*, whose discussion of the Son more probably derives from the contemporary debate over predestination and the divine decrees in Reformed dogmatics, in which Christology plays a defining role as it incontrovertibly does in Luther (see the discussions of Calvin's Christology in both Dowey and Muller). This anachronism in turn promotes a misreading of Milton's usage and argument that ultimately leads Hunter especially to discount the treatise altogether, as expedient, misleading, and impertinent to Milton's "real" Christocentric focus in *Paradise Lost*. The same problem obtains to a lesser extent in Patrides's *Milton and the Christian Tradition* (Oxford: Clarendon, 1966), where a similar lexical thematics tends to skew the conclusions the author draws from his always impressive erudition. I would argue the danger of such atomizing correlations of term to term, which tend to bypass the larger conceptual structure which organizes the sense of any given usage, either in the Fathers or in Milton. For one thing, there is nothing Platonizing about the *Christian Doctrine*: it resists metaphysics and the sort of speculative and symbolical exegesis that approach encourages, which might account for Hunter's aversion, who appears to regard every circumstantial argument the tract makes from the scriptural text as either flimsy or opportunistic.

14. See Muller, *Christ and the Decree*, 17–38, for Calvin's insistence on the primary role of Christ as mediator, as both the second person of the Trinity and the incarnate God, in the double decree of election and redemption. In short, predestination in Calvin does not entail a speculative recourse to a *Deus nudus absconditus*, intelligibly, positively possessed of the divine attributes. Dowey gives a somewhat different, compelling account of this Christocentric focus, once again emphasizing Calvin's *ordo cognoscendi* as "the limiting and controlling factor, prohibiting the believer from trying to reconstruct and comprehend the *ordo essendi* as if he were not both finite and sinful"; as in Luther, the only God with whom the believer has to do is "the gratuitously merciful redeemer in Christ" (*Knowledge of God*, 218–20):

> If we grant, then, that the element of sinfulness plays a greater role than mere finiteness in man's inability to receive the gospel, we must, however, go on to note that human creatureliness does act as a limit also to what faith knows. Calvin is justly called "the prophet of silence before God." His zeal in exhausting every syllable of what God has made known and in constantly advancing his knowledge is exceeded only by his firmness in calling an abrupt halt before God's "secrets." Salvation, while the fact of it and some qualities of it are knowable to the mind enlightened in faith, is finally mysterious in that it rests in God's secret, eternal decrees. (180)

Dowey exceptionally attends to the character of deity as *agape*, "gratuitous love," in Calvin, which matches Luther's passionate emphasis (208–9).

15. See Kendall, *English Calvinism*, esp. 1–41, for a critical account of supralapsarianism, the pastoral crisis it provoked, and the emergence of what was called "the practical

syllogism" and a voluntarist theology in English Calvinism, which sought to combat that crisis. Jaroslav Pelikan gives a lucid and succinct account of the theological issues, quoting Dowey, in *The Christian Tradition*, vol. 4, *Reformation of Church and Dogma (1300–1700)* (Chicago: Chicago U P, 1984), 217–44.

16. See Burrell, *Unknowable God*, who argues that Aquinas distinguishes essence from *esse* in God precisely to disrupt the causal logic of this Platonic emanation scheme, and thus to allow the exercise of human judgment. As Dowey observes (and Pelikan quotes): "Calvin's doctrine of the decrees, especially the decree of reprobation, cannot by a process of extrapolation be lifted out of its context and set above the doctrines of creation and redemption without being transmuted into a rationalistic metaphysic which would then change the nature of his entire theology. This process is just what Beza and subsequent Calvinistic orthodoxy brought about" (*Knowledge of God*, 218). Muller disputes this last conclusion.

17. B. A. Gerrish, "The Reformation and the Rise of Modern Science," in *The Old Protestantism and the New* (Edinburgh: T. & T. Clark, 1982), 170–73.

18. On the profound psychology that moves the mature Luther's rejection of Scholastic synteresis (as against the faculty of conscience), see von Loewenich, *Theology of the Cross*, 52–58.

19. *The New England Mind*, 192–95.

20. *Zettel*, #144.

21. Ambrose, *Wittgenstein's Lectures*, 31.

22. Ibid., 32.

23. Luther is rejecting the vulgar version of the fourfold method, which had rigidified by the time it reached his hands. It is important to remember that the prevalence of allegorical interpretation, from the Platonist Origen on, was itself a reaction against the extreme literalism that, for example, was used to promote Arian doctrine. One must nonetheless distinguish here the mantic or oracular sense of scripture, which thoroughly discounts the historical dimension of meaning, and in varying degrees affects allegorical exegesis from Patristics through Augustine up to renaissance versions of Kabbalism. On allegorical interpretation and the fourfold method, see the articles on scriptural exegesis by G.W.H. Lampe, Jean Leclercq, and Beryl Smalley in G.W.H. Lampe, ed., *The Cambridge History of the Bible*, vol. 2, *The West from the Fathers to the Reformation* (Cambridge: Cambridge U P, 1969), 155–216; Jack B. Rogers and Donald K. McKim, *The Authority and Interpretation of the Bible* (San Francisco: Harper & Row, 1979), 3–72; and (with due qualification for the author's striking prejudices) Frederic W. Farrar, *History of Interpretation* (1886; reprint, Grand Rapids, Mich.: Baker Book House, 1961), 47–303.

24. *Unknowable God*, 23.

25. As I mentioned earlier, Bennet, *Reviving Liberty*, esp. 94–117, and Hill, *English Revolution*, 306–16, give considered attention to Milton's brand of antinomianism.

26. Although he denies its force to Protestantism, Owen Barfield comments on this head: "I think it is true to say that, just by looking back through the Greek mind, we bring to life the apprehension of form in space as an image or representation, so by looking back through the Jewish mind, we bring to life the apprehension of form in time—that is, of events themselves, as images, whether of the past or future, or of a state of mind" (*Saving the Appearances*, 2nd ed. [Middleton, Conn.: Wesleyan U P, 1988], 150–51).

27. As von Loewenich observes of Luther's ethics: "In the works faith arrives at itself. Works are the self-realization of faith" (*Theology of the Cross*, 99). See also Paul Althaus,

The Ethics of Martin Luther, tr. Robert C. Schultz (Philadelphia: Fortress, 1972): "Faith, like human life itself, never stands still but is always energetically active in the present world. Luther does not think of faith as existing in and of itself and thus separate from the activity of life; he thinks of it only in terms of the concrete acts of life in specific existential situations. . . . At every moment throughout life, faith is summoned to concrete realization. 'Works' are nothing but the concrete realization of faith itself. Faith needs works—that is, concrete, specific acts of life—in order to be itself at any point" (17). By contrast, Marcuse argues that "Doer and deed[,] person and work are torn asunder: the person as such essentially never enters into the work, can never be fulfilled in the work, eternally precedes any and every work":

> The true human subject is never the subject of *praxis*. Thereby the person is relieved to a previously unknown degree from the responsibility for his praxis, while at the same time he has become free for all types of praxis: the person secure in his inner freedom and fullness can only now really throw himself into outer praxis, for he knows that in so doing nothing can basically happen to him. And the separation of deed and doer, person and praxis, already posits the 'double morality' which, in the form of the separation of 'office' and 'person' forms one of the foundation stones of Luther's ethics. (*From Luther to Popper*, tr. Joris De Bres [London: Verso, 1983], 56–78, esp. 58)

Niebuhr makes a comparable argument to Marcuse's, deprecating in Luther's politics "the complete severance between the final experience of grace and all the proximate possibilities of liberty and justice, which must be achieved in history" (*The Nature and Destiny of Man*, vol. 2, *Human Destiny* [Louisville: Westminster John Knox P, 1964], 192–93). Not coincidentally, Niebuhr's frequent counterexample is Milton, who proves that "the sectarian conception of the relation of the gospel to social problems is right and the Reformation is wrong." Again, I would distinguish here Luther's reactionary and expedient politics (since his very survival depended on the goodwill of the German princes) from the theology whose immediate outworking took an opposed shape that scandalized its author—the rise of Anabaptism and Calvinism and to a much lesser extent (as we understand now) the Peasants War. It remains an open question whether, in this case, Luther was his own best interpreter: certainly, his insistence on artificially sustaining and enforcing the antagonism between spiritual and civil values, as somehow manifesting the necessary distinction between God and the world, is variously perverse, and that not least because it identifies evil with a singular place (the world) and condition (the bodily or "external"), creating the very dualism against which he argues elsewhere.

28. Luther refers to catachresis in another but indicative sense, as the independent analogies or illustrations the exegete draws to emphasize the force of the scriptural text: for this interpretive usage, see his 1532 commentary on Psalm 51, where he engages in just such "catachresis," remarking that "Though it is not the true meaning, it is not an ungodly meaning either" (*LW* 12:346 and n.). The care with which Luther underscores this "abuse" of meaning signals that vehement respect not only for the sacred text's semantic integrity but also its intelligibility, so conspicuous in his controversy with Erasmus. I owe to Gretchen Bohach an understanding of catachresis as Luther uses it in his tract against purgatory.

29. For Luther's comparable emphasis on charity or love, see Althaus, *Ethics*, 10–16.

30. Rush Rhees, ed., *Recollections of Wittgenstein* (1981; reprint, Oxford: Oxford U P, 1984), 111.

31. Similarly, in keeping with the grammatical-historical method of exegesis (see below n.33), Luther observes that the elevation of the bread and the cup in the Catholic mass

"is either a survival of that Hebrew rite of lifting up what was received with thanksgiving and returned to God, or else it is an admonition to us to provoke us to faith in this testament which the priest has set forth and exhibited in the words of Christ, so that now he also shows us the sign of the testament. Thus the oblation of the bread properly accompanies the demonstrative 'this' in the words, 'this is my body,' and by the sign the priest addresses us gathered about him. . . . For it is faith that the priest ought to awaken in us by this act of elevation" (*LW* 36:53). Briefly, he argues meaning as usage both historically and occasionally, as against Jesus' words understood more or less magically, as working automatically or *ex opere operato*. For the latter conception in Britain, see Keith Thomas's *Religion and the Decline of Magic* (New York: Scribner's, 1971), 25–50; Eamon Duffy's revisionist account, *The Stripping of the Altars* (New Haven: Yale U P, 1992), esp. 266–87; and of course Marcel Mauss's *General Theory of Magic*, tr. Robert Brain (London: Routledge & Kegan Paul, 1972), 60–79, which draws heavily on the work of Frazer and E. B. Tylor for its model of magical representation.

32. *Bondage of the Will*, 231.

33. In observing the grammatical-historical method, Milton's exegetical approach closely resembles Luther's, summarized in the preface to his lectures on Isaiah (see Farrar, *History of Interpretation*, 331–32):

> Two things are necessary to explain the prophet. The first is a knowledge of grammar, and this may be regarded as having the greatest weight. The second is more necessary, namely, a knowledge of the historical background, not only as an understanding of the events themselves as expressed in letters and syllables but as at the same time embracing rhetoric and dialectic, so that the figures of speech and the circumstances may be carefully heeded. Therefore, having command of the grammar in the first place, you must quickly move on to the histories, namely, what those kings under whom Isaiah prophesied did; and these matters must be carefully examined and thoroughly studied. (*LW* 16:3)

While much has been written on Milton's theological arguments—overwhelmingly on the status he gives God's Son and the Christ—less has been said about the way he educes those arguments from the sacred text, from which I argue they gain their distinctive character. My point here is to remedy that omission, critical to a scripturalist theology like Milton's, which will argue a unitary model of divine revelation encompassing not only prophecy understood as scriptural exegesis, but also prophecy understood as providential history, from creation to incarnation to the *eschaton*. For Milton, deity observes the same manner of expression in both aspects of human experience and interpretation, with his Christology methodically reflecting how he believes meaning is manifest in text and history together, and the other way round. It is also important to recognize that the "literal" sense for such scripturalists is taken as usage (simply, the force of the grammatical and historical circumstances surrounding an utterance, as Milton argues), which when referred to the hidden God—*Deus absconditus* as well as *Deus crucifixus*—is always figurative.

Thus, where Luther, say, finds the preexistent Christ in Genesis, Milton would justify that reading this way: "No passage of Scripture is to be interpreted in more than one sense; in the Old Testament, however, this sense is sometimes a compound of the historical and typical, as in Hosea xi.1. compared with Matt.ii.15. 'out of Egypt have I called my son,' which may be explained in a double sense, as referring partly to the people of Israel, and partly to Christ in his infancy" (CM 16:263). In other words, Luther's reading is justified by the ancient precedent of prophetic interpretation of text and history together, here exemplified by both Hosea and Matthew, Judaic and Christian scriptures. For prophetic usage is at once figural (yet not reductively typical), recursive, and unitary, and as Erich

Auerbach has argued (*Mimesis*, esp. 3–49), an expressive practice integral to the very creation and assembly of Jewish and Christian scriptures, evident in every contribution of the (so-called) Elohist, Deuteronomist, and Priestly writers, as each generation reconceives and revises the significance of Israel's traditions and history. Unfortunately, we tend to understand the "literal" in an impoverished fashion that not only would preclude such usage, but is itself perversely the creation of scriptural allegorizing, evinced in the fourfold method but dating back to the Stoics, Philo, and Gnosticism, whose exegesis in varying degrees discounts the authority of the text's historical order of significance in favor of the flagrantly "spiritual" (on this head, see C. K. Barrett, "The Interpretation of the Old Testament in the New," in P. R. Ackroyd and C. F. Evans, eds., *The Cambridge History of the Bible*, vol. 1, *From the Beginnings to Jerome* [Cambridge: Cambridge U P, 1970], 377–411). For the grammatical-historical method from Chrysostom to Luther and Calvin, see Jack B. Rogers and Donald K. McKim, *Interpretation of the Bible*, 16–22, 75–116. For a sense of the sheer variety of opinion on Milton's exegesis, see the arguments put forward by Georgia Christopher, *Science of the Saints*; Hugh MacCallum, *Milton and the Sons of God*; Lewalski, *Milton's Brief Epic*; Stanley Fish, "Wanting a Supplement: The Question of Interpretation in Milton's Early Prose," in David Loewenstein and James Grantham Turner, eds., *Politics, Poetics, and Hermeneutics in Milton's Prose* (Cambridge: Cambridge U P, 1990), 41–68; Mary Nyquist, "Gynesis, Genesis, Exegesis, and the Formation of Milton's Eve," in Marjorie Garber, ed., *Cannibals, Witches, and Divorce* (Baltimore: Johns Hopkins U P, 1987), 147–208; Dayton Haskin, *Milton's Burden of Interpretation* (Philadelphia: U Pennsylvania P, 1994); and Jason Rosenblatt's *Torah and Law*, among others.

34. "Oblivious" is Masson's authoritative word, whose dismay and disapproval should guard Milton's apologists from undue extenuation. While he acknowledges that the divorce tract's flagrant imbalance, especially in the second edition, is owing in part to its polemical character (Milton pursuing the man's claims in a case of "mental cruelty" because the woman's had already been admitted by Beza and Paraeus, for example), Masson feels compelled to observe "that Milton, in his tract, writes wholly from the man's point of view, and in the man's interest, with a strange oblivion of the woman's": "Man being the superior being, and therefore, with the greater capacity of being pained or injured, God had pitied him, if unhappily married, more than the woman similarly situated. For him therefore, and not for the woman, there had been provided the right of divorce! This is not positively asserted, but it seems to be implied" (*Life of Milton*, 3:42–79, esp. 76–77). For the occasion and argument of the *Doctrine* in its two editions, see also William Parker, *Milton: A Biography*, ed. Gordon Campbell, 2nd ed., 2 vols. (Oxford: Clarendon, 1996), 1:226–48; Ernest Sirluck's introduction to volume 2 of the *Complete Prose Works of John Milton*, ed. Douglas Bush et al. (New Haven: Yale U P, 1959), 137–58; and Arthur Barker, *Puritan Dilemma*, 63–74. Both Sirluck and Barker, however, make the point that the important *exegetical* argument of the divorce tracts leads directly to the *Areopagitica*.

35. *Bondage of the Will*, 231.

36. I owe this reference to Georgia Christopher's *Science of the Saints*, 68n.

37. It is instructive to compare Calvin's reading of *Ezekiel*, in which he reads the prophetic allegory very much as Milton does: that is, he construes Ezekiel's vision as expressing deity's otherwise incomprehensible intent toward the world, not as supernatural entities. Further, Calvin emphasizes the incongruity, even grotesqueness, of the visions' figures—wheels with eyes, for example—to the divine purpose of disconcerting prophet and people alike so that they will attend but equally distinguish the "likeness" from its

significance, arguing that there is rather "an analogy or likeness to be maintained between this vision and the prophet's *teaching*" (*Calvin's Old Testament Commentaries: Ezekiel 1*, tr. D. Foxgrover and D. Martin [Grand Rapids, Mich.: Eerdmans, 1994], 23, my emphasis). So he observes that "When a word is spoken about God's works, we conceive what our reason can grasp and we want to limit God in some way to our imagination," which he calls "a depraved tendency inborn in us" (38). Accordingly, Calvin underscores how Ezekiel speaks circumspectly of *likeness* alone, not identity, in the prophet's vision of an enthroned figure in the heavens:

> It is worth observing that he says *he saw the likeness of an appearance*; we gather from this that he did not actually see the heavens, that the throne was not formed of any material, and that it was not really a natural human body. The prophet expresses these things clearly to prevent anyone imagining there is anything visible in God. Some fanatics conceived God to be corporeal, and from this passage someone might ignorantly conclude that God can be seen and confined to a place—seated like a human being. Lest any of these fabrications steal into people's minds, the prophet testifies that he saw neither a human body nor a material throne; what was offered to him were these forms or appearances. . . . One might ask why God assumes human form, both in this passage (that is, in this vision) and in others similar to it. I gladly embrace the opinion of the Fathers who say that this was a prelude to that mystery which was finally made known and which Paul extols magnificently when he exclaims, "this is a great mystery, that God at last was manifest in the flesh." Jerome's view that these words are said of the Father himself is harsh. We know that the Father never was clothed in human flesh. If he said simply that God was represented here, there would be nothing absurd. Remove all mention of persons, and it will be entirely true that the human being who sat on the throne was God.
>
> At the end of the chapter the prophet also testifies to this when he says this was the likeness of God's glory. There he uses the name "Yahweh," which expresses God's eternity and fundamental essence. It would be acceptable that God is represented in his figure. But what John says in chapter 12 must be added, that when Isaiah saw God seated on his throne, he saw the glory of Christ and was speaking of him. What I have already cited from the Fathers fully agrees with this, that whenever God appeared in human form, an obscure glimpse was given of that mystery which was at last made manifest in the person of Christ. (48–50)

In other words, deity can be expressed *figuratively* by a human form, yet in the understanding that this figure is no more like God than the visionary chariot, each conveying the divine glory but not deity as such. If there is a possible analogy here, it is to the Incarnation in the person of Jesus of Nazareth and still significantly parallactic—that is to say, it does not represent the nature of the Son as preexistent Christ, who is no more humanlike than the Father is, since both are deity in Calvin's Trinitarian view.

38. William Kerrigan has written substantially—and passionately—on Milton's idea and representation of prophecy and himself as prophet, in *The Prophetic Milton* (Charlottesville: U Virginia P, 1974). My account is perhaps less positive or supernaturalist than Kerrigan's, since I argue the character of prophecy in Milton's writings as human crisis and even tragedy—the almost intolerable burden that the absolute places upon the ordinary, as the Lord did Jeremiah. Milton's description in the *Apology* of Luther's predicament and his own evokes that burden, which the preface to the second book of *The Reason of Church Government* more fully describes, as I will argue in the next chapter.

39. *Bondage of the Will*, 203.

40. *The Return of Eden* (Toronto: U Toronto P, 1965), 111.

41. Brown, *Niebuhr*, 223. Niebuhr remarks that "the Christian doctrine of selfhood means that neither the life of the individual self nor the total drama of man's existence upon earth can be conceived in strictly rational terms of coherence." (223) At the same time, he criticizes Karl Barth for translating the necessary intelligibility of these things out of history: "His signs are all explicitly eschatological. They must have something of the aura of martyrdom about them. He bids the Church to wait until the issues are clear before it bears this heroic witness, just as he himself waited in witnessing against Hitlerism until the manifest injustices of a tyrannical state revealed their clearly idolatrous religious character. This is a religion, as a Catholic critic rightly observes, which is fashioned for the catacombs, and has little relation to the task of transfiguring the natural stuff of politics by the grace and wisdom of the gospel" (231). Niebuhr's sense of the inextricability of the gospel's imperatives from "the natural stuff of politics" is not unlike Milton's.

CHAPTER FOUR

1. Rupp and Watson, *Luther and Erasmus*, 64–74; *Bondage of the Will*, 229–35.

2. Rupp and Watson, *Luther and Erasmus*, 71.

3. *Bondage of the Will*, 231.

4. Ibid., 232–33.

5. Ibid., 83.

6. Ibid., 82–83.

7. *Fragility of Goodness*, 30.

8. *Aeschylus I: Oresteia*, tr. Richmond Lattimore (Chicago: Chicago U P, 1953), 40.

9. *Fragility of Goodness*, 45.

10. Ibid., 45.

11. *Grace Abounding to the Chief of Sinners*, ed. Roger Sharrock (Oxford: Clarendon P, 1962), 40–41.

12. Ibid., xxxiii.

13. Writing of Micaiah (1 Kings 22:9ff.), Isaiah, and Ezekiel, von Rad points out that in the very accounts given of their call, the prophets are assured of their own failure: "in no sense will the prophet's work lead to deliverance; it will only hasten on the inevitable disaster" (*OTT* 2:65). For that reason, among others, von Rad argues the prophets' separation from the institutional cult of Yahweh, which would stand to their dissent not only as the religious status quo, but also in its character as ritual, as an entirely opposed order of religious expression: "Their devastatingly negative outlook on the future of their work, and the way in which, without any illusions, they faced up to its complete failure, are again a factor which compels us to look for these prophets outside the cult. For cult always implies at least a minimum of effect; it is action which has beneficial results in one way or another" (*OTT* 2:65). For the proems of *Paradise Lost*, this discrimination raises the question of their status as ritual or prophecy—that is, the extent to which we take Milton's use of epic invocation as conventional or experimental, positive or ironic, magical or iconoclastic.

14. Again, von Rad argues that the seemingly irresistible compulsion under which the prophet labors is neither ecstatic nor subjugating; rather, it attends the individual's conscious decision to speak for God, an agreement to be bound by the divine word not only professedly but also somatically, viz., the bodily dimension of prophetic call and vision in

Isaiah, Ezekiel, and Jeremiah (see von Rad's discussion of prophetic freedom, *OTT* 2:70–79). The experience of God's word, in its character as divine fiat, cannot but bring with it such a sense of compulsion since its unique force is absolutely, ineluctably real.

15. Masson, *Life of Milton*, 4:530. As Masson observes, Milton was hardly the only sufferer in this correspondence: Williams, who was the early and grateful object of Coke's patronage (the motive behind his initial contact), was deemed a "villain" by Mrs. Sadleir; and his writings on toleration, along with Jeremy Taylor's sympathetic *Liberty of Prophesying*, she consigned to the flames. Masson believes that Milton was inured by this time to such vilification; I am dubious.

16. It is perhaps not coincidental that this revision of myth is typical of Euripides, Milton's tragedian, whose gods always manifest the terrible ambivalence Nussbaum remarks, as does the rationalism that would combat them. Jacob Burckhardt comments that "Euripides at times goes so far as actually to correct myth, and thus gives proof of the 'decay of mythical understanding.' This occurs for instance in the polemic against Aeschylus that he introduces into his *Electra* (508ff.); and in the same play the chorus of Argive women are made to explain quite openly (737ff.) that they themselves do not believe the story that Zeus, after the feast of Thyestes, altered the courses of the sun and stars—'but these tales of terror are salutary, because they heighten the glory of the heavenly powers'—which is as much as to say that such beliefs were good enough for the common people" (*The Greeks and Greek Civilization*, ed. Oswyn Murray, tr. Sheila Stern [New York: St. Martin's, 1998], 271). The example itself is interesting for what it says about Milton's sceptical affinity with Euripides, as well as the shift in sublunary phenomena after humanity's fall, which the Father ordains to illustrate the changed relation between divine and human, but also to parody Adam's slide into superstition.

17. *Milton's Epic and the Book of Psalms* (Princeton: Princeton U P, 1989).

18. "Milton and his Paraphrases of the Psalms," *Philological Quarterly* 4 (1925): 364–72.

19. *Epic and Psalms*, 138–48. This is of course the more usual way of understanding the proems, namely, as successful invocations precipitating the poet's/speaker's divine inspiration (signaled especially by the imagery of light) and the transcendence of his corrupt nature. See, for example, Anne Ferry's sensitive discussion of "the blind bard" in *Milton's Epic Voice* (1963; reprint, Chicago: U Chicago P, 1983), who herself invokes the language of the *Second Defense* and the instance of the man born blind but concludes in the indicative mood: "This is the light of divine inspiration shining within the purified heart of the blind bard, the light which is granted to him as fallen man when he prays for divine illumination to purge the mists obscuring his vision. It is a steadier light than the changing light of nature and it enables the blind bard to see beyond the colors and surfaces of things. It is a celestial not a mortal light" (33). In a more subjunctive and sublime mood, William Kerrigan gives an eloquently symbolic because psychoanalytical account of the speaker's/ Milton's lived paradox of sight in blindness, and the prophetic light (largely of the Romantic kind) that permits the poet an otherwise impossible originality, eventually identifying that light as *"the energy of wish-fulfillment unconditioned by a prior moment of satisfaction"*: "If Milton has this light within him as he illustrates and justifies its ways in a particular future, he would have access to the indefinite potential of an absolute origin, freed of the burden of anteriority in a radical sense: his would be the creative will that founds rather than repeats" (*The Sacred Complex*, 127–57, esp. 157). I obviously see a more conflicted and less majestic speaker, the voice of the psalms—what Claus Westermann calls "finite" humanity forever caught between time and desire (see below n.21).

20. Ibid., 65–75.

21. *Praise and Lament in the Psalms*, tr. Keith R. Crim and Richard N. Soulen (Atlanta: John Knox P, 1985), 263.

22. Ibid., 193–94.

23. Ibid., 268.

24. Ibid., 270–71.

25. To reiterate a point implicit in my discussion of Jeremiah: in the prophets, von Rad argues, "we are shown men who have become persons because God has addressed them and they have had to make a decision in his presence" (*OTT* 2:76). It is indicative that this novel predicament of individuality—or "personality"—entailed a significant formal innovation: namely, the use of the first person singular in a manner distinct from its collective and generalized use in cultic liturgy, since this "I" was profoundly particular and so deviant, articulating the historical circumstances of each person's call:

> The men who speak to us in these accounts were men who had been expressly called upon to abandon the fixed orders of religion which the majority of the people still considered valid—a tremendous step for a man of the ancient east to take—and because of it the prophets in their new and completely unprecedented situation, were faced with the need to justify themselves both in their own and in other people's eyes. The event of which the prophet tells burdened him with a commission, with knowledge and responsibility which placed him in complete isolation before God. It forced him to justify his exceptional status in the eyes of the majority. (*OTT* 2:54–55)

Inevitably, the self-justification that the prophet's dissent demands becomes a justification of the God whose vehement word is spoken, since the religious indecorum, even outrageousness of this species of exceptionalism can only be legitimated by the cultic deity itself. As von Rad says of Jeremiah, the novel liberty of his position allowed him to observe "a unique obedience, and yet it occasionally led him almost to the verge of blasphemy" (*OTT* 2:71–72). Accordingly, the account of the prophet's call—itself a poetic innovation—evokes such authority by claiming the equally exceptional behavior of God, who, rejecting the institutional means of religious expression, arbitrarily gives divine vision and speech to the individual then made dangerously singular, as it were, by that sudden, inscrutable intimacy:

> This was more than simply a new profession: it was a totally new way of life, even at the sociological level, to the extent that a call meant relinquishing normal social life and all the social and economic securities which this offered, and changing over instead to a condition where a man had nothing to depend upon, or, as we may put it, to a condition of dependence upon Jahweh and upon that security alone. "I do not sit blithely in the company of the merrymakers. Because thy hand is upon me, I sit alone; for thou hast filled me with indignation" (Jer.xv.17). (*OTT* 2:58)

And along with this seemingly perverse revolution in life and idea goes an expressive revolution, a liberty to experiment with the received forms of religious speech, whose results von Rad calls "perfectly daring": outrageous God, outrageous individuality, outrageous speech (*OTT* 2:76). Milton would seem to make a similar linkage between the religious predicament of his speakers and their indubitably experimental expressions, as here in the sonnet "When I consider how my light is spent"—a relation that strikingly reinvigorates the personality of the conventional lyric ego, while yet sustaining the artistic and ironic distinction between the speaker and himself.

26. This is hardly my discovery: it dates back to the undergraduate Milton course I took from Christopher Grose, to whom this book is dedicated and whose observations have become second nature to me and as it were sealed my fate. I can only recommend that the interested reader consult his *Milton's Epic Process* (New Haven: Yale U P, 1973), and *Milton and the Sense of Tradition* (New Haven: Yale U P, 1988).

27. On this head, it is significant for Milton's poetry that von Rad resists the ecstatic reading of prophetic vision, precisely because biblical prophecy entails the assertion, not the dissolution of personality: "when, in a way hitherto unknown in Israel and in the entire ancient east, the individual with his responsibility and power to make decisions came in prophecy to occupy the centre of the stage—one might almost say when the individual was discovered—it was only to be expected that it would be precisely in the event of the prophet's reception of revelation that this new factor would be apparent" (OTT 2:61). But because the prophet's unique knowledge remains historical, individual revelation does not mean idealist transcendence of self and its circumstances either:

> The purpose of the vision was not to impart knowledge of higher worlds. It was intended to open the prophet's eyes to coming events which were not only of a spiritual sort, but were also to be concrete realities in the objective world. Contrary to popular misconception, the prophets were not concerned with the being of God, but with future events which were about to occur in space and time—indeed, in Israel's own immediate surroundings. Yet even to the theologian this massive concentration upon historical events, as also the complete absence of any sort of "speculative" inclinations even in those visions where Jahweh is seen in person, must be a source of constant wonder. For example, Amos says that he saw Jahweh holding a plumb-line to a wall. But when Jahweh asked him what he saw, his answer was "a plumb-line" (Am.vii.7f.)! Again, in his fifth vision, where he sees Jahweh standing upon the altar, he shows an astonishing lack of interest in what Jahweh looked like (Am.ix.1). The same is also true of Isaiah's great throne vision (Is.vi). The first prophet to attempt anything like a detailed picture of the "glory of Jahweh" as it broke upon him from the realm of the transcendent at his call is Ezekiel. And yet how circumspect he too is as he describes what he perceived above the throne and "what was like as it were a human form" (Ezek.I.26ff.). (OTT 2:59)

It is not deity per se but the relation between God and the world, as it bears on the predicament of humanity, which consumes the prophets, as it does Milton's justification in *Paradise Lost*.

28. The locus classicus, so to speak, for the satanic "assault" of *Anfechtung* comes in Luther's 1535 lectures on Galatians, a description which speaks volumes here:

> But such is human weakness and misery that in the terrors of conscience and in the danger of death we look at nothing except our own works, our worthiness, and the Law. . . . Thus human reason cannot refrain from looking at active righteousness, that is, its own righteousness; nor can it shift its gaze to passive, that is, Christian righteousness, but it simply rests in the active righteousness. So deeply is this evil rooted in us, and so completely have we acquired this unhappy habit! Taking advantage of the weakness of our nature, Satan increases and aggravates these thoughts in us. Then it is impossible for the conscience to avoid being more seriously troubled, confounded, and frightened. For it is impossible for the human mind to conceive any comfort of itself, or to look only at grace amid its consciousness and terror of sin, or consistently to reject all discussion of works. To do this is beyond human power and

thought. Indeed, it is even beyond the Law of God. For although the Law is the best of all things in the world, it still cannot bring peace to a terrified conscience but makes it even sadder and drives it to despair. For by the Law sin becomes exceedingly sinful (Rom. 7:13). (*LW* 26:5)

29. Helen Darbishire, *Early Lives*, 291.

30. See Parker, *Milton*, 1:567–77; Masson, *Life of Milton*, 6:162–95.

31. Masson, *Life of Milton*, 6:628.

32. See ibid., 6:629–32, for Masson's evaluation of the two stories Richardson tells, including the remark attributed to Dryden (Darbishire, *Early Lives*, 295–96).

33. Ibid., 6:636.

34. Frank Allen Patterson, ed., *The Student's Milton*, rev. ed. (New York: Appleton-Century-Crofts, 1961), liii. Patterson points out that these lines (scarcely Dryden's best) were engraved without attribution beneath Milton's portrait in Tonson's edition.

35. Masson, *Life of Milton*, 6:752.

36. At this juncture, it seems significant to cite the marginalia Richardson quotes from a copy of *Eikonoklastes*, apparently written after the Restoration and while Milton was still alive (Darbishire, *Lives*, 276; Masson, *Life of Milton*, 6:717):

"Upon *John Milton's* not Suffering for His Traiterous Book
"when the Tryers were Executed 1660.
　　　"That thou Escapd'st that Vengeance which o'ertook,
"*Milton*, thy Regicides, and thy Own Book,
"was Clemency in *Charles* beyond compare,
"And yet thy Doom doth prove more Grevious farr.
"Old, Sickly, Poor, Stark Blind, thou Writ'st for Bread,
"So for to Live thou'dst call *Salmasius* from the Dead.

As Masson observes, while not "sunk into anything like destitution," Milton "was now, with all his new celebrity, as the author of *Paradise Lost*, *Paradise Regained*, and *Samson Agonistes*, a much poorer man than he had ever been before" and—it would appear—still infamous (*Life of Milton*, 6:718). For further vilifications contemporary with this one, see Parker, *Milton*, 1:568–71, who also suggests that, among the arguments made on his behalf in Parliament, was the one Milton himself vocally abhorred: that God had already punished him, with blindness. Parker has also collected in his *Milton's Contemporary Reputation* such classics of anti-Miltonism as *The Censure of the Rota upon Milton's Book* (1660) and Sir Roger L'Estrange's *No Blinde Guides* (1660) (1940; reprint, New York: Haskell House, 1971).

37. This is a comment that Aubrey makes: "He was visited much [by learned men]: more then he did desire" (Darbishire, *Early Lives*, 6). See also Masson, *Life of Milton*, 6:636–38.

38. *Lives of the Poets*, 1:102. The account of this treatment appears in Edward Phillips's biography; for analysis of that account, see Masson, *Life of Milton*, 6:446–49, and Parker, *Milton*, 1:585–86. Neither Masson nor Parker grants the story unqualified force, since neither loathes Milton as Dr. Johnson does.

39. *Permanence and Change*, 69–124, 91.

40. Ibid., 69.

41. *This New Yet Unapproachable America* (Albuquerque, N.M.: Living Batch P, 1989), 46–47.

42. Ibid., 44.

43. On this appropriation of Milton by Thoreau, Emerson, and Melville, see Robin Grey, *The Complicity of Imagination* (Cambridge: Cambridge U P, 1997), and more generally, K. P. Van Anglen, *The New England Milton* (University Park, Penn.: Pennsylvania State U P, 1993).

44. See his *Poetic Authority: Spenser, Milton, and Literary History* (New York: Columbia U P, 1983), which makes a comparable argument about the contingency or historical "accommodation" of Milton's truth but from a different methodical angle.

45. *Lives of the Poets,* 1:121.

46. Ibid., 1:98.

47. Remarking how biblical lament entails two orders of complaint against God—in early lament, that his present actions contradict his past, that is, the problem of absurdity; in the psalms proper, that he is remote or absent—Westermann puts the speaker's predicament this way: "For the lamenter it is not merely the isolated 'I' that is threatened by the power of death which one experiences in suffering; threatened as well is one's standing in the community; that is, what one means to others and what they mean to him. But also threatened is one's relationship with God and with it the meaning of life. This is what the 'Why?' of the complaint against God is all about" (*Praise and Lament,* 268). Because of the conceptual profundity of suffering evinced in the Judaic scriptures, Westermann refuses to subsume lament under petition, insisting on its generic integrity and, moreover, its connection with prophetic accusation. At the same time, he sees in the account of suffering "a movement towards God," with Job as its epitome:

> [Job] knows that his suffering is not punishment and that he can now no longer understand God. Forced into extreme isolation by friends who profess to speak in God's name, Job can do nothing but continue to hold on to a God he no longer understands. His lament is the language of one who clings to an incomprehensible God. . . . It is the bitter complaint of one who despairs, who has no one else to whom he can turn. He clings to God against God. . . . Doubt about God, even the kind of despair that can no longer understand God, receives in the lament a language that binds it to God, even as it accuses him. (273)

This analysis, I think, captures the speaker's vexed predicament in the proems of *Paradise Lost,* but it also attests once again to the force of Luther's *facere Deum:* in speaking to God, even in accusing him, we yet acknowledge and assert God in a tacit profession of faith. But if the psalmist's speech to God implicates a refusal to deny deity, it does not express assurance in that relationship; assurance waits instead upon a response to the enigma of suffering—what Westermann calls "the power of death at work within life"— which only deity can give (275). And that response for the speaker of Milton's poem consists in the tale that, despite his apprehension, he continues to tell.

48. It is appropriate here to reflect briefly on the symbolic force of such images, given the circumstances of their use. Both Michael Leib (*The Poetics of the Holy* [Chapel Hill: U North Carolina P, 1981]) and William Kerrigan (*The Sacred Complex*) have captured the iconic—both religious and psychodynamic—resonance of this language, which contributes an important dimension of the proems' meaning. Yet the circumstantial or rhetorical sense which Milton ascribes to scriptural statement argues that no single image can transcend the particular occasion of its use, or the peculiar attitude of its user, which is of course to challenge its semantic independence or generalization as symbol. We should think here about Milton's treatment of the Eucharist and the restricted force, neither magical nor symbolic, that he allows Christ's words of institution and sacramental signs

more largely. If we bring this hermeneutical caveat to the speaker's expressions—as Milton himself arguably does with *Lycidas* by adding the epigraph's last line in 1645 and abruptly shifting the poem's ostensible focus from pastoral elegy to prophetic satire—we are similarly constrained to acknowledge their contingent status (for such an approach to *Lycidas*, see my " 'Lycidas' and the Grammar of Revelation," *ELH* 58 [1991]: 779–808). By virtue of the speaker's predicament, the force of "light" in the proems becomes more dubious than real, and accordingly no argument for his or their supernaturalized or transcendent agency and authority. It seems to me that symbologies and thematic studies less nuanced and particular than Leib's or Kerrigan's tend to ignore those dramatic and methodical valences which Milton would regard as crucial, and which complicate the overt sense of any image. On this head, there is Stanley Fish's still more radical reading of the *Areopagitica* as self-consuming artifact, whose "lesson," he avers, is "that truth is not the property of any external form, even of a form that proclaims this very truth" ("Driving from the Letter: Truth and Indeterminacy in Milton's *Areopagitica*," in Mary Nyquist and Margaret W. Ferguson, eds., *Re-Membering Milton* [New York: Methuen, 1988], 234–54, esp. 243).

49. As Harold Bloom has told us, artistic imitation implicates artistic rivalry and resistance, which can here enforce the ironic distinction between speaker and poet insofar as that aspiration is made an index, as I believe it is here, of the speaker's religious state. But supercession of one's model can be its own reward: an instance would be Canto XXV of the *Inferno*, where the pilgrim proclaims the superior marvel of the metamorphosis he witnesses (over Lucan's imagery and Ovid's), and tacitly the superior ingenuity of the poet who composed it (94–102). Indeed, with Satan's serpentine metamorphosis, Georgia Christopher suggests that Milton seeks to supercede this very episode in Dante (*Science of the Saints*, 87).

50. Keeping in mind that he is distinct from *his* creator, it is well to remember that the speaker not only evokes the extraordinary achievements of these blind worthies but also, as with Bellerophon's madness and sometime death, their mythic tragedies which significantly occur at the hands of jealous gods. In each case, glory goes hand in hand with hubris and suffering; tragic contradiction attends them all (including, in one tradition, Homer). There is more trepidation, more fear and offense, in such allusions than may meet the eye.

51. Speaking of that first sight of Adam and Eve in Book Four, Summers remarks that
It is not only modern ideas of the equality of the sexes which may make this passage difficult for us; the democratic assumption that ideally every individual *should* be self-sufficient and our tendency to define "perfection" as eternal self-sufficiency complicate our difficulties further. But from the beginning of the poem Milton has done everything possible to make us realize that within his universe nothing is self-sufficient and immutable except God; that life is conceived as action and process rather than as static being; that any action or quality achieves value for good or evil only by means of its relationship to an all-embracing order which proceeds from God; and that "perfection" for a creature possessed of free will must mean that the individual is created properly for his role, "perfect" within his context and capable of the continuance of his relationships in time. (*The Muse's Method* [1962; reprint, Binghamton, N.Y.: Center for Medieval and Early Renaissance Studies, 1981], 95–96.

52. *Milton's Grand Style* (Oxford: Oxford U P, 1963), 69–72.

53. With no little difficulty, however. See, for example, Fish's acute argument about the dangers of causal thinking in *Paradise Lost* (with reference to Frye's impressive insight

which I cite in the following chapter). He says that we, along with the speaker, must resist such reasoning, even as he confesses that "The strain is considerable" (*Surprised by Sin*, 234–35).

CHAPTER FIVE

1. *Grand Style*, 18–19.
2. *Milton* (New York: Norton, 1966), 184.
3. I quote Pope's witticism from Irene Samuel's "The Dialogue in Heaven: A Reconsideration of *Paradise Lost*, III, 1–417," in Arthur Barker, *Modern Essays*, 233–45, esp. 233.
4. Responding to the disagreement between Addison and Dr. Johnson as to the merits of Miltonic decorum, Joseph Summers is particularly insightful about the motives of allegory in *Paradise Lost*:

> For a poet who rejected the opposition of matter against spirit, "the real and the sensible" against the intellectual and divine, such ambiguity was not a matter of intellectual confusion but for rejoicing. The poet was free to give all the physical particularity that he desired to his divine or satanic or abstract personages, but it was no part of his aim to lull the reader into a fictional identification of *this* reality with the material reality of everyday life. He wished to stimulate, develop, and then block the physical imagination. He used and then "broke" allegory. If the poem was to convey an image of reality as he believed it to exist, both in the universe and in any individual's experience, there could be no choice of a single naturalistic, or intellectual, or even symbolic vision. His reality was manifested in movement and in time, and the reader must perceive it through continual shifts in imagination and intellectual perspectives; for that, the mind *must* be shocked. (*Muse's Method*, 40–41)

Thomas Kranidas discusses declamation's use of *prosopopoia* to teach the expressive decorum behind the ethical appeal and characterization more largely; as compared with the conceptual sophistication Aristotle and Cicero brought to *ethopoeia*, he calls it "a mechanical and arid regularity" (*The Fierce Equation: A Study of Milton's Decorum* [The Hague: Mouton, 1965], 24). One cannot but feel that Milton, whose initial rhetorical education followed declamation's model, makes this formulaic sterility of *prosopopoeia* a reflexive meaning of Sin and Death and every other abstract personification in the poem—a cognate expression of that mentality he calls the law. In the matter of its ever exfoliating literary mode, Barbara Lewalski has brought her considerable scholarship to bear on the generic "encyclopedia" of *Paradise Lost*, where she argues persuasively that these generic shifts "present and promote complex and rigorous moral discriminations" (*"Paradise Lost" and the Rhetoric of Literary Forms* [Princeton: Princeton U P, 1985], 19).
5. On the conceptual impact of Sin and Death, as enacting both "the theological indifference of rhetorical figures which is a condition of correct interpretation and free will," and "the narrator's view that distance and division are not simply a consequence of the fall but are the structural conditions of prelapsarian experience," see Victoria Kahn's "Allegory, the Sublime, and the Rhetoric of Things Indifferent in *Paradise Lost*," in David Quint et al., eds., *Creative Imitation: New Essays on Renaissance Literature in Honor of Thomas M. Greene* (Binghamton: Center for Medieval and Early Renaissance Studies, SUNY Binghamton, 1992), 127–152. *Pace* Fish, she observes that this latitude or contingency of meaning, argued by the doctrine of things indifferent, offers a "theological equivalent of human rhetoric *in utramque partem*" (130–31).

6. *The Grotesque in Art and Literature* (1963; reprint, New York: McGraw-Hill, 1966), 179–89.

7. It is this figural sense of the law that Jason Rosenblatt (*Torah and Law*) does not understand in Paul or Milton's usage. I would certainly not disagree that Milton upholds the moral law, which he distinguishes from ritual observance, but that he upholds it as "Hebraic monism" against the putative "dualism" of a Hellenizing Paul I sincerely doubt. For one thing, Rosenblatt and Paul are not talking about the same thing or in the same way: in his own indicatively literal reading, Rosenblatt understands the law in Pauline usage as consistently referring to the Mosaic religious code, while Paul understands it to signify a religious mentality and way of reading the scriptural text which expounds that code. There is no conflict for Milton here, since he attacks the mentality and the reading, not the moral code, which is why one can enter Milton's heaven without knowledge of the Christ: what one must have is the understanding of divine revelation that not only Jesus but also (in Milton's view) the whole of scripture teaches, a reading that acknowledges the distinction between deity and its expressions. The same concept informs Luther's usage and both theologians follow Paul, who in his conflict with a conservative element in Galatia and Jerusalem challenges the argument that one must ritually become a Jew and be circumcised before one is properly a Christian. In that episode from Acts, which Milton in the *Areopagitica* adduces against the exclusive formalism of the Presbyterian censors (CM 4:308–9), a vacillating Peter is himself brought to relinquish—temporarily—the primacy and exclusivity of ritual forms: having dreamt that God thrice commands him to break the dietary laws, Peter admits the first gentile to the church, allowing that faith in God can exist where there is no observance of the ritual law (Acts 10–11). This distinction is the one Paul makes between the mentality of the gospel and the mentality of the law in Romans and Galatians, and it is the one Jesus (Matthew 9:13 and 12:1–8) draws between mercy and sacrifice after Hosea 6:6: "For I desire steadfast love and not sacrifice, / the knowledge of God, rather than burnt offerings." To recall the words of Samuel to Saul: "Has the LORD as great delight in burnt offerings and sacrifices, / as in obeying the voice of the Lord? / Behold, to obey is better than sacrifice, / and to hearken than the fat of rams" (1 Samuel 15:22). Taking Jesus as one, all three prophets (in the seventeenth-century sense of interpreters) exalt the attitude of heartfelt fidelity and obedience to the divine word over the ritual practice Samuel calls "divination" and "idolatry," where religious forms become an end in themselves and a magical placation of God (1 Samuel 15:23). This preference expresses something of what von Rad calls the "Deuteronomic picture of man, that is, of a man whose heart is perfect with Jahweh and who keeps Jahweh's statues and commandments with his whole heart" (*OTT* 1:345). But it is more truly typical of the psalmic, prophetic, and wisdom literature in the age of Israel's decline and exile, which raised with a new and terrible force the problem of human righteousness before God, and with it the question of religious practice. It is in these circumstances, von Rad explains, that Ezekiel "shatters the now rotten collectivism [of the cult], because it had become a comfortable refuge behind which people could hide from Jahweh. The prophet drags the individual out of this anonymity into the light and destroys every hidden security and false righteousness. If a man cannot rely on his own righteousness, so as to hide himself behind it from Jahweh, how much less can he rely on the righteousness of others" (*OTT* 1:394). In short, with the physical destruction of temple and nation, not only the collective performance of religious ordinance but also religious performance itself became an issue of fearful salience, attended by what von Rad describes as "the spiritualisation of many cultic ideas":

People talked of the circumcision of the heart, of praise as sacrifice, of prayer as incense, of God as the refuge of the soul of the pure in heart, etc.:

> Let my prayer be as incense,
> The lifting up of my hands as an evening sacrifice.
>
> (Ps. CXLI.2)

But these spiritualisations are only part of a very far-reaching process, namely, the intrusion of rational thinking into the patriarchal cultic world, of which we already got an idea in the theologising of the cult in Deuteronomy. These spiritualisations also make plain the way in which later Israel, *helped by its interpretive way of thinking*, laid hands upon the rites, in order once again to appropriate the world of the cult to itself in a living way. *Only here, therefore, did the question as to the "meaning" of the cultic usages become acute.* (OTT 1:396; my emphasis)

What Rosenblatt reduces prejudicially to a "typological" evisceration of the real by Pauline Christianity is an interpretive emphasis and expressive order demonstrably under way in Deuteronomy, undergoing an extraordinary development well through the prophets, to become the peculiar inheritance of the gospel Jesus for whom they serve as a regular proof text:

> Then Pharisees and scribes came to Jesus from Jerusalem and said, "Why do your disciples transgress the tradition of the elders? For they do not wash their hands when they eat." He answered them, "And why do you transgress the commandment of God for the sake of your tradition? For God commanded, 'Honor your father and your mother,' and, 'He who speaks evil of father or mother, let him surely die.' But you say, 'If any one tells his father or his mother, What you would have gained from me is given to God, he need not honor his father.' So, for the sake of your tradition, you have made void the word of God. You hypocrites! Well did Isaiah prophesy of you, when he said:
>
> > 'This people honors me with their lips,
> > but their heart is far from me;
> > in vain do they worship me,
> > teaching as doctrines the precepts of men.' "
> >
> > (Matthew 15:1–9)

In his distinction between law and gospel, Paul builds on this critical reconception of religious value and practice in Judaism. As for the extent of his Hellenizing (as compared, say, to the Johannine gospel), it has been the subject of decades of controversy, of a kind not unlike that Milton generates, and it is always worthy of further inquiry beyond the one study Rosenblatt cites on Paul. Indeed, from what I can tell, his Paul is really Augustine in disguise, who happily declares his Platonism in the *Confessions*; and since Milton was not much of an Augustinian nor—as I have argued—an allegorist in Augustine's fashion, he is unlikely to subscribe to the Augustinian argument Rosenblatt places in Paul's mouth. It is equally arguable whether either Paul's or Milton's typologies necessarily have the sort of sublimating, antipathetic and ahistorical effect for which Rosenblatt contends: Erich Auerbach, whose close and patient analysis of this subject remains incomparable in my view, demonstrates that figural expression, rather than abstracting, can invest the most profound value in the creatural and historical, even as naturalism can grow schematic and literalism empty and coercive. Milton himself dedicates *The Reason of Church Government* to making the latter point against the episcopal party, which he does in all the 1640s tracts whose exegetical argument Rosenblatt neglects. For more sophisticated discussions of Milton's typology than William Madsen's seminal argument, see Michael Fixler, Marshall Grossman, and Edward Tayler, who argue the historical integrity of type and antitype. Barbara Lewalski gives a balanced overview of typology's contemporary poetic uses, in *Protestant Poetics and the Seventeenth-Century Religious Lyric* ([Princeton: Princeton U P, 1979], esp. 111–44). I readily accept Hebraic influence on Milton, whose Protestant scripturalism ensures but also qualifies it, as did Selden's and Grotius's. Yet the prevailing tendency baldly to typify Plato and Paul, and indeed Christian theology more largely, does an injustice to the irreducible complexity of these writings, and in no way serves our understanding of Milton or the culture in which he wrote—a salutary reminder that I must be more careful in my treatment of Augustine, who yet stands behind both Luther and Calvin.

8. This order of signification also explains why "New *Presbyter* is but old *Priest* writ large" in Milton's sonnet "On the New Forcers of Conscience under the Long Parliament" (*LM* 14). As John Carey explains, Milton selects the Jewish ritual of phylacteries to express what he regards as the twin Presbyterian perversions of exegetical literalism and doctrinal coercion, in which the arbitrary enforcement of the letter brands the spirit as heretical, with the good called bad and the bad good in the manner of Luther's theologian of glory: "Men whose life, learning, faith and pure intent / Would have been held in high esteem with Paul / Must now be named and printed heretics" (*LM* 9–11). On this head, Carey refers to D. C. Dorian's thesis of a double reference for the phrase "baulk your ears": it is a topical allusion to Prynne's ears, twice mutilated for sedition under Laud and Charles I; but theologically, it may ascribe to the Presbyterians something like the Levitical prohibition against physical disfigurement in priests (Leviticus 21.17–23). For these "new forcers of conscience" in Milton's view equally exalt superficies over truth, human dogmas over divine meanings, conformity over faith. So after the fashion of the antiprelatical pamphlets, Milton's satire is once more directed against a religious mentality informing royalist and Presbyterian parties alike, entirely given over to the coercive rule of semblance and custom. And in the sensational example made of Prynne, that mentality indulges in something worse than verbal violence—the penal decorum which reciprocates heresy in opinion with disfigurement of the body, which is made to symbolize the consequences of dissent.

9. *Milton's God*, esp. 91–146.

10. *Return of Eden*, 99–101.

11. Ibid., 111.

12. *English Revolution*, 242–45.

13. It is essential to quote Empson's clinching comparison of the Father to the antics of latter-day dictators: "The picture of God in the poem, including perhaps even the high moments when he speaks at the end, is astonishingly like Uncle Joe Stalin; the same patience under an appearance of roughness, the same flashes of joviality, the same thorough unscrupulousness, the same real bad temper. It seems little use to puzzle ourselves whether Milton realized he was producing this effect, because it would follow in any case from what he had set himself to do" (*Milton's God*, 146).

14. To reiterate, Milton writes: "Let us then discard reason in sacred matters, and follow the doctrine of Holy Scripture exclusively. Accordingly, no one need expect that I should here premise a long metaphysical discussion and advocate in all its parts the drama of the personalities in the Godhead: since it is most evident, in the first place, from numberless passages of Scripture, that there is in reality but one true independent and supreme God [*Nos itaque in sacris rationi renuntiemus; quod divina scriptura docet, id unice sequamur. expectet igitur nemo dum hic longum ex metaphysicis apparatum praemittam, et personalitatum illud*

totum drama advocem, cum hoc primum ex plurimis sacrae scripturae locis clarrissimum sit, unum esse vere ac proprie atque a seipso summum Deum]" (CM 14:196–97). Those who seek metaphysical or ontological theses in the *Christian Doctrine* tend to disregard methodological qualifications like this—indeed, to ignore its integral order of statement even as the supralapsarians did with the *Institutes*—not least because they are focusing on singular passages, to the detriment of Milton's unitary argument. When Milton distinguishes the Son from God as being deity by imputation only, not substantially, and this succeeding his assertion that "both in the literal and figurative description of God, he is exhibited not as he really is, but in such a manner as may be within the scope of our comprehensions" [*Deum, non qualis in se est, sed qualem nos capere possumus, talem semper vel describi vel adumbrari*]," it follows that whatever scholastic phraseology Milton uses subsequently about deity can be read only as a way of speaking about the scriptural picture of God and scarcely as an analysis of deity per se (CM 14:31). It is interesting to remark how the figurative language of *Paradise Lost* itself is adduced in such enterprises, as though it were intended as a literal or a logical account of the real. Misconceiving the nature of Milton's justification may be the source of this practice; but it is also true that thematic readings tend to bestow primary status on epiphenomena. Even Maurice Kelley's otherwise salutary annotations to the Yale edition can conspire to encourage this interpretive fallacy—that Milton (and every theologian) uses scholastic terms in the same way. No theologian would agree.

15. Anne Ferry is quite wonderful on the satanic proclivity for allegory, arguing that Satan himself is finally a personification "because he no longer belongs to the world in which physical forms have reality and meaning," the logical outcome of what she regards as his degenerative disease of dissociation and abstraction (*Epic Voice*, 116–46). Although we both remark the phenomenon of abstract personification, she sees that effect as allegory's attenuation of the real, while I would argue that what we are seeing in Satan is rather a perverse hypostasis of meaning simultaneous with his engrossing substance: that is to say, its reification as against its incarnation, which fails to observe the ironic discrepancy between the evident sense of an image and its significance. In short, Ferry subscribes to the received opposition between metaphor or symbol on the one hand and allegory on the other, restricting Milton's use of incongruity or ironic discrepancy to a satire of the apostate, while preserving the "otherwise antiallegorical style of his epic" and what she regards as the enlightened metaphorics of the speaker: "[Milton] chose consistently to limit his allegory to parts of the poem relating only to fallen experience, and this choice is in keeping with the traditional notion that allegory is one means of accommodating truth to the limited and darkened minds of men" (131).

16. For that reason, I would have to say, that Stephen Fallon is of the devil's party without knowing it, since he takes the worlds of *Paradise Lost* to mean pretty much as Satan thinks they do. See his intriguing chapter on the allegory of Sin and Death in *Milton among the Philosophers*, 168–93, in which he banishes the merely figural from Milton's poem with these words: "Mediated truth is rejected in favor of direct truth. Even when using allegory, Milton guards the literal veracity of his poem." (183) Again, I think the argument for monism licenses a peculiar literality in reading Milton, which by complicated means turns the justification of *Paradise Lost* into a simple account of "the real," itself hypostasizing the sense of the poet's words.

17. Taking Satan and his legions as themselves an object on view, Georgia Christopher comments on the comic incongruity created by their supine position on hell's burning lake and their vaunting aspirations—"between defiant rhetoric and compliant posture, as well as the absurdity of heroic figures planning an attack while flat on their backs" (*Science*

of the Saints, 80). This indecorum, typical of Milton's hell, is itself significant of satanic anomy: that is, their unconscious divorce from epic's naturalized order as well as deity's design of creation, which it must be remembered are antipathetic decorums or grammars in Luther's sense. For the illogic that attends a disruption of natural order appears either ludicrous or terrible when the agency is satanic, while in God's hands it is miraculous.

18. Westermann observes that, in the psalms, the enemy of those lamenting is always one "separated from them at the deepest level of existence, that is, as one who no longer acknowledges God as God" (Praise and Lament, 191). "The evildoers (in the opinion of the lamenter) no longer take God seriously, and yet God does not condemn them": "The lamenter takes God seriously, yet the enemy is able to mock with impunity" (194). In this injustice, "lies the greatest temptation for the lamenter," namely, to disbelief—the temptation Satan presents to speaker and reader alike.

19. Hugh MacCallum is particularly good on this figural aspect of the Son's exaltation, as he is on the important nuances of Milton's theology more generally. See his Sons of God, esp. 71–87.

20. Merrill rightly recognizes that Satan's perversion of religious understanding stems in part from his "empirical objectivity," an exclusive focus on appearances which denies the accommodated character of religious language. The Father's logical absurdity will of course offend against Satan's empirical canon of truth. Merrill extends this analysis to the readers of Paradise Lost—especially Dennis Burden's The Logical Epic: A Study of the Argument of "Paradise Lost" (Cambridge, Mass.: Harvard U P, 1967)—whose literalism precludes their apprehending the parabolic dimension of Milton's argument: "A horizontal logician abhors strangeness because it has no place in his system; the vertical logician covets it because the system that governs him lies outside his understanding, and he is always eager for new disclosures. For the one, strangeness is inconsistency; for the other, it is insight" (Epic God-Talk, 83).

21. For the theological legacy on which Milton draws in his account of Satan's "separation" and its motives, see Stella Revard's The War in Heaven (Ithaca: Cornell U P, 1980), 28–85. She remarks:

> It is one of Milton's most remarkable paradoxes that the very decree that "causes" Satan to revolt might have been, had Satan listened to it carefully and without the blinding fury of his pride, the means to stay his revolt. For in the decree God is stating that ruin will result when a creature, a part, separates himself from the creation, the whole. God has named the Son to kingship so as to make manifest visually and symbolically the union upon which the vitality of his creation depends. The angelic essence must, if it is to retain its vigor, abide in God and, as Augustine has noted, look to be one with him. . . . It is an exercise of the angels that they understand the decree as a furtherance, not an impediment, to their desire for union. If, knowing God as a loving Creator, they see his decree as perverse, then they willfully misunderstand the universe and their part in it. (57)

On this head, Abdiel declares the angels are in the Son "more illustrious made, since he the head / One of our numbers thus reduced becomes. / His laws our laws, all honour to him done / Returns our own" (LM 5.842–45). The lines explicitly perform a paradox of grace in the Son's exaltation very like that Satan himself ineffectually confesses on Mt. Niphrates, where once again the creature is dignified by its frank dependency on God. But this ironic reciprocation remains perpetually incredible to the discrete, definitive mind of the apostate.

22. Rhees, Recollections, 107–8.

23. For this distinction between letter and spirit, which (as I mentioned above) informs Milton's concept of a double scripture, see Ebeling, *Luther*, 93–109. Milton very early conceived truthful language as engaging the whole person, not just conceptually but somatically and morally, which is one motive behind his deprecation of scholasticism in Prolusions Three and Seven, and undoubtedly a value drawn from his rhetorical education. His scripturalism could only deepen it, and for the reasons Ebeling explains in Luther's case, where "theology as the object of intellectual inquiry and theology as the sphere of a personal encounter, formed an indivisible unity" (95–96): "The Spirit is concealed in the letter. But this must be understood in a profound and theologically very significant sense. The letter is not a good word, for it is the law of the wrath of God. But the Spirit is a good word, good news, the gospel, because it is the word of grace. Or, to phrase it differently again: what the law says, and the events it recounts are mere words and signs. But the words and event of the gospel are reality, the very substance of what they describe" (99). Confounded by the ironic immanence or concealment of the divine word, creation for Satan is of course a "mere word," a dead letter, remaining unmoved even when he recognizes the veritable image of God in our first parents, which he of course misunderstands. Similarly, if hell contains only the desiccated remnants of meaning and identity— "O how fallen! how changed"—the abundant world beyond is no better, invariably taunting him with the malignant ingenuity of its maker, who not surprisingly precedes Satan wherever he goes (*LM* 1.84).

24. *The Origin of the German Tragic Drama*, tr. John Osborne (London: NLB, 1977). In her *Ruins of Allegory*, Catherine Gimelli Martin is the most recent critic bringing Benjamin's argument to bear on Milton. While I confine this phenomenon to Milton's speaker, his Satan and of course that other character, the now notorious reader of *Paradise Lost*, she extends pathological *allegoria* and its melancholy ruination to the poet himself, who confronts the disturbing threshold of modernity with peculiar consequences for his imagery—a sort of Newtonian shift from allegorical hieratics to the dimensions of space and time (thus defying Eliot). Although my approach to allegory has a different provenance and capacity, I do think Martin is entirely right to emphasize Angus Fletcher's point that irony and allegory are compatible, with ancient rhetoric properly making "irony a subcategory of allegory," as well as a modality that exceeds generic constraints (*Allegory*, 229–30; *Ruins of Allegory*, 17–18). Certainly, this is a considerable aspect of Benjamin's argument. It is also what Adorno understands as art's "crisis of illusion," in which the image is eclipsed even as it is created, not least to fend off the intrusion of some interpretive absolute that would reduce it (in Adorno's canon of value) to univocal symbol. In this sense, "aesthetic images are subject to the prohibition of graven images": "Works of art are not just allegories, but the catastrophic fulfillment of allegories. . . . The shocks [art] inflicts mark the explosion of its appearance. With these shocks appearance itself, formerly an unquestioned *a priori* of art, goes up in catastrophic smoke, fully revealing for the first time its true essence" (*Aesthetic Theory*, tr. C. Lenhardt [New York: Routledge & Kegan Paul, 1984], 153, 125). Arguing that Milton renders his language "almost designedly unallegorical," Maureen Quilligan by contrast associates allegory and ambiguity more generally in *Paradise Lost* with the postlapsarian condition, where I would make it integral to the experience of deity's distinction from the world, and so pervasive in creation both before and after the Fall (*The Language of Allegory* [Ithaca: Cornell U P, 1979], 179–82). This division between mimetic and allegorical expression in readings of the poem tends to render its meanings speciously schematic, even tractarian—the symbology created by an interpretive

absolute in Adorno's sense—with the usual result that the critic announces a preference for Dante or Spenser over Milton. Mindele Anne Treip discusses the backgrounds and possibilities of Miltonic allegory in her erudite and judicious *Allegorical Poetics and the Epic* (Lexington: U Kentucky P, 1994), whose argument equally recognizes the disturbance of any reductive allegory in *Paradise Lost*.

25. *German Tragic Drama*, 175.

26. Ibid, 200.

27. Ibid., 180–81.

28. Ibid., 192.

29. It is interesting that Satan would concede the Father's hegemony in this way, since it is the prerogative of conquest to devastate, even as the Greeks (and less frequently the Romans) in victory casually destroyed whole city-states—killing and enslaving their populations, burning and razing buildings, leaving not a trace of wonted life. To Satan, the very landscape of hell is intelligible on the heroic model, as the conqueror's right of desolation.

30. In *The Greeks and Greek Civilization*, Jacob Burckhardt describes the peculiar "liberation" of personality in fifth-century Greece as absolute self-assertion in pursuit of preeminence, that is to say, without regard for its human costs—Satan's version of godhead. Indeed, Burckhardt describes the Eteocles of Euripides' *Phoenician Women* in a way altogether salient for Milton's devil:

> What he wants, instead of reigning alternately with Polyneices according to law and previous agreement, is simply to retain power because he has it (504ff.); to possess supremacy, 'the highest divinity,' he would go to heaven or down to the underworld; to concede it to another and accept the lesser position, to serve voluntarily when he could rule, seems to him cowardice. He ends with the words:
>
> > If sin must be, the best is after all
> > To sin for power, and in all else be just.
> >
> > (*Phoenician Women* 524f.)
>
> This last proviso is thoroughly Athenian and reflects the attitude of a *polis* that can, with luck, rule for a while and perhaps pacify many other regions under its sway; if things go wrong and its power crumbles, the world may as well become a shambles. (244)

The ruination of the world as the sublime effect of the "titantic temperament" is something Satan both understands and expects of God, not least because he himself exemplifies that very principle. From the vantage of Burckhardt's astutely jaundiced account of the Greeks, the cliché of Satan as classical hero takes on new life: in his almost naive love of display and passion for monumentalizing self; his pleasure in the cunning lie and ingenious deceit; his incorrigible emotionalism (in nice contrast to Milton's God); like Plato's Callicles, his indifference to violence as the prerogative of the great-souled; his private pessimism and melancholy obsession with decline; and so forth. Reading Burckhardt, one cannot but feel that Milton, the student of the ancients, has anatomized in Satan the morbid history or pathology of heroism (which, as John Rumrich rightly argues, is evil in its abuse, not in itself), justifying the speaker's acquired aversion to its excesses and underscoring the perversity of Eve's sudden chivalry. Vernant and Vidal-Naquet argue that Greek tragedy itself expresses such complex ambivalence in its analysis of human being, which is understood in terms of the heroic *muthos*:

What is this being that tragedy describes as a *deinos*, an incomprehensible and baffling monster, both an agent and one acted upon, guilty and innocent, lucid and blind, whose industrious mind can dominate the whole of nature yet who is incapable of governing himself? What is the relationship of this man to the actions upon which we see him deliberate on the stage and for which he takes the initiative and responsibility but whose real meaning is beyond him and escapes him so that it is not so much the agent who explains the action but rather the action that, revealing its true significance after the event, recoils upon the agent and discloses what he is and what he has really, unwittingly, done? (*Myth and Tragedy*, 32)

31. I see the comparison as an altogether likely if tacit analogy of Milton's own making, which ironically implicates Satan's self-mystification in Books Five and Two—the devil himself as royal imago. On that head, Robert Fallon describes the monarchical imagery of *Paradise Lost* in apt relation to the French model in his *Divided Empire* (University Park: Pennsylvania State U P, 1995), although I would not be inclined to see heaven as a perfected hierarchy in Fallon's fashion —that is Satan's delusion. From this distance, what appears striking about Louis' court protocols is not so much their glorious excess as their patent and improbable artifice—their manufacture of hieratic significance for the most incongruously banal functions, all premised on the office's proximity to the royal presence. Louis' astonishing success in seducing by mere forms his once hostile but now credulous nobility remains a benchmark of propaganda, whose cynical calculation Rossellini captures in "The Rise to Power of Louis XIV." See also on this head Peter Burke's *The Fabrication of Louis XIV* (New Haven: Yale U P, 1992). One might add that Satan orchestrates his own portrait of martyred majesty, a theatrics of affliction which frequently exploits the iconics and illusionism Milton imputes to Charles and his propagandists in *Eikonoklastes*. Indeed, David Loewenstein makes royalism's "civil kinde of idolatry" the proper target of Milton's tract—its 'shrines,' 'masking scenes' and festival 'pageantry' disguising dubious political actualities—which requires him to reinterpret the king's image point by point and so to revise history (CM 5:68). See Loewenstein's *Drama of History*, 51–73.

32. Thus Frye:

The heaven of *Paradise Lost*, with God the supreme sovereign and the angels in a state of unquestioning obedience to his will, can only be set up on earth inside the individual's mind. The free man's mind is a dictatorship of reason obeyed by the will without argument: we go wrong only when we take these conceptions of kingship and service of freedom as *social* models. Absolute monarchs and their flunkeys on earth always follow the model of hell, not heaven. The cleavage between the conceptual and dramatic aspects of the Father clears up when we realize that the one is the opposite of the other. (*Return to Eden*, 111)

33. Once again, Frye makes a comparable point: "It follows that what man can do to achieve his own salvation, or even to achieve the social goals of reason and revelation, is largely negative. More precisely, it is, once more, iconoclastic. Man can demonstrate his willingness to be set free by knocking down his idols, but if he takes no advantage of the help then offered him, he will simply have to set new idols up, except that they will of course be the same old ones, error and custom" (ibid., 98).

34. *Idea of the Holy*, 52.

35. The most spectacular (as it were) of these similes comes at the end of Book One, an imagistic cataract where the speaker manages all but inadvertently to characterize his

own temptation to idolatry. He likens the optical illusion of the satanic's diminishing size to the sight of "faerie elves, / Whose midnight revels by a forest side / Or fountain some belated peasant sees, / Or dreams he sees": "they on their mirth and dance / Intent, with jocund music charm his ear; / At once with joy and fear his heart rebounds" (*LM* 1.775–88). We do not have merely an amelioration of the apostate angels through the speaker's feckless comparisons, whose superficial because merely visual likenesses here reduce the festivities of titanic supernaturalism to bucolic superstition. But this train of associated images also implies the insidious power of satanic appearance upon the speaker himself, by sight and sound seducing his ear (that peculiar Miltonic faculty of the soul) so that he can no longer distinguish illusion from actuality, real from apparent value, thus compromising any ostensible claims he makes to supernal authority.

36. *Lives of the Poets*, 1:112. Unacquainted with Freud, Johnson did not recognize guilt as a passion in his theory, although perhaps intuitively in his own melancholic life: hence his urgent pursuit of the decent and normative. Something like this could be said of Satan, who is a ferocious normalizer.

37. Georgia Christopher impressively develops the sense in which Satan is mad: "If classical epic is a skewed version of God's truth, the 'classical hero' of *Paradise Lost* is deranged" (*Science of the Saints*, 79–88). But her discussion and others like it do not do justice to Satan's real if attenuating attractions, which remain the attractions of the Hellenic ideal whose appeal has long disguised his gradual degeneracy from many readers—in the best tradition of Luther's white devil and Milton's own dialectical theodicy. Indeed, the poet has orchestrated this conflict of ethical ideals and expressive values precisely to emphasize the relative character of Satan's manifold "derangement"; for what is mad in heaven may not be madness on earth. On this head, Burckhardt comments that the *hamartia* of Sophocles' Ajax "is not defiance of the gods, only the awareness of extraordinary strength," and that centuries before Byronism, his madness was understood as the awesome extremity of a gigantic heroism:

> He incurs the undying hatred of Pallas for having refused her help in battle because the enemy would be unable to overcome him. This shows a pride beyond what was allowed to mortals, and following the savage ancient myth to which the poet links his psychological study, he is blinded and driven mad by Athena so that he kills cattle and herdsmen. But it is important to note that even in his right mind he intended to murder the generals of the Achaean army treacherously by night, simply because they denied him Achilles' weapons. . . . for Sophocles and the Athenians he remains an ideal figure deserving complete sympathy, and the facts of his pathological condition, as he and Tecmessa relate them, are intended to create a sublime effect. (*The Greeks*, 244)

Kenneth Gross provides a needful and eloquent counterbalance to the frequent implication that, as he says, "the heroic Satan (the Romantic Satan) is primarily an error of neophytes" and a figure that the knowing and equal reader can neatly resist ("Satan and the Romantic Satan: A Notebook," in Nyquist and Ferguson, *Re-membering Milton*, 318–41). Gross's argument is persuasive not least because he allows Blake and the two Shelleys, especially Percy Bysshe, the moral and conceptual complexity of their responses to Milton and his creation, which Gross himself extends in his own discussion. Indeed, precisely because they are psychological studies, the Satans of Arnold Stein (*The Art of Presence* [Berkeley: U California P, 1977]) and William Kerrigan (*The Sacred Complex*) sustain the same requisite complexity which can be lost to a more overt formalism.

38. *Milton's God*, 110–11.

39. *Return of Eden*, 101.

40. Empson is self-conscious and determined in this enterprise, which is why his reading remains so apt and worthy of reiteration:

I am not denying, what Milton regularly asserts, that Satan fell out of pride and envy; but as Satan believes God to be a usurper he genuinely does believe him to be envious. As soon as we waive our metaphysical presumptions, we easily recognize that the motivation will be complex as in human affairs. In another case, resisting Charles I for example, the emotional forces actuating Satan could have made him work for the public good with increasingly public-spirited sentiments. As has often been pointed out, he is in the wrong solely because of an intellectual error; and we are ill-equipped to feel certain that we ourselves, in his place, would have decided rightly from the right motives. (*Milton's God*, 40)

41. *Return of Eden*, 99.

42. There is of course the ambiguous reference "towards either throne" at 3.350, which could suggest two discrete locations to which the angels bow, or in their single movement, exactly the contrary; but the implication is that the same figure inhabits both, as expressing in turn the *opus alienum* and *opus proprium* of deity—God's alien and God's proper revelation.

43. Unlike many readers, Empson is perfectly clear about Milton's theology on this point, even as he argues that the poet's scripturalism demanded the figure of the Father: "Milton would also consider that even this way of writing about God, though the best, was very limited because God was ineffable; in the *De Doctrina*, he is inclined to think that no man or angel could see God, and that God could only act through the agency of the Son. . . . Yet he was determined to present the whole of the relevant text of Genesis, however literally false in his own opinion; as by making God walk in the Garden, or punish the race of serpents" (*Milton's God*, 92–93). Frye makes the same observation: "In Milton, God the Father, in flagrant defiance of Milton's own theology, which tells us that we can know nothing about the Father except through the human incarnation of the Son, does speak, and with disastrous consequences. The rest of the poem hardly recovers from his speech, and there are few difficulties in the appreciation of *Paradise Lost* that are not directly connected with it" (*Return of Eden*, 99). On this issue of Milton's depiction of the Father and God's passibility in general—that is, his self-representation as an intelligible and intelligibly feeling *person*—see Michael Lieb's important essay "Reading God: Milton and the Anthropopathetic Tradition" (*Milton Studies* 25 [1989]: 213–43), where he argues that *Paradise Lost* makes the hermeneutical problem of interpreting God *as passible* into a singular challenge of the reader's faith, which consists in acknowledging and crediting the accommodated, anthropomorphic picture deity provides of itself in scripture. He then concludes that "the theopathetic dimensions of the Father are consummated in the Son," who both confirms and renders them recognizable (236). Lieb also enlists Lactantius's treatise on the anger of God as arguing precisely this position on scriptural anthropomorphism, to which he gives full and complementary discussion in his " 'Hate in Heav'n': Milton and the *Odium Dei*," *ELH* 53 (1986): 519–39.

Yet I would diverge from his account in arguing (after Empson and Frye) for Milton's emphasis on the conceptual and moral difficulty that this challenge of reading the Father involves, which I believe has its expression in the ambivalent character of allegory in *Paradise Lost*. Lieb is right to resist the implication that Milton's anthropomorphism is a mere figment of human sin, the effect of our resistance to what Empson calls divine "ineffa-bility": as the poet himself says of the scriptural God, he is all we know of deity—Luther's God-for-us—whose effects we cannot simply count and discount as more or less objective, depending on whether faith or sin views them. This is the one criticism Lieb rightly levels at Georgia Christopher's argument, which—as he himself observes—is otherwise strikingly apposite in its theological analysis of Milton, not to mention Luther and Calvin. But both Christopher and Lieb are inclined to overlook the intractable predicament of faith itself, which cannot render either scripture's or Milton's personification of deity seamlessly, transparently, and in a manner mystically true to the believer. As Luther argues, and Christopher tends to downplay, we must make God *against* the appearances of divine irrationality, injustice, and outrageousness—appearances which, like suffering itself, are humanly real and true as they are to the speaker of *Paradise Lost*, who would otherwise have no compelling motive to justify God's ways (see Christopher, *Science of the Saints*, 101–19, for this tacit amelioration of Lutheran *facere Deum*). To underscore Empson's point, the metaphysics (and for that matter mysticism) of divine transcendence allows us to evade the full force of Satan's case against God, as it does the obscene demand God makes of Abraham, or the terrible sufferings of Jesus. Here the conceptual works unfortu-nately to circumvent the moral, something I don't think Milton would wish.

I must take note of the fact that Christopher herself, in this matter of God's speech, invokes Wittgenstein's remark about talking lions—Wittgenstein appearing at interesting intervals throughout Milton criticism: indicatively, she uses it to emphasize divine impassi-bility, as Lieb contends, in that "A vast gulf separates God's speech from Satan's because his words do not imply a familiar psychic life as do those of Satan and Adam" (112). While she is right to apply this distinction after Luther, as precluding ontological specula-tion (112–13), she neglects the perplexity to which Wittgenstein points: that is, of ascer-taining the possibility and range of understanding since the lion *is talking in our sense of that word*. Wittgenstein asks not only at what threshold of expression understanding of the other is confounded, but what are the consequences of that confusion for any relation-ship with a mind different from our own:

> If I see someone writhing in pain with evident cause I do not think: all the same, his feelings are hidden from me.
>
> We also say of some people that they are transparent to us. It is, however, important as regards this observation that one human being can be a complete enigma to an-other. We learn this when we come into a strange country with entirely strange traditions; and, what is more, even given a mastery of the country's language. We do not *understand* the people. (And not because of not knowing what they are saying to themselves.) We cannot find our feet with them.
>
> "I cannot know what is going on in him" is above all a *picture*. It is the convincing expression of a conviction. It does not give the reasons for the conviction. *They* are not readily accessible.
>
> If a lion could talk, we could not understand him. (*PI* p.223)

Taken as punctuating this sequence of remarks, the talking yet unintelligible lion would seem instead to have an ironic function for Wittgenstein, since he is describing how the sceptic enlists the fallacy of the mind's hiddenness, its concealment by the body, to justify refusing what the body—and human language—does express of another mind. As Cavell comments here, with passionate conviction we construe our "incapacity or unwillingness to interpret [the body] or to judge it accurately, to draw the right connections" as an impenetrable opacity, a barrier erected against our proper knowledge. But the contrary is the case; for "What hides the mind is not the body but the mind itself": "If something separates us, comes between us, that can only be a particular aspect or stance of the mind itself, a particular *way* in which we relate, or are related . . . to one another—our positions, our attitudes, with reference to one another" (CR 368–69). On the model of the "dark places of scripture," we can refuse the knowledge revelation offers because we find its expressions strange, disorienting, and in that sense, unintelligible; and in a move curiously related to the transcendental turn of speculation, we can make our estrangement from the manner of God's speech justify a sceptical decision not to understand what it says. Luther describes Erasmus as doing something equivalent; and Satan makes this refusal after a fashion, when he insists that Abdiel offer evidence that the angelic were not self-made— in short, that Abdiel deliver up the memory or person of God himself as proof. Satan thus rejects the same revelation of deity's presence that conscience finds sufficient in the *Christian Doctrine*, simply because it is oblique, deflected, mediated, and, what is worse, without the personal touch for which the apostate Adam also yearns. So we might refuse to understand a talking lion by virtue of its sheer anomaly, rendering a real difference insurmountable at the expense of viable knowledge and relationship. We do so because that decision, as Cavell would put it, still recognizes something true about the circumstances of understanding both lion and God, which is that their speech is incoherent with our assumptions about meaning—how we think deity's anthropomorphic picture should signify, which is to say positively or at least familiarly. When it doesn't, we can't help but be startled, not to say shocked, by this sometimes elusive, sometimes inescapable discrepancy, like Wittgenstein's stranger in a strange land; and so we should be, since the rupture of presumptive meaning entails suffering for faithful and sinner alike. Moreover, what Cavell argues for human relationship is still more profoundly true for the religious: "we are answerable for everything that comes between us; if not for causing it then for continuing it; if not for denying it then for affirming it; if not for it then to it" (CR 369).

A theological adept in every other respect, Christopher tellingly finds no place in her discussion for the precipitant of Luther's conversion and his theology, namely, *Anfechtung*—the episodic crisis of faith fomented by deity's *opus alienum*. As Alister McGrath argues, "In order for the Christian to progress in his spiritual life, he must continually be forced back to the foot of the cross, to begin it all over again (*semper a novo incipiere*)— and this takes place through the continued experience of *Anfechtung*":

> It must be emphasized that Luther does not regard *Anfechtung* as a purely subjective state of the individual. Two aspects of the concept can be distinguished, although they are inseparable: the *objective* assault of spiritual forces upon the believer, and the *subjective* anxiety and doubt which arise within him as a consequence of these assaults. Most significantly of all, as we have already noted, God himself must be recognized as the ultimate source of *Anfechtung*: it is his *opus alienum*, which is intended to destroy man's self-confidence and complacency, and reduce him to a state of utter despair and humiliation, in order that he may finally turn to God, devoid of all the obstacles to justification which formerly existed. (*Theology of the Cross*, 170–71)

So it is hardly surprising that Christopher would use Wittgenstein's remark to draw the boundary of the distinction between human and divine, yet without contemplating what it is like fully to experience that distinction, and what is equally terrifying, one's complete responsibility to it. But in *Paradise Lost*, despair is more than a word. The element of conversion Christopher perfectly understands as "the act of discovery—'the sense of finding' that was so important in the literary experience of the Reformation" entails only notional costs in her argument, while the "event-making, crisis-bearing property of God's word" produces (if you will forgive the phrase) no more than a wondrous and inevitable triumph over the father of lies (*Science of the Saints*, 120). For the same reason, she can raise the problem posed by the Father's figure but accounts for its methodical offense only incidentally, as the usual doctrinaire or poetic ineptitude. It follows that the apostasy of Christopher's Satan will appear unnecessary, uncalled for, the willful aberration of a madman, and the speaker of *Paradise Lost* no Samson struggling with his God but a cipher of the poet's own presumptively transcendent understanding.

44. "Dialogue in Heaven," in Barker, *Milton*, 234.

45. *Surprised by Sin*, 61–71.

46. *Leviathan*, 220.

47. Ibid., 217. Hobbes argues in several places that we simply cannot confuse philosophy with theology, the pictures we have of God with deity, our knowledge of a person with that person per se, and indeed our necessary ordering of the world with what may actually be the case. In the first chapter of *De Corpore*, Hobbes says that because God and the things of God, like angels or revelation or religious doctrine, have none of the attributes which permit our knowing them as such, they cannot be the subject of philosophy as the discipline of what we know, not what we believe. Because the relation between cause and effect cannot be calculated in the case of God as "the eternal, ingenerable, and incomprehensible"; since angels "are thought to be neither bodies nor properties of bodies," and thus not susceptible of rational manipulation or reckoning in Hobbes's sense; since we cannot infer the doctrine of God by "natural reason," we cannot apply to these things the method of knowledge or its characteristics of truth or falsity (*Human Nature and De Corpore Politico*, ed. and tr. J. C. A. Gaskin [Oxford: Oxford U P, World's Classics, 1994], 191–92). In other words, they belong to an entirely separate order of meaning that effectively precludes "scientific" understanding, much less our usual forms of analysis. Again, in the third set of objections to Descartes's *Meditations*, Hobbes comments:

> when one thinks of an Angel, what is noticed in the mind is now the image of a flame, now that of a fair winged child, and this, I may be sure, has no likeness to an Angel, and hence is not the idea of an Angel. But believing that created beings exist that are the ministers of God, invisible and immaterial, we give the name Angel to this object of belief, this supposed being, though the idea used in imagining an Angel is, nevertheless constructed out of the ideas of visible things.
>
> It is the same way with the most holy name of God; we have no image, no idea corresponding to it. Hence we are forbidden to worship God in the form of an image, lest we should think we could conceive Him who is inconceivable. (*The Philosophical Works of Descartes*, tr. Elizabeth S. Haldane and G. R. T. Ross, 2 vols. [Cambridge: Cambridge U P, 1970], 2:67)

Hobbes's point is Wittgenstein's, namely, that the pictures we have of *res non apparentes*, whether deity or the soul, do not structure the things they convey. On the contrary, they are in a manner signs without substance, images without objects, what Benjamin in speaking of allegory has called monograms of essence but not essence in a mask. That is to say, they are tokens we use to indicate the presence, not the nature of something that exceeds the possibilities of our knowledge.

48. *Milton*, 182.

49. *Return of Eden*, 102.

50. *Language, Hermeneutic, and Word of God* (New York: Harper & Row, 1966), 146. Besides Frye's comment (see below n.60), the original discussion of Miltonic parable comes in John M. Evan's *"Paradise Lost" and the Genesis Tradition* (Oxford: Clarendon, 1968). But see also Merrill (*Epic God-Talk*, 18–31, who remarks:

> The parable of the Prodigal Son, for example, concerns the relation between God and Man, but it tells us very little about the essential nature of God. Instead, it urges that if we look on God as if he were a father, our attitude toward Him is appropriate. Such an attitudinally-based similitude is not simply a matter of encouraging one to pretend that God is a father, but that what he means by this is "to be explained in terms of human attitudes: I believe that God is *such that* the attitude appropriate to Him is similar to that which is appropriate towards a human father." Again, we can savor the consonance of this parabolic logic with Milton's position: ". . . in the literal and figurative descriptions of God, he is exhibited not as he really is . . . [but] as he desires we should conceive [Him]." Parabolic similarities are different from analogical ones, [Donald] Evans urges, because they are "self-involving" rather than neutral, or, as logical docetism would contend, "self-destructive." The parable, in other words, involves one logically in something more than mere assent to fact and something less than capitulation to a logic of obedience. It is, in short, an incarnational mode. (27)

51. Funk, *Word of God*, 152.

52. Ibid., 156.

53. Ibid., 161.

54. Ibid., 158.

55. Ibid., 160.

56. *Wisdom in Israel*, tr. James D. Martin (Valley Forge, Penn.: Trinity P International, 1972), 70.

57. Ibid., 249.

58. Ibid., 67.

59. Ibid., 73.

60. Frye makes the same point, again with regard to the challenge revelation presents to reason: "Reason is subordinate to a higher principle than itself: revelation, coming directly from the Word of God, which emancipates and fulfils the reason and gives it a basis to work on which the reason could not achieve by itself. The point at which revelation impinges on reason is the point at which discursive understanding begins to be intuitive: the point of the emblematic vision or parable, which is the normal unit in the teaching of Jesus. The story of the fall of Satan is a parable to Adam, giving him the kind of knowledge he needs in the only form appropriate to a free man" (*Return to Eden*, 74).

CHAPTER SIX

1. *Art of Presence*, 142–43.

2. It is important to recognize that all arguments for Milton's monism or animist materialism assume an emanation scheme linking the nature of deity as "spirit" to the nature of its creation, a scheme usually dependent on that passage in the *Christian Doctrine* where Milton argues that matter was not created ex nihilo but from God: "Nor did St. Paul hesitate to attribute to God something corporeal [*Quin et corporale quiddam Deo attribuere non ipse dubitavit Paulus*]; Col.ii.9. 'in him dwelleth all the fulness of the Godhead bodily' " (CM 15:24–25). Once again, this argument is philological, not ontological, and as such

it refers to the *image of God* in scripture, not to deity per se. I will reiterate the point that Milton's theological treatise, like Calvin's, has an epistemological order; and that we must take Book One's seventh chapter in the light of its first, where Milton concludes: "It is better therefore to contemplate the Deity, and to conceive of him, not with reference to human passions [anthropopathy], that is, after the manner of men, who are never weary of forming subtle imaginations respecting him, but after the manner of Scripture, that is, in the way wherein God has offered himself to our contemplation" (CM 14:33). As Milton uses anthropopathy here, he asserts that there is no essential or even analogical relation between deity itself and the anthropomorphic picture provided to us, since the distinction of creator from creature prohibits such a relation. However, we are to treat that picture *as if* God were how he describes himself, as an act of faith in Luther's sense. To reiterate, "In arguing thus, we do not say that God is in fashion like unto man in all his parts and members, but that as far as we are concerned to know, he is of that form which he attributes to himself in the sacred writings. If therefore we persist in entertaining a different conception of the Deity than that which it is to be presumed he desires should be cherished, insasmuch as he has himself disclosed it to us, we frustrate the purposes of God instead of rendering him submissive obedience" (CM 14:37). That creation itself is material, Milton avers, and ascribes to heaven as well both material and historical existence (CM 15:34–35). But as I will shortly clarify, creation is not God any more than heaven is; nor—to take the case from another angle—is the Spirit of God, who "being actually and numerically distinct from God himself, cannot possibly be essentially one God with him whose Spirit he is (except on certain strange and absurd hypotheses, which have no foundation in Holy Scripture, but were devised by human ingenuity for the sole purpose of supporting this particular doctrine)" (CM 14:379).

3. Regina Schwartz rightly argues the dialectical as against mythic character of Milton's creation account, demonstrating not only the paradox of chaos but also, through that paradox, the peculiar discrepancy between what Luther calls natural and religious expression, where what looks like an entity figures an occasion of faith and choice. The question that the psalmist and Milton's speaker put to God—what is the cause of human suffering, of *human* evil?—receives a discrepant order of response signaling this distinction, as Schwartz contends for Job: "But in its deepest sense, that question is never answered in its own terms. Instead, Milton turns from the question to an assertion—of providence. The same pattern obtains in the Book of Job, where, of all of Milton's Biblical models, the theodical issue is most pressing. Job also begins asking why he suffers, and his question is 'answered' in a very different key, with an assertion of divine omnipotence, and with what must have been especially striking for Milton, an assertion of creation" (*Remembering and Repeating*, 36).

On the model of Job, the creation Raphael pictures is not a cosmos but a religious and parabolic meaning for Adam and Eve to apprehend: namely, the distinction between creator and creature, as signaled here by divine illogic. It is a picture which effectively defies the presumption of metaphysical scrutiny, shifting the idiom of understanding from objects and causes to attitudes and relations, or as Schwartz puts it, to an assertion of faith in divine providence—that God brings good out of evil—like that order of assertion with which Luther parries both Erasmus's scepticism and its transcendental refusal to allow the intelligibility of religious truth in this life.

4. *Theology*, 2:125.

5. *Anthropology of the Old Testament*, tr. Margaret Kohl (1974; reprint, Mifflintown, Penn.: Sigler P, 1996), 24–25. See also von Rad, who remarks that "the Hebrews did not distinguish between the intellectual and vital functions of the body," and recommends that *nepes* not be translated as "soul" (*OTT* 1:153). This is a way of speaking about the whole human person, but as von Rad cautions, it is not ontological but anthropological talk: "There is absolutely no unity in the ideas of the Old Testament about the nature of man. And, of course, uniformity is not to be expected there, because in the source material the body of ideas with which we meet derive from the most diverse periods and circles, and Israel felt even less need to unify these anthropological concepts or to reduce them to a norm than she did with her theological traditions" (*OTT* 1:152–53).

6. Wolff, *Anthropology*, 22.

7. Ibid., 20. As always, it seems clear that one can trace Milton's supposed heresy—in this case, mortalism—to a scriptural usage as against a metaphysical concept.

8. Ibid., 32.

9. Wolff calls this tropological process the *"stereometry* of expression": "Stereometric thinking thus simultaneously presupposes a synopsis of the members and organs of the human body with their capacities and function. It is *synthetic* thinking, which by naming the part of the body means its function. . . . The member and its efficacious action are synthesized. With a relatively small vocabulary, through which he names things and particularly the parts of the body, the Hebrew can and must express a multiplicity of fine nuances by extracting from the context of the sentence the possibilities, activities, qualities or experiences of what is named" (ibid., 8). It is this sort of analysis that Milton brings to the word "fornication": such usage represents the configuration of human experience and understanding—how we know and describe ourselves—not monism.

10. Ibid., 33.

11. On this head, Wolff comments that the word *basar*, usually translated as "flesh," refers not only to the mortal body humanity shares with the animals, but also to "what binds people together and what can then be almost a legal term for 'relationship' " or commonality: "Gen. 2.24 can say of man that he will 'cleave to his wife and they will become one [*basar*],' that is to say, a common body, a 'fellowship for life' " (29). Thus the creatural vulnerability of the body is extended to include the moral dimension of human life: "Ethical frailty is added to the frailty of the creature," with the result that *basar* understood as "flesh" "does not only mean the powerlessness of the mortal creature but also the feebleness of his faithfulness and obedience to the will of God" (31).

12. Wilhelm Pauck, ed. and tr., *Luther: Lectures on Romans* (Philadelphia: Westminster, 1961), 212–13. As quoted, Jacob Preus in the American Luther translates *utrunque* as "twofold idea"; I include Pauck's "dialectic" since it expresses the rhetorical sense which I believe Luther intends here.

13. The beauty and glory attending God's image in humanity is assumed, but it is of a kind always expressive of deity, as John Rumrich argues in *Matter of Glory*, having its source in the relation between self and God, each rightly understood and valued. While retailing the perfections that inhered in our first parents, Luther nonetheless observes that "when we speak about that image, we are speaking about something unknown. Not only have we no experience of it, but we continually experience the opposite; and so we hear nothing but bare words" (*LW* 1:63). He then makes this indicative analogy between our knowledge of the *selem elohim* and Moses' sight of God's *kabod* or glory from behind—the

posteriora: "What we are stating faith and the Word teach, which, as if from a distance, point out the glory of the divine image" (*LW* 1:65). Rumrich sensitively discusses how death is the existential foil of that different moral glory or splendor and complex heroism our first parents attain at the end of *Paradise Lost*, in emulation of the Son's sacrifice as the perfect image of God.

14. Charles Taylor, *Sources of the Self: The Making of the Modern Identity* (Cambridge, Mass.: Harvard U P, 1989), 34.

15. In his reading of Genesis, Luther offers an excursus on anthropomorphia, concluding that "This is the first stage of error, when men disregard God as He has enveloped Himself and become incarnate, and seek to scrutinize the unveiled God" (*LW* 2:47):

> God in His essence is altogether unknowable; nor is it possible to define or put into words what He is, though we burst in the effort.
>
> It is for this reason that God lowers Himself to the level of our weak comprehension and presents Himself to us in images, *in coverings, as it were, in simplicity adapted to a child, that in some measure it may be possible for Him to be known by us.* . . . for we cannot define what God is in His nature. Yet we can define what He is not, namely, that He is not a voice, not a dove, not water, not bread, and not wine. Nevertheless, He presents Himself to us in these visible forms, deals with us, and puts these forms before us to keep us from degenerating into erratic and vagabond spirits who indeed carry on discussions about God but who are profoundly ignorant of Him as of One who cannot be comprehended in His unveiled majesty. . . . He says: "Man shall not see Me and live." Therefore he puts before us an image of Himself, because He shows Himself to us in such a manner that we can grasp Him. In the New Testament we have Baptism, the Lord's Supper, absolution, and the ministry of the Word.
>
> These, in the terminology of the scholastics, are "the will of the sign," and these we must consider when we want to know God's will. The other is His "will of good pleasure," the essential will of God or His unveiled majesty, which is God Himself. From this the eyes must turn away, for it cannot be grasped. In God there is sheer Deity, and the essence of God is his Transcendent wisdom and omnipotent power. These attributes are altogether beyond the grasp of reason. . . . This will is unsearchable, and God did not want to give us an insight into it in this life. He merely wanted to indicate it by means of some coverings: Baptism, the Word, the Sacrament of the Altar. These are the divine images and "the will of the sign." Through them God deals with us within the range of our comprehension. Therefore these alone must engage our attention. (*LW* 2:45–47, my emphasis)

Luther's "will of the sign" is what Milton and Calvin understand when they read Ezekiel: its images do not describe entities but meanings—the will of God for humanity—expressed in the precisely *sheltering* figures of sacramental signs and the scriptural word. For the "covering" of accommodated language—God as he has "enveloped" and "incarnated" himself in scriptural expressions—protects us from the annihilating force of divine will per se, which cannot be known "in this life." Despite appearances, this argument does not entail a negative or mystical theology, since Luther does not want us to meditate what deity is not—an empty revelation. On the contrary, he wants us to address God as he pictures himself, an anthropomorphic imagery inflected by his intelligible and—as Luther stipulates—conditional intent: "This will, they say, is not almighty," for we are at liberty to accept or reject it as communicated either by the law or sacraments (*LW* 2:47). In other words, in the very "covering" or accommodation of divine meanings, which describes the distinction between deity and the world, consists in humanity's freedom to choose or reject knowledge of God. Any attempt to circumvent the dialectic of divine expression, as a meaning concealed beneath its opposite, is an exercise in religious futility: so Luther comments (with religious enthusiasts in mind) that "those who boast of visions, revelations, and enlightenments and follow them are either overwhelmed by God's majesty or remain in utter ignorance of God" (*LW* 2:46). Here again we have a case against direct inspiration that can be extended to Milton, who understands scriptural anthropomorphism comparably, further subverting the magical or ecstatic force of invocation presumed for the author or speaker of *Paradise Lost*.

16. "Life in the Garden: Freedom and the Image of God in Paradise Lost," *Journal of Religion* 60 (1980): 247–71, esp. 255. Yu cites both Bonhoeffer and Karl Barth as arguing for the *imago Dei* no *analogia entis* but rather an *analogia relationis*, consisting in the attribute of freedom as "a relationship between two persons," in Bonhoeffer's phrase (255). Moreover, Yu vigorously and appropriately contrasts Milton's concept of the divine image with Augustine's, who in that perpetually definitive tract on the trinity understands it as singular intellectual entity and self-relation exclusive to the man (255–57).

17. In what MacCallum calls the Son's second exaltation in Book Three, the birth is not the Son's begetting but his incarnation as the Christ—"Both God and man, Son both of God and man" (*LM* 3.316)—a new degree of mediation which may explain why this heavenly episode more completely emphasizes the Son's status as *image*: as "The radiant image of his glory" (*LM* 3.63); "Beyond compare the Son of God was seen / Most glorious, in him all his Father shone / Substantially expressed, and in his face / Divine compassion visibly appeared" (*LM* 3. 138–41); "Son who art alone / My word, my wisdom, and effectual might, / All has thou spoken as my thoughts are, all / As my eternal purpose hath decreed" (*LM* 3.169–72); "Adore the Son, and honour him *as me*" (*LM* 3.343, my emphasis); and of course "Begotten Son, divine similitude, / In whose conspicuous countenance, without cloud / Made visible, the Almighty Father shines, / Whom else no creature can behold" (*LM* 3.384–87).

18. Wolff, *Anthropology*, 159–60.

19. Again, Wolff speculates that the use of the word for likeness "is perhaps intended to guard against the misunderstanding that correspondence indicates identity only, and not differentiation within the similarity as well" (161). This is certainly how Calvin understands the phrase, "likeness of an appearance," in Ezekiel: "appearance" underscores the degree of mediation between divine and human, which is expressed in Genesis by the relation, "in our image, *after* our likeness." What humanity resembles in this interpretation is not deity per se but its perceptible expression.

20. *Sources of the Self*, 35.

21. Ibid., 34.

22. Along with von Rad, Wolff remarks that "It is precisely in his function as ruler that he is God's image," even as the Son is the Father's vice-gerent: "In the ancient East the setting up of the king's statue was the equivalent to the proclamation of his domination over the sphere in which the state was erected (cf. Dan. 3.1, 5f.). . . . Accordingly man is set in the midst of creation as God's statue. He is evidence that God is the Lord of creation; but as God's steward he also exerts his rule, fulfilling his task not in arbitrary despotism but as a responsible agent. *His rule and his duty to rule are not autonomous; they are copies*" (*Anthropology*, 160–61, my emphasis).

23. *Jacob Arminius*, 60.

24. On the status of natural law in Milton, see especially Bennet, *Reviving Liberty*: "The humanist antinomian had available the entire law of nature to order the moral vision with which he or she viewed the elements of a particular situation. . . . Released from all positive laws, the Christian must build his or her moral judgment, inner authority, through the discernment of the valid hierarchy of natural laws that apply in particular ethical situations" (108).

25. Responding to the language of Genesis 1:27—"So God created man in his own image, in the image of God he created him"—Phyllis Trible remarks: "The identity of vocabulary, *God* and 'the image of God,' establishes a similarity in meaning at the same time that the word *the-image-of* stresses the difference between Creator and created. More-over, the lack of any formal parallelism between these two elements of the poem suggests further their semantic disparity. This difference between 'God' and 'the image of God' witnesses to the transcendence and freedom of the deity" (*God and the Rhetoric of Sexuality* [Philadelphia: Fortress, 1978], 20–21).

26. This is a version of that libertinism, at once intellectual and erotic, which is the other sexual and interpretive polarity besides mere procreative functionalism, both of which the speaker attacks in Book Four in his paean to "wedded love" (LM 4.744–70). In Comus's fashion, the libertine exhibits the tyranny of consumption, in which the world is merely the pleasurable extension of narcissistic desire: there is no other person, no interrelation, only proliferating and ultimately indifferent consumables, since the be-loved's "absolute" value is readily transferred to another once the lover is satiated. In effect, the beloved is simultaneously objectified by the lover and assimilated to self, so that what the lover adores—in the manner of all narcissists—is his or her own projected image, like Satan with Sin, or Eve with her own reflection. James Turner insightfully discusses the analyses of Augustine, Aquinas, and Luther, each of whom address the coin-cidence of sin and erotic excess in Genesis: see his *One Flesh: Paradisal Marriage and Sexual Relations in the Age of Milton* (Oxford: Clarendon, 1987), esp. 49–95, where he also argues the interesting polarities of interpretive libertinism.

27. Thus Milton in *The Tenure of Kings and Magistrates* offers a genesis of governments: No man, who knows ought, can be so stupid to deny that all men naturally were borne free, being the image and resemblance of God himself, and where by privilege above all the creatures, born to command and not to obey; and that they liv'd so. Till from the root of *Adams* transgression, falling among themselves to doe wrong and violence, and foreseeing that such courses must needs tend to the destruction of them all, they agreed by common league to bind each other from mutual injury, and joyntly to defend themselves against any that gave disturbance or opposition to such agreement. Hence came Cities, Townes and Common-wealths. And because no faith in all was found sufficiently binding, they saw it needfull to ordaine som authori-tie, that might restrain by force and punishment what was violated against peace and common right. This autoritie and power of self-defence and preservation being originally and naturally in every one of them, and unitedly in them all, for ease, for order, and least each man should be his own partial Judge, they communicated and deriv'd either to one, whom for the eminence of his wisdom and integritie they chose above the rest, or to more than one whom they thought of equal deserving: the first was call'd a King; the other Magistrates. Not to be thir Lords and Maisters (though afterward those names in som places were giv'n voluntarily to such as had been Au-thors of inestimable good to the people) but, to be thir Deputies and Commissioners,

to execute, by vertue of thir intrusted power, that justice which else every man by the bond of nature and of Cov'nant must have executed for himself, and for one another. And to him that shall consider well why among free Persons, one man by civil right should beare autority and jurisdiction over another, no other end or reason can be imaginable. (CM 5:8–9)

Milton's affinities with the republicanism of Algernon Sidney are impressive, with Sidney offering an account of tyranny in the *Court Maxims* but especially the *Discourses*, which echoes Milton's emphasis on the tyrant as narcissist and consumer—an ancient topos: "surely no Christian Prince, not drunk with high mind, and prouder than those Pagan *Caesars* that deifi'd themselves, would arrogate so unreasonably above human condition, or derogate so basely from a whole Nation of men his Brethren, as if for him only subsisting, and to serve his glory; valuing them in comparison of his owne brute will and pleasure, no more than so many beasts, or vermin under his Feet, not to be reasond with, but to be trod on; among whom there might be found so many thousand Men for wisdom, vertue, nobleness of mind, and all other respects, but the fortune of his dignity, farr above him" (CM 5:12–13). On this latter head, see my essay " 'Our Author, Who Delights in Monsters': Sidney's *Discourses* on Political Imagoes and Royalist Iconography," in Derek Hirst and Richard Strier, eds., *Writing and Engagement in 17th-Century England* (Cambridge: Cambridge U P, 1999), 165–87.

28. Turner is specially sensitive to the insoluble tension between mutuality and subordination in marriage, in Milton but also in Protestant exegesis and doctrine more generally: see *One Flesh*, 96–123, 215–26, 281–87. Diane McColley also gives an intelligently balanced account of the same problem in her *Milton's Eve* (U Illinois P, 1983), 22–57.

29. To recall what Perez Zagorin terms the "aristocratic" Milton in *The Ready and Easy Way*: "For the ground and basis of every just and free government (since men have smarted so oft for commiting all to one person) is a general councel of ablest men, chosen by the people to consult of public affairs from time to time for the common good" (CM 6:125–26). Further, he recommends that this council be "a perpetual Senate" (CM 6:128), "permitting only those of them who are rightly qualifi'd, to nominat as many as they will; and out of that number others of a better breeding, to chuse a less number more judiciously, till after a third or fourth sifting and refining of exactest choice, they only be left chosen who are the due number, and seem by most voices the worthiest" (CM 6:131)—in short, the republican sort of aristocracy. On this head, see Zagorin's *A History of Political Thought in the English Revolution* (London: Routledge & Kegan Paul, 1954) and *Milton: Aristocrat & Rebel* (Rochester, N.Y.: D. S. Brewer, 1992), as well as Fixler, *Kingdoms of God*, 133–71.

30. Wolff remarks that Genesis is "a demythologized world, such as the creation account displays in general, and to some extent polemically, in its countering of the myths of the surrounding world. All and everything that is to be found in the world is revealed as being God's creation; consequently, for the man who has grasped this, there is neither a divine earth, nor divine beasts, nor divine constellations, nor any other divine spheres basically inaccessible to man" (*Anthropology*, 162). Were matter animated, or conscious life supernaturalized, Adam would not refuse the equality of the beasts.

31. *Rhetoric of Sexuality*, 15, 79–82. In her otherwise admirable essay, "Gynesis, Genesis," Mary Nyquist has criticized Trible's reading of Genesis rather unfairly—although she does not simply disregard Trible's account, as the strict parameters of her model ensures Kristeva would do. Nyquist charges Trible with formalist presuppositions which she herself displays, since her own argument depends on just such an assumption: namely, that in a

sequence, "the temporally later term then becomes the superior, being both more perfect than and necessary to its predecessor" (159). Although she sees her own analysis in a critical relation to that idea, the fact remains that Nyquist uses it no less instrumentally than Trible does her Hebrew parallel structures and moreover gives it no contingent but an essential value—of patriarchalism and, specifically, the shape of bourgeois subjectivity. Moreover, as this maneuver should suggest, Nyquist reads symbolically (since she appears—like many of the rest of us—not to read Hebrew), which is no less formalist a tack than Trible reading form-critically or what she calls rhetorically. Finally, Nyquist's is a negative theology, and like all negative theologies (of which poststructuralism can become one), it retains the *modus cognoscendi* of the phallologocentrism it would refute—in this case, the method of *analogia entis*. We cannot of course escape analogy, nor should we: the issue is how we use it, and I don't find Trible more culpable than Nyquist in this regard—if culpability plays any role here.

32. Ian Maclean, *The Renaissance Notion of Woman* (Cambridge: Cambridge U P, 1980), 71.

33. Again, Wolff is helpful here:

The context makes it clear that no individual at all is meant. The continuation in I.26b '(Let us make *'adam*) so that *they* may have dominion . . .' points to a plural. Thus *'adam*' is unquestionably to be understood in a collective sense; God wants to create *mankind*. Dominion over the world is not to be made over to great individuals, but to the community. Psalm 8 says that man is crowned to rule over all creation, surprising though it at first seems (v.4) that it should just be man, in view of the mighty works of the Creator which are to be seen in the heavens (v.3). . . . It is precisely man in his littleness that God has cared for and has called to be plenipotentiary. No member of mankind is to be excluded from this authority. (*Anthropology*, 161)

As he goes on to remark, "the lordship of man over man is a falsification of the image of God," which is of course how Satan understands dominion (164).

34. Ibid., 162. It is worth quoting at length what Wolff says about the second creation account:

The premise of the Yahwist's story about the Garden of Eden is also a love relationship between man and woman which is crowned with happiness. This aspect can be shown as a continuous thread running right through the whole. (1) The state of being alone is expressly stated by Yahweh as not being good for the man (2.18a). (2) From the very beginning man's partner is defined as the help fit for him (v.18b); this presupposes the social character of the differences between the sexes. (3) Help of this kind is not to be found in the animal world; man is distinguished from that world by his superiority in possessing language (the naming of the beasts); and he remains lonely in the midst of it (vv.19f.). (4) The partner who really corresponds to man is not created out of the earth, like the first man (v.7) and the animals (v.19); she comes from the rib of man himself; thus man and woman belong together qualitatively in a completely different degree from the way in which they belong to other created beings; it is only man and woman together who represent the whole man. . . . (5) Unique though their solidarity is, man and woman none the less stand in genuine contrast to one another. The woman is formed during man's deep sleep (v.21) and is only brought to man when she is a complete, independent person (on *bw'* in v.22b as the end of the leading home of the bride cf. Judg. 12.9). (6) Whereas man only gives the animals names (v.20), *in the discovery of his wife he arrives at a true expression of himself; with his bridegroom's exultation the Yahwist quotes man's speech for the first time; next to the formula of relationship stands the derivation of the name 'issa ('woman') from 'is ('man'), which bring out both the unity of nature and the difference in sex.* The note of exultation—'this at last!'—announces the fulfillment of a long desired happiness. (7) Love is essentially marked by the personal yearning for one another; even the powerful bonds of the family group are burst apart (v.24a) and in man's 'cleaving' to his wife the original physical unity is realized anew (v.24b). (8) *Shame in the form of embarrassment and inhibition only penetrates the duality of man and woman as the result of their mistrust towards God and their disobedience towards his word* (cf. v.25b with 3.7–11)." (171–72, my emphasis).

35. *Rhetoric of Sexuality*, 100–102.

36. Ibid., 96–97.

37. For a range of views on the productive or deleterious effect of that disrupted reverie, see Grossman, *Authors to Themselves*, 83ff.; Nyquist, "Gynesis, Genesis," 192ff.; McColley, *Milton's Eve*, 74ff.; Summers, *Muse's Method*, 97ff.; Kerrigan, *Sacred Complex*, 69ff.; Richard Corum, "In White Ink: *Paradise Lost* and Milton's Ideas of Women," in Julia Walker, ed., *Milton and the Idea of Woman* (Urbana: U Illinois P, 1988), 120–47; Stein, *Answerable Presence*, 95ff.; Christine Froula's "When Eve Reads Milton: Undoing the Canonical Economy," *Critical Inquiry* 10 (1983), 321–47; and Christopher, *Science of the Saints*, 147ff.

38. *Anthropology*, 174–75.

39. *Rhetoric of Sexuality*, 81.

40. *Theology*, 1:252. Wolff's account of erotic disharmony, which runs throughout Genesis, also argues that "The uniqueness of Yahweh's love relationship to Israel meant a fundamental prohibition on adultery (Ex. 20.3, 14)," which Hosea's predicament outrageously underscores and which Eve in a manner transgresses insofar as she allows Satan as the serpent to usurp Adam's (and by extension, God's) role in *Paradise Lost* (*Anthropology*, 173).

41. See Eichrodt, *Theology*, 1:253–54.

42. Ibid., 1:251–52.

43. Both Wolff and Eichrodt remark Israel's resistance to literally erotic expressions of God, which they agree lies in its conscious separation of Yahwism from surrounding nature or fertility religions, especially the Canaanite practice of cult prostitutes in which the supernatural is sexually incorporated. It is a refusal that equally reinforces the distinction between deity and its expressions. Moreover, in the prophets' erotic parables, Eichrodt comments that "The impulsive and compulsive character of merely natural love is replaced by *deliberate direction of the will and readiness for action,* evinced in God's choice of one particular people before all others and his faithfulness to the task of training them" (ibid., 1:252, my emphasis)—a freedom from necessity and a liberty to choose which Milton makes integral to the erotic relation of our first parents and its educative power.

44. *Wisdom in Israel*, 67–68.

45. Although he calls it "peripheral," Arnold Stein offers a remarkable synopsis of the problem and its implication for Milton's Eden:

The poet, we may observe, goes out of his way to relate the problems of feeling and knowing happiness to problems of obedience and of love and of knowledge. He deliberately assigns to the perfect bliss of Adam and Eve a formal declaration that no further growth will be possible during the present stage of their existence, and this is intended as part of the trial of obedience.

Knowledge has limits but the limits are not all of one kind, are not exclusively related to the external or quantitative, or to the infinite or divine or "other." The limits also define (or reflect) human nature by postulating a moral wisdom in which proper knowledge has a reciprocal function and serves the good life. Of this last the forbidden tree is a master symbol. Love is different, without limits in reference to God (unlike knowledge) but nevertheless limited by the disciplines of direction and control. Love as mercy may shine first and last, but not without satisfying an intellectual middle ground. This ground in turn cannot be separable from the ultimate purposes of God. Such reasoning, though it is peripheral to Milton's main enterprise, seems to require recognizing the concept of the "hidden God" whose nature, as many have thought, is only in part manifested in Scripture, the order of the world, and the reasoned interpretations of the sages. That God exists rather in the commanding "nothingness" of deity, in the pregnant omissions of Scripture, and may be traced in the varied efforts of "negative theology," and in the long record of human compulsion to attempt thoughts of the unthinkable and of the inexpressible.

For the most part Milton's "great argument" clearly chooses not to enter such regions, but nevertheless marks their borders and does not act as if what lies beyond is a barren abyss empty of meaning. (*Art of Presence*, 145)

46. Ibid., 72–73.

47. Significantly, this is Luther's point in his reading of the Edenic trees and their fruit, distinguishing once again between sign and word, sacrament and testament, a physical and a religious reality:

This tree was not deadly by nature; it was deadly because it was stated to be so by the Word of God. . . . In this manner this one tree—or that particular kind of several trees in the midst of Paradise—killed Adam for not obeying the Word of God, not indeed because of its nature but because it had been so laid down by the Word of God. . . . To our reason it appears very ludicrous for one fruit to be so injurious that the entire human race, in an almost infinite series, perished and died an eternal death. But the fruit did not have this power. Adam did indeed put his teeth into the fruit, but actually he put his teeth into a sting. This God had forbidden; this was disobedience to God. This is the true cause of the evil, namely, that Adam sins against God, disregards His order, and obeys Satan. The tree of the knowledge of good and evil was a good tree; it produced very fine fruit. But because the prohibition is added and man is disobedient, it becomes more injurious than any poison. (*LW* 1:95–96)

48. *Theology*, 1:375.

49. The frequency of this magical leap, a crude symbology that derives the supernatural nature of a thing from its appearance, is felicitously demonstrated in *The Malleus Maleficarum*. Kramer and Sprenger not only make and elaborate the same argument about Adam's rib—"bent as it were in a contrary direction to a man," which "defect" makes woman "an imperfect animal, [who] always deceives" (44)—but also go on to argue that David's harping cured Saul not by its musical therapy but because "it was made in the sign of a cross, being a cross of wood with the strings stretched across" (41).

50. *The Grotesque*, 181.

51. *A Midsummer Night's Dream* (5.1.2–22), in G. Blakemore Evans et al., eds., *The Riverside Shakespeare* (Boston: Houghton Mifflin, 1974), 242.

52. Although he understands the faculty and *res non apparentes* in idealist terms, this is Paul Stevens's argument in "Milton and the Icastic Imagination," *Milton Studies* 20 (1984): 43–73: "For Milton, imagination at its highest potential is not simply a necessary evil—the means by which those of soft and delicious temper may be brought to look upon truth. It is a God-given faculty which has a specific purpose in assisting man toward knowledge of his Maker. It is certainly true that imagination divorced from judgment, fancy uninformed by reason, leads to delusion. But the *educated* imagination is the peculiar instrument of grace. It provides the psychological mechanism by which we come to see and believe the evidence of things not seen" (44).

INDEX